FABLES: THE DELUXE EDITION

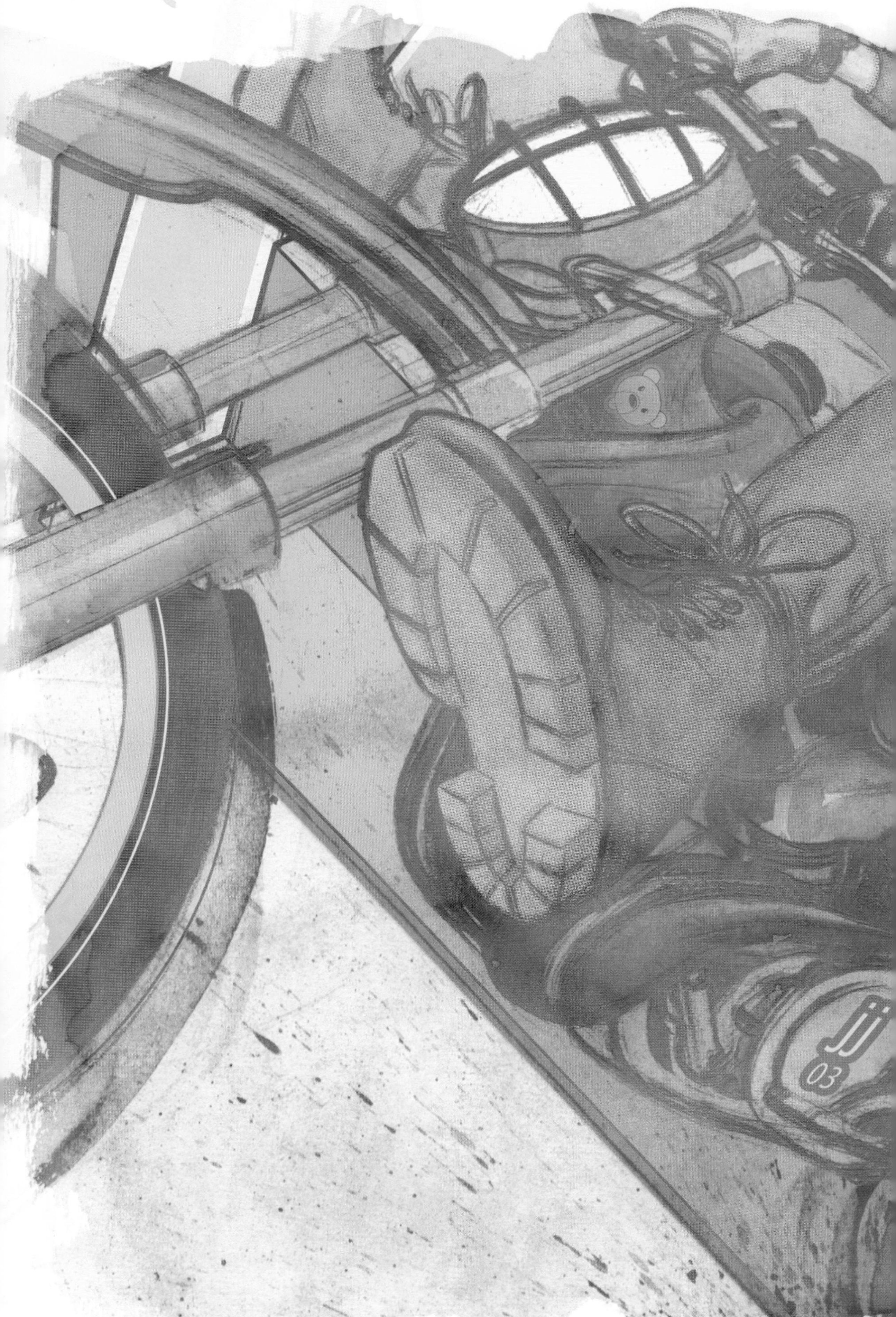
jj
03

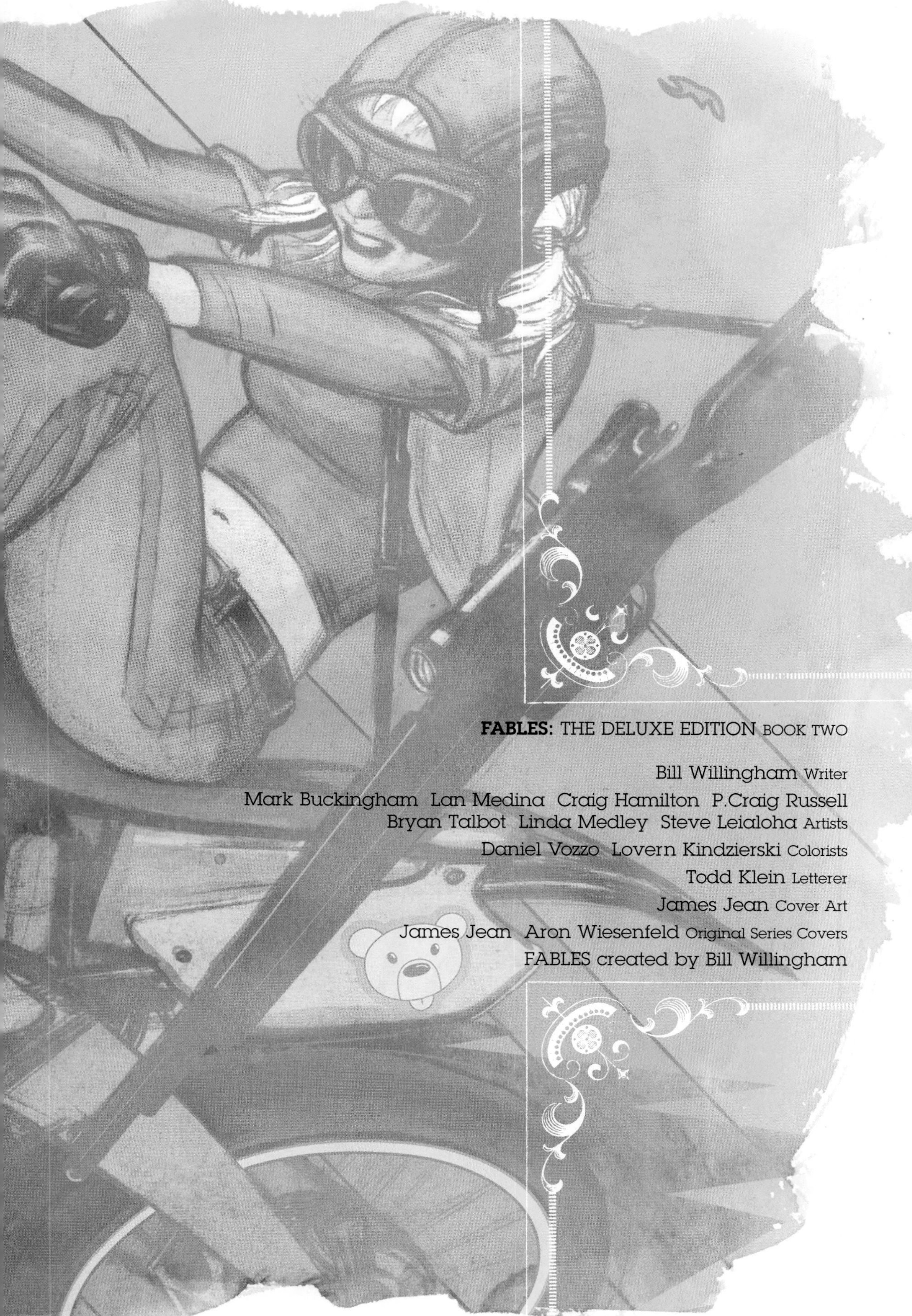

FABLES: THE DELUXE EDITION BOOK TWO

Bill Willingham Writer

Mark Buckingham Lan Medina Craig Hamilton P.Craig Russell Bryan Talbot Linda Medley Steve Leialoha Artists

Daniel Vozzo Lovern Kindzierski Colorists

Todd Klein Letterer

James Jean Cover Art

James Jean Aron Wiesenfeld Original Series Covers

FABLES created by Bill Willingham

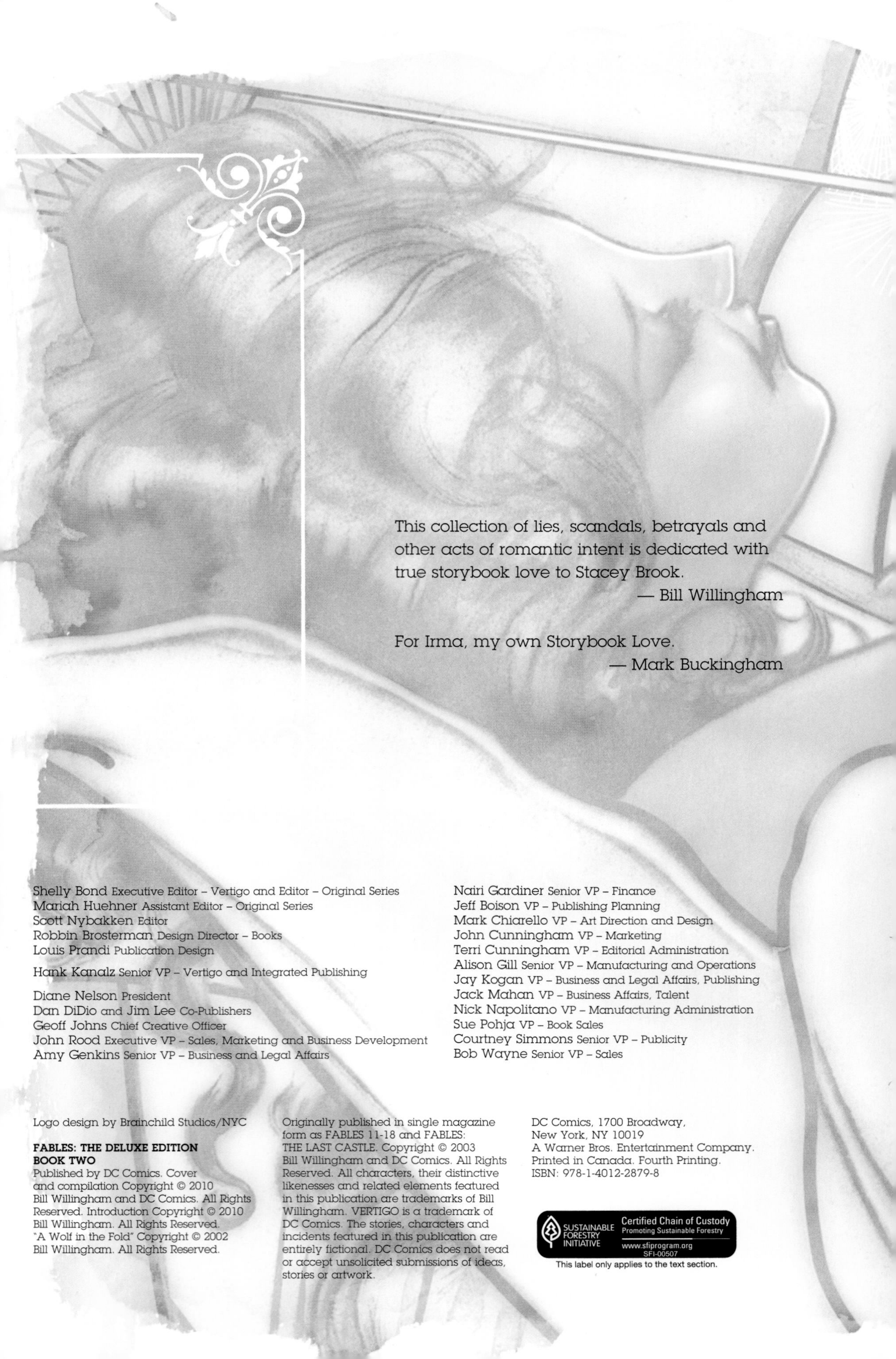

This collection of lies, scandals, betrayals and
other acts of romantic intent is dedicated with
true storybook love to Stacey Brook.
— Bill Willingham

For Irma, my own Storybook Love.
— Mark Buckingham

Shelly Bond Executive Editor – Vertigo and Editor – Original Series
Mariah Huehner Assistant Editor – Original Series
Scott Nybakken Editor
Robbin Brosterman Design Director – Books
Louis Prandi Publication Design

Hank Kanalz Senior VP – Vertigo and Integrated Publishing

Diane Nelson President
Dan DiDio and Jim Lee Co-Publishers
Geoff Johns Chief Creative Officer
John Rood Executive VP – Sales, Marketing and Business Development
Amy Genkins Senior VP – Business and Legal Affairs

Nairi Gardiner Senior VP – Finance
Jeff Boison VP – Publishing Planning
Mark Chiarello VP – Art Direction and Design
John Cunningham VP – Marketing
Terri Cunningham VP – Editorial Administration
Alison Gill Senior VP – Manufacturing and Operations
Jay Kogan VP – Business and Legal Affairs, Publishing
Jack Mahan VP – Business Affairs, Talent
Nick Napolitano VP – Manufacturing Administration
Sue Pohja VP – Book Sales
Courtney Simmons Senior VP – Publicity
Bob Wayne Senior VP – Sales

Logo design by Brainchild Studios/NYC

**FABLES: THE DELUXE EDITION
BOOK TWO**
Published by DC Comics. Cover
and compilation Copyright © 2010
Bill Willingham and DC Comics. All Rights
Reserved. Introduction Copyright © 2010
Bill Willingham. All Rights Reserved.
"A Wolf in the Fold" Copyright © 2002
Bill Willingham. All Rights Reserved.

Originally published in single magazine
form as FABLES 11-18 and FABLES:
THE LAST CASTLE. Copyright © 2003
Bill Willingham and DC Comics. All Rights
Reserved. All characters, their distinctive
likenesses and related elements featured
in this publication are trademarks of Bill
Willingham. VERTIGO is a trademark of
DC Comics. The stories, characters and
incidents featured in this publication are
entirely fictional. DC Comics does not read
or accept unsolicited submissions of ideas,
stories or artwork.

DC Comics, 1700 Broadway,
New York, NY 10019
A Warner Bros. Entertainment Company.
Printed in Canada. Fourth Printing.
ISBN: 978-1-4012-2879-8

Table of Contents

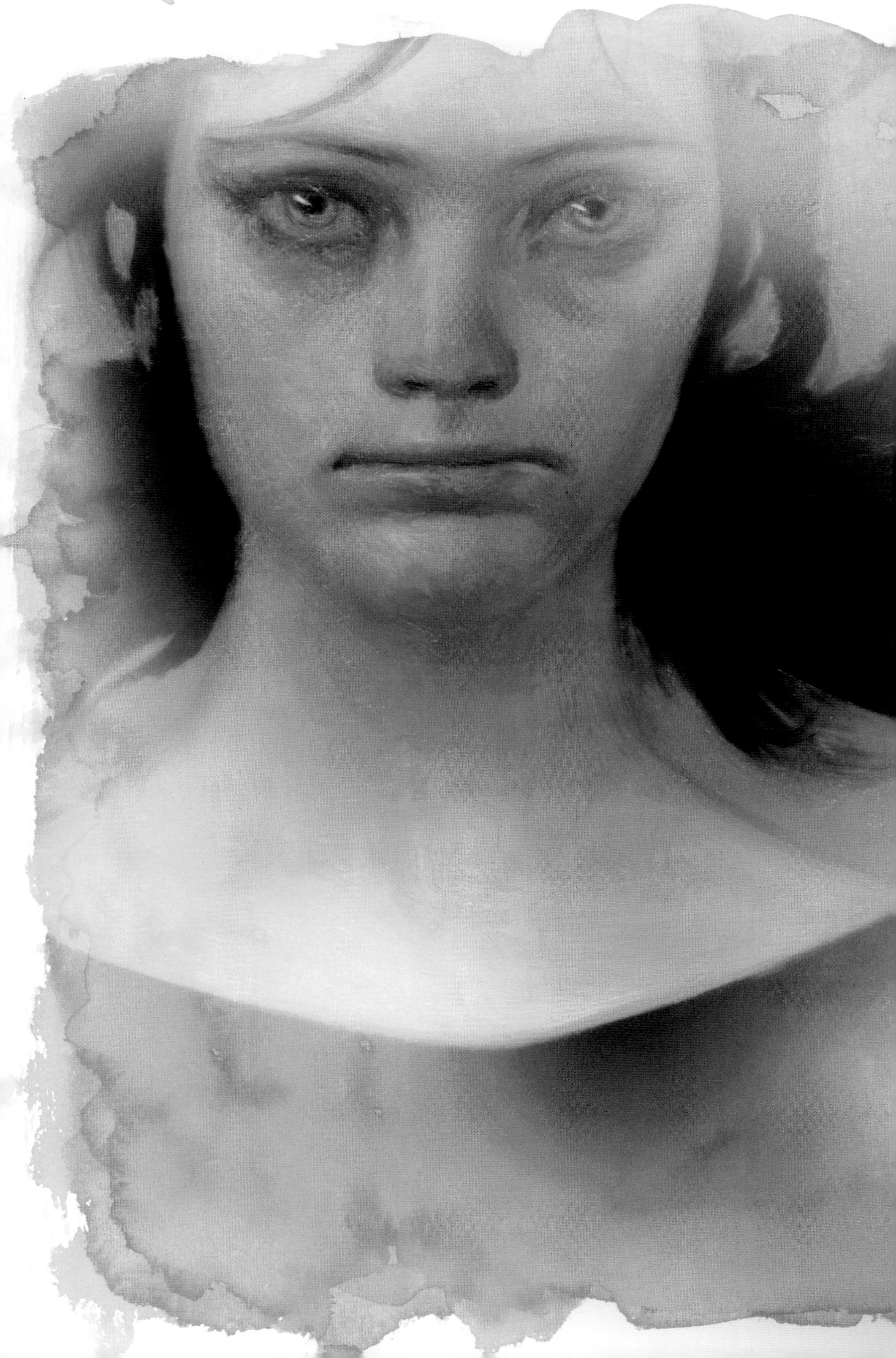

Story Time

What defines humanity? Forget all those silly scientific designations — *Homo erectus*? So what if we can walk upright? A bear can do as much. Monkeys, beavers, chipmunks, bugs and birds can. Penguins and emus and a dozen other kinds of bird even gave up flight to do it. My cat can do it for a step or two (and let me tell you, he looks adorable when he does). Even lizards can run along on two feet, to woo the ladies and intimidate enemies. Maybe we can do it a little better than the average bear, but the ability to walk on our two hind legs isn't unique to mankind.

No, what really makes us special, what separates us from the other beasts, is our never-ending capacity for spinning yarns.

We tell stories to live, to love, to prosper and to fail. A house doesn't get built until someone — the architect or the wise old man of the village — first tells the story of how it will be built. And the architect doesn't even begin his story until he hears one from the young new couple, eager and scared and nervous and excited, telling him the story of the sort of home they want. Stories within stories within stories, or nothing gets done.

Money isn't real. It's a story we tell each other to convince us it has worth. An agreed-upon fiction. The laws we live under are the stories we tell ourselves about the kinds of people that we want to be — that we expect to be. And our stories matter. Interrupt the story by breaking one of those laws (try one of the big ones, just for fun) and you'll find out how important they are. Every road and every step along it begins with a story.

And it isn't just the practical side of our lives that is ruled by the stories we tell. Our fictions move us to do great things, things worth doing for no better reason than that there's poetry in us. We dream before we do. Generations before we physically set foot on the moon, the storytellers got us there first. In the distant past we spun tall tales about impossible lost continents like Lemuria and Hy-Brasil, and then we went out and found them in fact. Stories precede everything we do. That's our most basic nature, and we couldn't escape it if we tried.

I'm in the storytelling profession, and it's an honest trade. But I didn't build the tales you're about to read alone. Not by a long shot. I was joined by men and women of amazing talent and remarkable ability — so remarkable, in fact, that I'm moved to remark on it. Mark Buckingham, Steve Leialoha, Craig Hamilton, P. Craig Russell, Bryan Talbot, Lan Medina, Linda Medley, Danny Vozzo, Lovern Kindzierski, Todd Klein, Aron Wiesenfeld and James Jean — each worked on one or more of the tales in this volume. Master storytellers all, they've conspired with me here to spin some whoppers about a group of people who are living stories — tall tales made flesh. In a page or two we'll begin. We'll watch them struggle for true love, attempt heroic deeds and perpetrate terrible betrayals. Let us choose sides and join in their battles and schemes.

And while we're at it, let's not forget that just because these characters are the magical stuff of raw story in human form, it doesn't mean that they're mere fantasy — in fact, they're as real as we are. Each and every one of us, fictional or not, is a member in good standing of the species *Homo fabula* — the Storytelling People.

— Bill Willingham

9 September 2010

In the woods, by the river, just below the limestone cliffs

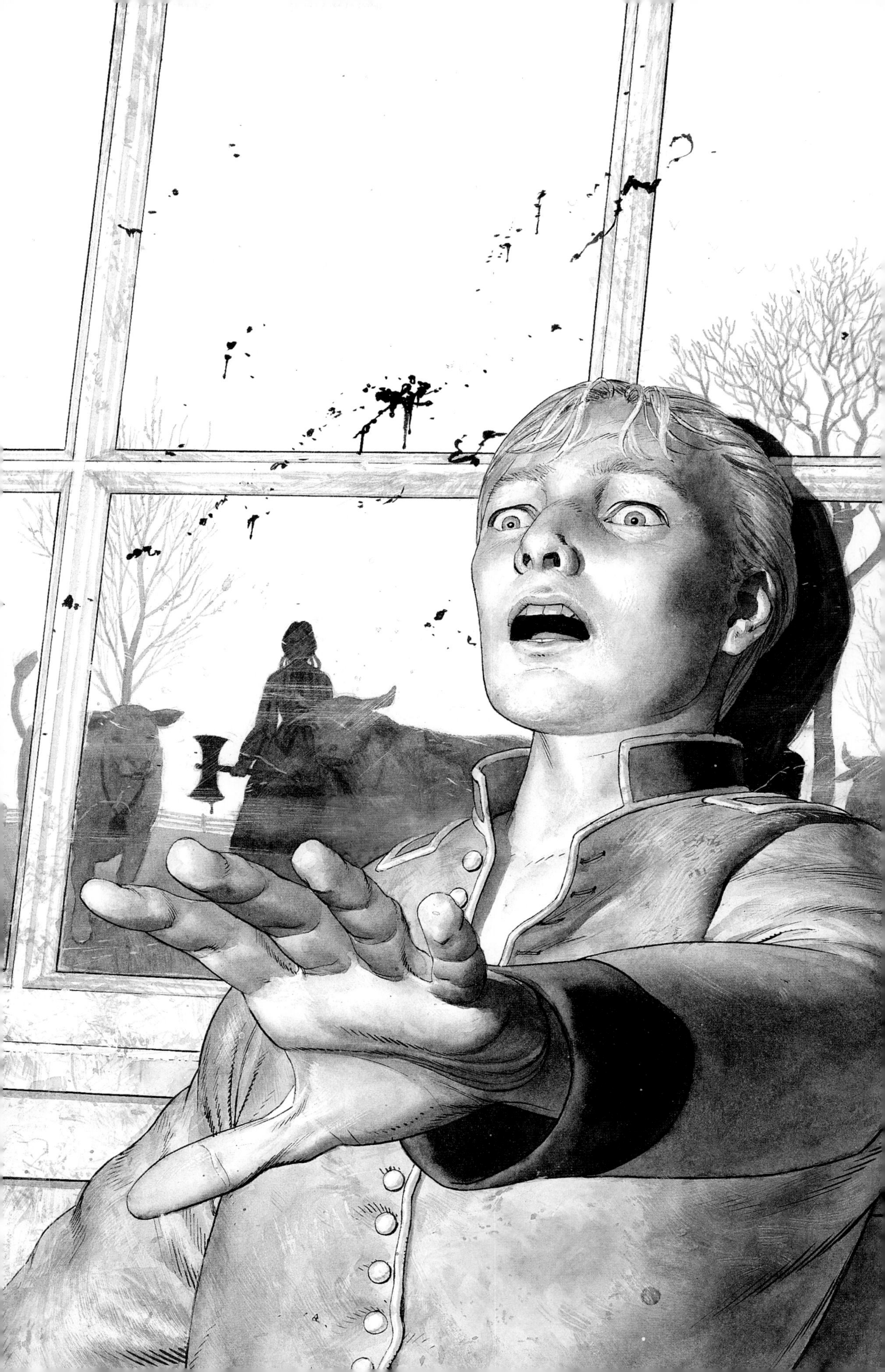

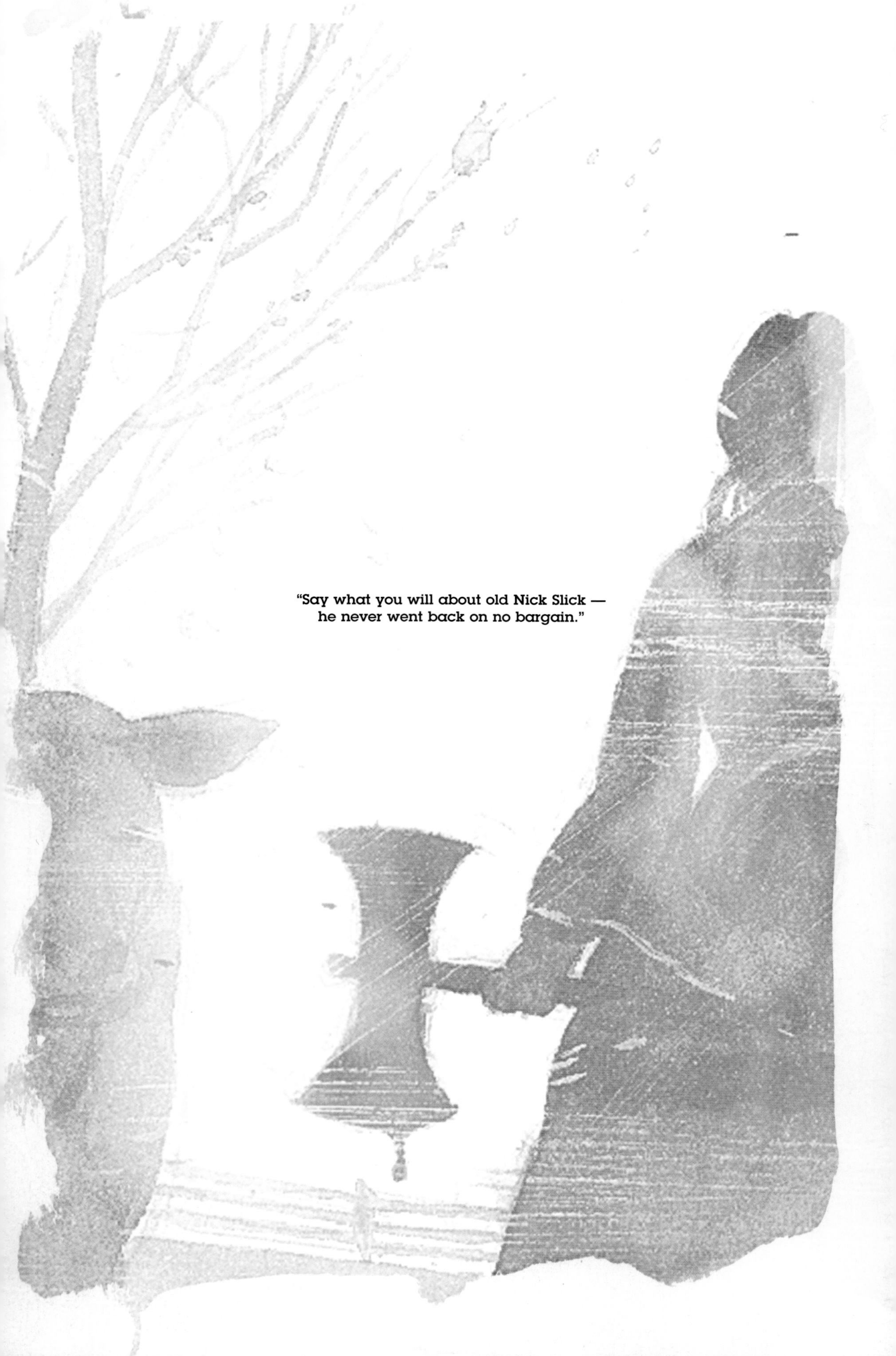
"Say what you will about old Nick Slick —
he never went back on no bargain."

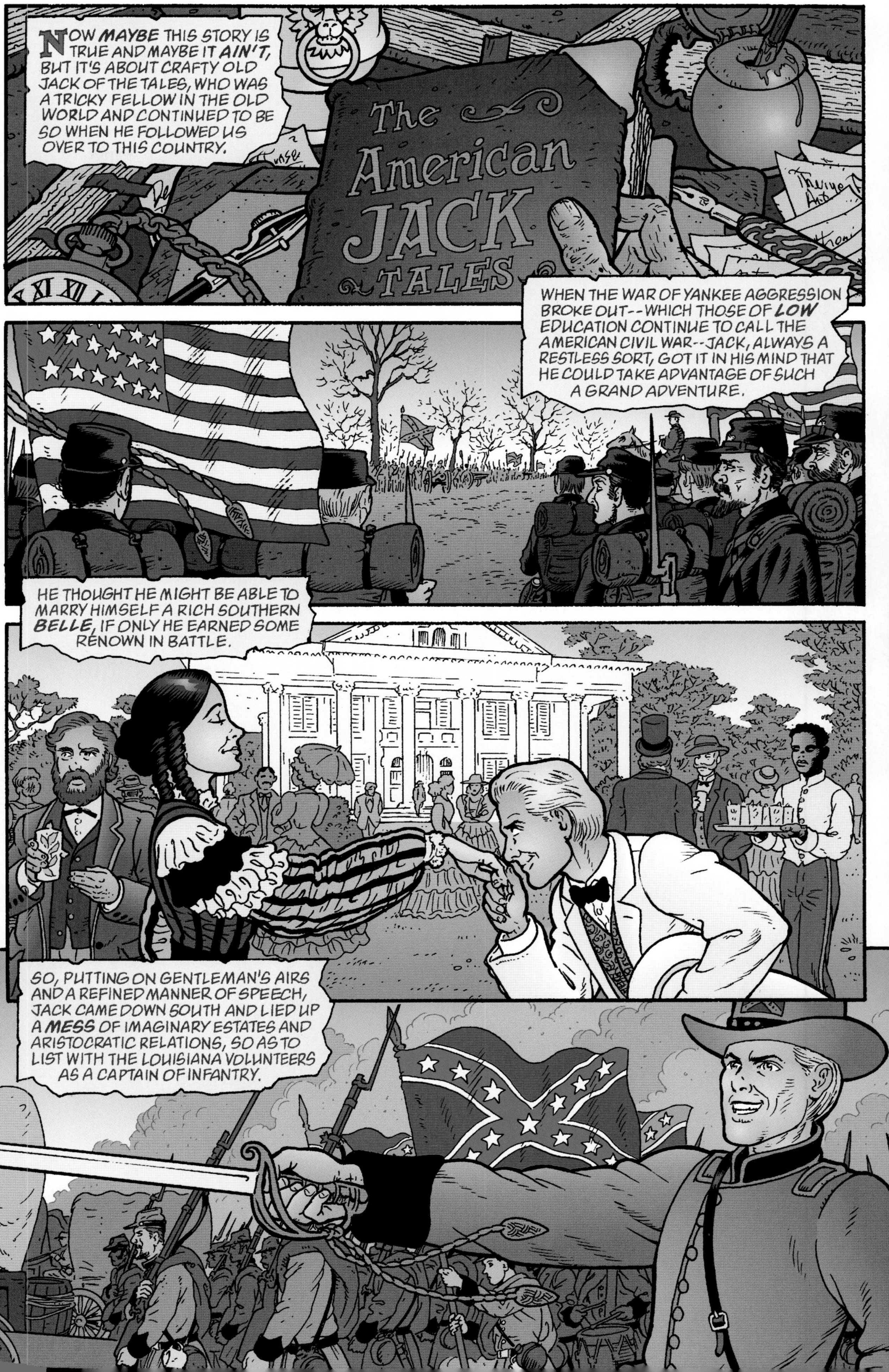
NOW MAYBE THIS STORY IS TRUE AND MAYBE IT AIN'T, BUT IT'S ABOUT CRAFTY OLD JACK OF THE TALES, WHO WAS A TRICKY FELLOW IN THE OLD WORLD AND CONTINUED TO BE SO WHEN HE FOLLOWED US OVER TO THIS COUNTRY.
The American JACK TALES
WHEN THE WAR OF YANKEE AGGRESSION BROKE OUT--WHICH THOSE OF LOW EDUCATION CONTINUE TO CALL THE AMERICAN CIVIL WAR--JACK, ALWAYS A RESTLESS SORT, GOT IT IN HIS MIND THAT HE COULD TAKE ADVANTAGE OF SUCH A GRAND ADVENTURE.
HE THOUGHT HE MIGHT BE ABLE TO MARRY HIMSELF A RICH SOUTHERN BELLE, IF ONLY HE EARNED SOME RENOWN IN BATTLE.
SO, PUTTING ON GENTLEMAN'S AIRS AND A REFINED MANNER OF SPEECH, JACK CAME DOWN SOUTH AND LIED UP A MESS OF IMAGINARY ESTATES AND ARISTOCRATIC RELATIONS, SO AS TO LIST WITH THE LOUISIANA VOLUNTEERS AS A CAPTAIN OF INFANTRY.

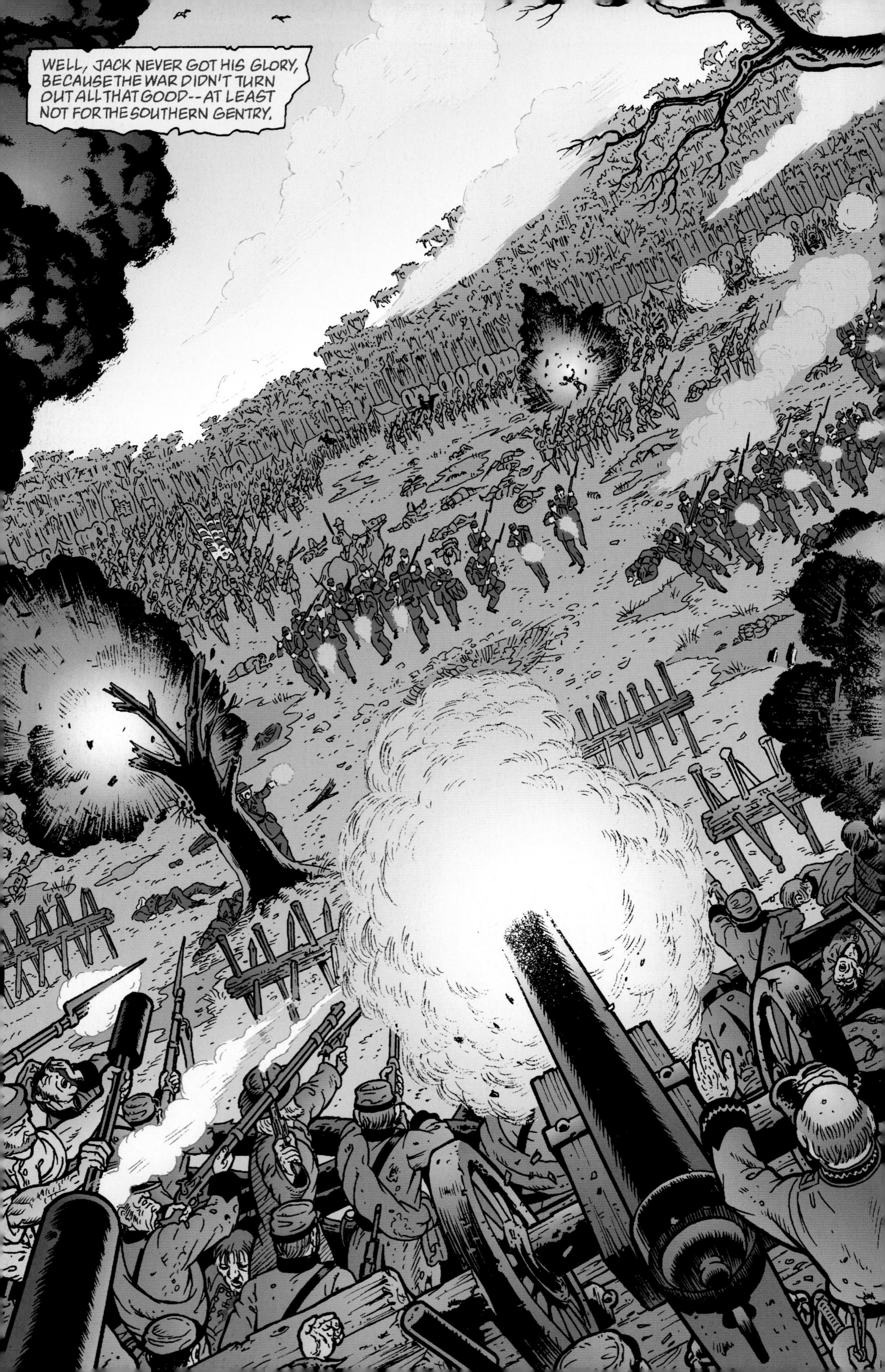
WELL, JACK NEVER GOT HIS GLORY, BECAUSE THE WAR DIDN'T TURN OUT ALL THAT GOOD--AT LEAST NOT FOR THE SOUTHERN GENTRY.

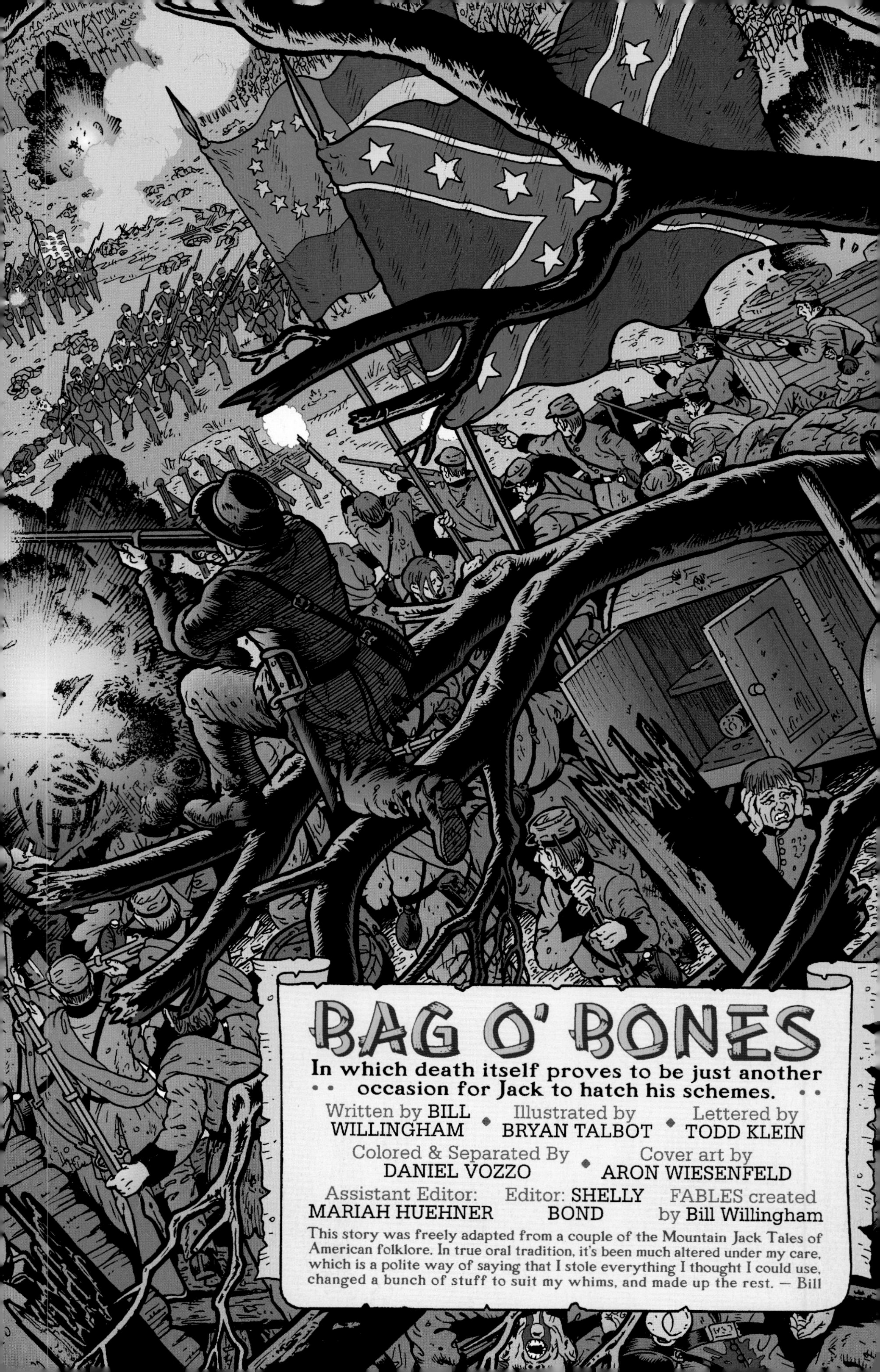
BAG O' BONES
In which death itself proves to be just another occasion for Jack to hatch his schemes.
Written by BILL WILLINGHAM
Illustrated by BRYAN TALBOT
Lettered by TODD KLEIN
Colored & Separated By DANIEL VOZZO
Cover art by ARON WIESENFELD
Assistant Editor: MARIAH HUEHNER
Editor: SHELLY BOND
FABLES created by Bill Willingham
This story was freely adapted from a couple of the Mountain Jack Tales of American folklore. In true oral tradition, it's been much altered under my care, which is a polite way of saying that I stole everything I thought I could use, changed a bunch of stuff to suit my whims, and made up the rest. — Bill

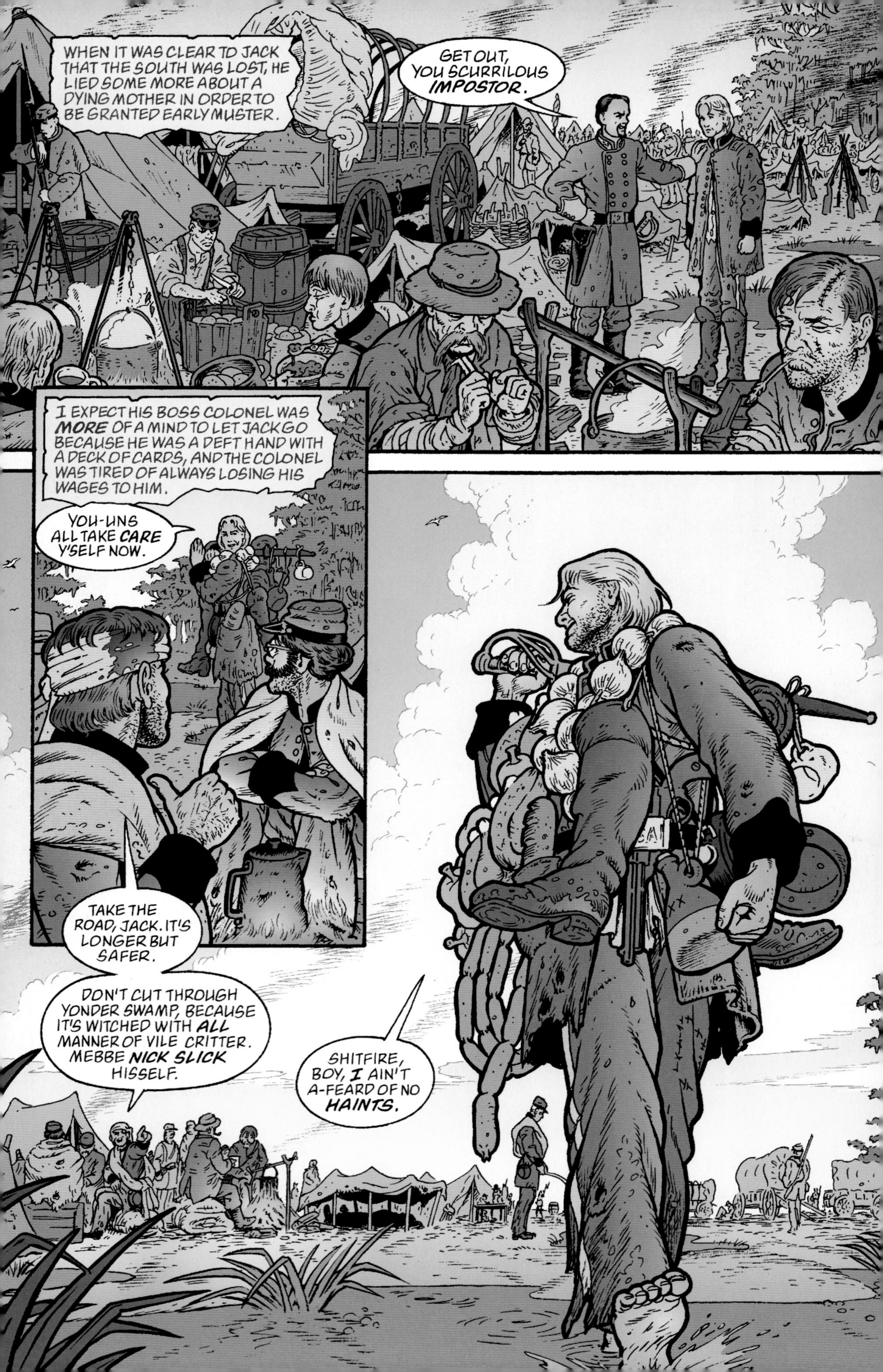
WHEN IT WAS CLEAR TO JACK THAT THE SOUTH WAS LOST, HE LIED SOME MORE ABOUT A DYING MOTHER IN ORDER TO BE GRANTED EARLY MUSTER.
GET OUT, YOU SCURRILOUS IMPOSTOR.
I EXPECT HIS BOSS COLONEL WAS MORE OF A MIND TO LET JACK GO BECAUSE HE WAS A DEFT HAND WITH A DECK OF CARDS, AND THE COLONEL WAS TIRED OF ALWAYS LOSING HIS WAGES TO HIM.
YOU-UNS ALL TAKE CARE Y'SELF NOW.
TAKE THE ROAD, JACK. IT'S LONGER BUT SAFER.
DON'T CUT THROUGH YONDER SWAMP, BECAUSE IT'S WITCHED WITH ALL MANNER OF VILE CRITTER. MEBBE NICK SLICK HISSELF.
SHITFIRE, BOY, I AIN'T A-FEARD OF NO HAINTS.

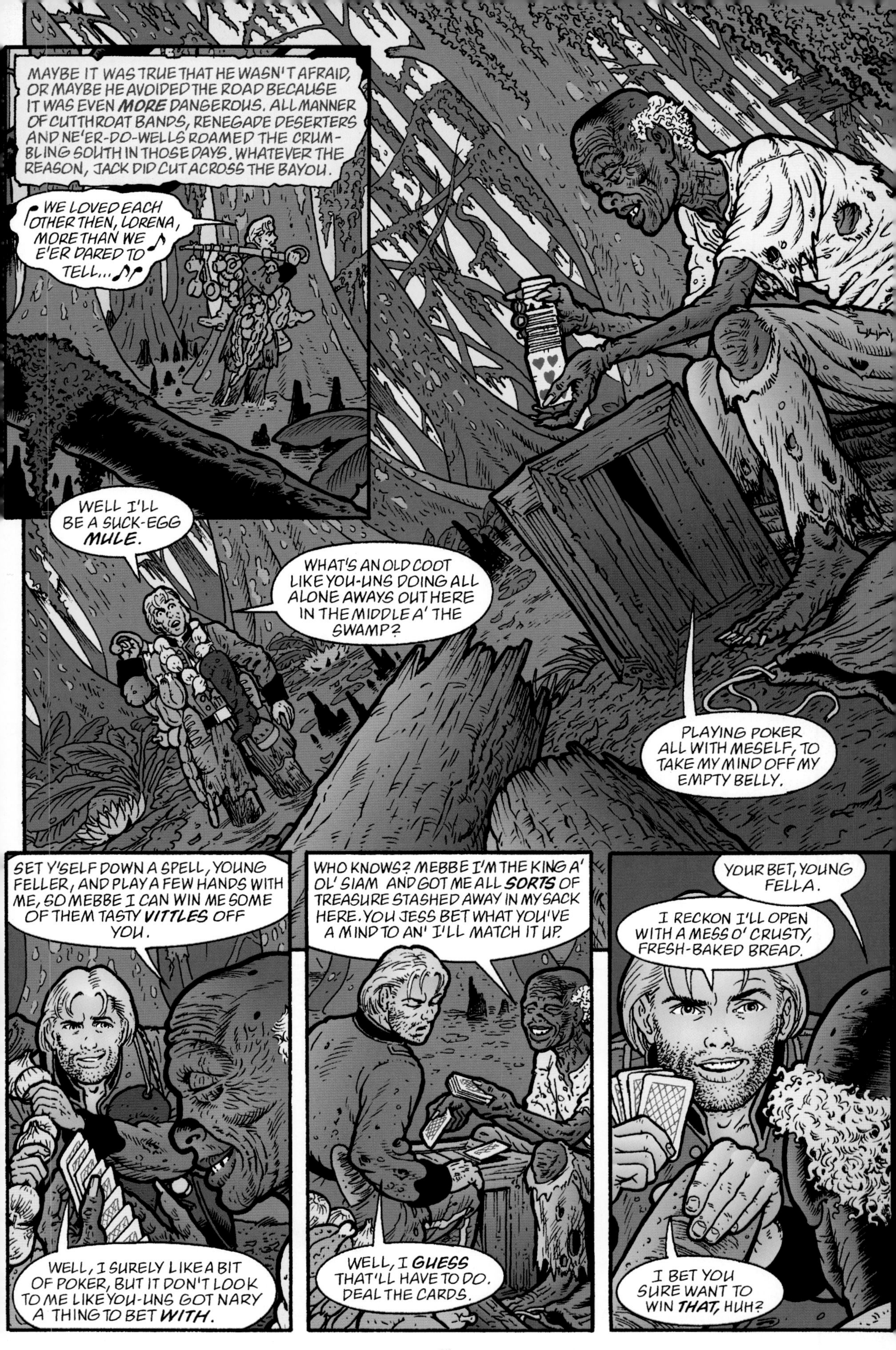

MAYBE IT WAS TRUE THAT HE WASN'T AFRAID, OR MAYBE HE AVOIDED THE ROAD BECAUSE IT WAS EVEN MORE DANGEROUS. ALL MANNER OF CUTTHROAT BANDS, RENEGADE DESERTERS AND NE'ER-DO-WELLS ROAMED THE CRUMBLING SOUTH IN THOSE DAYS. WHATEVER THE REASON, JACK DID CUT ACROSS THE BAYOU.
♪ WE LOVED EACH OTHER THEN, LORENA, MORE THAN WE ♪ E'ER DARED TO TELL... ♪♪
WELL I'LL BE A SUCK-EGG MULE.
WHAT'S AN OLD COOT LIKE YOU-UNS DOING ALL ALONE AWAYS OUT HERE IN THE MIDDLE A' THE SWAMP?
PLAYING POKER ALL WITH MESELF, TO TAKE MY MIND OFF MY EMPTY BELLY.
SET Y'SELF DOWN A SPELL, YOUNG FELLER, AND PLAY A FEW HANDS WITH ME, SO MEBBE I CAN WIN ME SOME OF THEM TASTY VITTLES OFF YOU.
WELL, I SURELY LIKE A BIT OF POKER, BUT IT DON'T LOOK TO ME LIKE YOU-UNS GOT NARY A THING TO BET WITH.
WHO KNOWS? MEBBE I'M THE KING A' OL' SIAM AND GOT ME ALL SORTS OF TREASURE STASHED AWAY IN MY SACK HERE. YOU JESS BET WHAT YOU'VE A MIND TO AN' I'LL MATCH IT UP.
WELL, I GUESS THAT'LL HAVE TO DO. DEAL THE CARDS.
YOUR BET, YOUNG FELLA.
I RECKON I'LL OPEN WITH A MESS O' CRUSTY, FRESH-BAKED BREAD.
I BET YOU SURE WANT TO WIN THAT, HUH?

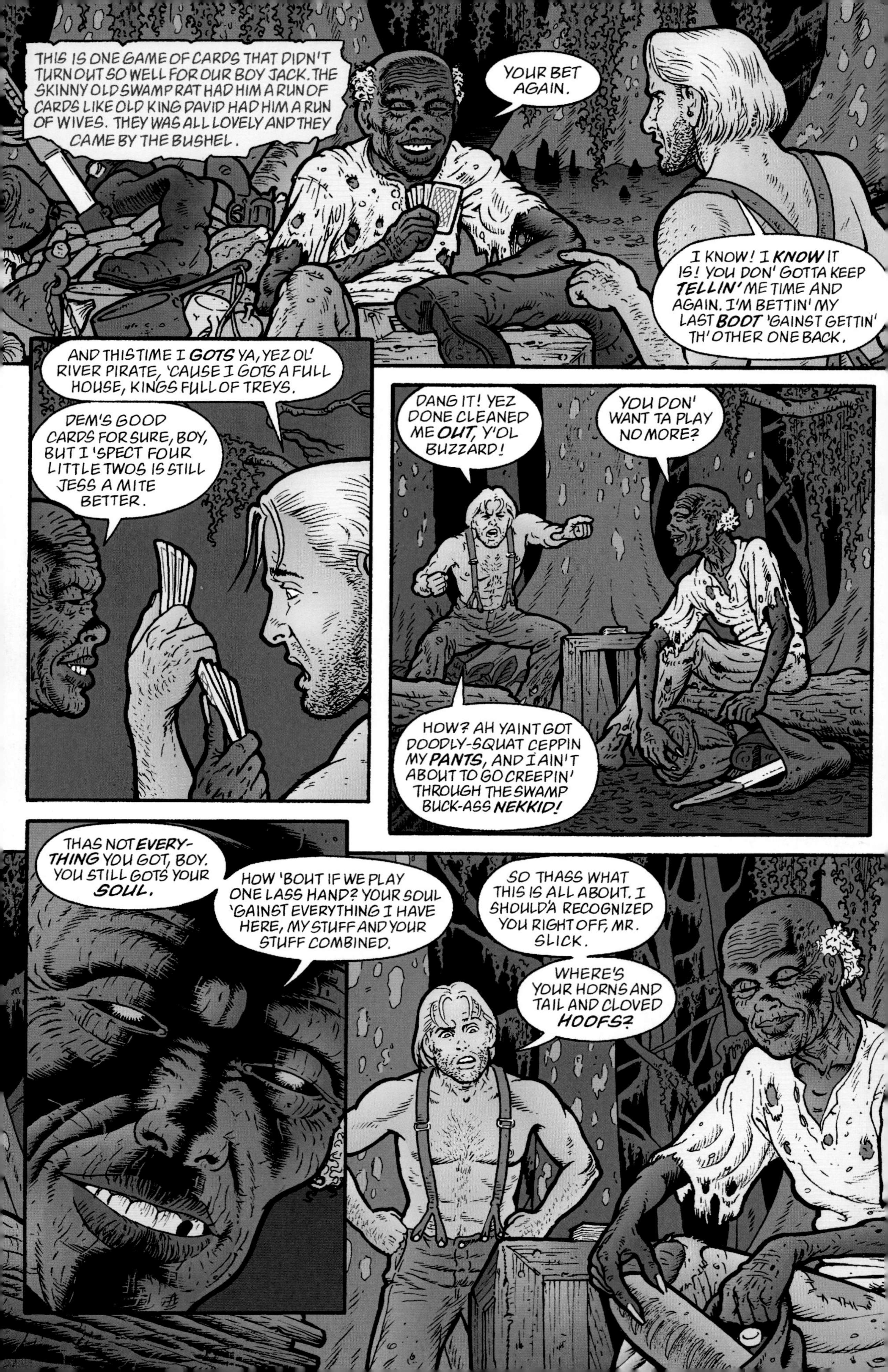
THIS IS ONE GAME OF CARDS THAT DIDN'T TURN OUT SO WELL FOR OUR BOY JACK. THE SKINNY OLD SWAMP RAT HAD HIM A RUN OF CARDS LIKE OLD KING DAVID HAD HIM A RUN OF WIVES. THEY WAS ALL LOVELY AND THEY CAME BY THE BUSHEL.
YOUR BET AGAIN.
I KNOW! I KNOW IT IS! YOU DON' GOTTA KEEP TELLIN' ME TIME AND AGAIN. I'M BETTIN' MY LAST BOOT 'GAINST GETTIN' TH' OTHER ONE BACK.
AND THIS TIME I GOTS YA, YEZ OL' RIVER PIRATE, 'CAUSE I GOTS A FULL HOUSE, KINGS FULL OF TREYS.
DEM'S GOOD CARDS FOR SURE, BOY, BUT I 'SPECT FOUR LITTLE TWOS IS STILL JESS A MITE BETTER.
DANG IT! YEZ DONE CLEANED ME OUT, Y'OL BUZZARD!
YOU DON' WANT TA PLAY NO MORE?
HOW? AH YAINT GOT DOODLY-SQUAT CEPPIN MY PANTS, AND I AIN'T ABOUT TO GO CREEPIN' THROUGH THE SWAMP BUCK-ASS NEKKID!
THAS NOT EVERYTHING YOU GOT, BOY. YOU STILL GOTS YOUR SOUL.
HOW 'BOUT IF WE PLAY ONE LASS HAND? YOUR SOUL 'GAINST EVERYTHING I HAVE HERE, MY STUFF AND YOUR STUFF COMBINED.
SO THASS WHAT THIS IS ALL ABOUT. I SHOULD'A RECOGNIZED YOU RIGHT OFF, MR. SLICK.
WHERE'S YOUR HORNS AND TAIL AND CLOVED HOOFS?

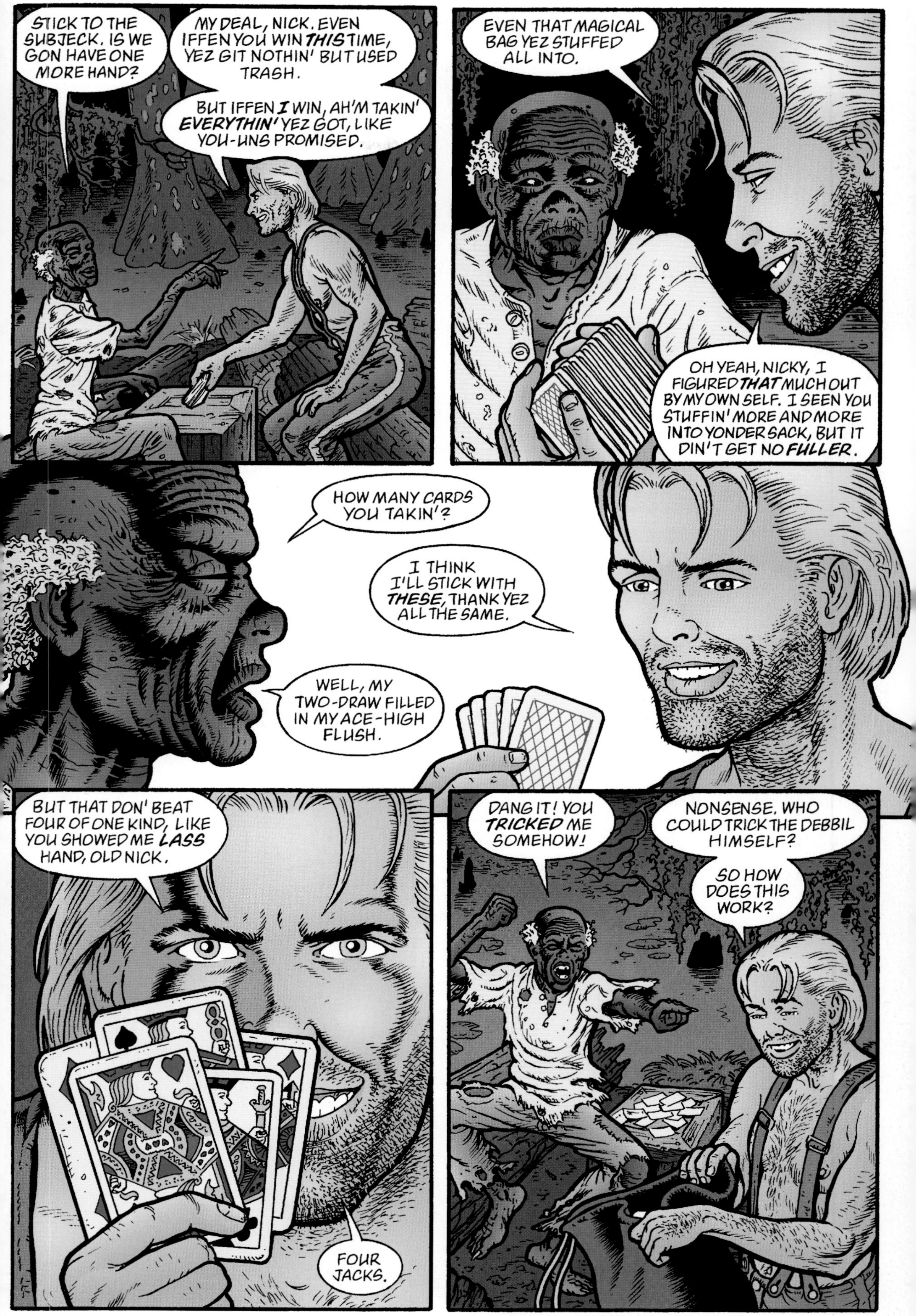
STICK TO THE SUBJECK. IS WE GON HAVE ONE MORE HAND?
MY DEAL, NICK. EVEN IFFEN YOU WIN THIS TIME, YEZ GIT NOTHIN' BUT USED TRASH.
BUT IFFEN I WIN, AH'M TAKIN' EVERYTHIN' YEZ GOT, LIKE YOU-UNS PROMISED.
EVEN THAT MAGICAL BAG YEZ STUFFED ALL INTO.
OH YEAH, NICKY, I FIGURED THAT MUCH OUT BY MY OWN SELF. I SEEN YOU STUFFIN' MORE AND MORE INTO YONDER SACK, BUT IT DIN'T GET NO FULLER.
HOW MANY CARDS YOU TAKIN'?
I THINK I'LL STICK WITH THESE, THANK YEZ ALL THE SAME.
WELL, MY TWO-DRAW FILLED IN MY ACE-HIGH FLUSH.
BUT THAT DON' BEAT FOUR OF ONE KIND, LIKE YOU SHOWED ME LASS HAND, OLD NICK.
FOUR JACKS.
DANG IT! YOU TRICKED ME SOMEHOW!
NONSENSE. WHO COULD TRICK THE DEBBIL HIMSELF?
SO HOW DOES THIS WORK?

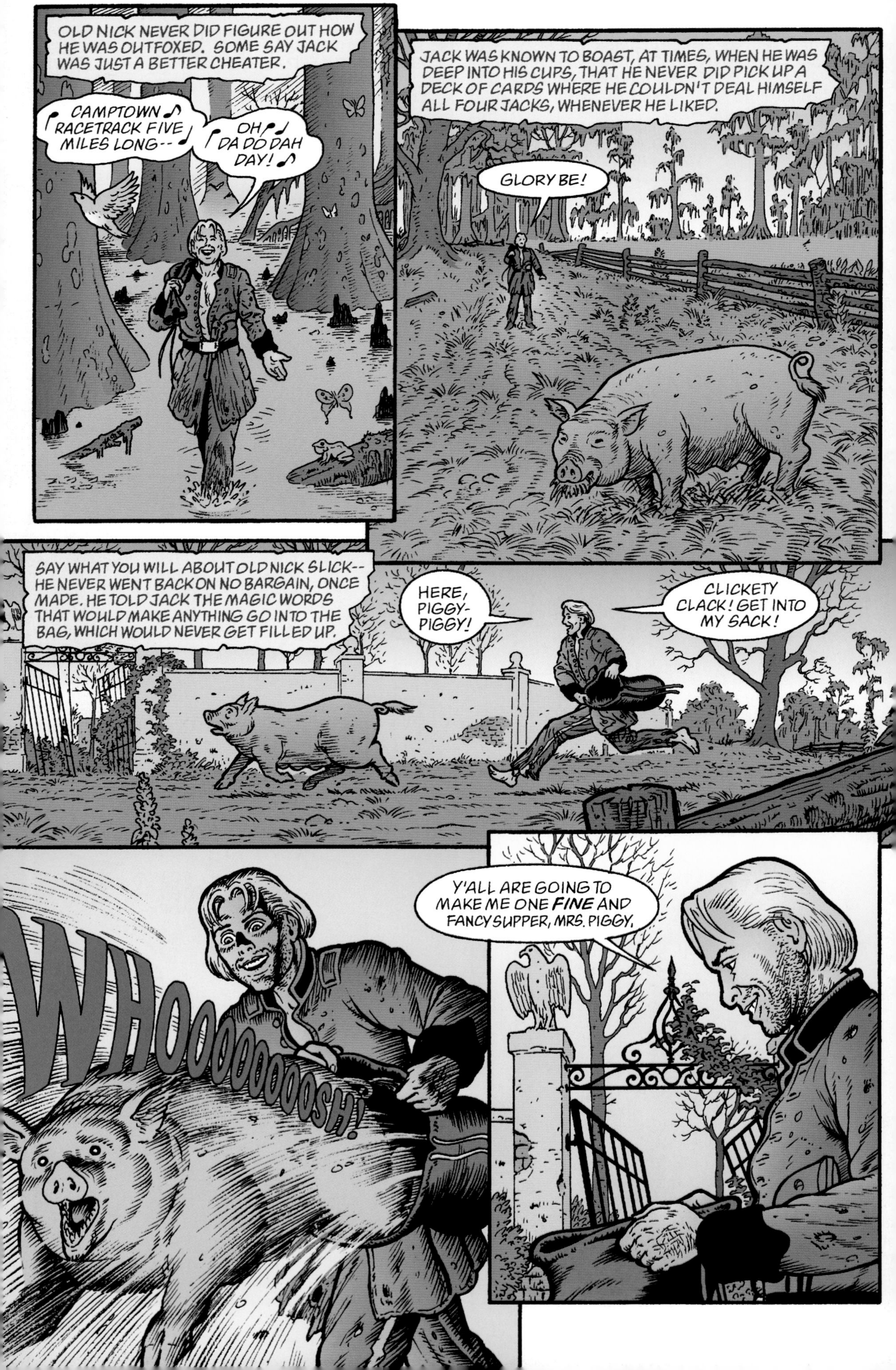
OLD NICK NEVER DID FIGURE OUT HOW HE WAS OUTFOXED. SOME SAY JACK WAS JUST A BETTER CHEATER.
CAMPTOWN RACETRACK FIVE MILES LONG--
OH DA DO DAH DAY!
JACK WAS KNOWN TO BOAST, AT TIMES, WHEN HE WAS DEEP INTO HIS CUPS, THAT HE NEVER DID PICK UP A DECK OF CARDS WHERE HE COULDN'T DEAL HIMSELF ALL FOUR JACKS, WHENEVER HE LIKED.
GLORY BE!
SAY WHAT YOU WILL ABOUT OLD NICK SLICK-- HE NEVER WENT BACK ON NO BARGAIN, ONCE MADE. HE TOLD JACK THE MAGIC WORDS THAT WOULD MAKE ANYTHING GO INTO THE BAG, WHICH WOULD NEVER GET FILLED UP.
HERE, PIGGY-PIGGY!
CLICKETY CLACK! GET INTO MY SACK!
WHOOOOOOOOOSH!
Y'ALL ARE GOING TO MAKE ME ONE FINE AND FANCY SUPPER, MRS. PIGGY.

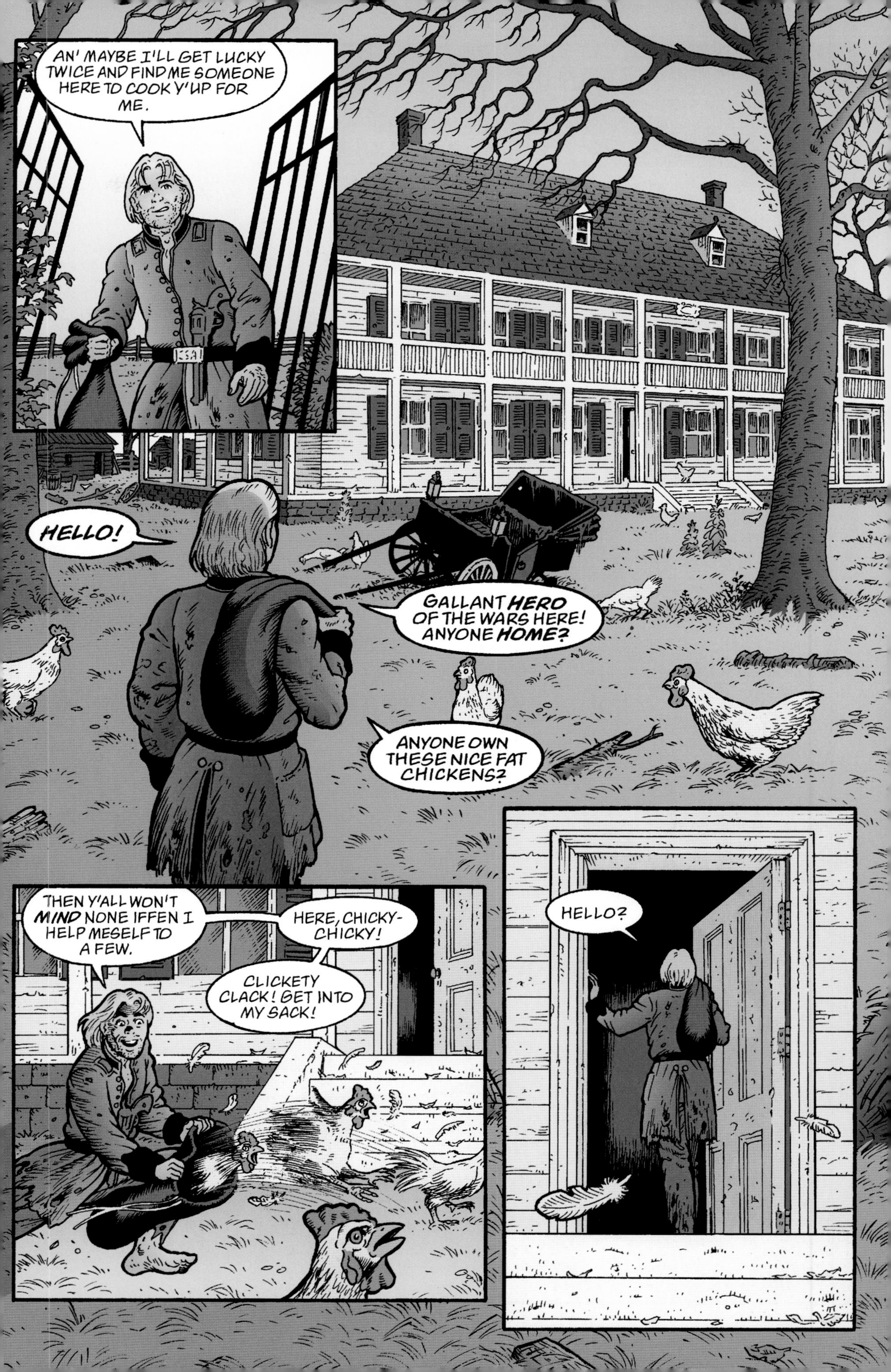
AN' MAYBE I'LL GET LUCKY TWICE AND FIND ME SOMEONE HERE TO COOK Y'UP FOR ME.
HELLO!
GALLANT HERO OF THE WARS HERE! ANYONE HOME?
ANYONE OWN THESE NICE FAT CHICKENS?
THEN Y'ALL WON'T MIND NONE IFFEN I HELP MESELF TO A FEW.
HERE, CHICKY-CHICKY!
CLICKETY CLACK! GET INTO MY SACK!
HELLO?

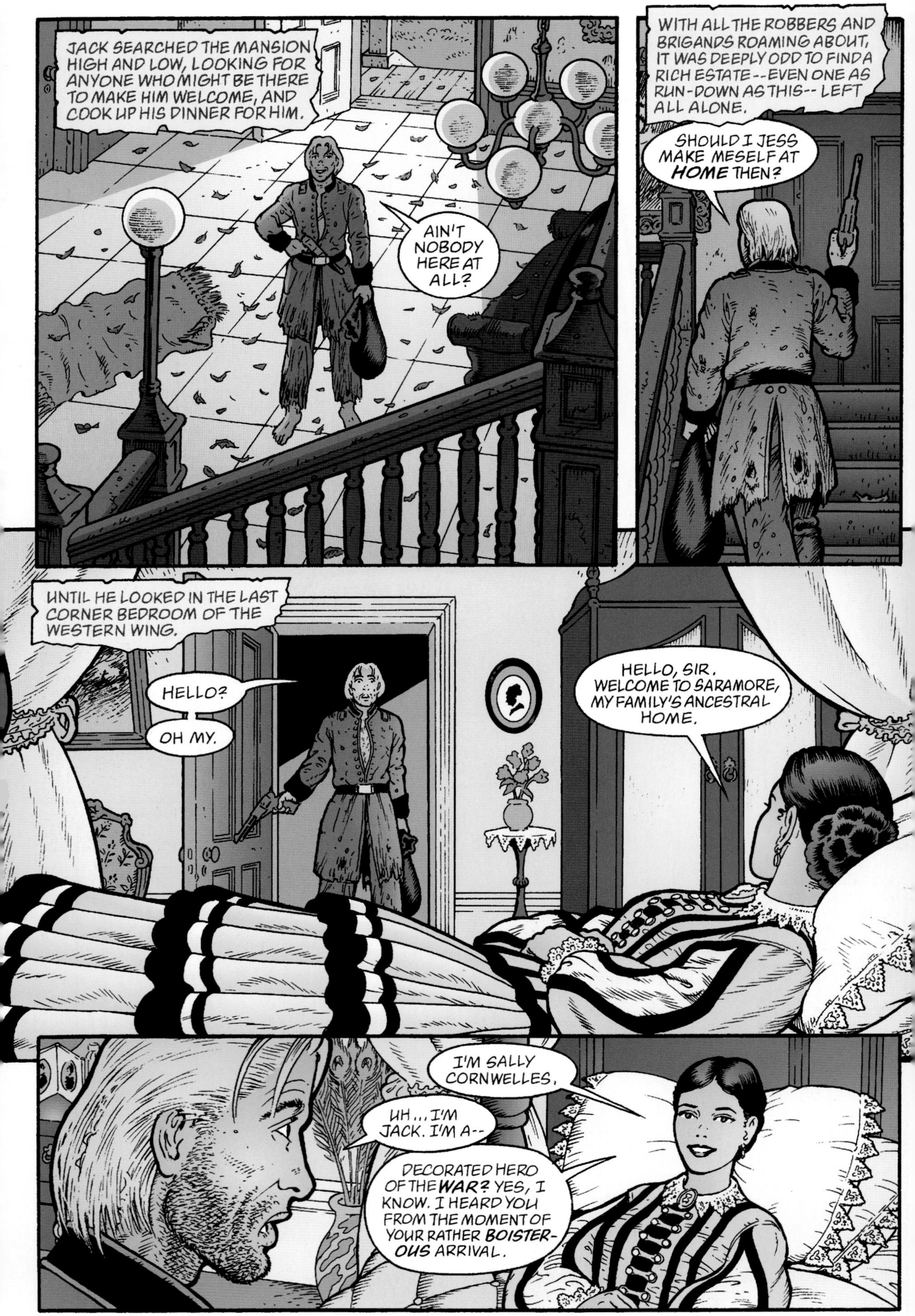
JACK SEARCHED THE MANSION HIGH AND LOW, LOOKING FOR ANYONE WHO MIGHT BE THERE TO MAKE HIM WELCOME, AND COOK UP HIS DINNER FOR HIM.
AIN'T NOBODY HERE AT ALL?
WITH ALL THE ROBBERS AND BRIGANDS ROAMING ABOUT, IT WAS DEEPLY ODD TO FIND A RICH ESTATE -- EVEN ONE AS RUN-DOWN AS THIS -- LEFT ALL ALONE.
SHOULD I JESS MAKE MESELF AT HOME THEN?
UNTIL HE LOOKED IN THE LAST CORNER BEDROOM OF THE WESTERN WING.
HELLO?
OH MY.
HELLO, SIR. WELCOME TO SARAMORE, MY FAMILY'S ANCESTRAL HOME.
I'M SALLY CORNWELLES.
UH ... I'M JACK. I'M A--
DECORATED HERO OF THE WAR? YES, I KNOW. I HEARD YOU FROM THE MOMENT OF YOUR RATHER BOISTER-OUS ARRIVAL.

THEN WHY DIN'T YOU-UNS **ANSWER** NOTHIN'?

A YOUNG LADY OF GOOD **BREEDING** DOESN'T SCREAM OUT HER GREETINGS LIKE SOME UNEDUCATED **HOOLIGAN**.

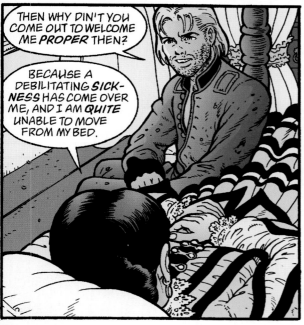

THEN WHY DIN'T YOU COME OUT TO WELCOME ME **PROPER** THEN?

BECAUSE A DEBILITATING **SICK-NESS** HAS COME OVER ME, AND I AM **QUITE** UNABLE TO MOVE FROM MY BED.

YOUAH SICK?

DON'T FRET. IT'S NOT **CONTAGIOUS**. AT LEAST IT'S ONLY EVER AFFECTED MEMBERS OF MY FAMILY BEFORE.

WHEREAH THEY? YOUAH FAMILY?

ALL GONE NOW, VICTIMS OF THE SAME MORTAL AFFLICTION. I'M THE LAST OF THE CORNWELLES LINE.

NO GENTLEMAN WOULD **HAVE** ME, KNOWING THAT MY CONDITION WOULD DETERIORATE UNTIL I WAS LEFT LIKE THIS.

WE HAVE THE REPUTATION OF BEING CURSED. I'M SURPRISED YOU WERE **BRAVE** ENOUGH TO VENTURE ONTO OUR LANDS. WE'RE RUMORED TO BE **HAUNTED**, DON'T YOU KNOW?

AN' THE SLAVES?

ALL RUN OFF OR SOLD **LONG** AGO. MY NAN STAYED WITH ME, OF COURSE. BRAVE AND LOYAL NAN. BUT WITH DEATH ONLY **HOURS** AWAY NOW, I SET HER FREE THIS MORNING.

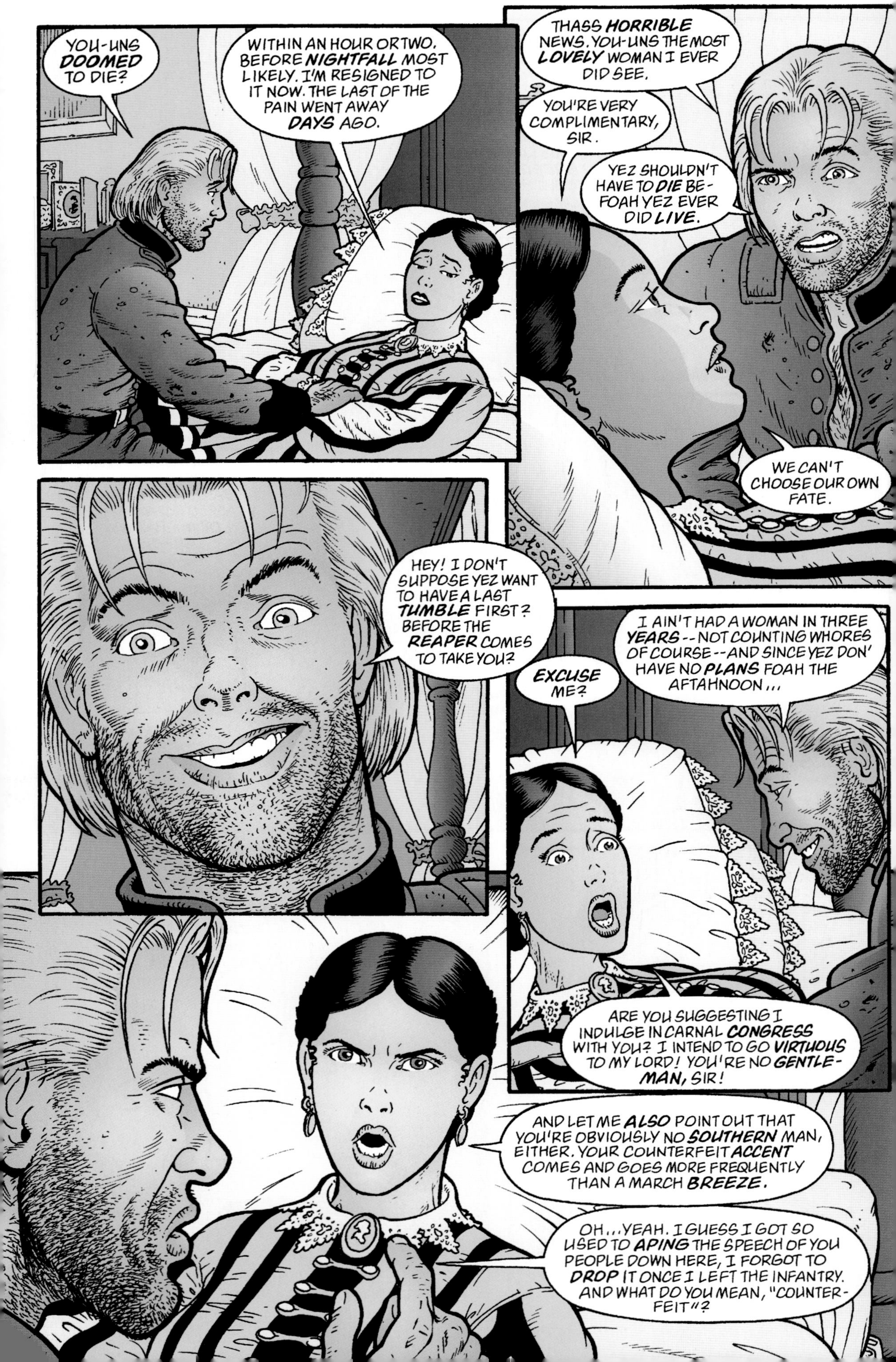
YOU-UNS DOOMED TO DIE?
WITHIN AN HOUR OR TWO. BEFORE NIGHTFALL MOST LIKELY. I'M RESIGNED TO IT NOW. THE LAST OF THE PAIN WENT AWAY DAYS AGO.
THASS HORRIBLE NEWS. YOU-UNS THE MOST LOVELY WOMAN I EVER DID SEE.
YOU'RE VERY COMPLIMENTARY, SIR.
YEZ SHOULDN'T HAVE TO DIE BE-FOAH YEZ EVER DID LIVE.
WE CAN'T CHOOSE OUR OWN FATE.
HEY! I DON'T SUPPOSE YEZ WANT TO HAVE A LAST TUMBLE FIRST? BEFORE THE REAPER COMES TO TAKE YOU?
I AIN'T HAD A WOMAN IN THREE YEARS -- NOT COUNTING WHORES OF COURSE -- AND SINCE YEZ DON' HAVE NO PLANS FOAH THE AFTAHNOON...
EXCUSE ME?
ARE YOU SUGGESTING I INDULGE IN CARNAL CONGRESS WITH YOU? I INTEND TO GO VIRTUOUS TO MY LORD! YOU'RE NO GENTLE-MAN, SIR!
AND LET ME ALSO POINT OUT THAT YOU'RE OBVIOUSLY NO SOUTHERN MAN, EITHER. YOUR COUNTERFEIT ACCENT COMES AND GOES MORE FREQUENTLY THAN A MARCH BREEZE.
OH... YEAH. I GUESS I GOT SO USED TO APING THE SPEECH OF YOU PEOPLE DOWN HERE, I FORGOT TO DROP IT ONCE I LEFT THE INFANTRY. AND WHAT DO YOU MEAN, "COUNTER-FEIT"?

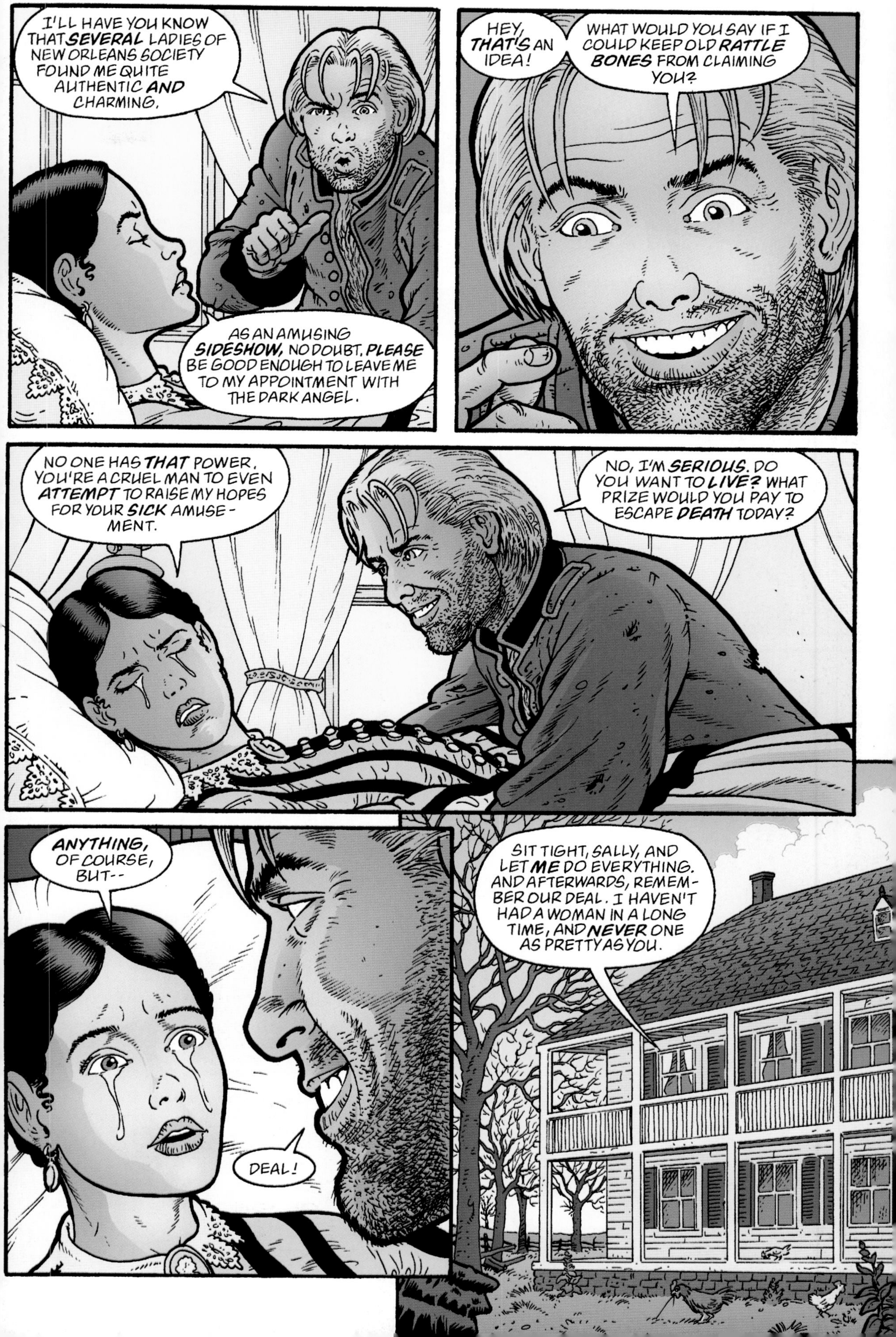
I'LL HAVE YOU KNOW THAT SEVERAL LADIES OF NEW ORLEANS SOCIETY FOUND ME QUITE AUTHENTIC AND CHARMING.
AS AN AMUSING SIDESHOW, NO DOUBT. PLEASE BE GOOD ENOUGH TO LEAVE ME TO MY APPOINTMENT WITH THE DARK ANGEL.
HEY, THAT'S AN IDEA!
WHAT WOULD YOU SAY IF I COULD KEEP OLD RATTLE BONES FROM CLAIMING YOU?
NO ONE HAS THAT POWER. YOU'RE A CRUEL MAN TO EVEN ATTEMPT TO RAISE MY HOPES FOR YOUR SICK AMUSE-MENT.
NO, I'M SERIOUS. DO YOU WANT TO LIVE? WHAT PRIZE WOULD YOU PAY TO ESCAPE DEATH TODAY?
ANYTHING, OF COURSE, BUT--
DEAL!
SIT TIGHT, SALLY, AND LET ME DO EVERYTHING. AND AFTERWARDS, REMEM-BER OUR DEAL. I HAVEN'T HAD A WOMAN IN A LONG TIME, AND NEVER ONE AS PRETTY AS YOU.

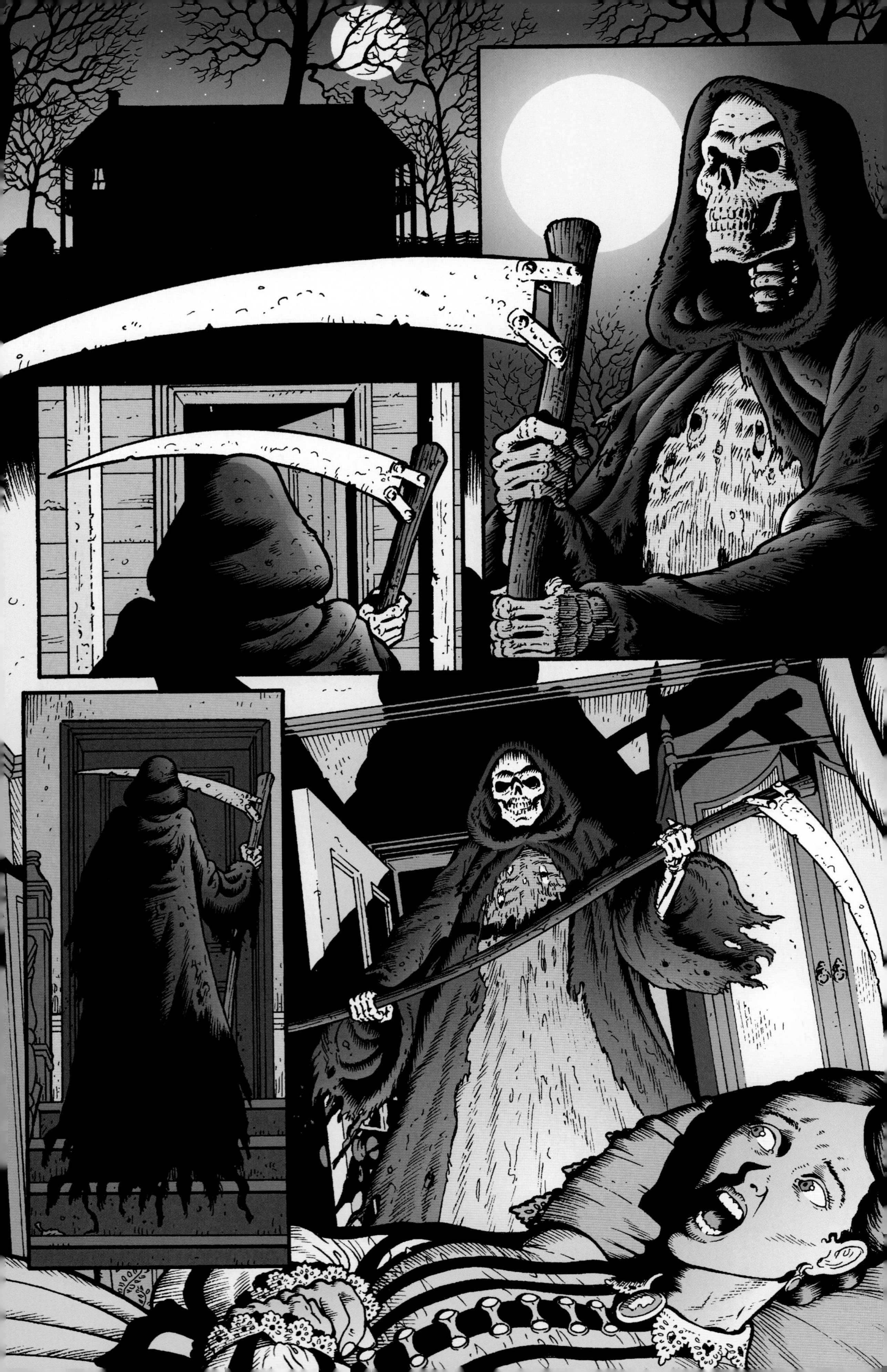

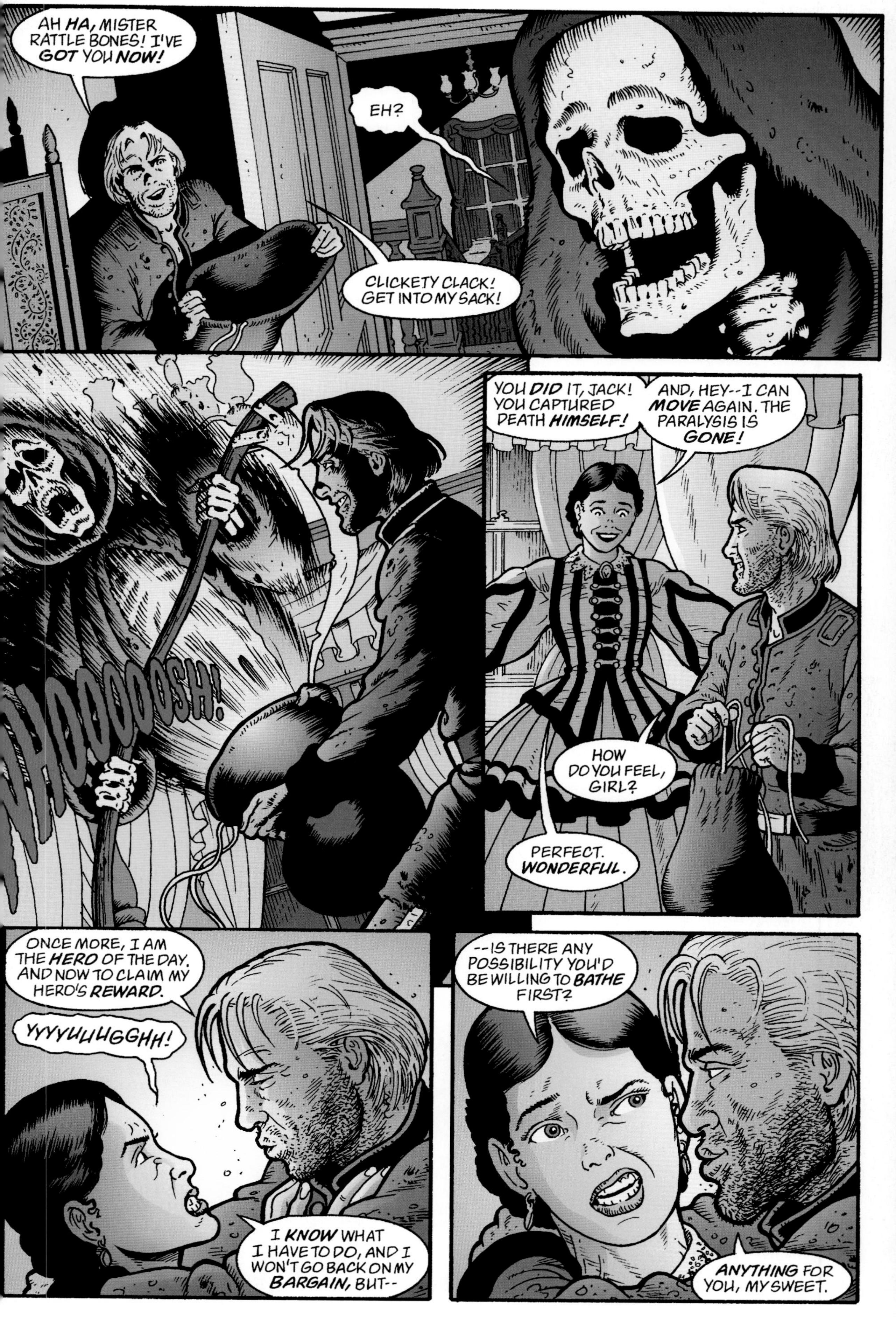

AH HA, MISTER RATTLE BONES! I'VE GOT YOU NOW!
EH?
CLICKETY CLACK! GET INTO MY SACK!
WHOOOOOSH!
YOU DID IT, JACK! YOU CAPTURED DEATH HIMSELF!
AND, HEY--I CAN MOVE AGAIN. THE PARALYSIS IS GONE!
HOW DO YOU FEEL, GIRL?
PERFECT. WONDERFUL.
ONCE MORE, I AM THE HERO OF THE DAY. AND NOW TO CLAIM MY HERO'S REWARD.
YYYYUUUGGHH!
I KNOW WHAT I HAVE TO DO, AND I WON'T GO BACK ON MY BARGAIN, BUT--
--IS THERE ANY POSSIBILITY YOU'D BE WILLING TO BATHE FIRST?
ANYTHING FOR YOU, MY SWEET.

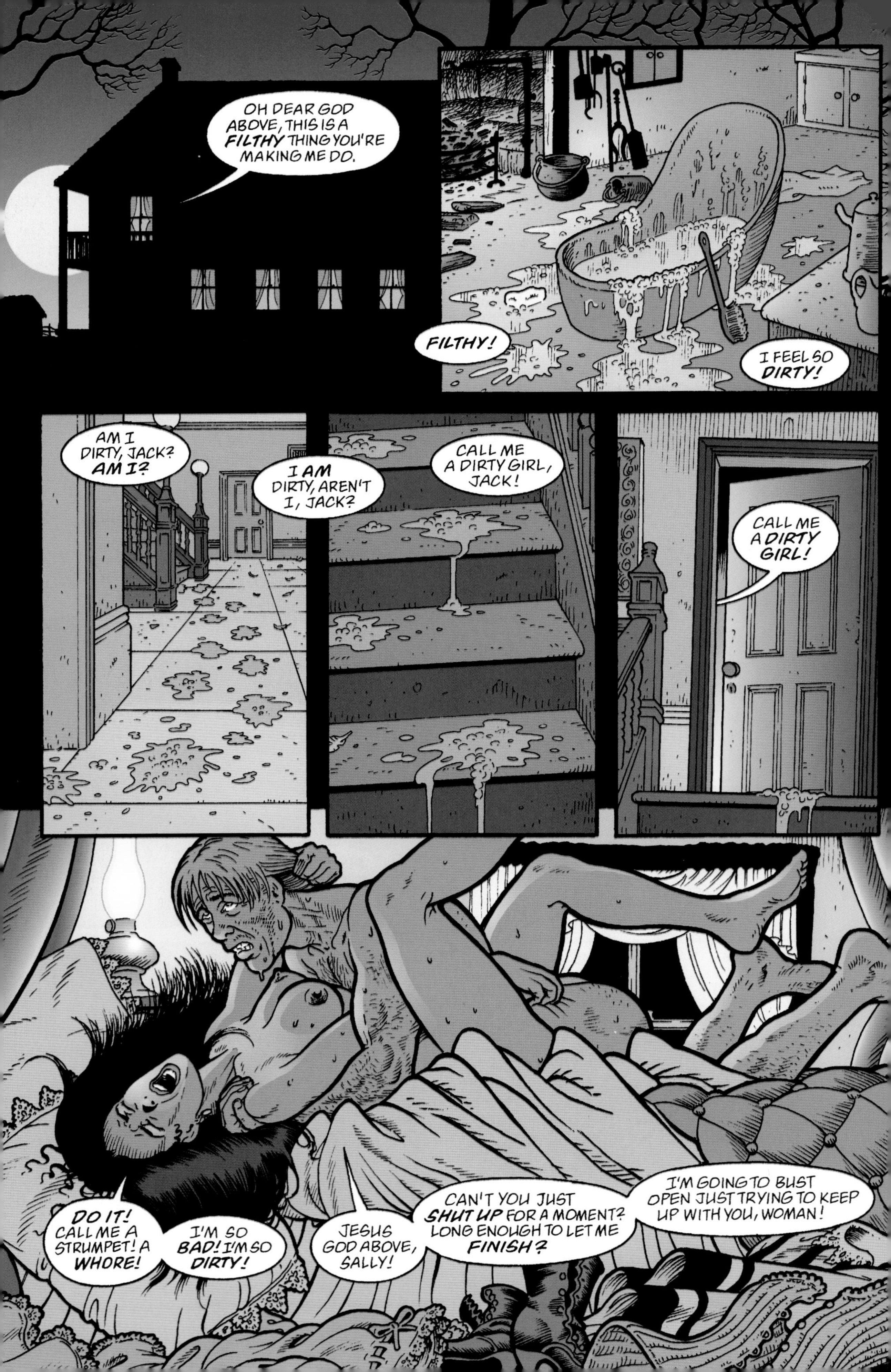
OH DEAR GOD ABOVE, THIS IS A FILTHY THING YOU'RE MAKING ME DO.
FILTHY!
I FEEL SO DIRTY!
AM I DIRTY, JACK? AM I?
I AM DIRTY, AREN'T I, JACK?
CALL ME A DIRTY GIRL, JACK!
CALL ME A DIRTY GIRL!
DO IT! CALL ME A STRUMPET! A WHORE!
I'M SO BAD! I'M SO DIRTY!
JESUS GOD ABOVE, SALLY!
CAN'T YOU JUST SHUT UP FOR A MOMENT? LONG ENOUGH TO LET ME FINISH?
I'M GOING TO BUST OPEN JUST TRYING TO KEEP UP WITH YOU, WOMAN!

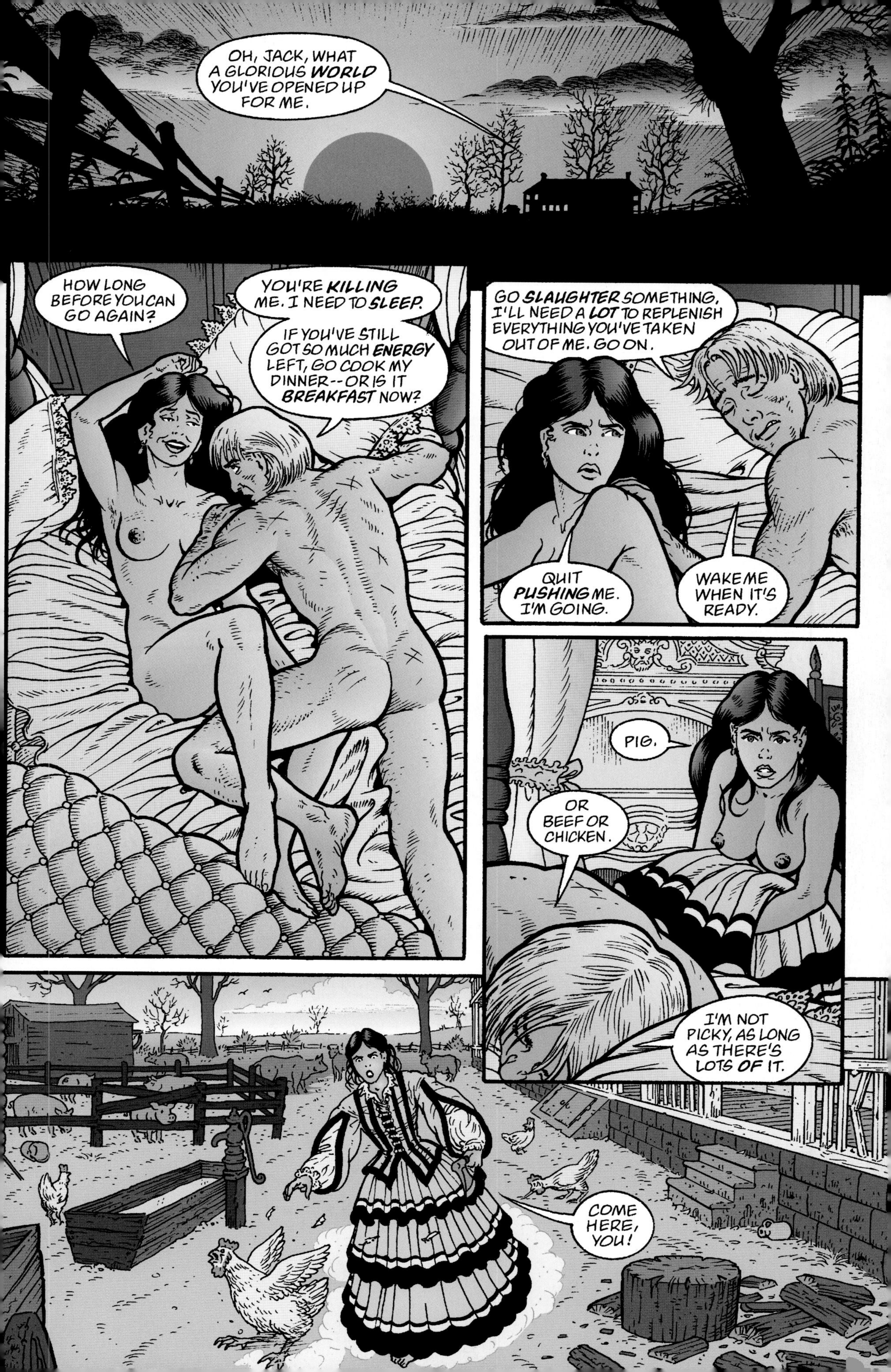
OH, JACK, WHAT A GLORIOUS WORLD YOU'VE OPENED UP FOR ME.
HOW LONG BEFORE YOU CAN GO AGAIN?
YOU'RE KILLING ME. I NEED TO SLEEP.
IF YOU'VE STILL GOT SO MUCH ENERGY LEFT, GO COOK MY DINNER--OR IS IT BREAKFAST NOW?
GO SLAUGHTER SOMETHING, I'LL NEED A LOT TO REPLENISH EVERYTHING YOU'VE TAKEN OUT OF ME. GO ON.
QUIT PUSHING ME. I'M GOING.
WAKE ME WHEN IT'S READY.
PIG.
OR BEEF OR CHICKEN.
I'M NOT PICKY, AS LONG AS THERE'S LOTS OF IT.
COME HERE, YOU!

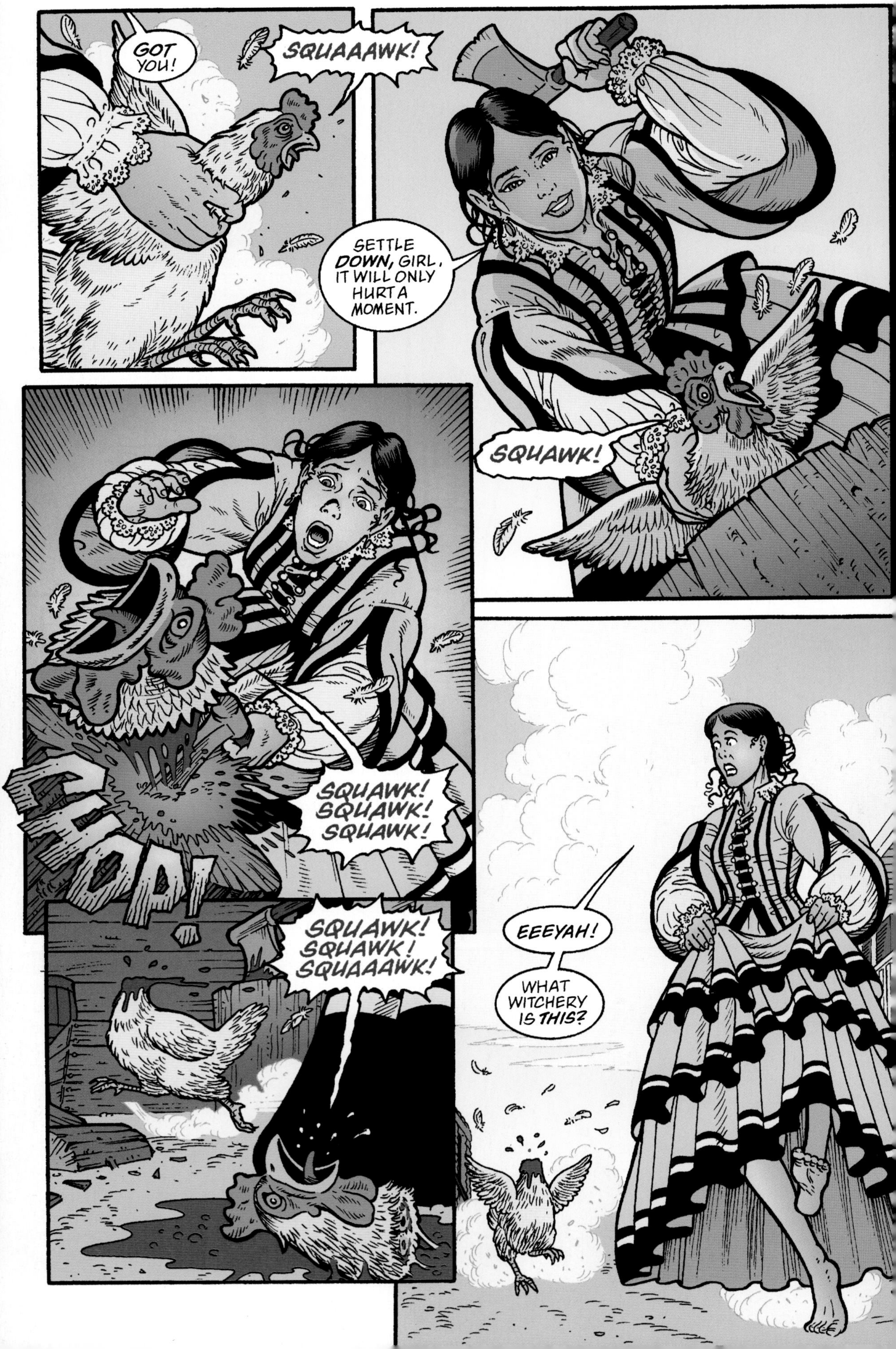
GOT YOU!
SQUAAAWK!
SETTLE DOWN, GIRL, IT WILL ONLY HURT A MOMENT.
SQUAWK!
SQUAWK! SQUAWK! SQUAWK!
SQUAWK! SQUAWK! SQUAAAWK!
EEEYAH!
WHAT WITCHERY IS THIS?

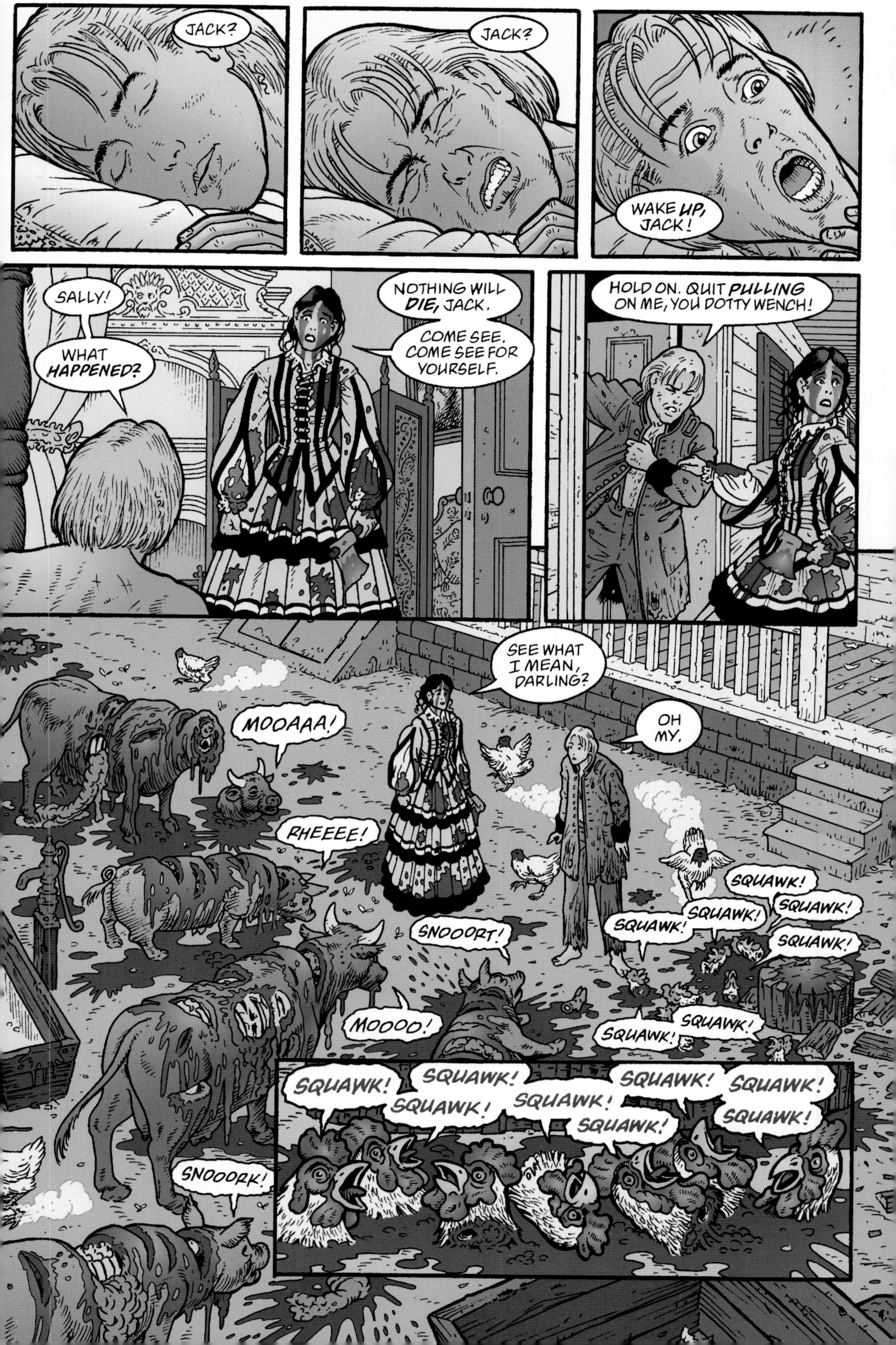
JACK?
JACK?
WAKE UP, JACK!
SALLY!
WHAT HAPPENED?
NOTHING WILL DIE, JACK.
COME SEE. COME SEE FOR YOURSELF.
HOLD ON. QUIT PULLING ON ME, YOU DOTTY WENCH!
SEE WHAT I MEAN, DARLING?
OH MY.
MOOAAA!
RHEEEE!
SNOOORT!
SQUAWK!
SQUAWK!
SQUAWK!
SQUAWK!
MOOOO!
SQUAWK!
SQUAWK!
SNOOORK!
SQUAWK!
SQUAWK!
SQUAWK!
SQUAWK!
SQUAWK!
SQUAWK!
SQUAWK!
SQUAWK!

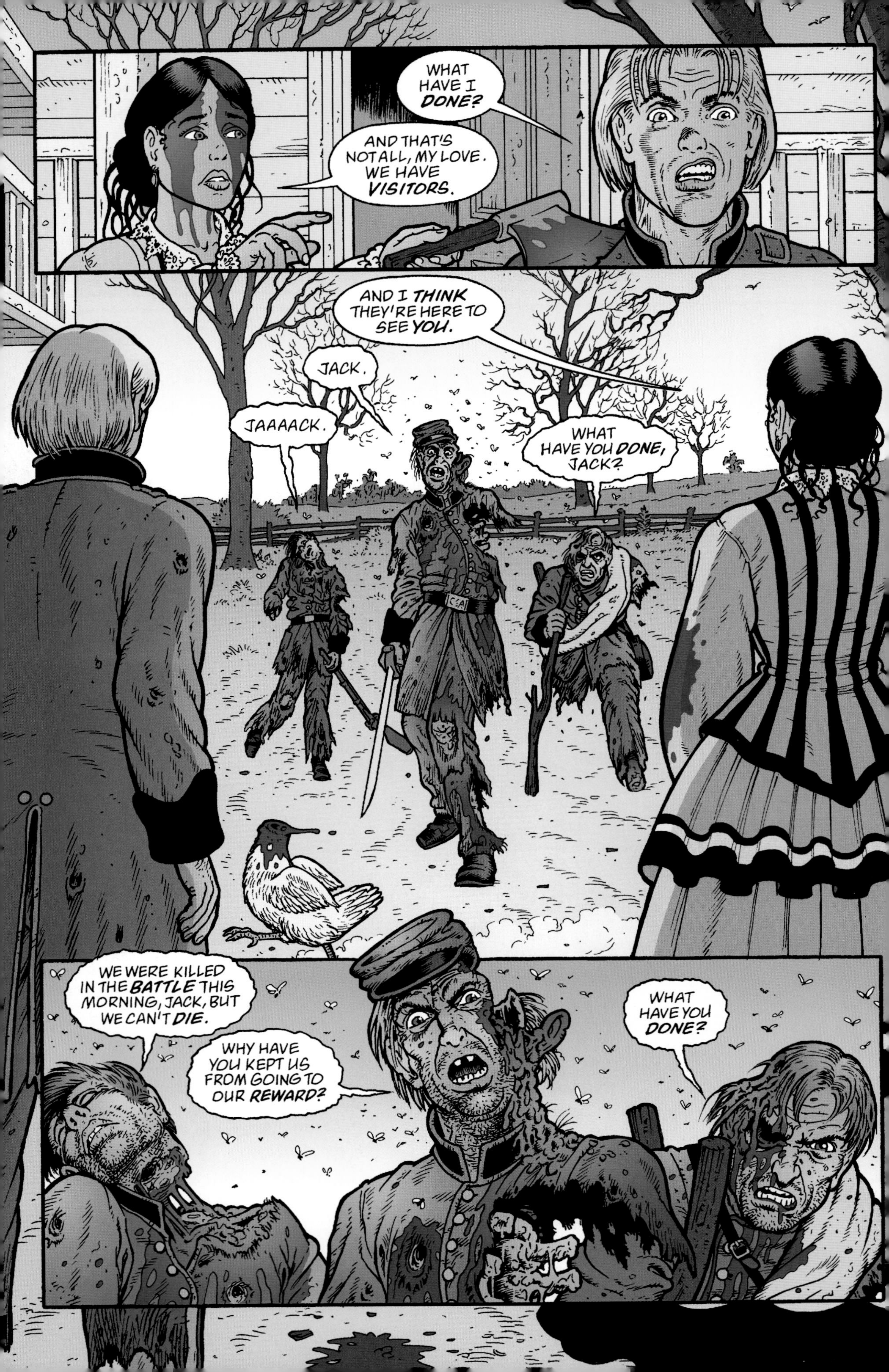
WHAT HAVE I DONE?
AND THAT'S NOT ALL, MY LOVE. WE HAVE VISITORS.
AND I THINK THEY'RE HERE TO SEE YOU.
JACK.
JAAAACK.
WHAT HAVE YOU DONE, JACK?
WE WERE KILLED IN THE BATTLE THIS MORNING, JACK, BUT WE CAN'T DIE.
WHY HAVE YOU KEPT US FROM GOING TO OUR REWARD?
WHAT HAVE YOU DONE?

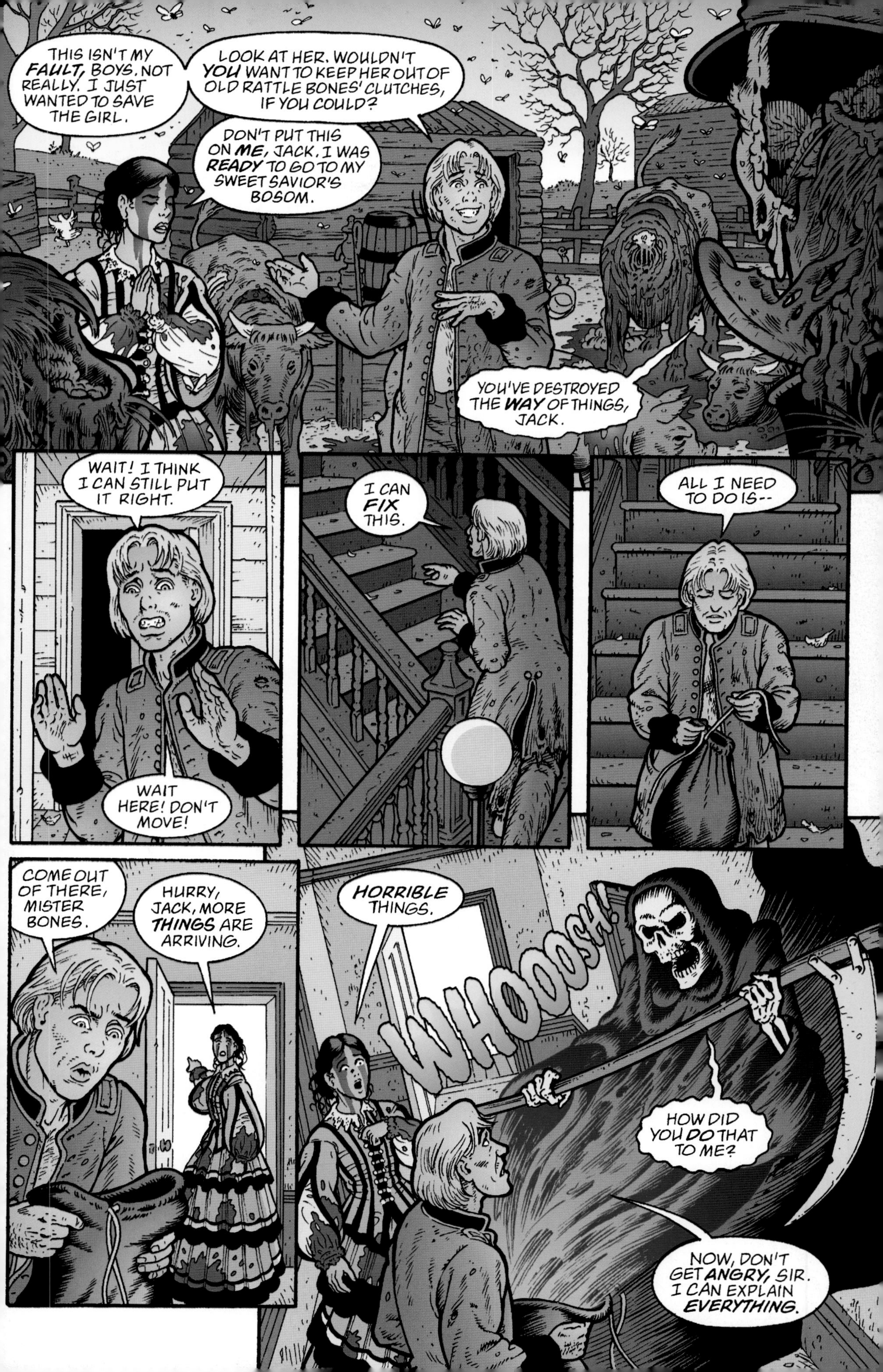
THIS ISN'T MY FAULT, BOYS. NOT REALLY. I JUST WANTED TO SAVE THE GIRL.
LOOK AT HER. WOULDN'T YOU WANT TO KEEP HER OUT OF OLD RATTLE BONES' CLUTCHES, IF YOU COULD?
DON'T PUT THIS ON ME, JACK. I WAS READY TO GO TO MY SWEET SAVIOR'S BOSOM.
YOU'VE DESTROYED THE WAY OF THINGS, JACK.
WAIT! I THINK I CAN STILL PUT IT RIGHT.
WAIT HERE! DON'T MOVE!
I CAN FIX THIS.
ALL I NEED TO DO IS--
COME OUT OF THERE, MISTER BONES.
HURRY, JACK, MORE THINGS ARE ARRIVING.
HORRIBLE THINGS.
WHOOOSH!
HOW DID YOU DO THAT TO ME?
NOW, DON'T GET ANGRY, SIR. I CAN EXPLAIN EVERYTHING.

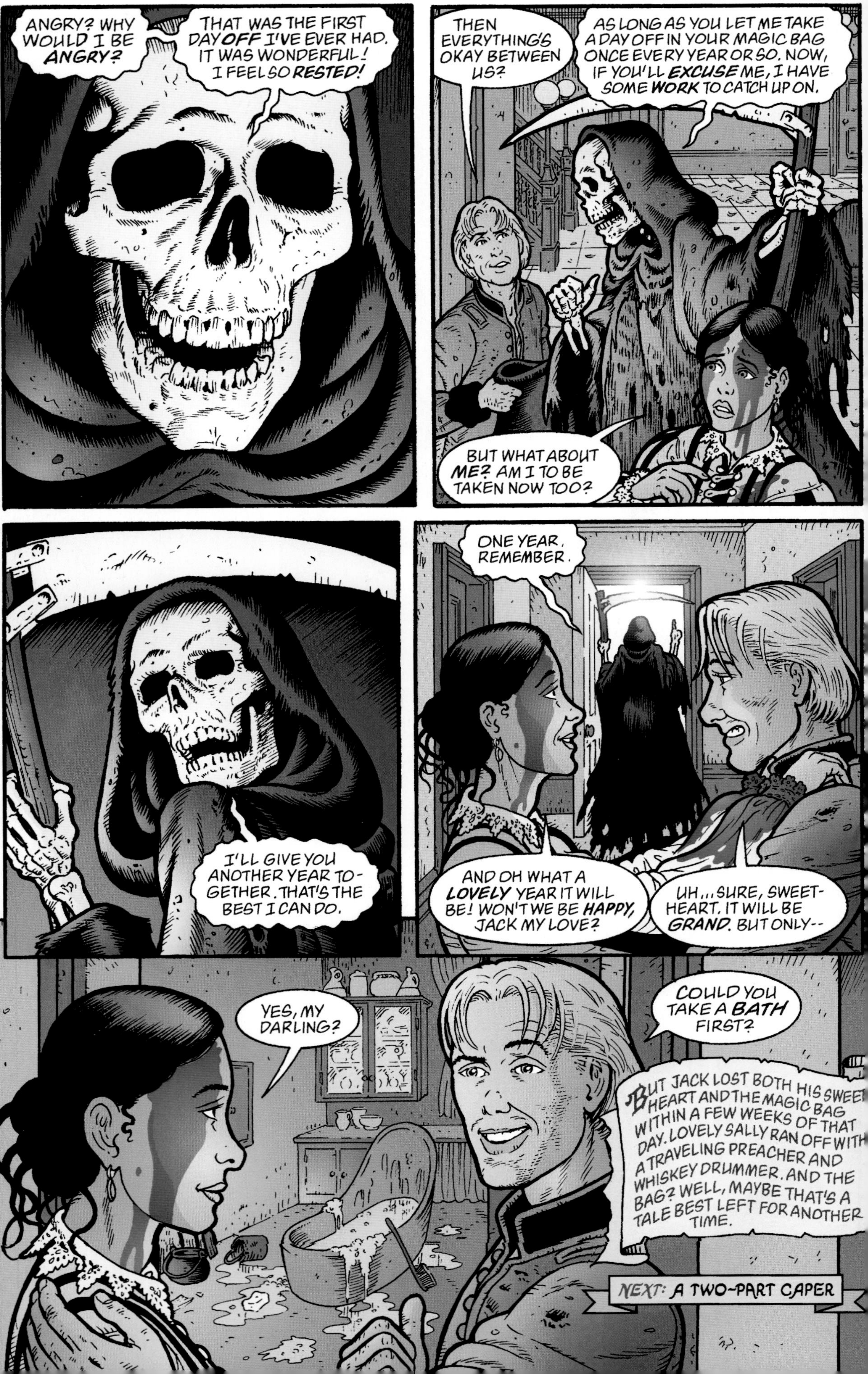
ANGRY? WHY WOULD I BE ANGRY?
THAT WAS THE FIRST DAY OFF I'VE EVER HAD. IT WAS WONDERFUL! I FEEL SO RESTED!
THEN EVERYTHING'S OKAY BETWEEN US?
AS LONG AS YOU LET ME TAKE A DAY OFF IN YOUR MAGIC BAG ONCE EVERY YEAR OR SO. NOW, IF YOU'LL EXCUSE ME, I HAVE SOME WORK TO CATCH UP ON.
BUT WHAT ABOUT ME? AM I TO BE TAKEN NOW TOO?
I'LL GIVE YOU ANOTHER YEAR TOGETHER. THAT'S THE BEST I CAN DO.
ONE YEAR. REMEMBER.
AND OH WHAT A LOVELY YEAR IT WILL BE! WON'T WE BE HAPPY, JACK MY LOVE?
UH... SURE, SWEETHEART. IT WILL BE GRAND. BUT ONLY--
YES, MY DARLING?
COULD YOU TAKE A BATH FIRST?
BUT JACK LOST BOTH HIS SWEETHEART AND THE MAGIC BAG WITHIN A FEW WEEKS OF THAT DAY. LOVELY SALLY RAN OFF WITH A TRAVELING PREACHER AND WHISKEY DRUMMER. AND THE BAG? WELL, MAYBE THAT'S A TALE BEST LEFT FOR ANOTHER TIME.
NEXT: A TWO-PART CAPER

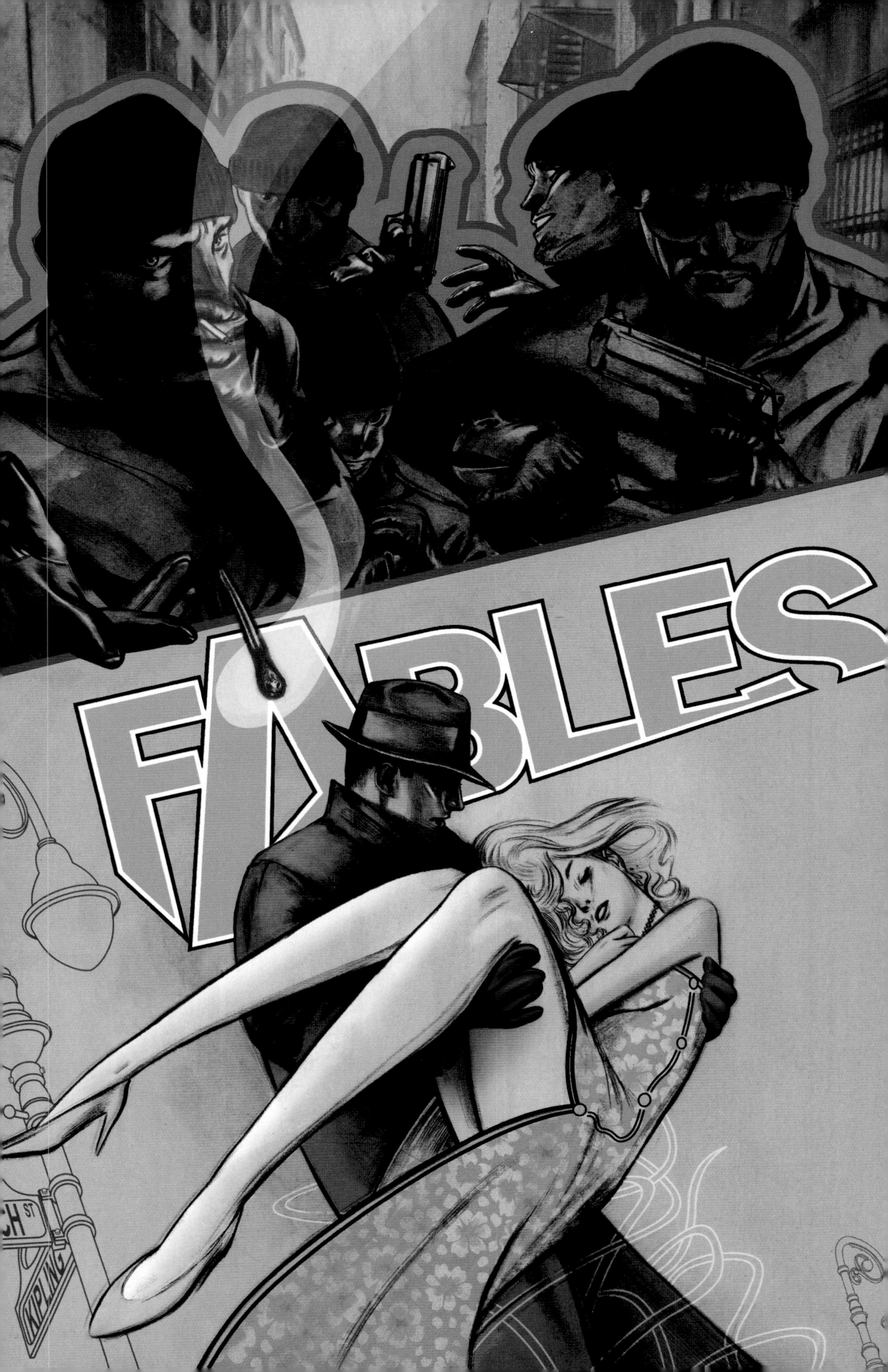
FABLES
CH ST
KIPLING

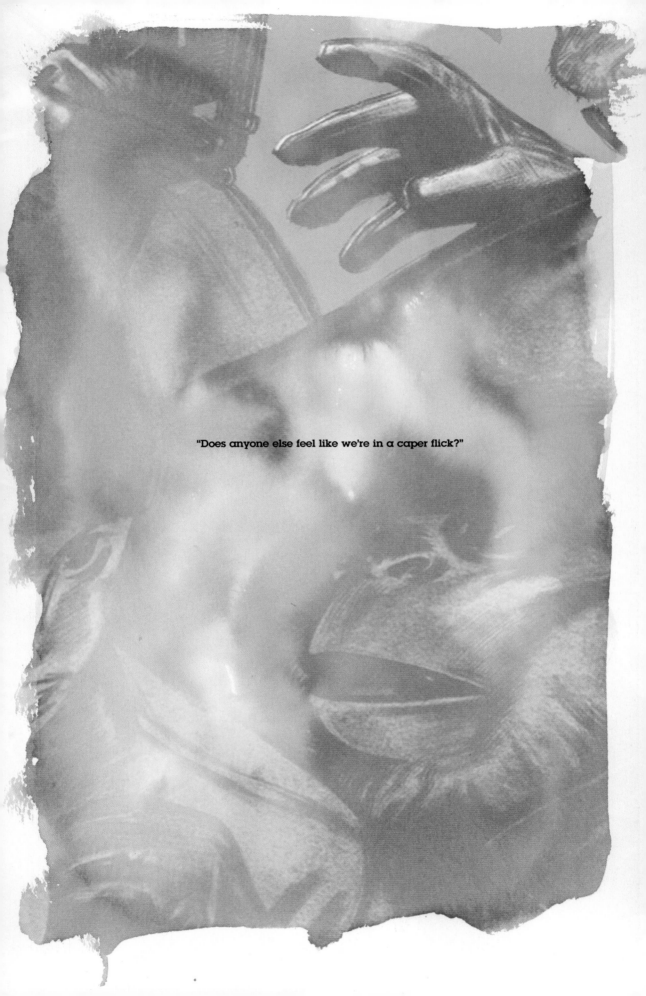

"Does anyone else feel like we're in a caper flick?"

HERE'S A NASTY LITTLE WINTER'S TALE...

THIS IS SERIOUS, BRIAR ROSE.

YOU FELL ASLEEP AGAIN, IN THE MIDDLE OF TIFFANY'S.

I COULDN'T *HELP* IT, BIGBY.

I PRICKED MY FINGER ON A DIAMOND PIN AT THE JEWELRY COUNTER.

CAUSING THE ENTIRE *SALES* FLOOR TO FALL ASLEEP *WITH* YOU?

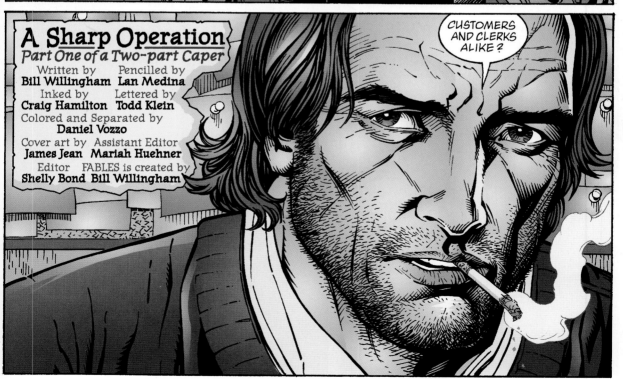

A Sharp Operation
Part One of a Two-part Caper

Written by — Bill Willingham
Pencilled by — Lan Medina
Inked by — Craig Hamilton
Lettered by — Todd Klein
Colored and Separated by — Daniel Vozzo
Cover art by — James Jean
Assistant Editor — Mariah Huehner
Editor — Shelly Bond
FABLES is created by Bill Willingham

CUSTOMERS AND CLERKS ALIKE?

UNFORTUNATELY THAT'S THE WAY THE OLD ENCHANTMENT **WORKS.** FIRST I PRICK MY FINGER ON SOMETHING AND FALL ASLEEP, THEN EVERYONE AROUND ME FALLS ASLEEP, AND THEN THE THORN FOREST STARTS GROWING AROUND WHATEVER **BUILDING** I HAPPEN TO BE IN.

WE GOT **LUCKY** THIS TIME. THEY THINK SOME KIND OF **GAS** LEAK CAUSED IT, BUT WE **CAN'T** HAVE INCIDENTS LIKE THIS. NOT OUT AMONG THE BLOODY **MUNDYS.**

I DON'T THINK THE ENCHANTMENT **CARES** WHERE I AM, OR AMONGST **WHOM.**

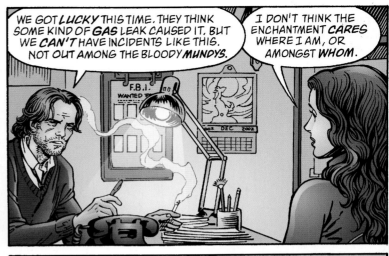

I THOUGHT IT WAS ENDED FOR ALL TIME BACK IN THE HOME- LANDS, WHEN PRINCE CHARMING **KISSED** ME -- BUT APPARENTLY ALL **THAT** DOES IS RESET THE SPELL TO ITS STARTING POSITION.

IT'S AN ENDLESS CYCLE.

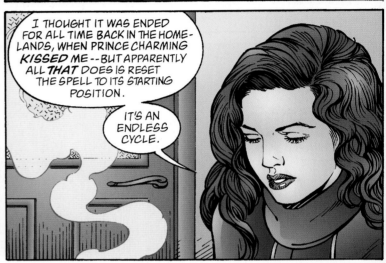

THEN YOU'RE JUST GOING TO HAVE TO **STOP** PRICK- ING YOUR FINGERS. YOU'RE STILL WEALTHY ENOUGH. GET SOME WORKMEN TO GO THROUGH YOUR APART- MENT AND REMOVE ALL THE ROUGH EDGES AND SHARP CORNERS.

AND WHEN YOU GO OUT, WEAR GLOVES. **THICK** ONES.

THAT MIGHT WORK WHILE WINTER LASTS, BUT NOT WHEN SPRING COMES.

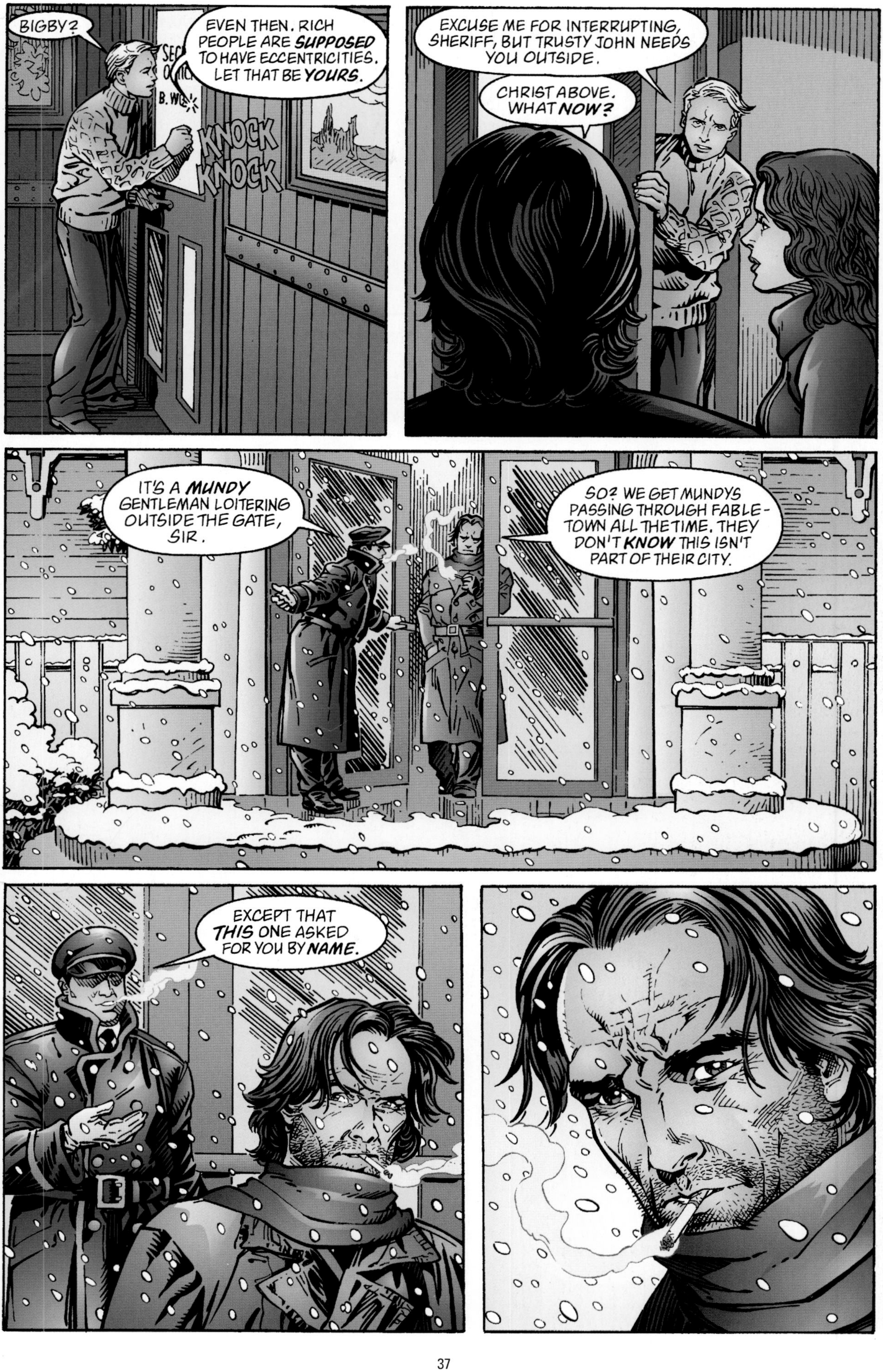
BIGBY?
EVEN THEN. RICH PEOPLE ARE SUPPOSED TO HAVE ECCENTRICITIES. LET THAT BE YOURS.
B. WO
KNOCK KNOCK
EXCUSE ME FOR INTERRUPTING, SHERIFF, BUT TRUSTY JOHN NEEDS YOU OUTSIDE.
CHRIST ABOVE. WHAT NOW?
IT'S A MUNDY GENTLEMAN LOITERING OUTSIDE THE GATE, SIR.
SO? WE GET MUNDYS PASSING THROUGH FABLE-TOWN ALL THE TIME. THEY DON'T KNOW THIS ISN'T PART OF THEIR CITY.
EXCEPT THAT THIS ONE ASKED FOR YOU BY NAME.

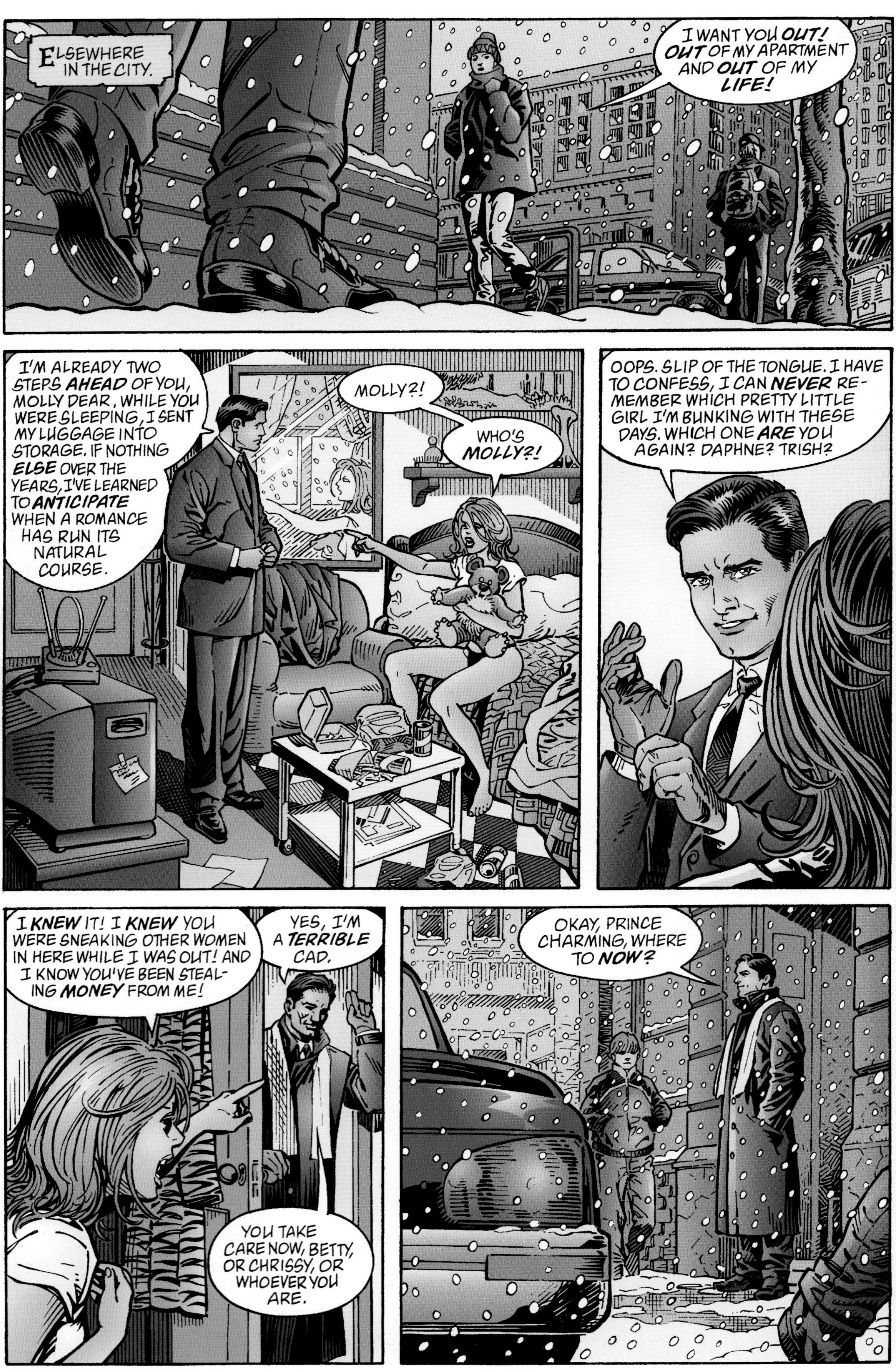
ELSEWHERE IN THE CITY.
I WANT YOU OUT! OUT OF MY APARTMENT AND OUT OF MY LIFE!
I'M ALREADY TWO STEPS AHEAD OF YOU, MOLLY DEAR, WHILE YOU WERE SLEEPING, I SENT MY LUGGAGE INTO STORAGE. IF NOTHING ELSE OVER THE YEARS, I'VE LEARNED TO ANTICIPATE WHEN A ROMANCE HAS RUN ITS NATURAL COURSE.
MOLLY?!
WHO'S MOLLY?!
OOPS. SLIP OF THE TONGUE. I HAVE TO CONFESS, I CAN NEVER RE-MEMBER WHICH PRETTY LITTLE GIRL I'M BUNKING WITH THESE DAYS. WHICH ONE ARE YOU AGAIN? DAPHNE? TRISH?
I KNEW IT! I KNEW YOU WERE SNEAKING OTHER WOMEN IN HERE WHILE I WAS OUT! AND I KNOW YOU'VE BEEN STEAL-ING MONEY FROM ME!
YES, I'M A TERRIBLE CAD.
YOU TAKE CARE NOW, BETTY, OR CHRISSY, OR WHOEVER YOU ARE.
OKAY, PRINCE CHARMING, WHERE TO NOW?

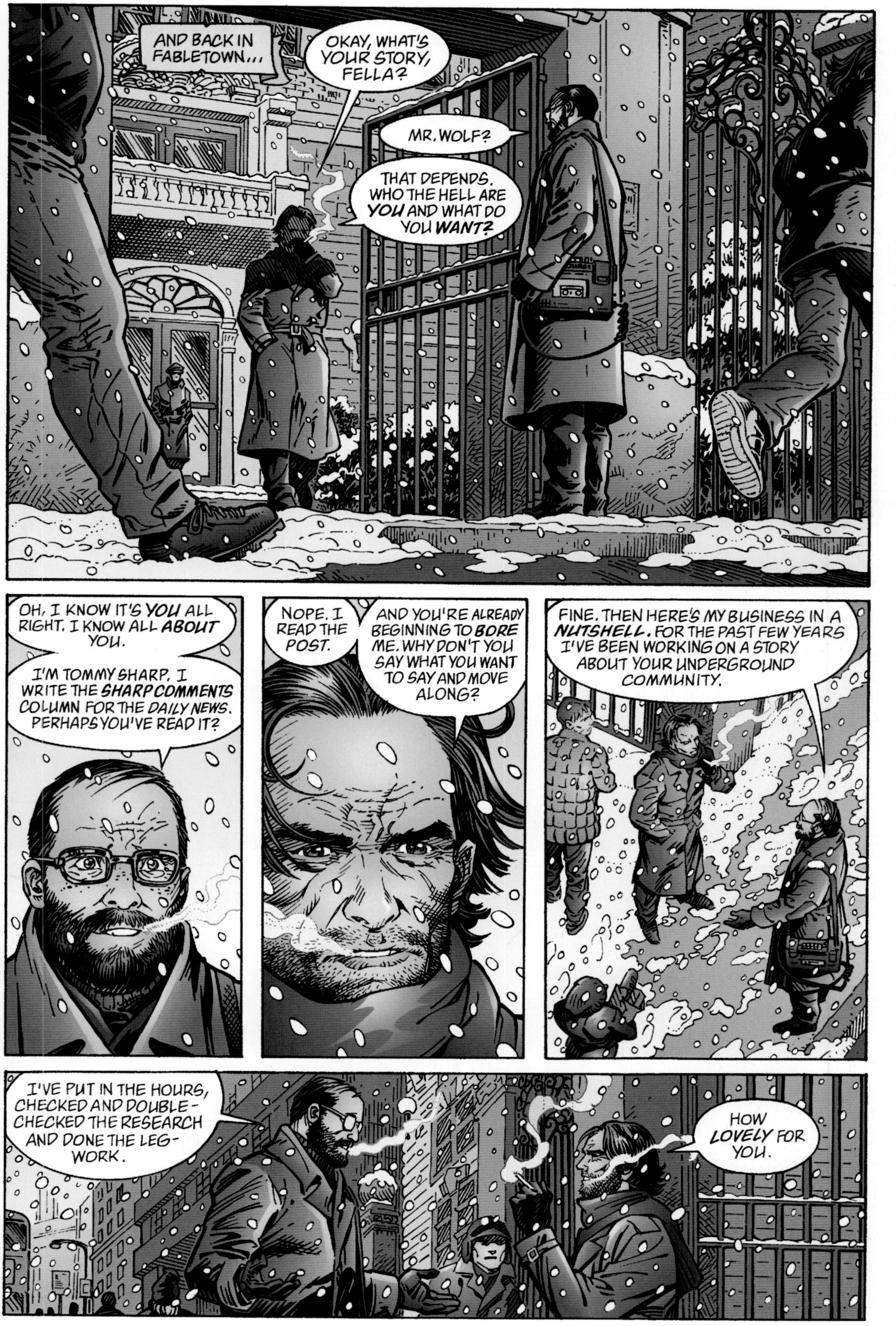
AND BACK IN FABLETOWN...
OKAY, WHAT'S YOUR STORY, FELLA?
MR. WOLF?
THAT DEPENDS. WHO THE HELL ARE YOU AND WHAT DO YOU WANT?
OH, I KNOW IT'S YOU ALL RIGHT. I KNOW ALL ABOUT YOU.
I'M TOMMY SHARP. I WRITE THE SHARP COMMENTS COLUMN FOR THE DAILY NEWS. PERHAPS YOU'VE READ IT?
NOPE. I READ THE POST.
AND YOU'RE ALREADY BEGINNING TO BORE ME. WHY DON'T YOU SAY WHAT YOU WANT TO SAY AND MOVE ALONG?
FINE. THEN HERE'S MY BUSINESS IN A NUTSHELL. FOR THE PAST FEW YEARS I'VE BEEN WORKING ON A STORY ABOUT YOUR UNDERGROUND COMMUNITY.
I'VE PUT IN THE HOURS, CHECKED AND DOUBLE-CHECKED THE RESEARCH AND DONE THE LEG-WORK.
HOW LOVELY FOR YOU.

I KNOW ALL YOUR **SECRETS.**

THEN YOU'RE WAY AHEAD OF ME.

AND, AS A JOURNAL-ISTIC **COURTESY,** I'VE DECIDED TO FINALLY **REVEAL** MYSELF--COME OUT OF THE SHADOWS, SO TO SPEAK--

--IN ORDER TO GIVE YOU AN OPPORTUNITY TO RESPOND, BEFORE I **PRINT** MY STORY.

RESPOND TO **WHAT?** SO FAR YOU'VE ONLY BABBLED **NONSENSE.**

TAKE THAT **EVASIVE** TACK IF YOU LIKE, BUT I KNOW WHAT I **KNOW.**

GET THAT THING OUT FROM UNDER MY NOSE.

YOU'RE A COMMUNITY OF **IMMORTALS**-- PROBABLY.

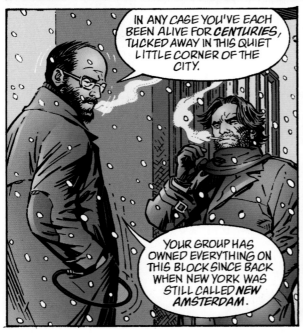

IN ANY CASE YOU'VE EACH BEEN ALIVE FOR **CENTURIES,** TUCKED AWAY IN THIS QUIET LITTLE CORNER OF THE CITY.

YOUR GROUP HAS OWNED EVERYTHING ON THIS BLOCK SINCE BACK WHEN NEW YORK WAS STILL CALLED **NEW AMSTERDAM.**

I'VE GOT **RECORDS.** I'VE COMPILED PERSONAL **HISTORIES.** I'VE DUG UP PICTURES OF A NUMBER OF YOU--DATING BACK TO THE VERY BEGINNINGS OF PHOTOGRAPHIC TECHNOLOGY--AND NOT A **ONE** OF YOU HAS AGED A **DAY.**

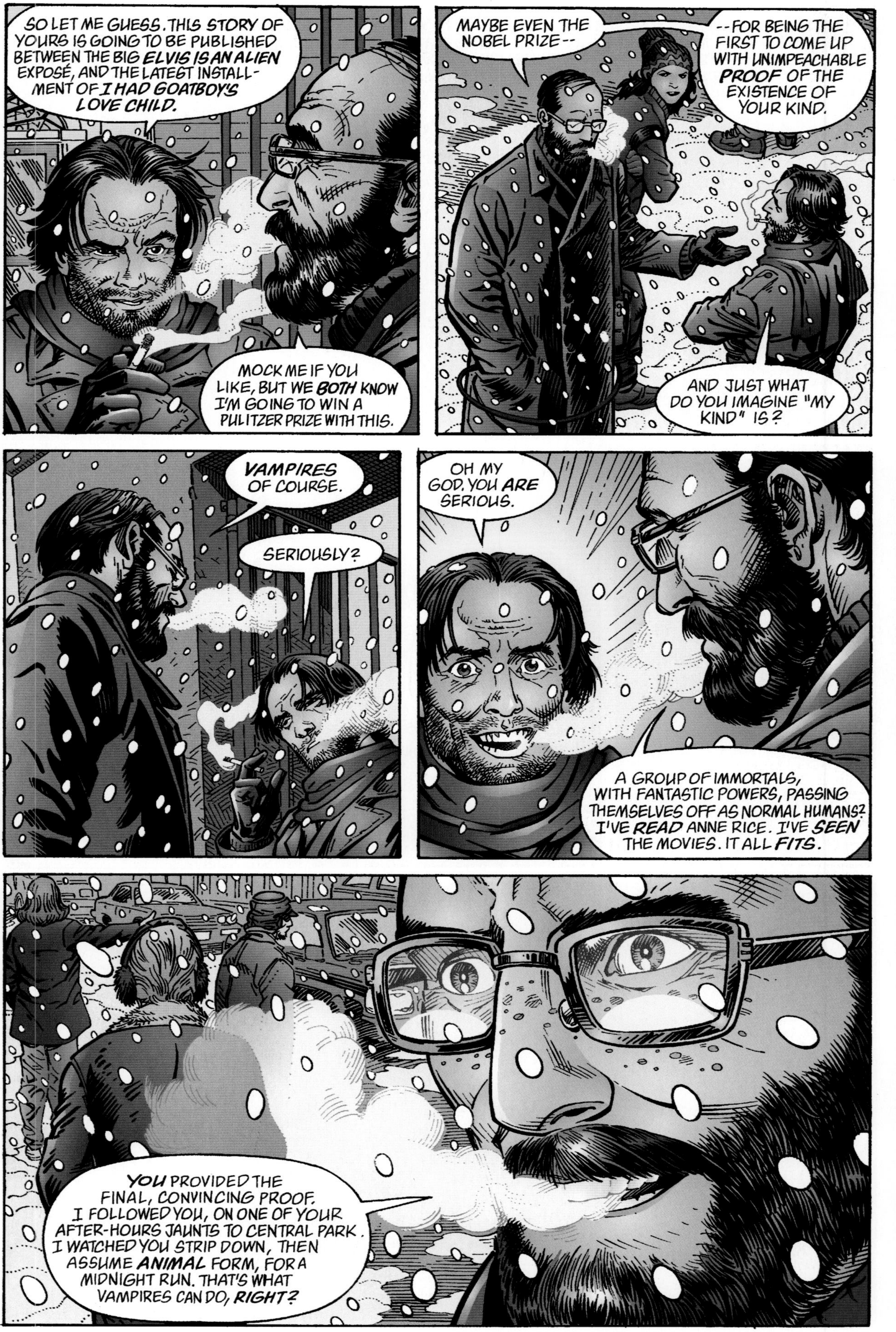
SO LET ME GUESS. THIS STORY OF YOURS IS GOING TO BE PUBLISHED BETWEEN THE BIG ELVIS IS AN ALIEN EXPOSÉ, AND THE LATEST INSTALLMENT OF I HAD GOATBOY'S LOVE CHILD.
MOCK ME IF YOU LIKE, BUT WE BOTH KNOW I'M GOING TO WIN A PULITZER PRIZE WITH THIS.
MAYBE EVEN THE NOBEL PRIZE --
-- FOR BEING THE FIRST TO COME UP WITH UNIMPEACHABLE PROOF OF THE EXISTENCE OF YOUR KIND.
AND JUST WHAT DO YOU IMAGINE "MY KIND" IS?
VAMPIRES OF COURSE.
SERIOUSLY?
OH MY GOD. YOU ARE SERIOUS.
A GROUP OF IMMORTALS, WITH FANTASTIC POWERS, PASSING THEMSELVES OFF AS NORMAL HUMANS? I'VE READ ANNE RICE. I'VE SEEN THE MOVIES. IT ALL FITS.
YOU PROVIDED THE FINAL, CONVINCING PROOF. I FOLLOWED YOU, ON ONE OF YOUR AFTER-HOURS JAUNTS TO CENTRAL PARK. I WATCHED YOU STRIP DOWN, THEN ASSUME ANIMAL FORM, FOR A MIDNIGHT RUN. THAT'S WHAT VAMPIRES CAN DO, RIGHT?

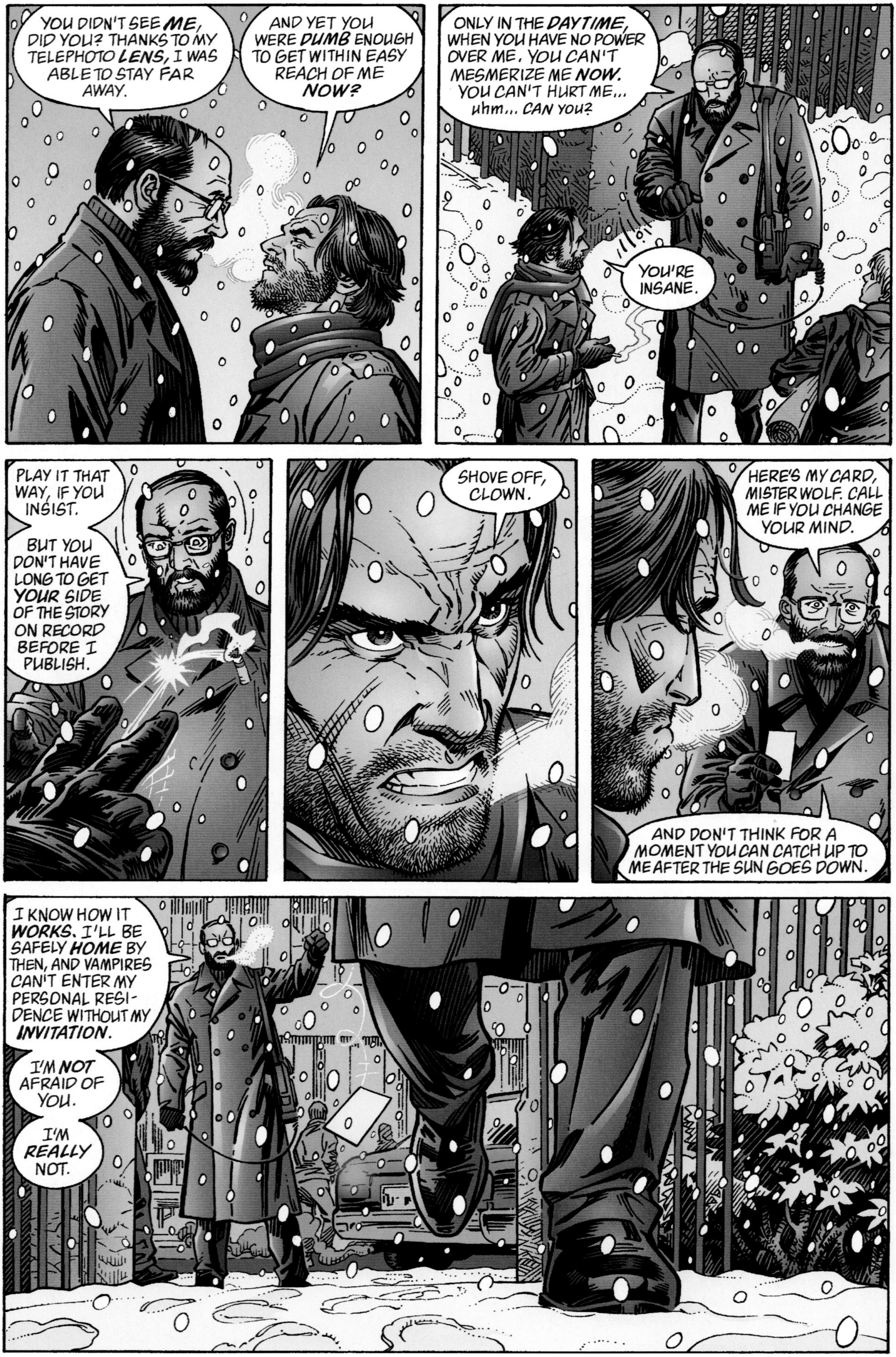
YOU DIDN'T SEE ME, DID YOU? THANKS TO MY TELEPHOTO LENS, I WAS ABLE TO STAY FAR AWAY.
AND YET YOU WERE DUMB ENOUGH TO GET WITHIN EASY REACH OF ME NOW?
ONLY IN THE DAYTIME, WHEN YOU HAVE NO POWER OVER ME. YOU CAN'T MESMERIZE ME NOW. YOU CAN'T HURT ME... uhm... CAN YOU?
YOU'RE INSANE.
PLAY IT THAT WAY, IF YOU INSIST.
BUT YOU DON'T HAVE LONG TO GET YOUR SIDE OF THE STORY ON RECORD BEFORE I PUBLISH.
SHOVE OFF, CLOWN.
HERE'S MY CARD, MISTER WOLF. CALL ME IF YOU CHANGE YOUR MIND.
AND DON'T THINK FOR A MOMENT YOU CAN CATCH UP TO ME AFTER THE SUN GOES DOWN.
I KNOW HOW IT WORKS. I'LL BE SAFELY HOME BY THEN, AND VAMPIRES CAN'T ENTER MY PERSONAL RESIDENCE WITHOUT MY INVITATION.
I'M NOT AFRAID OF YOU.
I'M REALLY NOT.

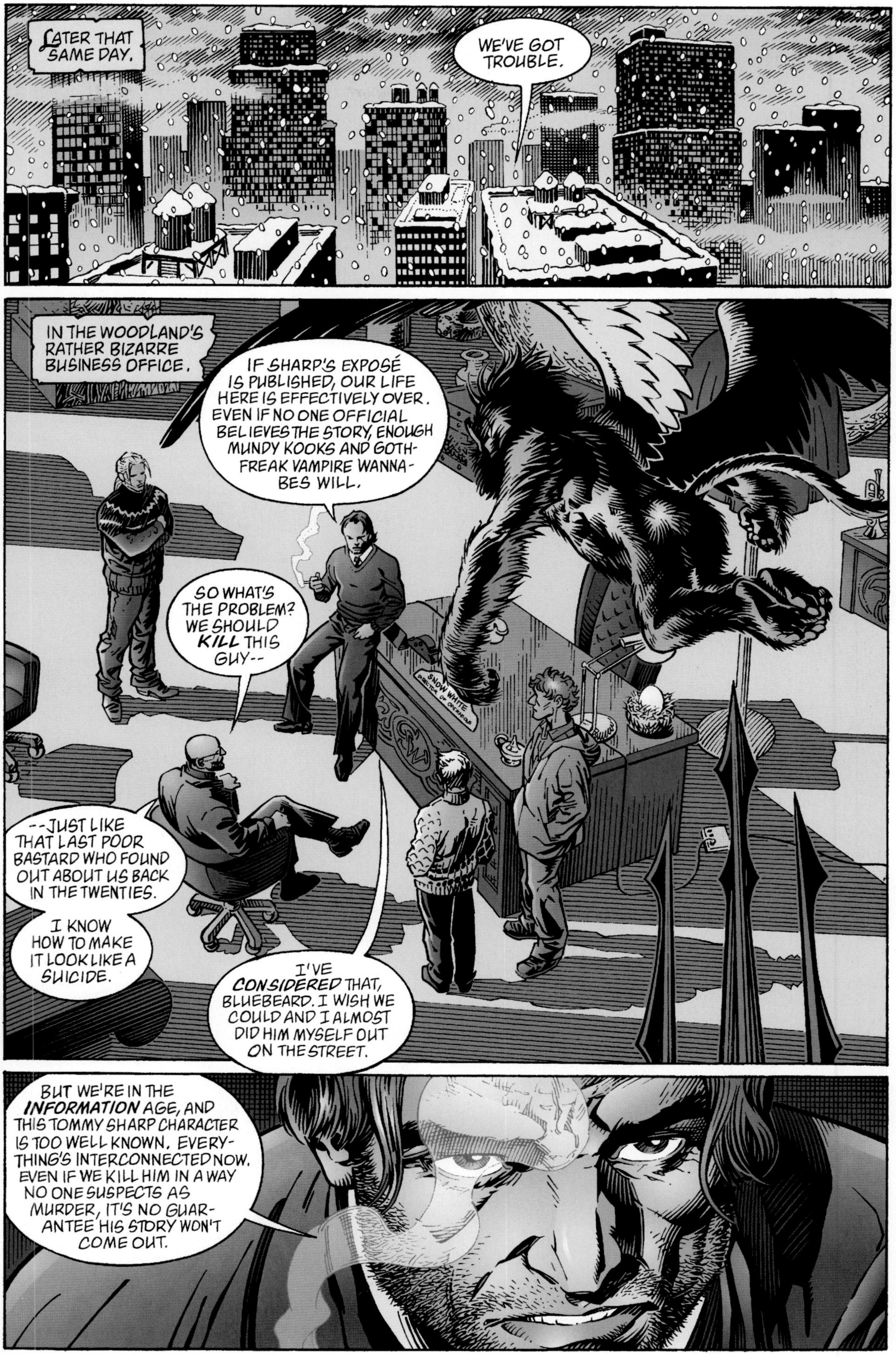
LATER THAT SAME DAY.
WE'VE GOT TROUBLE.
IN THE WOODLAND'S RATHER BIZARRE BUSINESS OFFICE.
IF SHARP'S EXPOSÉ IS PUBLISHED, OUR LIFE HERE IS EFFECTIVELY OVER. EVEN IF NO ONE OFFICIAL BELIEVES THE STORY, ENOUGH MUNDY KOOKS AND GOTH-FREAK VAMPIRE WANNA-BES WILL.
SO WHAT'S THE PROBLEM? WE SHOULD KILL THIS GUY--
SNOW WHITE
--JUST LIKE THAT LAST POOR BASTARD WHO FOUND OUT ABOUT US BACK IN THE TWENTIES.
I KNOW HOW TO MAKE IT LOOK LIKE A SUICIDE.
I'VE CONSIDERED THAT, BLUEBEARD. I WISH WE COULD AND I ALMOST DID HIM MYSELF OUT ON THE STREET.
BUT WE'RE IN THE INFORMATION AGE, AND THIS TOMMY SHARP CHARACTER IS TOO WELL KNOWN. EVERY-THING'S INTERCONNECTED NOW. EVEN IF WE KILL HIM IN A WAY NO ONE SUSPECTS AS MURDER, IT'S NO GUAR-ANTEE HIS STORY WON'T COME OUT.

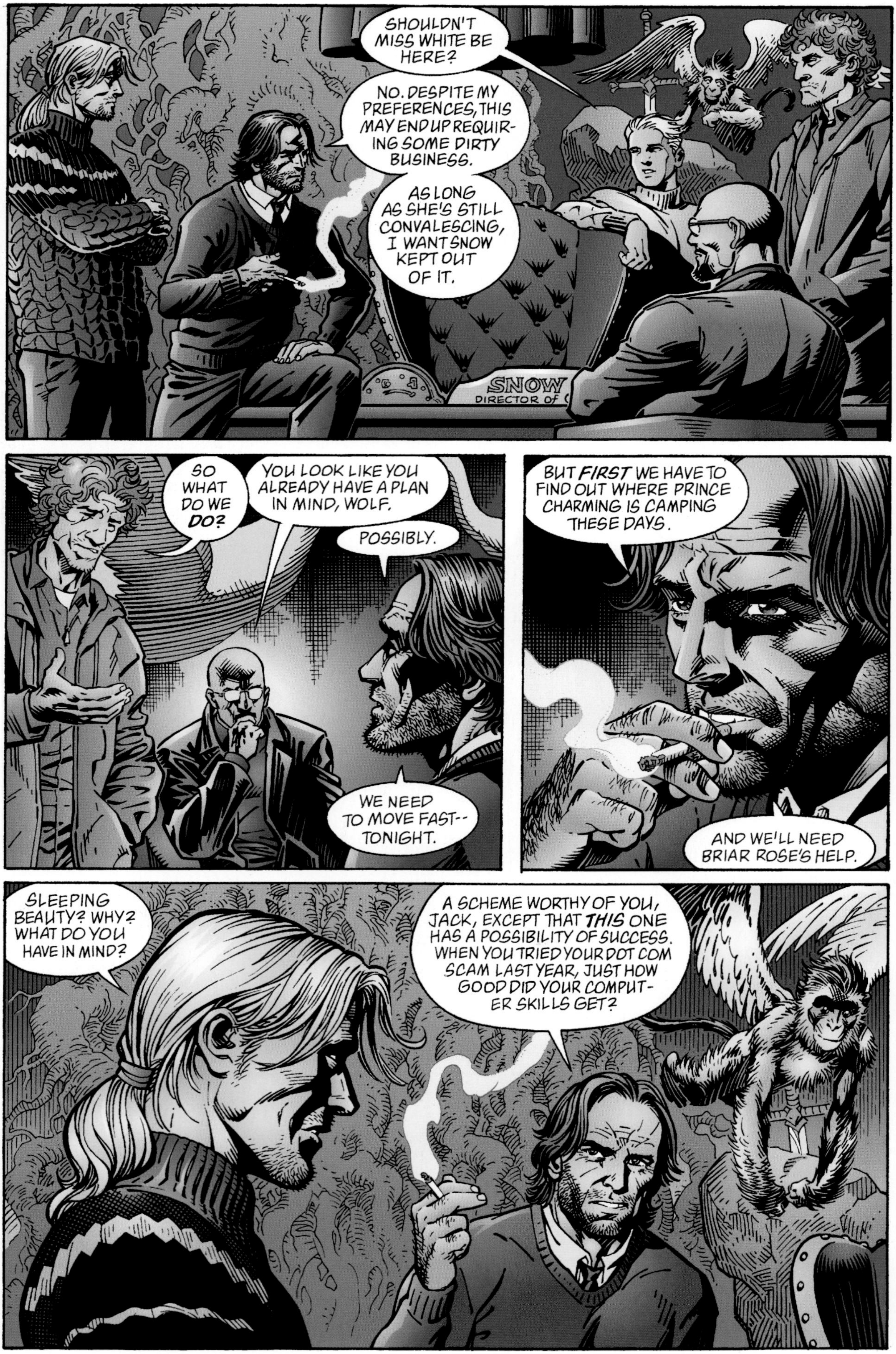
SHOULDN'T MISS WHITE BE HERE?
NO. DESPITE MY PREFERENCES, THIS MAY END UP REQUIRING SOME DIRTY BUSINESS.
AS LONG AS SHE'S STILL CONVALESCING, I WANT SNOW KEPT OUT OF IT.
SNOW
DIRECTOR OF
SO WHAT DO WE DO?
YOU LOOK LIKE YOU ALREADY HAVE A PLAN IN MIND, WOLF.
POSSIBLY.
WE NEED TO MOVE FAST-- TONIGHT.
BUT FIRST WE HAVE TO FIND OUT WHERE PRINCE CHARMING IS CAMPING THESE DAYS.
AND WE'LL NEED BRIAR ROSE'S HELP.
SLEEPING BEAUTY? WHY? WHAT DO YOU HAVE IN MIND?
A SCHEME WORTHY OF YOU, JACK, EXCEPT THAT THIS ONE HAS A POSSIBILITY OF SUCCESS. WHEN YOU TRIED YOUR DOT COM SCAM LAST YEAR, JUST HOW GOOD DID YOUR COMPUTER SKILLS GET?

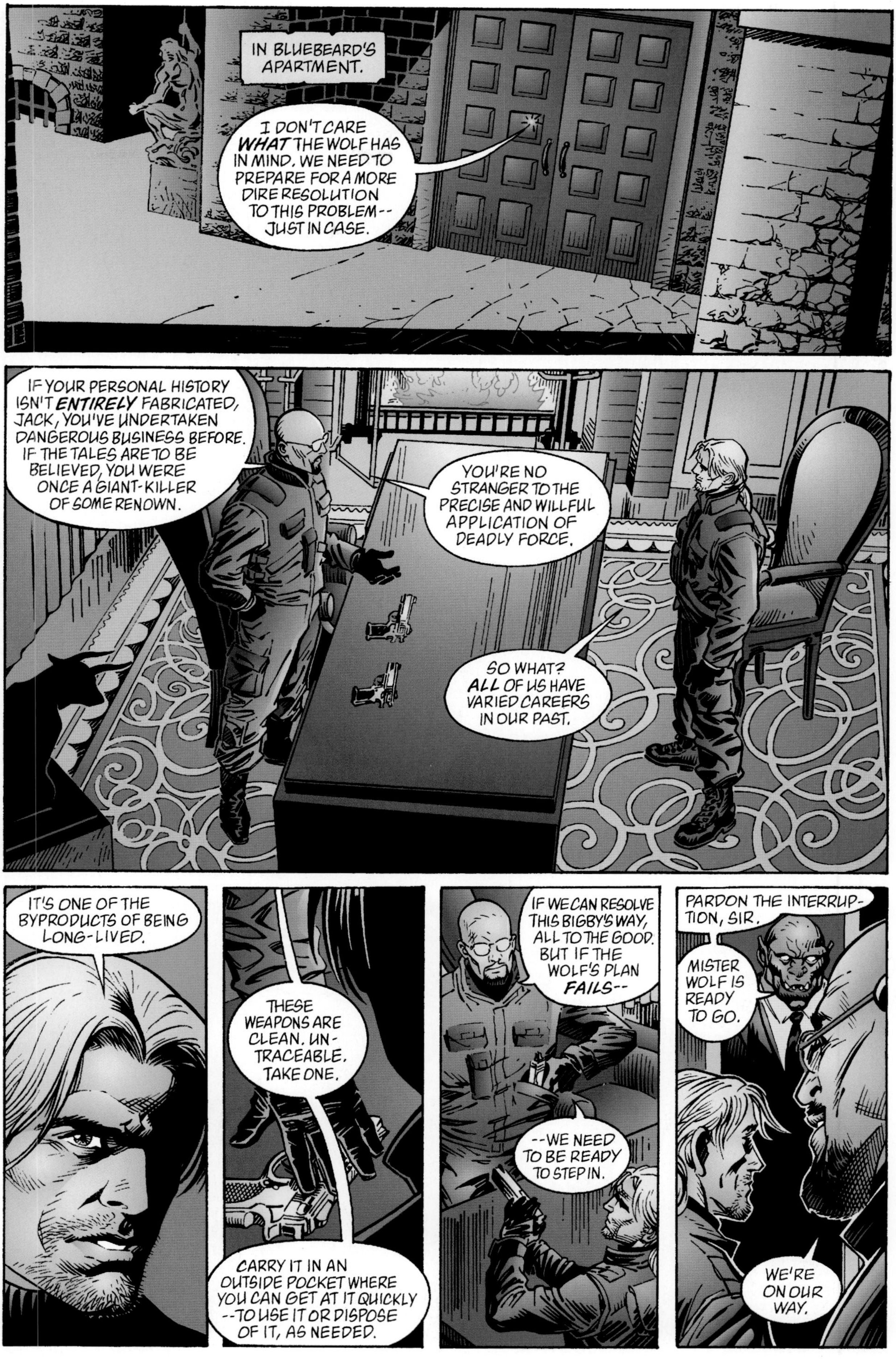
IN BLUEBEARD'S APARTMENT.
I DON'T CARE WHAT THE WOLF HAS IN MIND. WE NEED TO PREPARE FOR A MORE DIRE RESOLUTION TO THIS PROBLEM-- JUST IN CASE.
IF YOUR PERSONAL HISTORY ISN'T ENTIRELY FABRICATED, JACK, YOU'VE UNDERTAKEN DANGEROUS BUSINESS BEFORE. IF THE TALES ARE TO BE BELIEVED, YOU WERE ONCE A GIANT-KILLER OF SOME RENOWN.
YOU'RE NO STRANGER TO THE PRECISE AND WILLFUL APPLICATION OF DEADLY FORCE.
SO WHAT? ALL OF US HAVE VARIED CAREERS IN OUR PAST.
IT'S ONE OF THE BYPRODUCTS OF BEING LONG-LIVED.
THESE WEAPONS ARE CLEAN. UNTRACEABLE. TAKE ONE.
CARRY IT IN AN OUTSIDE POCKET WHERE YOU CAN GET AT IT QUICKLY --TO USE IT OR DISPOSE OF IT, AS NEEDED.
IF WE CAN RESOLVE THIS BIGBY'S WAY, ALL TO THE GOOD. BUT IF THE WOLF'S PLAN FAILS--
--WE NEED TO BE READY TO STEP IN.
PARDON THE INTERRUPTION, SIR.
MISTER WOLF IS READY TO GO.
WE'RE ON OUR WAY.

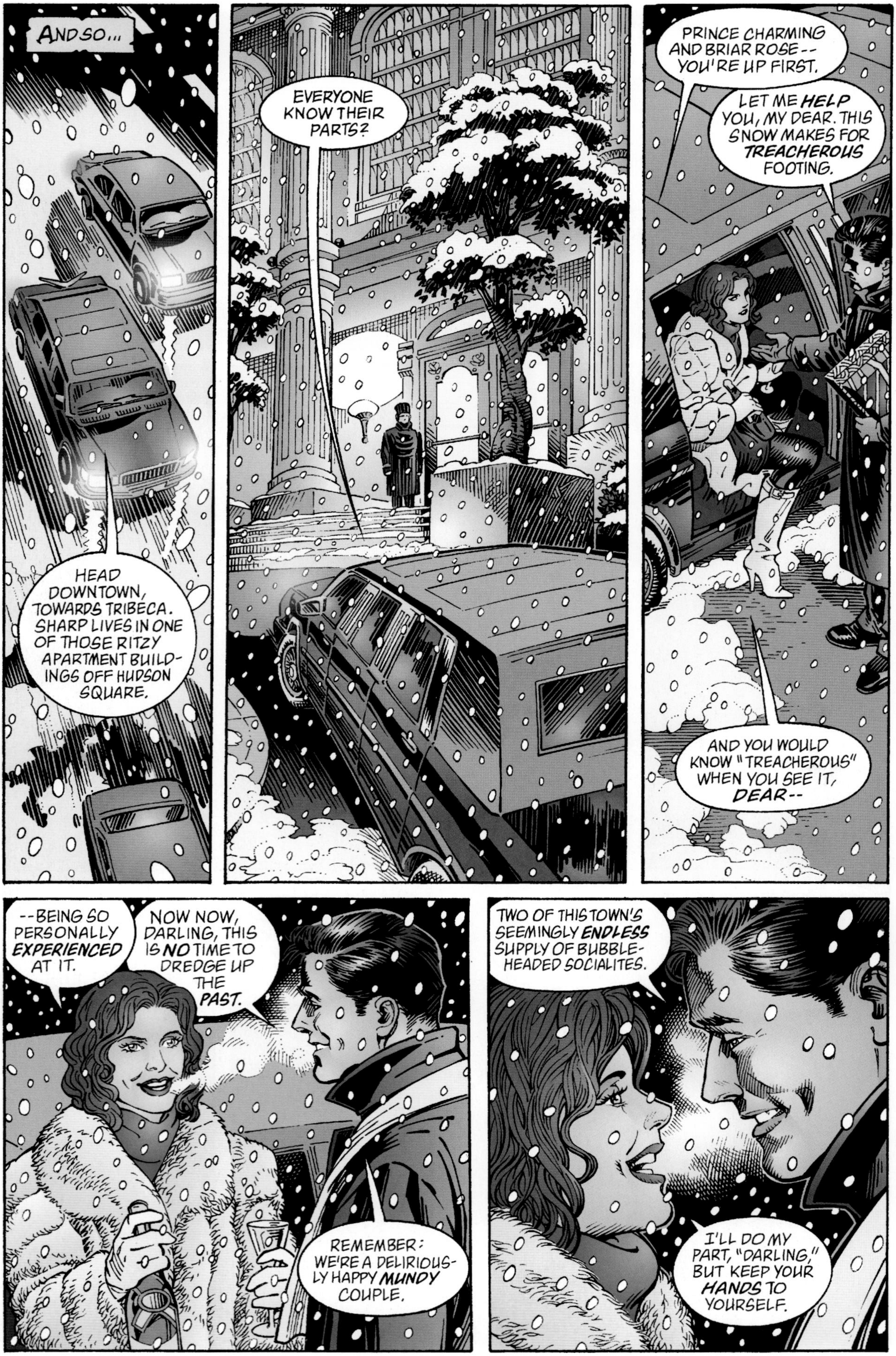
AND SO...
HEAD DOWNTOWN, TOWARDS TRIBECA. SHARP LIVES IN ONE OF THOSE RITZY APARTMENT BUILDINGS OFF HUDSON SQUARE.
EVERYONE KNOW THEIR PARTS?
PRINCE CHARMING AND BRIAR ROSE -- YOU'RE UP FIRST.
LET ME HELP YOU, MY DEAR. THIS SNOW MAKES FOR TREACHEROUS FOOTING.
AND YOU WOULD KNOW "TREACHEROUS" WHEN YOU SEE IT, DEAR --
-- BEING SO PERSONALLY EXPERIENCED AT IT.
NOW NOW, DARLING, THIS IS NO TIME TO DREDGE UP THE PAST.
REMEMBER: WE'RE A DELIRIOUSLY HAPPY MUNDY COUPLE.
TWO OF THIS TOWN'S SEEMINGLY ENDLESS SUPPLY OF BUBBLE-HEADED SOCIALITES.
I'LL DO MY PART, "DARLING," BUT KEEP YOUR HANDS TO YOURSELF.

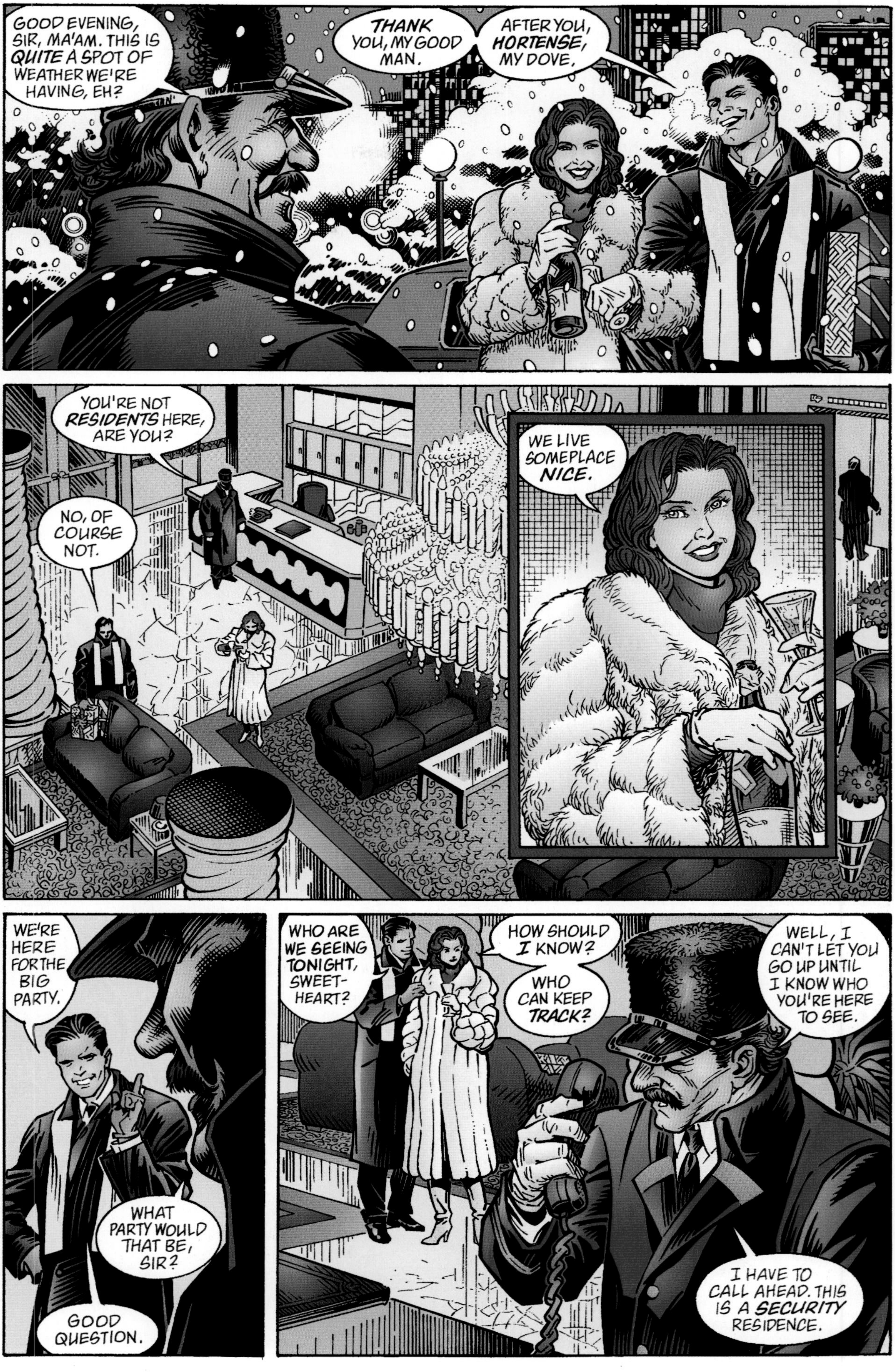
GOOD EVENING, SIR, MA'AM. THIS IS QUITE A SPOT OF WEATHER WE'RE HAVING, EH?
THANK YOU, MY GOOD MAN.
AFTER YOU, HORTENSE, MY DOVE.
YOU'RE NOT RESIDENTS HERE, ARE YOU?
NO, OF COURSE NOT.
WE LIVE SOMEPLACE NICE.
WE'RE HERE FOR THE BIG PARTY.
WHAT PARTY WOULD THAT BE, SIR?
GOOD QUESTION.
WHO ARE WE SEEING TONIGHT, SWEET-HEART?
HOW SHOULD I KNOW?
WHO CAN KEEP TRACK?
WELL, I CAN'T LET YOU GO UP UNTIL I KNOW WHO YOU'RE HERE TO SEE.
I HAVE TO CALL AHEAD. THIS IS A SECURITY RESIDENCE.

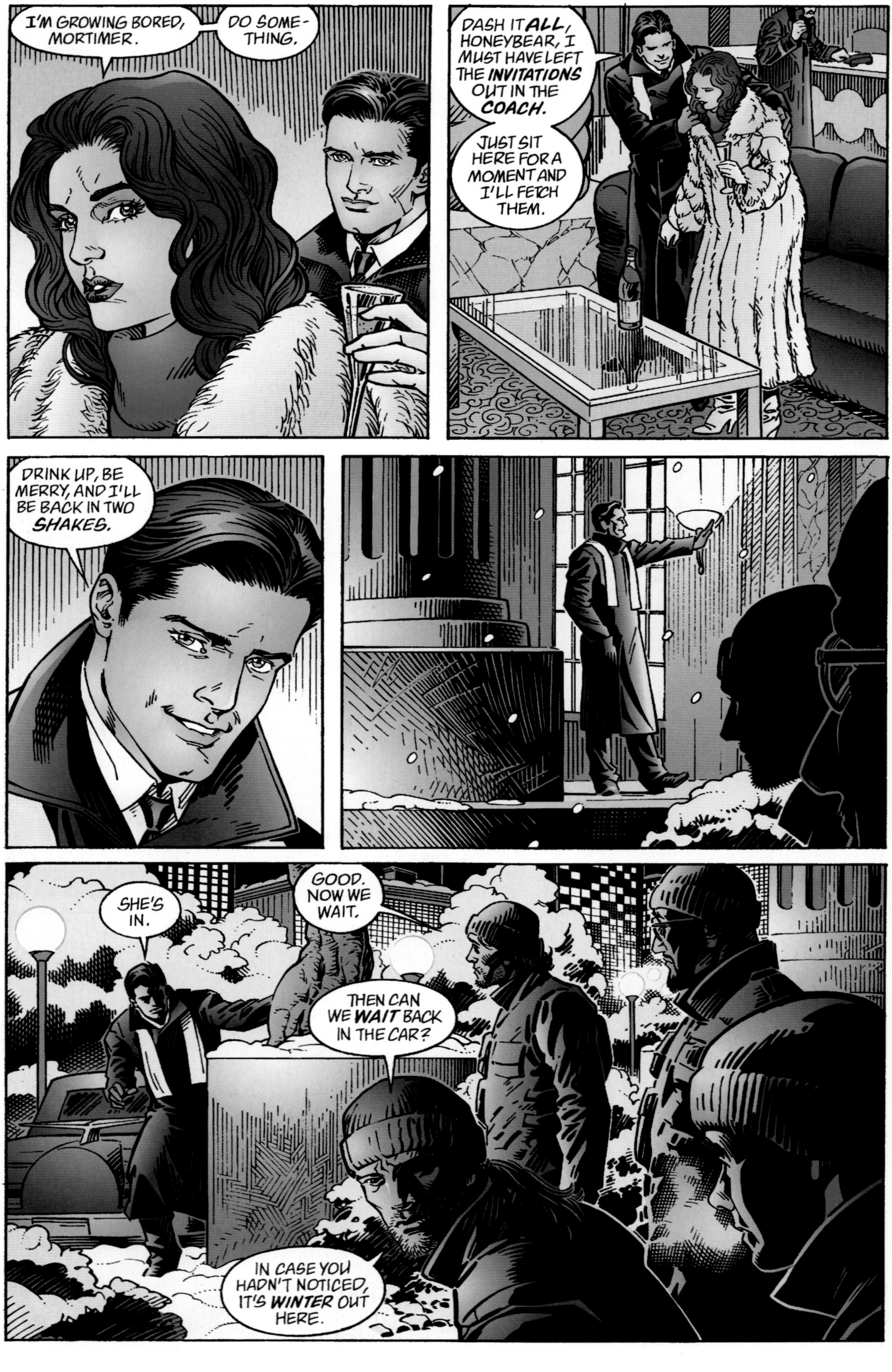
I'M GROWING BORED, MORTIMER.
DO SOME-THING.
DASH IT ALL, HONEYBEAR, I MUST HAVE LEFT THE INVITATIONS OUT IN THE COACH.
JUST SIT HERE FOR A MOMENT AND I'LL FETCH THEM.
DRINK UP, BE MERRY, AND I'LL BE BACK IN TWO SHAKES.
SHE'S IN.
GOOD. NOW WE WAIT.
THEN CAN WE WAIT BACK IN THE CAR?
IN CASE YOU HADN'T NOTICED, IT'S WINTER OUT HERE.

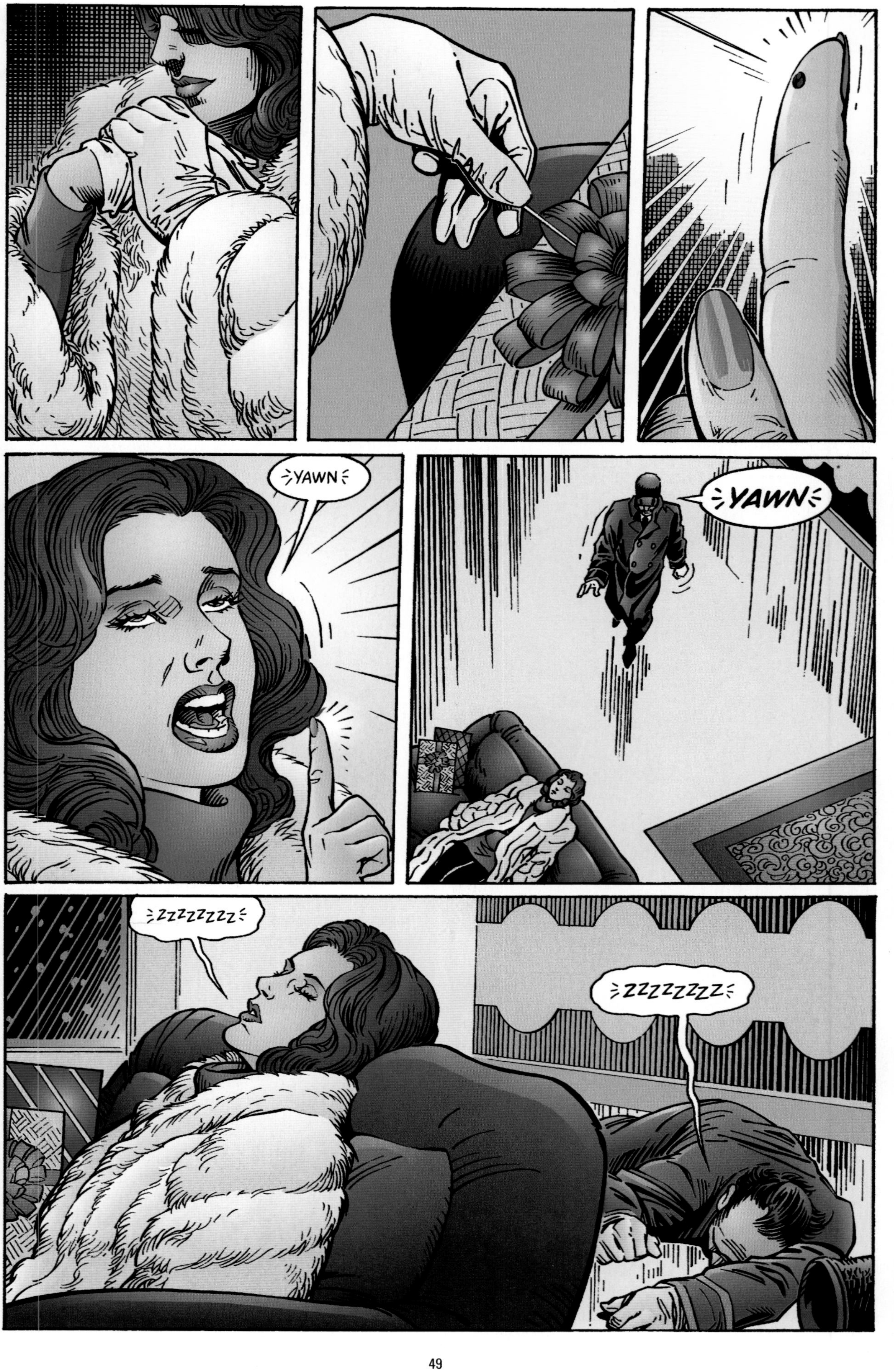
YAWN
YAWN
ZZZZZZZZ
ZZZZZZZZ

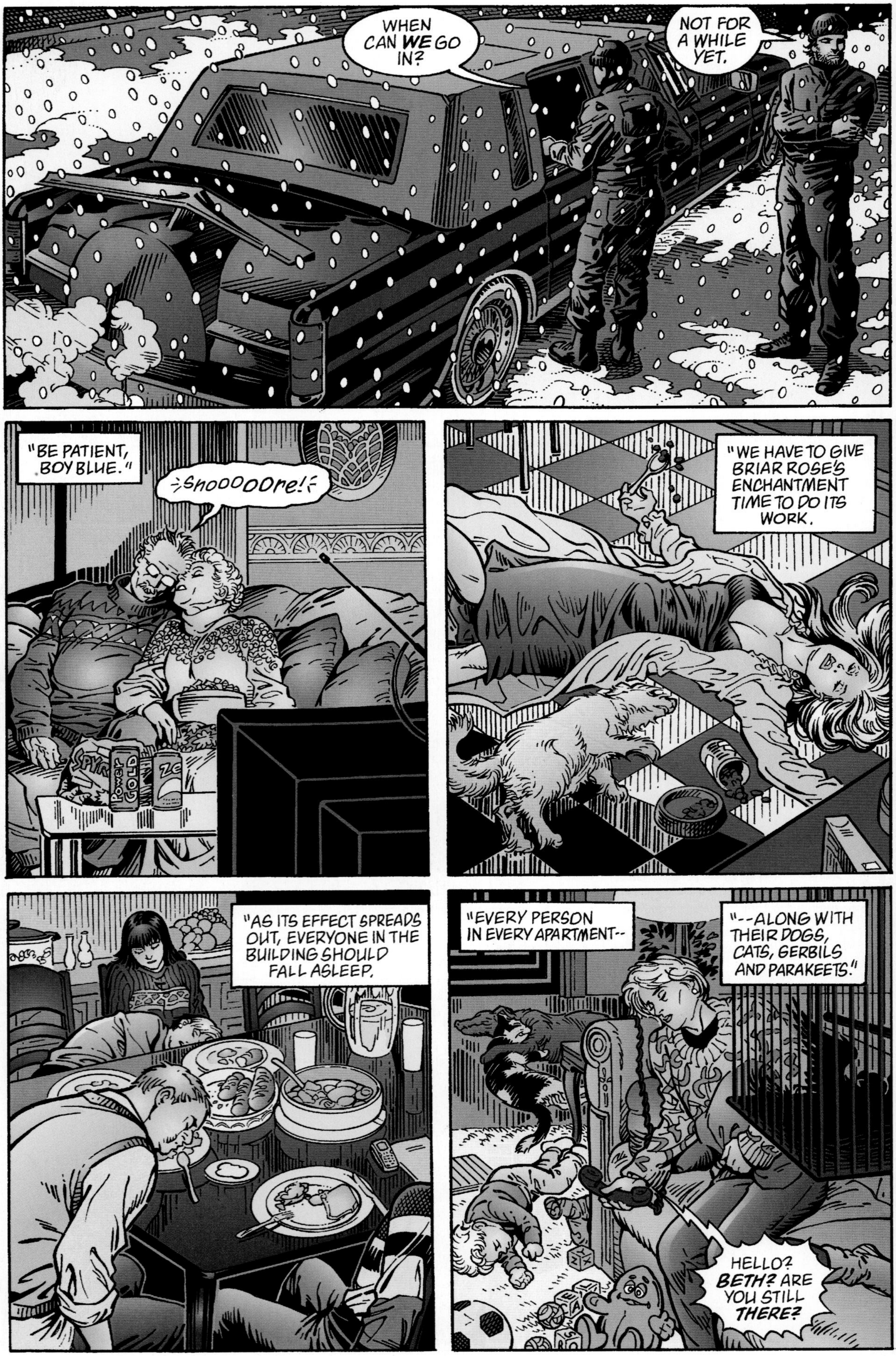
WHEN CAN WE GO IN?
NOT FOR A WHILE YET.
"BE PATIENT, BOY BLUE."
SNOOOOORE!
"WE HAVE TO GIVE BRIAR ROSE'S ENCHANTMENT TIME TO DO ITS WORK.
"AS ITS EFFECT SPREADS OUT, EVERYONE IN THE BUILDING SHOULD FALL ASLEEP.
"EVERY PERSON IN EVERY APARTMENT--
"--ALONG WITH THEIR DOGS, CATS, GERBILS AND PARAKEETS."
HELLO? BETH? ARE YOU STILL THERE?

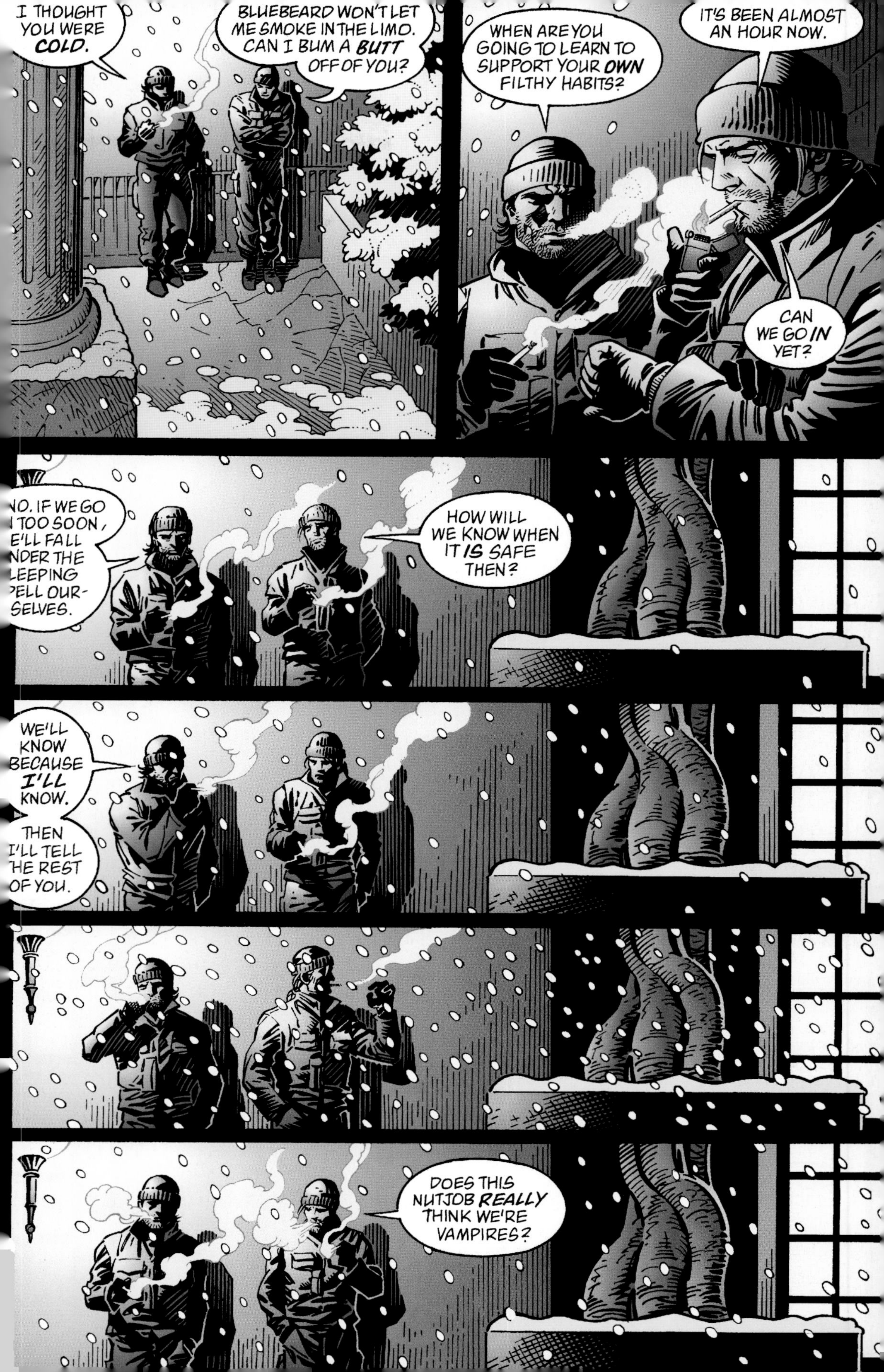
I THOUGHT YOU WERE COLD.
BLUEBEARD WON'T LET ME SMOKE IN THE LIMO. CAN I BUM A BUTT OFF OF YOU?
WHEN ARE YOU GOING TO LEARN TO SUPPORT YOUR OWN FILTHY HABITS?
IT'S BEEN ALMOST AN HOUR NOW.
CAN WE GO IN YET?
NO. IF WE GO IN TOO SOON, WE'LL FALL UNDER THE SLEEPING SPELL OURSELVES.
HOW WILL WE KNOW WHEN IT IS SAFE THEN?
WE'LL KNOW BECAUSE I'LL KNOW.
THEN I'LL TELL THE REST OF YOU.
DOES THIS NUTJOB REALLY THINK WE'RE VAMPIRES?

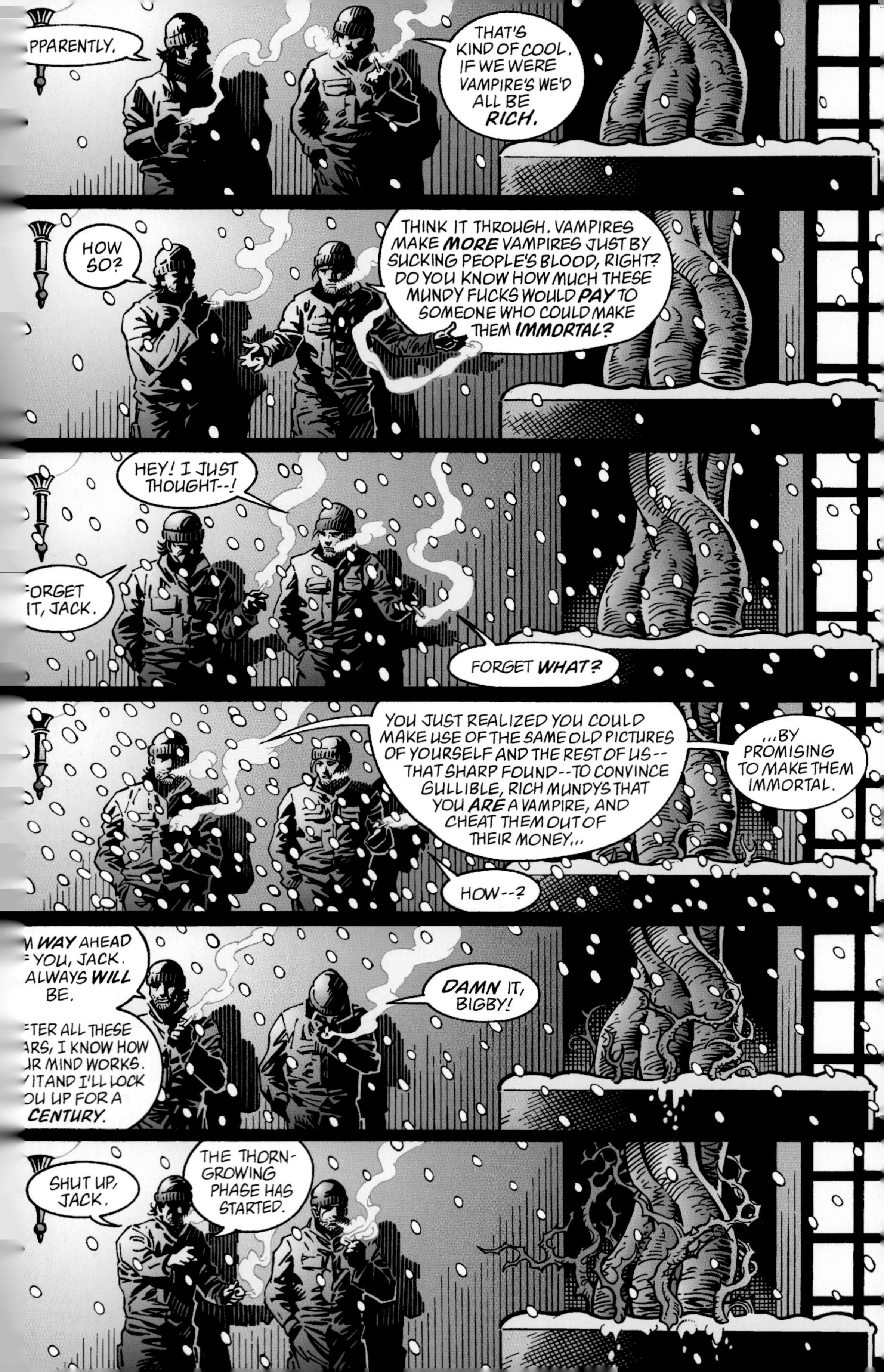
PPARENTLY.
THAT'S KIND OF COOL. IF WE WERE VAMPIRE'S WE'D ALL BE RICH.
HOW SO?
THINK IT THROUGH. VAMPIRES MAKE MORE VAMPIRES JUST BY SUCKING PEOPLE'S BLOOD, RIGHT? DO YOU KNOW HOW MUCH THESE MUNDY FUCKS WOULD PAY TO SOMEONE WHO COULD MAKE THEM IMMORTAL?
HEY! I JUST THOUGHT--!
ORGET IT, JACK.
FORGET WHAT?
YOU JUST REALIZED YOU COULD MAKE USE OF THE SAME OLD PICTURES OF YOURSELF AND THE REST OF US--THAT SHARP FOUND--TO CONVINCE GULLIBLE, RICH MUNDYS THAT YOU ARE A VAMPIRE, AND CHEAT THEM OUT OF THEIR MONEY...
...BY PROMISING TO MAKE THEM IMMORTAL.
HOW--?
M WAY AHEAD F YOU, JACK. ALWAYS WILL BE.
FTER ALL THESE ARS, I KNOW HOW UR MIND WORKS. Y IT AND I'LL LOCK OU UP FOR A CENTURY.
DAMN IT, BIGBY!
SHUT UP, JACK.
THE THORN-GROWING PHASE HAS STARTED.

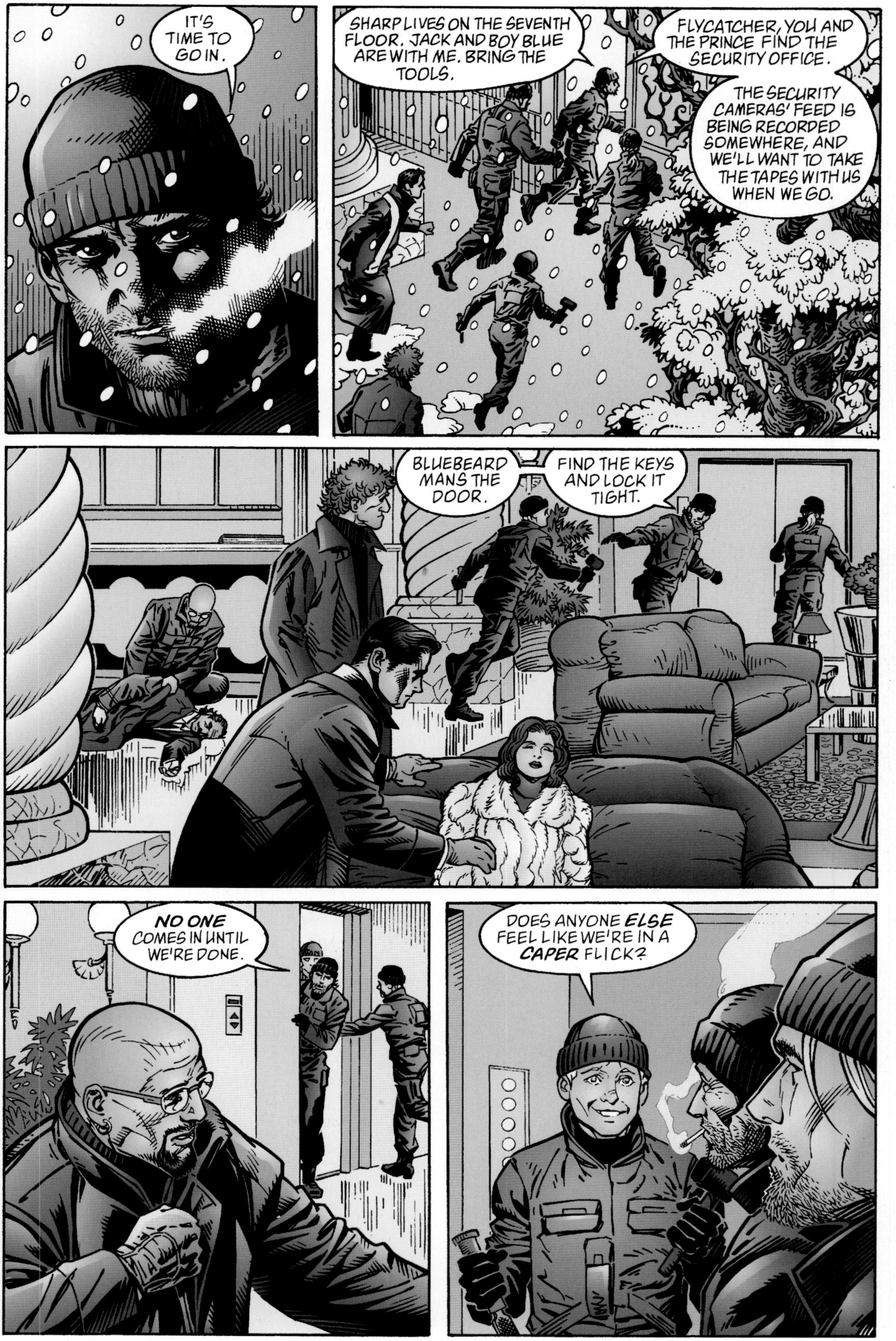
IT'S TIME TO GO IN.
SHARP LIVES ON THE SEVENTH FLOOR. JACK AND BOY BLUE ARE WITH ME. BRING THE TOOLS.
FLYCATCHER, YOU AND THE PRINCE FIND THE SECURITY OFFICE.
THE SECURITY CAMERAS' FEED IS BEING RECORDED SOMEWHERE, AND WE'LL WANT TO TAKE THE TAPES WITH US WHEN WE GO.
BLUEBEARD MANS THE DOOR.
FIND THE KEYS AND LOCK IT TIGHT.
NO ONE COMES IN UNTIL WE'RE DONE.
DOES ANYONE ELSE FEEL LIKE WE'RE IN A CAPER FLICK?

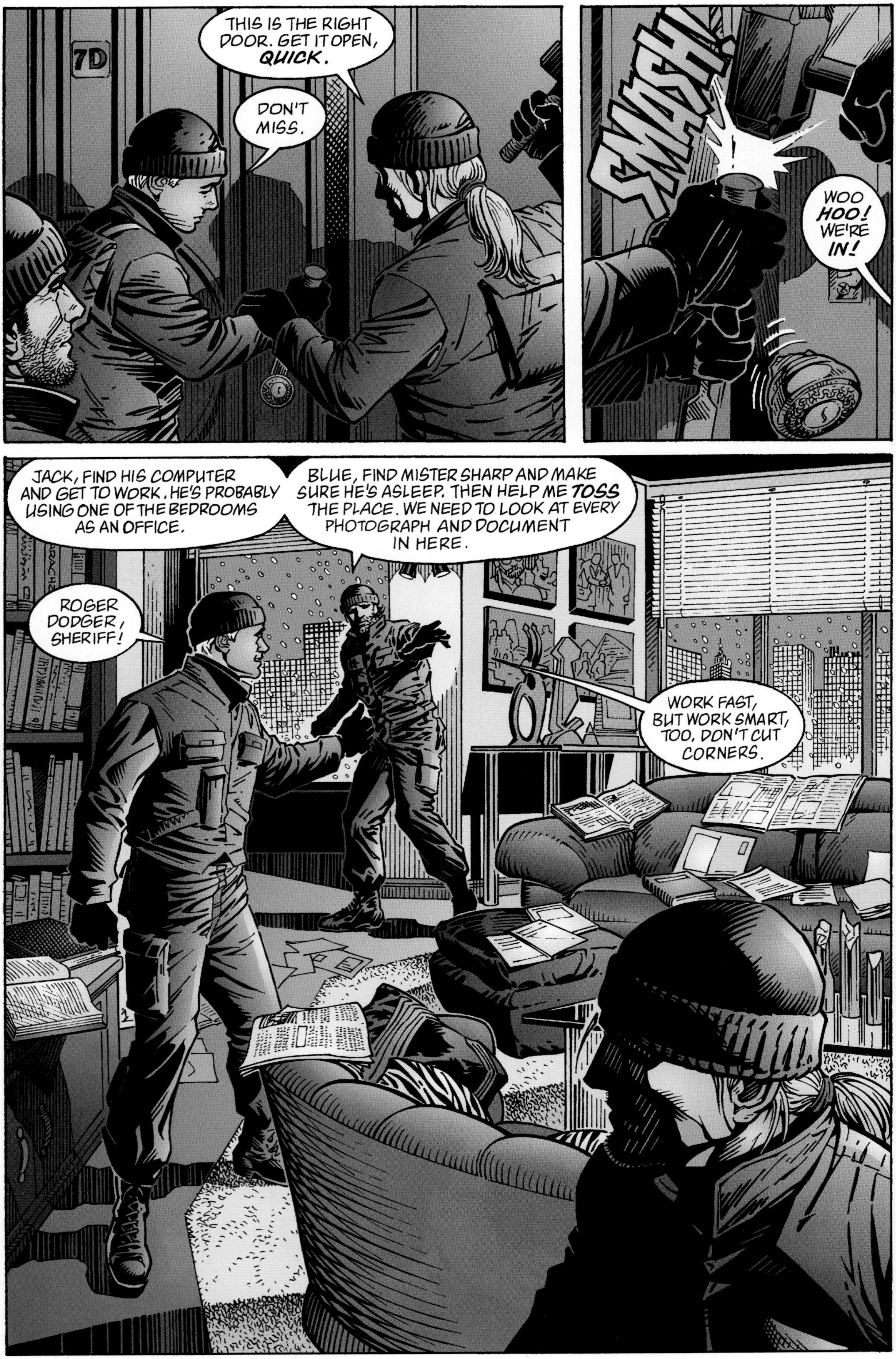
7D
THIS IS THE RIGHT DOOR. GET IT OPEN, QUICK.
DON'T MISS.
SMASH
WOO HOO! WE'RE IN!
JACK, FIND HIS COMPUTER AND GET TO WORK. HE'S PROBABLY USING ONE OF THE BEDROOMS AS AN OFFICE.
BLUE, FIND MISTER SHARP AND MAKE SURE HE'S ASLEEP. THEN HELP ME TOSS THE PLACE. WE NEED TO LOOK AT EVERY PHOTOGRAPH AND DOCUMENT IN HERE.
ROGER DODGER, SHERIFF!
WORK FAST, BUT WORK SMART, TOO, DON'T CUT CORNERS.

AND **SING OUT** IF YOU START GETTING SLEEPY. WE CAN'T AFFORD TO BE CAUGHT HERE.

LOOK AT YOU, TOMMY.

PLEASE, **GOD**, LET THERE BE A CAMERA HERE. WE NEED A **PICTURE** OF THIS.

≈ZZZZZZZZZZZZ≈

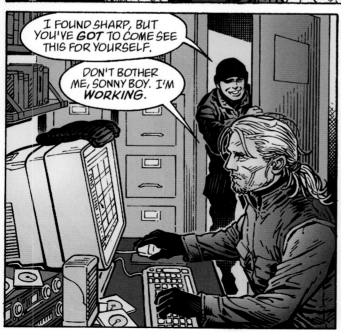

I FOUND SHARP, BUT YOU'VE **GOT** TO COME SEE THIS FOR YOURSELF.

DON'T BOTHER ME, SONNY BOY. I'M **WORKING**.

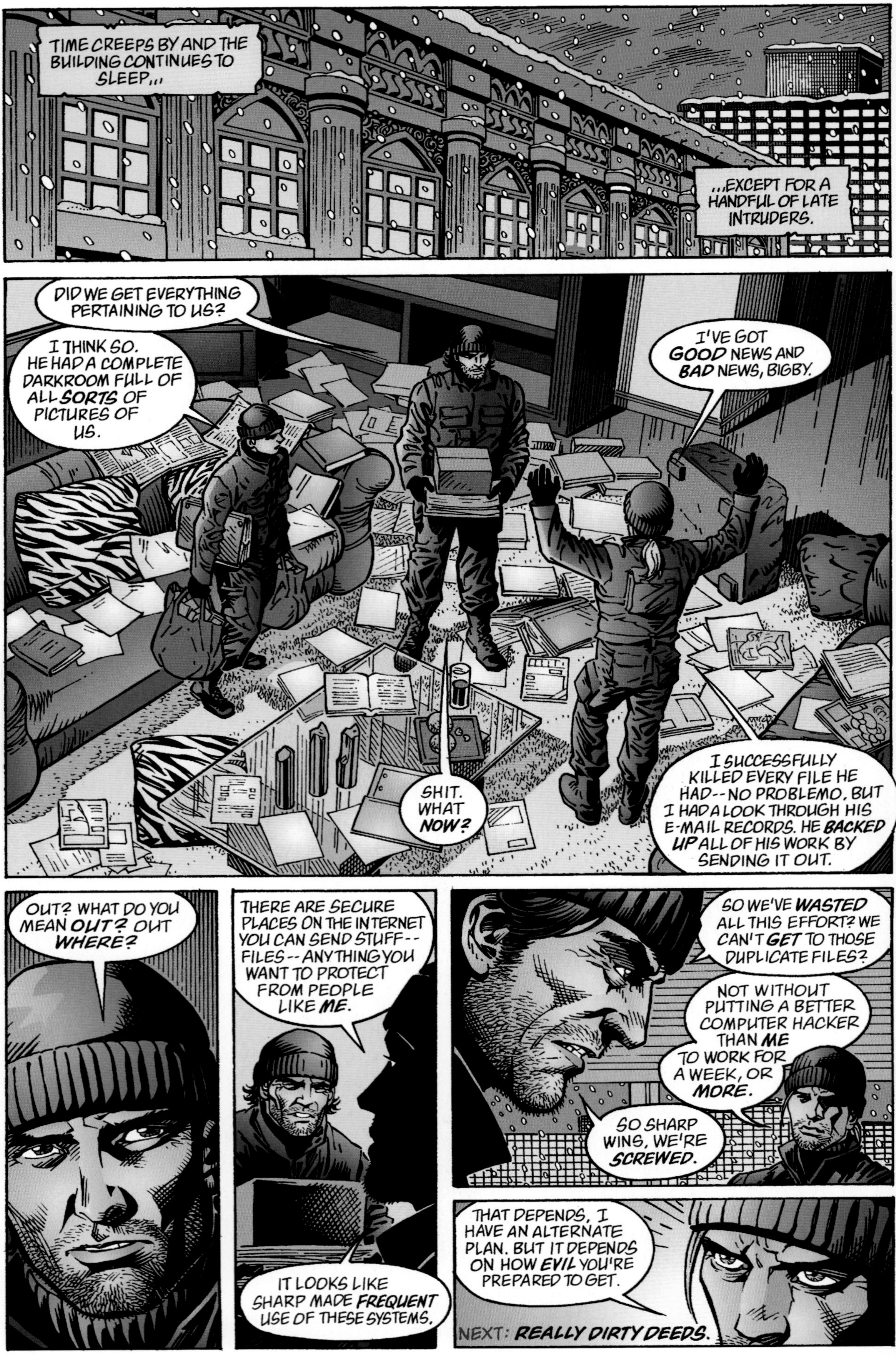

TIME CREEPS BY AND THE BUILDING CONTINUES TO SLEEP...
...EXCEPT FOR A HANDFUL OF LATE INTRUDERS.
DID WE GET EVERYTHING PERTAINING TO US?
I THINK SO. HE HAD A COMPLETE DARKROOM FULL OF ALL SORTS OF PICTURES OF US.
I'VE GOT GOOD NEWS AND BAD NEWS, BIGBY.
I SUCCESSFULLY KILLED EVERY FILE HE HAD--NO PROBLEMO. BUT I HAD A LOOK THROUGH HIS E-MAIL RECORDS. HE BACKED UP ALL OF HIS WORK BY SENDING IT OUT.
SHIT. WHAT NOW?
OUT? WHAT DO YOU MEAN OUT? OUT WHERE?
THERE ARE SECURE PLACES ON THE INTERNET YOU CAN SEND STUFF--FILES--ANYTHING YOU WANT TO PROTECT FROM PEOPLE LIKE ME.
IT LOOKS LIKE SHARP MADE FREQUENT USE OF THESE SYSTEMS.
SO WE'VE WASTED ALL THIS EFFORT? WE CAN'T GET TO THOSE DUPLICATE FILES?
NOT WITHOUT PUTTING A BETTER COMPUTER HACKER THAN ME TO WORK FOR A WEEK, OR MORE.
SO SHARP WINS. WE'RE SCREWED.
THAT DEPENDS. I HAVE AN ALTERNATE PLAN. BUT IT DEPENDS ON HOW EVIL YOU'RE PREPARED TO GET.
NEXT: REALLY DIRTY DEEDS.

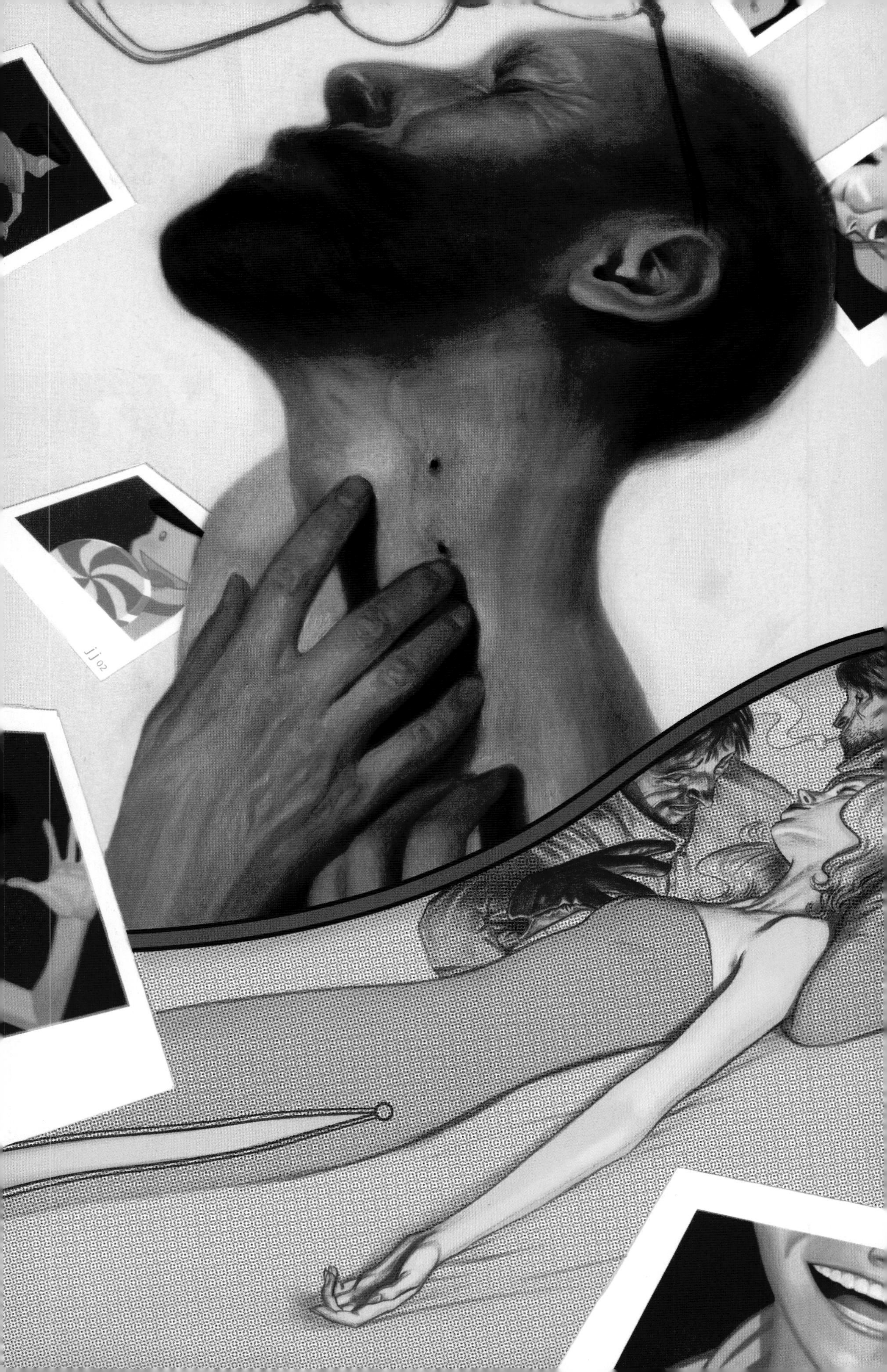
JJ 02

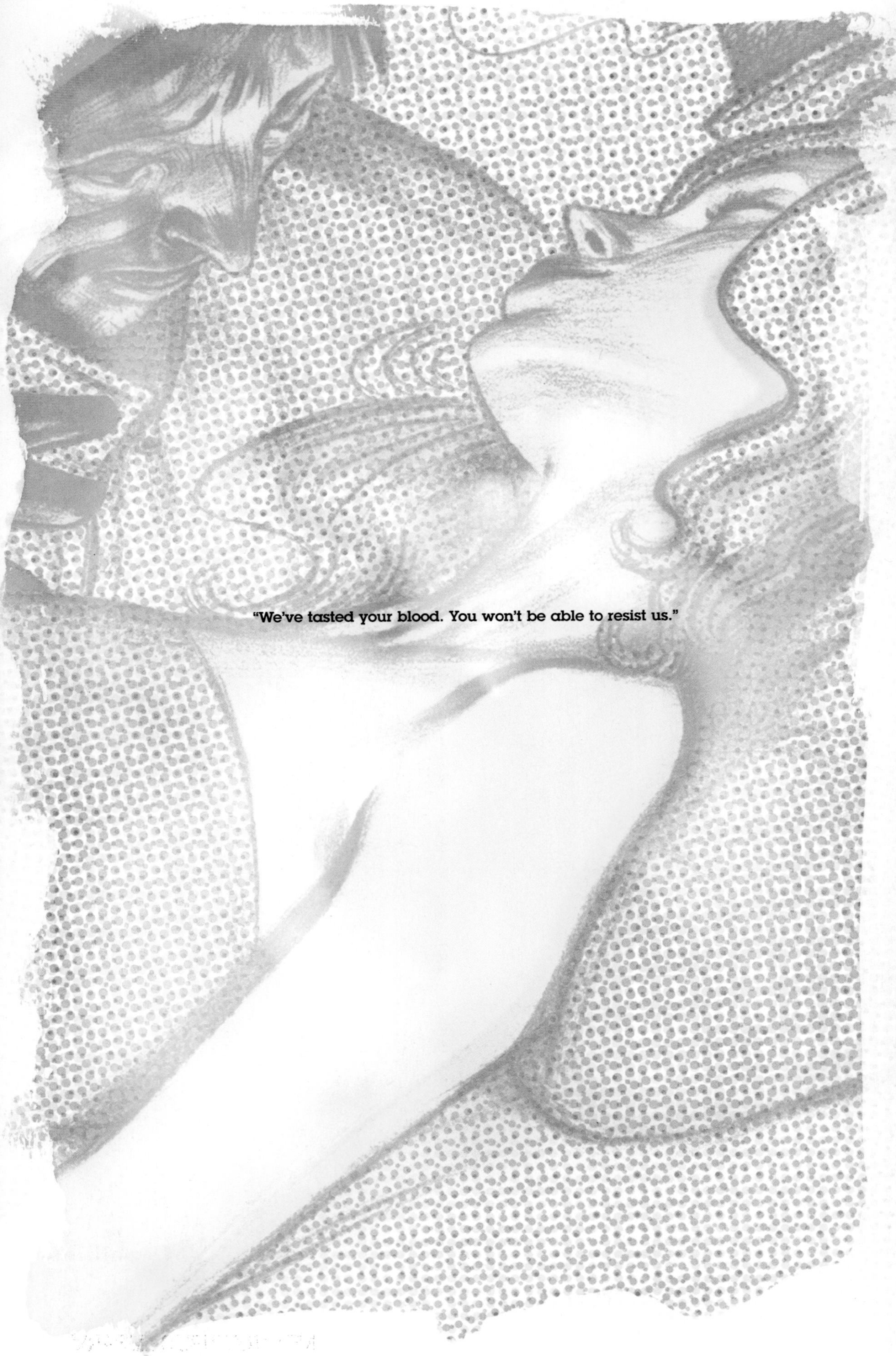

"We've tasted your blood. You won't be able to resist us."

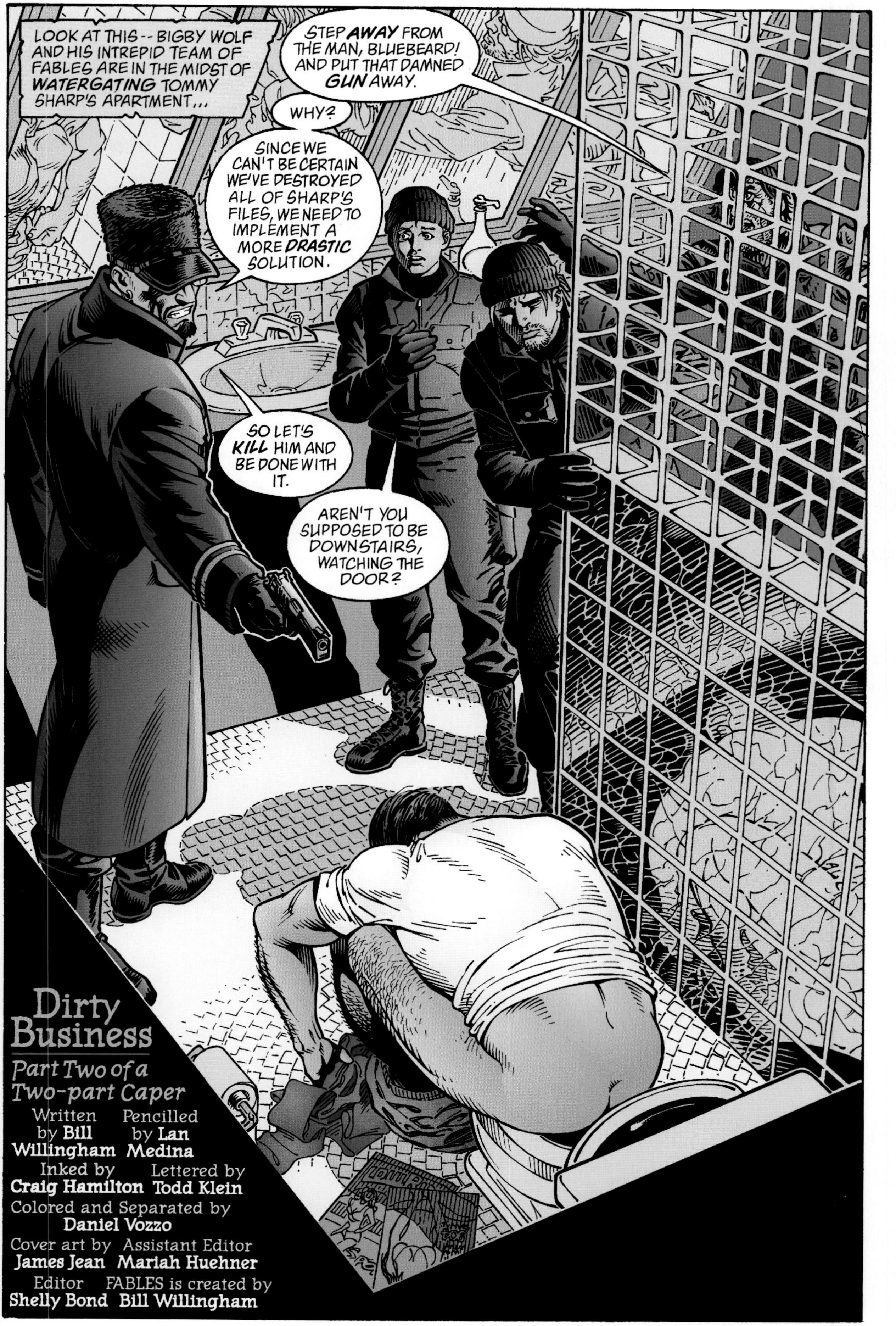
LOOK AT THIS -- BIGBY WOLF AND HIS INTREPID TEAM OF FABLES ARE IN THE MIDST OF WATERGATING TOMMY SHARP'S APARTMENT...
STEP AWAY FROM THE MAN, BLUEBEARD! AND PUT THAT DAMNED GUN AWAY.
WHY?
SINCE WE CAN'T BE CERTAIN WE'VE DESTROYED ALL OF SHARP'S FILES, WE NEED TO IMPLEMENT A MORE DRASTIC SOLUTION.
SO LET'S KILL HIM AND BE DONE WITH IT.
AREN'T YOU SUPPOSED TO BE DOWNSTAIRS, WATCHING THE DOOR?
Dirty Business
Part Two of a Two-part Caper
Written by Bill Willingham
Pencilled by Lan Medina
Inked by Craig Hamilton
Lettered by Todd Klein
Colored and Separated by Daniel Vozzo
Cover art by James Jean
Assistant Editor Mariah Huehner
Editor Shelly Bond
FABLES is created by Bill Willingham

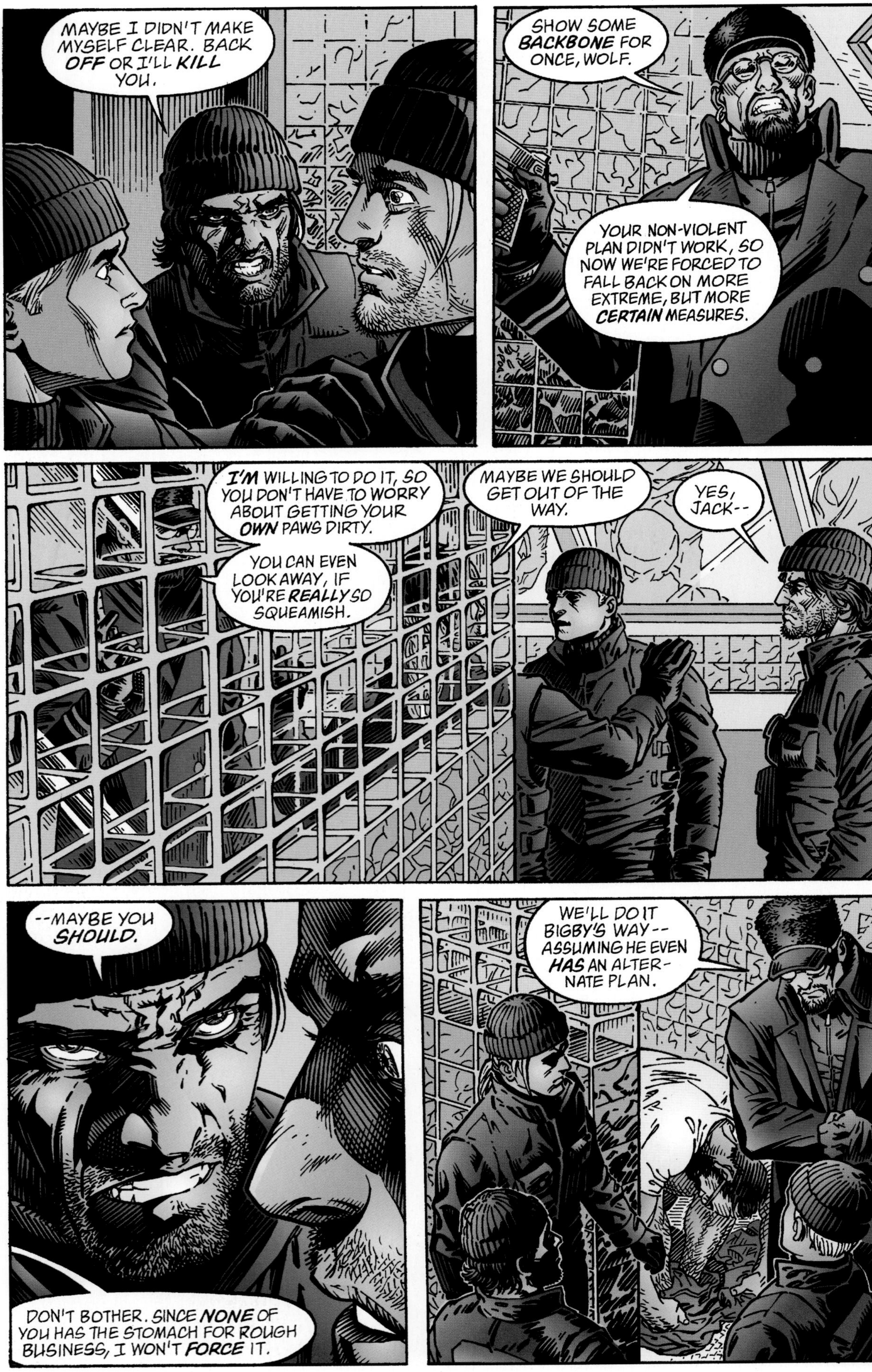
MAYBE I DIDN'T MAKE MYSELF CLEAR. BACK OFF OR I'LL KILL YOU.
SHOW SOME BACKBONE FOR ONCE, WOLF.
YOUR NON-VIOLENT PLAN DIDN'T WORK, SO NOW WE'RE FORCED TO FALL BACK ON MORE EXTREME, BUT MORE CERTAIN MEASURES.
I'M WILLING TO DO IT, SO YOU DON'T HAVE TO WORRY ABOUT GETTING YOUR OWN PAWS DIRTY.
YOU CAN EVEN LOOK AWAY, IF YOU'RE REALLY SO SQUEAMISH.
MAYBE WE SHOULD GET OUT OF THE WAY.
YES, JACK--
--MAYBE YOU SHOULD.
DON'T BOTHER. SINCE NONE OF YOU HAS THE STOMACH FOR ROUGH BUSINESS, I WON'T FORCE IT.
WE'LL DO IT BIGBY'S WAY--ASSUMING HE EVEN HAS AN ALTERNATE PLAN.

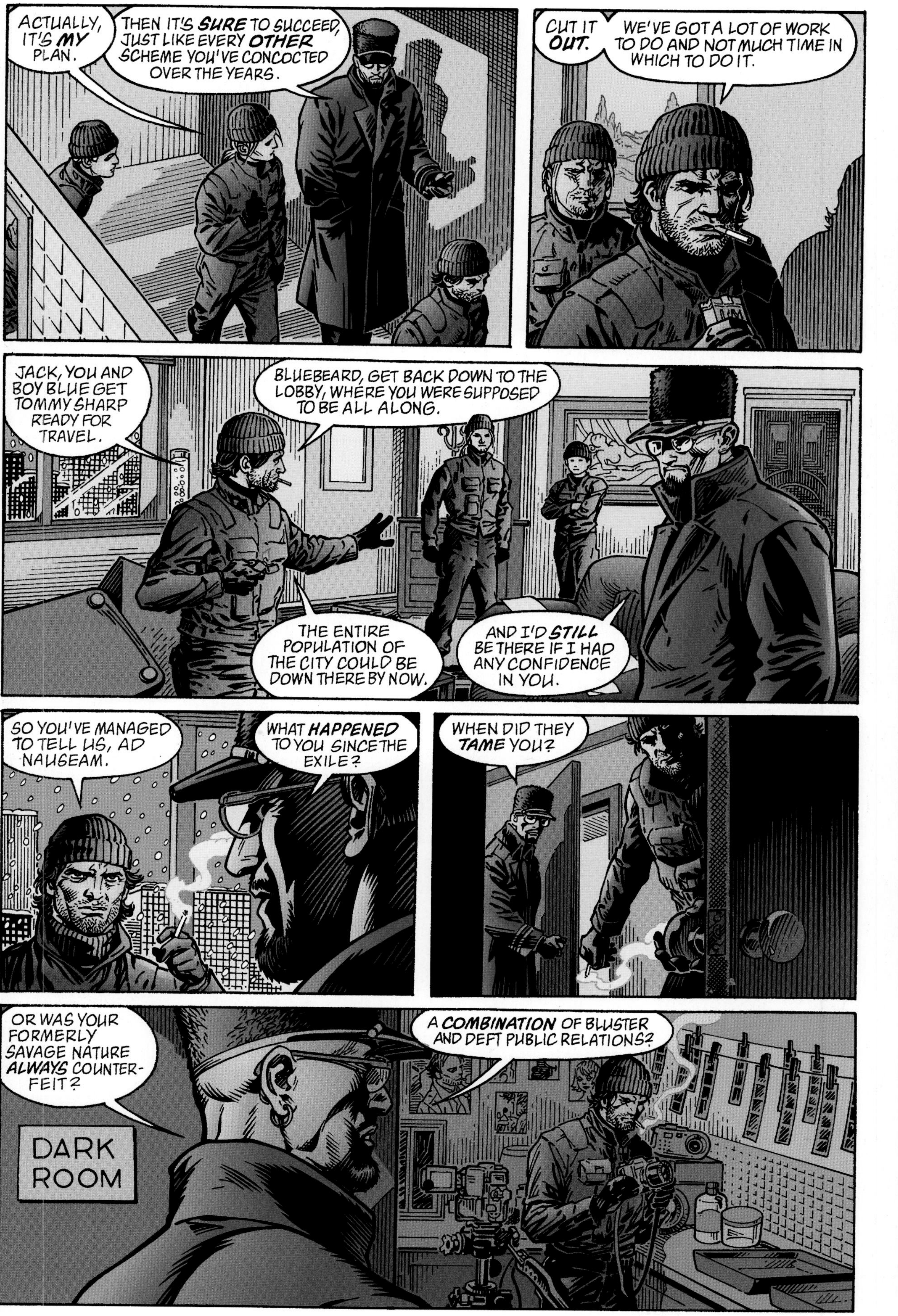
ACTUALLY, IT'S MY PLAN.
THEN IT'S SURE TO SUCCEED, JUST LIKE EVERY OTHER SCHEME YOU'VE CONCOCTED OVER THE YEARS.
CUT IT OUT.
WE'VE GOT A LOT OF WORK TO DO AND NOT MUCH TIME IN WHICH TO DO IT.
JACK, YOU AND BOY BLUE GET TOMMY SHARP READY FOR TRAVEL.
BLUEBEARD, GET BACK DOWN TO THE LOBBY, WHERE YOU WERE SUPPOSED TO BE ALL ALONG.
THE ENTIRE POPULATION OF THE CITY COULD BE DOWN THERE BY NOW.
AND I'D STILL BE THERE IF I HAD ANY CONFIDENCE IN YOU.
SO YOU'VE MANAGED TO TELL US, AD NAUSEAM.
WHAT HAPPENED TO YOU SINCE THE EXILE?
WHEN DID THEY TAME YOU?
OR WAS YOUR FORMERLY SAVAGE NATURE ALWAYS COUNTER-FEIT?
A COMBINATION OF BLUSTER AND DEFT PUBLIC RELATIONS?
DARK ROOM

DON'T PUSH THIS ANY FURTHER.

OR YOU'LL RIP MY **THROAT** OUT, OR **KILL** ME, OR BLAH BLAH BLAH?

YOU'VE SAID IT ALL BEFORE, WOLF.

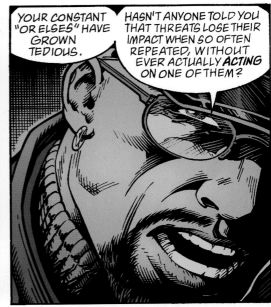

YOUR CONSTANT "OR ELSES" HAVE GROWN TEDIOUS.

HASN'T ANYONE TOLD YOU THAT THREATS LOSE THEIR IMPACT WHEN SO OFTEN REPEATED, WITHOUT EVER ACTUALLY **ACTING** ON ONE OF THEM?

I HAVEN'T **NEEDED** TO ACT, BECAUSE YOU'VE ALWAYS BACKED DOWN AND ALWAYS **WILL**.

SURE, YOU'RE A TERROR WHEN GUTTING UNARMED **BRIDES** ON THEIR WEDDING NIGHT, OR GUNNING DOWN AN UNCONSCIOUS MAN ON A **TOILET**.

YOU'RE A **COWARD**, BLUEBEARD, HIDING BEHIND A LIFETIME OF WEALTH AND PRIVILEGE.

NOW, UNLESS YOU'RE PREPARED TO THROW **DOWN**...

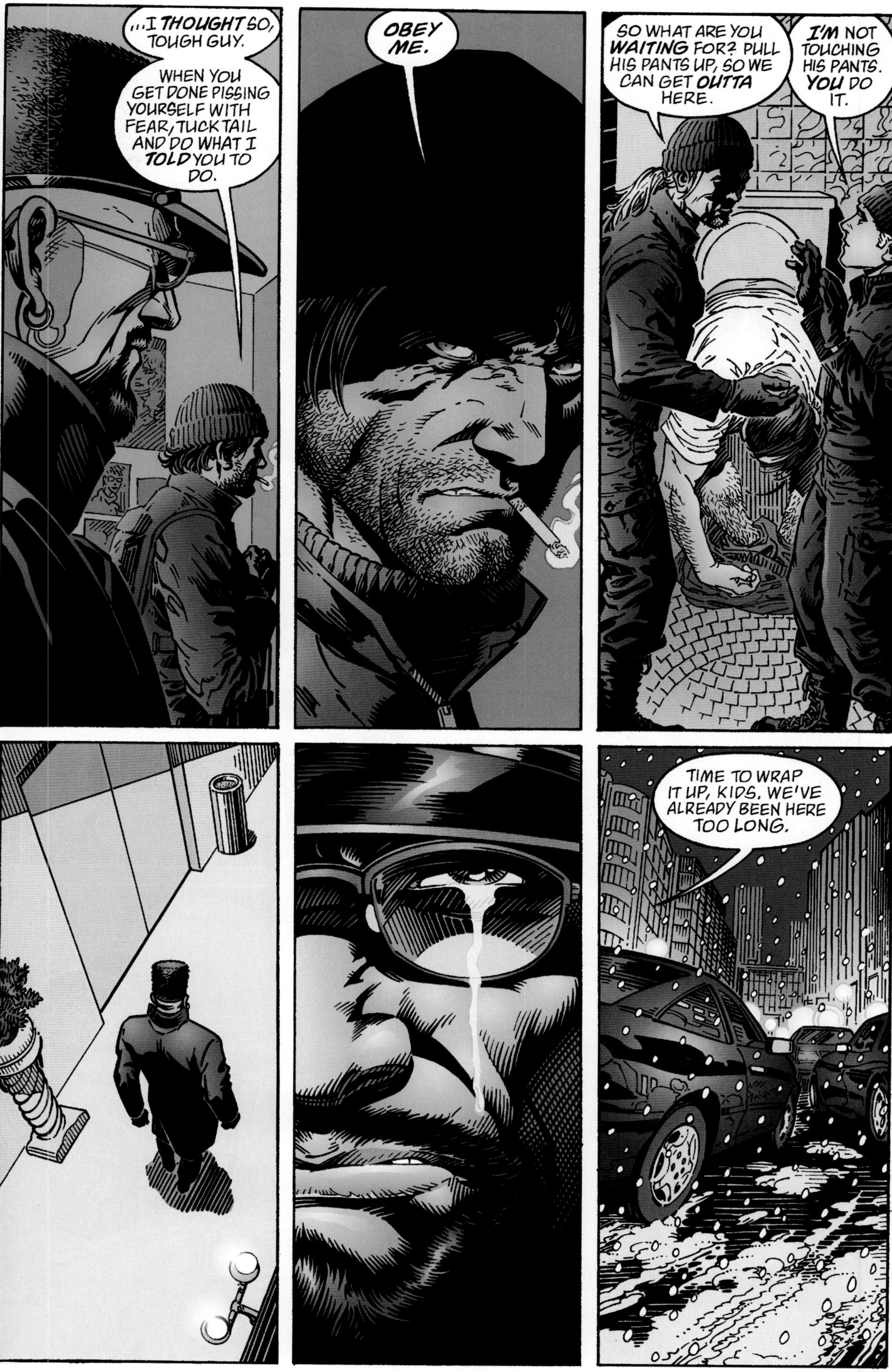
...I THOUGHT SO, TOUGH GUY.
WHEN YOU GET DONE PISSING YOURSELF WITH FEAR, TUCK TAIL AND DO WHAT I TOLD YOU TO DO.
OBEY ME.
SO WHAT ARE YOU WAITING FOR? PULL HIS PANTS UP, SO WE CAN GET OUTTA HERE.
I'M NOT TOUCHING HIS PANTS. YOU DO IT.
TIME TO WRAP IT UP, KIDS. WE'VE ALREADY BEEN HERE TOO LONG.

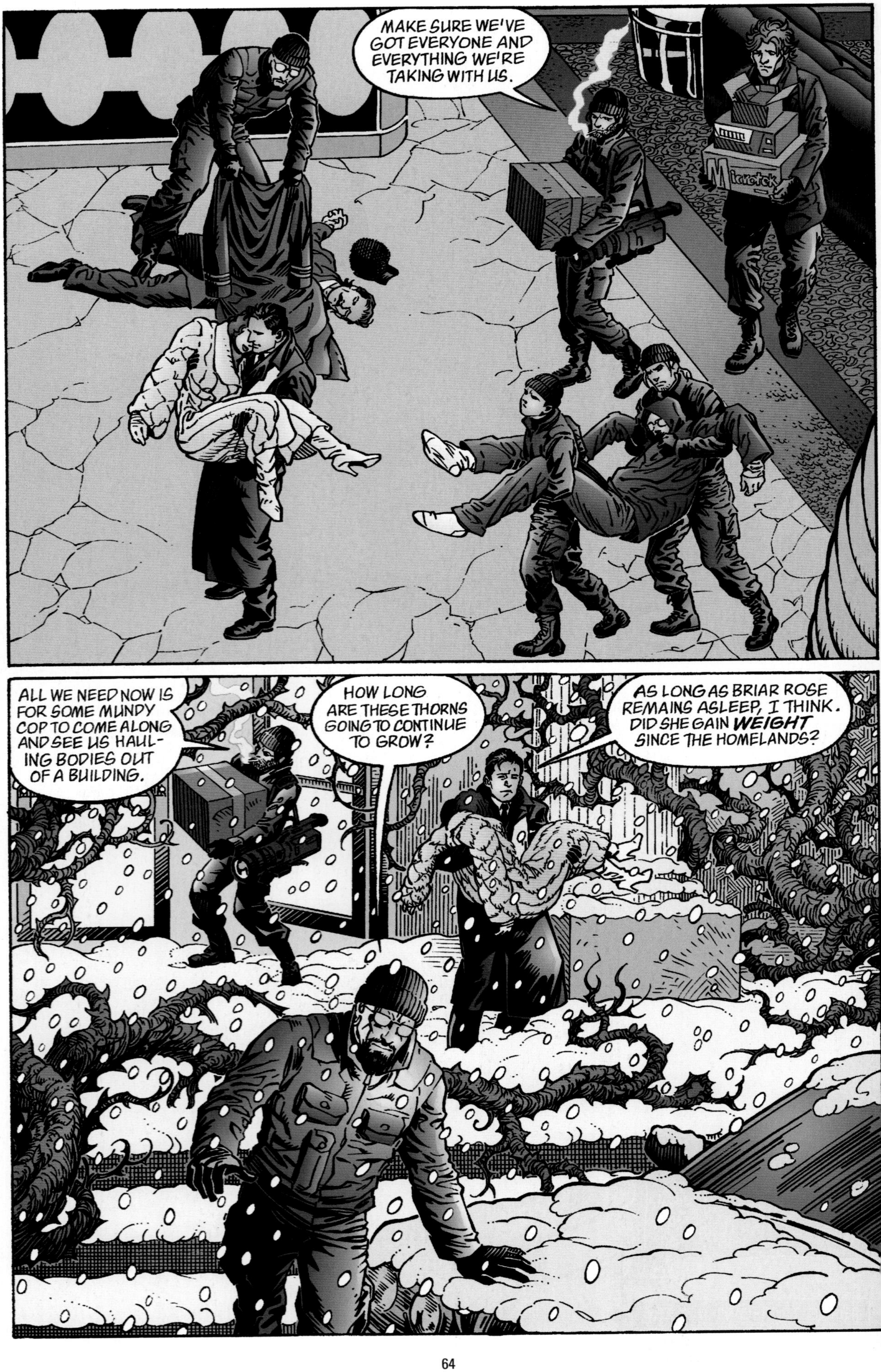
MAKE SURE WE'VE GOT EVERYONE AND EVERYTHING WE'RE TAKING WITH US.
ALL WE NEED NOW IS FOR SOME MUNDY COP TO COME ALONG AND SEE US HAULING BODIES OUT OF A BUILDING.
HOW LONG ARE THESE THORNS GOING TO CONTINUE TO GROW?
AS LONG AS BRIAR ROSE REMAINS ASLEEP, I THINK. DID SHE GAIN WEIGHT SINCE THE HOMELANDS?

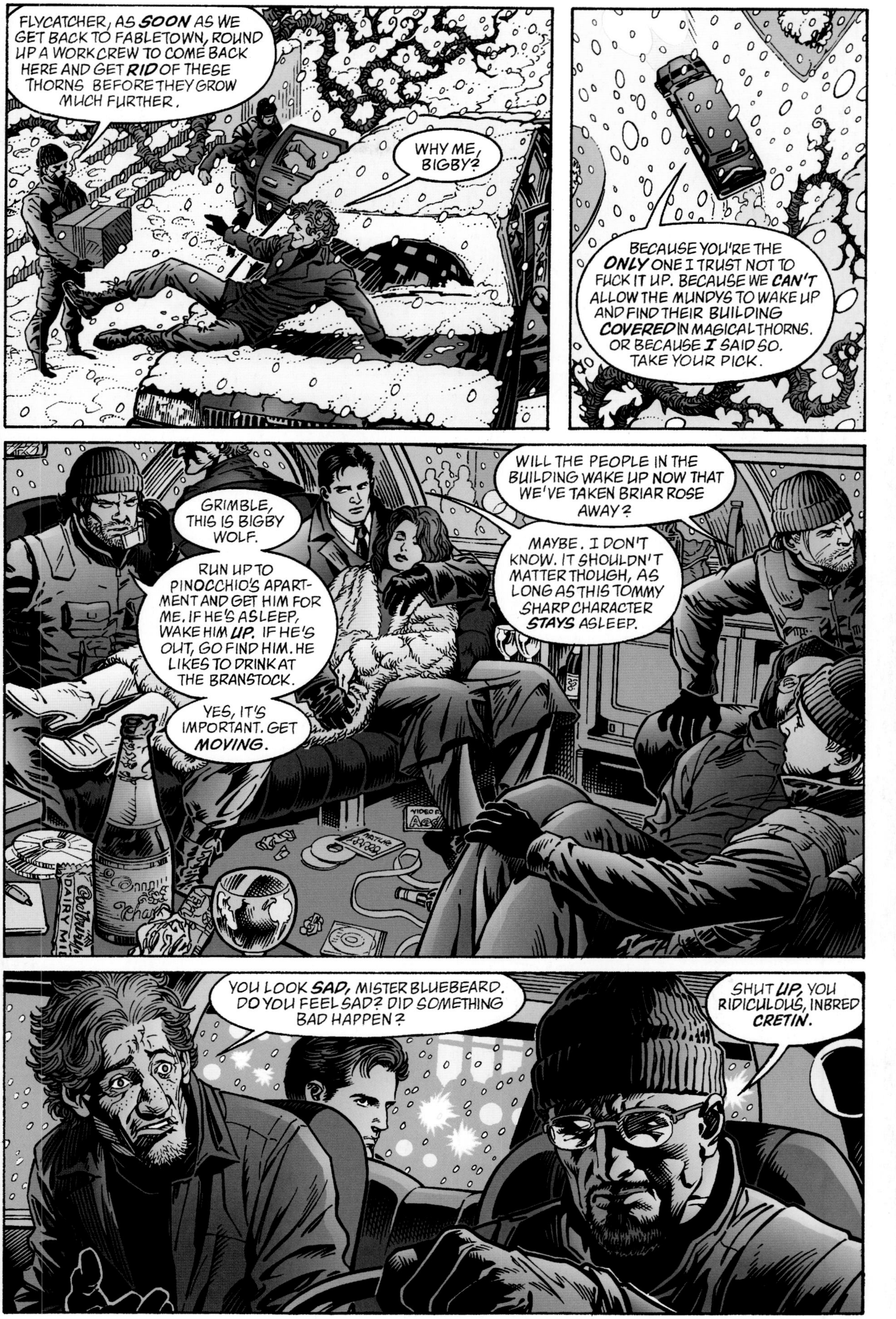
FLYCATCHER, AS SOON AS WE GET BACK TO FABLETOWN, ROUND UP A WORKCREW TO COME BACK HERE AND GET RID OF THESE THORNS BEFORE THEY GROW MUCH FURTHER.
WHY ME, BIGBY?
BECAUSE YOU'RE THE ONLY ONE I TRUST NOT TO FUCK IT UP. BECAUSE WE CAN'T ALLOW THE MUNDYS TO WAKE UP AND FIND THEIR BUILDING COVERED IN MAGICAL THORNS. OR BECAUSE I SAID SO. TAKE YOUR PICK.
GRIMBLE, THIS IS BIGBY WOLF.
RUN UP TO PINOCCHIO'S APARTMENT AND GET HIM FOR ME. IF HE'S ASLEEP, WAKE HIM UP. IF HE'S OUT, GO FIND HIM. HE LIKES TO DRINK AT THE BRANSTOCK.
YES, IT'S IMPORTANT. GET MOVING.
WILL THE PEOPLE IN THE BUILDING WAKE UP NOW THAT WE'VE TAKEN BRIAR ROSE AWAY?
MAYBE. I DON'T KNOW. IT SHOULDN'T MATTER THOUGH, AS LONG AS THIS TOMMY SHARP CHARACTER STAYS ASLEEP.
YOU LOOK SAD, MISTER BLUEBEARD. DO YOU FEEL SAD? DID SOMETHING BAD HAPPEN?
SHUT UP, YOU RIDICULOUS, INBRED CRETIN.

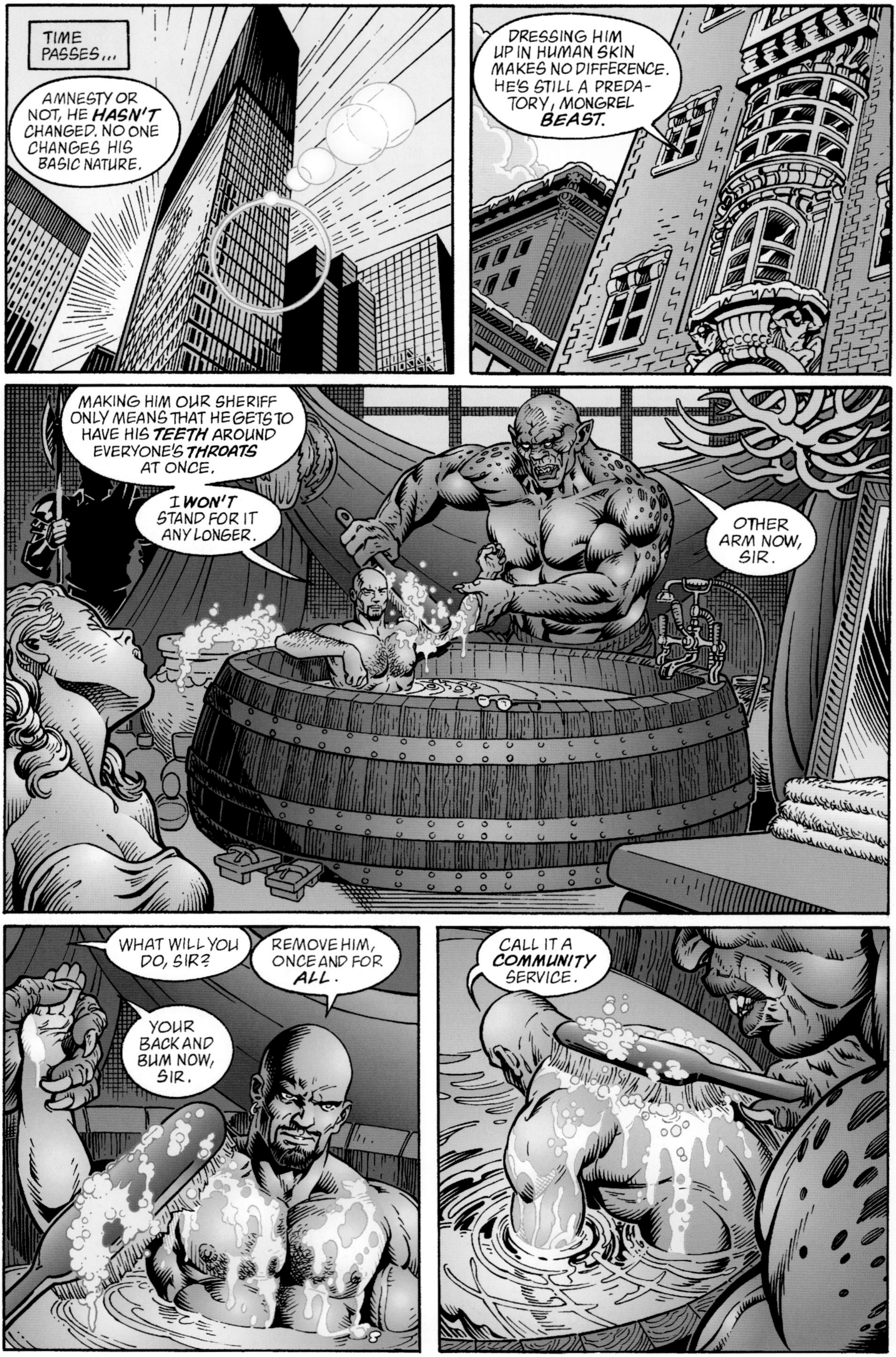

TIME PASSES...
AMNESTY OR NOT, HE **HASN'T** CHANGED. NO ONE CHANGES HIS BASIC NATURE.
DRESSING HIM UP IN HUMAN SKIN MAKES NO DIFFERENCE. HE'S STILL A PREDATORY, MONGREL **BEAST**.
MAKING HIM OUR SHERIFF ONLY MEANS THAT HE GETS TO HAVE HIS **TEETH** AROUND EVERYONE'S **THROATS** AT ONCE.
I **WON'T** STAND FOR IT ANY LONGER.
OTHER ARM NOW, SIR.
WHAT WILL YOU DO, SIR?
REMOVE HIM, ONCE AND FOR **ALL**.
YOUR BACK AND BUM NOW, SIR.
CALL IT A **COMMUNITY** SERVICE.

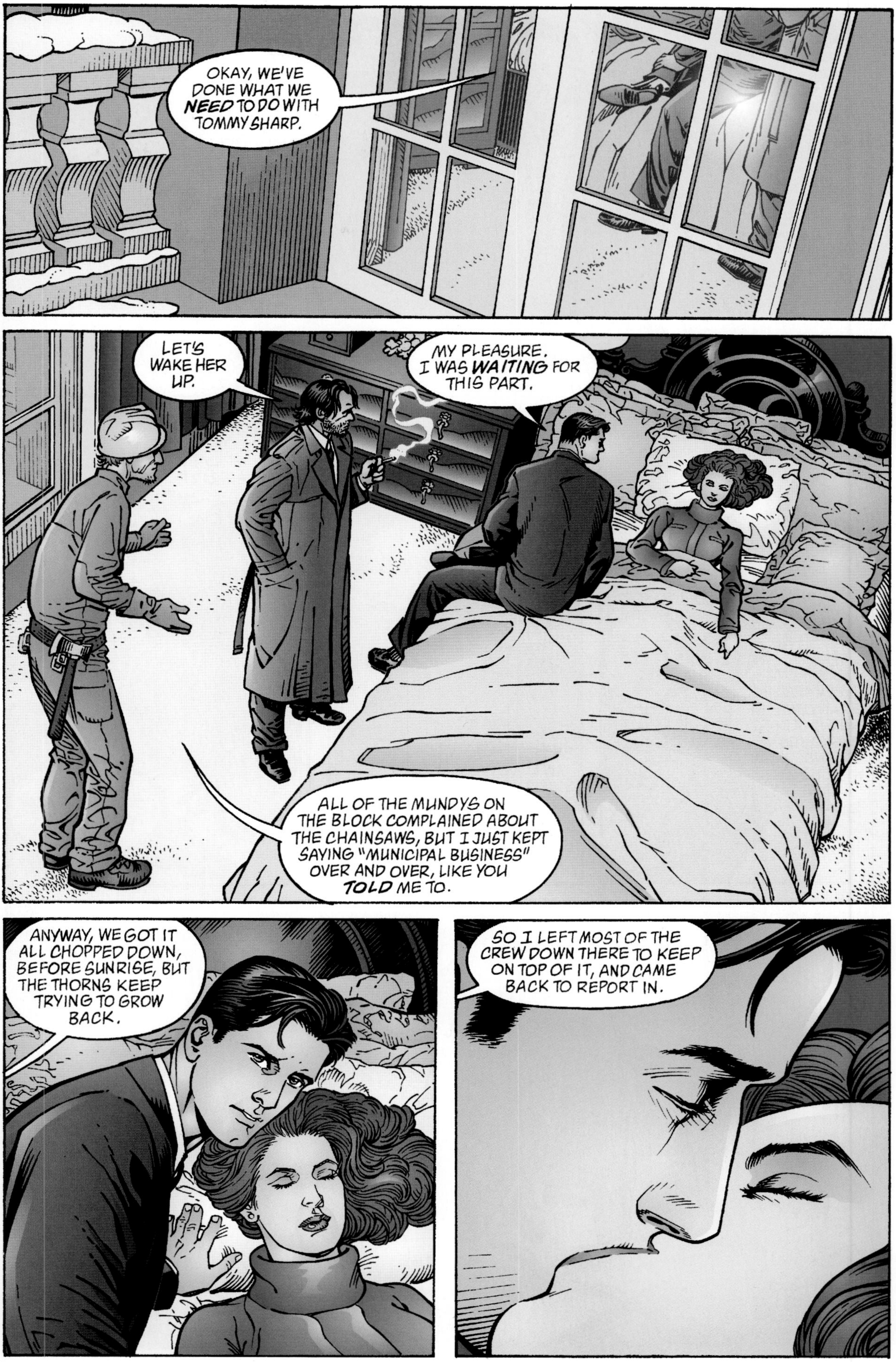
OKAY, WE'VE DONE WHAT WE NEED TO DO WITH TOMMY SHARP.
LET'S WAKE HER UP.
MY PLEASURE. I WAS WAITING FOR THIS PART.
ALL OF THE MUNDYS ON THE BLOCK COMPLAINED ABOUT THE CHAINSAWS, BUT I JUST KEPT SAYING "MUNICIPAL BUSINESS" OVER AND OVER, LIKE YOU TOLD ME TO.
ANYWAY, WE GOT IT ALL CHOPPED DOWN, BEFORE SUNRISE, BUT THE THORNS KEEP TRYING TO GROW BACK.
SO I LEFT MOST OF THE CREW DOWN THERE TO KEEP ON TOP OF IT, AND CAME BACK TO REPORT IN.

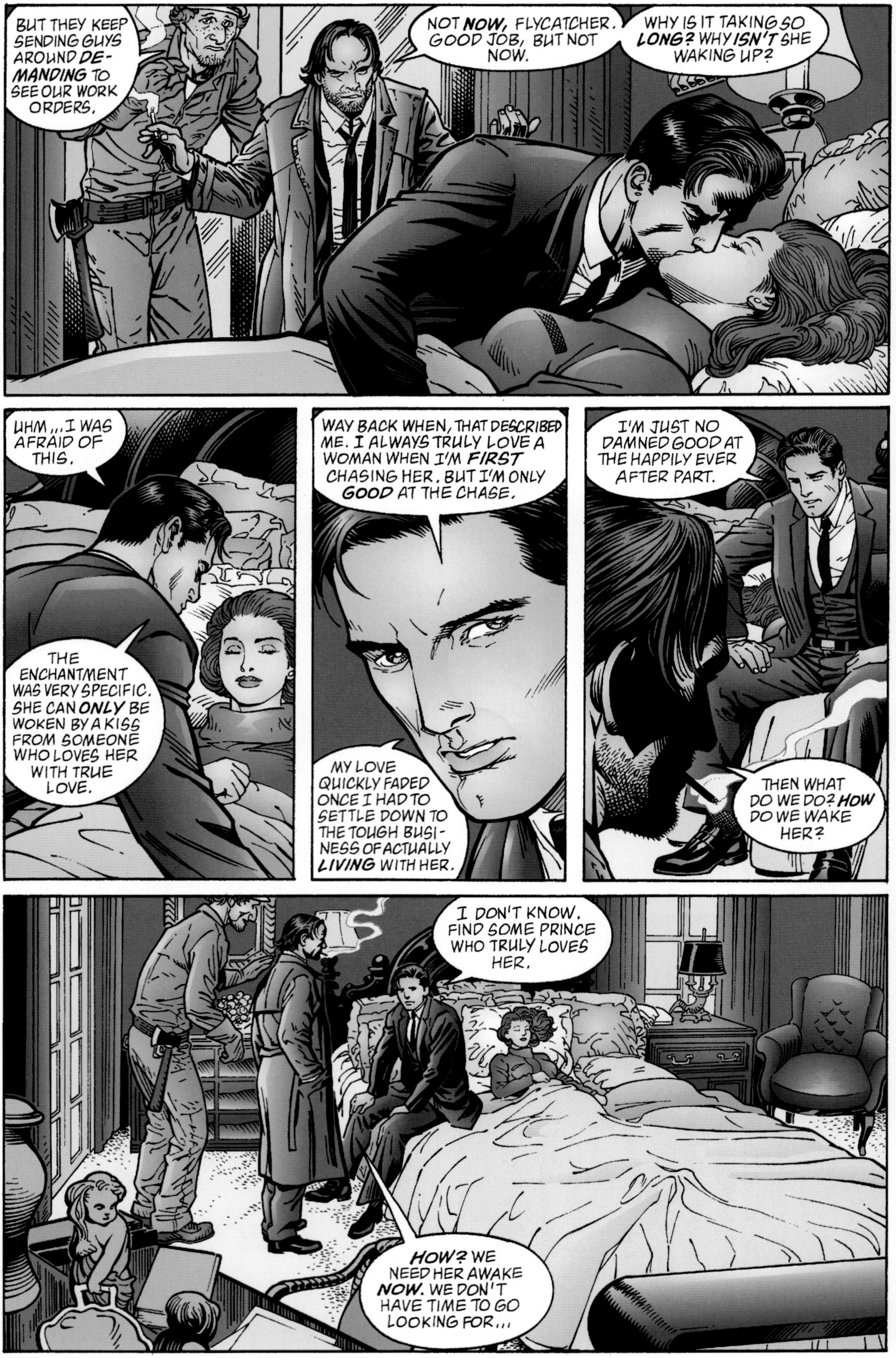
BUT THEY KEEP SENDING GUYS AROUND DE-MANDING TO SEE OUR WORK ORDERS.
NOT NOW, FLYCATCHER. GOOD JOB, BUT NOT NOW.
WHY IS IT TAKING SO LONG? WHY ISN'T SHE WAKING UP?
UHM... I WAS AFRAID OF THIS.
THE ENCHANTMENT WAS VERY SPECIFIC. SHE CAN ONLY BE WOKEN BY A KISS FROM SOMEONE WHO LOVES HER WITH TRUE LOVE.
WAY BACK WHEN, THAT DESCRIBED ME. I ALWAYS TRULY LOVE A WOMAN WHEN I'M FIRST CHASING HER. BUT I'M ONLY GOOD AT THE CHASE.
MY LOVE QUICKLY FADED ONCE I HAD TO SETTLE DOWN TO THE TOUGH BUSI-NESS OF ACTUALLY LIVING WITH HER.
I'M JUST NO DAMNED GOOD AT THE HAPPILY EVER AFTER PART.
THEN WHAT DO WE DO? HOW DO WE WAKE HER?
I DON'T KNOW. FIND SOME PRINCE WHO TRULY LOVES HER.
HOW? WE NEED HER AWAKE NOW. WE DON'T HAVE TIME TO GO LOOKING FOR...

EXCUSE ME, MISTER WOLF. *I* COULD TRY.

NOT NOW, FLY. THIS IS GROWN-UP TALK. WE NEED TO BE *SERIOUS* NOW.

BUT *I* *AM* SERIOUS. YOU NEED A PRINCE AND I'M A PRINCE. MAYBE NOT A VERY HANDSOME ONE, BUT I'M AWFULLY FOND OF MISS BRIAR. I MEAN SHE'S... I TAKE ONE LOOK AT HER AND I WANT TO...

...WHO WOULDN'T?

WHAT THE HELL. WHY NOT? GIVE IT A SHOT.

ARE YOU OUT OF YOUR *MIND?* HE'S AN *IMBECILE!*

LET HIM TRY. WHAT COULD IT *HURT?*

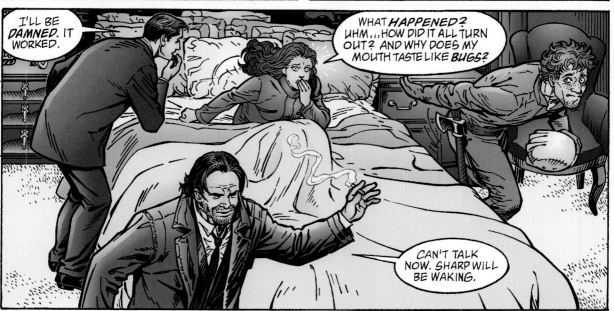

I'LL BE *DAMNED.* IT WORKED.

WHAT *HAPPENED?* UHM... HOW DID IT ALL TURN OUT? AND WHY DOES MY MOUTH TASTE LIKE *BUGS?*

CAN'T TALK NOW. SHARP WILL BE WAKING.

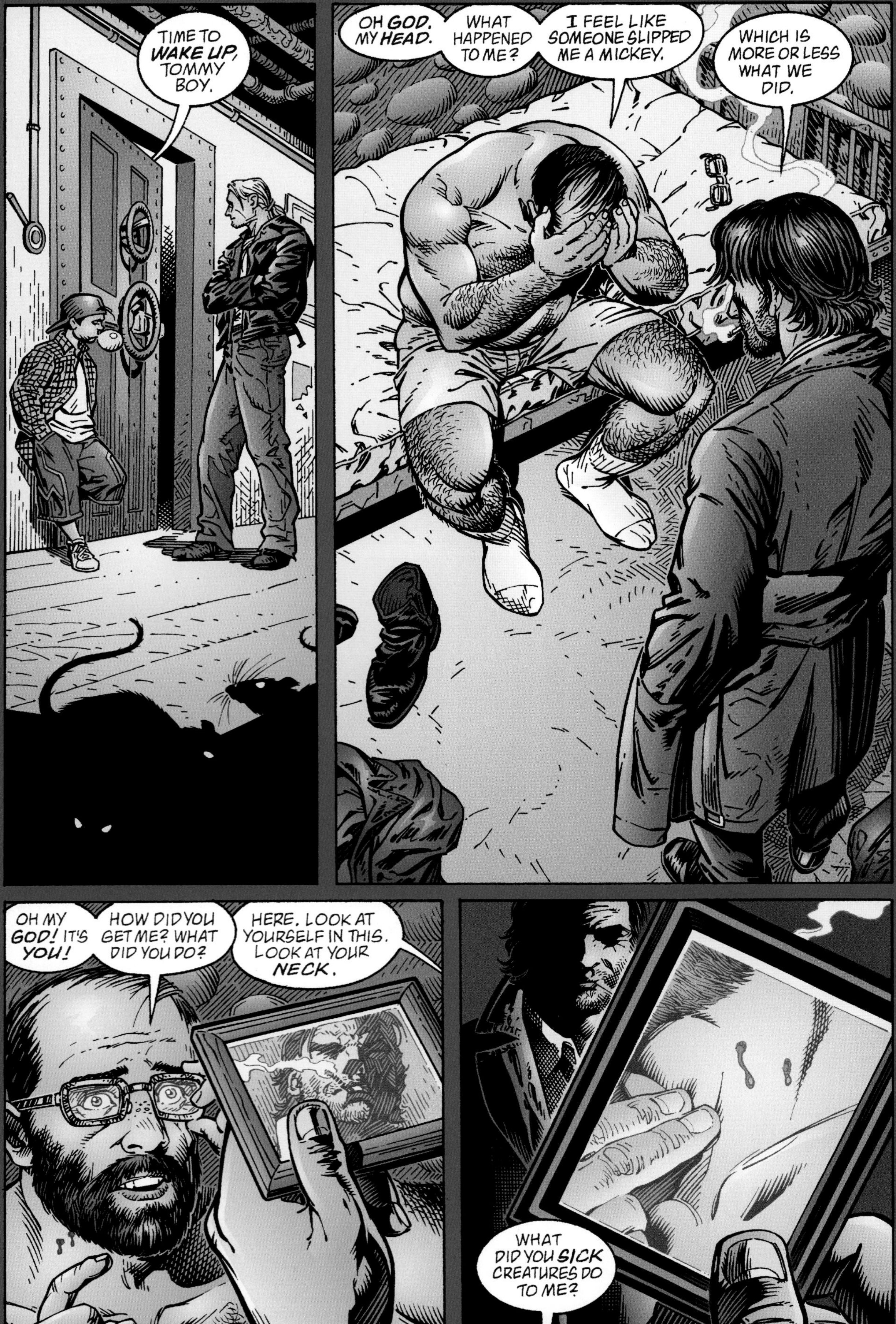
TIME TO WAKE UP, TOMMY BOY.
OH GOD. MY HEAD.
WHAT HAPPENED TO ME?
I FEEL LIKE SOMEONE SLIPPED ME A MICKEY.
WHICH IS MORE OR LESS WHAT WE DID.
OH MY GOD! IT'S YOU!
HOW DID YOU GET ME? WHAT DID YOU DO?
HERE. LOOK AT YOURSELF IN THIS. LOOK AT YOUR NECK.
WHAT DID YOU SICK CREATURES DO TO ME?

YOU FIGURED OUT WE'RE VAMPIRES, TOMMY. YOU KNOW WHAT WE DID. WE DRANK YOUR BLOOD.

OH DEAR LORDY.

NOT ALL THAT MUCH. NOT ENOUGH TO CHANGE YOU INTO ONE OF US. *RELAX*. YOU WON'T BE GROWING FANGS OR AVOIDING ITALIAN FOOD.

BUT NOW WE'LL BE ABLE TO KEEP TABS ON YOU, AND CONTROL YOU IF WE HAVE TO. YOU'VE SEEN THE MOVIES, YOU *KNOW* HOW THAT WORKS.

I ONLY WANTED A BIG STORY. I DIDN'T *MEAN* ANYTHING.

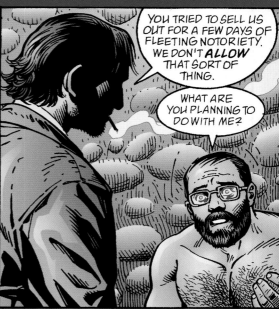

YOU TRIED TO SELL US OUT FOR A FEW DAYS OF FLEETING NOTORIETY. WE DON'T *ALLOW* THAT SORT OF THING.

WHAT ARE YOU PLANNING TO DO WITH ME?

NOTHING, AS LONG AS YOU BEHAVE. BUT IF YOU EXPOSE US, WE'LL MAKE YOU DO SOMETHING *FATAL* TO YOURSELF. HANG YOURSELF. SLIT YOUR WRISTS IN THE BATH.

WHATEVER STRIKES OUR *FANCY* AT THE TIME. WE'VE TASTED YOUR *BLOOD*. YOU WON'T BE ABLE TO RESIST US.

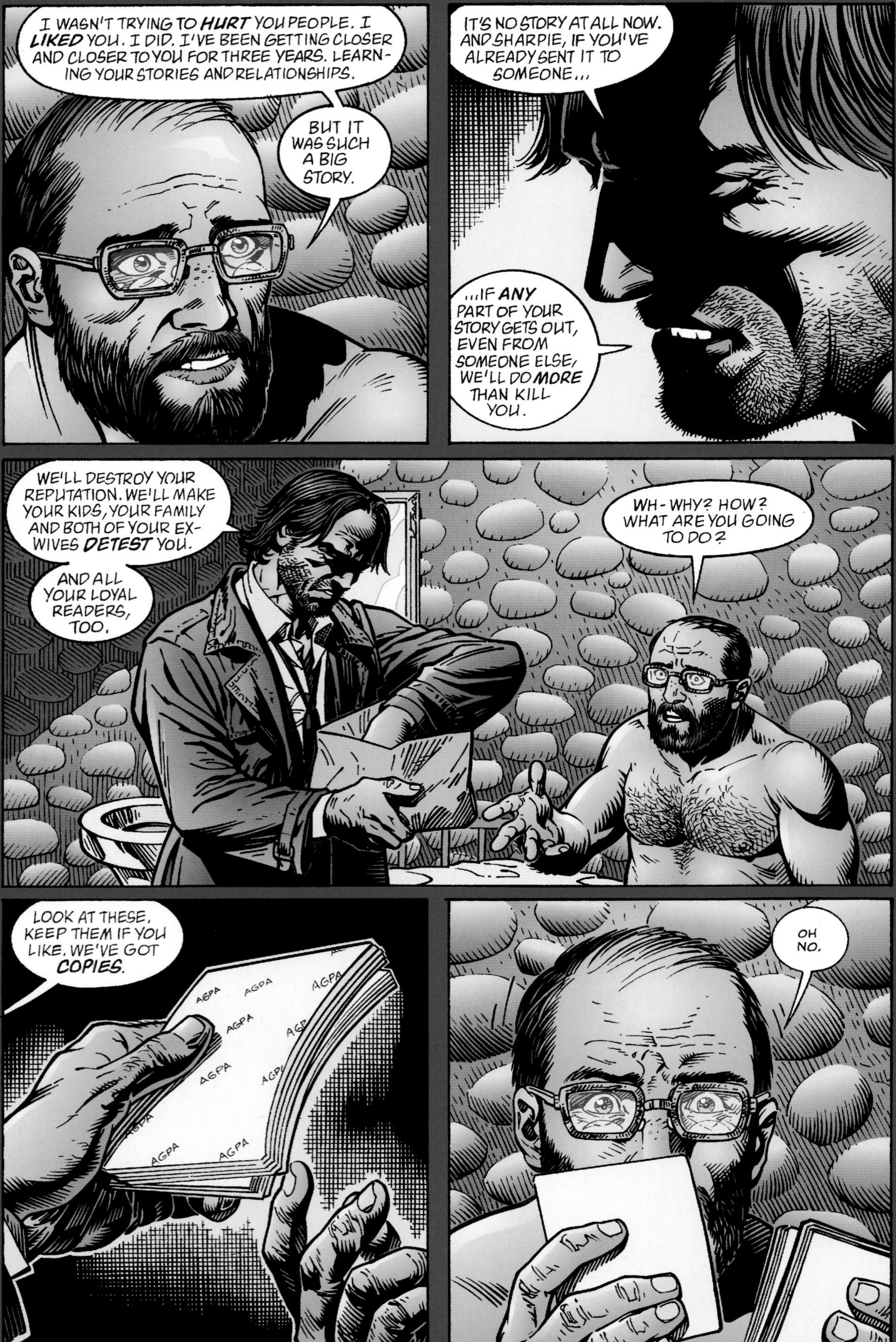
I WASN'T TRYING TO HURT YOU PEOPLE. I LIKED YOU. I DID. I'VE BEEN GETTING CLOSER AND CLOSER TO YOU FOR THREE YEARS. LEARNING YOUR STORIES AND RELATIONSHIPS.
BUT IT WAS SUCH A BIG STORY.
IT'S NO STORY AT ALL NOW. AND SHARPIE, IF YOU'VE ALREADY SENT IT TO SOMEONE...
...IF ANY PART OF YOUR STORY GETS OUT, EVEN FROM SOMEONE ELSE, WE'LL DO MORE THAN KILL YOU.
WE'LL DESTROY YOUR REPUTATION. WE'LL MAKE YOUR KIDS, YOUR FAMILY AND BOTH OF YOUR EX-WIVES DETEST YOU.
AND ALL YOUR LOYAL READERS, TOO.
WH- WHY? HOW? WHAT ARE YOU GOING TO DO?
LOOK AT THESE. KEEP THEM IF YOU LIKE. WE'VE GOT COPIES.
AGPA
OH NO.

WHAT HAVE YOU **DONE?**

WHAT DID YOU MAKE ME **DO?**

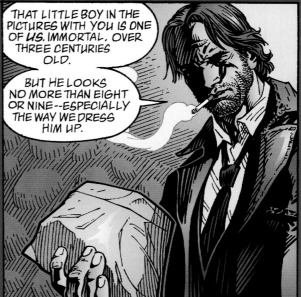

THAT LITTLE BOY IN THE PICTURES WITH YOU IS ONE OF *US.* IMMORTAL, OVER THREE CENTURIES OLD.

BUT HE LOOKS NO MORE THAN EIGHT OR NINE--ESPECIALLY THE WAY WE DRESS HIM UP.

I *NEVER* DID THIS. I'M NOT--

I *COULDN'T* HAVE.

WHAT WILL PEOPLE THINK OF YOU WHEN THESE GET OUT? EVEN IN OUR LIBERTINE ERA THIS SORT OF CONDUCT IS NOTHING SHORT OF *DISGUSTING.*

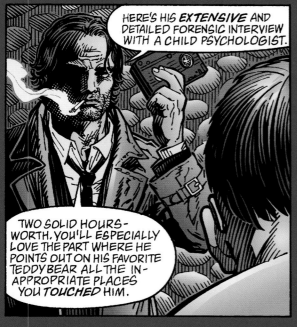

HERE'S HIS *EXTENSIVE* AND DETAILED FORENSIC INTERVIEW WITH A CHILD PSYCHOLOGIST.

TWO SOLID HOURS-WORTH. YOU'LL ESPECIALLY LOVE THE PART WHERE HE POINTS OUT ON HIS FAVORITE TEDDY BEAR ALL THE IN-APPROPRIATE PLACES YOU *TOUCHED* HIM.

HE'S *VERY* CONVINCING.

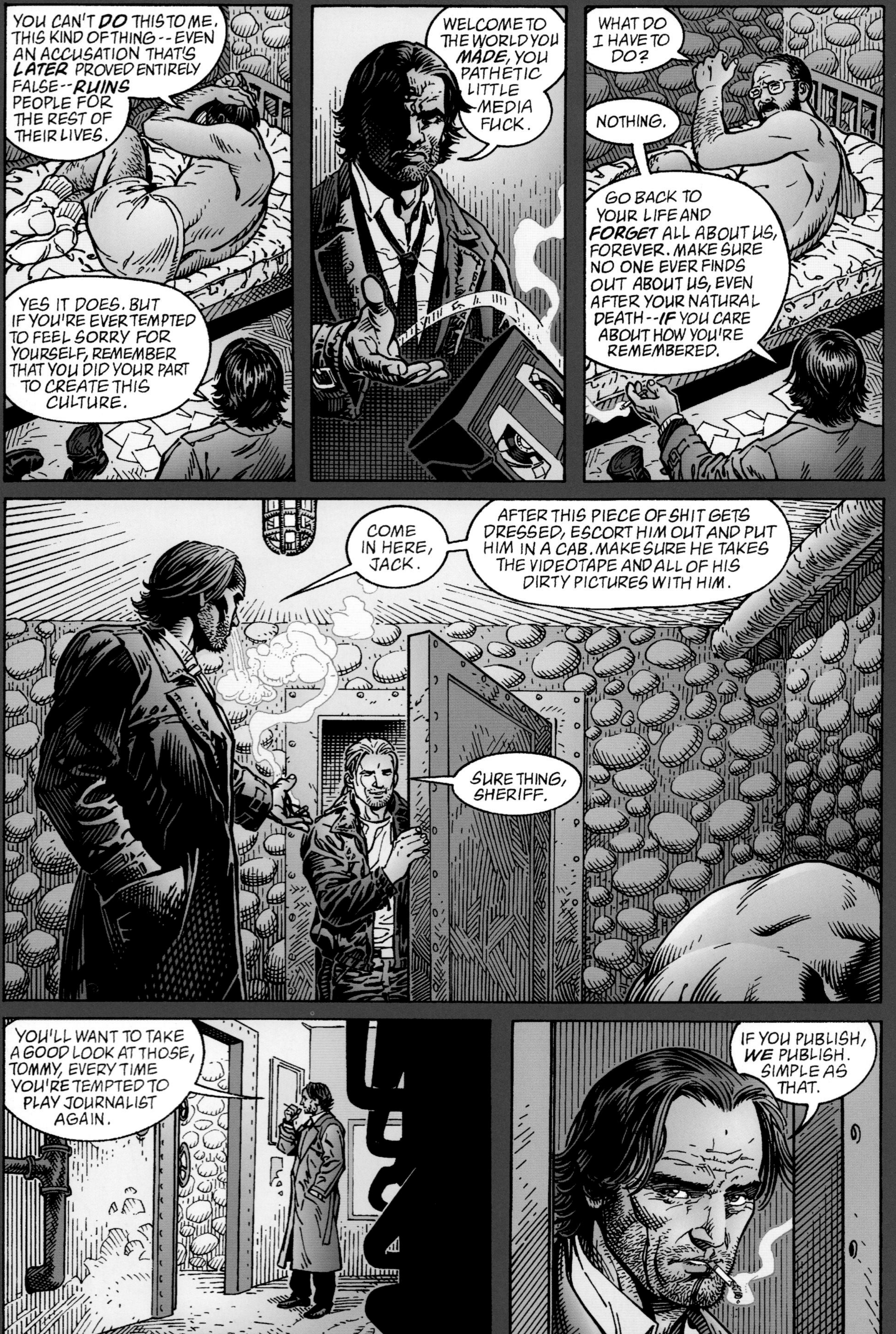
YOU CAN'T DO THIS TO ME. THIS KIND OF THING -- EVEN AN ACCUSATION THAT'S LATER PROVED ENTIRELY FALSE--RUINS PEOPLE FOR THE REST OF THEIR LIVES.
YES IT DOES. BUT IF YOU'RE EVER TEMPTED TO FEEL SORRY FOR YOURSELF, REMEMBER THAT YOU DID YOUR PART TO CREATE THIS CULTURE.
WELCOME TO THE WORLD YOU MADE, YOU PATHETIC LITTLE MEDIA FUCK.
WHAT DO I HAVE TO DO?
NOTHING.
GO BACK TO YOUR LIFE AND FORGET ALL ABOUT US, FOREVER. MAKE SURE NO ONE EVER FINDS OUT ABOUT US, EVEN AFTER YOUR NATURAL DEATH--IF YOU CARE ABOUT HOW YOU'RE REMEMBERED.
COME IN HERE, JACK.
AFTER THIS PIECE OF SHIT GETS DRESSED, ESCORT HIM OUT AND PUT HIM IN A CAB. MAKE SURE HE TAKES THE VIDEOTAPE AND ALL OF HIS DIRTY PICTURES WITH HIM.
SURE THING, SHERIFF.
YOU'LL WANT TO TAKE A GOOD LOOK AT THOSE, TOMMY, EVERY TIME YOU'RE TEMPTED TO PLAY JOURNALIST AGAIN.
IF YOU PUBLISH, WE PUBLISH. SIMPLE AS THAT.

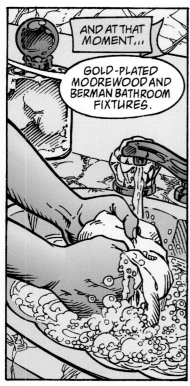

AND AT THAT MOMENT...

GOLD-PLATED MOOREWOOD AND BERMAN BATHROOM FIXTURES.

VENETIAN MARBLE TILES AND COUNTER-TOPS.

ETRUSCAN STATUARY.

SUNG DYNASTY CERAMICS. OH, BRIAR, MY LOST LOVE--

--YOU *HAVE* DONE WELL FOR YOURSELF.

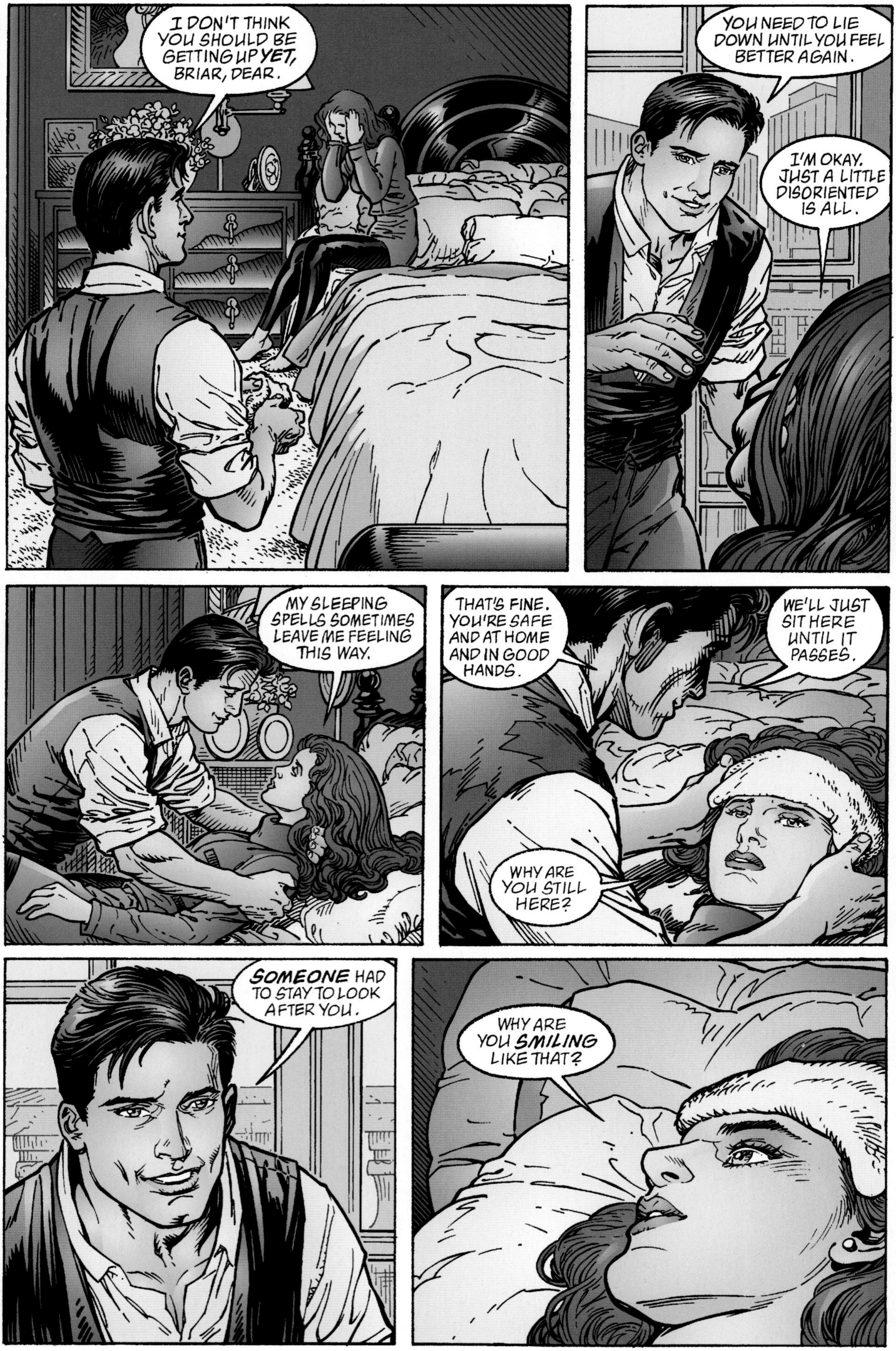
I DON'T THINK YOU SHOULD BE GETTING UP **YET**, BRIAR, DEAR.
YOU NEED TO LIE DOWN UNTIL YOU FEEL BETTER AGAIN.
I'M OKAY. JUST A LITTLE DISORIENTED IS ALL.
MY SLEEPING SPELLS SOMETIMES LEAVE ME FEELING THIS WAY.
THAT'S FINE. YOU'RE SAFE AND AT HOME AND IN GOOD HANDS.
WE'LL JUST SIT HERE UNTIL IT PASSES.
WHY ARE YOU STILL HERE?
SOMEONE HAD TO STAY TO LOOK AFTER YOU.
WHY ARE YOU **SMILING** LIKE THAT?

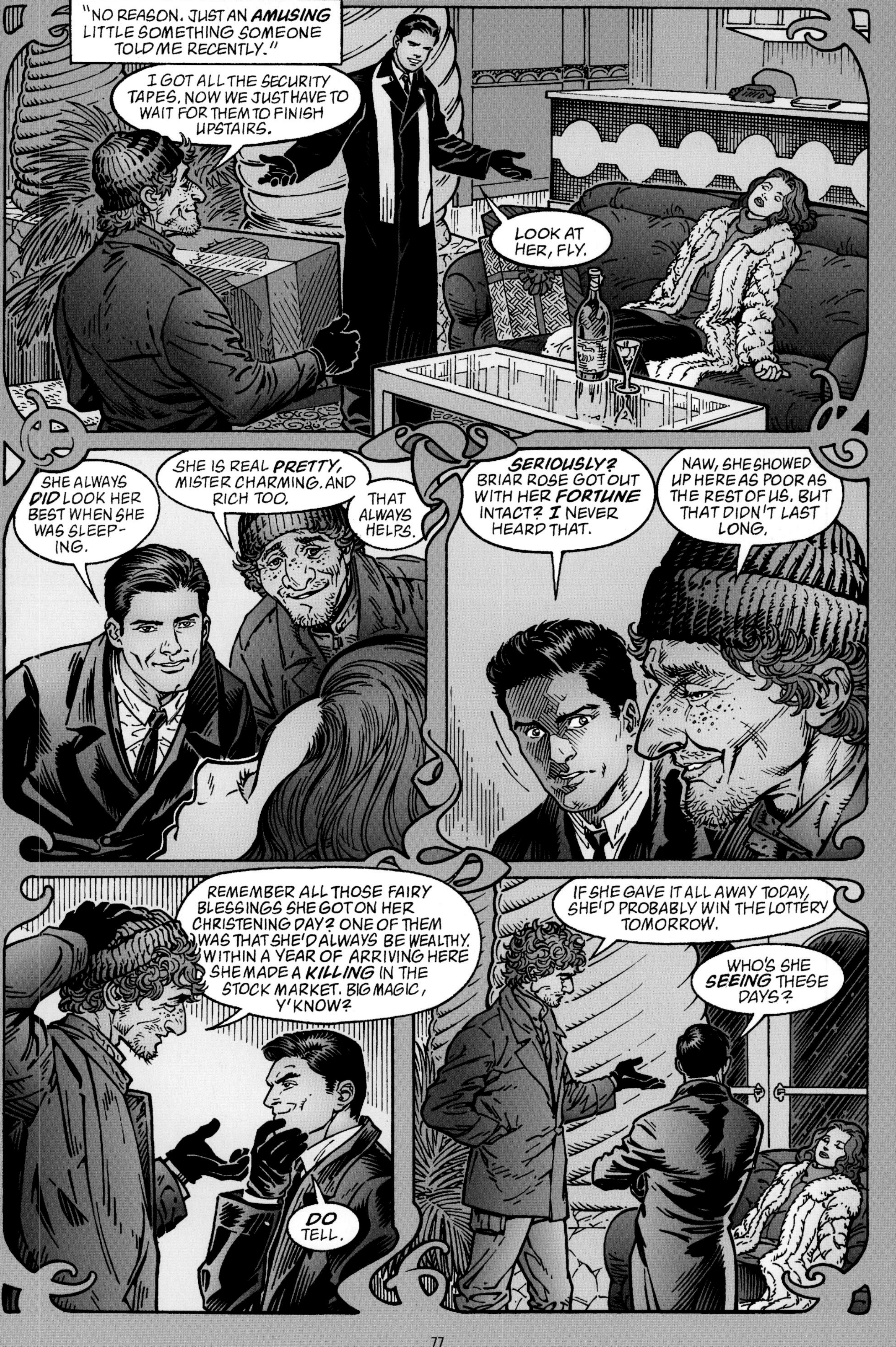
"NO REASON. JUST AN AMUSING LITTLE SOMETHING SOMEONE TOLD ME RECENTLY."
I GOT ALL THE SECURITY TAPES. NOW WE JUST HAVE TO WAIT FOR THEM TO FINISH UPSTAIRS.
LOOK AT HER, FLY.
SHE ALWAYS DID LOOK HER BEST WHEN SHE WAS SLEEP-ING.
SHE IS REAL PRETTY, MISTER CHARMING. AND RICH TOO.
THAT ALWAYS HELPS.
SERIOUSLY? BRIAR ROSE GOT OUT WITH HER FORTUNE INTACT? I NEVER HEARD THAT.
NAW, SHE SHOWED UP HERE AS POOR AS THE REST OF US. BUT THAT DIDN'T LAST LONG.
REMEMBER ALL THOSE FAIRY BLESSINGS SHE GOT ON HER CHRISTENING DAY? ONE OF THEM WAS THAT SHE'D ALWAYS BE WEALTHY. WITHIN A YEAR OF ARRIVING HERE SHE MADE A KILLING IN THE STOCK MARKET. BIG MAGIC, Y'KNOW?
DO TELL.
IF SHE GAVE IT ALL AWAY TODAY, SHE'D PROBABLY WIN THE LOTTERY TOMORROW.
WHO'S SHE SEEING THESE DAYS?

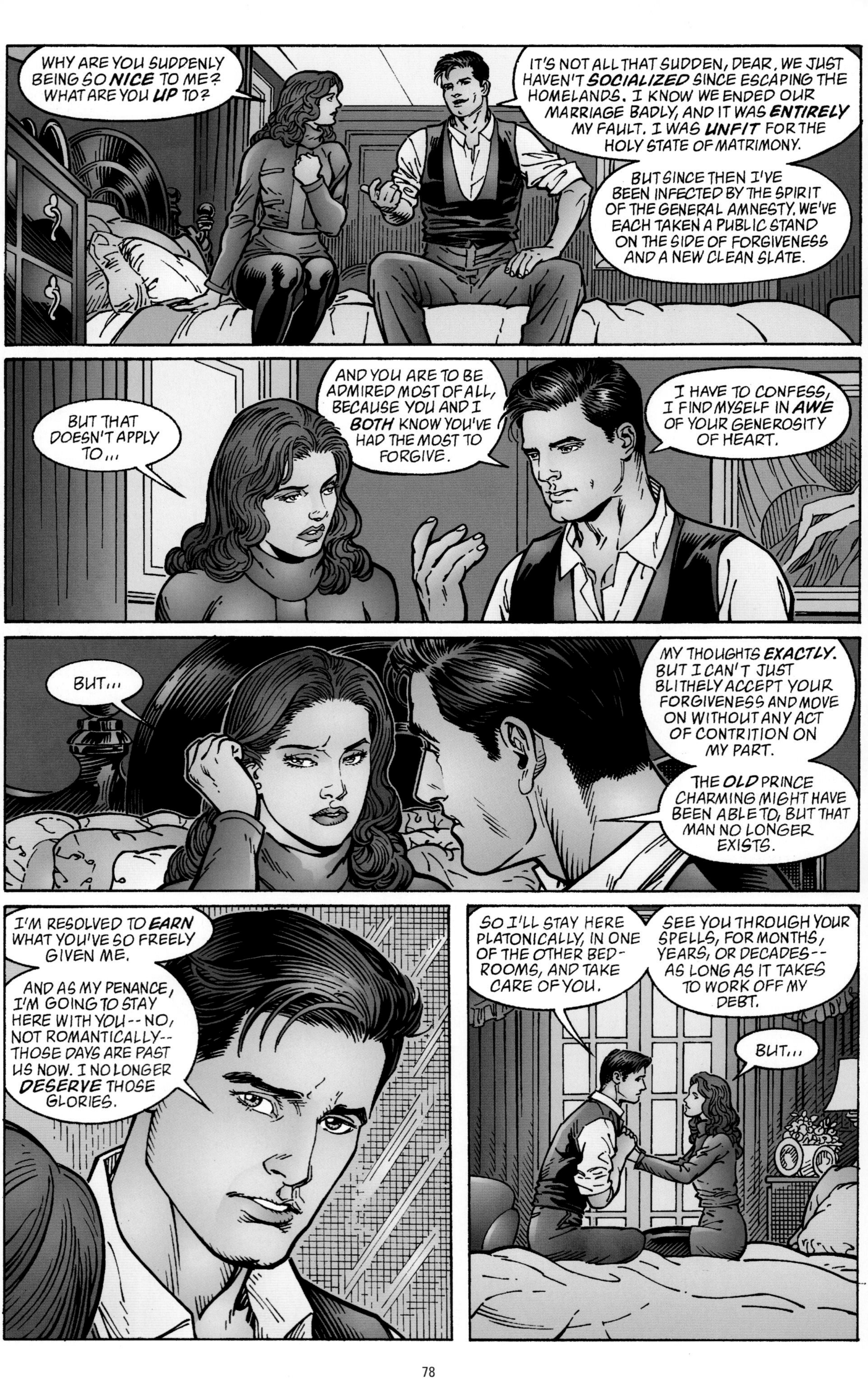
WHY ARE YOU SUDDENLY BEING SO NICE TO ME? WHAT ARE YOU UP TO?
IT'S NOT ALL THAT SUDDEN, DEAR, WE JUST HAVEN'T SOCIALIZED SINCE ESCAPING THE HOMELANDS. I KNOW WE ENDED OUR MARRIAGE BADLY, AND IT WAS ENTIRELY MY FAULT. I WAS UNFIT FOR THE HOLY STATE OF MATRIMONY.
BUT SINCE THEN I'VE BEEN INFECTED BY THE SPIRIT OF THE GENERAL AMNESTY. WE'VE EACH TAKEN A PUBLIC STAND ON THE SIDE OF FORGIVENESS AND A NEW CLEAN SLATE.
BUT THAT DOESN'T APPLY TO...
AND YOU ARE TO BE ADMIRED MOST OF ALL, BECAUSE YOU AND I BOTH KNOW YOU'VE HAD THE MOST TO FORGIVE.
I HAVE TO CONFESS, I FIND MYSELF IN AWE OF YOUR GENEROSITY OF HEART.
BUT...
MY THOUGHTS EXACTLY. BUT I CAN'T JUST BLITHELY ACCEPT YOUR FORGIVENESS AND MOVE ON WITHOUT ANY ACT OF CONTRITION ON MY PART.
THE OLD PRINCE CHARMING MIGHT HAVE BEEN ABLE TO, BUT THAT MAN NO LONGER EXISTS.
I'M RESOLVED TO EARN WHAT YOU'VE SO FREELY GIVEN ME.
AND AS MY PENANCE, I'M GOING TO STAY HERE WITH YOU--NO, NOT ROMANTICALLY--THOSE DAYS ARE PAST US NOW. I NO LONGER DESERVE THOSE GLORIES.
SO I'LL STAY HERE PLATONICALLY, IN ONE OF THE OTHER BED-ROOMS, AND TAKE CARE OF YOU.
SEE YOU THROUGH YOUR SPELLS, FOR MONTHS, YEARS, OR DECADES--AS LONG AS IT TAKES TO WORK OFF MY DEBT.
BUT...

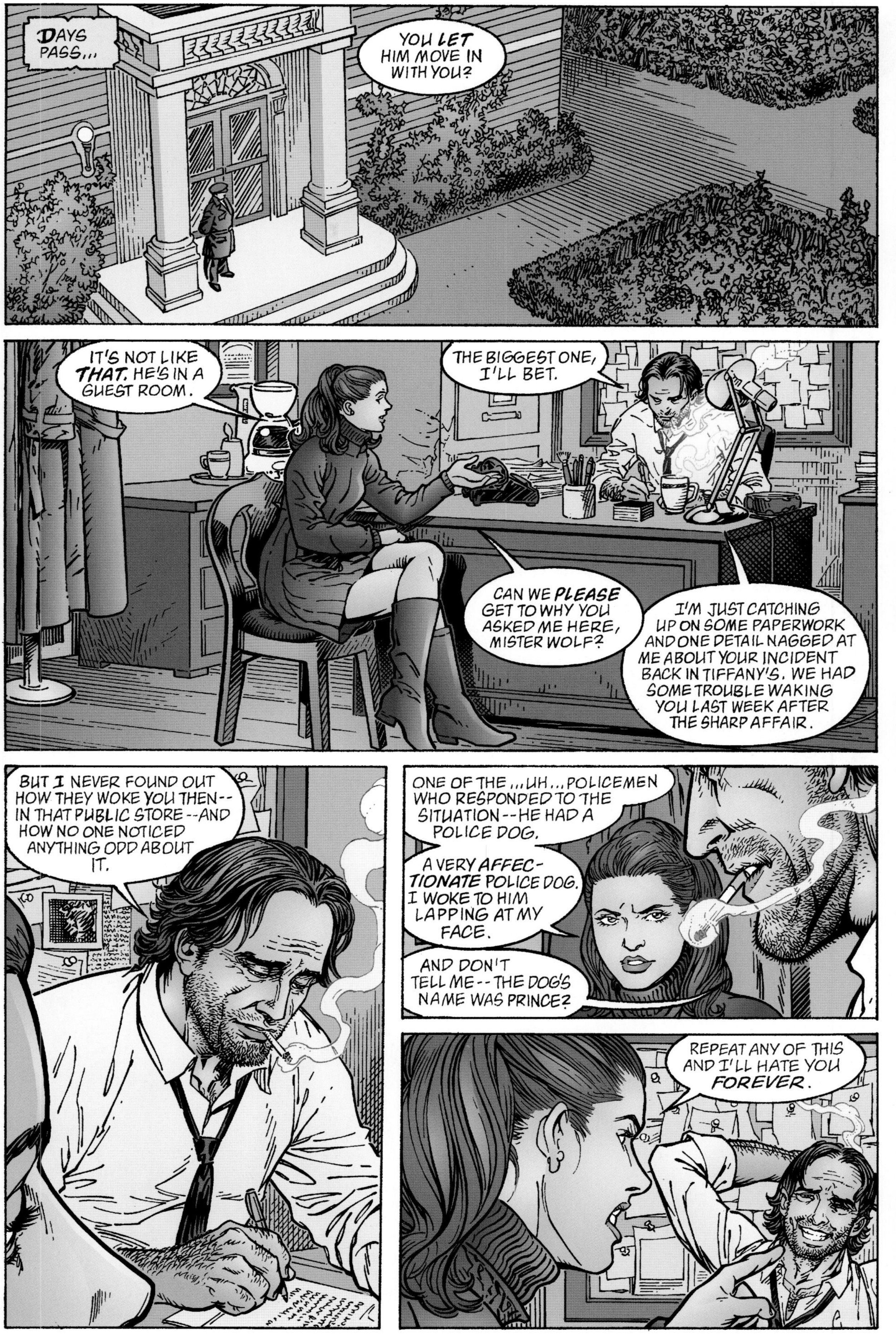
DAYS PASS...
YOU LET HIM MOVE IN WITH YOU?
IT'S NOT LIKE THAT. HE'S IN A GUEST ROOM.
THE BIGGEST ONE, I'LL BET.
CAN WE PLEASE GET TO WHY YOU ASKED ME HERE, MISTER WOLF?
I'M JUST CATCHING UP ON SOME PAPERWORK AND ONE DETAIL NAGGED AT ME ABOUT YOUR INCIDENT BACK IN TIFFANY'S. WE HAD SOME TROUBLE WAKING YOU LAST WEEK AFTER THE SHARP AFFAIR.
BUT I NEVER FOUND OUT HOW THEY WOKE YOU THEN-- IN THAT PUBLIC STORE --AND HOW NO ONE NOTICED ANYTHING ODD ABOUT IT.
ONE OF THE ...UH... POLICEMEN WHO RESPONDED TO THE SITUATION --HE HAD A POLICE DOG.
A VERY AFFECTIONATE POLICE DOG. I WOKE TO HIM LAPPING AT MY FACE.
AND DON'T TELL ME -- THE DOG'S NAME WAS PRINCE?
REPEAT ANY OF THIS AND I'LL HATE YOU FOREVER.

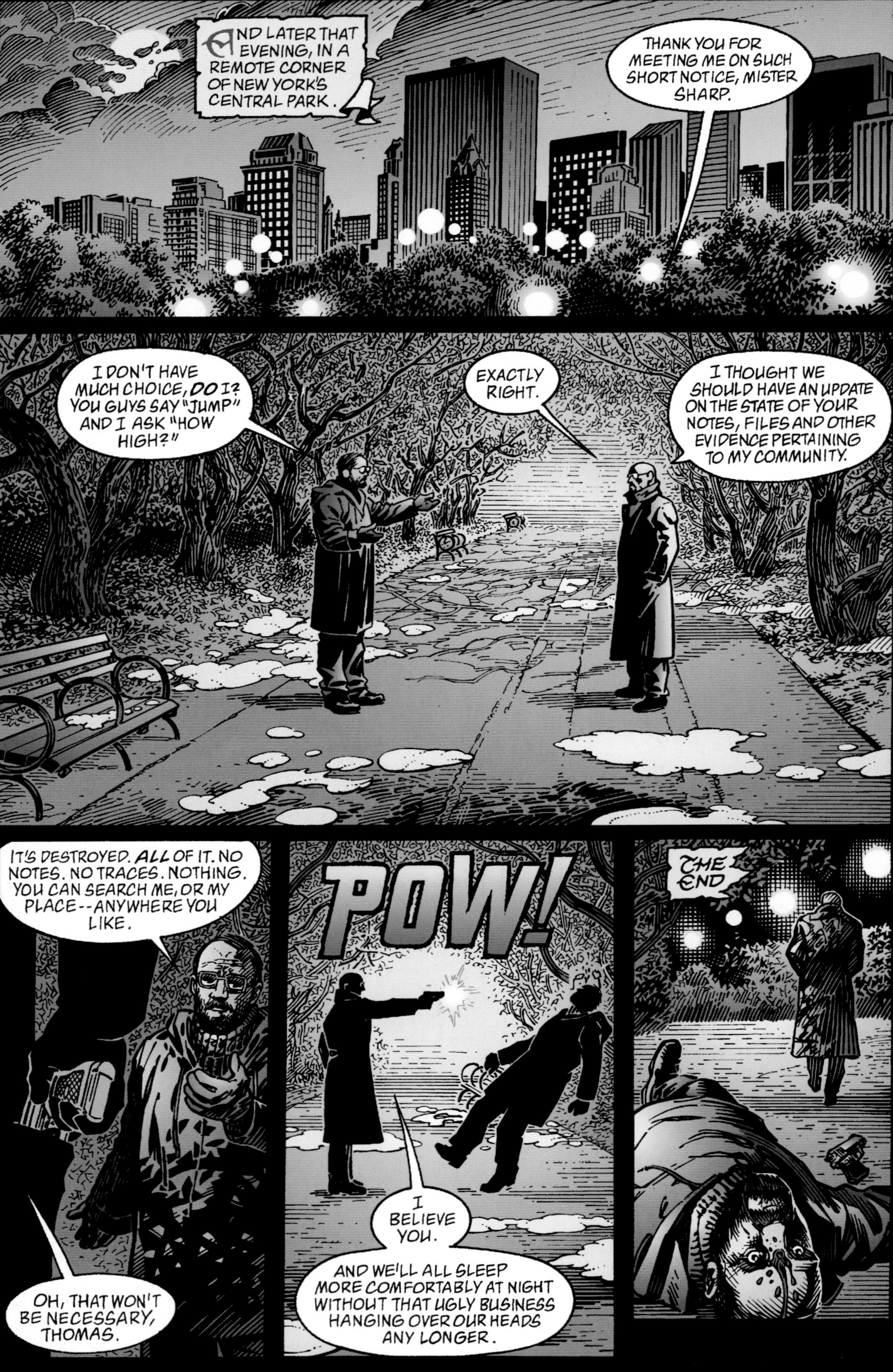
AND LATER THAT EVENING, IN A REMOTE CORNER OF NEW YORK'S CENTRAL PARK.
THANK YOU FOR MEETING ME ON SUCH SHORT NOTICE, MISTER SHARP.
I DON'T HAVE MUCH CHOICE, DO I? YOU GUYS SAY "JUMP" AND I ASK "HOW HIGH?"
EXACTLY RIGHT.
I THOUGHT WE SHOULD HAVE AN UPDATE ON THE STATE OF YOUR NOTES, FILES AND OTHER EVIDENCE PERTAINING TO MY COMMUNITY.
IT'S DESTROYED. ALL OF IT. NO NOTES. NO TRACES. NOTHING. YOU CAN SEARCH ME, OR MY PLACE--ANYWHERE YOU LIKE.
OH, THAT WON'T BE NECESSARY, THOMAS.
POW!
I BELIEVE YOU.
AND WE'LL ALL SLEEP MORE COMFORTABLY AT NIGHT WITHOUT THAT UGLY BUSINESS HANGING OVER OUR HEADS ANY LONGER.
THE END

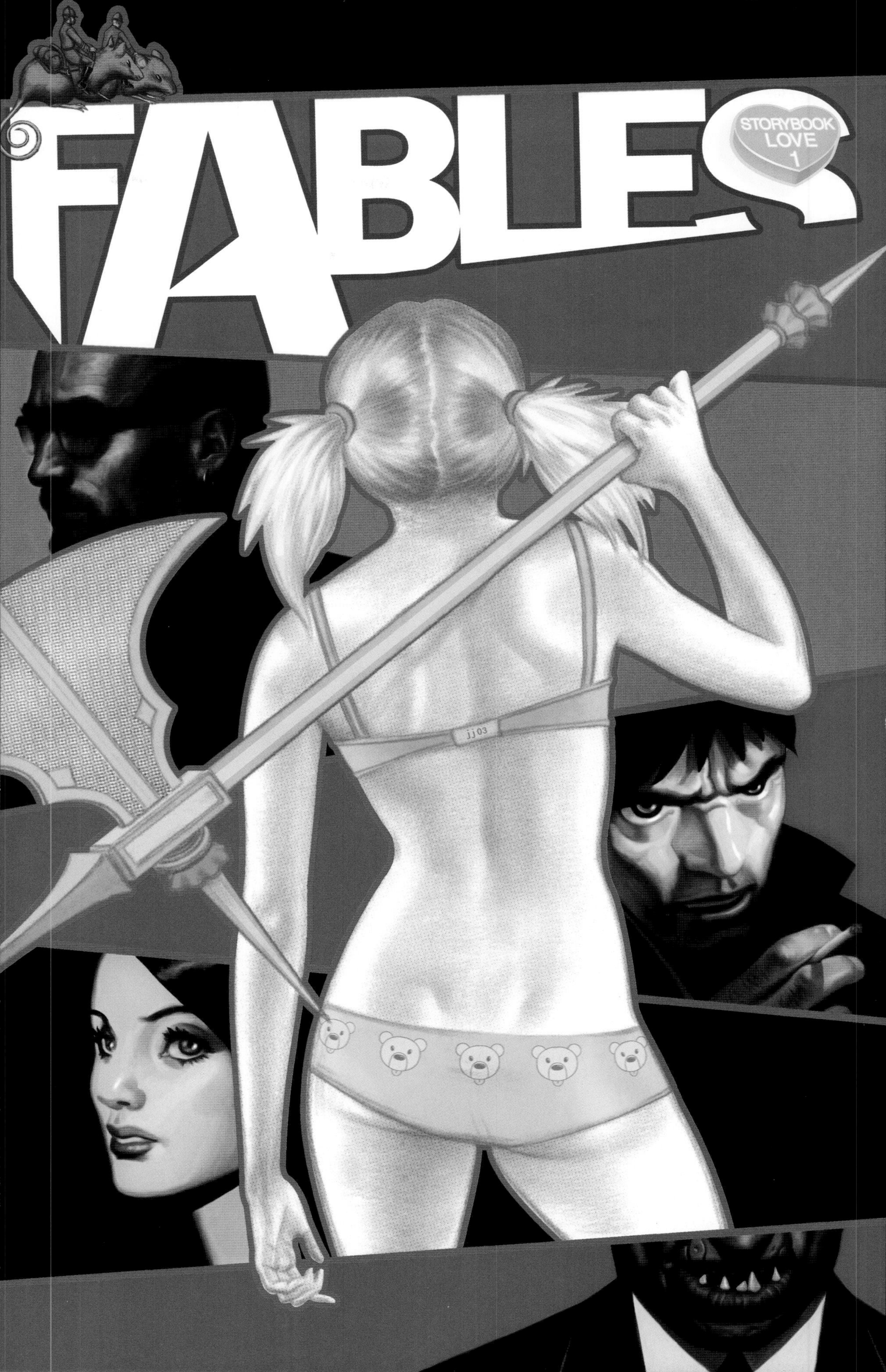
FABLES
STORYBOOK LOVE
1
jj 03

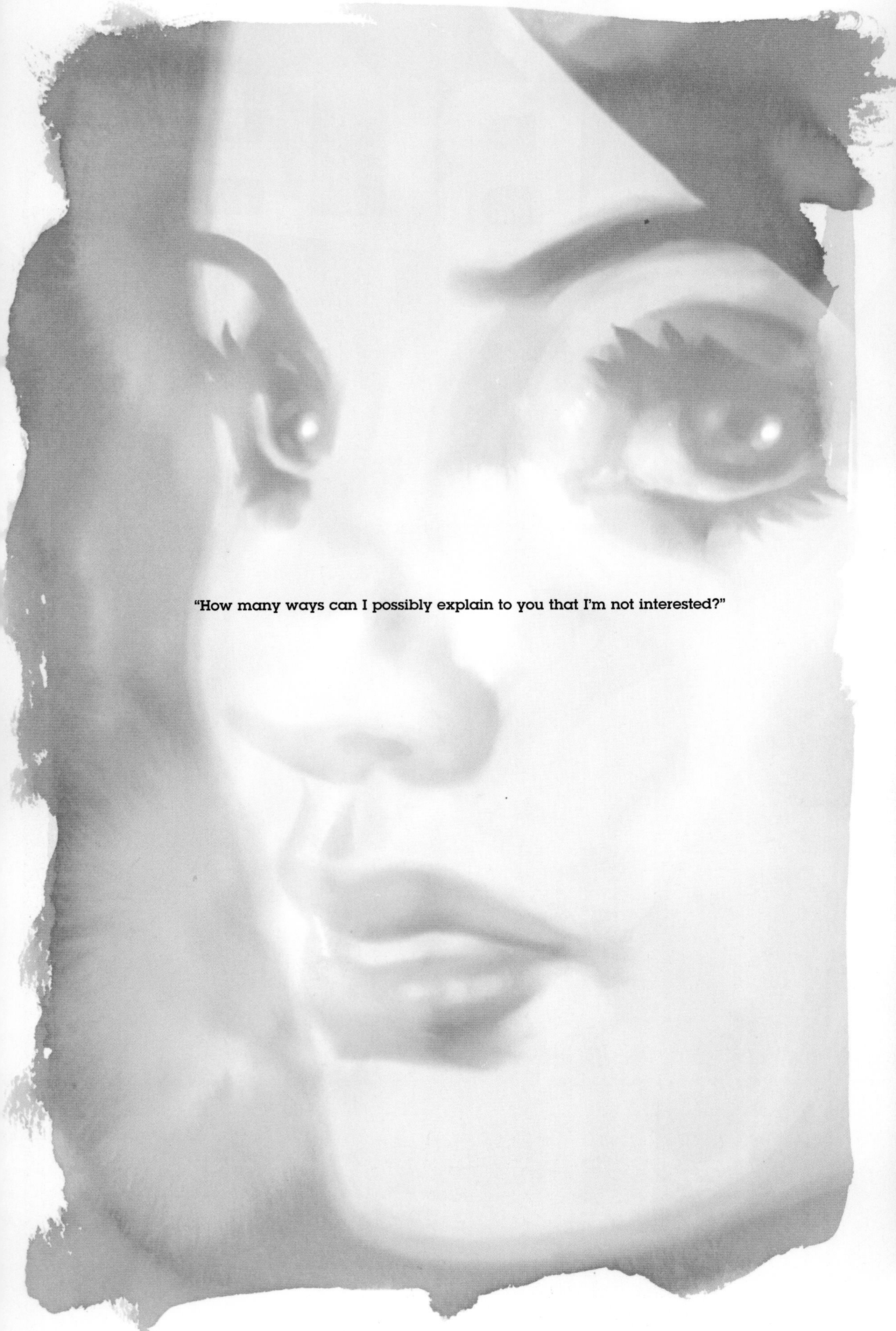
"How many ways can I possibly explain to you that I'm not interested?"

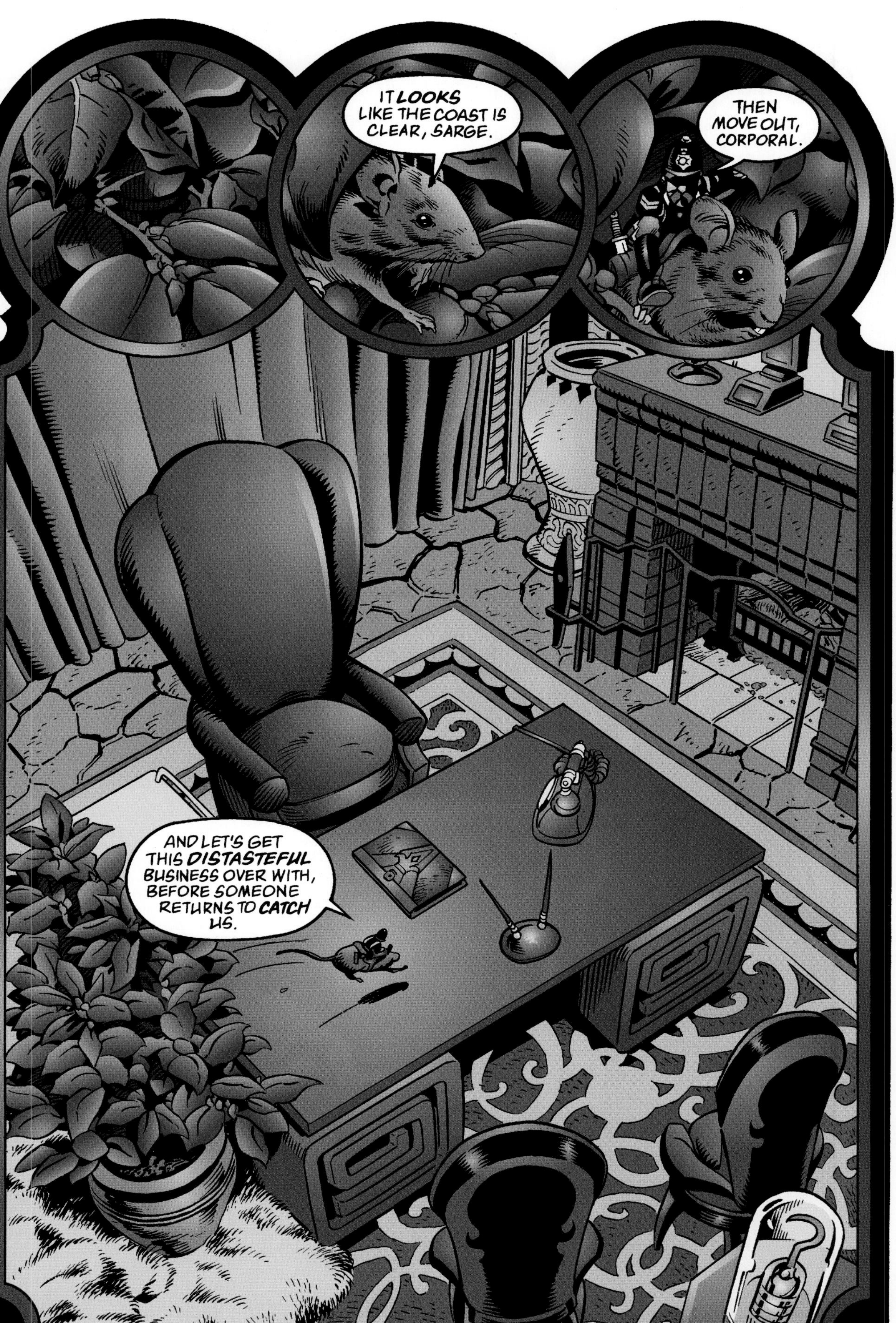
IT LOOKS LIKE THE COAST IS CLEAR, SARGE.
THEN MOVE OUT, CORPORAL.
AND LET'S GET THIS DISTASTEFUL BUSINESS OVER WITH, BEFORE SOMEONE RETURNS TO CATCH US.

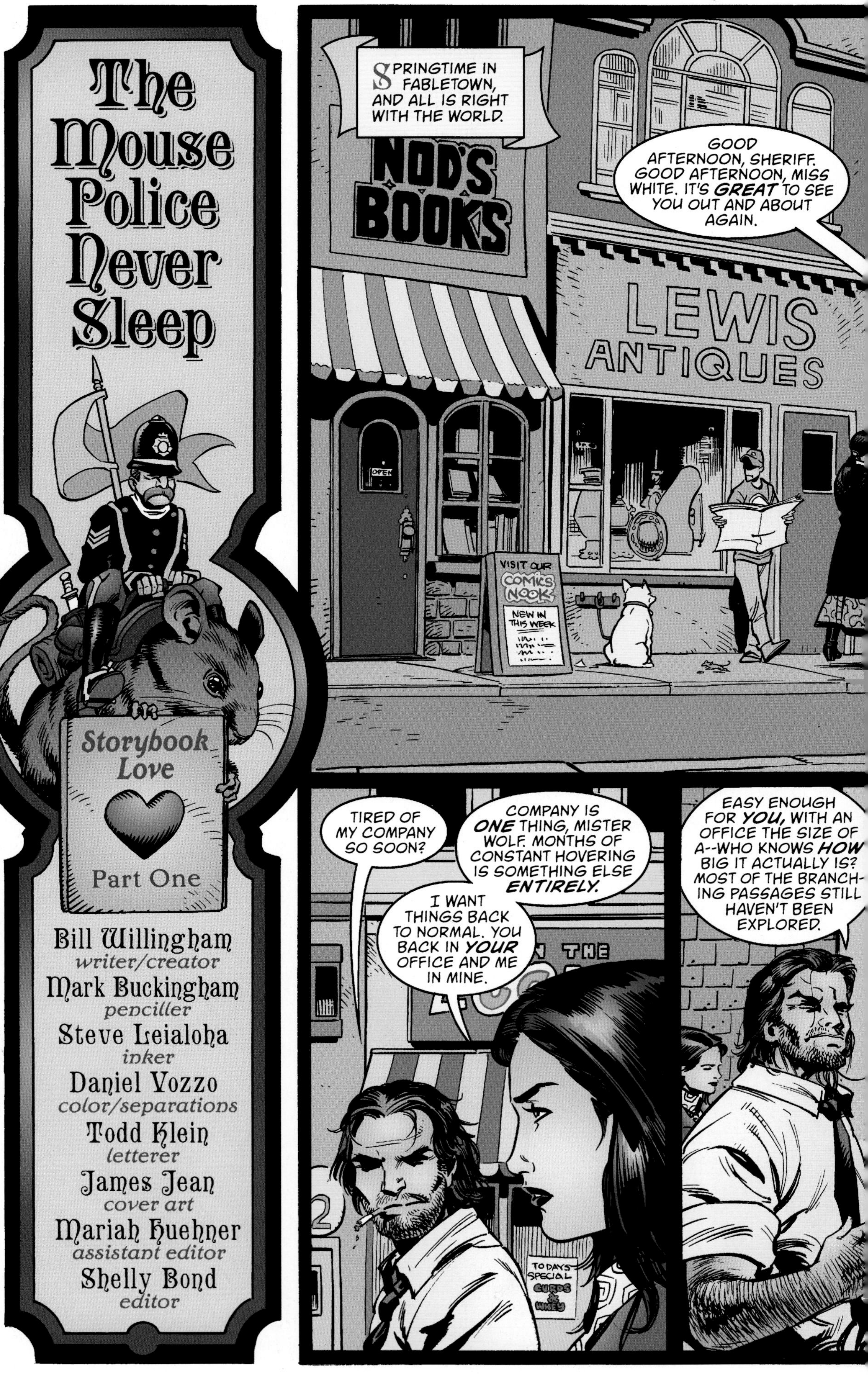
The Mouse Police Never Sleep
Storybook Love
Part One
Bill Willingham
writer/creator
Mark Buckingham
penciller
Steve Leialoha
inker
Daniel Vozzo
color/separations
Todd Klein
letterer
James Jean
cover art
Mariah Huehner
assistant editor
Shelly Bond
editor
SPRINGTIME IN FABLETOWN, AND ALL IS RIGHT WITH THE WORLD.
NOD'S BOOKS
LEWIS ANTIQUES
OPEN
VISIT OUR COMICS NOOK
NEW IN THIS WEEK
GOOD AFTERNOON, SHERIFF. GOOD AFTERNOON, MISS WHITE. IT'S GREAT TO SEE YOU OUT AND ABOUT AGAIN.
TIRED OF MY COMPANY SO SOON?
COMPANY IS ONE THING, MISTER WOLF. MONTHS OF CONSTANT HOVERING IS SOMETHING ELSE ENTIRELY.
I WANT THINGS BACK TO NORMAL. YOU BACK IN YOUR OFFICE AND ME IN MINE.
TODAY'S SPECIAL CURDS & WHEY
EASY ENOUGH FOR YOU, WITH AN OFFICE THE SIZE OF A--WHO KNOWS HOW BIG IT ACTUALLY IS? MOST OF THE BRANCHING PASSAGES STILL HAVEN'T BEEN EXPLORED.

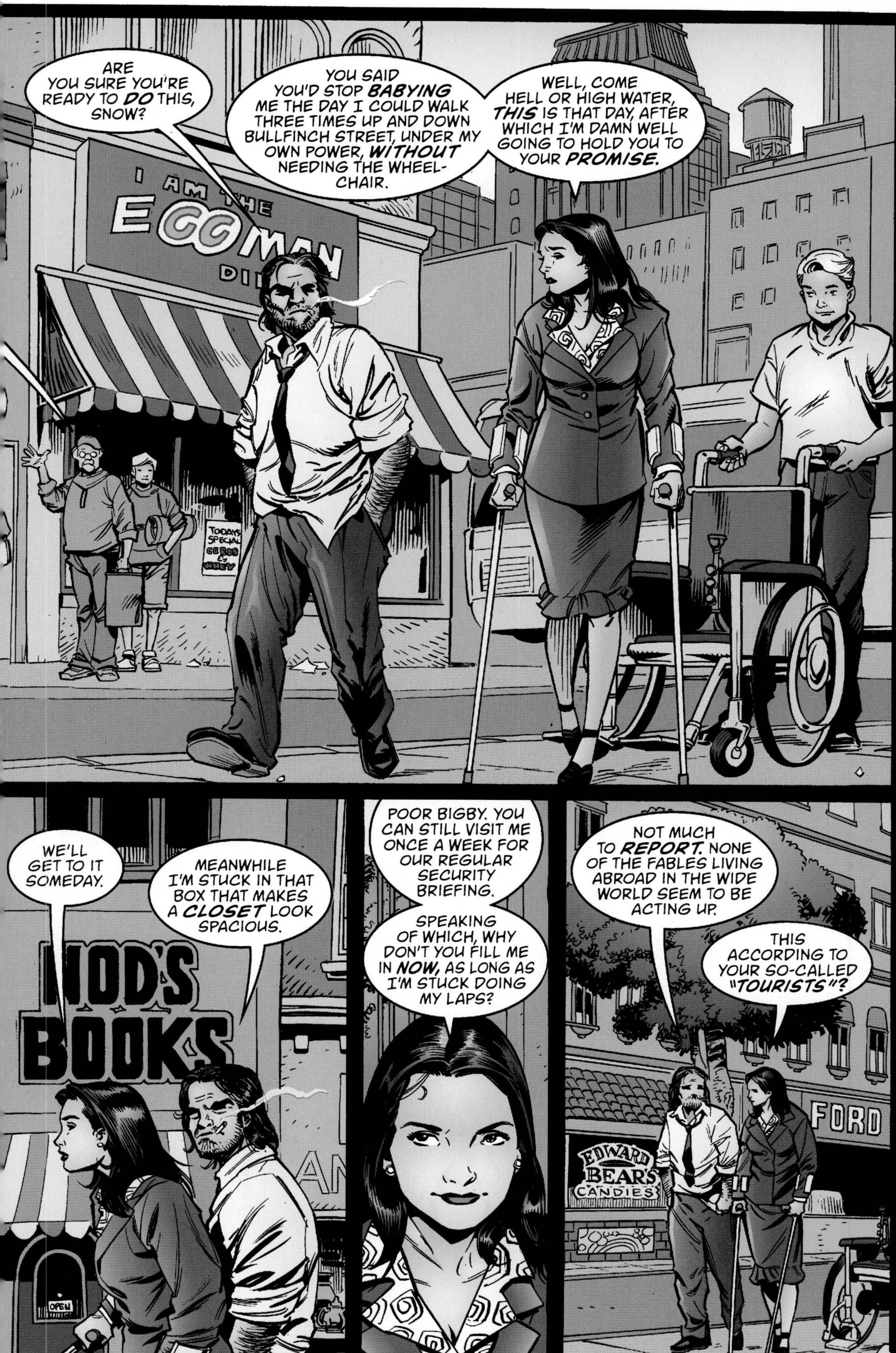
ARE YOU SURE YOU'RE READY TO DO THIS, SNOW?
YOU SAID YOU'D STOP BABYING ME THE DAY I COULD WALK THREE TIMES UP AND DOWN BULLFINCH STREET, UNDER MY OWN POWER, WITHOUT NEEDING THE WHEEL-CHAIR.
WELL, COME HELL OR HIGH WATER, THIS IS THAT DAY, AFTER WHICH I'M DAMN WELL GOING TO HOLD YOU TO YOUR PROMISE.
I AM THE EGGMAN
TODAYS SPECIAL CURDS & WHEY
NOD'S BOOKS
WE'LL GET TO IT SOMEDAY.
MEANWHILE I'M STUCK IN THAT BOX THAT MAKES A CLOSET LOOK SPACIOUS.
OPEN
POOR BIGBY. YOU CAN STILL VISIT ME ONCE A WEEK FOR OUR REGULAR SECURITY BRIEFING.
SPEAKING OF WHICH, WHY DON'T YOU FILL ME IN NOW, AS LONG AS I'M STUCK DOING MY LAPS?
NOT MUCH TO REPORT. NONE OF THE FABLES LIVING ABROAD IN THE WIDE WORLD SEEM TO BE ACTING UP.
THIS ACCORDING TO YOUR SO-CALLED "TOURISTS"?
EDWARD BEAR'S CANDIES
FORD

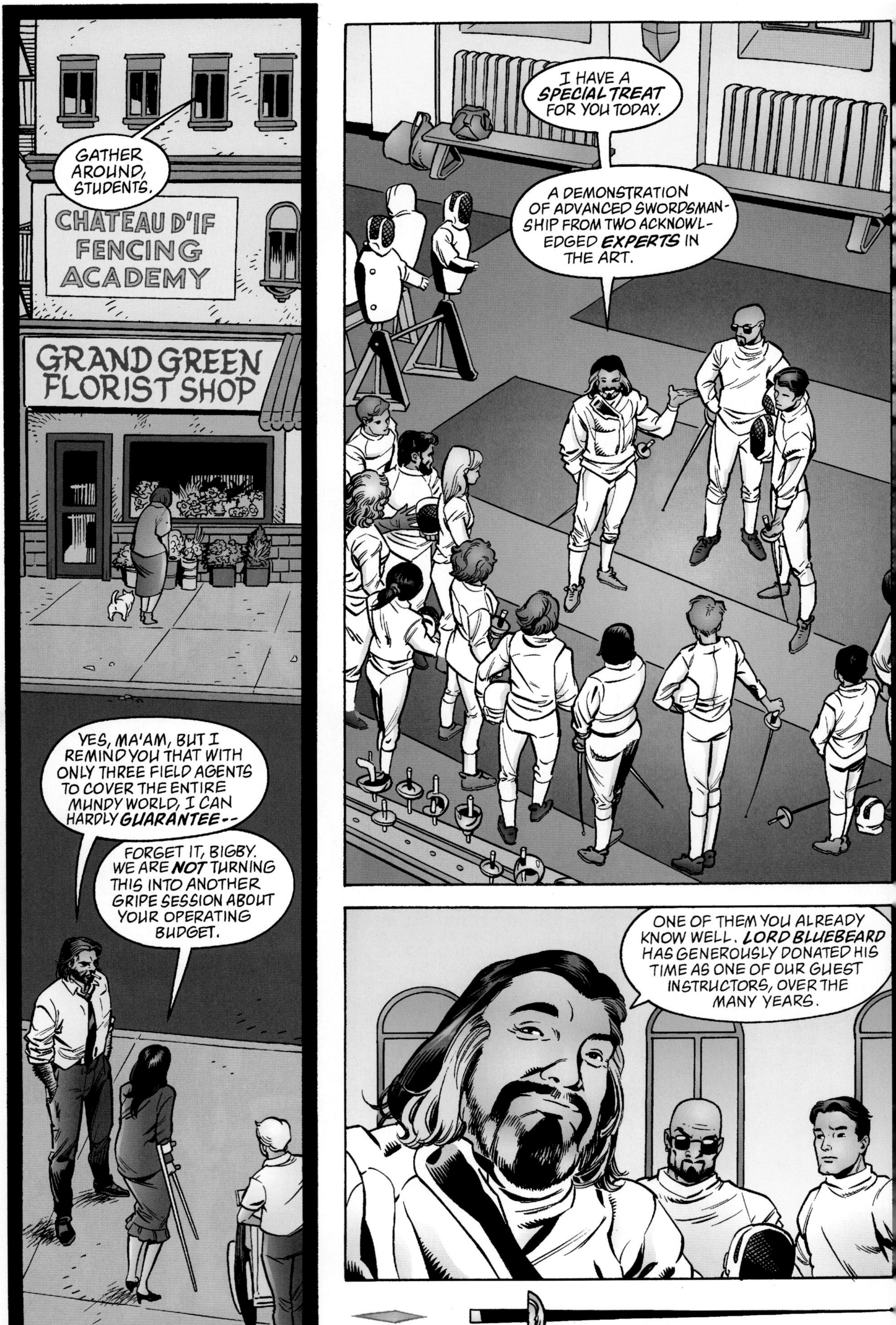
GATHER AROUND, STUDENTS.
CHATEAU D'IF FENCING ACADEMY
GRAND GREEN FLORIST SHOP
YES, MA'AM, BUT I REMIND YOU THAT WITH ONLY THREE FIELD AGENTS TO COVER THE ENTIRE MUNDY WORLD, I CAN HARDLY GUARANTEE--
FORGET IT, BIGBY. WE ARE NOT TURNING THIS INTO ANOTHER GRIPE SESSION ABOUT YOUR OPERATING BUDGET.
I HAVE A SPECIAL TREAT FOR YOU TODAY.
A DEMONSTRATION OF ADVANCED SWORDSMANSHIP FROM TWO ACKNOWLEDGED EXPERTS IN THE ART.
ONE OF THEM YOU ALREADY KNOW WELL. LORD BLUEBEARD HAS GENEROUSLY DONATED HIS TIME AS ONE OF OUR GUEST INSTRUCTORS, OVER THE MANY YEARS.

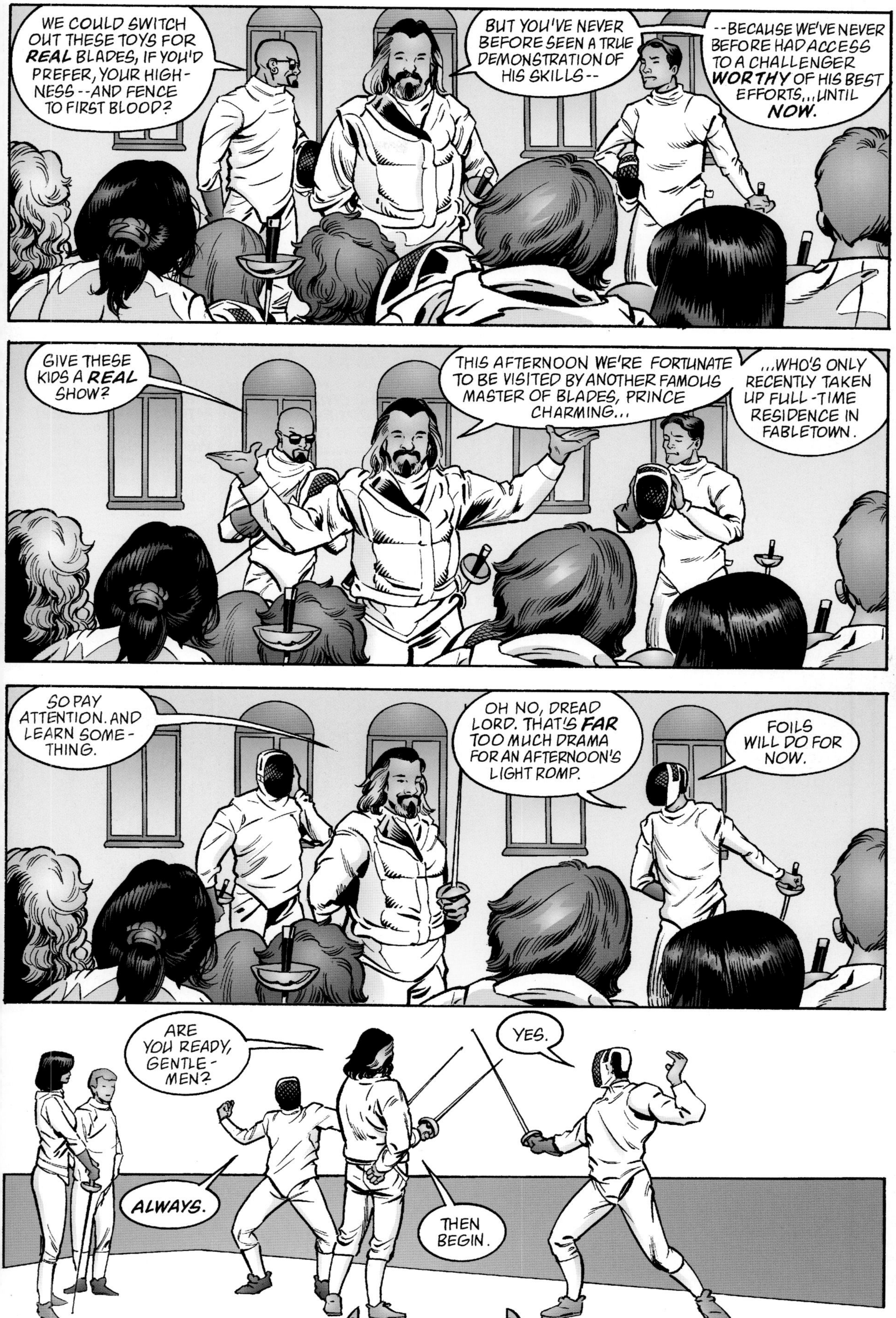
WE COULD SWITCH OUT THESE TOYS FOR REAL BLADES, IF YOU'D PREFER, YOUR HIGH-NESS--AND FENCE TO FIRST BLOOD?
BUT YOU'VE NEVER BEFORE SEEN A TRUE DEMONSTRATION OF HIS SKILLS--
--BECAUSE WE'VE NEVER BEFORE HAD ACCESS TO A CHALLENGER WORTHY OF HIS BEST EFFORTS... UNTIL NOW.
GIVE THESE KIDS A REAL SHOW?
THIS AFTERNOON WE'RE FORTUNATE TO BE VISITED BY ANOTHER FAMOUS MASTER OF BLADES, PRINCE CHARMING...
...WHO'S ONLY RECENTLY TAKEN UP FULL-TIME RESIDENCE IN FABLETOWN.
SO PAY ATTENTION. AND LEARN SOME-THING.
OH NO, DREAD LORD. THAT'S FAR TOO MUCH DRAMA FOR AN AFTERNOON'S LIGHT ROMP.
FOILS WILL DO FOR NOW.
ARE YOU READY, GENTLE-MEN?
YES.
ALWAYS.
THEN BEGIN.

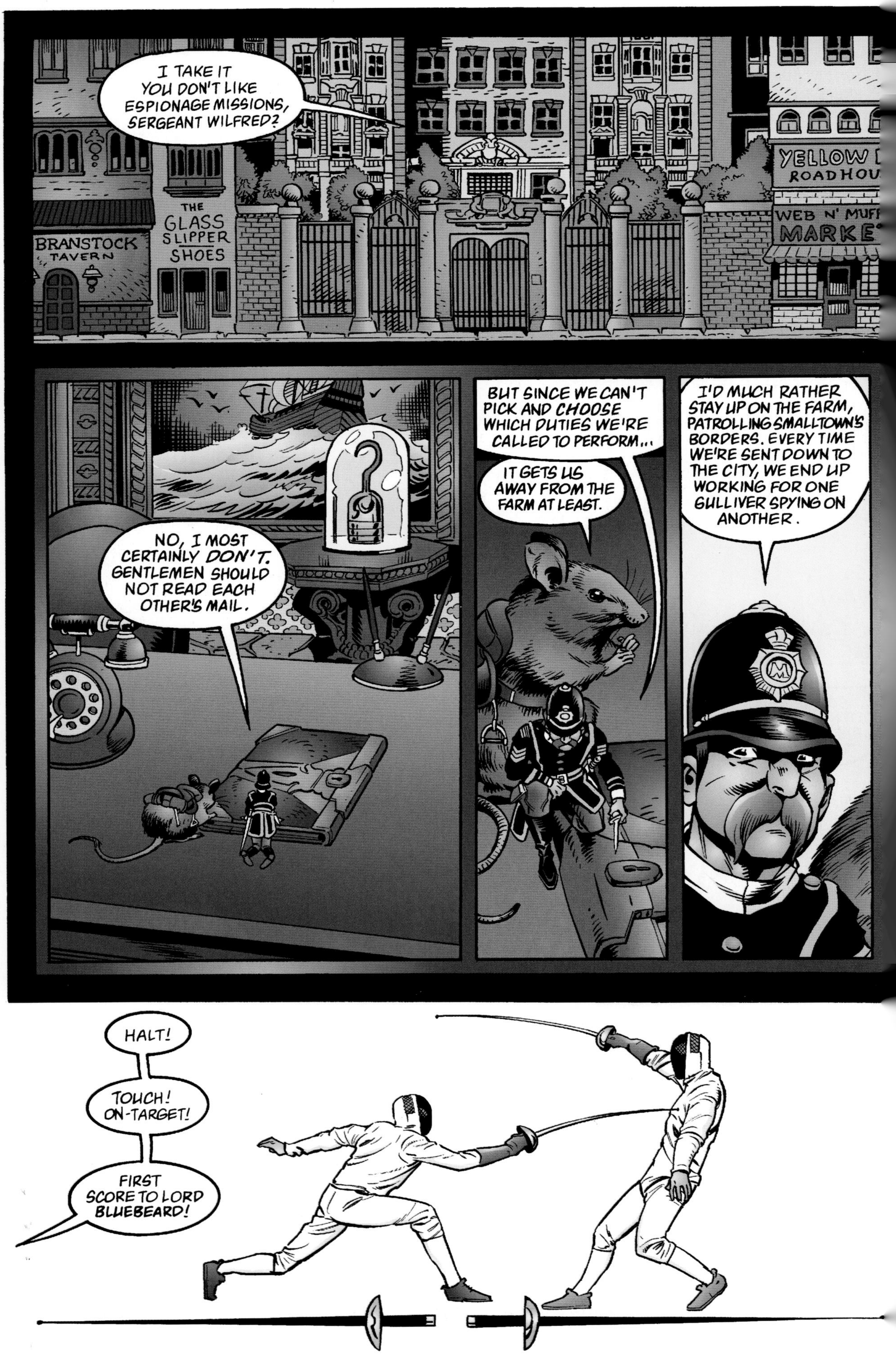
I TAKE IT YOU DON'T LIKE ESPIONAGE MISSIONS, SERGEANT WILFRED?
BRANSTOCK TAVERN
THE GLASS SLIPPER SHOES
NO, I MOST CERTAINLY DON'T. GENTLEMEN SHOULD NOT READ EACH OTHER'S MAIL.
BUT SINCE WE CAN'T PICK AND CHOOSE WHICH DUTIES WE'RE CALLED TO PERFORM...
IT GETS US AWAY FROM THE FARM AT LEAST.
I'D MUCH RATHER STAY UP ON THE FARM, PATROLLING SMALLTOWN'S BORDERS. EVERY TIME WE'RE SENT DOWN TO THE CITY, WE END UP WORKING FOR ONE GULLIVER SPYING ON ANOTHER.
HALT!
TOUCH! ON-TARGET!
FIRST SCORE TO LORD BLUEBEARD!

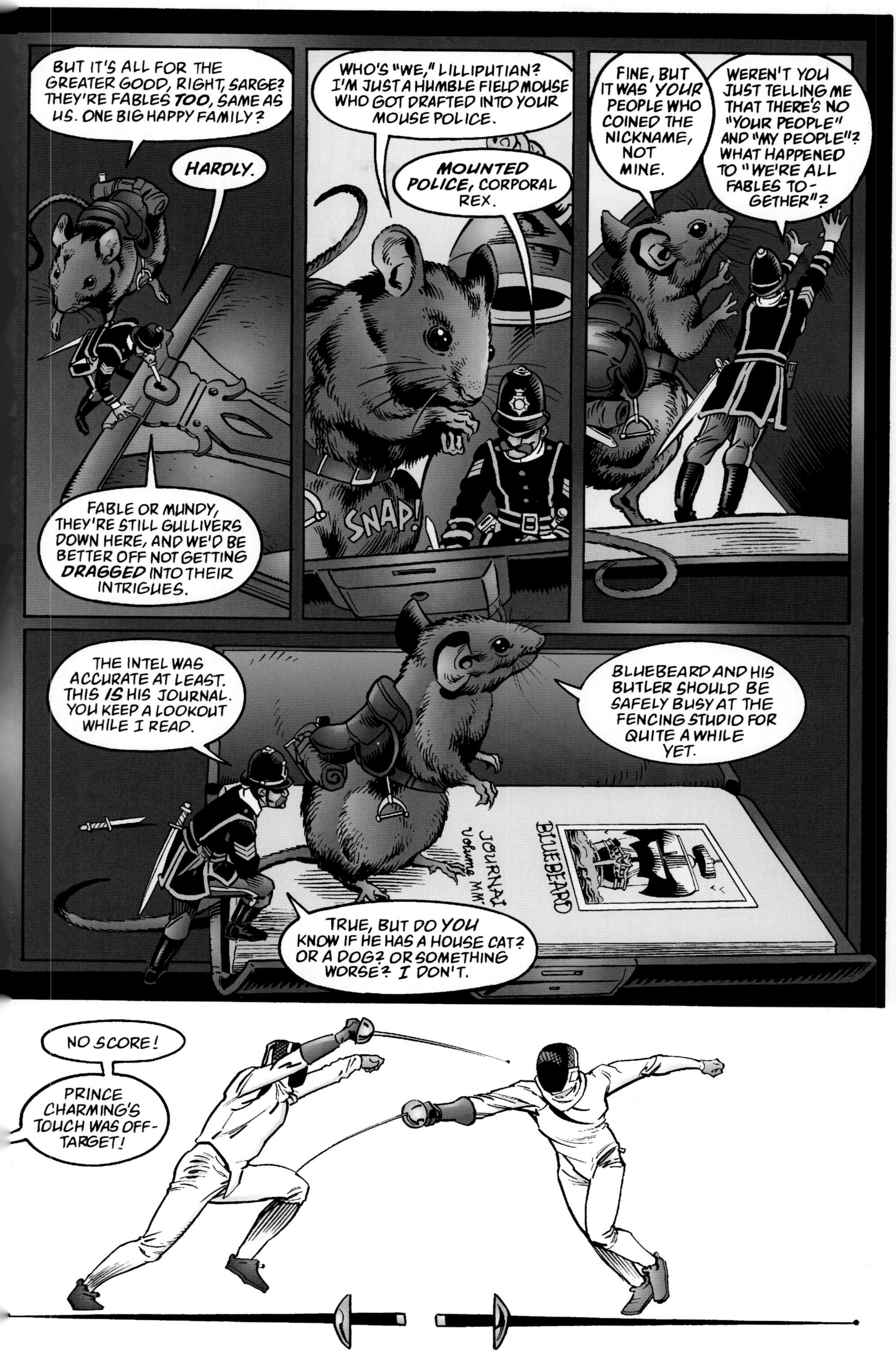

BUT IT'S ALL FOR THE GREATER GOOD, RIGHT, SARGE? THEY'RE FABLES TOO, SAME AS US. ONE BIG HAPPY FAMILY?
HARDLY.
FABLE OR MUNDY, THEY'RE STILL GULLIVERS DOWN HERE, AND WE'D BE BETTER OFF NOT GETTING DRAGGED INTO THEIR INTRIGUES.
WHO'S "WE," LILLIPUTIAN? I'M JUST A HUMBLE FIELD MOUSE WHO GOT DRAFTED INTO YOUR MOUSE POLICE.
MOUNTED POLICE, CORPORAL REX.
SNAP!
FINE, BUT IT WAS YOUR PEOPLE WHO COINED THE NICKNAME, NOT MINE.
WEREN'T YOU JUST TELLING ME THAT THERE'S NO "YOUR PEOPLE" AND "MY PEOPLE"? WHAT HAPPENED TO "WE'RE ALL FABLES TO-GETHER"?
THE INTEL WAS ACCURATE AT LEAST. THIS IS HIS JOURNAL. YOU KEEP A LOOKOUT WHILE I READ.
BLUEBEARD AND HIS BUTLER SHOULD BE SAFELY BUSY AT THE FENCING STUDIO FOR QUITE A WHILE YET.
JOURNAL
BLUEBEARD
TRUE, BUT DO YOU KNOW IF HE HAS A HOUSE CAT? OR A DOG? OR SOMETHING WORSE? I DON'T.
NO SCORE!
PRINCE CHARMING'S TOUCH WAS OFF-TARGET!

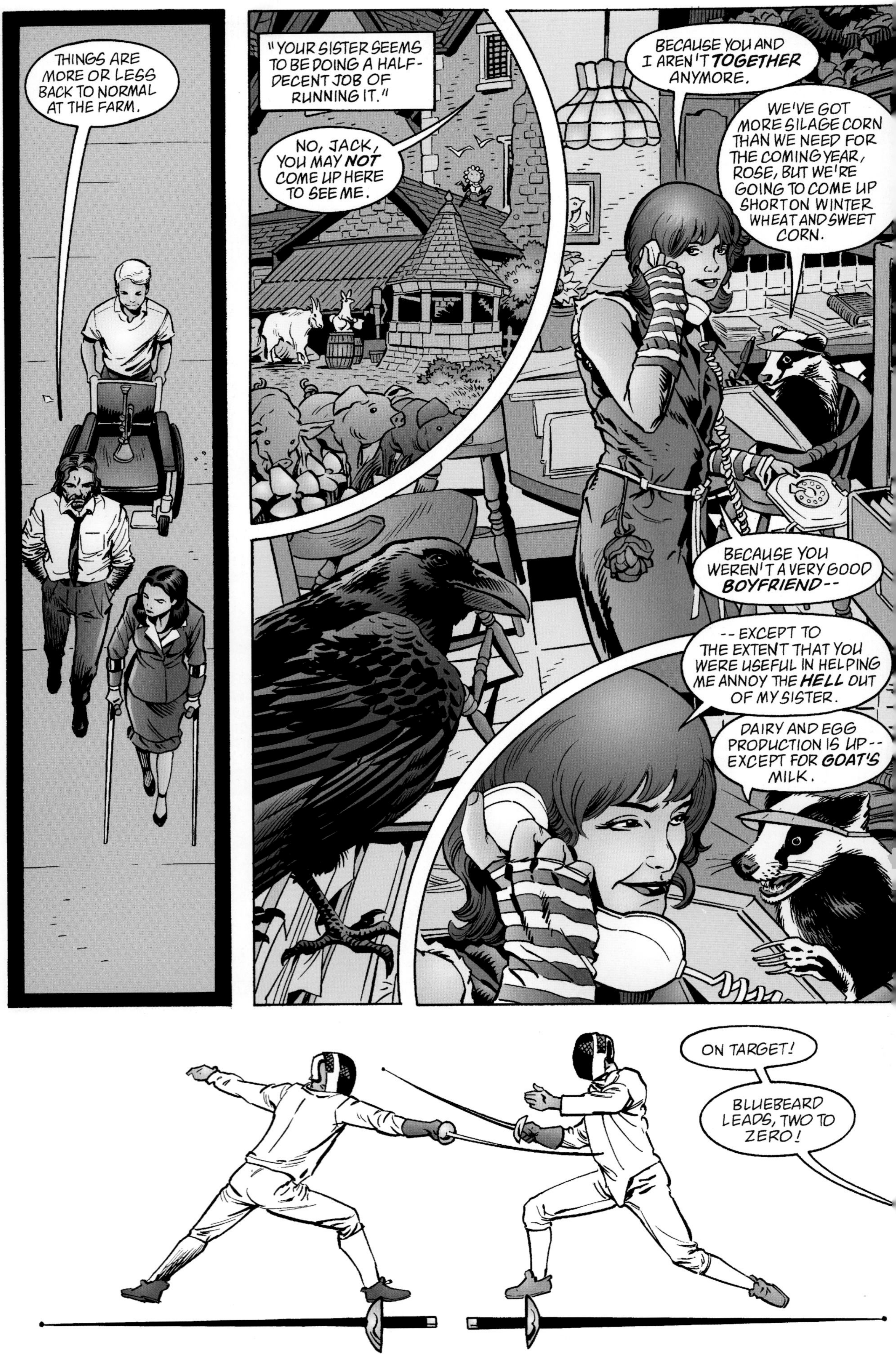
THINGS ARE MORE OR LESS BACK TO NORMAL AT THE FARM.
"YOUR SISTER SEEMS TO BE DOING A HALF-DECENT JOB OF RUNNING IT."
NO, JACK, YOU MAY NOT COME UP HERE TO SEE ME.
BECAUSE YOU AND I AREN'T TOGETHER ANYMORE.
WE'VE GOT MORE SILAGE CORN THAN WE NEED FOR THE COMING YEAR, ROSE, BUT WE'RE GOING TO COME UP SHORT ON WINTER WHEAT AND SWEET CORN.
BECAUSE YOU WEREN'T A VERY GOOD BOYFRIEND--
--EXCEPT TO THE EXTENT THAT YOU WERE USEFUL IN HELPING ME ANNOY THE HELL OUT OF MY SISTER.
DAIRY AND EGG PRODUCTION IS UP--EXCEPT FOR GOAT'S MILK.
ON TARGET!
BLUEBEARD LEADS, TWO TO ZERO!

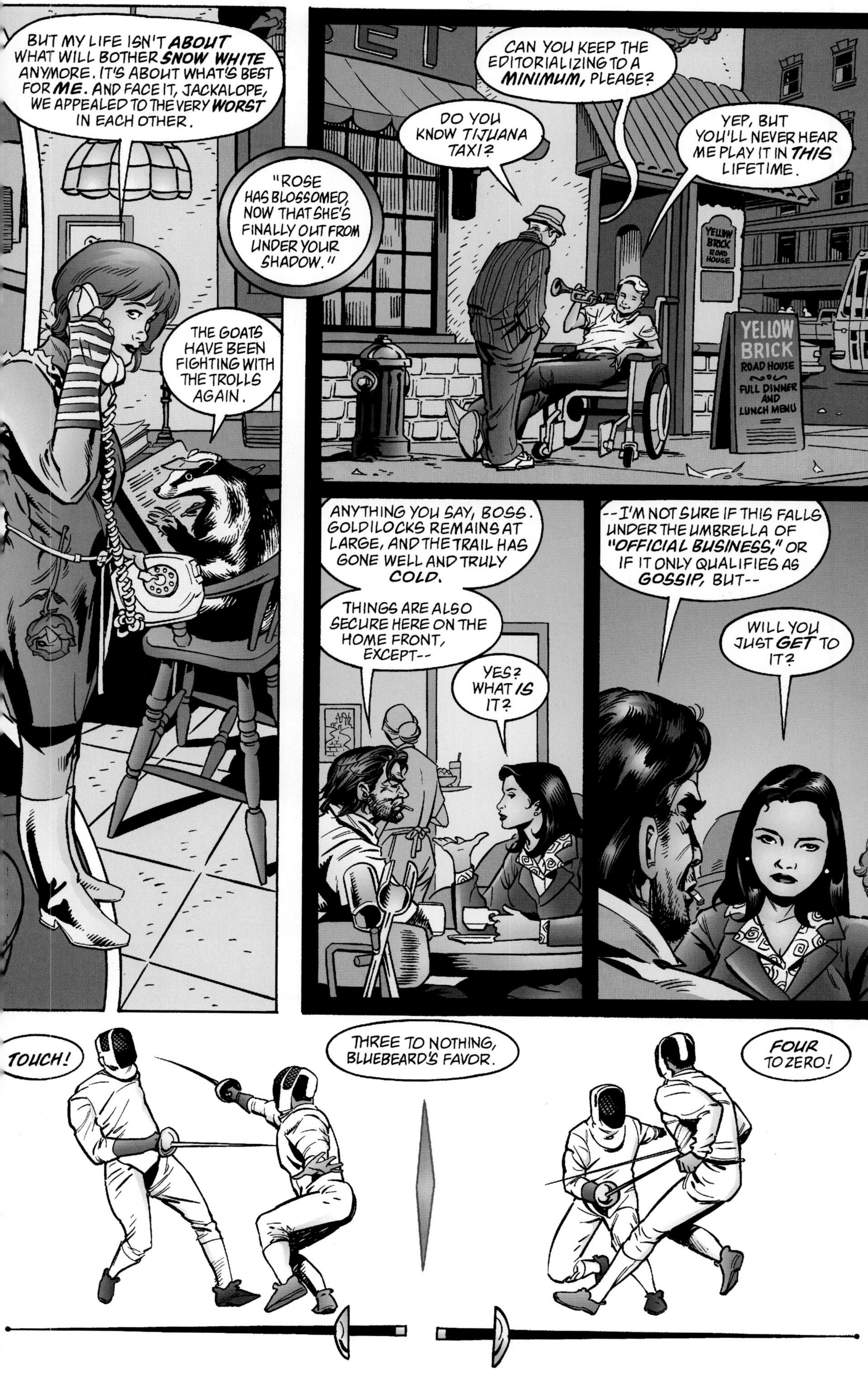
BUT MY LIFE ISN'T ABOUT WHAT WILL BOTHER SNOW WHITE ANYMORE. IT'S ABOUT WHAT'S BEST FOR ME. AND FACE IT, JACKALOPE, WE APPEALED TO THE VERY WORST IN EACH OTHER.
"ROSE HAS BLOSSOMED, NOW THAT SHE'S FINALLY OUT FROM UNDER YOUR SHADOW."
THE GOATS HAVE BEEN FIGHTING WITH THE TROLLS AGAIN.
CAN YOU KEEP THE EDITORIALIZING TO A MINIMUM, PLEASE?
DO YOU KNOW TIJUANA TAXI?
YEP, BUT YOU'LL NEVER HEAR ME PLAY IT IN THIS LIFETIME.
YELLOW BRICK ROAD HOUSE
YELLOW BRICK ROAD HOUSE FULL DINNER AND LUNCH MENU
ANYTHING YOU SAY, BOSS. GOLDILOCKS REMAINS AT LARGE, AND THE TRAIL HAS GONE WELL AND TRULY COLD.
THINGS ARE ALSO SECURE HERE ON THE HOME FRONT, EXCEPT--
YES? WHAT IS IT?
--I'M NOT SURE IF THIS FALLS UNDER THE UMBRELLA OF "OFFICIAL BUSINESS," OR IF IT ONLY QUALIFIES AS GOSSIP, BUT--
WILL YOU JUST GET TO IT?
TOUCH!
THREE TO NOTHING, BLUEBEARD'S FAVOR.
FOUR TO ZERO!

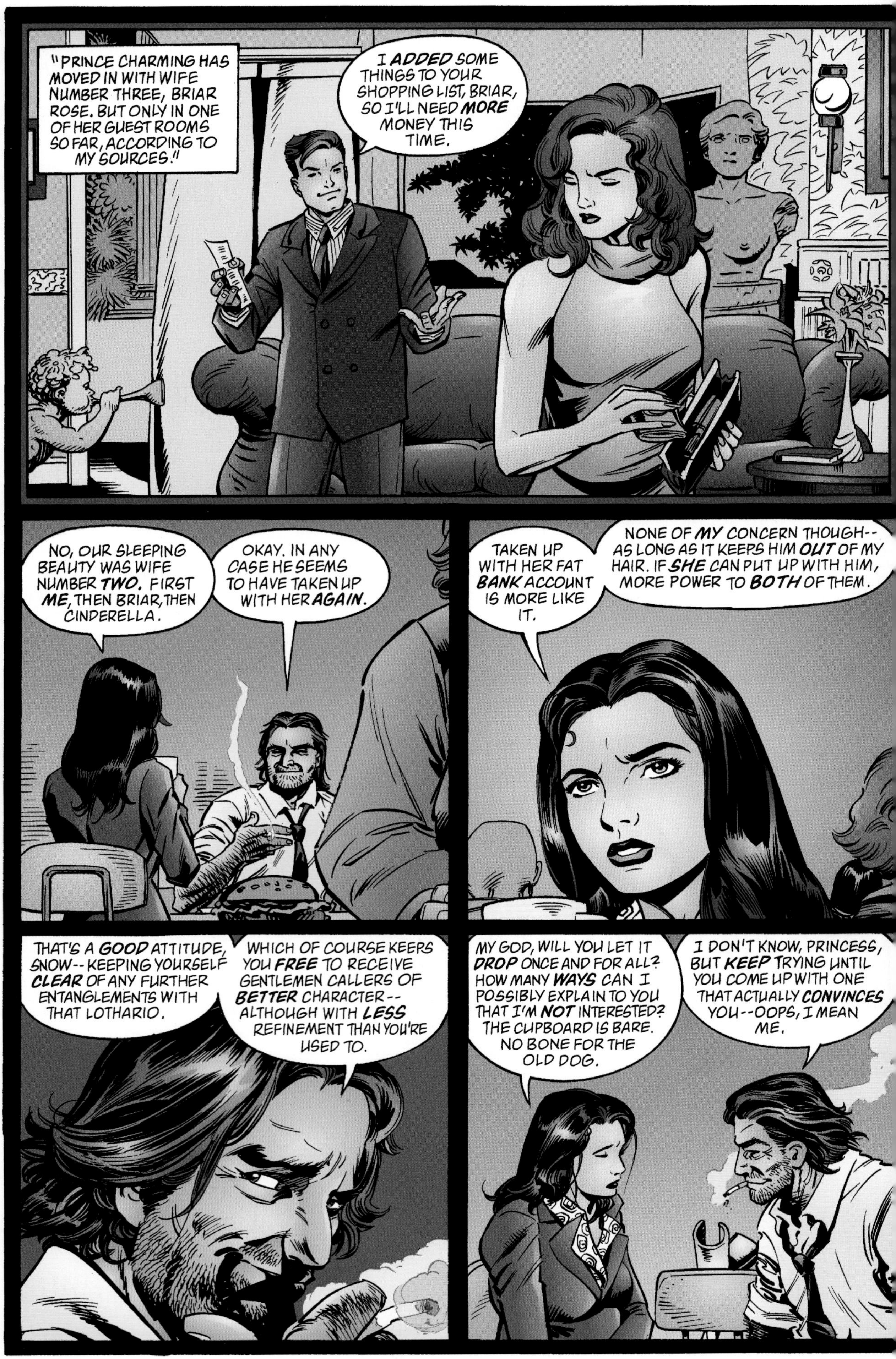
"PRINCE CHARMING HAS MOVED IN WITH WIFE NUMBER THREE, BRIAR ROSE. BUT ONLY IN ONE OF HER GUEST ROOMS SO FAR, ACCORDING TO MY SOURCES."
I ADDED SOME THINGS TO YOUR SHOPPING LIST, BRIAR, SO I'LL NEED MORE MONEY THIS TIME.
NO, OUR SLEEPING BEAUTY WAS WIFE NUMBER TWO. FIRST ME, THEN BRIAR, THEN CINDERELLA.
OKAY. IN ANY CASE HE SEEMS TO HAVE TAKEN UP WITH HER AGAIN.
TAKEN UP WITH HER FAT BANK ACCOUNT IS MORE LIKE IT.
NONE OF MY CONCERN THOUGH--AS LONG AS IT KEEPS HIM OUT OF MY HAIR. IF SHE CAN PUT UP WITH HIM, MORE POWER TO BOTH OF THEM.
THAT'S A GOOD ATTITUDE, SNOW--KEEPING YOURSELF CLEAR OF ANY FURTHER ENTANGLEMENTS WITH THAT LOTHARIO.
WHICH OF COURSE KEEPS YOU FREE TO RECEIVE GENTLEMEN CALLERS OF BETTER CHARACTER--ALTHOUGH WITH LESS REFINEMENT THAN YOU'RE USED TO.
MY GOD, WILL YOU LET IT DROP ONCE AND FOR ALL? HOW MANY WAYS CAN I POSSIBLY EXPLAIN TO YOU THAT I'M NOT INTERESTED? THE CUPBOARD IS BARE. NO BONE FOR THE OLD DOG.
I DON'T KNOW, PRINCESS, BUT KEEP TRYING UNTIL YOU COME UP WITH ONE THAT ACTUALLY CONVINCES YOU--OOPS, I MEAN ME.

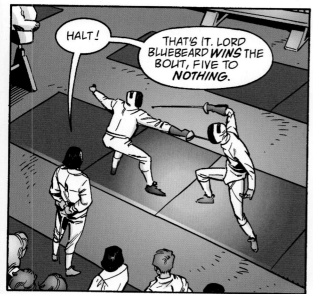

HALT!

THAT'S IT. LORD BLUEBEARD *WINS* THE BOUT, FIVE TO *NOTHING*.

HA! A CLEAN SWEEP!

CONGRATULATIONS, BLUEBEARD.

YOU DID *FINE*, OF COURSE. YOU WERE JUST OUT OF PRACTICE. HARD TO TRAIN, WHAT WITH YOUR RECENT TRAVELS.

WELL DONE. NOTHING TO BE *ASHAMED* OF.

SURE. FINE.

NOW, IF YOU'LL EXCUSE ME--

I SUPPOSE HIS HIGHNESS WILL GET OVER IT, GIVEN TIME.

COME ALONG, HOBBES. IT'S GETTING *LATE* AND I WANT YOU TO DRAW ME A BATH BEFORE SUPPER.

VERY GOOD, SIR.

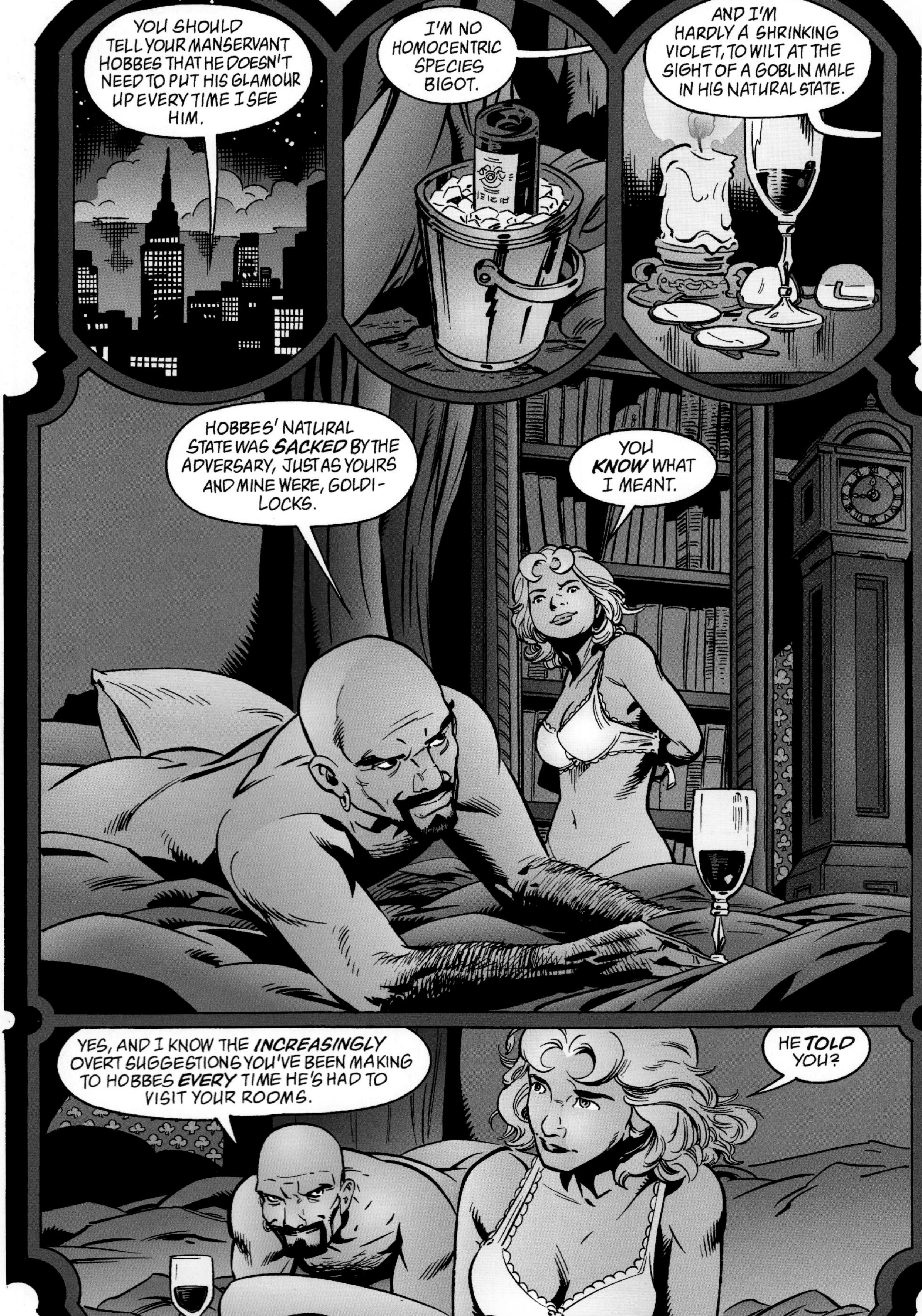
YOU SHOULD TELL YOUR MANSERVANT HOBBES THAT HE DOESN'T NEED TO PUT HIS GLAMOUR UP EVERY TIME I SEE HIM.
I'M NO HOMOCENTRIC SPECIES BIGOT.
AND I'M HARDLY A SHRINKING VIOLET, TO WILT AT THE SIGHT OF A GOBLIN MALE IN HIS NATURAL STATE.
HOBBES' NATURAL STATE WAS SACKED BY THE ADVERSARY, JUST AS YOURS AND MINE WERE, GOLDI-LOCKS.
YOU KNOW WHAT I MEANT.
YES, AND I KNOW THE INCREASINGLY OVERT SUGGESTIONS YOU'VE BEEN MAKING TO HOBBES EVERY TIME HE'S HAD TO VISIT YOUR ROOMS.
HE TOLD YOU?

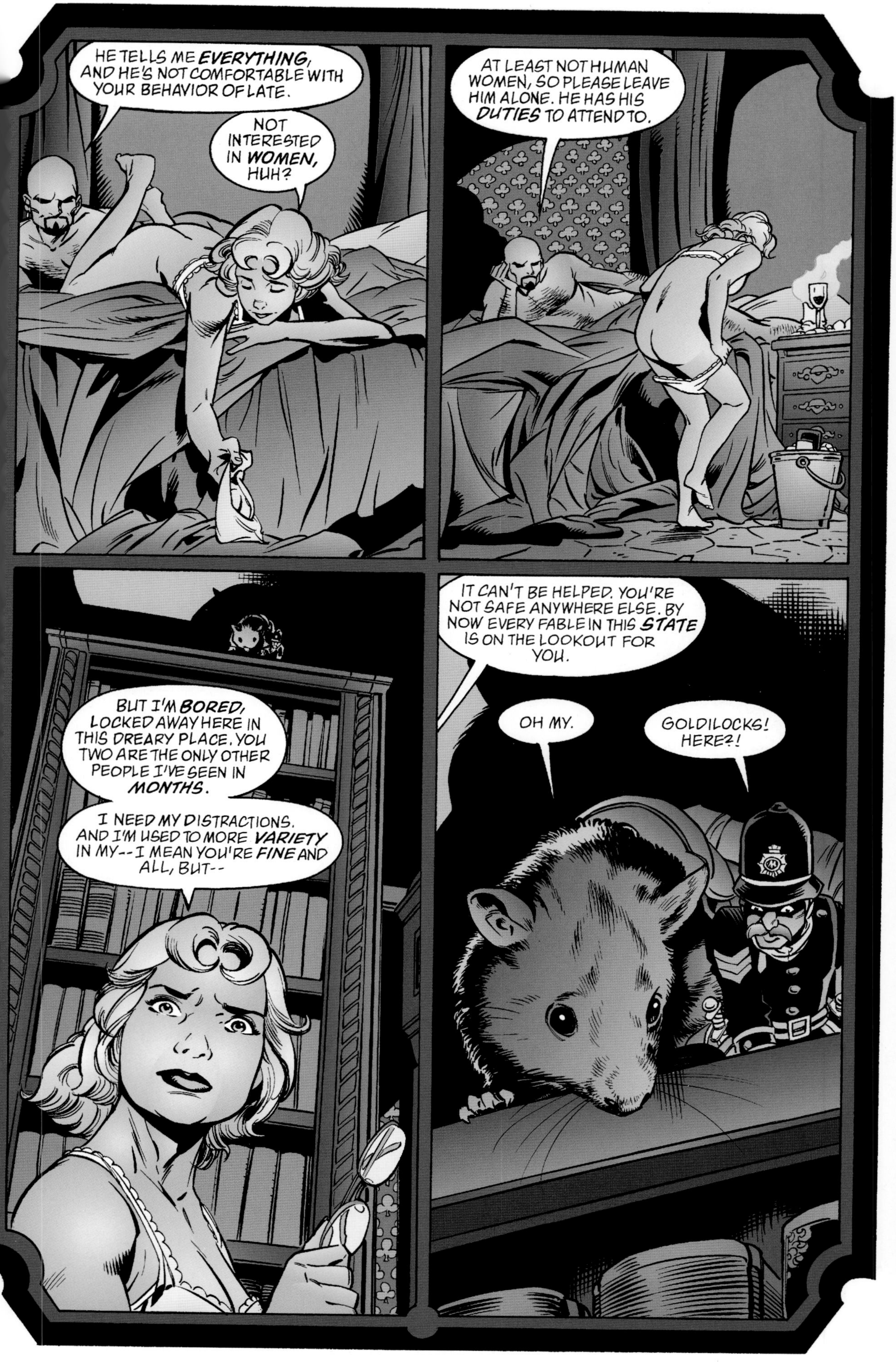
HE TELLS ME EVERYTHING, AND HE'S NOT COMFORTABLE WITH YOUR BEHAVIOR OF LATE.
NOT INTERESTED IN WOMEN, HUH?
AT LEAST NOT HUMAN WOMEN, SO PLEASE LEAVE HIM ALONE. HE HAS HIS DUTIES TO ATTEND TO.
BUT I'M BORED, LOCKED AWAY HERE IN THIS DREARY PLACE. YOU TWO ARE THE ONLY OTHER PEOPLE I'VE SEEN IN MONTHS.
I NEED MY DISTRACTIONS. AND I'M USED TO MORE VARIETY IN MY--I MEAN YOU'RE FINE AND ALL, BUT--
IT CAN'T BE HELPED. YOU'RE NOT SAFE ANYWHERE ELSE. BY NOW EVERY FABLE IN THIS STATE IS ON THE LOOKOUT FOR YOU.
OH MY.
GOLDILOCKS! HERE?!

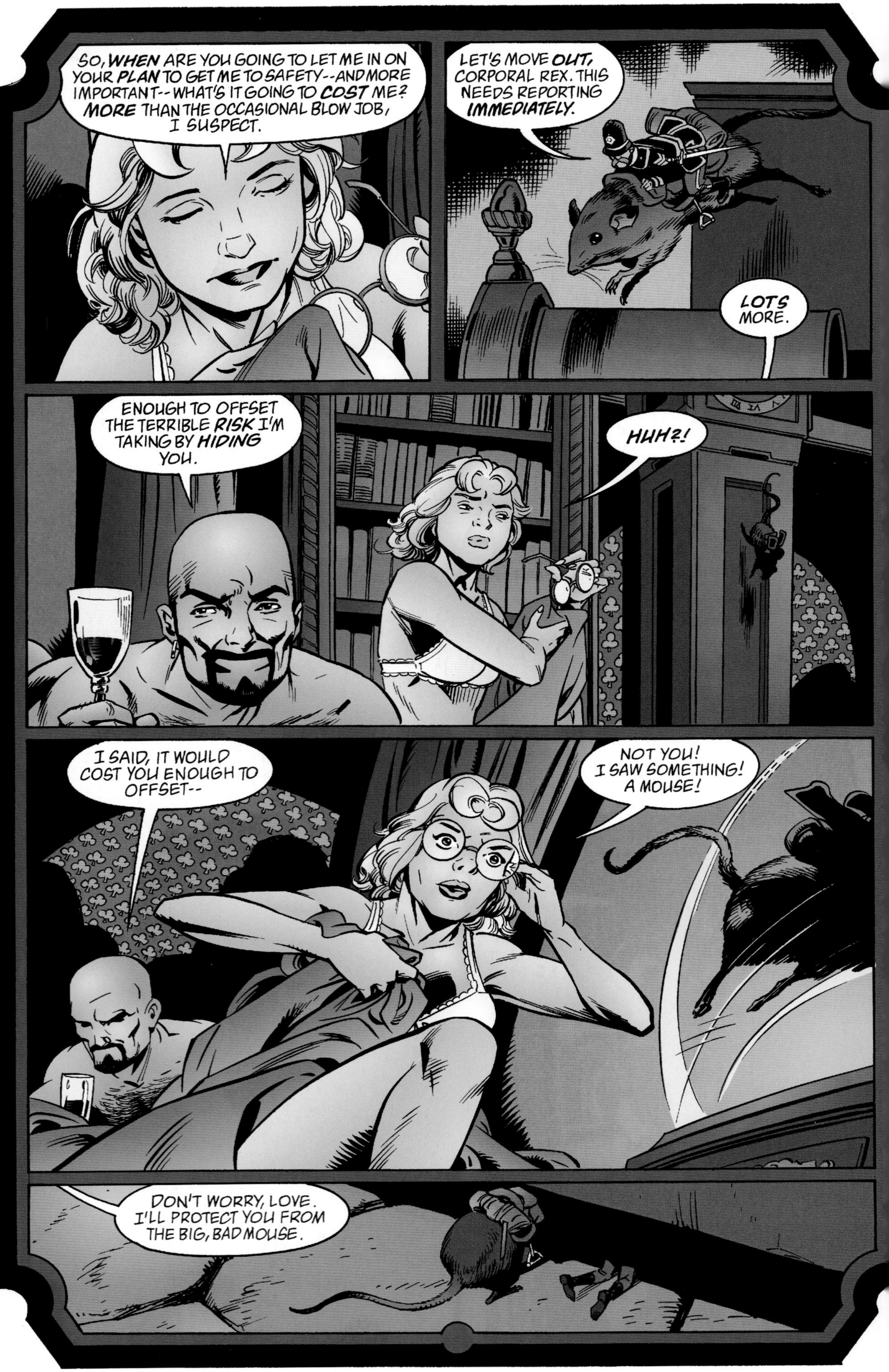

SO, WHEN ARE YOU GOING TO LET ME IN ON YOUR PLAN TO GET ME TO SAFETY--AND MORE IMPORTANT--WHAT'S IT GOING TO COST ME? MORE THAN THE OCCASIONAL BLOW JOB, I SUSPECT.
LET'S MOVE OUT, CORPORAL REX. THIS NEEDS REPORTING IMMEDIATELY.
LOTS MORE.
ENOUGH TO OFFSET THE TERRIBLE RISK I'M TAKING BY HIDING YOU.
HUH?!
I SAID, IT WOULD COST YOU ENOUGH TO OFFSET--
NOT YOU! I SAW SOMETHING! A MOUSE!
DON'T WORRY, LOVE. I'LL PROTECT YOU FROM THE BIG, BAD MOUSE.

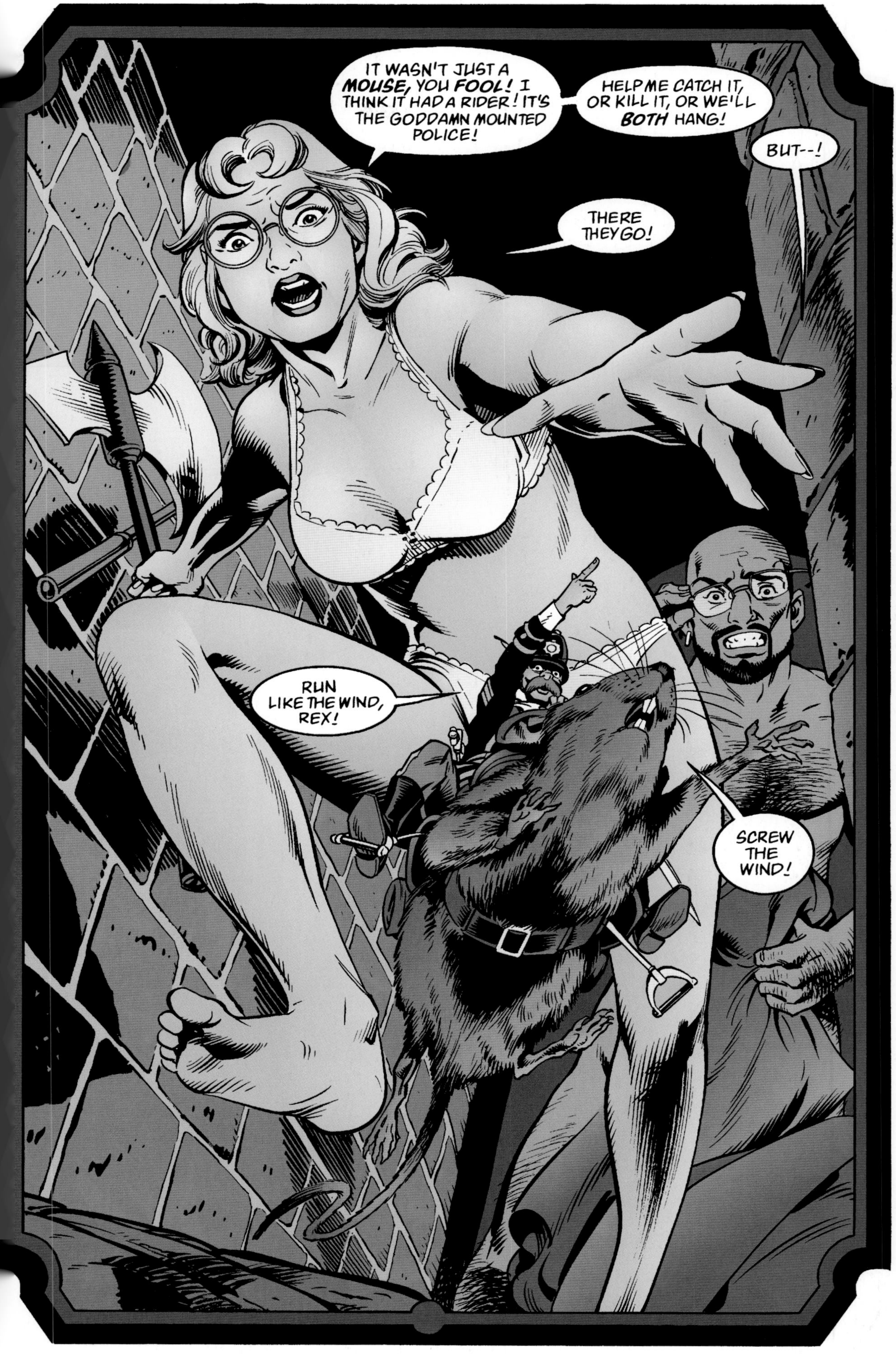
IT WASN'T JUST A MOUSE, YOU FOOL! I THINK IT HAD A RIDER! IT'S THE GODDAMN MOUNTED POLICE!
HELP ME CATCH IT, OR KILL IT, OR WE'LL BOTH HANG!
BUT--!
THERE THEY GO!
RUN LIKE THE WIND, REX!
SCREW THE WIND!

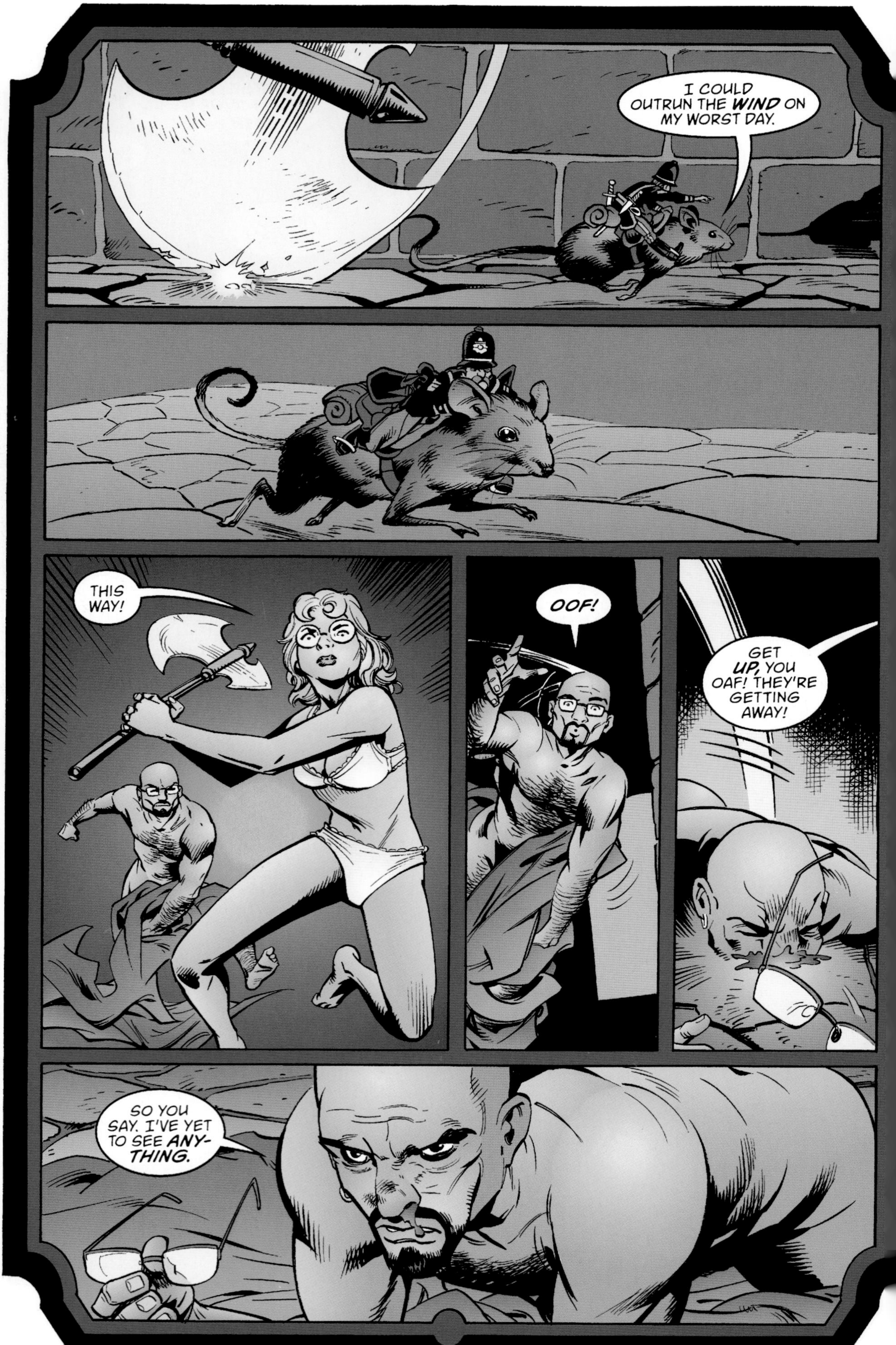
I COULD OUTRUN THE **WIND** ON MY WORST DAY.
THIS WAY!
OOF!
GET **UP,** YOU OAF! THEY'RE GETTING AWAY!
SO YOU SAY. I'VE YET TO SEE **ANY-THING.**

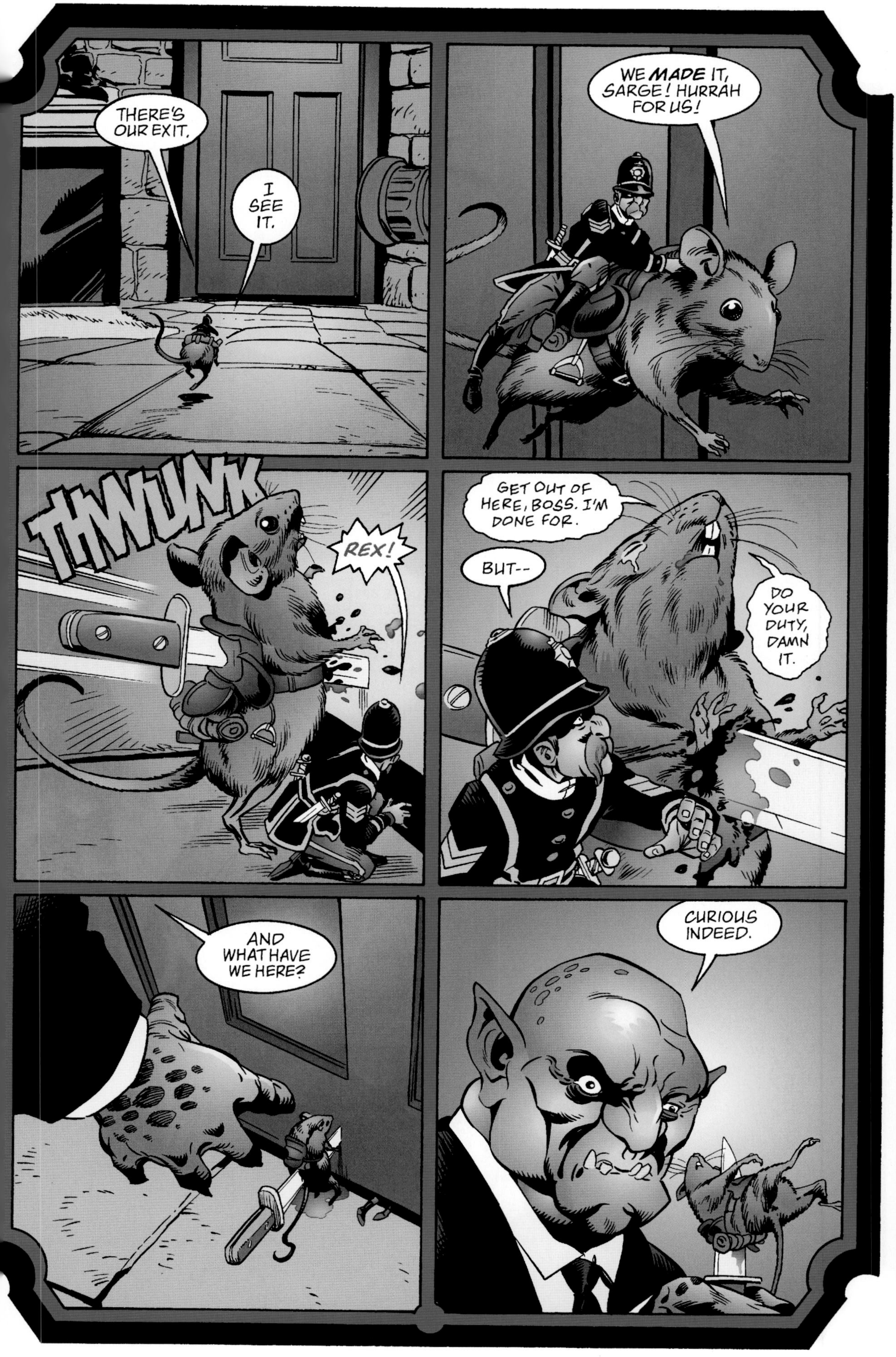
THERE'S OUR EXIT.
I SEE IT.
WE MADE IT, SARGE! HURRAH FOR US!
THWUNK
REX!
GET OUT OF HERE, BOSS. I'M DONE FOR.
BUT--
DO YOUR DUTY, DAMN IT.
AND WHAT HAVE WE HERE?
CURIOUS INDEED.

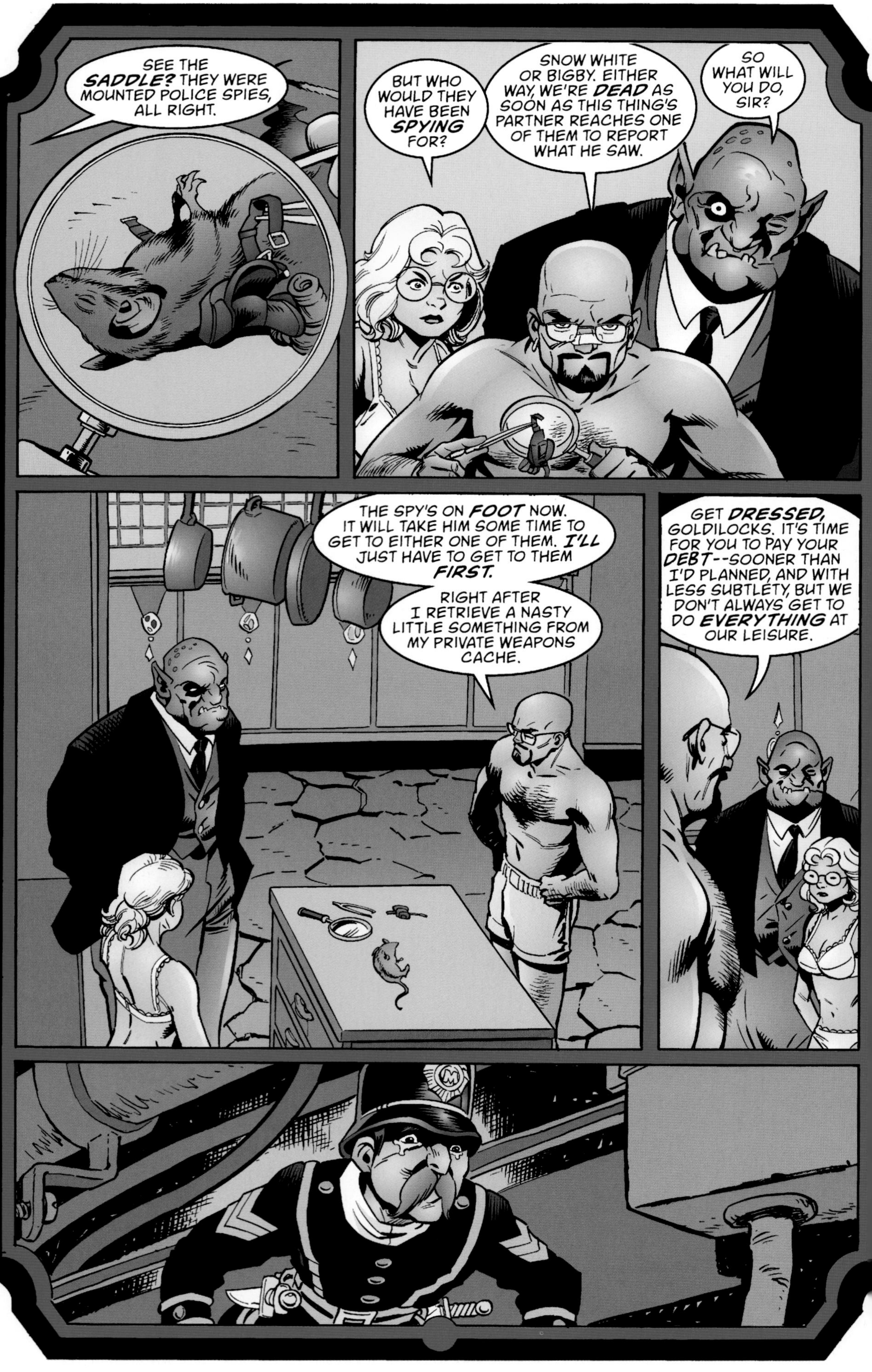
SEE THE SADDLE? THEY WERE MOUNTED POLICE SPIES, ALL RIGHT.
BUT WHO WOULD THEY HAVE BEEN SPYING FOR?
SNOW WHITE OR BIGBY. EITHER WAY, WE'RE DEAD AS SOON AS THIS THING'S PARTNER REACHES ONE OF THEM TO REPORT WHAT HE SAW.
SO WHAT WILL YOU DO, SIR?
THE SPY'S ON FOOT NOW. IT WILL TAKE HIM SOME TIME TO GET TO EITHER ONE OF THEM. I'LL JUST HAVE TO GET TO THEM FIRST.
RIGHT AFTER I RETRIEVE A NASTY LITTLE SOMETHING FROM MY PRIVATE WEAPONS CACHE.
GET DRESSED, GOLDILOCKS. IT'S TIME FOR YOU TO PAY YOUR DEBT--SOONER THAN I'D PLANNED, AND WITH LESS SUBTLETY, BUT WE DON'T ALWAYS GET TO DO EVERYTHING AT OUR LEISURE.

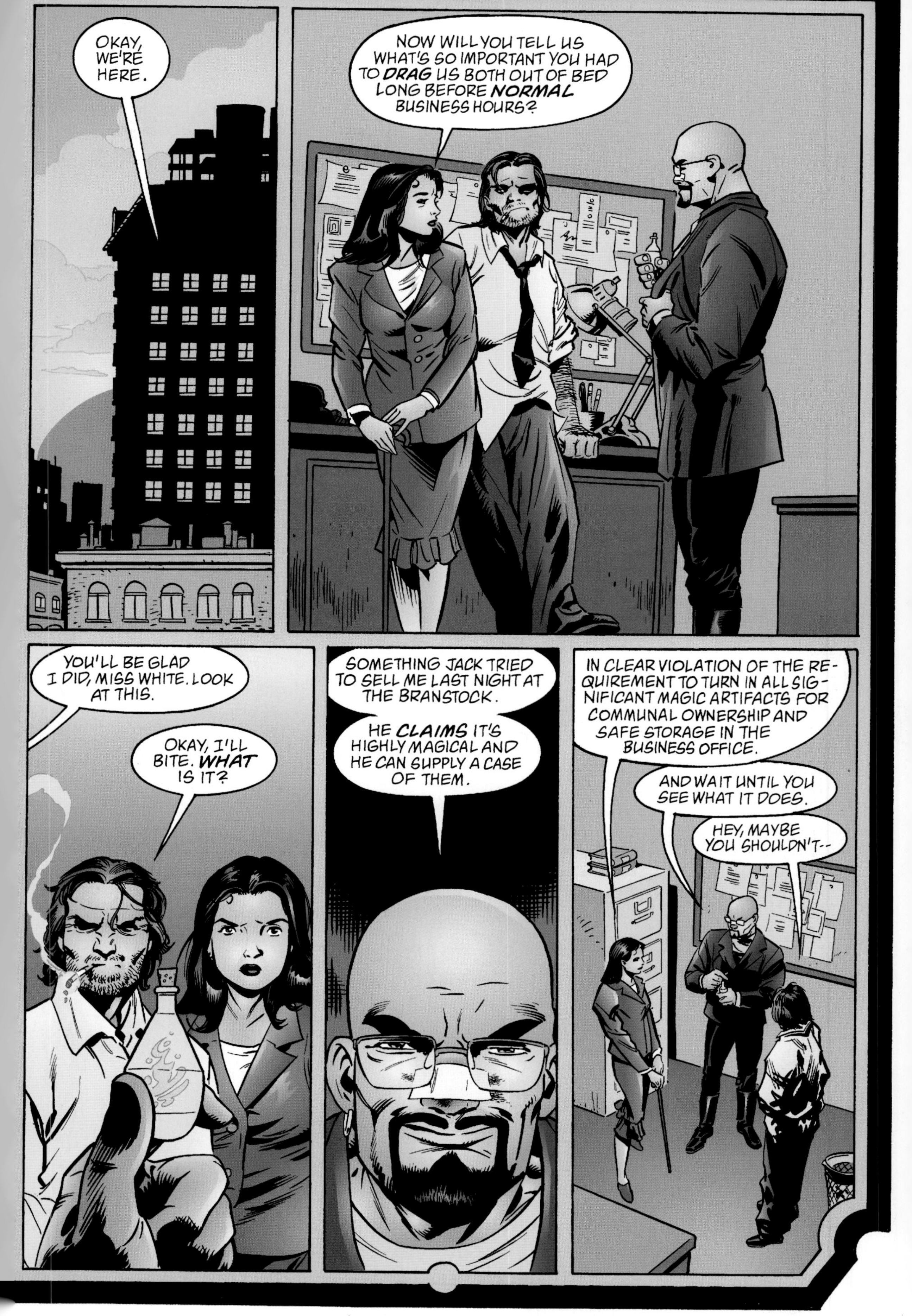

OKAY, WE'RE HERE.
NOW WILL YOU TELL US WHAT'S SO IMPORTANT YOU HAD TO DRAG US BOTH OUT OF BED LONG BEFORE NORMAL BUSINESS HOURS?
YOU'LL BE GLAD I DID, MISS WHITE. LOOK AT THIS.
OKAY, I'LL BITE. WHAT IS IT?
SOMETHING JACK TRIED TO SELL ME LAST NIGHT AT THE BRANSTOCK.
HE CLAIMS IT'S HIGHLY MAGICAL AND HE CAN SUPPLY A CASE OF THEM.
IN CLEAR VIOLATION OF THE REQUIREMENT TO TURN IN ALL SIGNIFICANT MAGIC ARTIFACTS FOR COMMUNAL OWNERSHIP AND SAFE STORAGE IN THE BUSINESS OFFICE.
AND WAIT UNTIL YOU SEE WHAT IT DOES.
HEY, MAYBE YOU SHOULDN'T--

--DO THAT.

SON OF A--

ALL BETTER NOW? LISTEN UP THEN. HERE ARE YOUR ORDERS FOR THE NEXT FEW DAYS...

A BIT LATER...

AND REMEMBER, IF BY CHANCE YOU MANAGE TO SURVIVE, EVERYTHING WAS JACK'S FAULT.

SECURITY OFFICE

B. WOLF

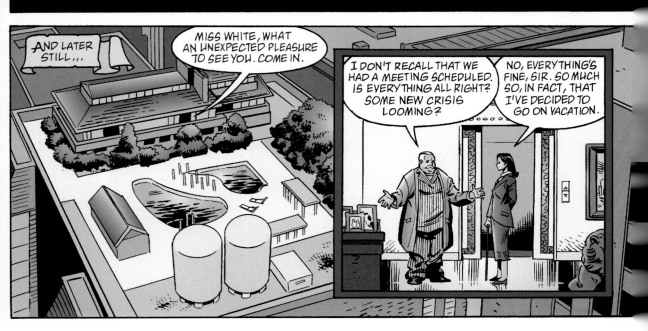

AND LATER STILL...

MISS WHITE, WHAT AN UNEXPECTED PLEASURE TO SEE YOU. COME IN.

I DON'T RECALL THAT WE HAD A MEETING SCHEDULED. IS EVERYTHING ALL RIGHT? SOME NEW CRISIS LOOMING?

NO, EVERYTHING'S FINE, SIR. SO MUCH SO, IN FACT, THAT I'VE DECIDED TO GO ON VACATION.

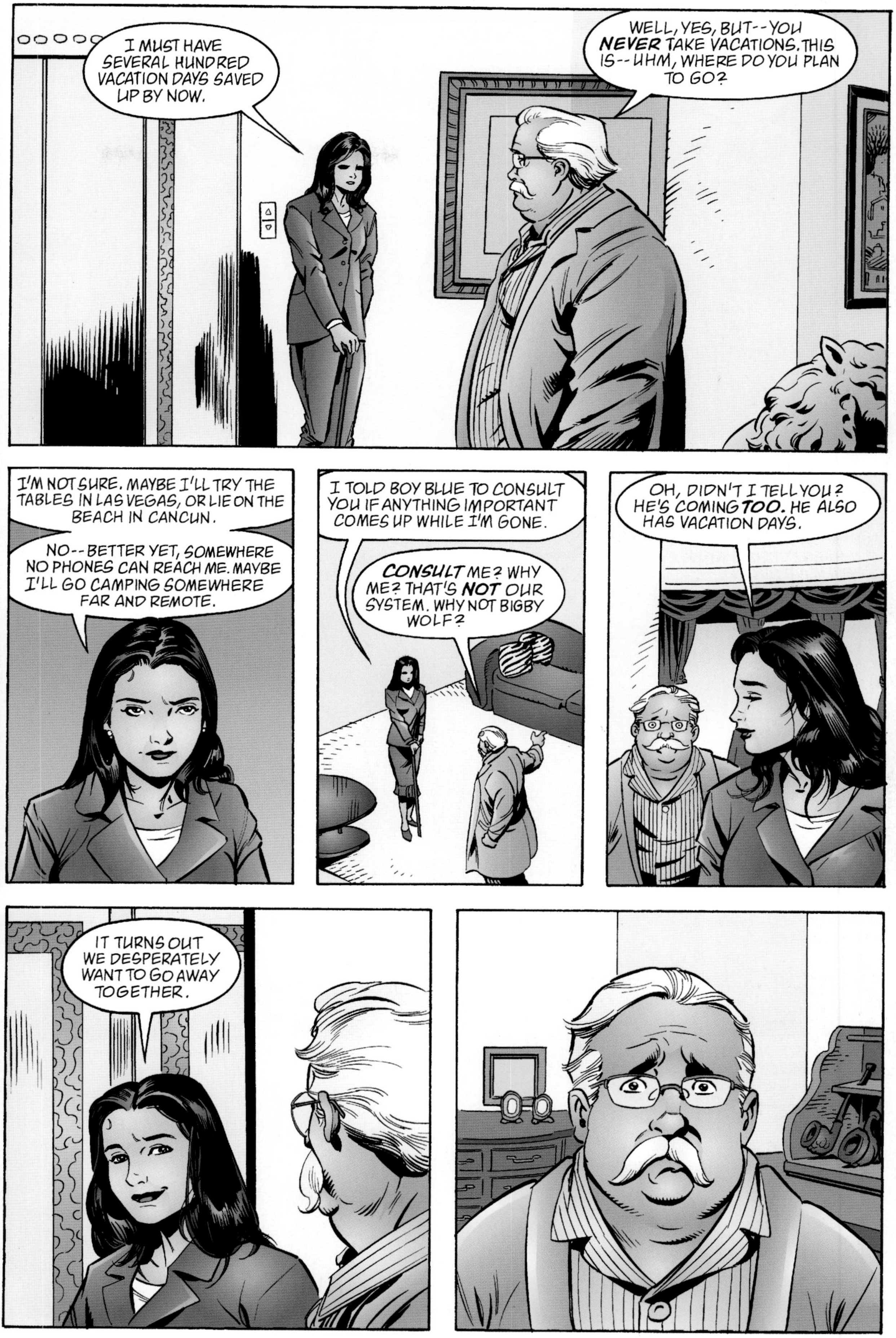
I MUST HAVE SEVERAL HUNDRED VACATION DAYS SAVED UP BY NOW.
WELL, YES, BUT--YOU NEVER TAKE VACATIONS. THIS IS--UHM, WHERE DO YOU PLAN TO GO?
I'M NOT SURE. MAYBE I'LL TRY THE TABLES IN LAS VEGAS, OR LIE ON THE BEACH IN CANCUN.
NO--BETTER YET, SOMEWHERE NO PHONES CAN REACH ME. MAYBE I'LL GO CAMPING SOMEWHERE FAR AND REMOTE.
I TOLD BOY BLUE TO CONSULT YOU IF ANYTHING IMPORTANT COMES UP WHILE I'M GONE.
CONSULT ME? WHY ME? THAT'S NOT OUR SYSTEM. WHY NOT BIGBY WOLF?
OH, DIDN'T I TELL YOU? HE'S COMING TOO. HE ALSO HAS VACATION DAYS.
IT TURNS OUT WE DESPERATELY WANT TO GO AWAY TOGETHER.

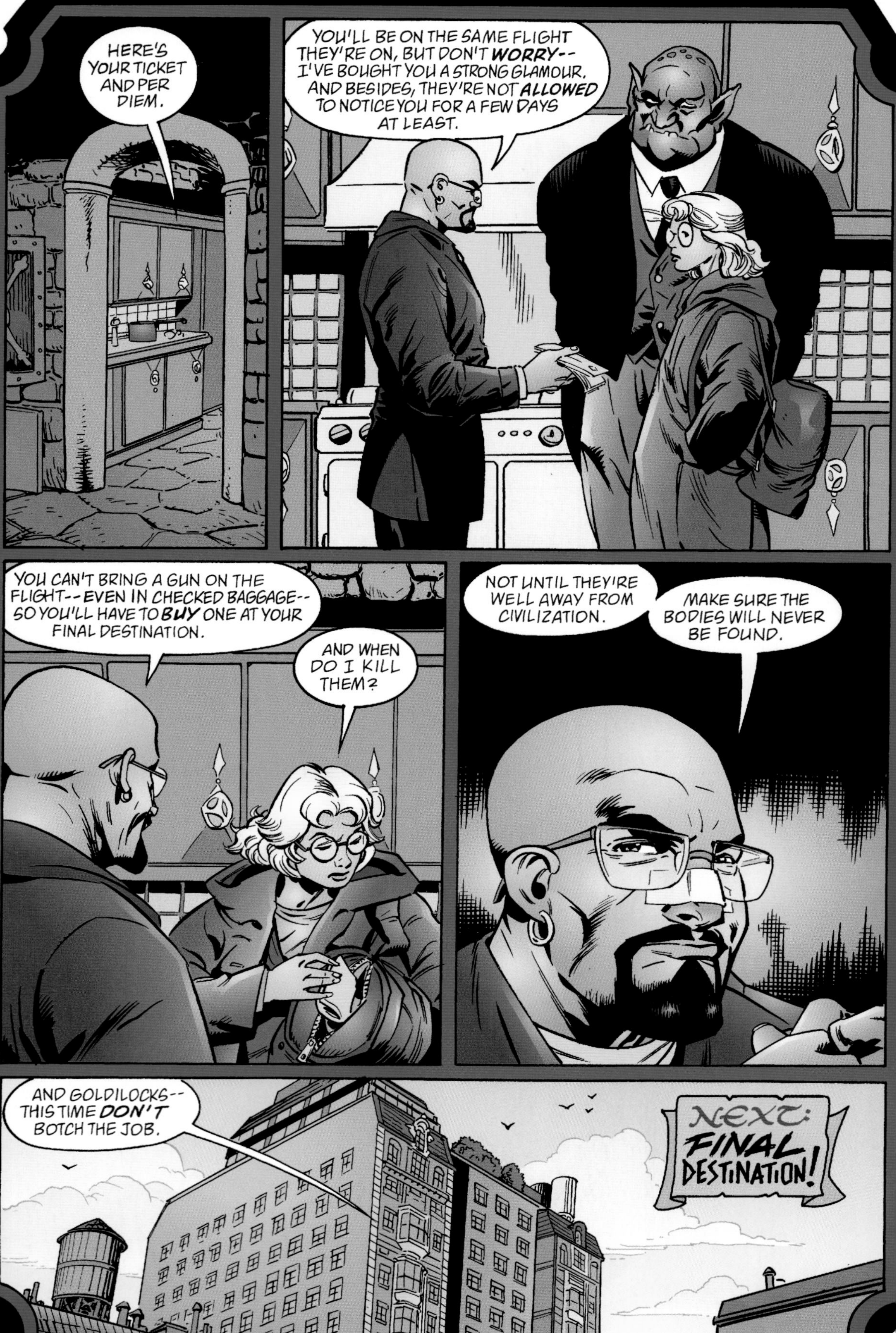
HERE'S YOUR TICKET AND PER DIEM.
YOU'LL BE ON THE SAME FLIGHT THEY'RE ON, BUT DON'T WORRY-- I'VE BOUGHT YOU A STRONG GLAMOUR. AND BESIDES, THEY'RE NOT ALLOWED TO NOTICE YOU FOR A FEW DAYS AT LEAST.
YOU CAN'T BRING A GUN ON THE FLIGHT--EVEN IN CHECKED BAGGAGE-- SO YOU'LL HAVE TO BUY ONE AT YOUR FINAL DESTINATION.
AND WHEN DO I KILL THEM?
NOT UNTIL THEY'RE WELL AWAY FROM CIVILIZATION.
MAKE SURE THE BODIES WILL NEVER BE FOUND.
AND GOLDILOCKS-- THIS TIME DON'T BOTCH THE JOB.
NEXT: FINAL DESTINATION!

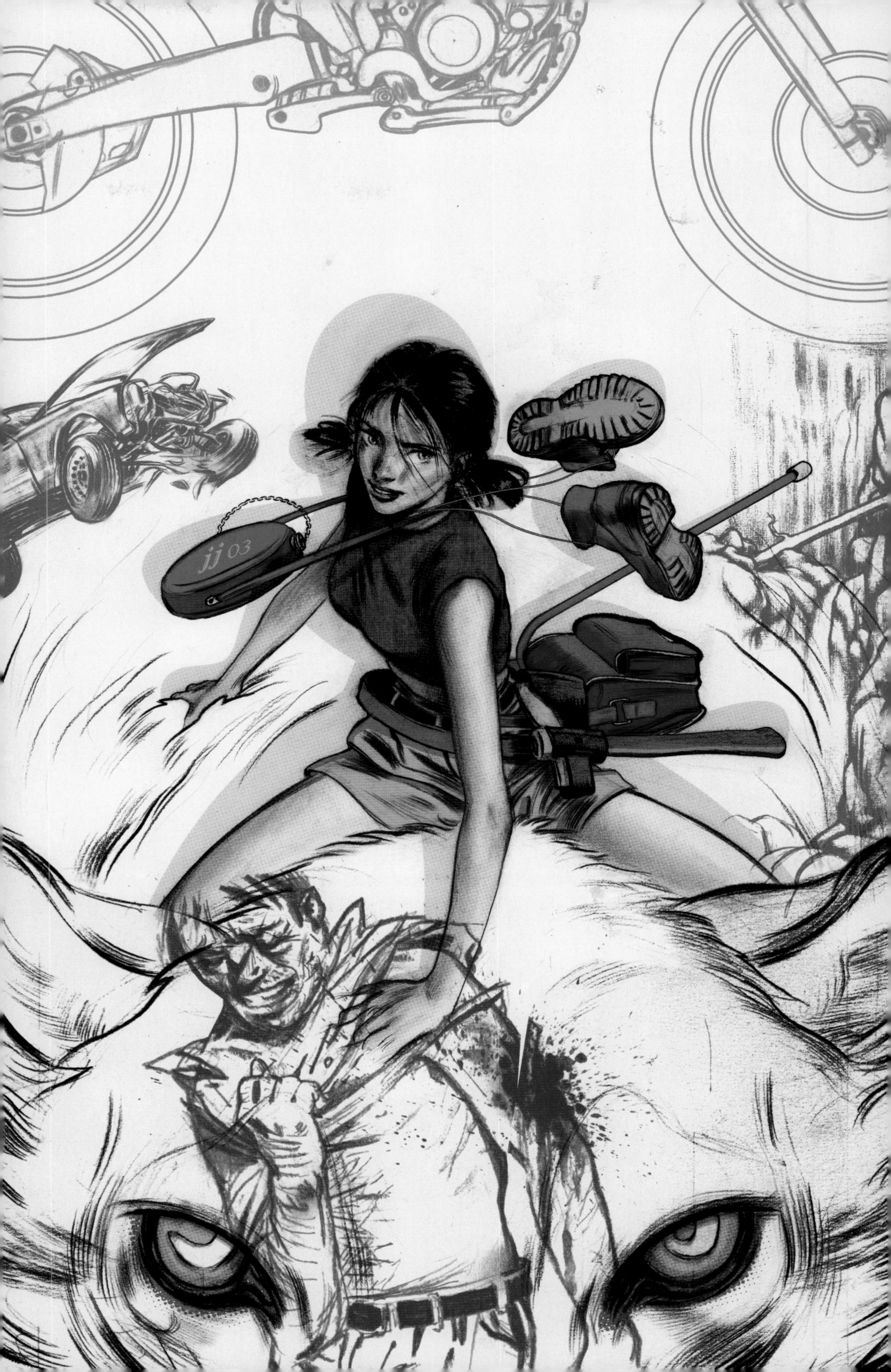
jj 03

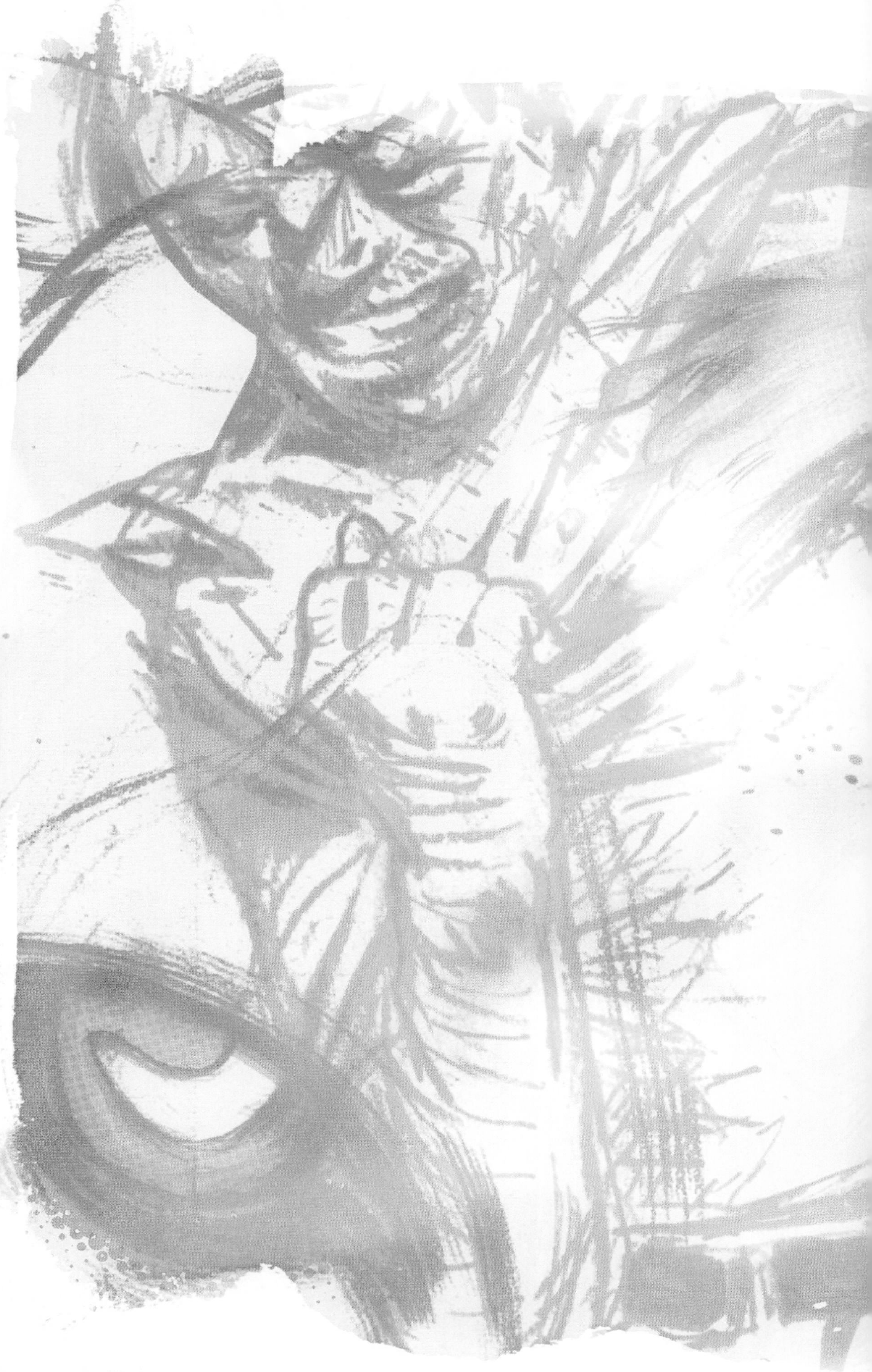

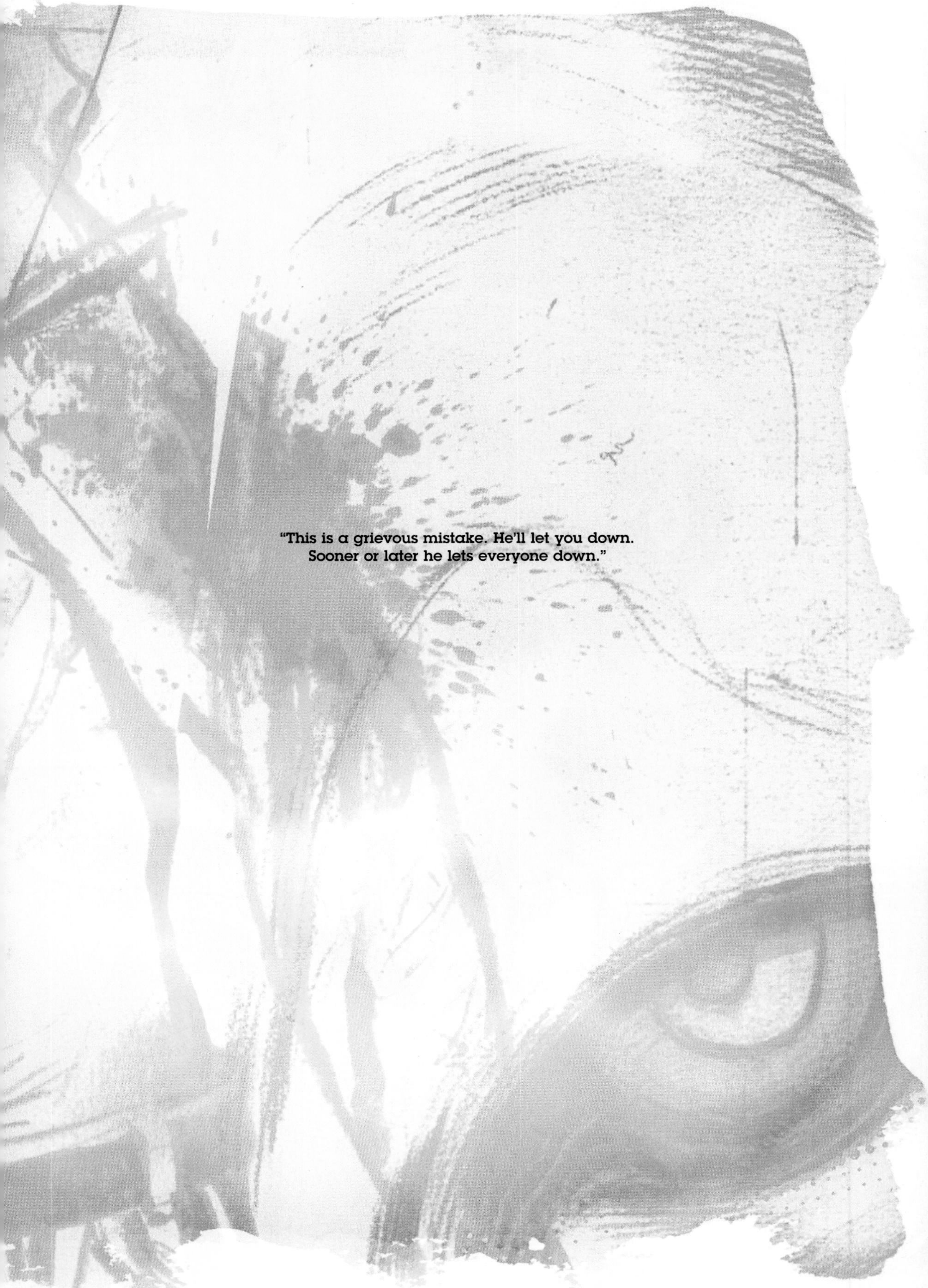

"This is a grievous mistake. He'll let you down.
Sooner or later he lets everyone down."

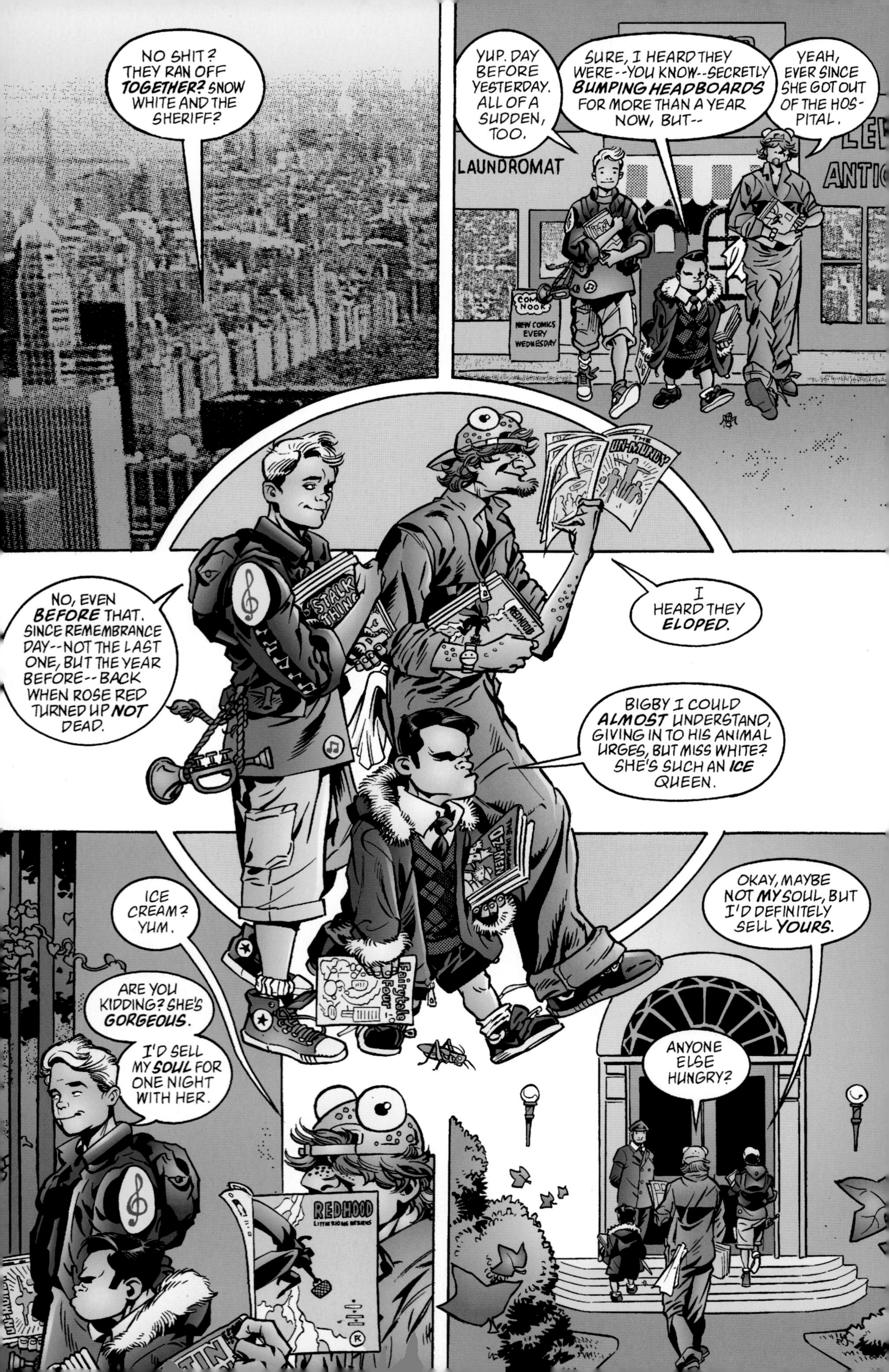

NO SHIT? THEY RAN OFF TOGETHER? SNOW WHITE AND THE SHERIFF?
YUP. DAY BEFORE YESTERDAY. ALL OF A SUDDEN, TOO.
SURE, I HEARD THEY WERE--YOU KNOW--SECRETLY BUMPING HEADBOARDS FOR MORE THAN A YEAR NOW, BUT--
YEAH, EVER SINCE SHE GOT OUT OF THE HOS-PITAL.
LAUNDROMAT
COMIC NOOK
NEW COMICS EVERY WEDNESDAY
NO, EVEN BEFORE THAT. SINCE REMEMBRANCE DAY--NOT THE LAST ONE, BUT THE YEAR BEFORE--BACK WHEN ROSE RED TURNED UP NOT DEAD.
I HEARD THEY ELOPED.
BIGBY I COULD ALMOST UNDERSTAND, GIVING IN TO HIS ANIMAL URGES, BUT MISS WHITE? SHE'S SUCH AN ICE QUEEN.
ICE CREAM? YUM.
ARE YOU KIDDING? SHE'S GORGEOUS.
I'D SELL MY SOUL FOR ONE NIGHT WITH HER.
OKAY, MAYBE NOT MY SOUL, BUT I'D DEFINITELY SELL YOURS.
ANYONE ELSE HUNGRY?
THE UN-MUNDY
STALK THING
Fairytale Four
REDHOOD

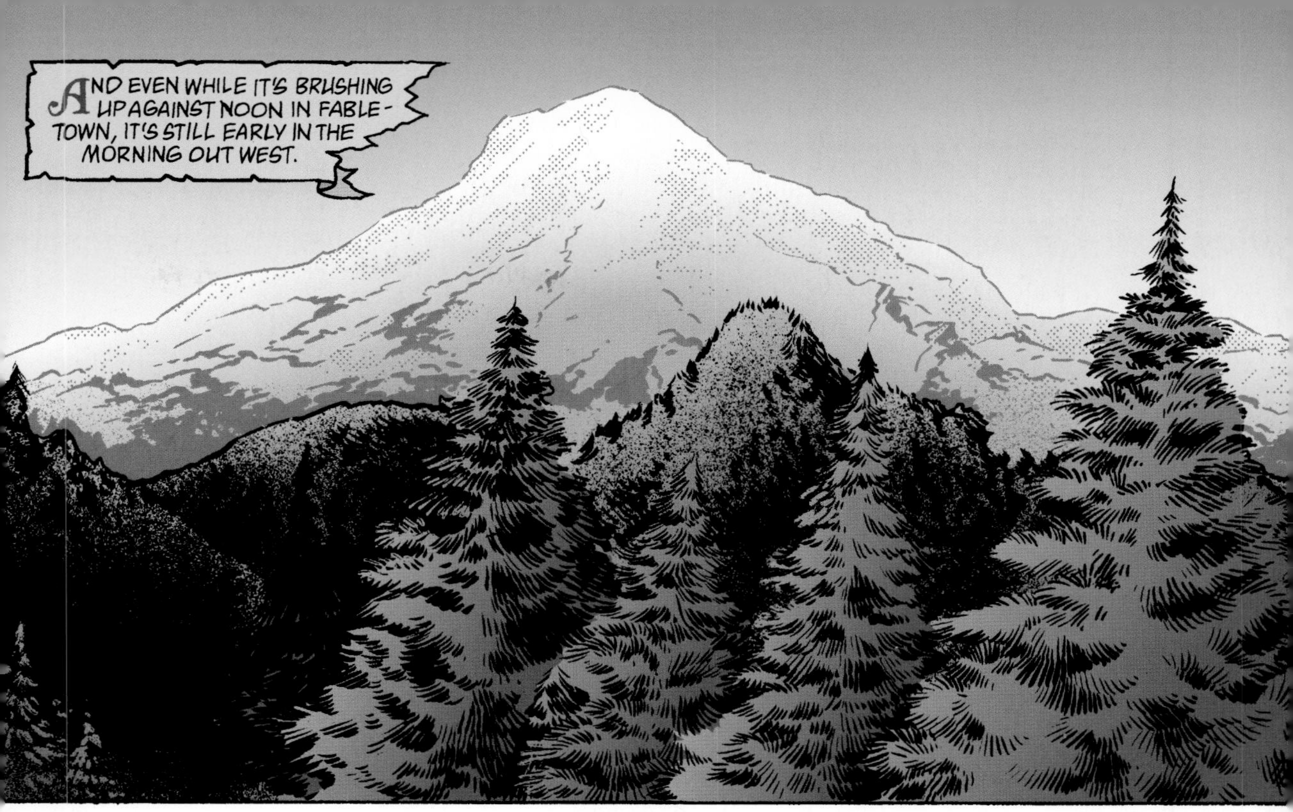
And even while it's brushing up against noon in Fabletown, it's still early in the morning out west.

Into the Woods

Storybook Love

Part Two

Bill Willingham
writer/creator

Mark Buckingham
penciller

Steve Leialoha
inker

Daniel Vozzo
color/separations

Todd Klein
lettering

James Jean
cover art

Mariah Huehner
assistant editor

Shelly Bond
editor

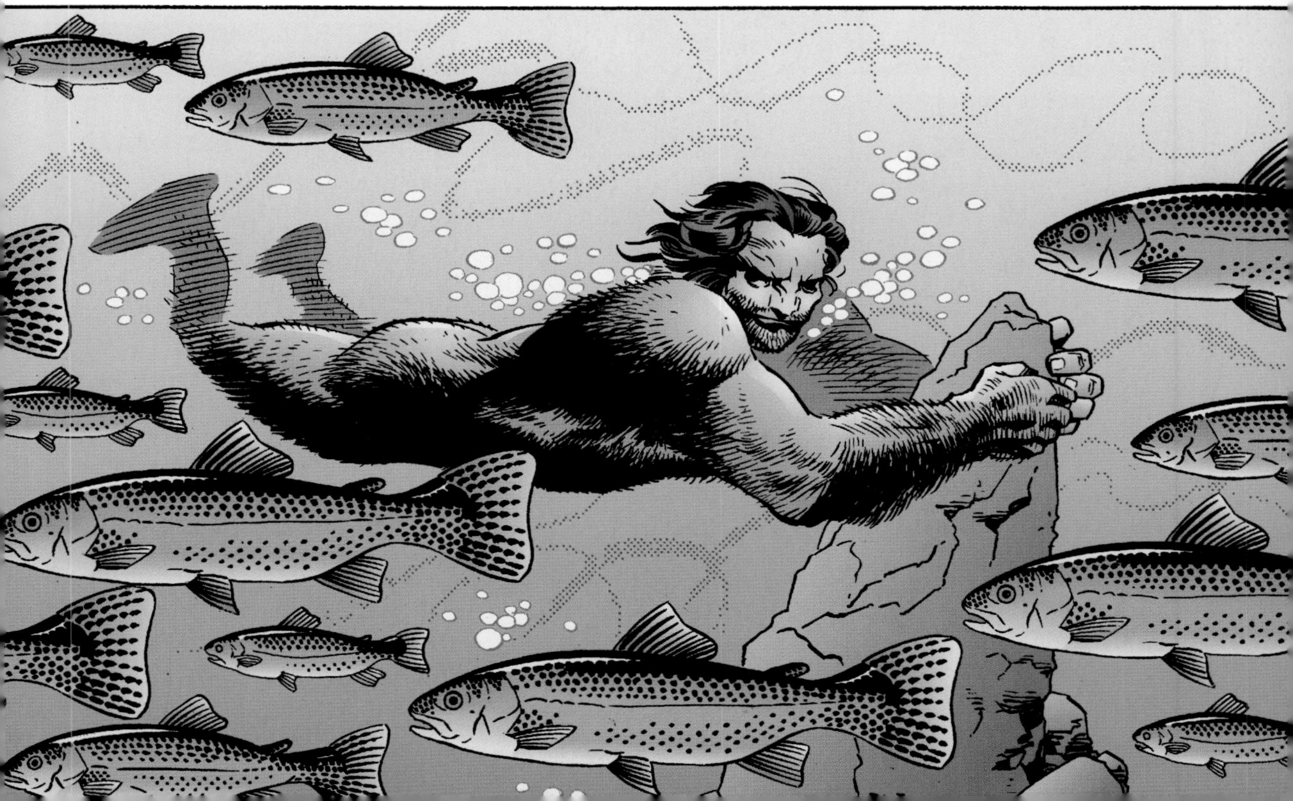

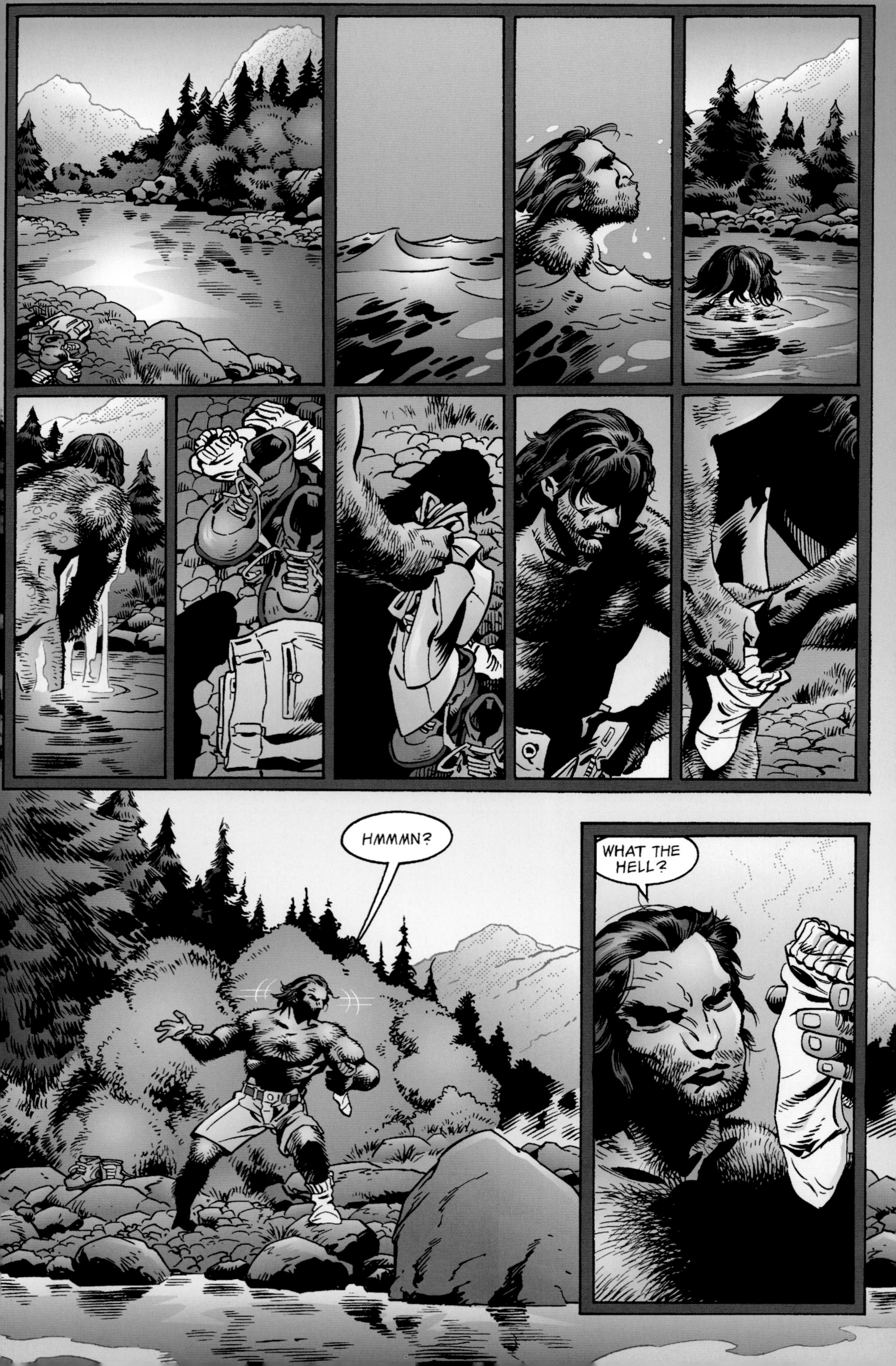
HMMMN?
WHAT THE HELL?

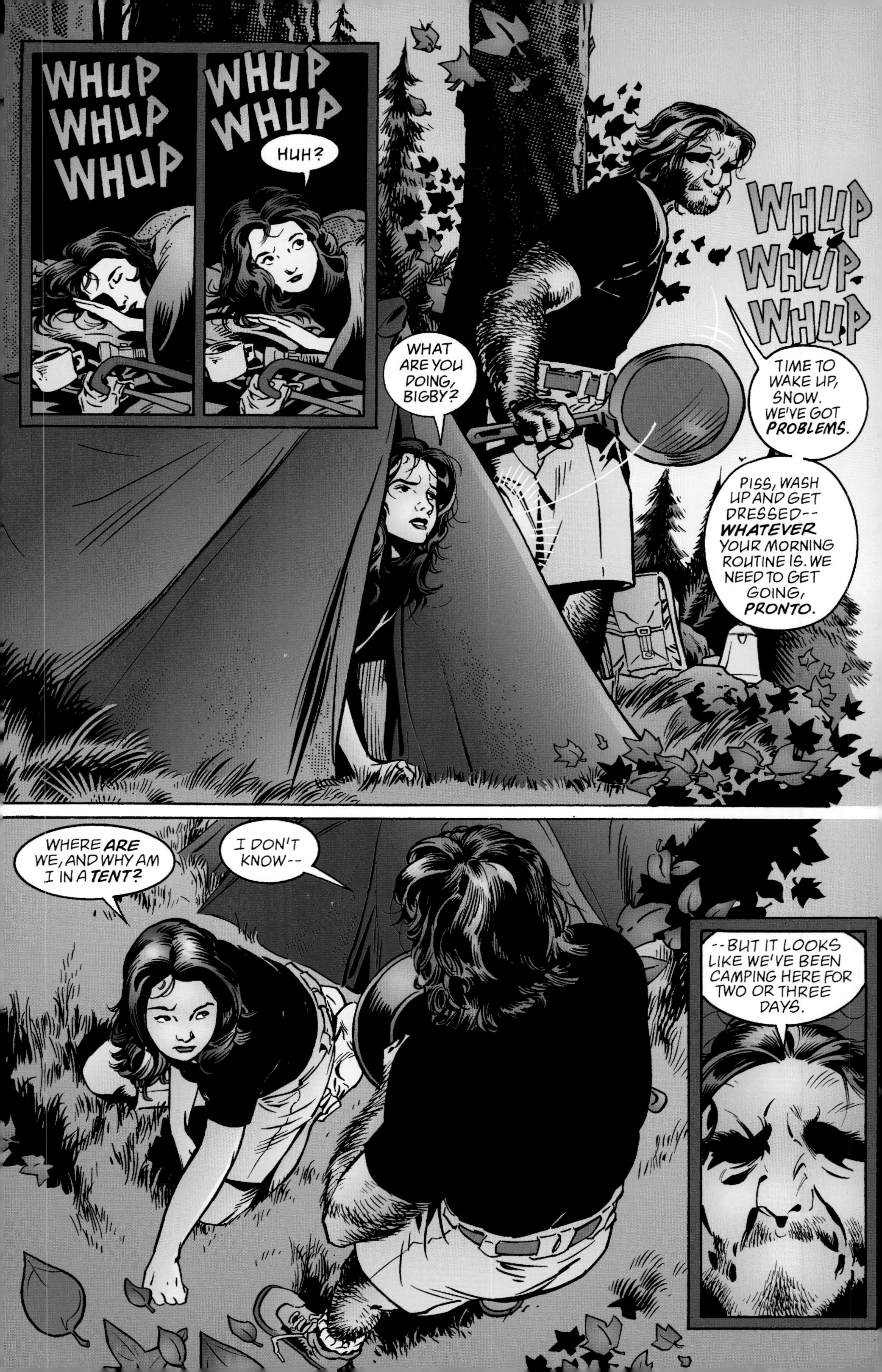
WHUP WHUP WHUP
WHUP WHUP
HUH?
WHAT ARE YOU DOING, BIGBY?
WHUP WHUP WHUP
TIME TO WAKE UP, SNOW. WE'VE GOT PROBLEMS.
PISS, WASH UP AND GET DRESSED-- WHATEVER YOUR MORNING ROUTINE IS. WE NEED TO GET GOING, PRONTO.
WHERE ARE WE, AND WHY AM I IN A TENT?
I DON'T KNOW--
--BUT IT LOOKS LIKE WE'VE BEEN CAMPING HERE FOR TWO OR THREE DAYS.

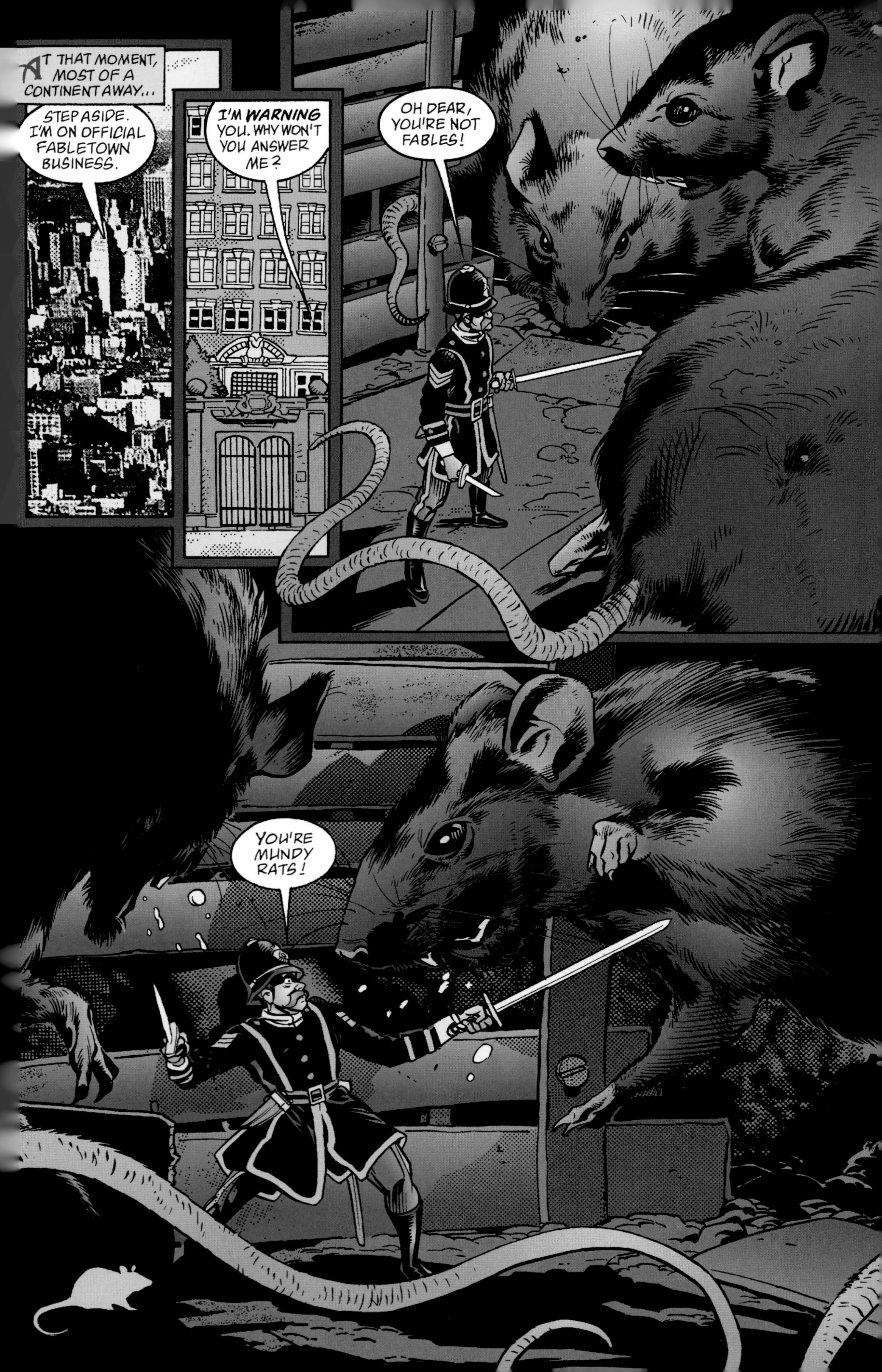
AT THAT MOMENT, MOST OF A CONTINENT AWAY...
STEP ASIDE. I'M ON OFFICIAL FABLETOWN BUSINESS.
I'M WARNING YOU. WHY WON'T YOU ANSWER ME?
OH DEAR, YOU'RE NOT FABLES!
YOU'RE MUNDY RATS!

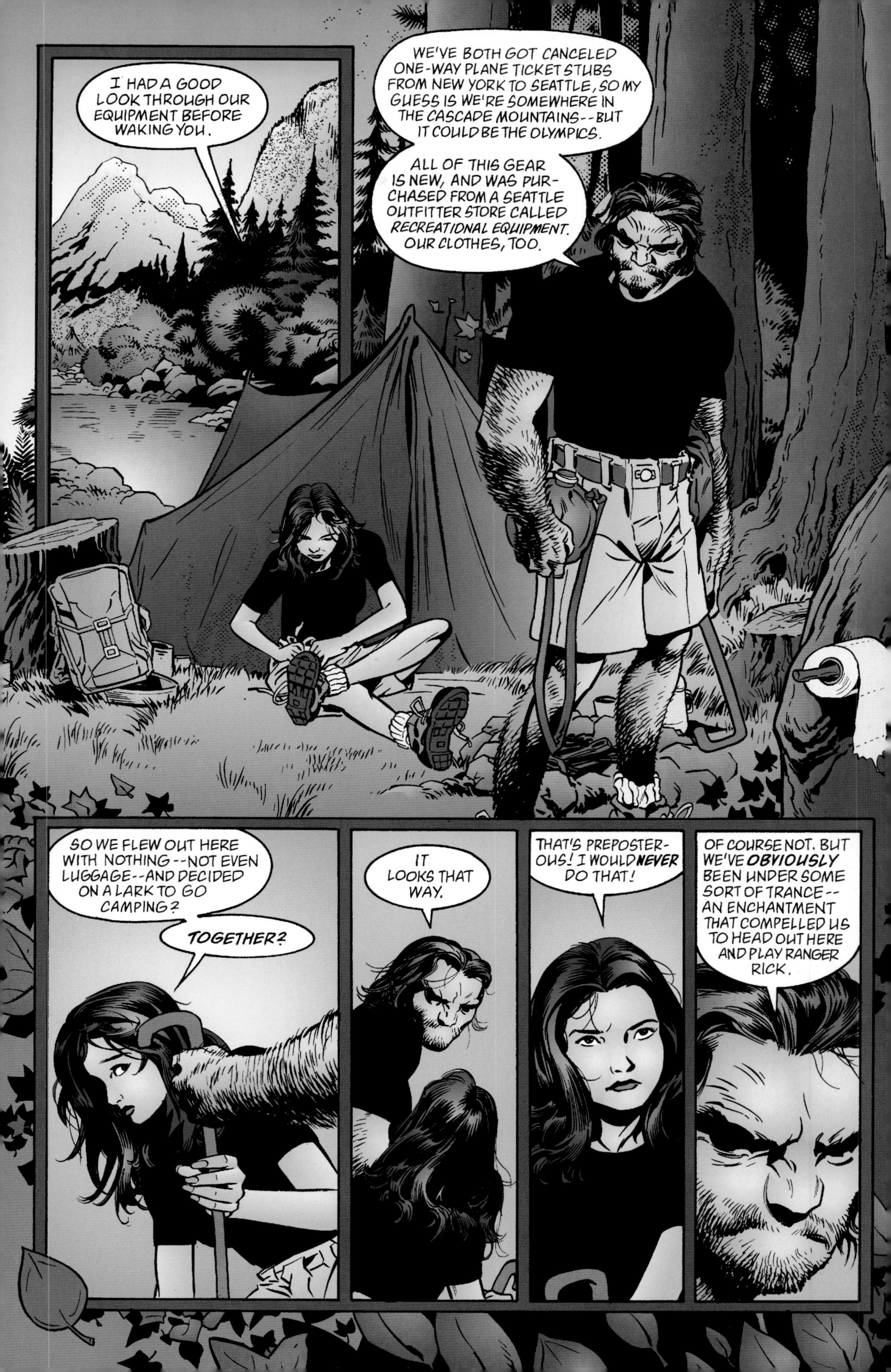
I HAD A GOOD LOOK THROUGH OUR EQUIPMENT BEFORE WAKING YOU.
WE'VE BOTH GOT CANCELED ONE-WAY PLANE TICKET STUBS FROM NEW YORK TO SEATTLE, SO MY GUESS IS WE'RE SOMEWHERE IN THE CASCADE MOUNTAINS--BUT IT COULD BE THE OLYMPICS.
ALL OF THIS GEAR IS NEW, AND WAS PURCHASED FROM A SEATTLE OUTFITTER STORE CALLED RECREATIONAL EQUIPMENT. OUR CLOTHES, TOO.
SO WE FLEW OUT HERE WITH NOTHING--NOT EVEN LUGGAGE--AND DECIDED ON A LARK TO GO CAMPING?
TOGETHER?
IT LOOKS THAT WAY.
THAT'S PREPOSTEROUS! I WOULD NEVER DO THAT!
OF COURSE NOT. BUT WE'VE OBVIOUSLY BEEN UNDER SOME SORT OF TRANCE--AN ENCHANTMENT THAT COMPELLED US TO HEAD OUT HERE AND PLAY RANGER RICK.

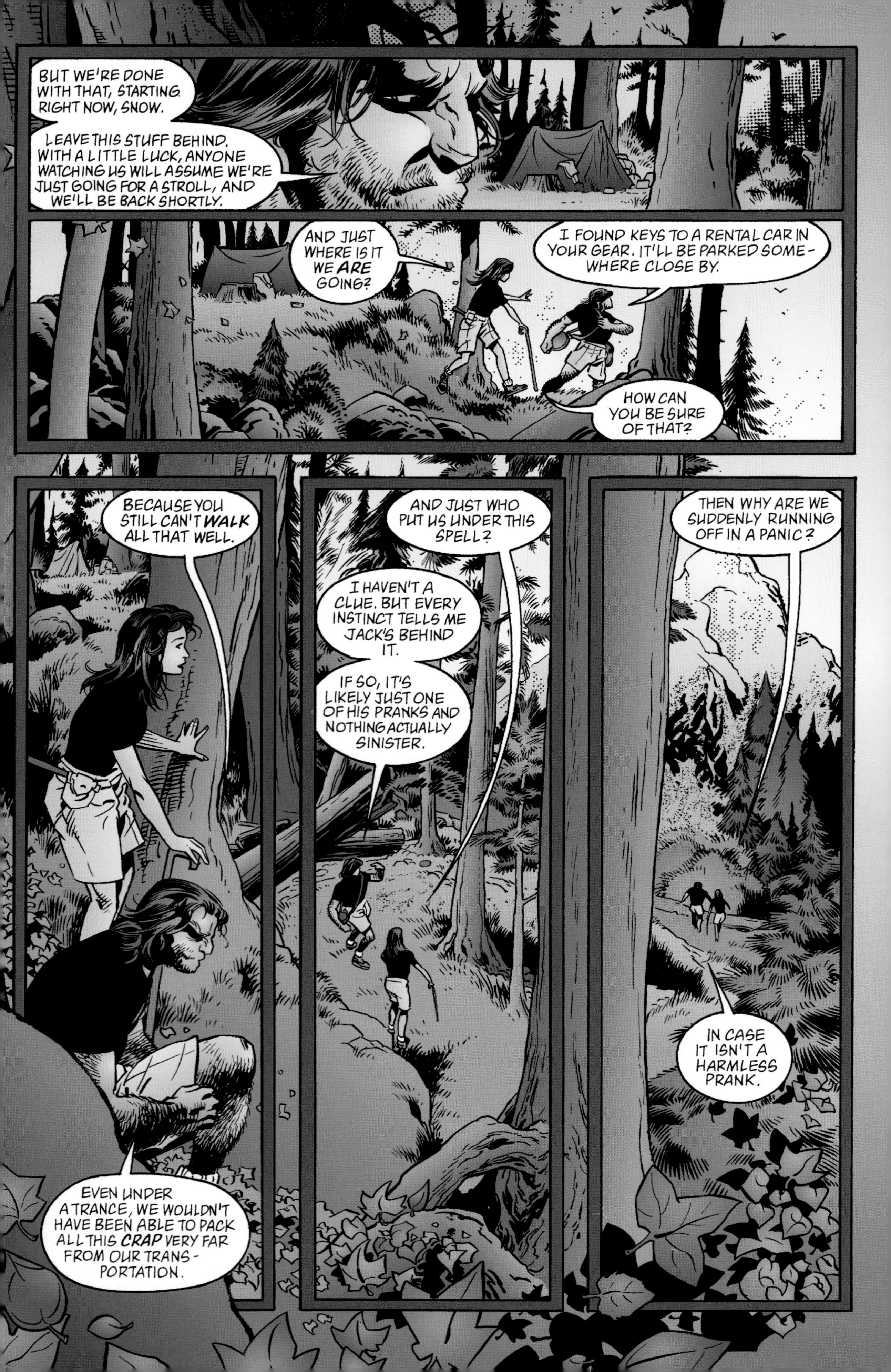
BUT WE'RE DONE WITH THAT, STARTING RIGHT NOW, SNOW.
LEAVE THIS STUFF BEHIND. WITH A LITTLE LUCK, ANYONE WATCHING US WILL ASSUME WE'RE JUST GOING FOR A STROLL, AND WE'LL BE BACK SHORTLY.
AND JUST WHERE IS IT WE *ARE* GOING?
I FOUND KEYS TO A RENTAL CAR IN YOUR GEAR. IT'LL BE PARKED SOME-WHERE CLOSE BY.
HOW CAN YOU BE SURE OF THAT?
BECAUSE YOU STILL CAN'T *WALK* ALL THAT WELL.
EVEN UNDER A TRANCE, WE WOULDN'T HAVE BEEN ABLE TO PACK ALL THIS *CRAP* VERY FAR FROM OUR TRANS-PORTATION.
AND JUST WHO PUT US UNDER THIS SPELL?
I HAVEN'T A CLUE. BUT EVERY INSTINCT TELLS ME JACK'S BEHIND IT.
IF SO, IT'S LIKELY JUST ONE OF HIS PRANKS AND NOTHING ACTUALLY SINISTER.
THEN WHY ARE WE SUDDENLY RUNNING OFF IN A PANIC?
IN CASE IT ISN'T A HARMLESS PRANK.

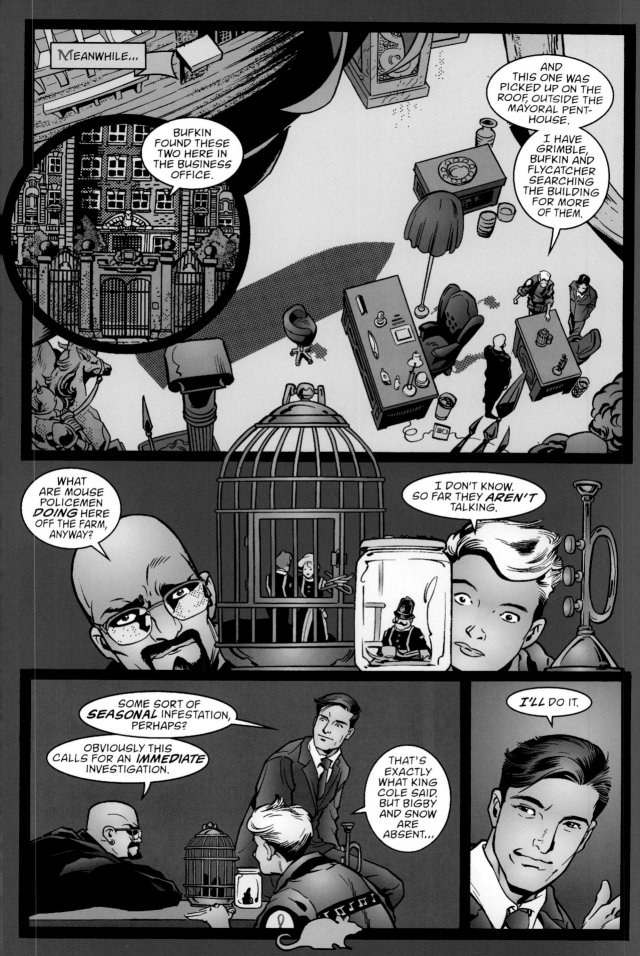

MEANWHILE...

BUFKIN FOUND THESE TWO HERE IN THE BUSINESS OFFICE.

AND THIS ONE WAS PICKED UP ON THE ROOF, OUTSIDE THE MAYORAL PENT-HOUSE.

I HAVE GRIMBLE, BUFKIN AND FLYCATCHER SEARCHING THE BUILDING FOR MORE OF THEM.

WHAT ARE MOUSE POLICEMEN *DOING* HERE OFF THE FARM, ANYWAY?

I DON'T KNOW. SO FAR THEY *AREN'T* TALKING.

SOME SORT OF *SEASONAL* INFESTATION, PERHAPS?

OBVIOUSLY THIS CALLS FOR AN *IMMEDIATE* INVESTIGATION.

THAT'S EXACTLY WHAT KING COLE SAID. BUT BIGBY AND SNOW ARE ABSENT...

I'LL DO IT.

WHY YOU? THIS DUTY REQUIRES SOMEONE WITH PROVEN STATUS IN THE COMMUNITY--

--SOMEONE MORE INVESTED IN OUR LONG-TERM PROSPERITY.

IT'S HARDLY A JOB WE CAN TRUST TO A NEWLY ARRIVED *COMMONER.*

NOW WAIT A MINUTE, BLUEBEARD, WE CAN ARGUE MY OTHER MERITS, BUT I *AM* A PRINCE AGAIN.

I BOUGHT MY TITLE BACK FROM JACK, THE DAY AFTER HE WON THE ONLINE AUCTION.

SNOW WHITE
~DIRECTOR OF OPERATIONS~

HOWEVER...

THAT MAY BE TECHNICALLY TRUE, BUT ONCE A TITLE HAS BEEN BOUGHT AND SOLD A FEW TIMES, LIKE SOME COMMODITY, IT LOSES ITS CACHET.

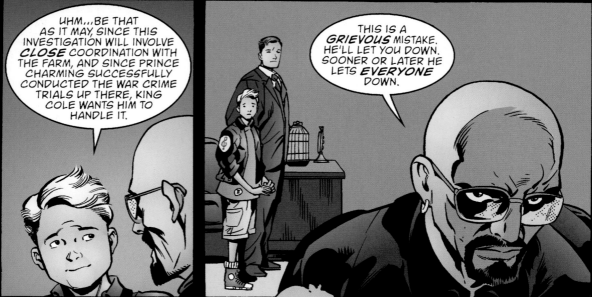

UHM...BE THAT AS IT MAY, SINCE THIS INVESTIGATION WILL INVOLVE *CLOSE* COORDINATION WITH THE FARM, AND SINCE PRINCE CHARMING SUCCESSFULLY CONDUCTED THE WAR CRIME TRIALS UP THERE, KING COLE WANTS HIM TO HANDLE IT.

THIS IS A *GRIEVOUS* MISTAKE. HE'LL LET YOU DOWN. SOONER OR LATER HE LETS *EVERYONE* DOWN.

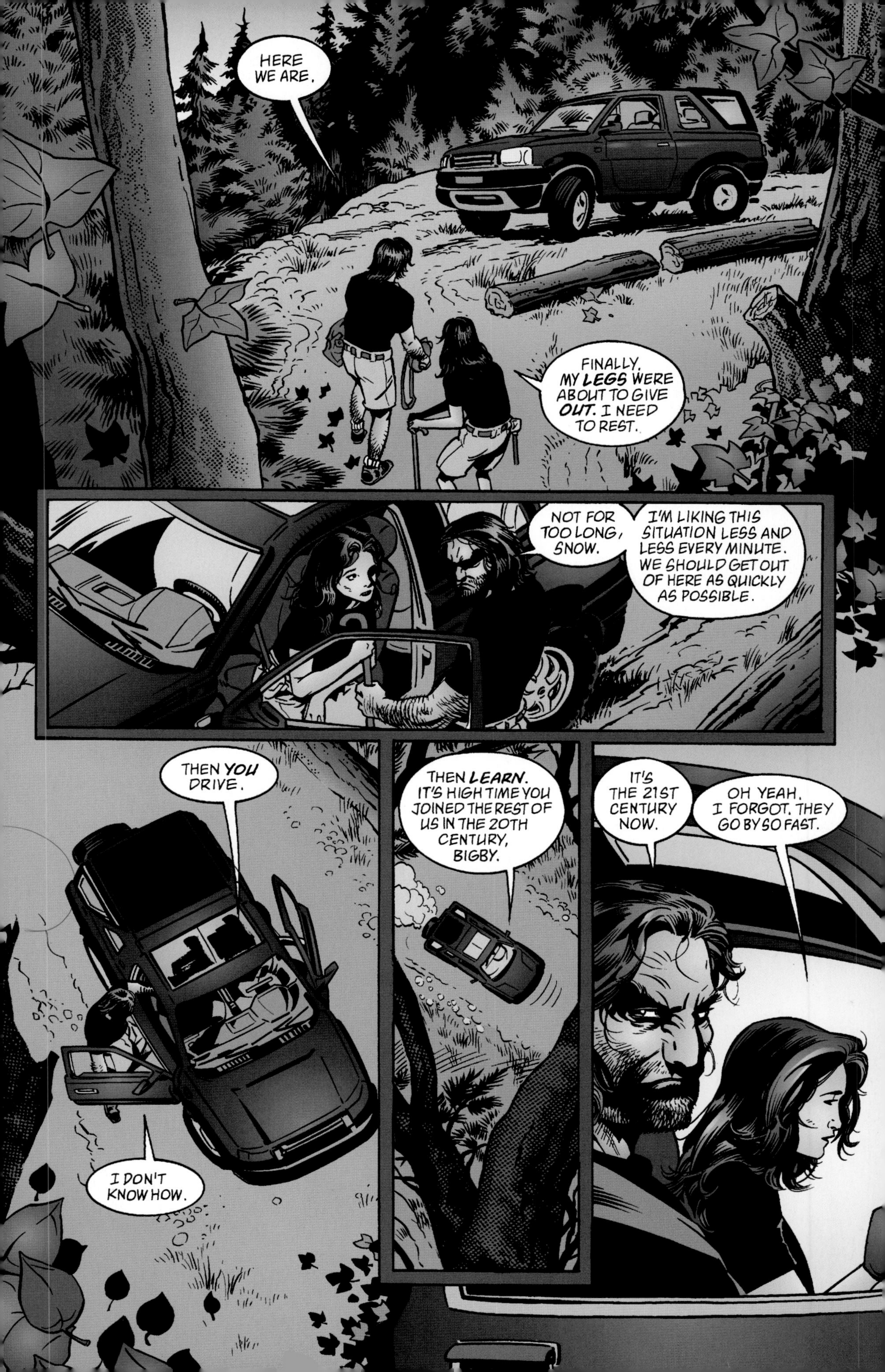
HERE WE ARE.
FINALLY. MY LEGS WERE ABOUT TO GIVE OUT. I NEED TO REST.
NOT FOR TOO LONG, SNOW.
I'M LIKING THIS SITUATION LESS AND LESS EVERY MINUTE. WE SHOULD GET OUT OF HERE AS QUICKLY AS POSSIBLE.
THEN YOU DRIVE.
I DON'T KNOW HOW.
THEN LEARN. IT'S HIGH TIME YOU JOINED THE REST OF US IN THE 20TH CENTURY, BIGBY.
IT'S THE 21ST CENTURY NOW.
OH YEAH. I FORGOT. THEY GO BY SO FAST.

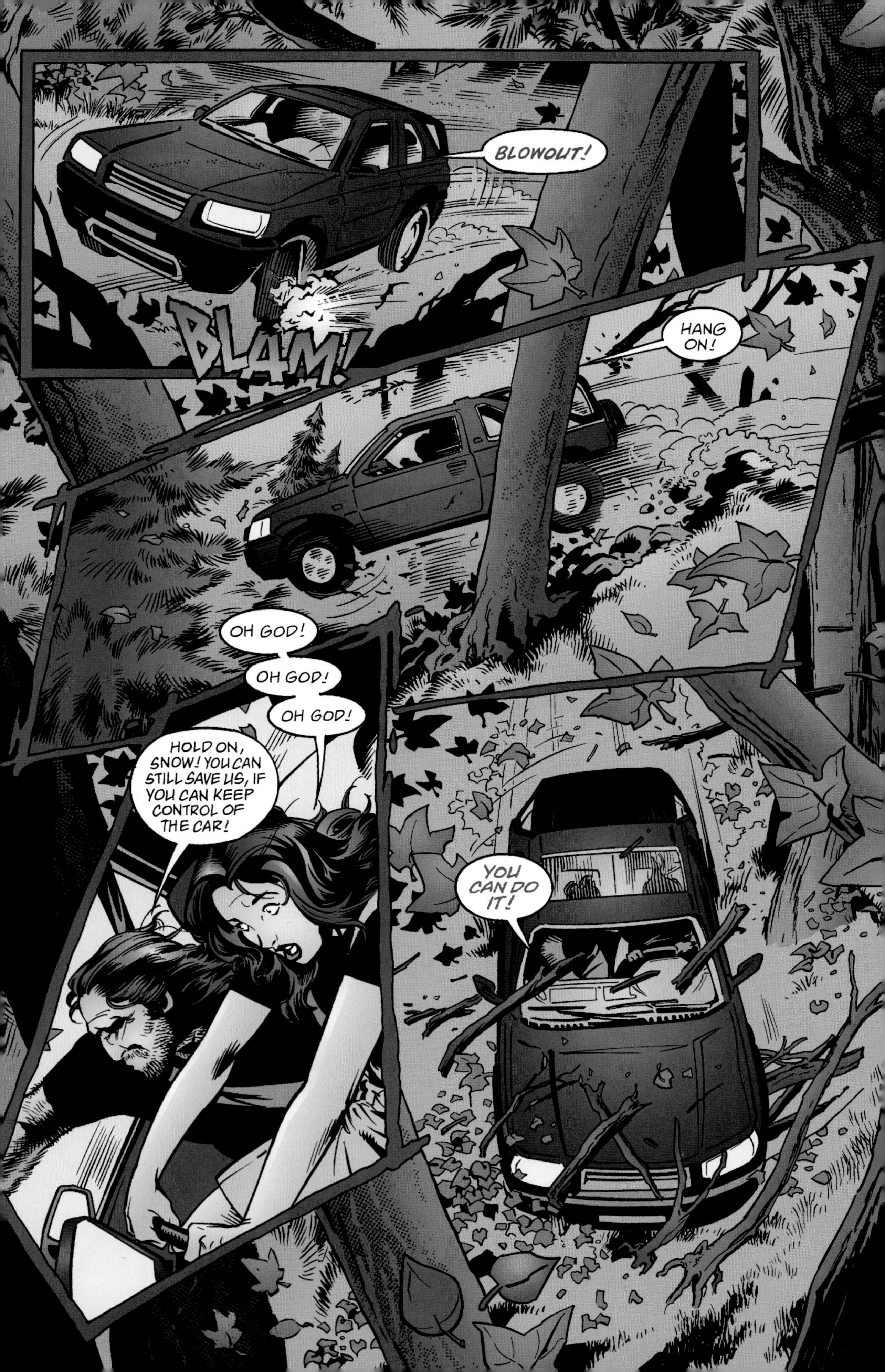
BLOWOUT!
BLAM!
HANG ON!
OH GOD!
OH GOD!
OH GOD!
HOLD ON, SNOW! YOU CAN STILL SAVE US, IF YOU CAN KEEP CONTROL OF THE CAR!
YOU CAN DO IT!

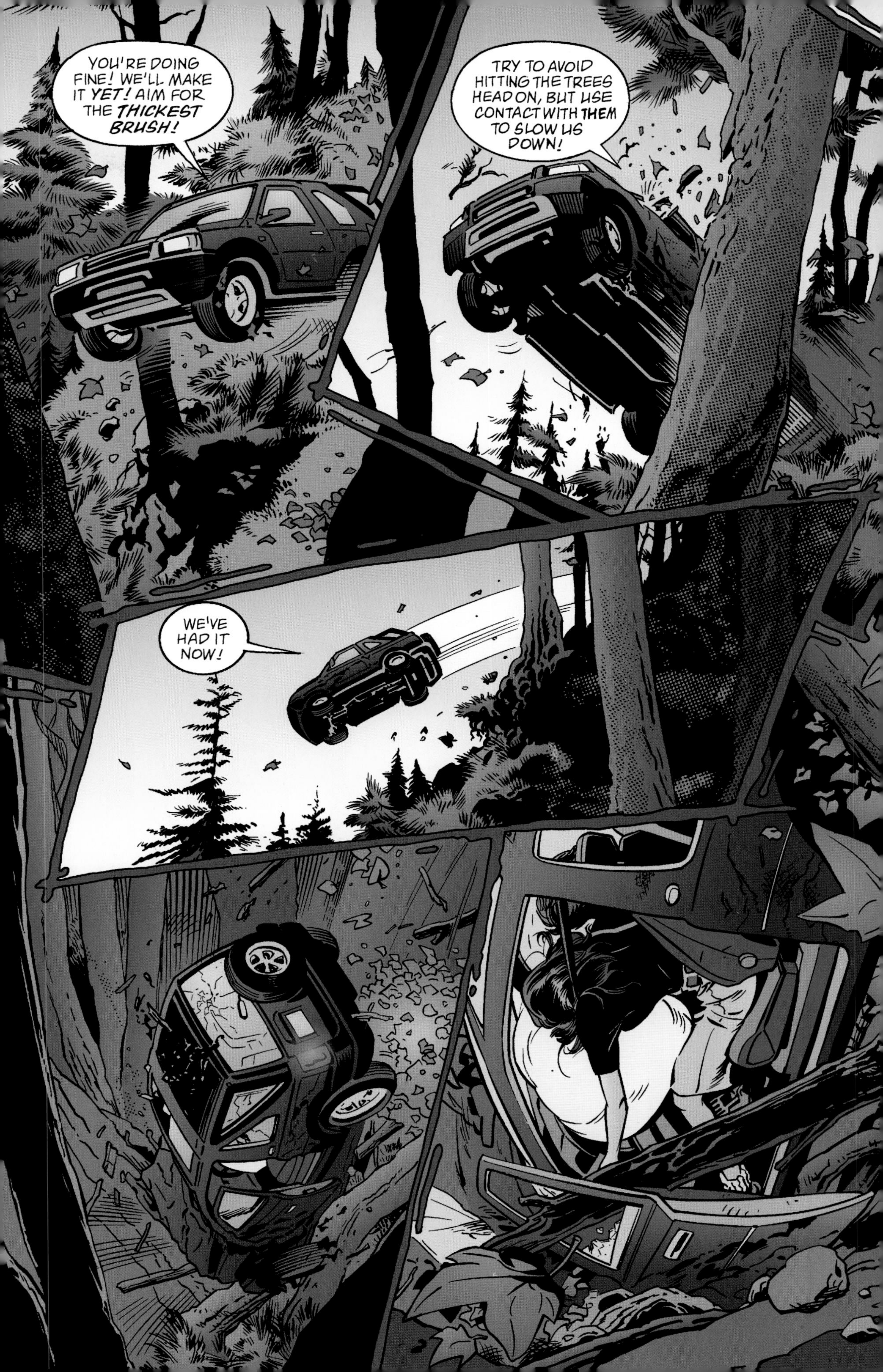
YOU'RE DOING FINE! WE'LL MAKE IT YET! AIM FOR THE THICKEST BRUSH!
TRY TO AVOID HITTING THE TREES HEAD ON, BUT USE CONTACT WITH THEM TO SLOW US DOWN!
WE'VE HAD IT NOW!

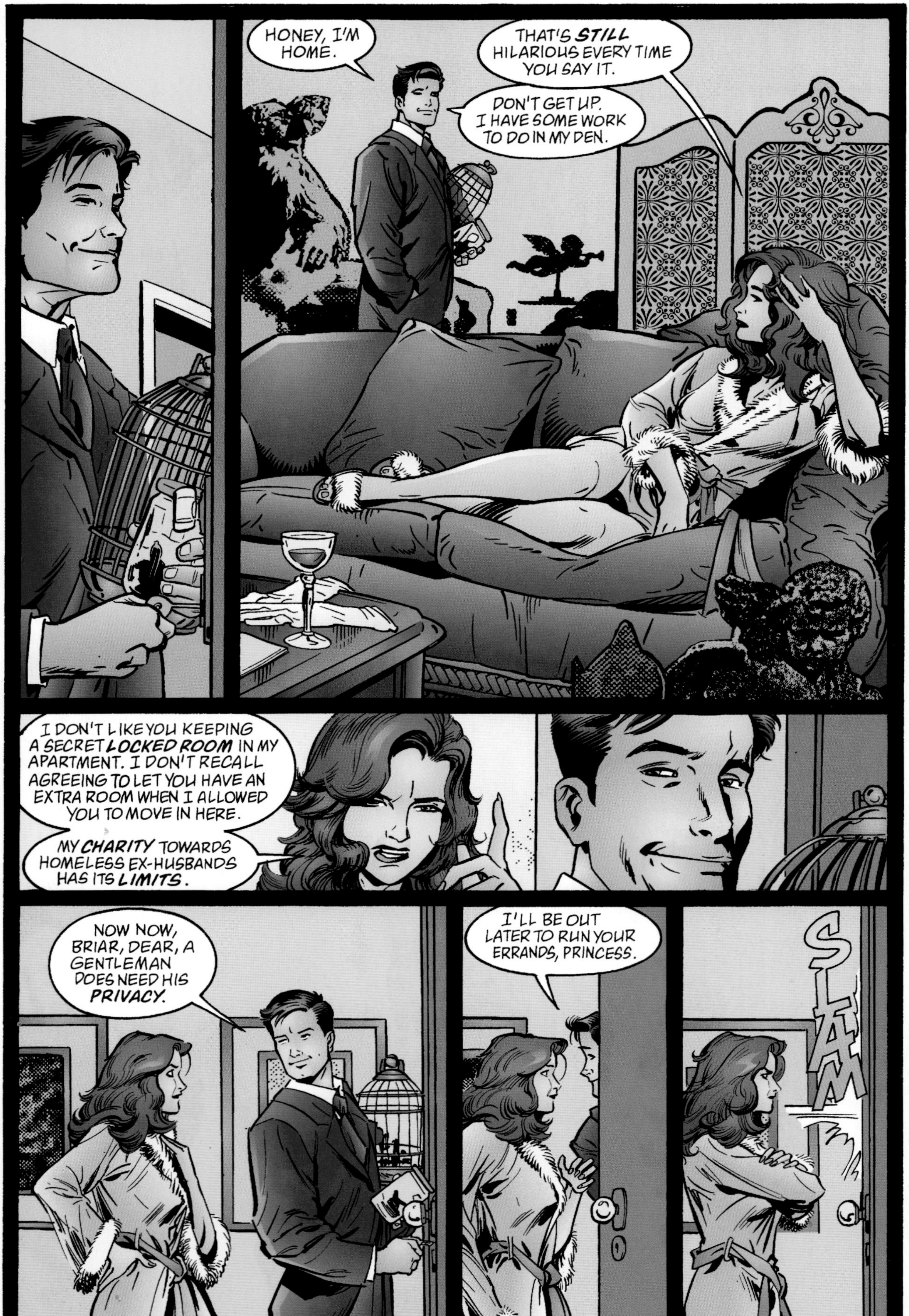
HONEY, I'M HOME.
THAT'S STILL HILARIOUS EVERY TIME YOU SAY IT.
DON'T GET UP. I HAVE SOME WORK TO DO IN MY DEN.
I DON'T LIKE YOU KEEPING A SECRET LOCKED ROOM IN MY APARTMENT. I DON'T RECALL AGREEING TO LET YOU HAVE AN EXTRA ROOM WHEN I ALLOWED YOU TO MOVE IN HERE.
MY CHARITY TOWARDS HOMELESS EX-HUSBANDS HAS ITS LIMITS.
NOW NOW, BRIAR, DEAR, A GENTLEMAN DOES NEED HIS PRIVACY.
I'LL BE OUT LATER TO RUN YOUR ERRANDS, PRINCESS.
SLAM

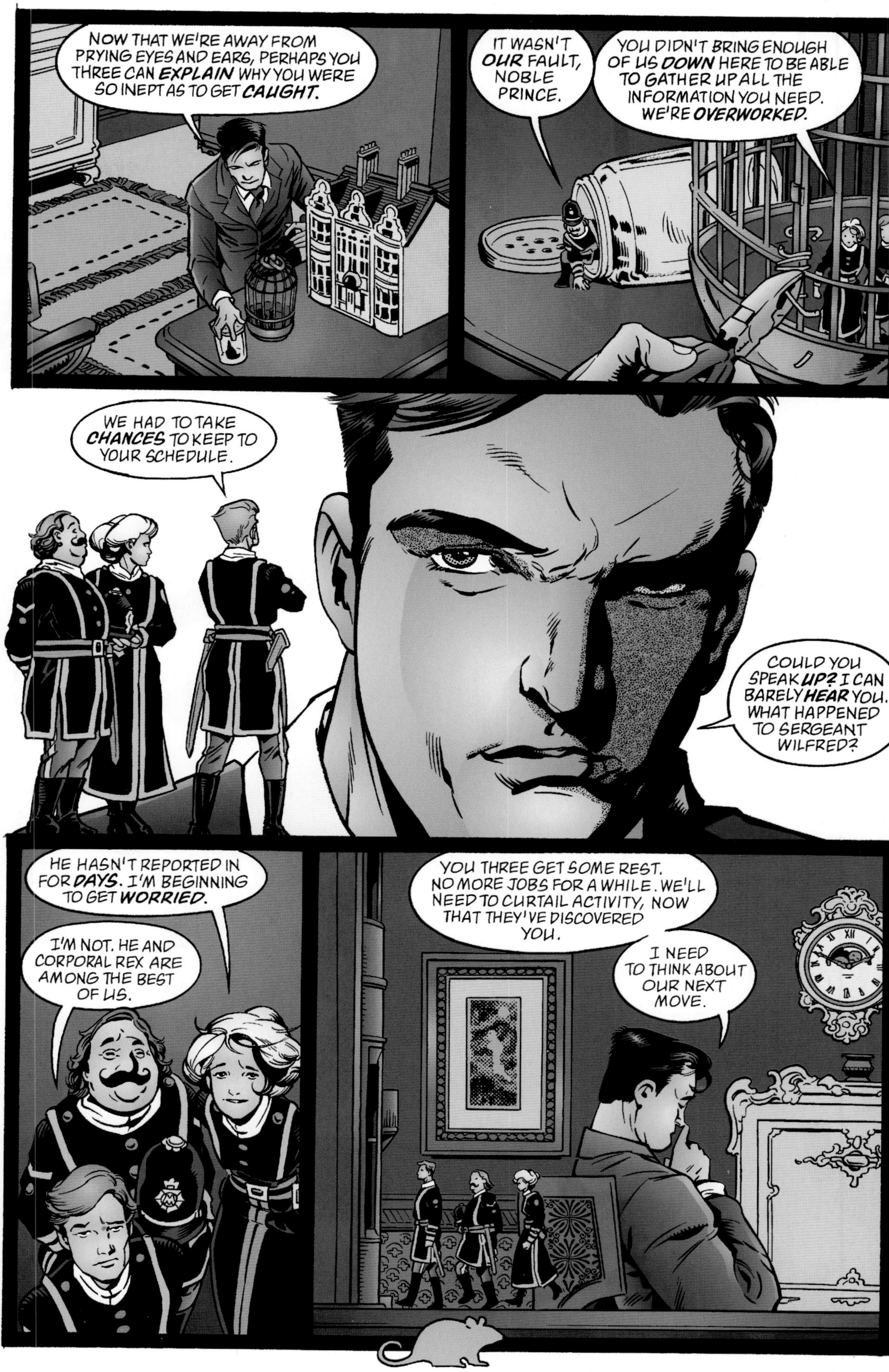
NOW THAT WE'RE AWAY FROM PRYING EYES AND EARS, PERHAPS YOU THREE CAN EXPLAIN WHY YOU WERE SO INEPT AS TO GET CAUGHT.
IT WASN'T OUR FAULT, NOBLE PRINCE.
YOU DIDN'T BRING ENOUGH OF US DOWN HERE TO BE ABLE TO GATHER UP ALL THE INFORMATION YOU NEED. WE'RE OVERWORKED.
WE HAD TO TAKE CHANCES TO KEEP TO YOUR SCHEDULE.
COULD YOU SPEAK UP? I CAN BARELY HEAR YOU. WHAT HAPPENED TO SERGEANT WILFRED?
HE HASN'T REPORTED IN FOR DAYS. I'M BEGINNING TO GET WORRIED.
I'M NOT. HE AND CORPORAL REX ARE AMONG THE BEST OF US.
YOU THREE GET SOME REST. NO MORE JOBS FOR A WHILE. WE'LL NEED TO CURTAIL ACTIVITY, NOW THAT THEY'VE DISCOVERED YOU.
I NEED TO THINK ABOUT OUR NEXT MOVE.

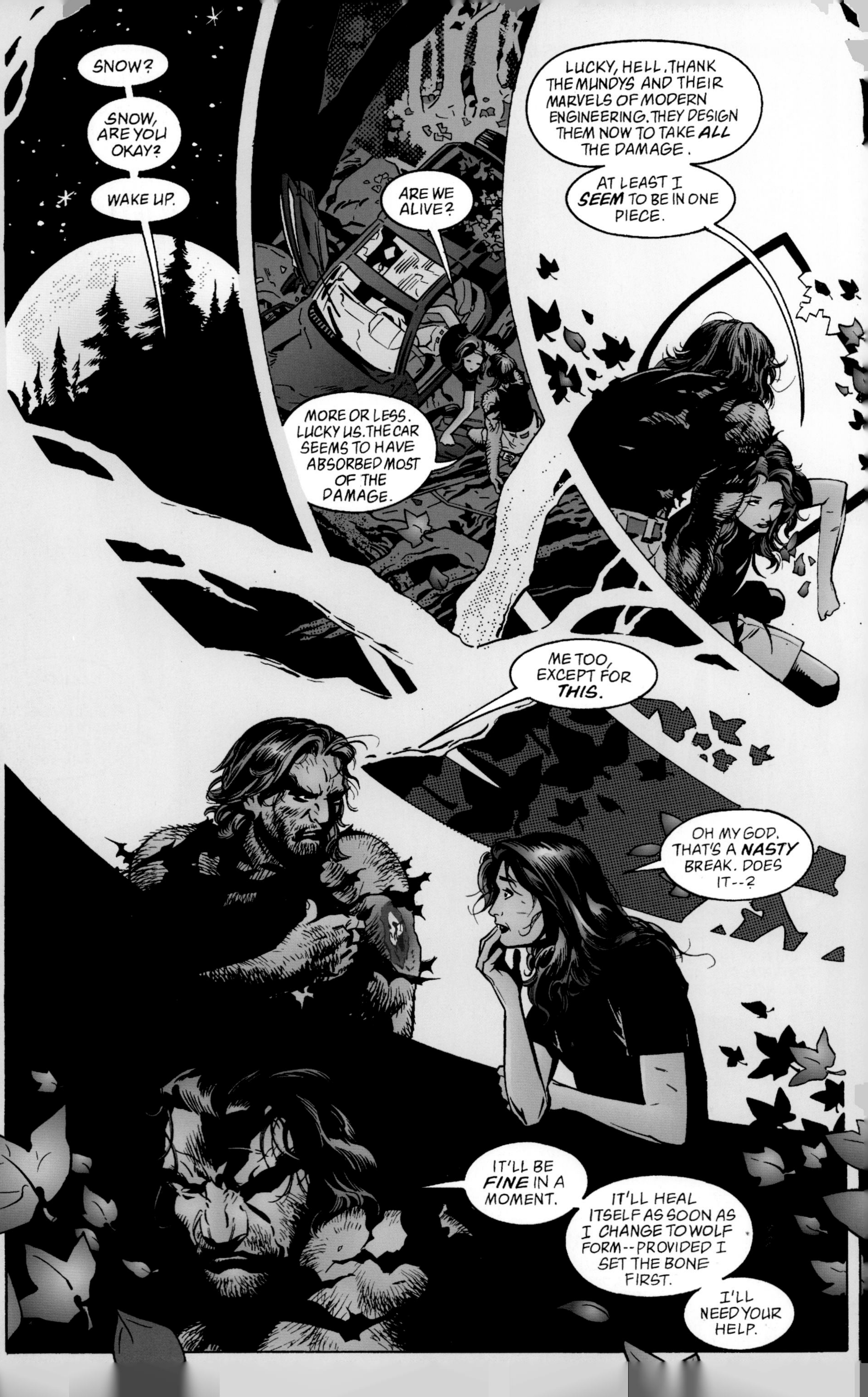
SNOW?
SNOW, ARE YOU OKAY?
WAKE UP.
ARE WE ALIVE?
MORE OR LESS. LUCKY US. THE CAR SEEMS TO HAVE ABSORBED MOST OF THE DAMAGE.
LUCKY, HELL. THANK THE MUNDYS AND THEIR MARVELS OF MODERN ENGINEERING. THEY DESIGN THEM NOW TO TAKE **ALL** THE DAMAGE.
AT LEAST I **SEEM** TO BE IN ONE PIECE.
ME TOO, EXCEPT FOR **THIS**.
OH MY GOD. THAT'S A **NASTY** BREAK. DOES IT--?
IT'LL BE **FINE** IN A MOMENT.
IT'LL HEAL ITSELF AS SOON AS I CHANGE TO WOLF FORM--PROVIDED I SET THE BONE FIRST.
I'LL NEED YOUR HELP.

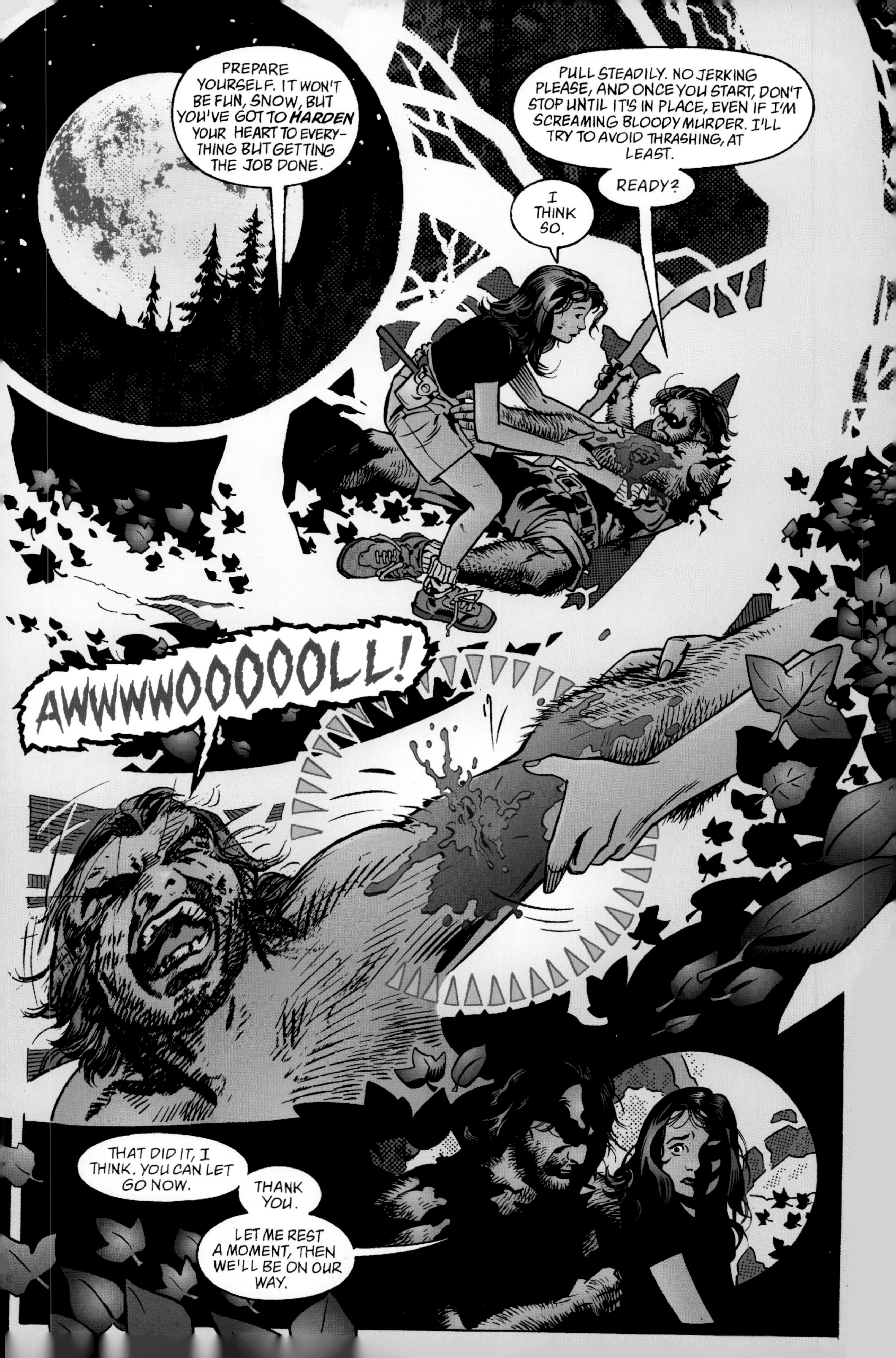
PREPARE YOURSELF. IT WON'T BE FUN, SNOW, BUT YOU'VE GOT TO **HARDEN** YOUR HEART TO EVERY-THING BUT GETTING THE JOB DONE.
PULL STEADILY. NO JERKING PLEASE, AND ONCE YOU START, DON'T STOP UNTIL IT'S IN PLACE, EVEN IF I'M SCREAMING BLOODY MURDER. I'LL TRY TO AVOID THRASHING, AT LEAST.
READY?
I THINK SO.
AWWWOOOOOLL!
THAT DID IT, I THINK. YOU CAN LET GO NOW.
THANK YOU.
LET ME REST A MOMENT, THEN WE'LL BE ON OUR WAY.

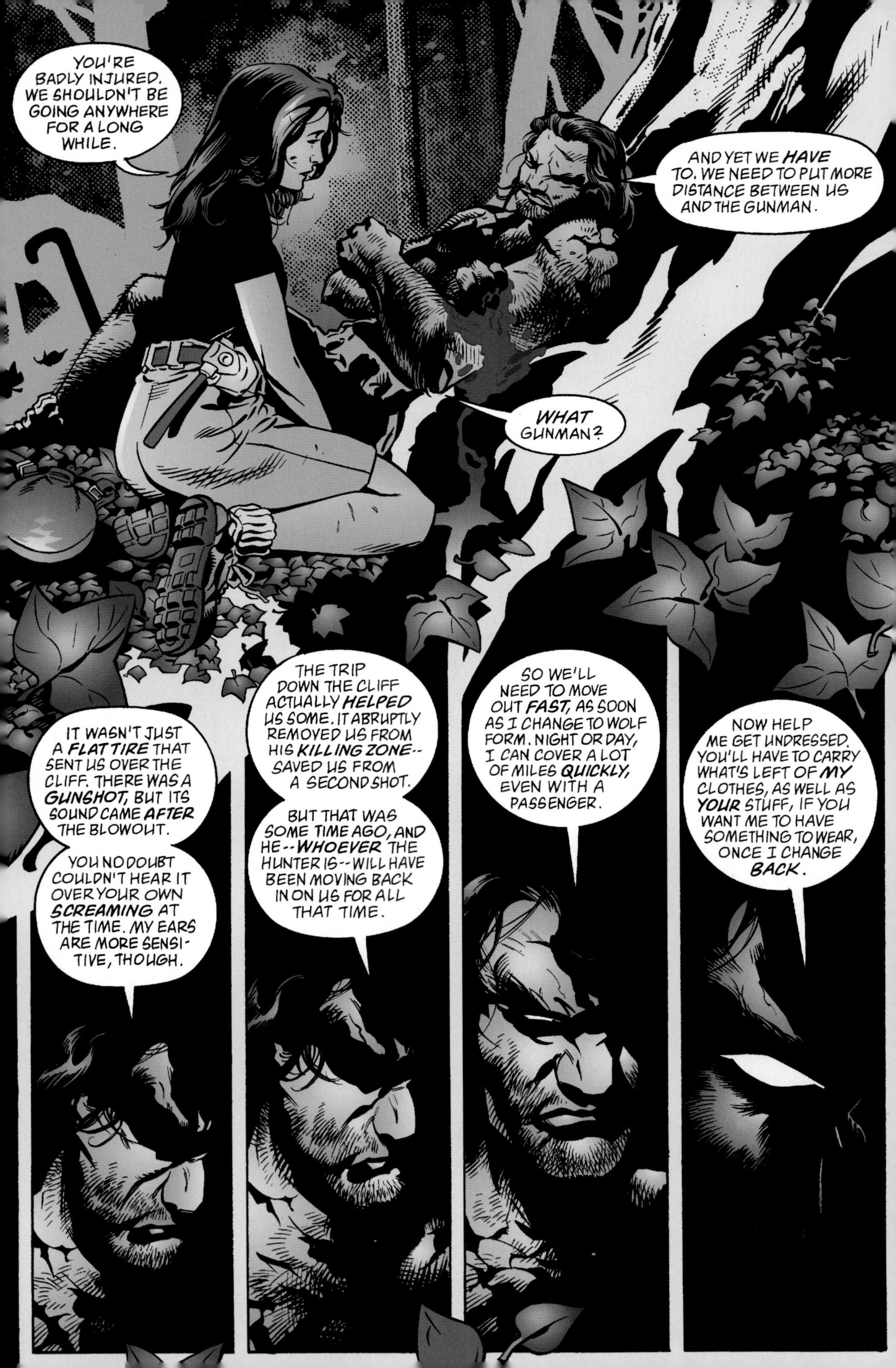

YOU'RE BADLY INJURED. WE SHOULDN'T BE GOING ANYWHERE FOR A LONG WHILE.
AND YET WE HAVE TO. WE NEED TO PUT MORE DISTANCE BETWEEN US AND THE GUNMAN.
WHAT GUNMAN?
IT WASN'T JUST A FLAT TIRE THAT SENT US OVER THE CLIFF. THERE WAS A GUNSHOT, BUT ITS SOUND CAME AFTER THE BLOWOUT.
YOU NO DOUBT COULDN'T HEAR IT OVER YOUR OWN SCREAMING AT THE TIME. MY EARS ARE MORE SENSI-TIVE, THOUGH.
THE TRIP DOWN THE CLIFF ACTUALLY HELPED US SOME. IT ABRUPTLY REMOVED US FROM HIS KILLING ZONE-- SAVED US FROM A SECOND SHOT.
BUT THAT WAS SOME TIME AGO, AND HE--WHOEVER THE HUNTER IS--WILL HAVE BEEN MOVING BACK IN ON US FOR ALL THAT TIME.
SO WE'LL NEED TO MOVE OUT FAST, AS SOON AS I CHANGE TO WOLF FORM. NIGHT OR DAY, I CAN COVER A LOT OF MILES QUICKLY, EVEN WITH A PASSENGER.
NOW HELP ME GET UNDRESSED. YOU'LL HAVE TO CARRY WHAT'S LEFT OF MY CLOTHES, AS WELL AS YOUR STUFF, IF YOU WANT ME TO HAVE SOMETHING TO WEAR, ONCE I CHANGE BACK.

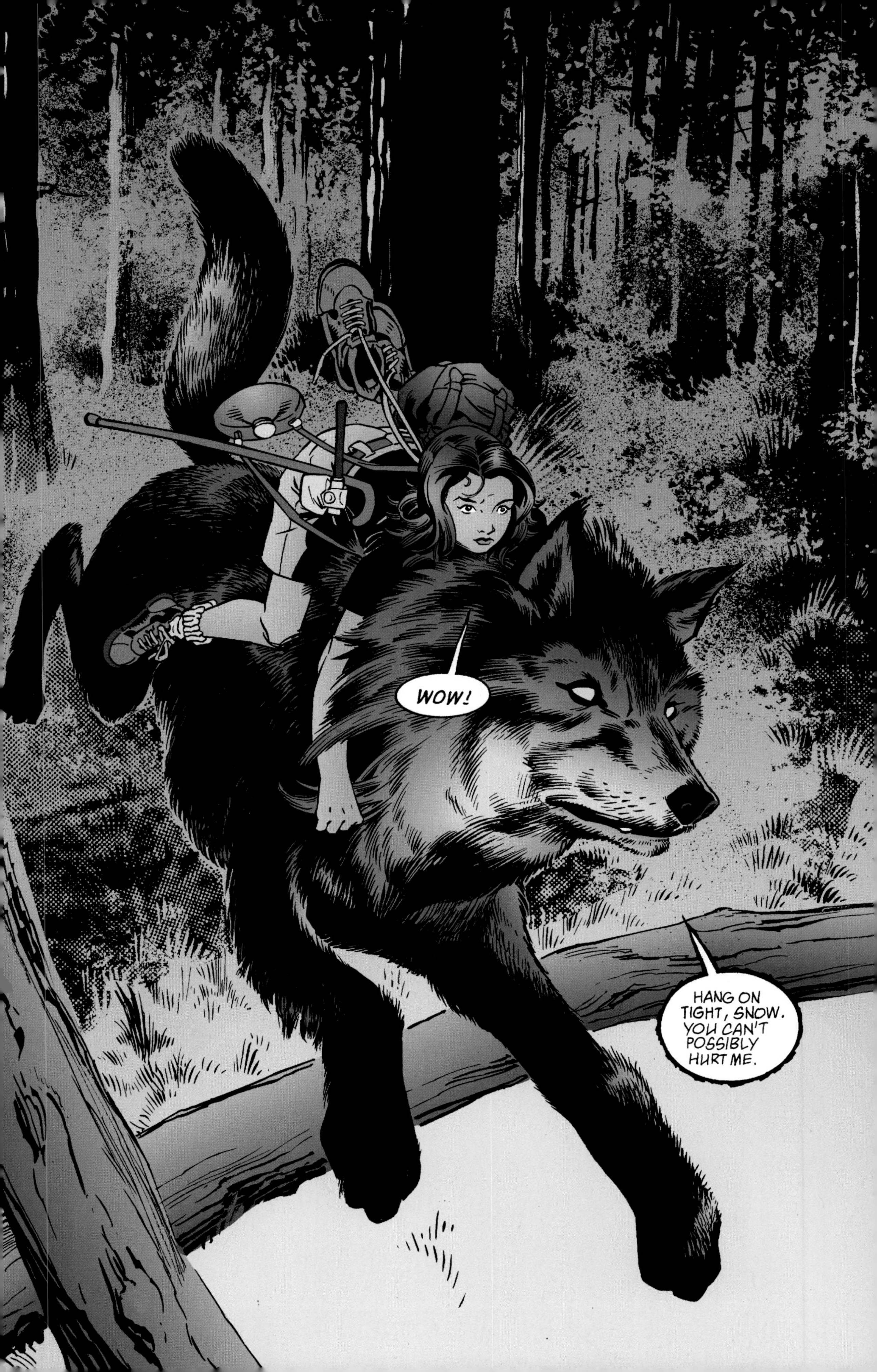
WOW!
HANG ON TIGHT, SNOW. YOU CAN'T POSSIBLY HURT ME.

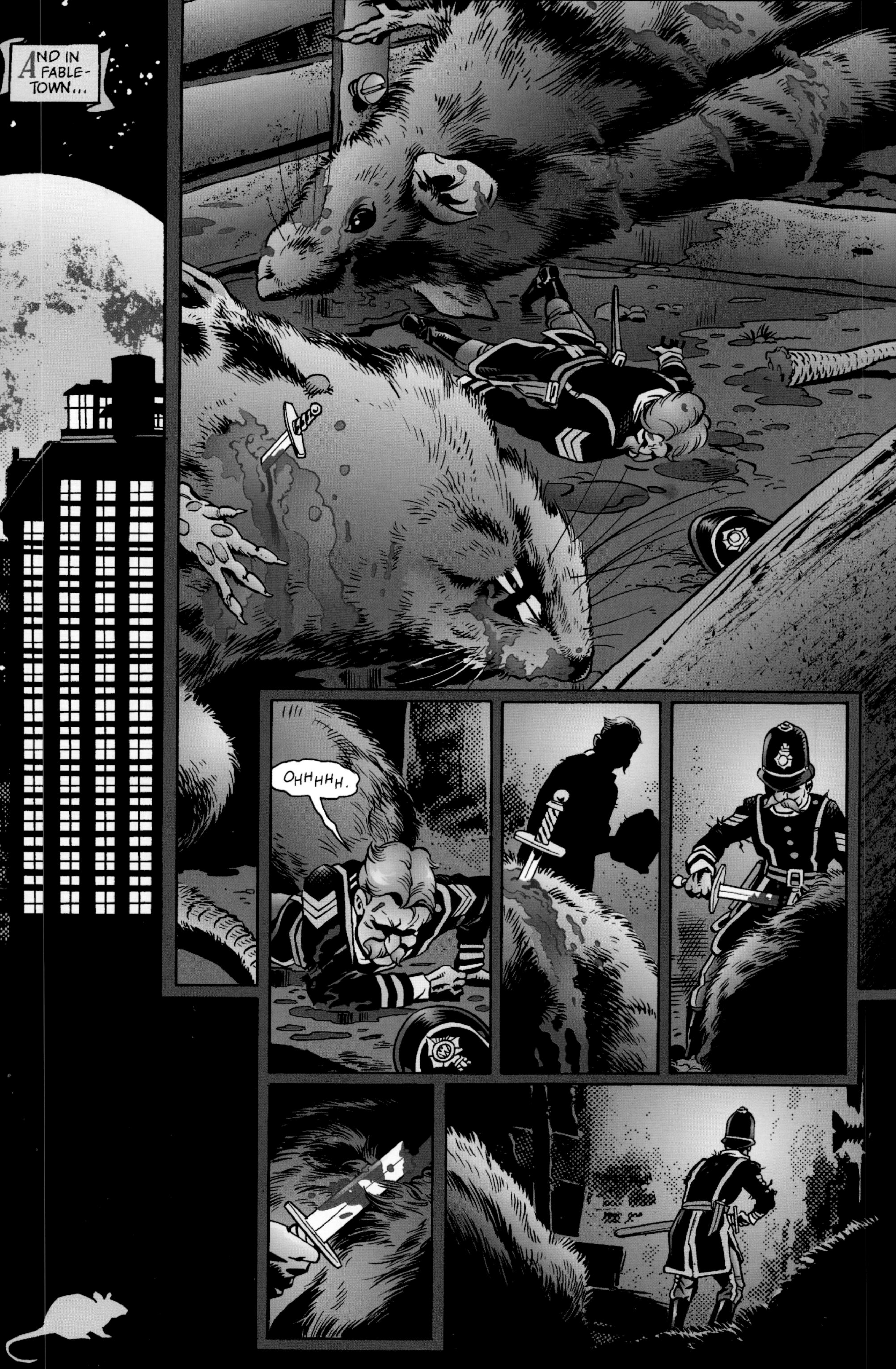
And in Fable-town...
OHHHHH.

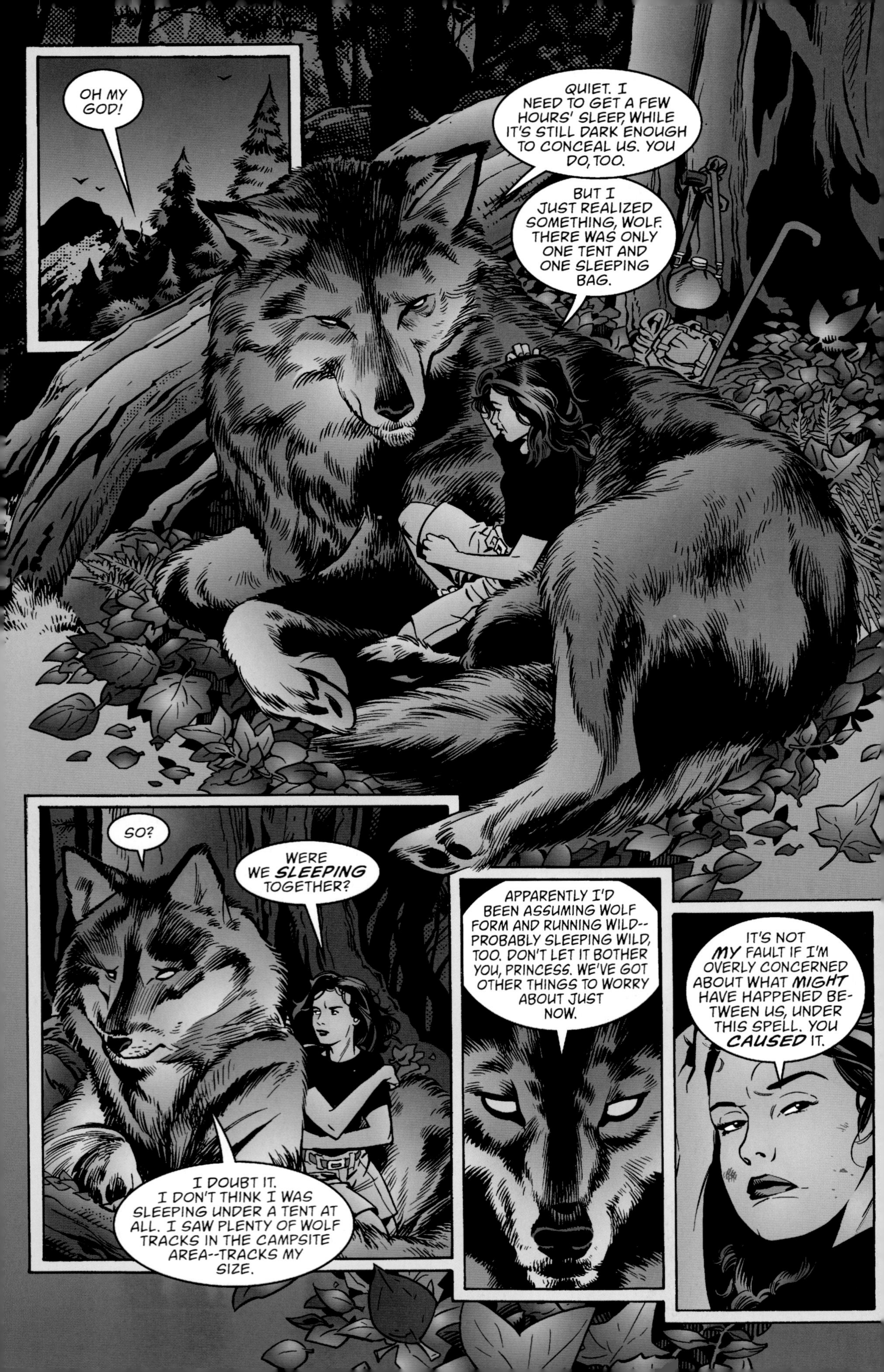
OH MY GOD!
QUIET. I NEED TO GET A FEW HOURS' SLEEP, WHILE IT'S STILL DARK ENOUGH TO CONCEAL US. YOU DO, TOO.
BUT I JUST REALIZED SOMETHING, WOLF. THERE WAS ONLY ONE TENT AND ONE SLEEPING BAG.
SO?
WERE WE SLEEPING TOGETHER?
I DOUBT IT. I DON'T THINK I WAS SLEEPING UNDER A TENT AT ALL. I SAW PLENTY OF WOLF TRACKS IN THE CAMPSITE AREA--TRACKS MY SIZE.
APPARENTLY I'D BEEN ASSUMING WOLF FORM AND RUNNING WILD--PROBABLY SLEEPING WILD, TOO. DON'T LET IT BOTHER YOU, PRINCESS. WE'VE GOT OTHER THINGS TO WORRY ABOUT JUST NOW.
IT'S NOT MY FAULT IF I'M OVERLY CONCERNED ABOUT WHAT MIGHT HAVE HAPPENED BETWEEN US, UNDER THIS SPELL. YOU CAUSED IT.

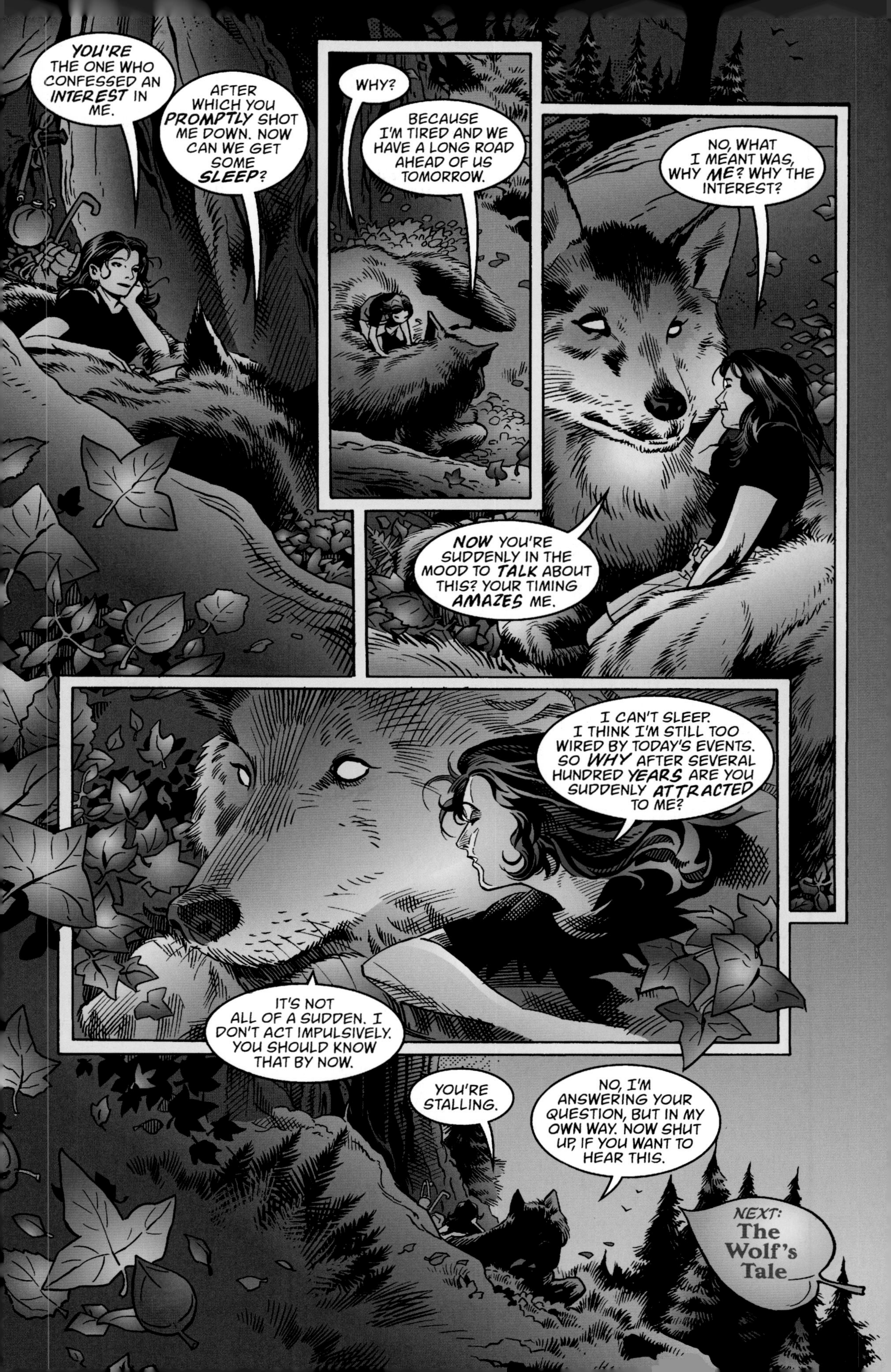
YOU'RE THE ONE WHO CONFESSED AN INTEREST IN ME.
AFTER WHICH YOU PROMPTLY SHOT ME DOWN. NOW CAN WE GET SOME SLEEP?
WHY?
BECAUSE I'M TIRED AND WE HAVE A LONG ROAD AHEAD OF US TOMORROW.
NO, WHAT I MEANT WAS, WHY ME? WHY THE INTEREST?
NOW YOU'RE SUDDENLY IN THE MOOD TO TALK ABOUT THIS? YOUR TIMING AMAZES ME.
I CAN'T SLEEP. I THINK I'M STILL TOO WIRED BY TODAY'S EVENTS. SO WHY AFTER SEVERAL HUNDRED YEARS ARE YOU SUDDENLY ATTRACTED TO ME?
IT'S NOT ALL OF A SUDDEN. I DON'T ACT IMPULSIVELY. YOU SHOULD KNOW THAT BY NOW.
YOU'RE STALLING.
NO, I'M ANSWERING YOUR QUESTION, BUT IN MY OWN WAY. NOW SHUT UP, IF YOU WANT TO HEAR THIS.
NEXT: The Wolf's Tale

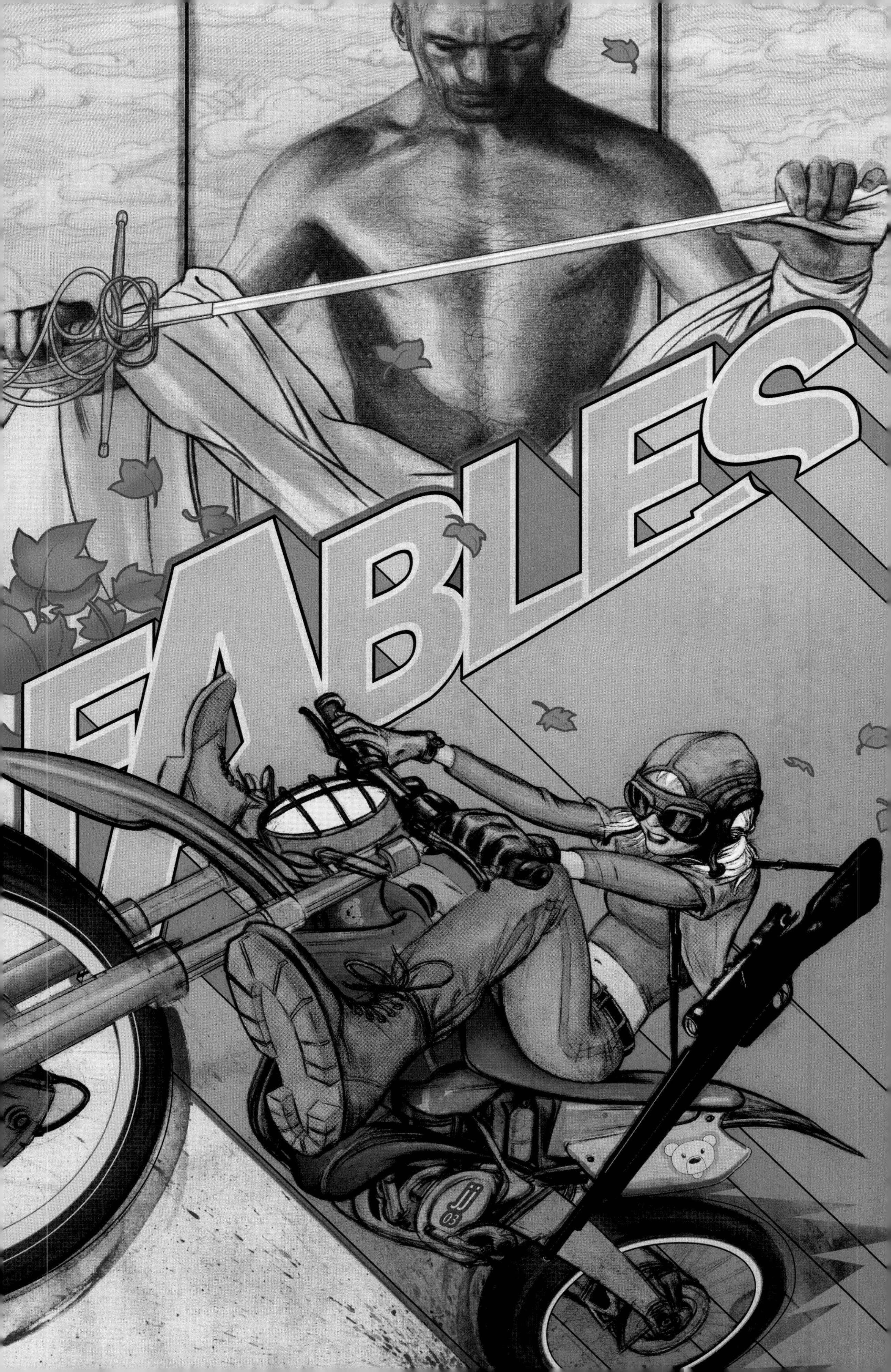
FABLES
JJ
03

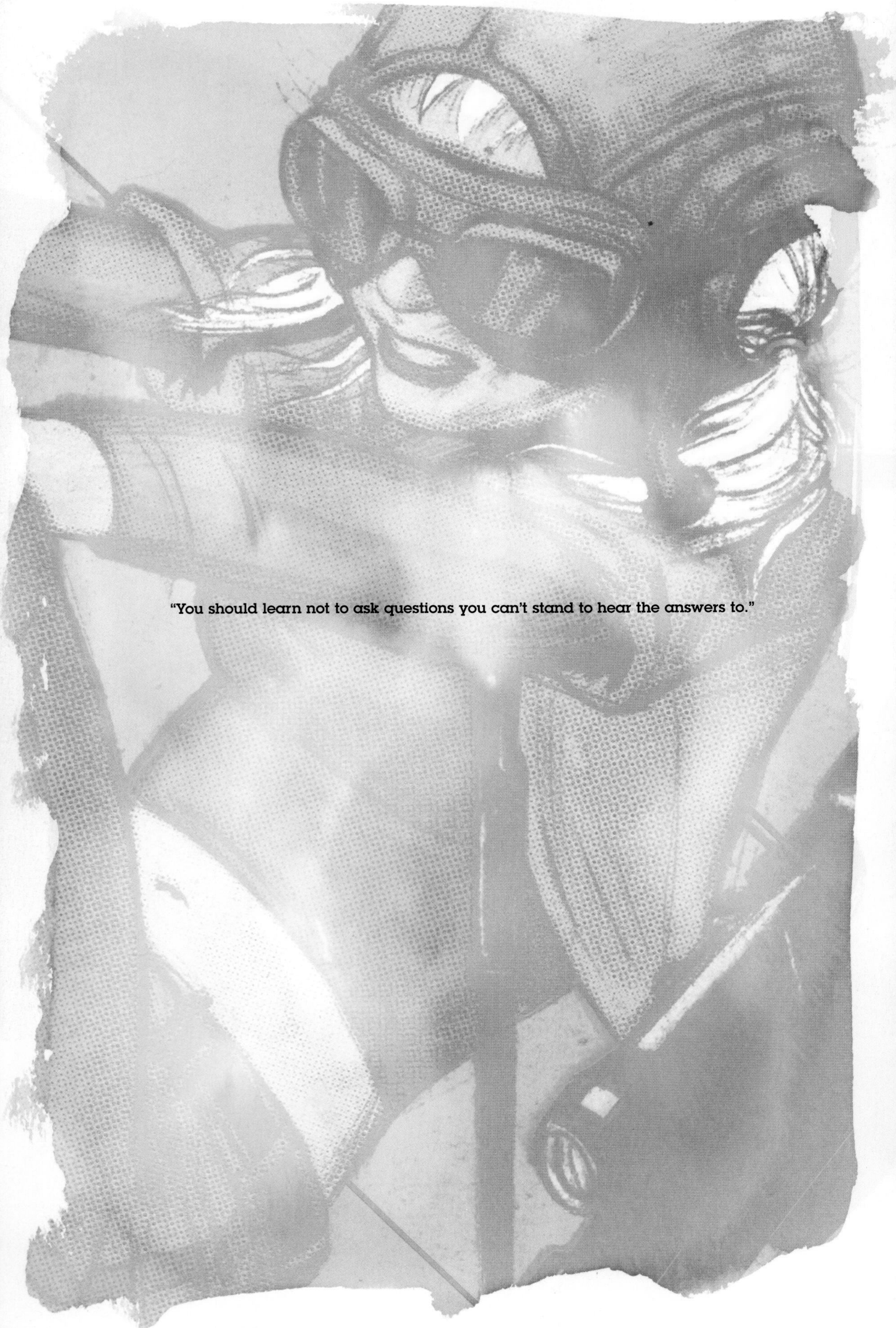
"You should learn not to ask questions you can't stand to hear the answers to."

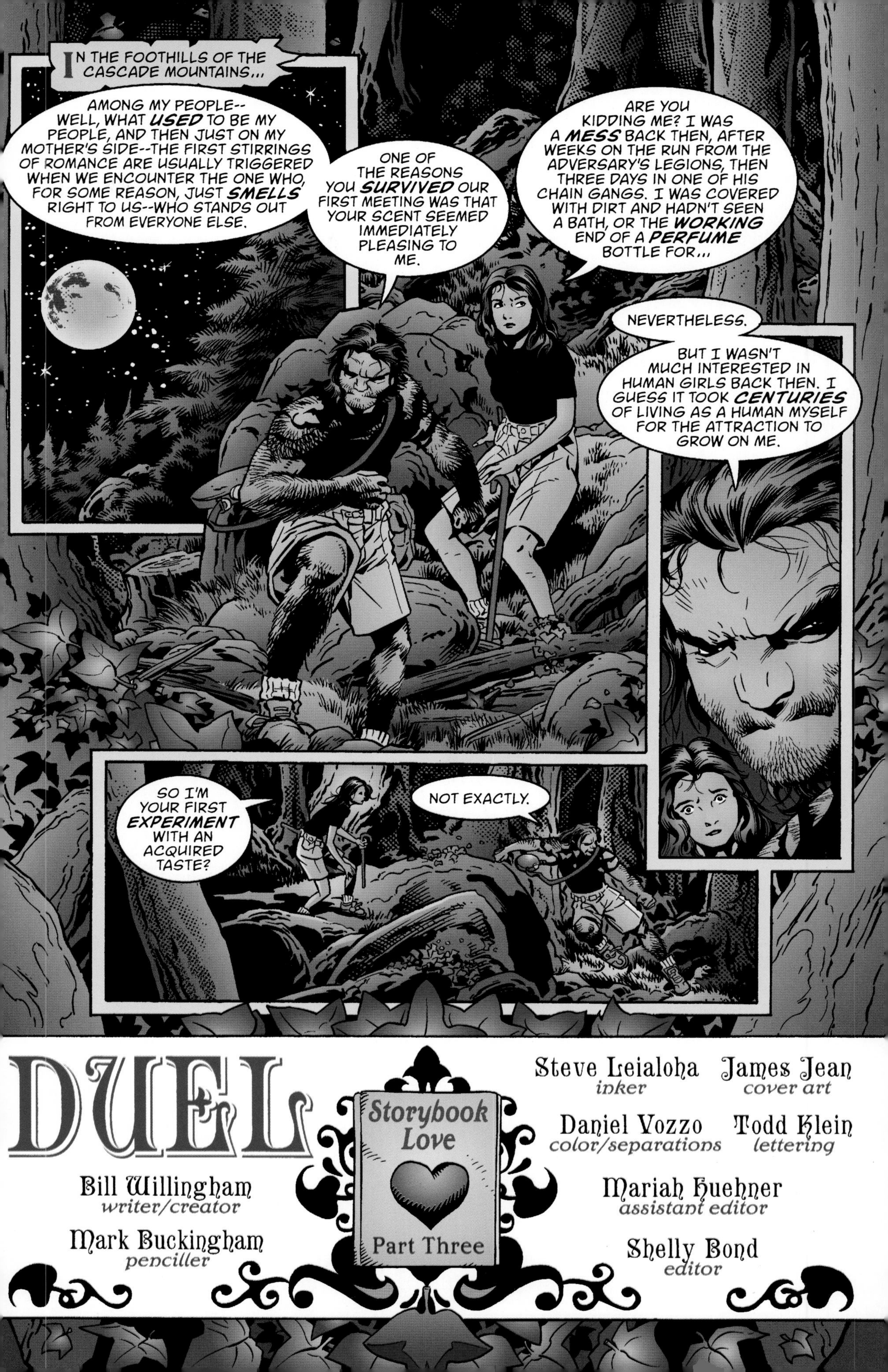

IN THE FOOTHILLS OF THE CASCADE MOUNTAINS...
AMONG MY PEOPLE-- WELL, WHAT USED TO BE MY PEOPLE, AND THEN JUST ON MY MOTHER'S SIDE--THE FIRST STIRRINGS OF ROMANCE ARE USUALLY TRIGGERED WHEN WE ENCOUNTER THE ONE WHO, FOR SOME REASON, JUST SMELLS RIGHT TO US--WHO STANDS OUT FROM EVERYONE ELSE.
ONE OF THE REASONS YOU SURVIVED OUR FIRST MEETING WAS THAT YOUR SCENT SEEMED IMMEDIATELY PLEASING TO ME.
ARE YOU KIDDING ME? I WAS A MESS BACK THEN, AFTER WEEKS ON THE RUN FROM THE ADVERSARY'S LEGIONS, THEN THREE DAYS IN ONE OF HIS CHAIN GANGS. I WAS COVERED WITH DIRT AND HADN'T SEEN A BATH, OR THE WORKING END OF A PERFUME BOTTLE FOR...
NEVERTHELESS.
BUT I WASN'T MUCH INTERESTED IN HUMAN GIRLS BACK THEN. I GUESS IT TOOK CENTURIES OF LIVING AS A HUMAN MYSELF FOR THE ATTRACTION TO GROW ON ME.
SO I'M YOUR FIRST EXPERIMENT WITH AN ACQUIRED TASTE?
NOT EXACTLY.

DUEL

Storybook Love

Part Three

Bill Willingham *writer/creator*

Mark Buckingham *penciller*

Steve Leialoha *inker*

James Jean *cover art*

Daniel Vozzo *color/separations*

Todd Klein *lettering*

Mariah Huehner *assistant editor*

Shelly Bond *editor*

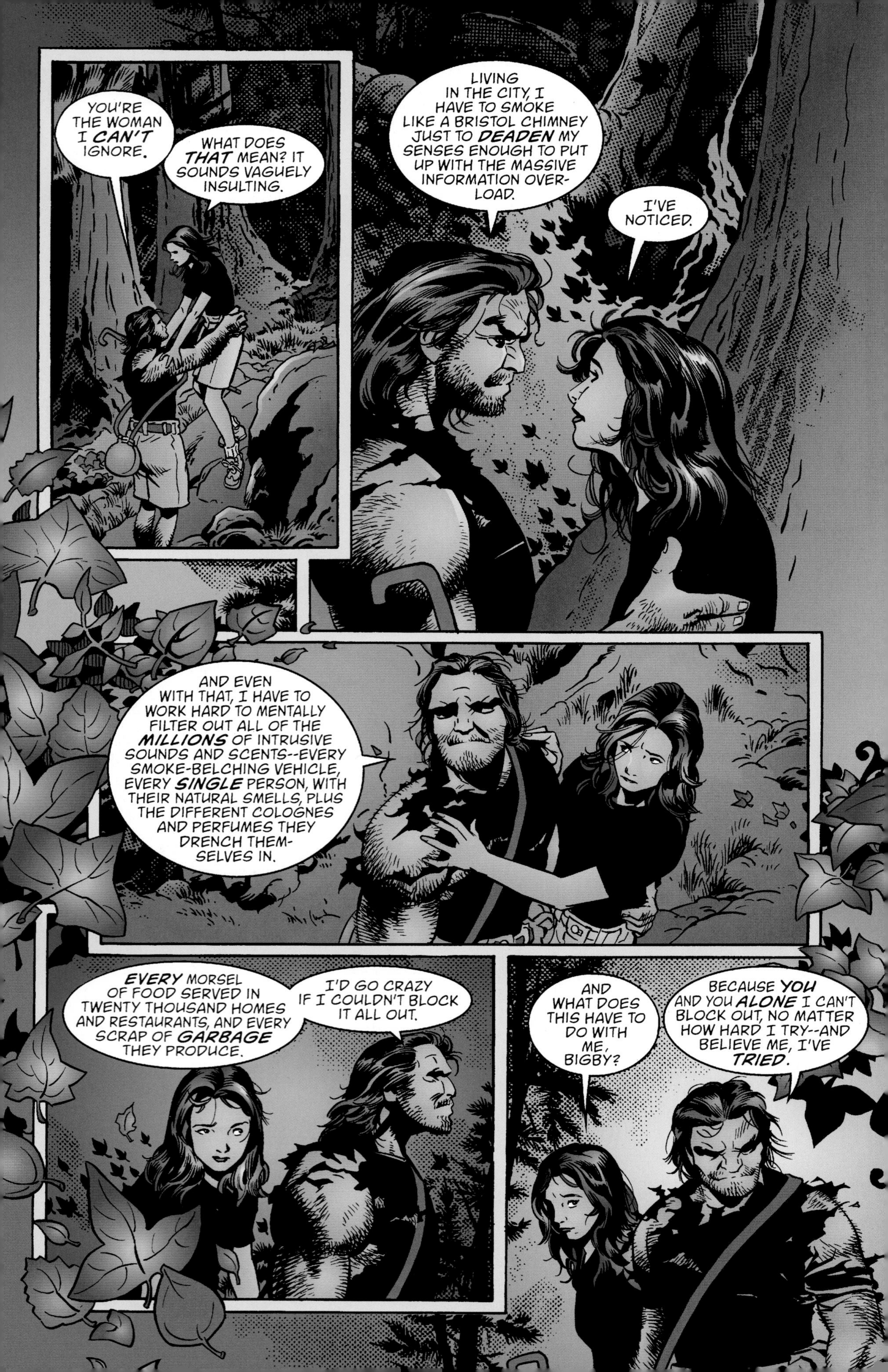
YOU'RE THE WOMAN I CAN'T IGNORE.
WHAT DOES THAT MEAN? IT SOUNDS VAGUELY INSULTING.
LIVING IN THE CITY, I HAVE TO SMOKE LIKE A BRISTOL CHIMNEY JUST TO DEADEN MY SENSES ENOUGH TO PUT UP WITH THE MASSIVE INFORMATION OVER-LOAD.
I'VE NOTICED.
AND EVEN WITH THAT, I HAVE TO WORK HARD TO MENTALLY FILTER OUT ALL OF THE MILLIONS OF INTRUSIVE SOUNDS AND SCENTS--EVERY SMOKE-BELCHING VEHICLE, EVERY SINGLE PERSON, WITH THEIR NATURAL SMELLS, PLUS THE DIFFERENT COLOGNES AND PERFUMES THEY DRENCH THEM-SELVES IN.
EVERY MORSEL OF FOOD SERVED IN TWENTY THOUSAND HOMES AND RESTAURANTS, AND EVERY SCRAP OF GARBAGE THEY PRODUCE.
I'D GO CRAZY IF I COULDN'T BLOCK IT ALL OUT.
AND WHAT DOES THIS HAVE TO DO WITH ME, BIGBY?
BECAUSE YOU AND YOU ALONE I CAN'T BLOCK OUT, NO MATTER HOW HARD I TRY--AND BELIEVE ME, I'VE TRIED.

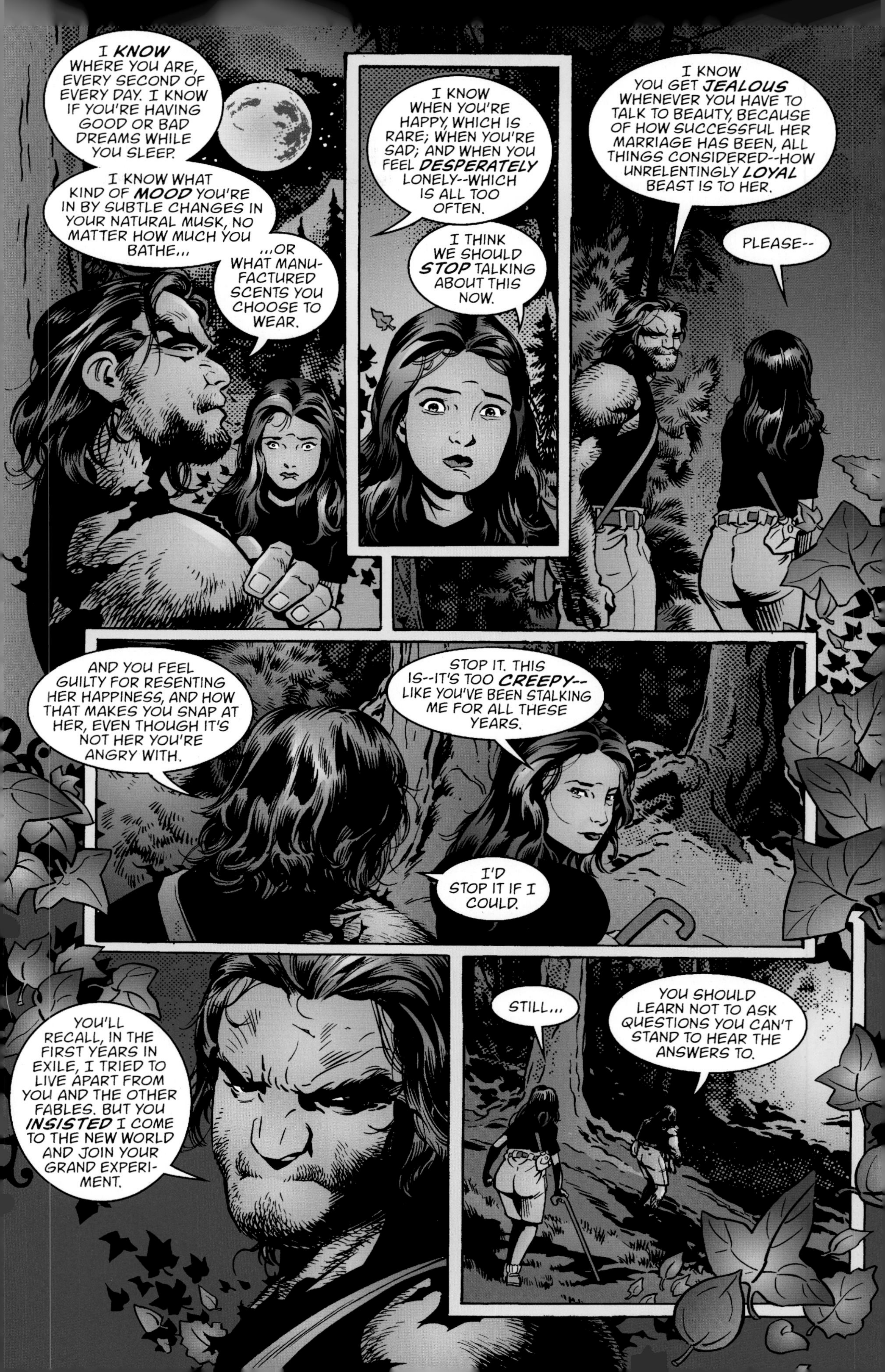
I KNOW WHERE YOU ARE, EVERY SECOND OF EVERY DAY. I KNOW IF YOU'RE HAVING GOOD OR BAD DREAMS WHILE YOU SLEEP.
I KNOW WHAT KIND OF MOOD YOU'RE IN BY SUBTLE CHANGES IN YOUR NATURAL MUSK, NO MATTER HOW MUCH YOU BATHE...
...OR WHAT MANU-FACTURED SCENTS YOU CHOOSE TO WEAR.
I KNOW WHEN YOU'RE HAPPY, WHICH IS RARE; WHEN YOU'RE SAD; AND WHEN YOU FEEL DESPERATELY LONELY--WHICH IS ALL TOO OFTEN.
I THINK WE SHOULD STOP TALKING ABOUT THIS NOW.
I KNOW YOU GET JEALOUS WHENEVER YOU HAVE TO TALK TO BEAUTY, BECAUSE OF HOW SUCCESSFUL HER MARRIAGE HAS BEEN, ALL THINGS CONSIDERED--HOW UNRELENTINGLY LOYAL BEAST IS TO HER.
PLEASE--
AND YOU FEEL GUILTY FOR RESENTING HER HAPPINESS, AND HOW THAT MAKES YOU SNAP AT HER, EVEN THOUGH IT'S NOT HER YOU'RE ANGRY WITH.
STOP IT. THIS IS--IT'S TOO CREEPY--LIKE YOU'VE BEEN STALKING ME FOR ALL THESE YEARS.
I'D STOP IT IF I COULD.
YOU'LL RECALL, IN THE FIRST YEARS IN EXILE, I TRIED TO LIVE APART FROM YOU AND THE OTHER FABLES. BUT YOU INSISTED I COME TO THE NEW WORLD AND JOIN YOUR GRAND EXPERI-MENT.
STILL...
YOU SHOULD LEARN NOT TO ASK QUESTIONS YOU CAN'T STAND TO HEAR THE ANSWERS TO.

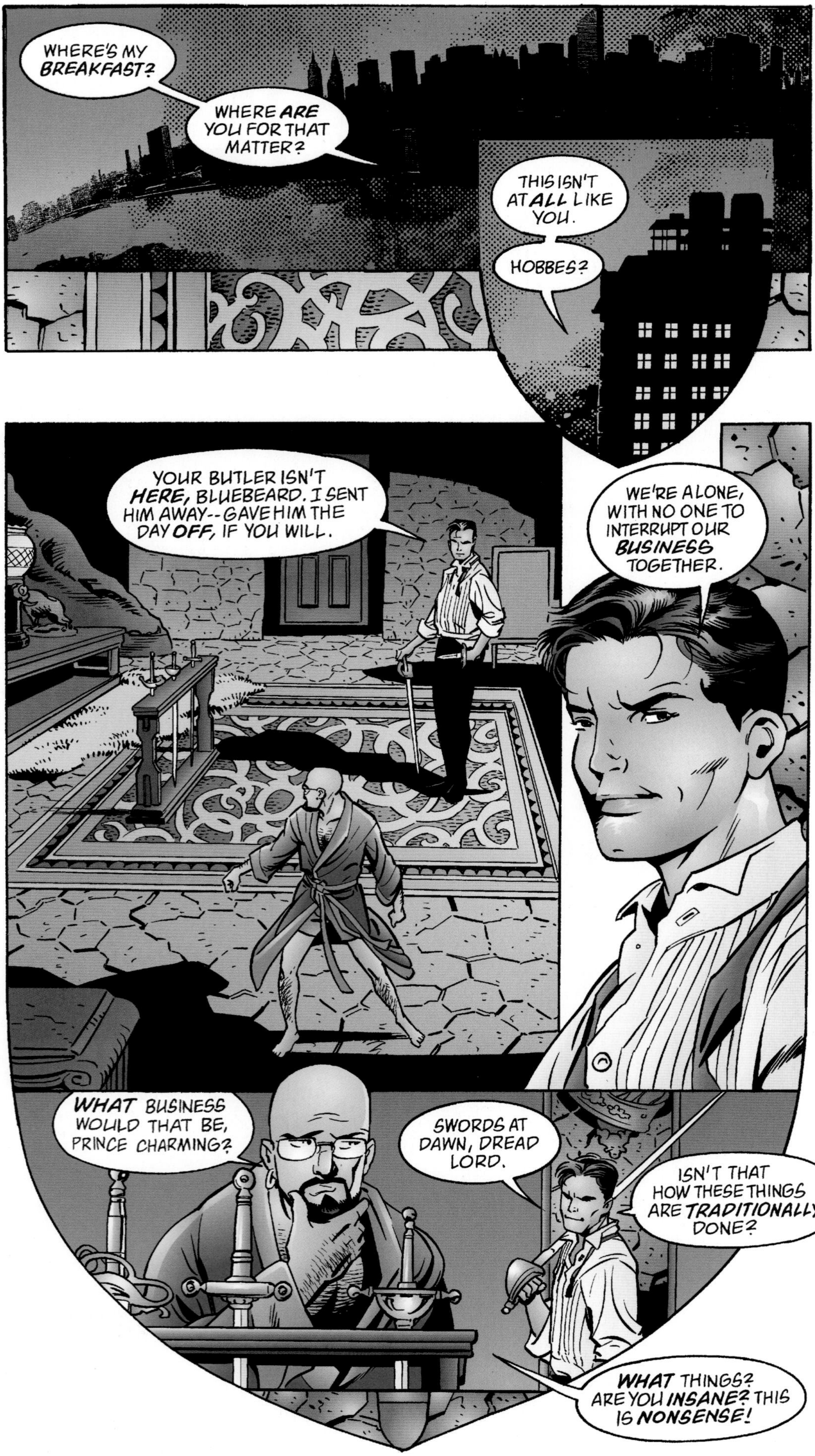
WHERE'S MY BREAKFAST?
WHERE ARE YOU FOR THAT MATTER?
THIS ISN'T AT ALL LIKE YOU.
HOBBES?
YOUR BUTLER ISN'T HERE, BLUEBEARD. I SENT HIM AWAY--GAVE HIM THE DAY OFF, IF YOU WILL.
WE'RE ALONE, WITH NO ONE TO INTERRUPT OUR BUSINESS TOGETHER.
WHAT BUSINESS WOULD THAT BE, PRINCE CHARMING?
SWORDS AT DAWN, DREAD LORD.
ISN'T THAT HOW THESE THINGS ARE TRADITIONALLY DONE?
WHAT THINGS? ARE YOU INSANE? THIS IS NONSENSE!

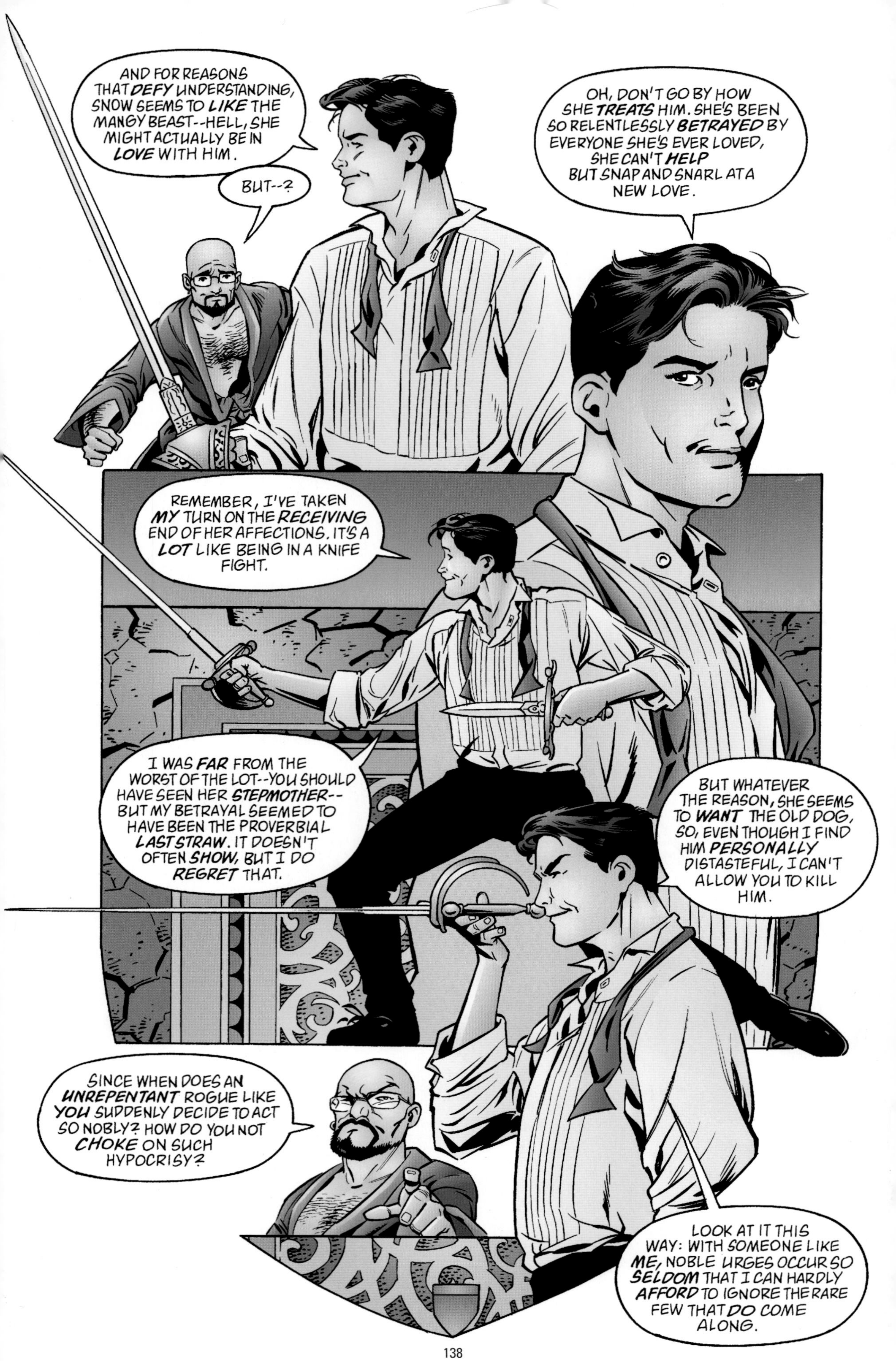
AND FOR REASONS THAT DEFY UNDERSTANDING, SNOW SEEMS TO LIKE THE MANGY BEAST--HELL, SHE MIGHT ACTUALLY BE IN LOVE WITH HIM.
BUT--?
OH, DON'T GO BY HOW SHE TREATS HIM. SHE'S BEEN SO RELENTLESSLY BETRAYED BY EVERYONE SHE'S EVER LOVED, SHE CAN'T HELP BUT SNAP AND SNARL AT A NEW LOVE.
REMEMBER, I'VE TAKEN MY TURN ON THE RECEIVING END OF HER AFFECTIONS. IT'S A LOT LIKE BEING IN A KNIFE FIGHT.
I WAS FAR FROM THE WORST OF THE LOT--YOU SHOULD HAVE SEEN HER STEPMOTHER--BUT MY BETRAYAL SEEMED TO HAVE BEEN THE PROVERBIAL LAST STRAW. IT DOESN'T OFTEN SHOW, BUT I DO REGRET THAT.
BUT WHATEVER THE REASON, SHE SEEMS TO WANT THE OLD DOG, SO, EVEN THOUGH I FIND HIM PERSONALLY DISTASTEFUL, I CAN'T ALLOW YOU TO KILL HIM.
SINCE WHEN DOES AN UNREPENTANT ROGUE LIKE YOU SUDDENLY DECIDE TO ACT SO NOBLY? HOW DO YOU NOT CHOKE ON SUCH HYPOCRISY?
LOOK AT IT THIS WAY: WITH SOMEONE LIKE ME, NOBLE URGES OCCUR SO SELDOM THAT I CAN HARDLY AFFORD TO IGNORE THE RARE FEW THAT DO COME ALONG.

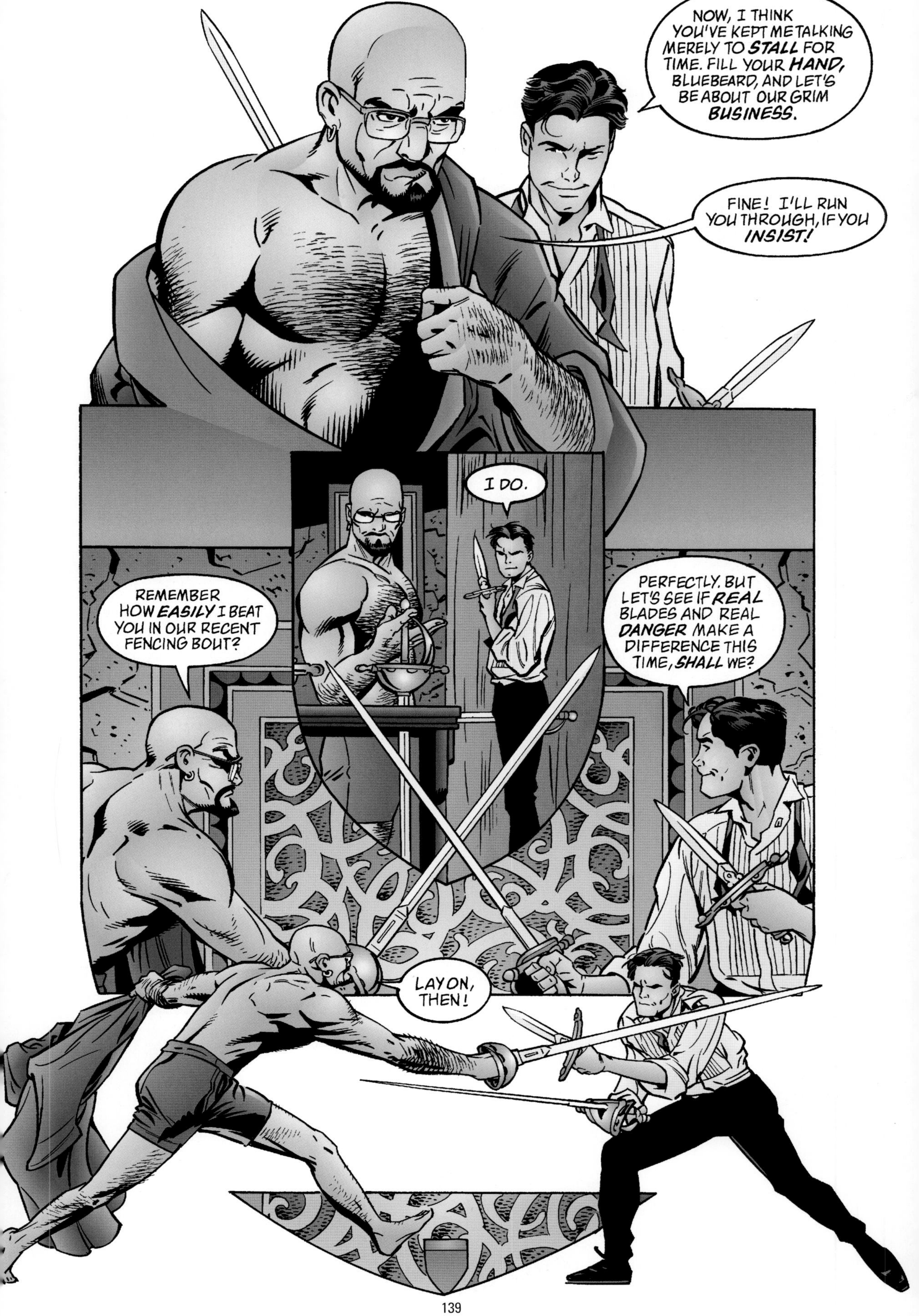
NOW, I THINK YOU'VE KEPT ME TALKING MERELY TO STALL FOR TIME. FILL YOUR HAND, BLUEBEARD, AND LET'S BE ABOUT OUR GRIM BUSINESS.
FINE! I'LL RUN YOU THROUGH, IF YOU INSIST!
REMEMBER HOW EASILY I BEAT YOU IN OUR RECENT FENCING BOUT?
I DO.
PERFECTLY. BUT LET'S SEE IF REAL BLADES AND REAL DANGER MAKE A DIFFERENCE THIS TIME, SHALL WE?
LAY ON, THEN!

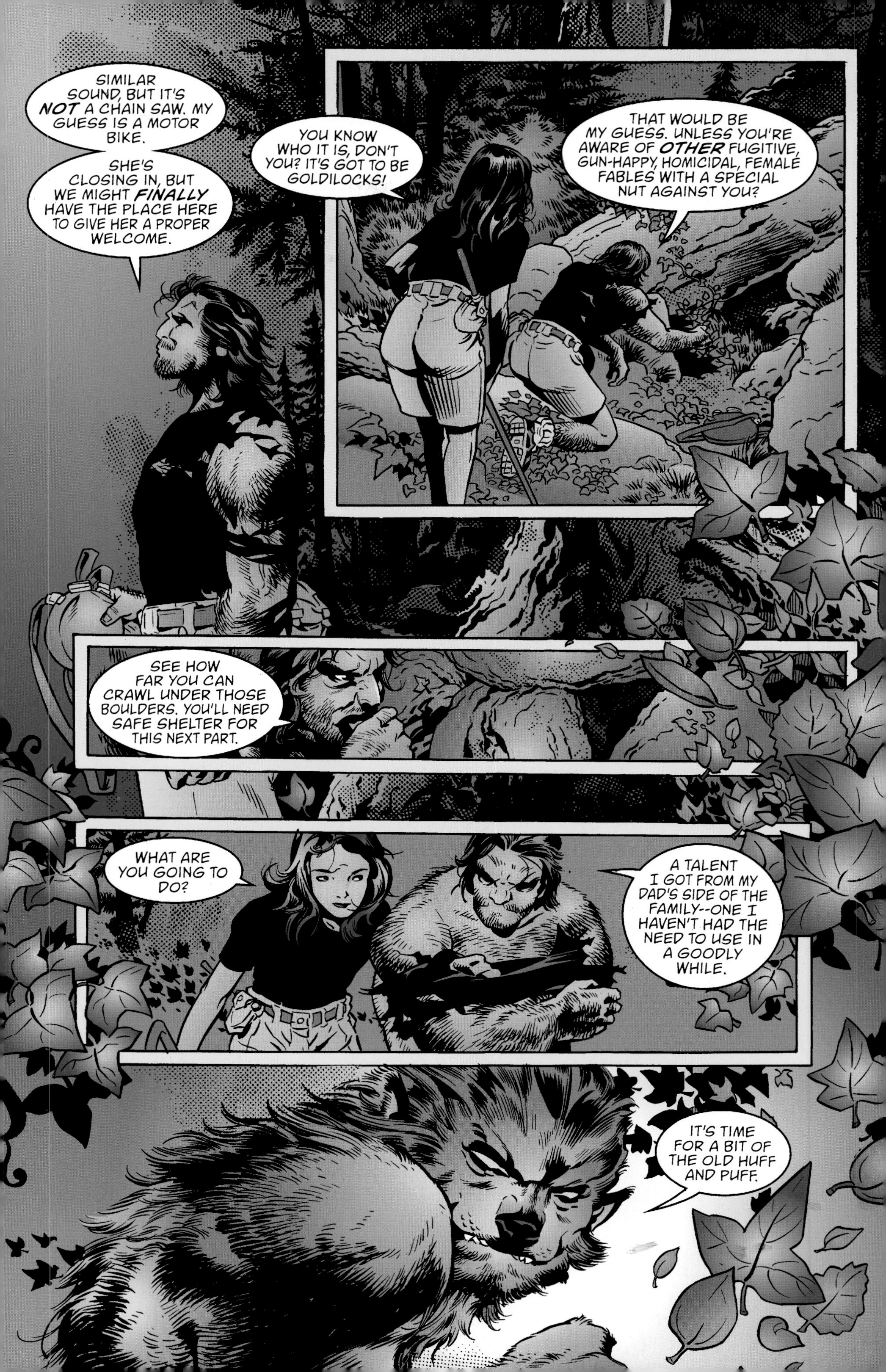
SIMILAR SOUND, BUT IT'S NOT A CHAIN SAW. MY GUESS IS A MOTOR BIKE.
SHE'S CLOSING IN, BUT WE MIGHT FINALLY HAVE THE PLACE HERE TO GIVE HER A PROPER WELCOME.
YOU KNOW WHO IT IS, DON'T YOU? IT'S GOT TO BE GOLDILOCKS!
THAT WOULD BE MY GUESS. UNLESS YOU'RE AWARE OF OTHER FUGITIVE, GUN-HAPPY, HOMICIDAL, FEMALE FABLES WITH A SPECIAL NUT AGAINST YOU?
SEE HOW FAR YOU CAN CRAWL UNDER THOSE BOULDERS. YOU'LL NEED SAFE SHELTER FOR THIS NEXT PART.
WHAT ARE YOU GOING TO DO?
A TALENT I GOT FROM MY DAD'S SIDE OF THE FAMILY--ONE I HAVEN'T HAD THE NEED TO USE IN A GOODLY WHILE.
IT'S TIME FOR A BIT OF THE OLD HUFF AND PUFF.

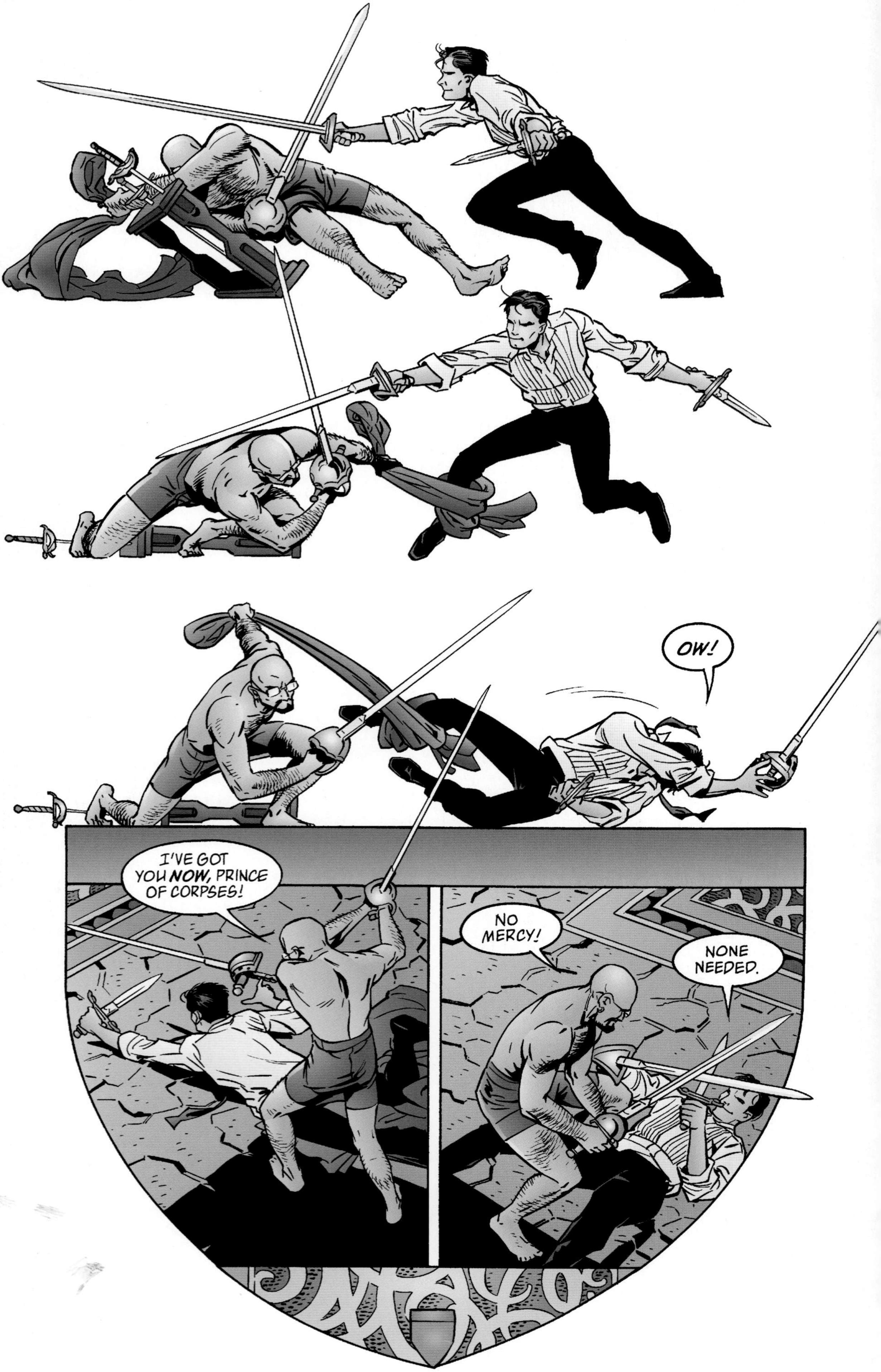
OW!
I'VE GOT YOU NOW, PRINCE OF CORPSES!
NO MERCY!
NONE NEEDED.

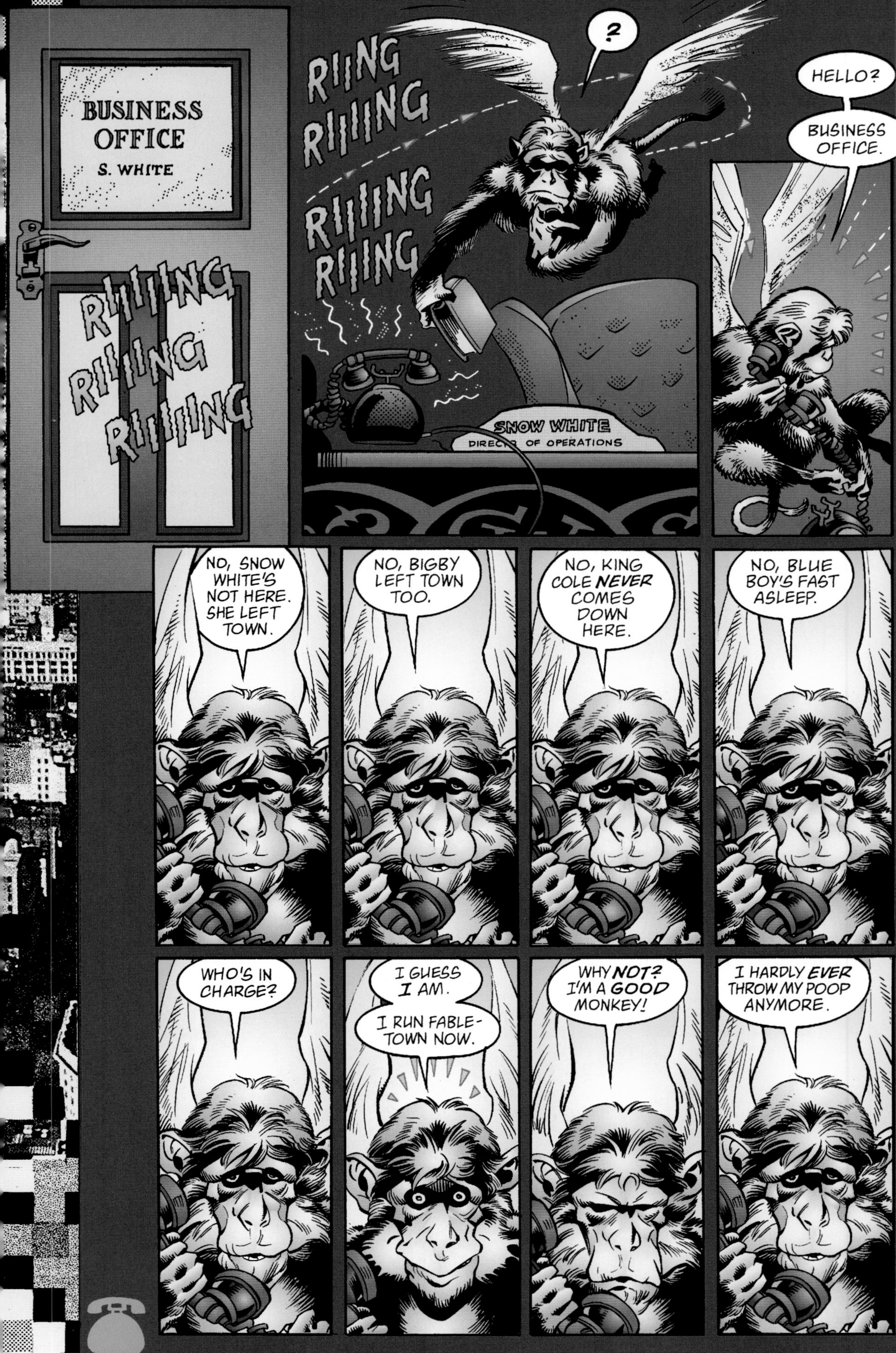
BUSINESS OFFICE
S. WHITE
RIIIING RIIIING RIIIING
RIIING RIIIING RIIIING RIIING
?
SNOW WHITE
DIRECTOR OF OPERATIONS
HELLO?
BUSINESS OFFICE.
NO, SNOW WHITE'S NOT HERE. SHE LEFT TOWN.
NO, BIGBY LEFT TOWN TOO.
NO, KING COLE NEVER COMES DOWN HERE.
NO, BLUE BOY'S FAST ASLEEP.
WHO'S IN CHARGE?
I GUESS I AM.
I RUN FABLE-TOWN NOW.
WHY NOT? I'M A GOOD MONKEY!
I HARDLY EVER THROW MY POOP ANYMORE.

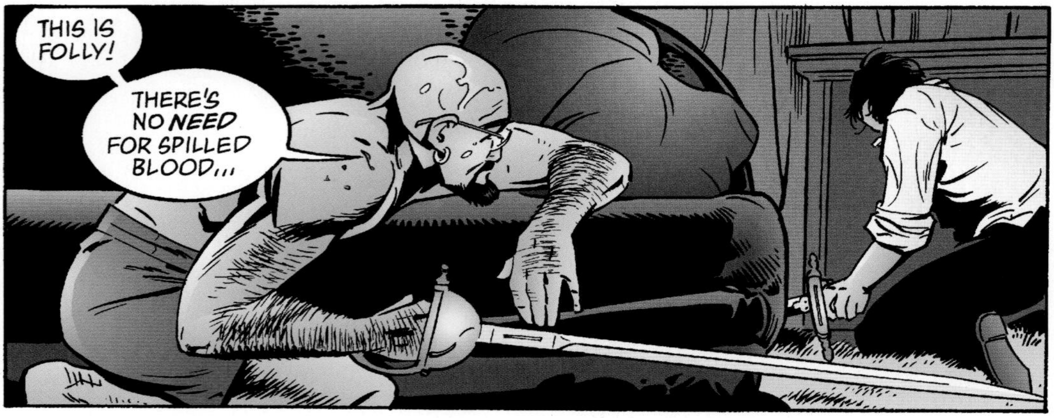
THIS IS FOLLY!
THERE'S NO NEED FOR SPILLED BLOOD...

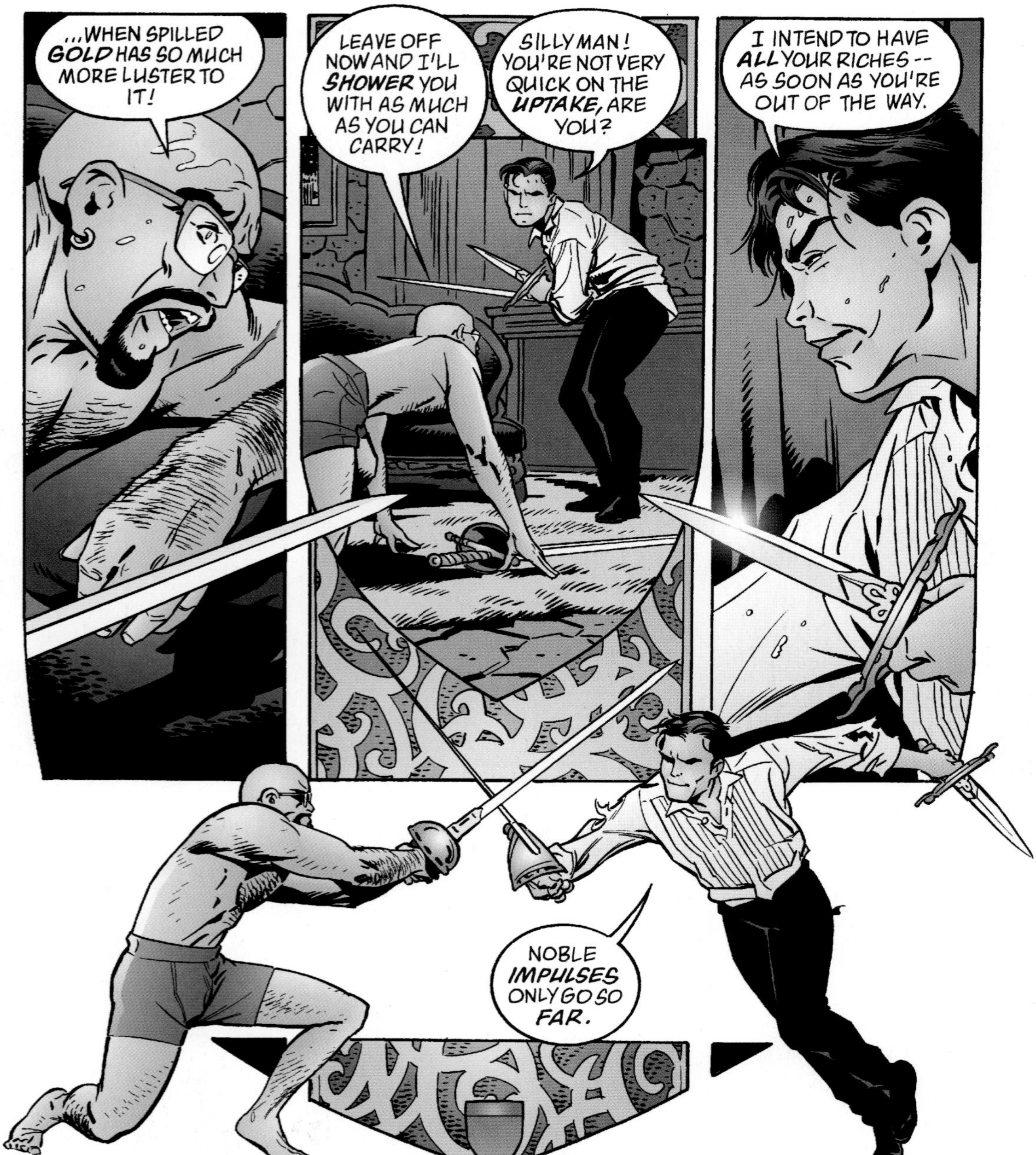
...WHEN SPILLED GOLD HAS SO MUCH MORE LUSTER TO IT!
LEAVE OFF NOW AND I'LL SHOWER YOU WITH AS MUCH AS YOU CAN CARRY!
SILLY MAN! YOU'RE NOT VERY QUICK ON THE UPTAKE, ARE YOU?
I INTEND TO HAVE ALL YOUR RICHES -- AS SOON AS YOU'RE OUT OF THE WAY.
NOBLE IMPULSES ONLY GO SO FAR.

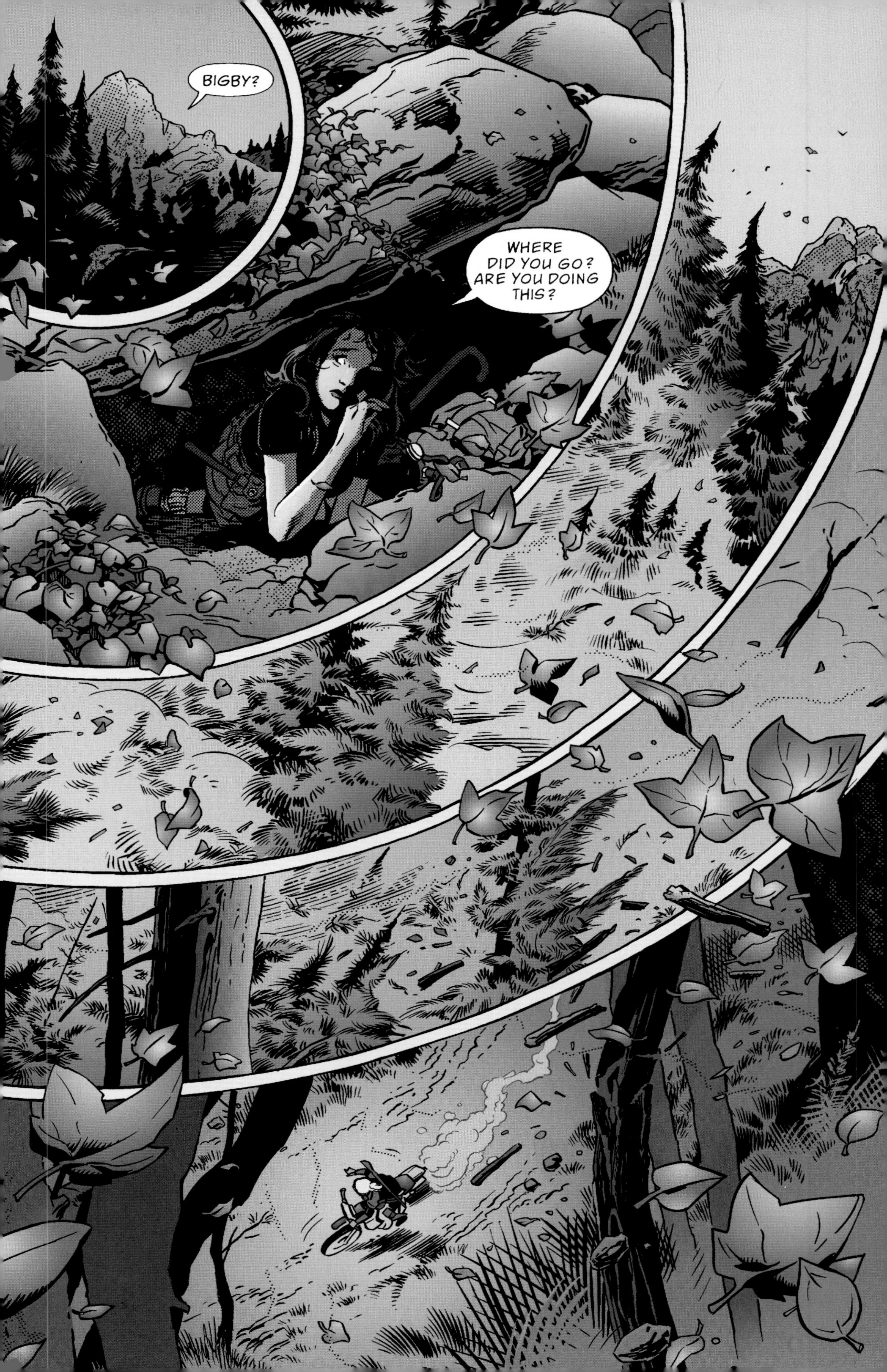
BIGBY?
WHERE DID YOU GO? ARE YOU DOING THIS?

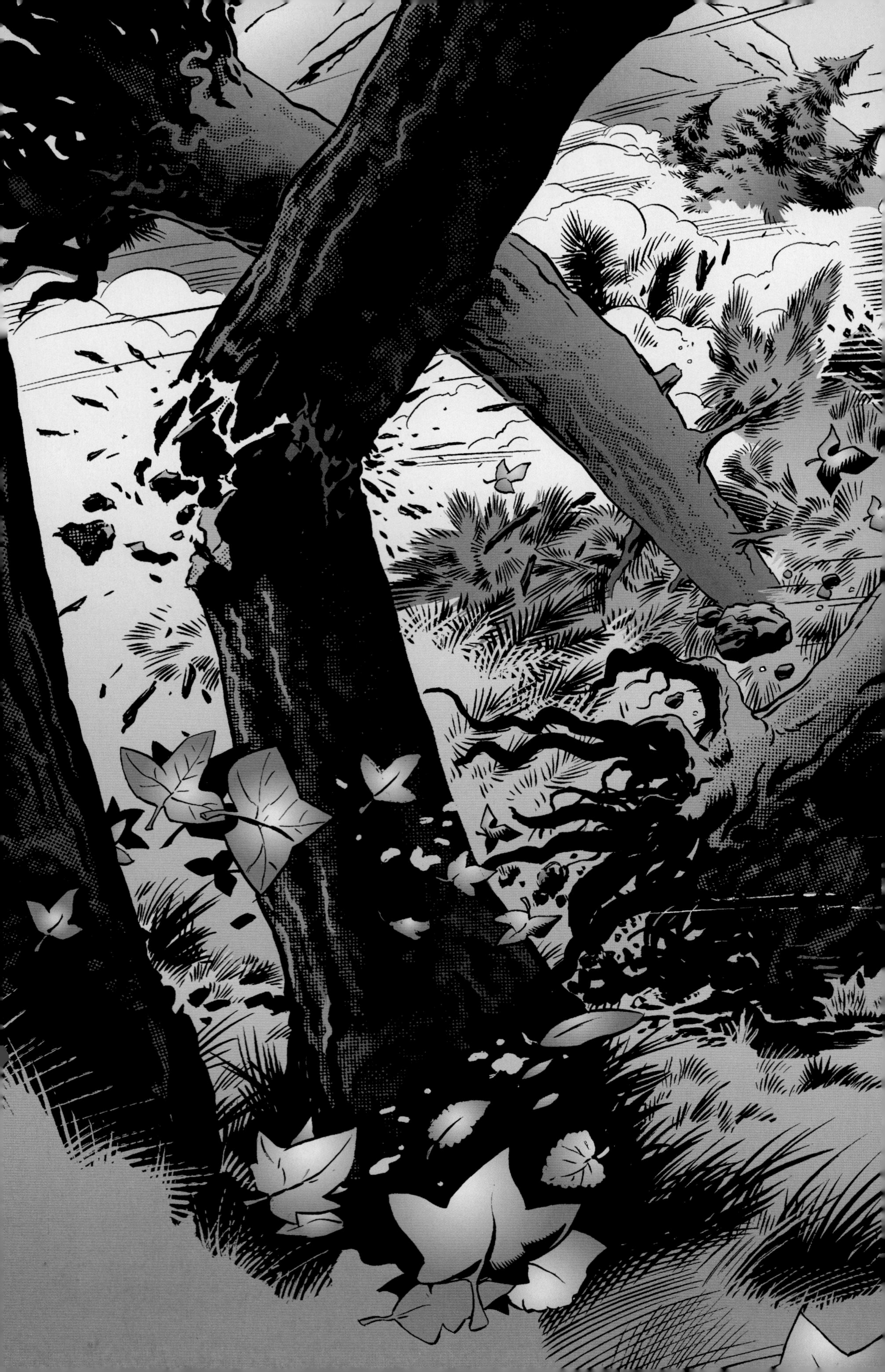

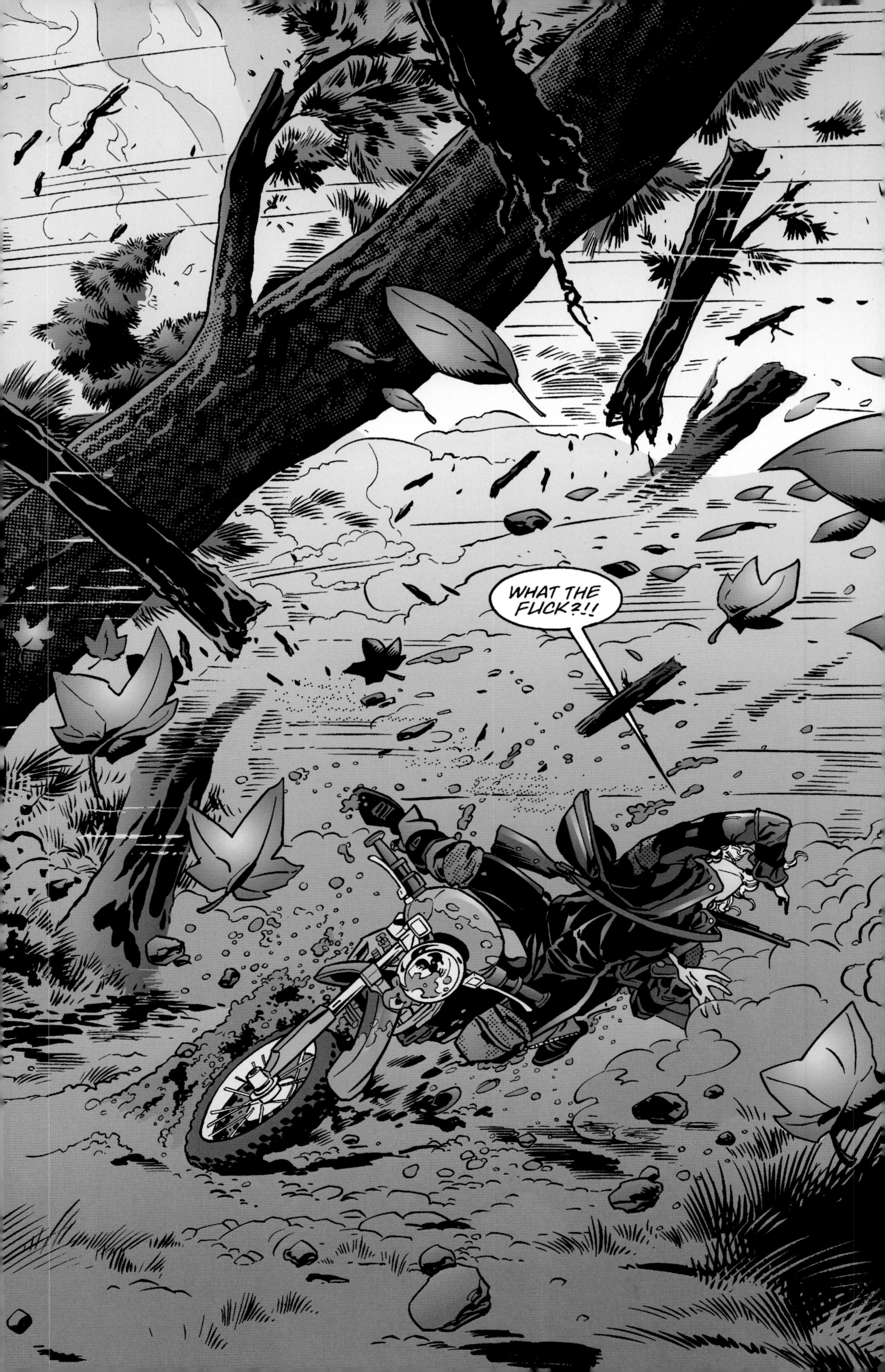
WHAT THE FUCK?!!

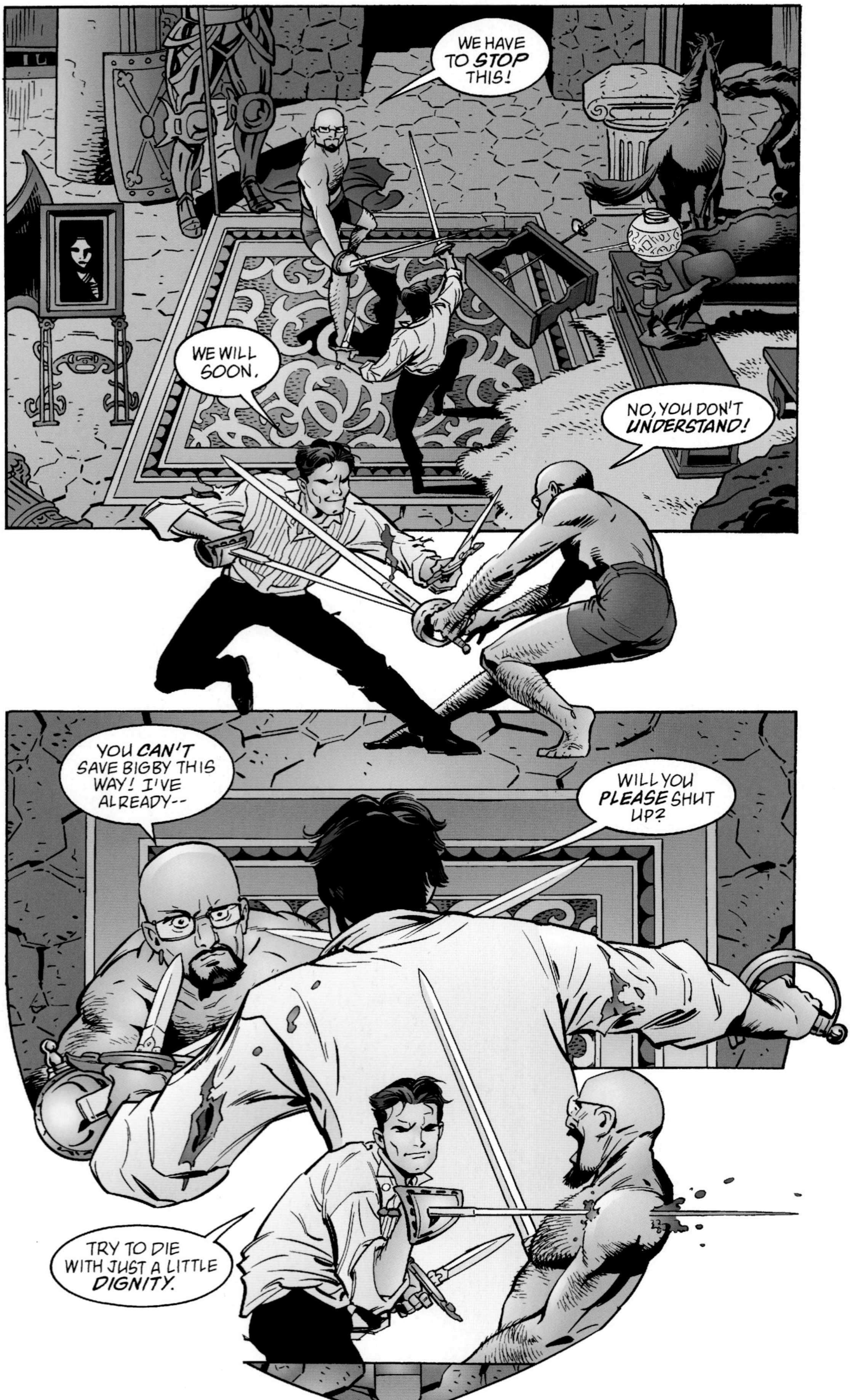
WE HAVE TO STOP THIS!
WE WILL SOON.
NO, YOU DON'T UNDERSTAND!
YOU CAN'T SAVE BIGBY THIS WAY! I'VE ALREADY--
WILL YOU PLEASE SHUT UP?
TRY TO DIE WITH JUST A LITTLE DIGNITY.

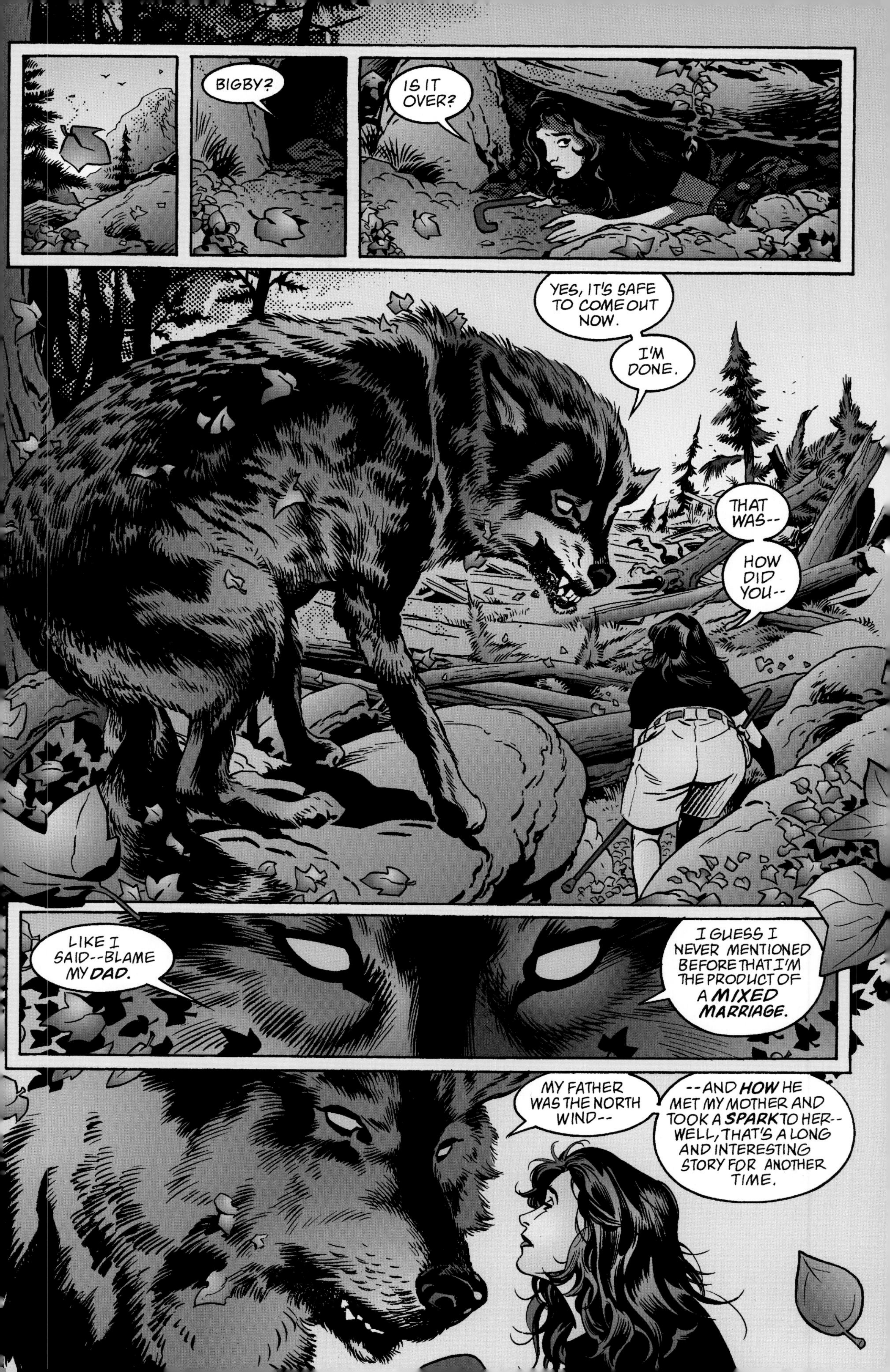
BIGBY?
IS IT OVER?
YES, IT'S SAFE TO COME OUT NOW.
I'M DONE.
THAT WAS--
HOW DID YOU--
LIKE I SAID--BLAME MY DAD.
I GUESS I NEVER MENTIONED BEFORE THAT I'M THE PRODUCT OF A MIXED MARRIAGE.
MY FATHER WAS THE NORTH WIND--
--AND HOW HE MET MY MOTHER AND TOOK A SPARK TO HER--WELL, THAT'S A LONG AND INTERESTING STORY FOR ANOTHER TIME.

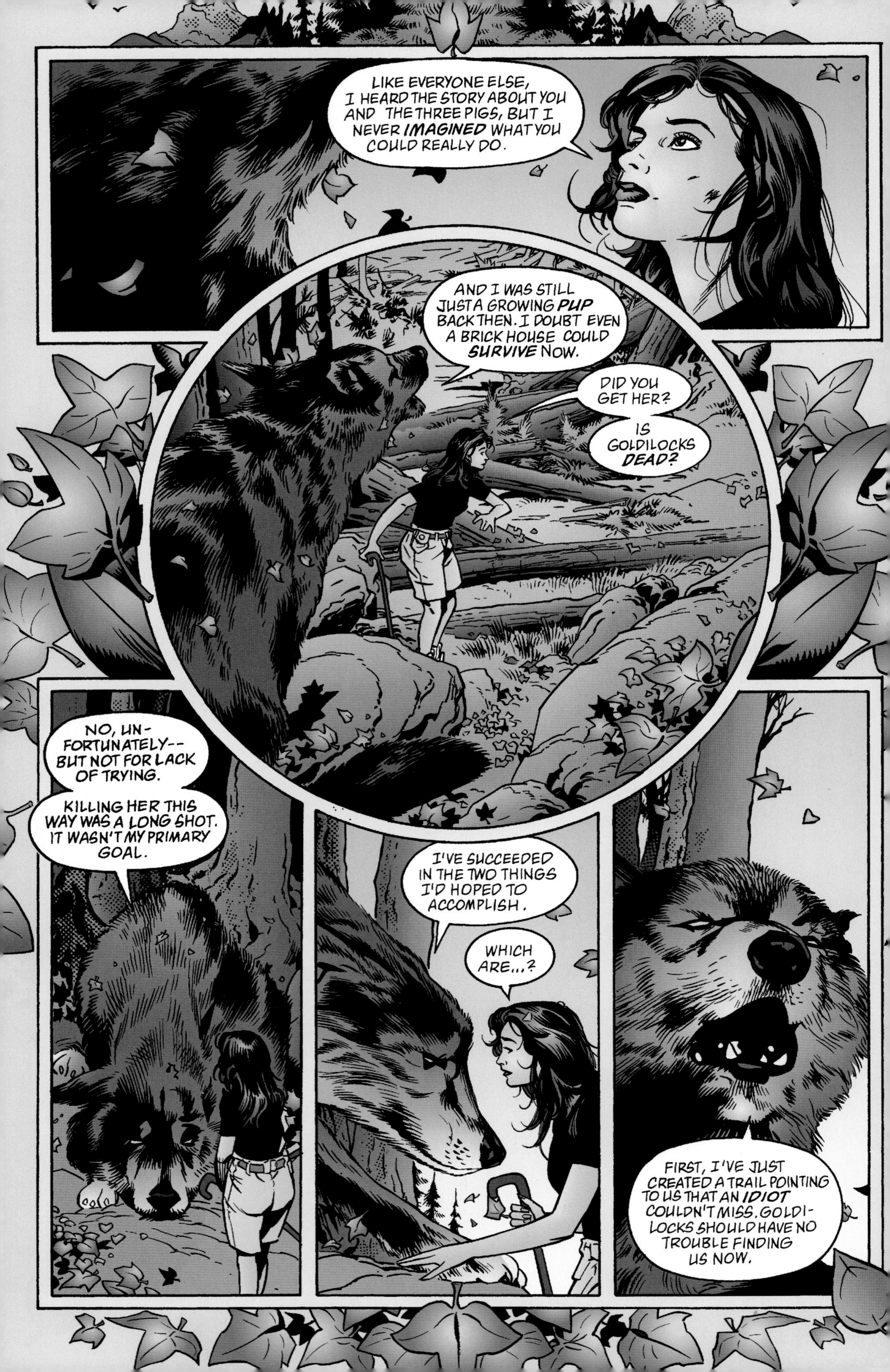
LIKE EVERYONE ELSE, I HEARD THE STORY ABOUT YOU AND THE THREE PIGS, BUT I NEVER IMAGINED WHAT YOU COULD REALLY DO.
AND I WAS STILL JUST A GROWING PUP BACK THEN. I DOUBT EVEN A BRICK HOUSE COULD SURVIVE NOW.
DID YOU GET HER?
IS GOLDILOCKS DEAD?
NO, UN-FORTUNATELY-- BUT NOT FOR LACK OF TRYING.
KILLING HER THIS WAY WAS A LONG SHOT. IT WASN'T MY PRIMARY GOAL.
I'VE SUCCEEDED IN THE TWO THINGS I'D HOPED TO ACCOMPLISH.
WHICH ARE...?
FIRST, I'VE JUST CREATED A TRAIL POINTING TO US THAT AN IDIOT COULDN'T MISS. GOLDI-LOCKS SHOULD HAVE NO TROUBLE FINDING US NOW.

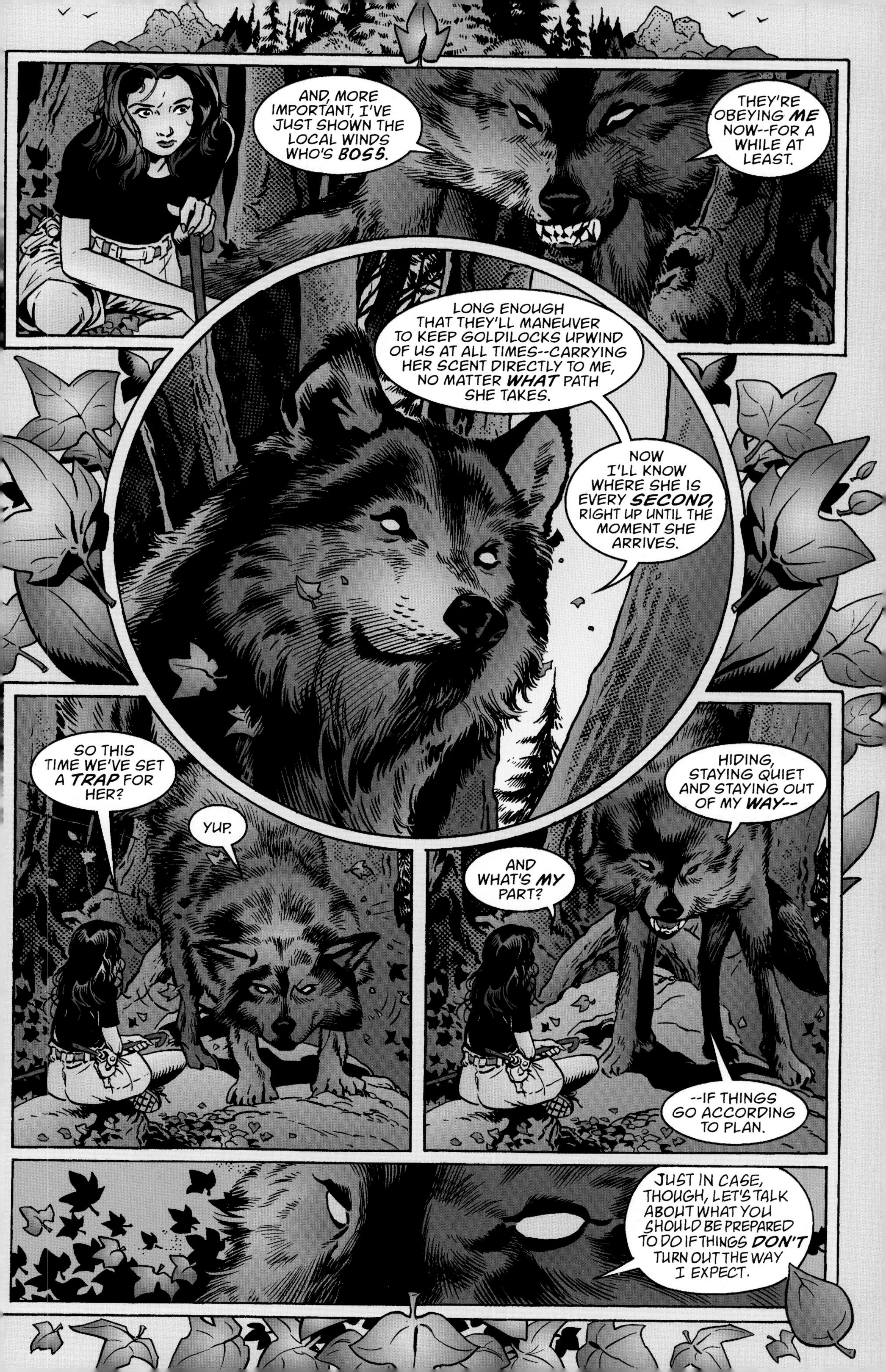
AND, MORE IMPORTANT, I'VE JUST SHOWN THE LOCAL WINDS WHO'S BOSS.
THEY'RE OBEYING ME NOW--FOR A WHILE AT LEAST.
LONG ENOUGH THAT THEY'LL MANEUVER TO KEEP GOLDILOCKS UPWIND OF US AT ALL TIMES--CARRYING HER SCENT DIRECTLY TO ME, NO MATTER WHAT PATH SHE TAKES.
NOW I'LL KNOW WHERE SHE IS EVERY SECOND, RIGHT UP UNTIL THE MOMENT SHE ARRIVES.
SO THIS TIME WE'VE SET A TRAP FOR HER?
YUP.
AND WHAT'S MY PART?
HIDING, STAYING QUIET AND STAYING OUT OF MY WAY--
--IF THINGS GO ACCORDING TO PLAN.
JUST IN CASE, THOUGH, LET'S TALK ABOUT WHAT YOU SHOULD BE PREPARED TO DO IF THINGS DON'T TURN OUT THE WAY I EXPECT.

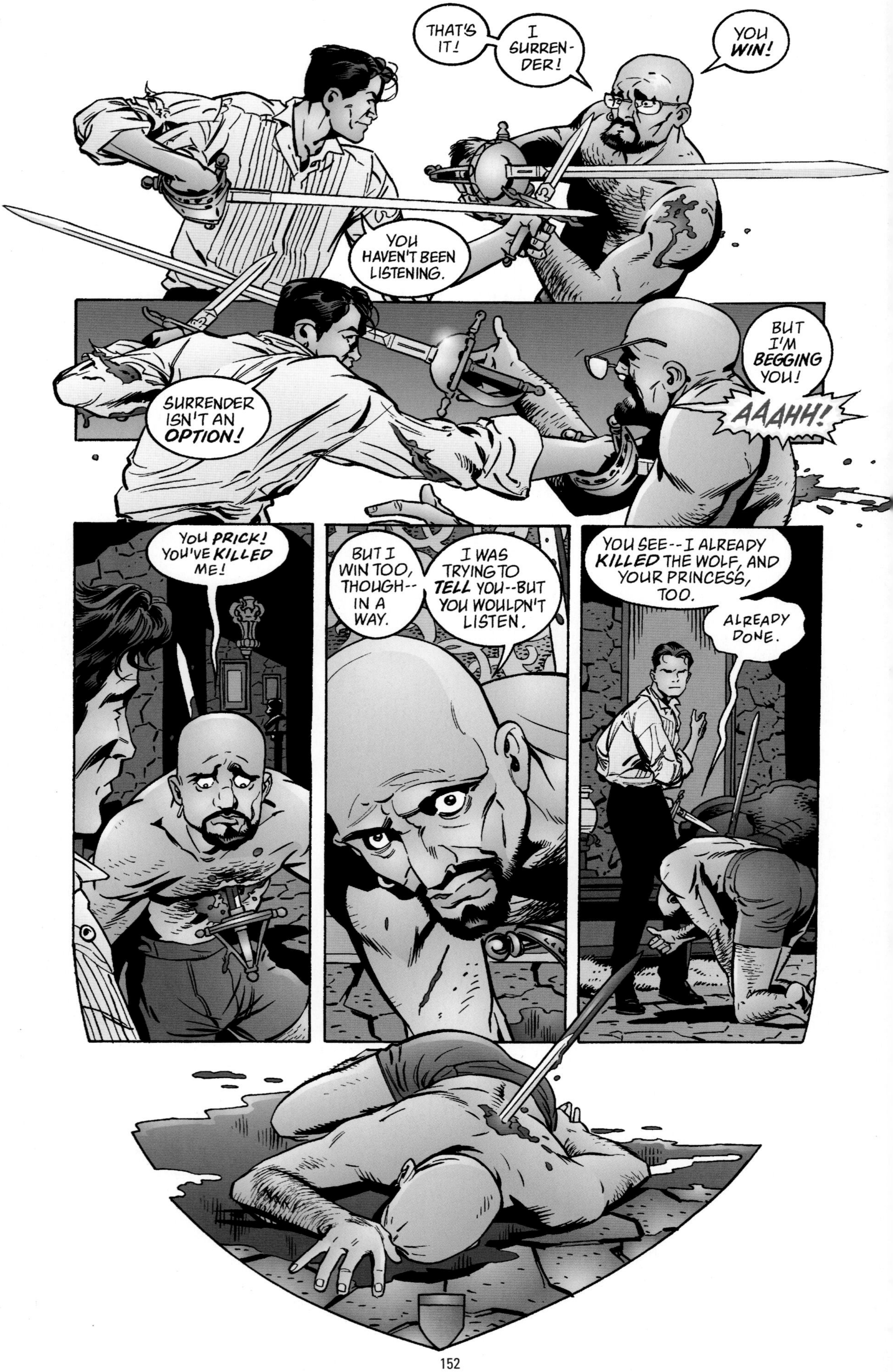
THAT'S IT!
I SURRENDER!
YOU WIN!
YOU HAVEN'T BEEN LISTENING.
SURRENDER ISN'T AN OPTION!
BUT I'M BEGGING YOU!
AAAHH!
YOU PRICK! YOU'VE KILLED ME!
BUT I WIN TOO, THOUGH-- IN A WAY.
I WAS TRYING TO TELL YOU--BUT YOU WOULDN'T LISTEN.
YOU SEE--I ALREADY KILLED THE WOLF, AND YOUR PRINCESS, TOO.
ALREADY DONE.

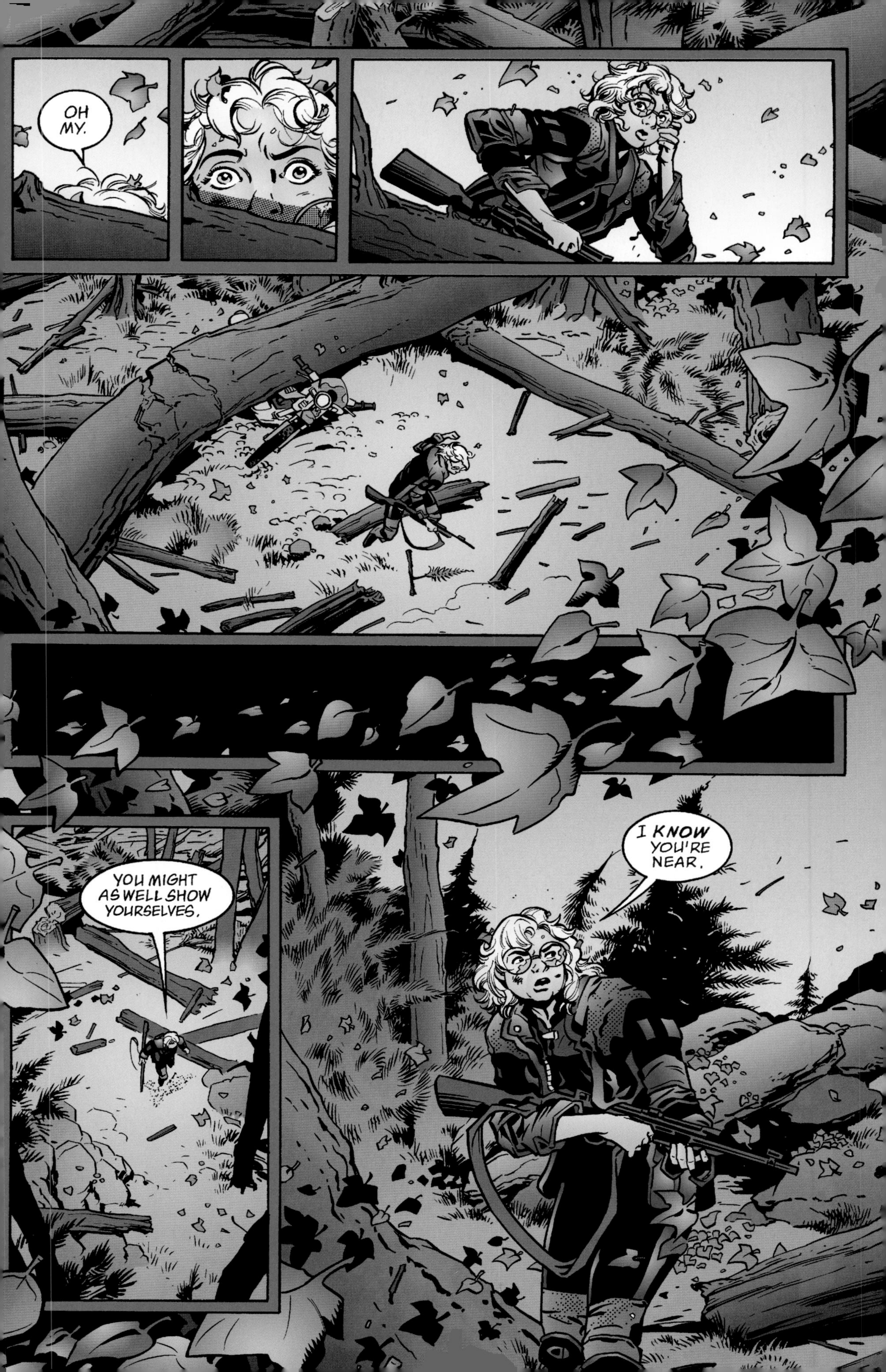
OH MY.
YOU MIGHT AS WELL SHOW YOURSELVES.
I KNOW YOU'RE NEAR.

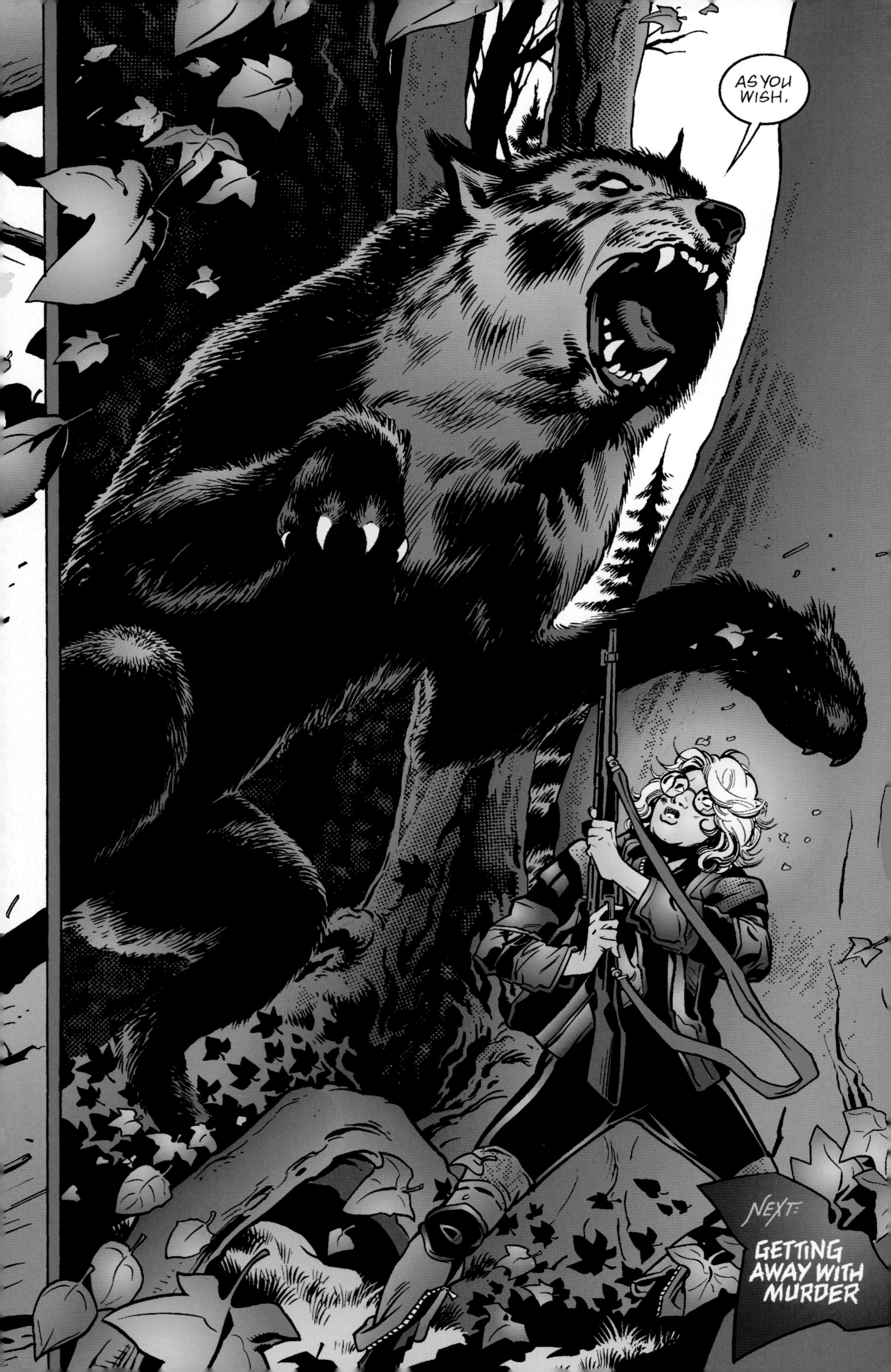
AS YOU WISH.
NEXT:
GETTING AWAY WITH MURDER

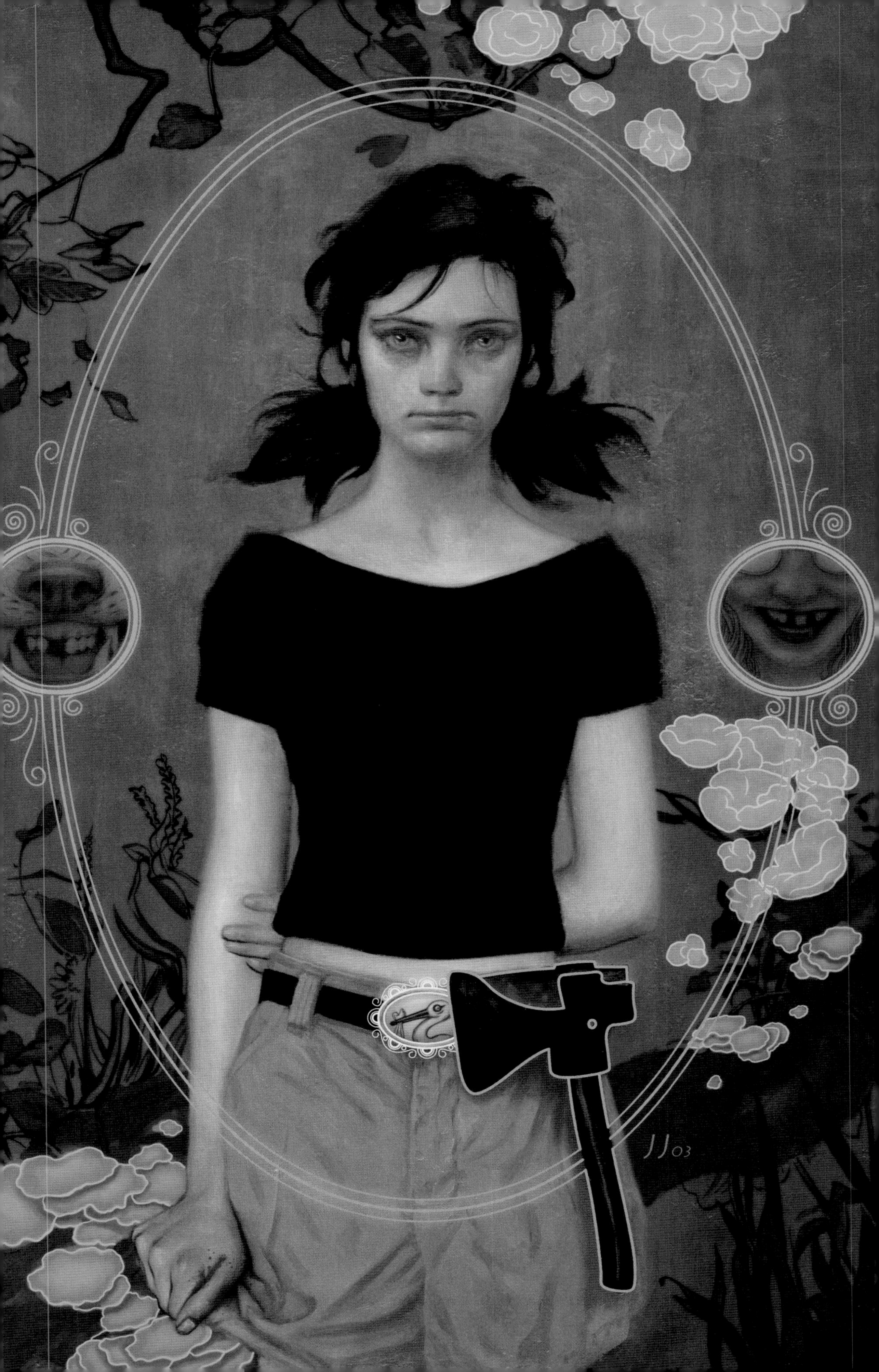

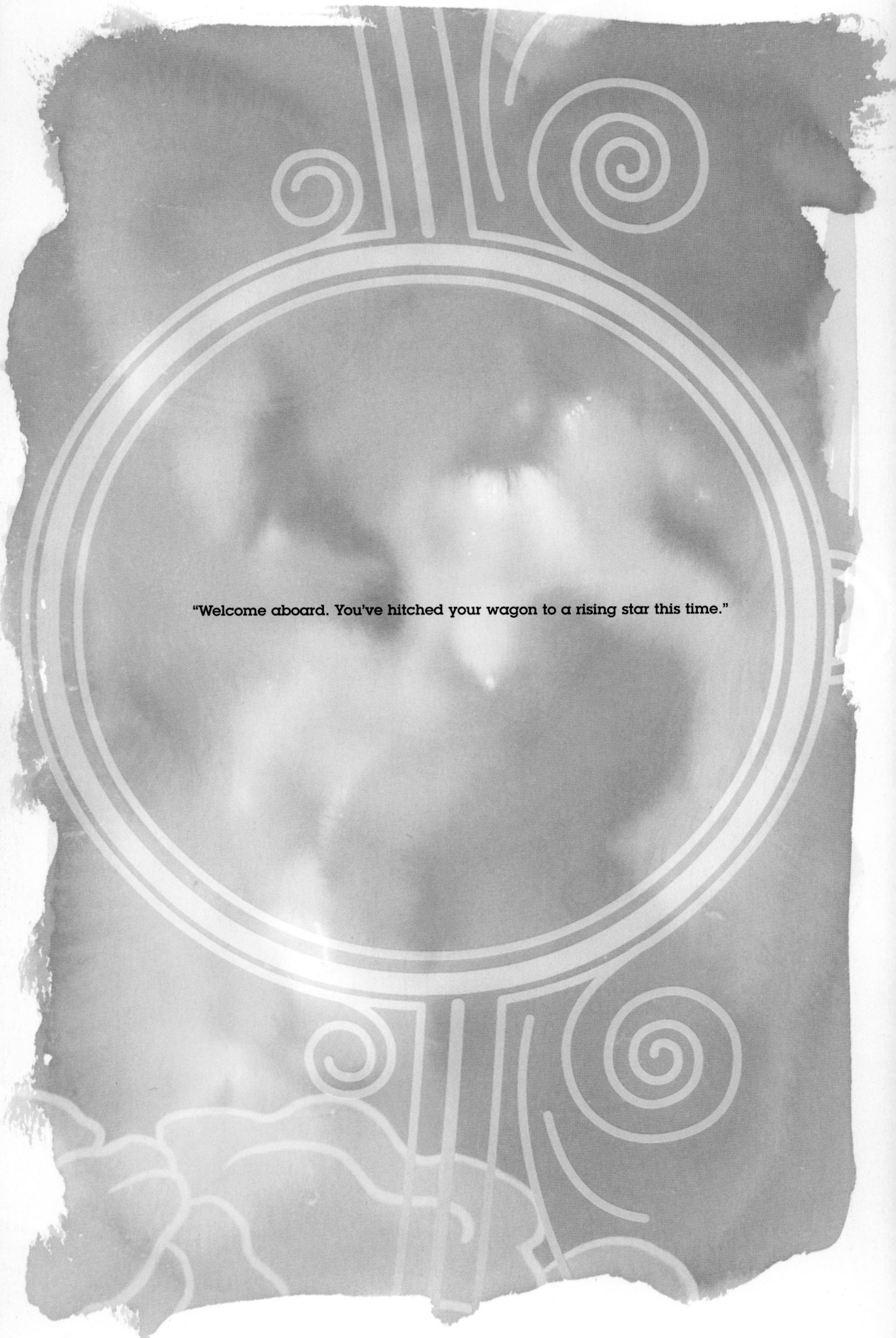
"Welcome aboard. You've hitched your wagon to a rising star this time."

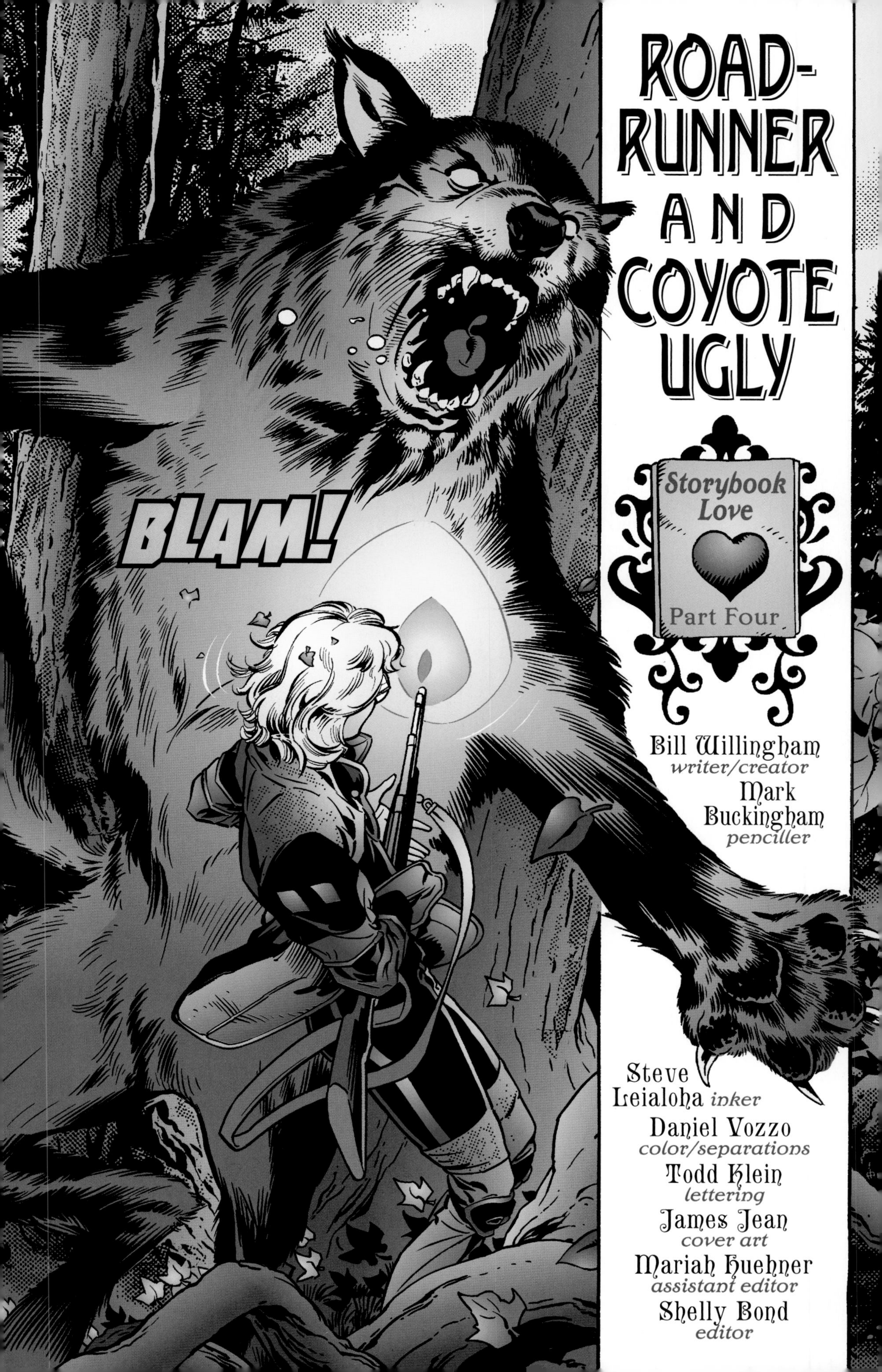
BLAM!
ROAD-RUNNER AND COYOTE UGLY
Storybook Love
Part Four
Bill Willingham writer/creator
Mark Buckingham penciller
Steve Leialoha inker
Daniel Vozzo color/separations
Todd Klein lettering
James Jean cover art
Mariah Huehner assistant editor
Shelly Bond editor

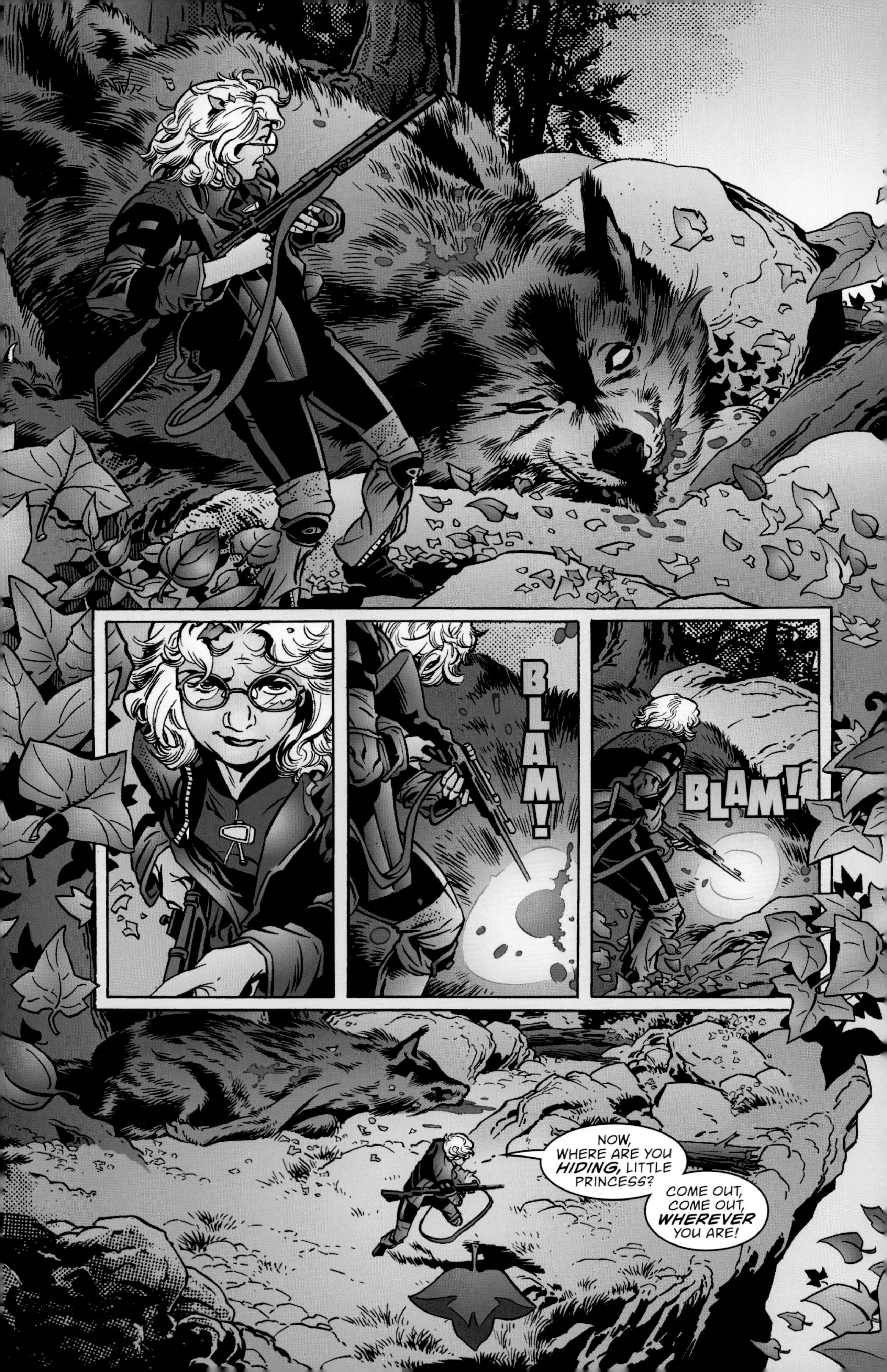
BLAM!
BLAM!!
NOW, WHERE ARE YOU *HIDING,* LITTLE PRINCESS?
COME OUT, COME OUT, ***WHEREVER*** YOU ARE!

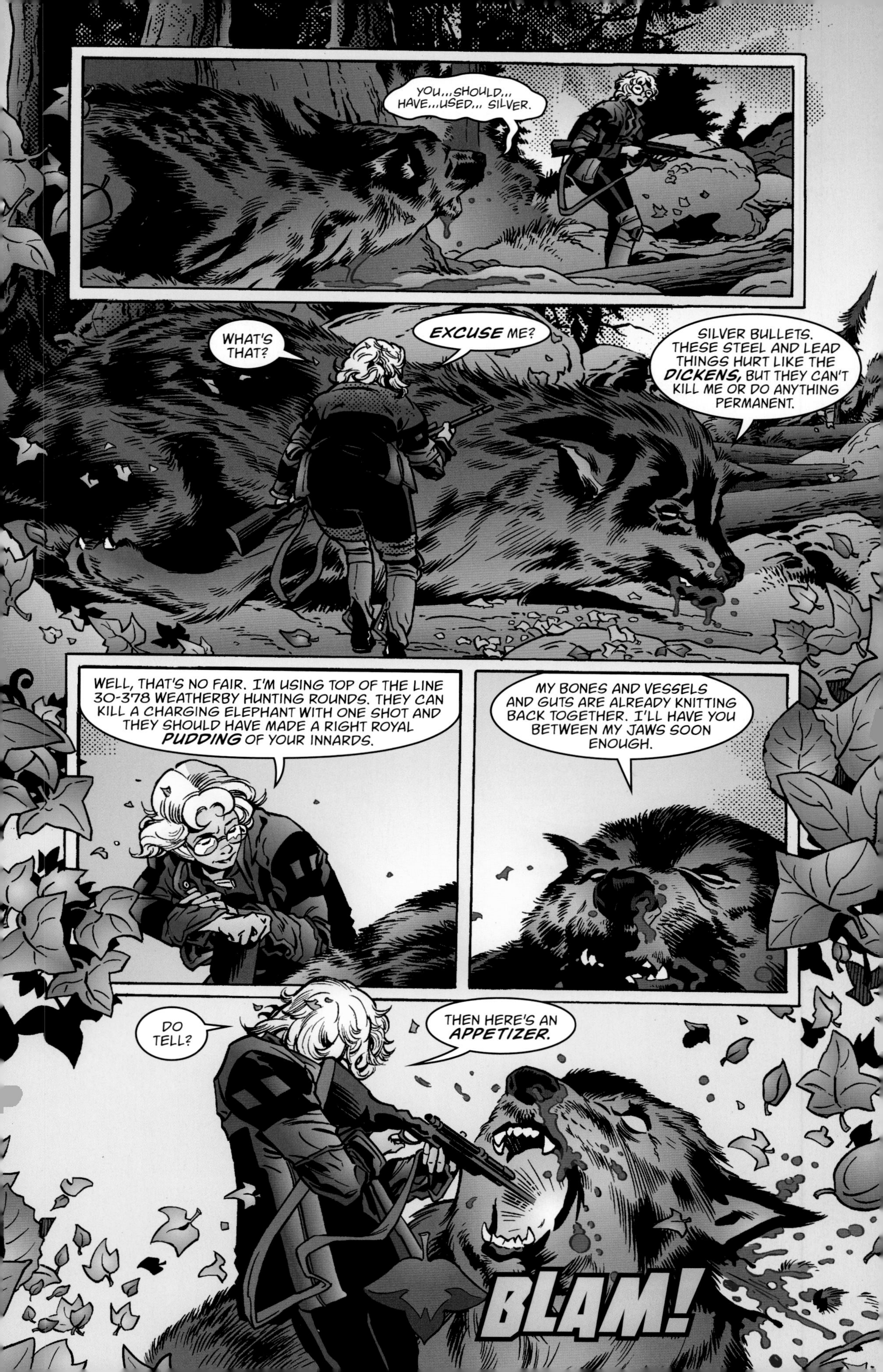
YOU... SHOULD... HAVE... USED... SILVER.
WHAT'S THAT?
EXCUSE ME?
SILVER BULLETS. THESE STEEL AND LEAD THINGS HURT LIKE THE DICKENS, BUT THEY CAN'T KILL ME OR DO ANYTHING PERMANENT.
WELL, THAT'S NO FAIR. I'M USING TOP OF THE LINE 30-378 WEATHERBY HUNTING ROUNDS. THEY CAN KILL A CHARGING ELEPHANT WITH ONE SHOT AND THEY SHOULD HAVE MADE A RIGHT ROYAL PUDDING OF YOUR INNARDS.
MY BONES AND VESSELS AND GUTS ARE ALREADY KNITTING BACK TOGETHER. I'LL HAVE YOU BETWEEN MY JAWS SOON ENOUGH.
DO TELL?
THEN HERE'S AN APPETIZER.
BLAM!

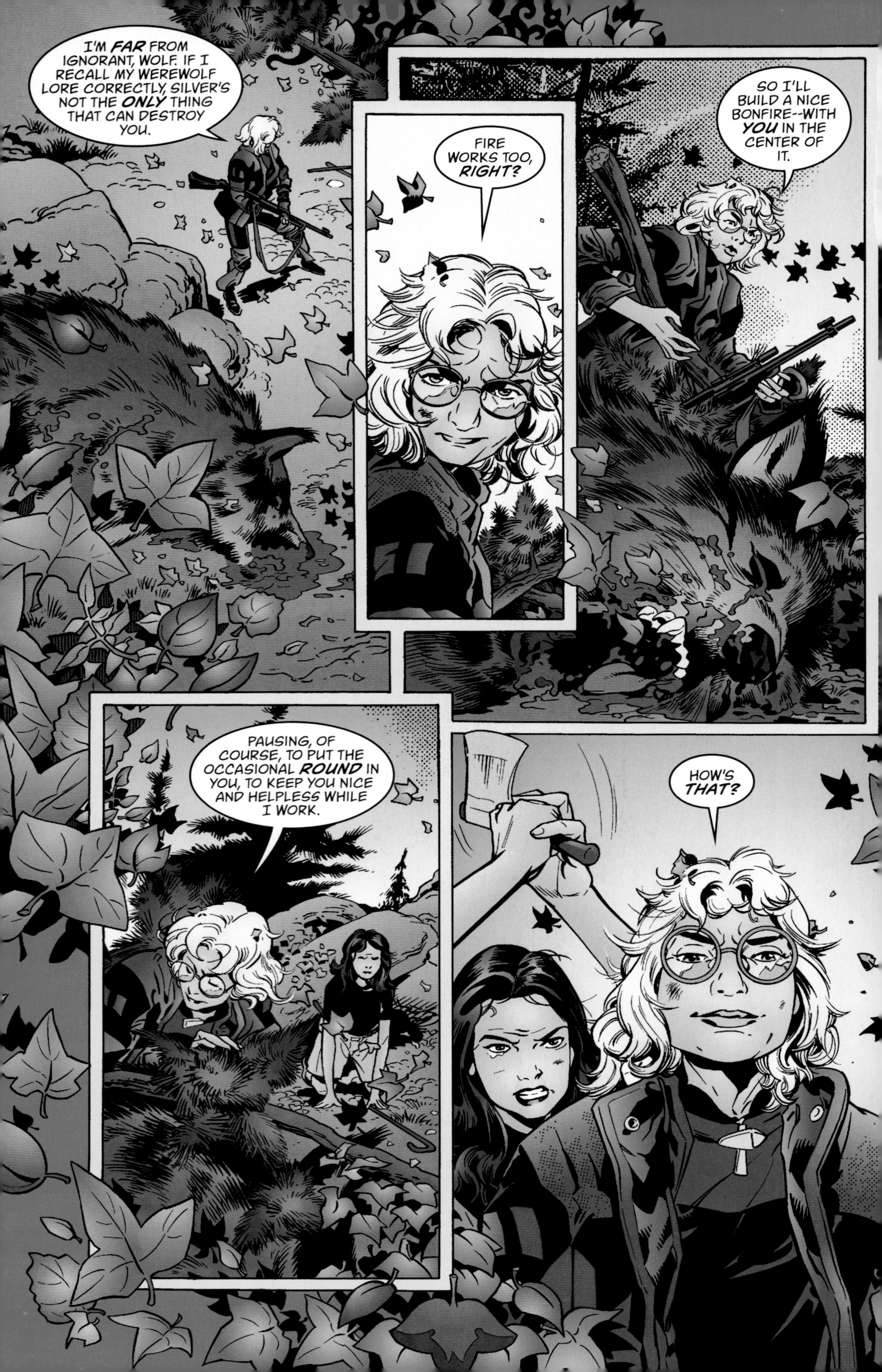
I'M FAR FROM IGNORANT, WOLF. IF I RECALL MY WEREWOLF LORE CORRECTLY, SILVER'S NOT THE ONLY THING THAT CAN DESTROY YOU.
FIRE WORKS TOO, RIGHT?
SO I'LL BUILD A NICE BONFIRE--WITH YOU IN THE CENTER OF IT.
PAUSING, OF COURSE, TO PUT THE OCCASIONAL ROUND IN YOU, TO KEEP YOU NICE AND HELPLESS WHILE I WORK.
HOW'S THAT?

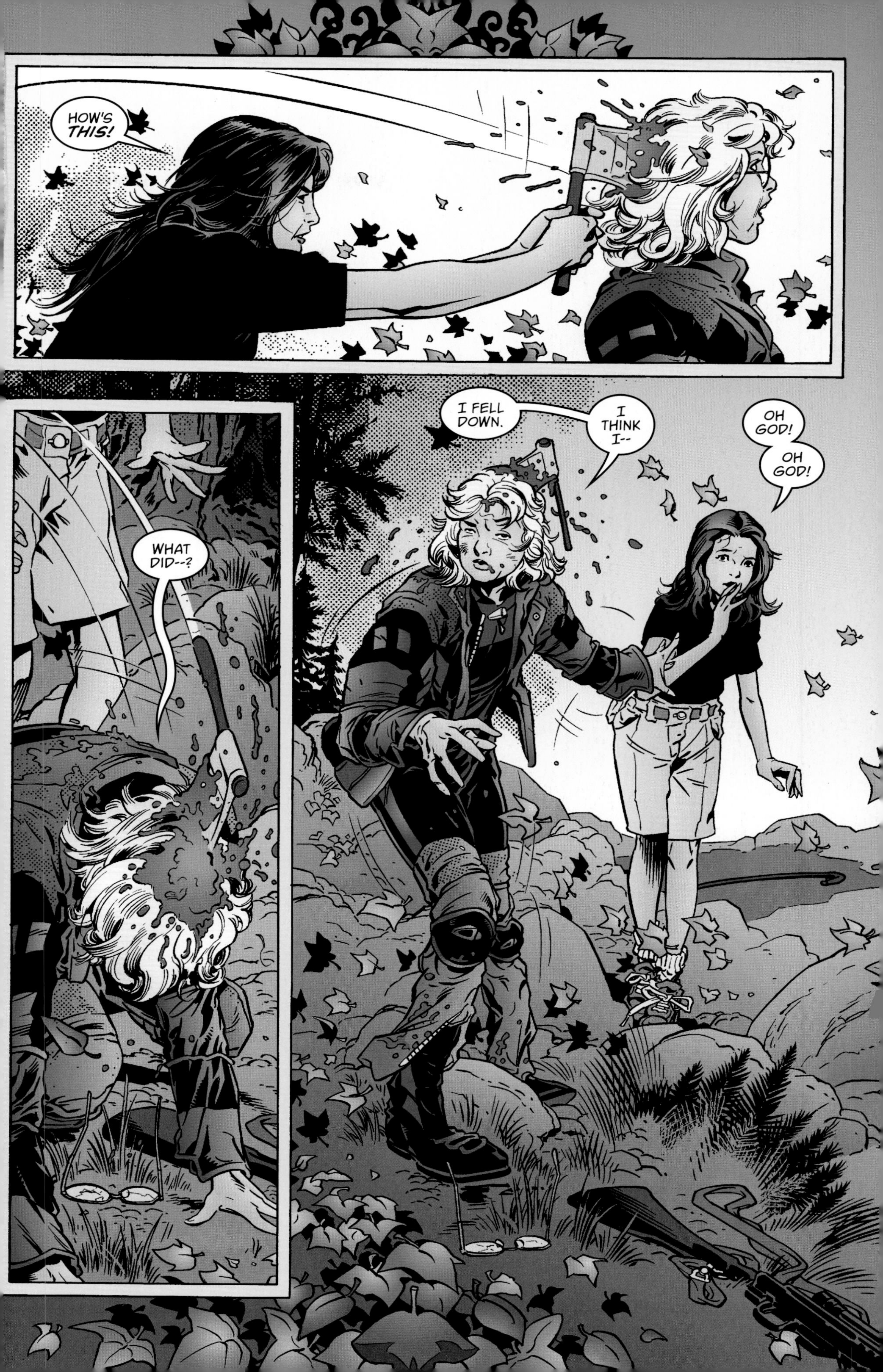
HOW'S THIS!
WHAT DID--?
I FELL DOWN.
I THINK I--
OH GOD!
OH GOD!

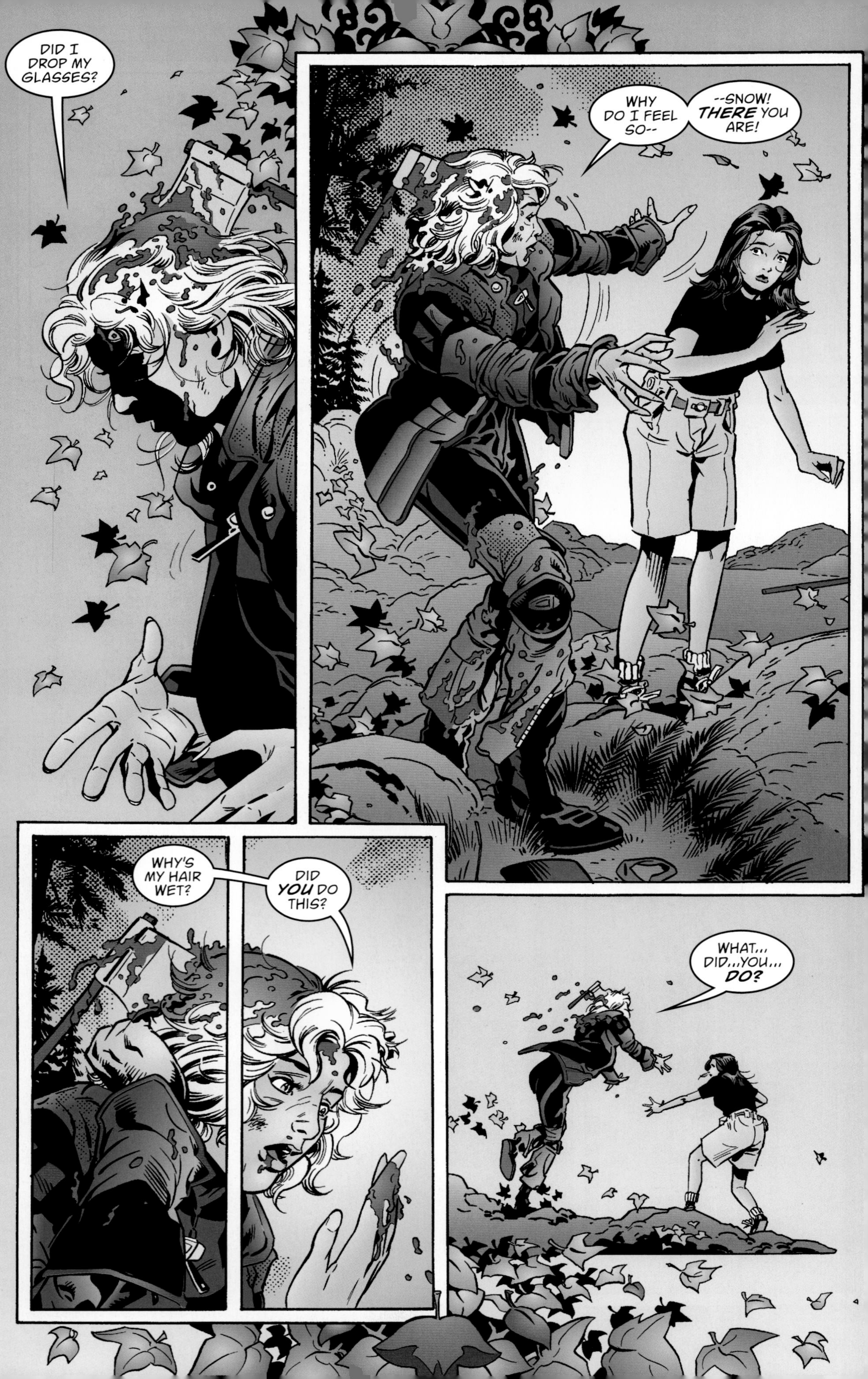
DID I DROP MY GLASSES?
WHY DO I FEEL SO--
--SNOW! THERE YOU ARE!
WHY'S MY HAIR WET?
DID YOU DO THIS?
WHAT... DID...YOU... DO?

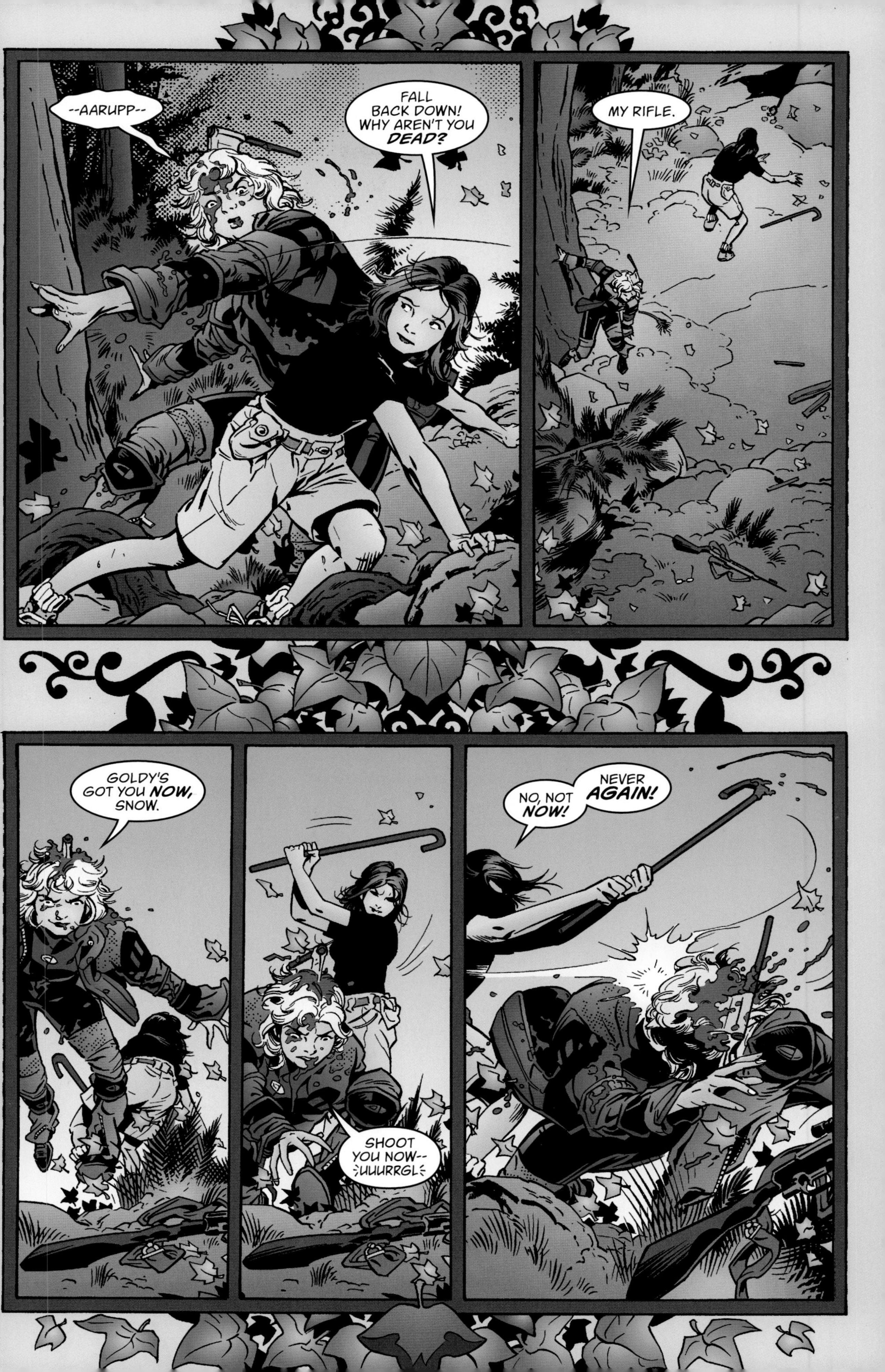

--AARUPP--
FALL BACK DOWN! WHY AREN'T YOU DEAD?
MY RIFLE.
GOLDY'S GOT YOU NOW, SNOW.
SHOOT YOU NOW-- UUURRGL
NO, NOT NOW!
NEVER AGAIN!

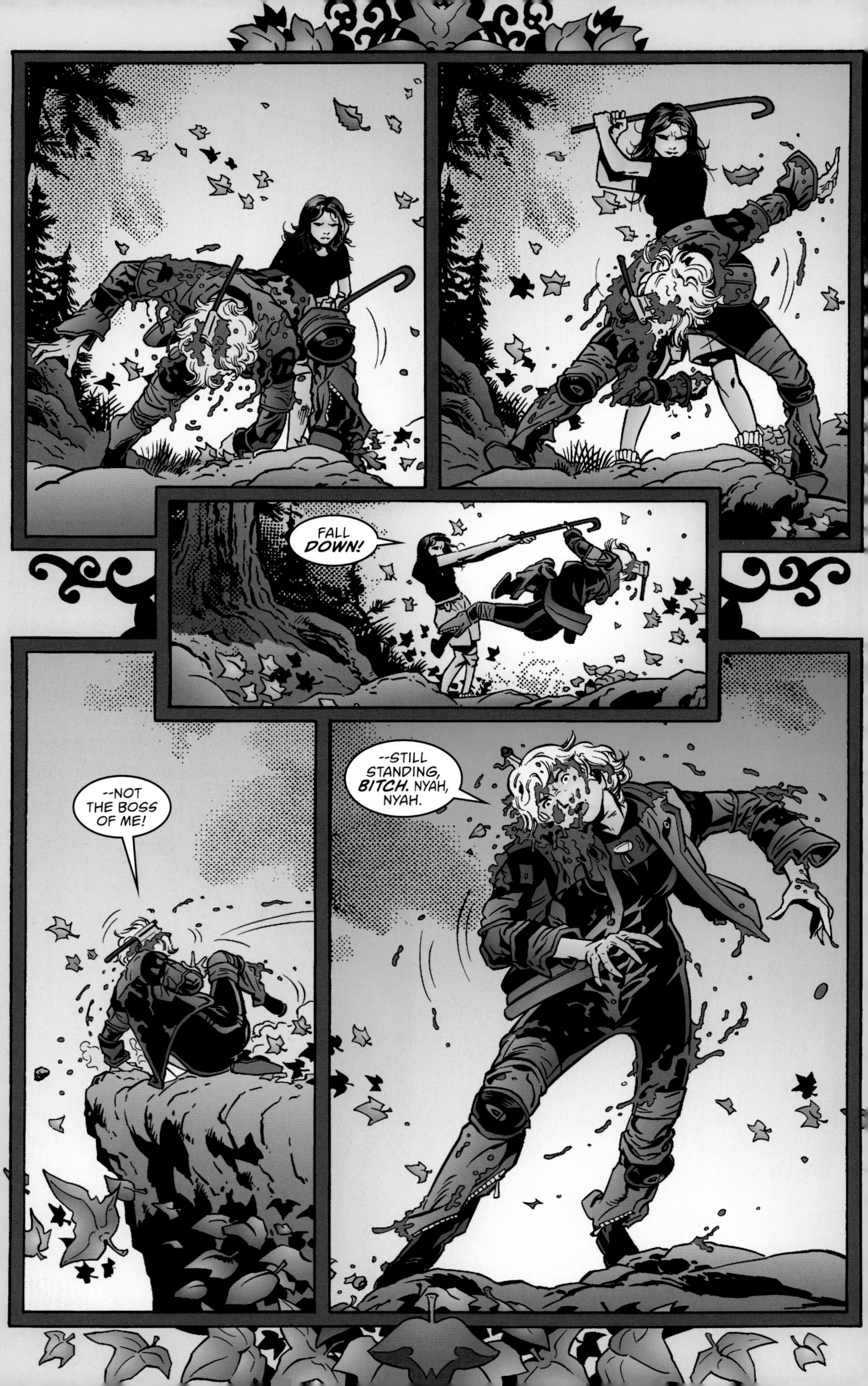
FALL DOWN!
--NOT THE BOSS OF ME!
--STILL STANDING, BITCH. NYAH, NYAH.

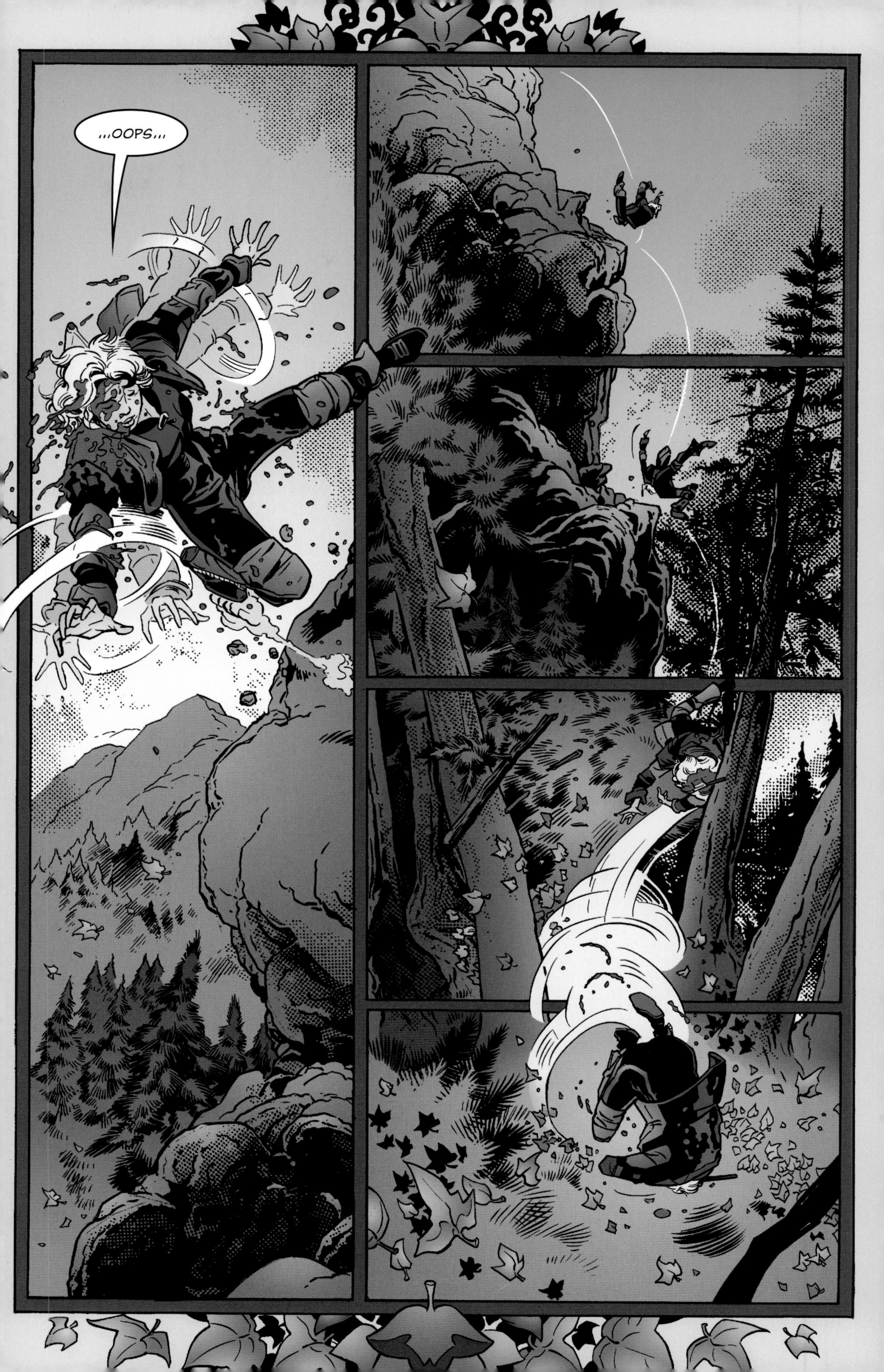
...OOPS...

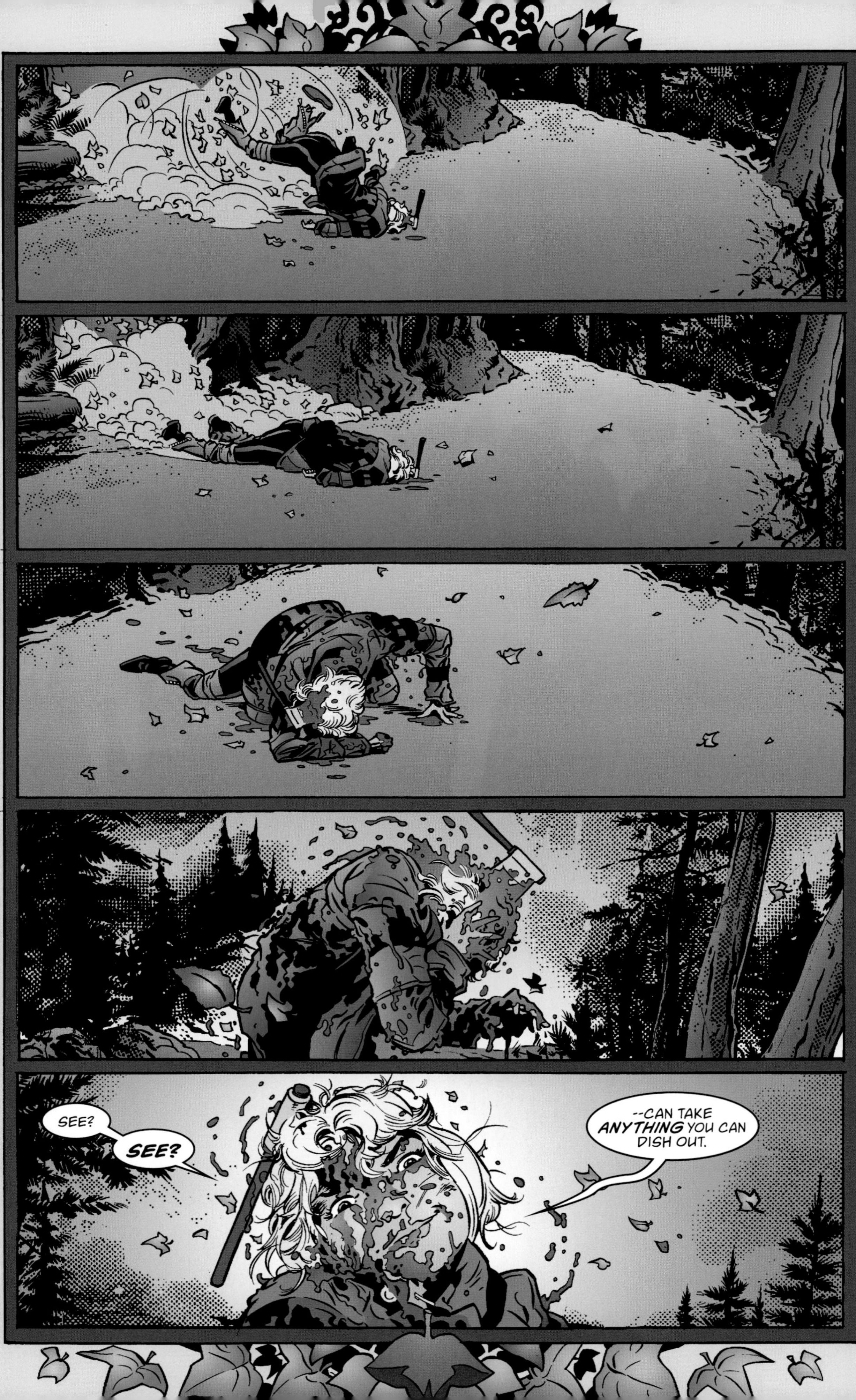
SEE?
SEE?
--CAN TAKE ANYTHING YOU CAN DISH OUT.

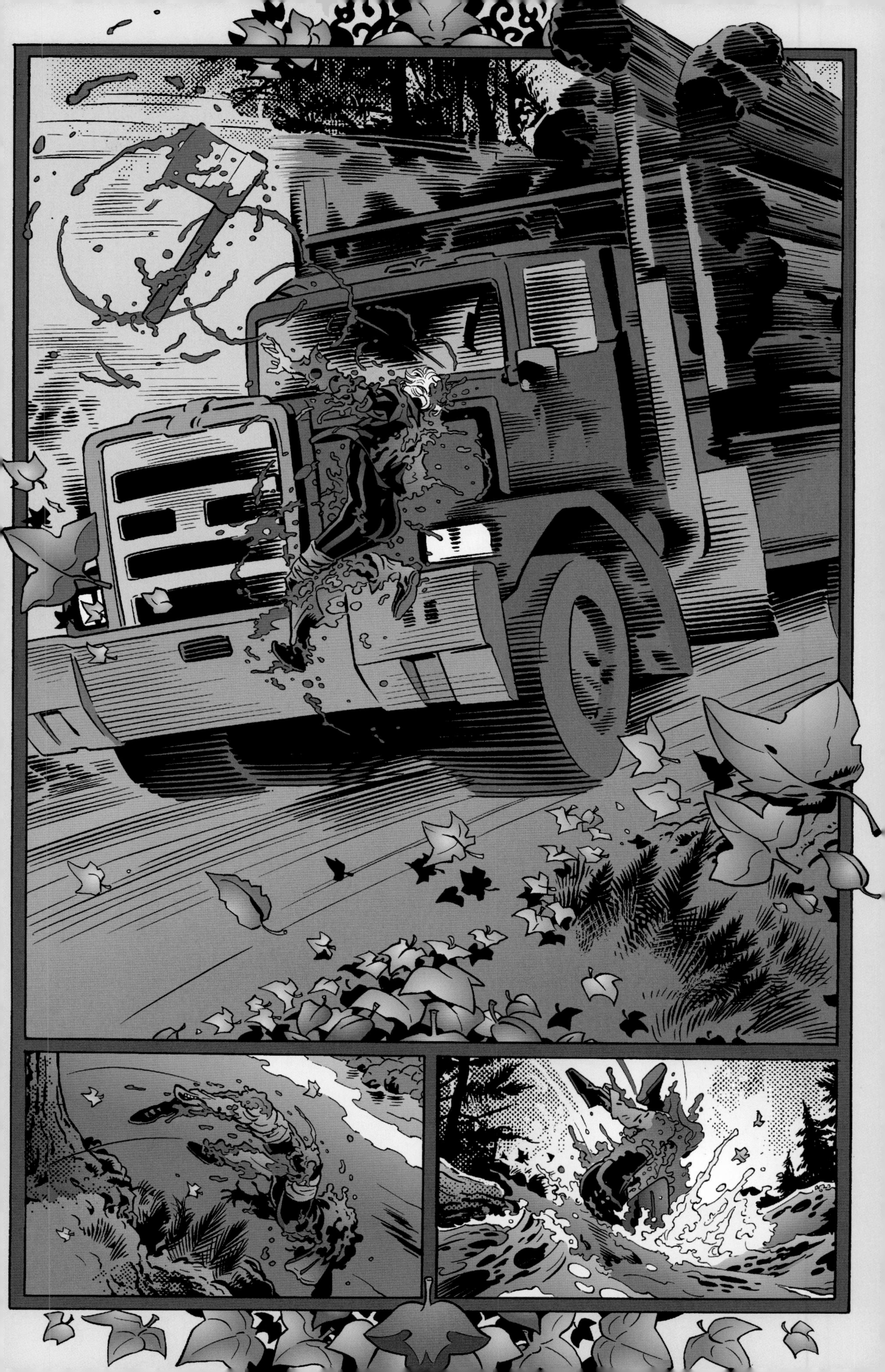

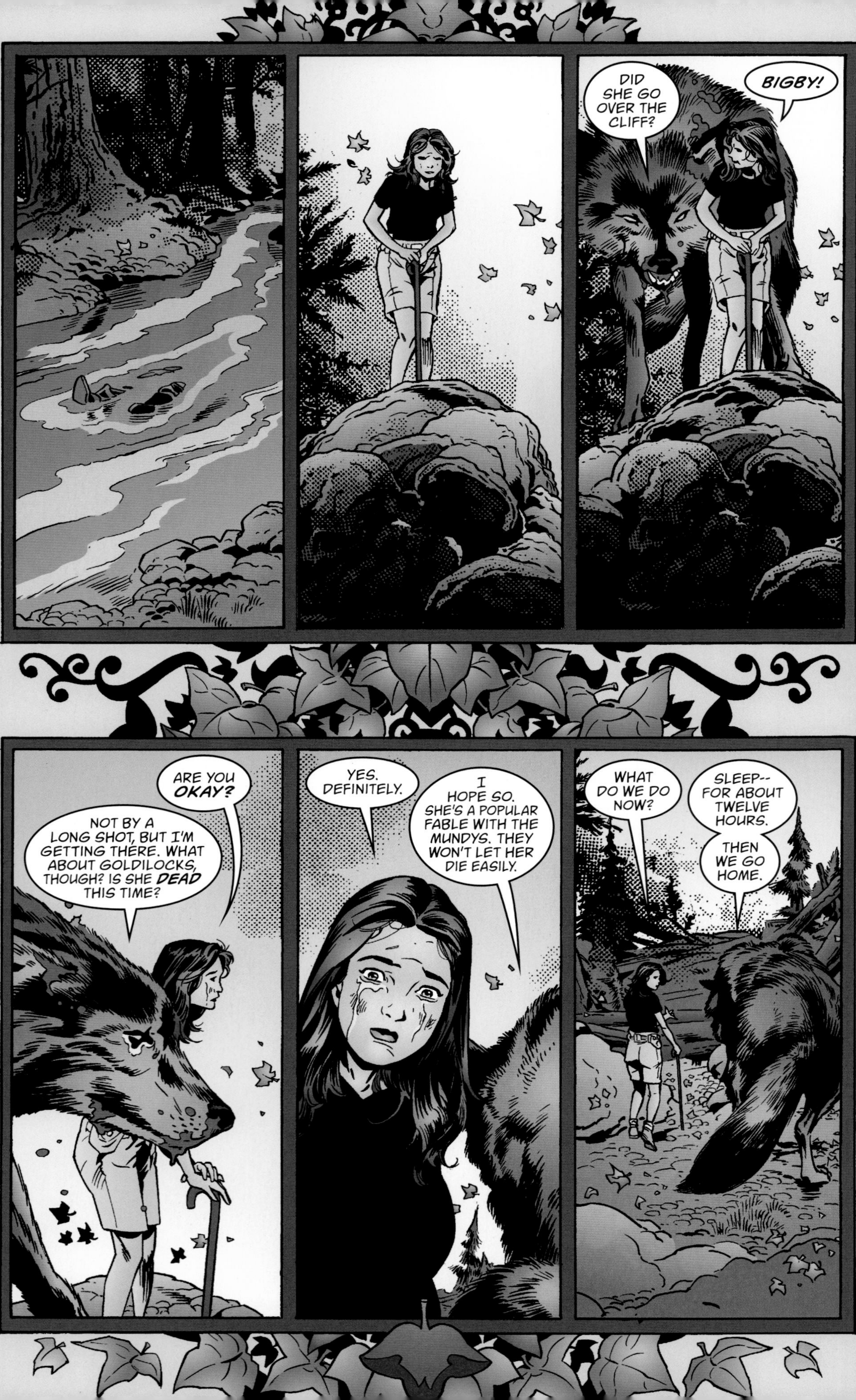
DID SHE GO OVER THE CLIFF?
BIGBY!
ARE YOU OKAY?
NOT BY A LONG SHOT, BUT I'M GETTING THERE. WHAT ABOUT GOLDILOCKS, THOUGH? IS SHE DEAD THIS TIME?
YES. DEFINITELY.
I HOPE SO. SHE'S A POPULAR FABLE WITH THE MUNDYS. THEY WON'T LET HER DIE EASILY.
WHAT DO WE DO NOW?
SLEEP-- FOR ABOUT TWELVE HOURS.
THEN WE GO HOME.

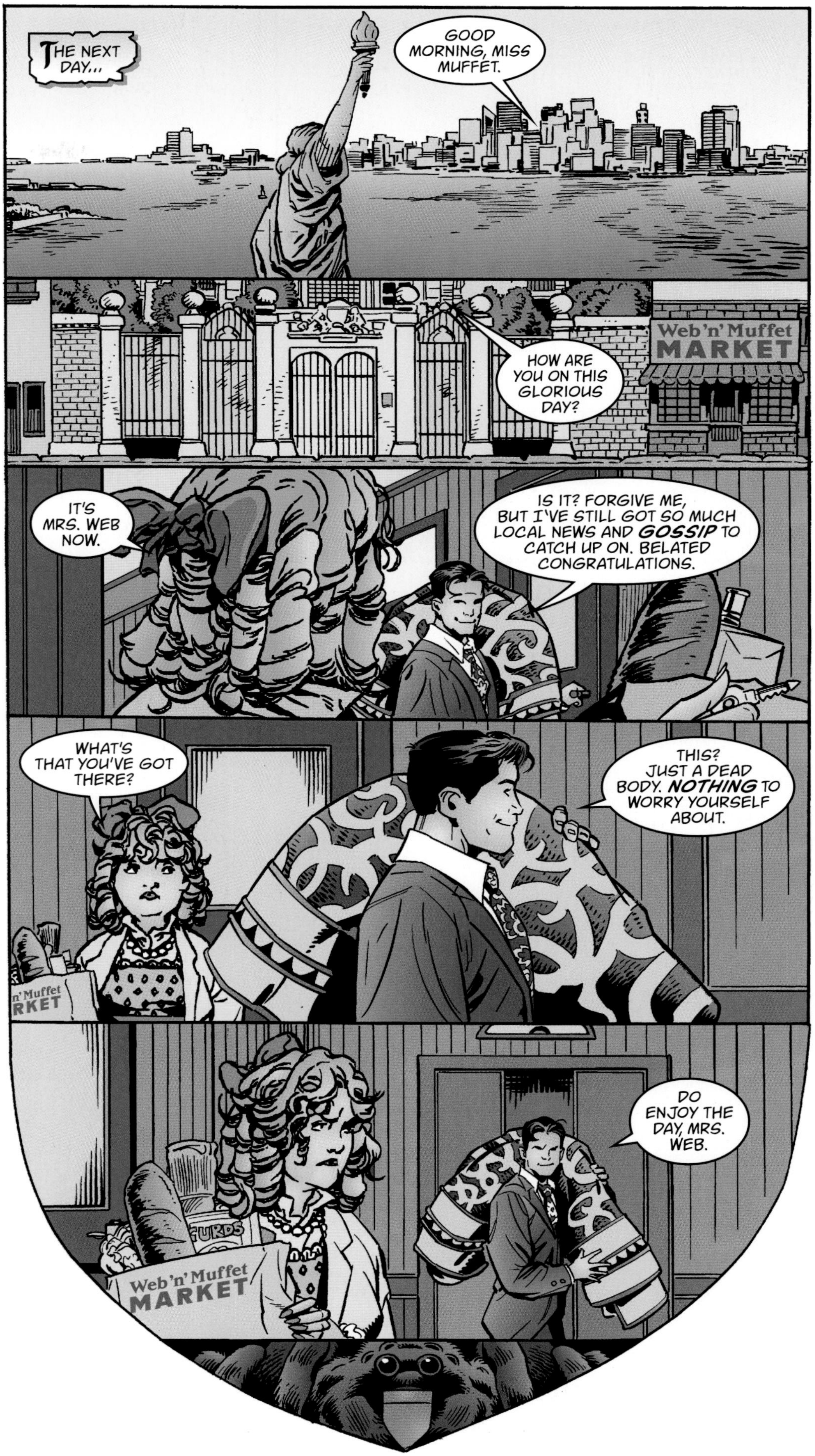
THE NEXT DAY...
GOOD MORNING, MISS MUFFET.
Web'n' Muffet MARKET
HOW ARE YOU ON THIS GLORIOUS DAY?
IT'S MRS. WEB NOW.
IS IT? FORGIVE ME, BUT I'VE STILL GOT SO MUCH LOCAL NEWS AND GOSSIP TO CATCH UP ON. BELATED CONGRATULATIONS.
WHAT'S THAT YOU'VE GOT THERE?
THIS? JUST A DEAD BODY. NOTHING TO WORRY YOURSELF ABOUT.
DO ENJOY THE DAY, MRS. WEB.
Web'n' Muffet MARKET

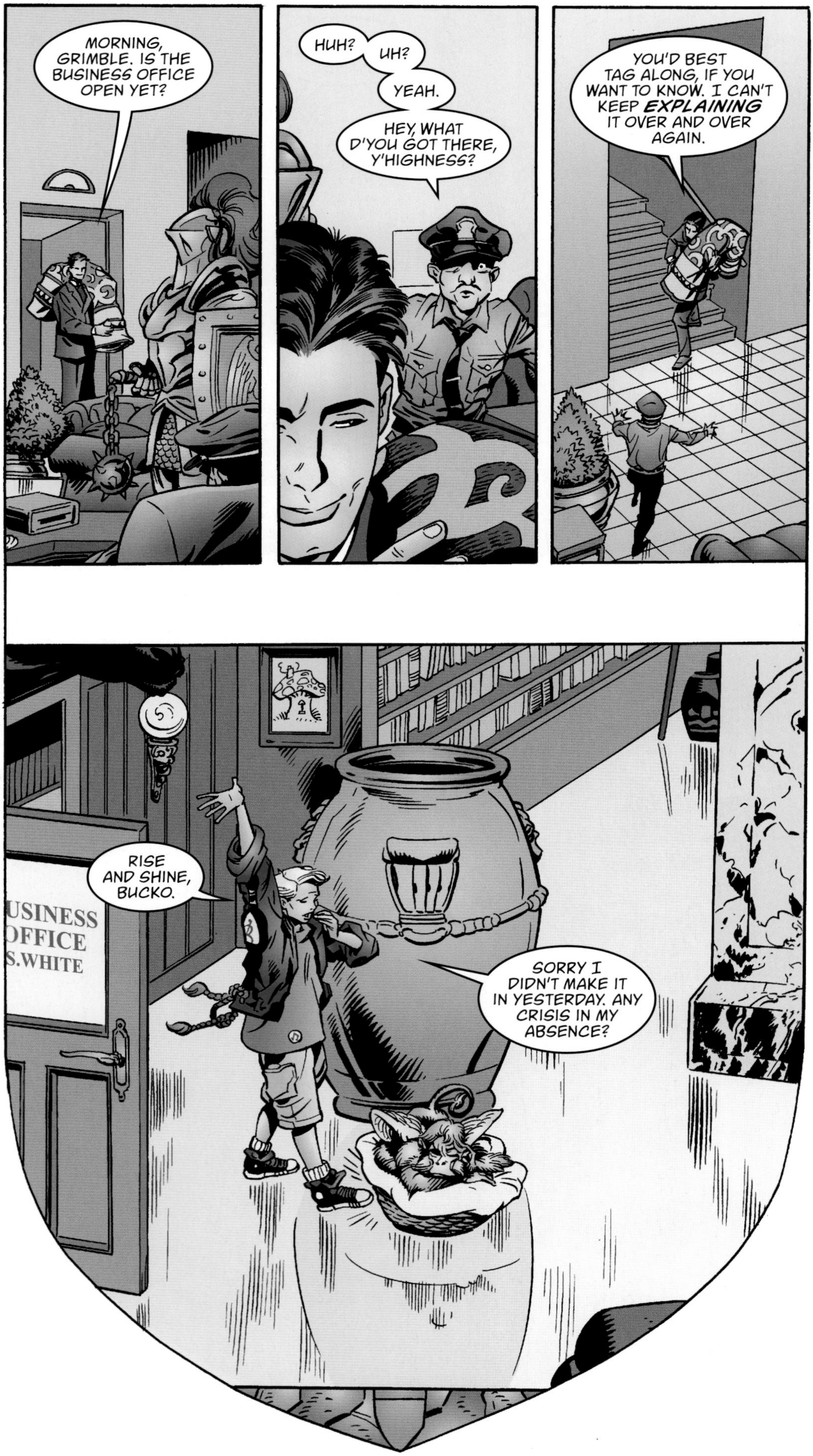
MORNING, GRIMBLE. IS THE BUSINESS OFFICE OPEN YET?
HUH?
UH?
YEAH.
HEY, WHAT D'YOU GOT THERE, Y'HIGHNESS?
YOU'D BEST TAG ALONG, IF YOU WANT TO KNOW. I CAN'T KEEP EXPLAINING IT OVER AND OVER AGAIN.
USINESS OFFICE S.WHITE
RISE AND SHINE, BUCKO.
SORRY I DIDN'T MAKE IT IN YESTERDAY. ANY CRISIS IN MY ABSENCE?

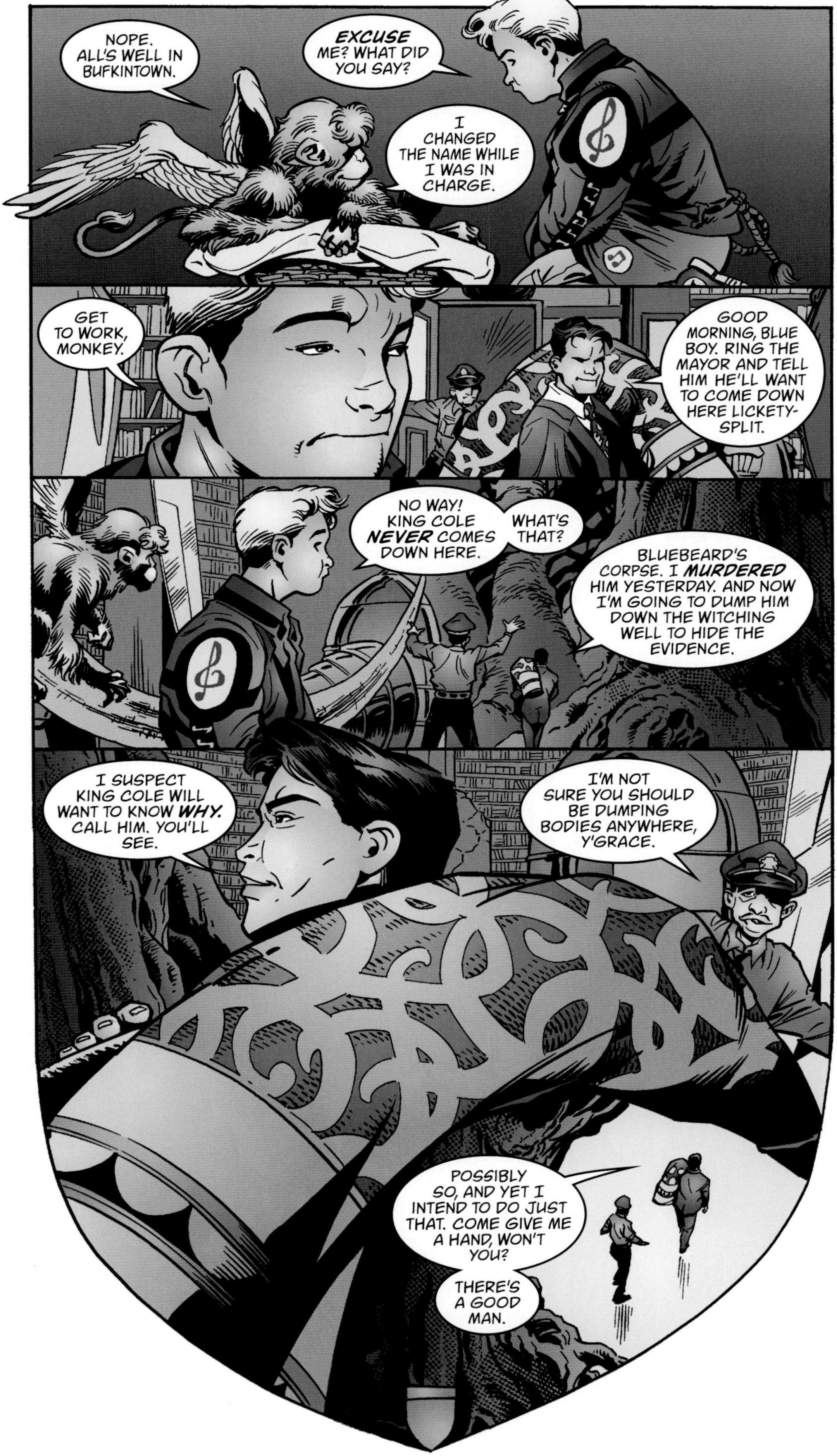
NOPE. ALL'S WELL IN BUFKINTOWN.
EXCUSE ME? WHAT DID YOU SAY?
I CHANGED THE NAME WHILE I WAS IN CHARGE.
GET TO WORK, MONKEY.
GOOD MORNING, BLUE BOY. RING THE MAYOR AND TELL HIM HE'LL WANT TO COME DOWN HERE LICKETY-SPLIT.
NO WAY! KING COLE NEVER COMES DOWN HERE.
WHAT'S THAT?
BLUEBEARD'S CORPSE. I MURDERED HIM YESTERDAY. AND NOW I'M GOING TO DUMP HIM DOWN THE WITCHING WELL TO HIDE THE EVIDENCE.
I SUSPECT KING COLE WILL WANT TO KNOW WHY. CALL HIM. YOU'LL SEE.
I'M NOT SURE YOU SHOULD BE DUMPING BODIES ANYWHERE, Y'GRACE.
POSSIBLY SO, AND YET I INTEND TO DO JUST THAT. COME GIVE ME A HAND, WON'T YOU?
THERE'S A GOOD MAN.

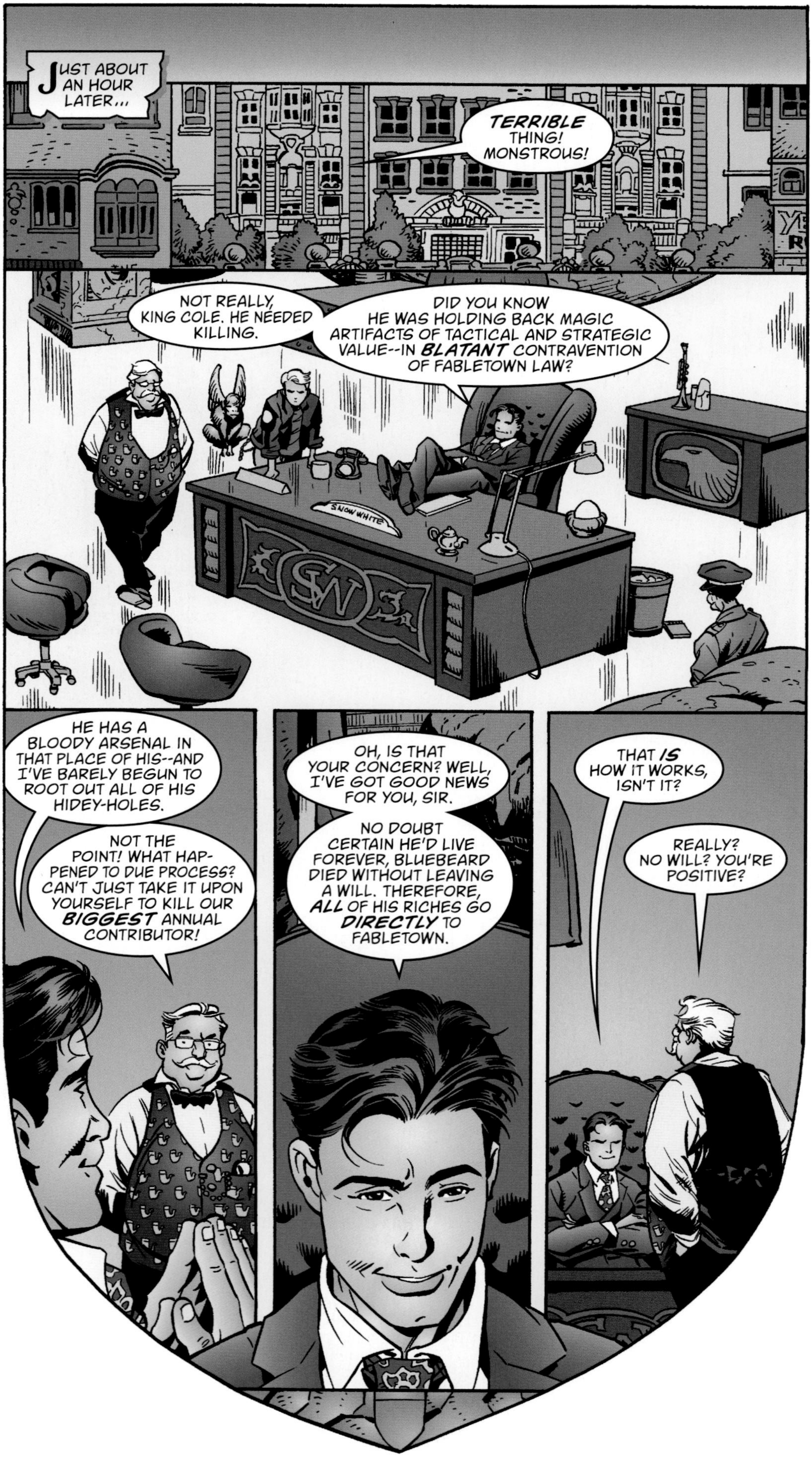

JUST ABOUT AN HOUR LATER...
TERRIBLE THING! MONSTROUS!
NOT REALLY, KING COLE. HE NEEDED KILLING.
DID YOU KNOW HE WAS HOLDING BACK MAGIC ARTIFACTS OF TACTICAL AND STRATEGIC VALUE--IN BLATANT CONTRAVENTION OF FABLETOWN LAW?
SNOW WHITE
HE HAS A BLOODY ARSENAL IN THAT PLACE OF HIS--AND I'VE BARELY BEGUN TO ROOT OUT ALL OF HIS HIDEY-HOLES.
NOT THE POINT! WHAT HAPPENED TO DUE PROCESS? CAN'T JUST TAKE IT UPON YOURSELF TO KILL OUR BIGGEST ANNUAL CONTRIBUTOR!
OH, IS THAT YOUR CONCERN? WELL, I'VE GOT GOOD NEWS FOR YOU, SIR.
NO DOUBT CERTAIN HE'D LIVE FOREVER, BLUEBEARD DIED WITHOUT LEAVING A WILL. THEREFORE, ALL OF HIS RICHES GO DIRECTLY TO FABLETOWN.
THAT IS HOW IT WORKS, ISN'T IT?
REALLY? NO WILL? YOU'RE POSITIVE?

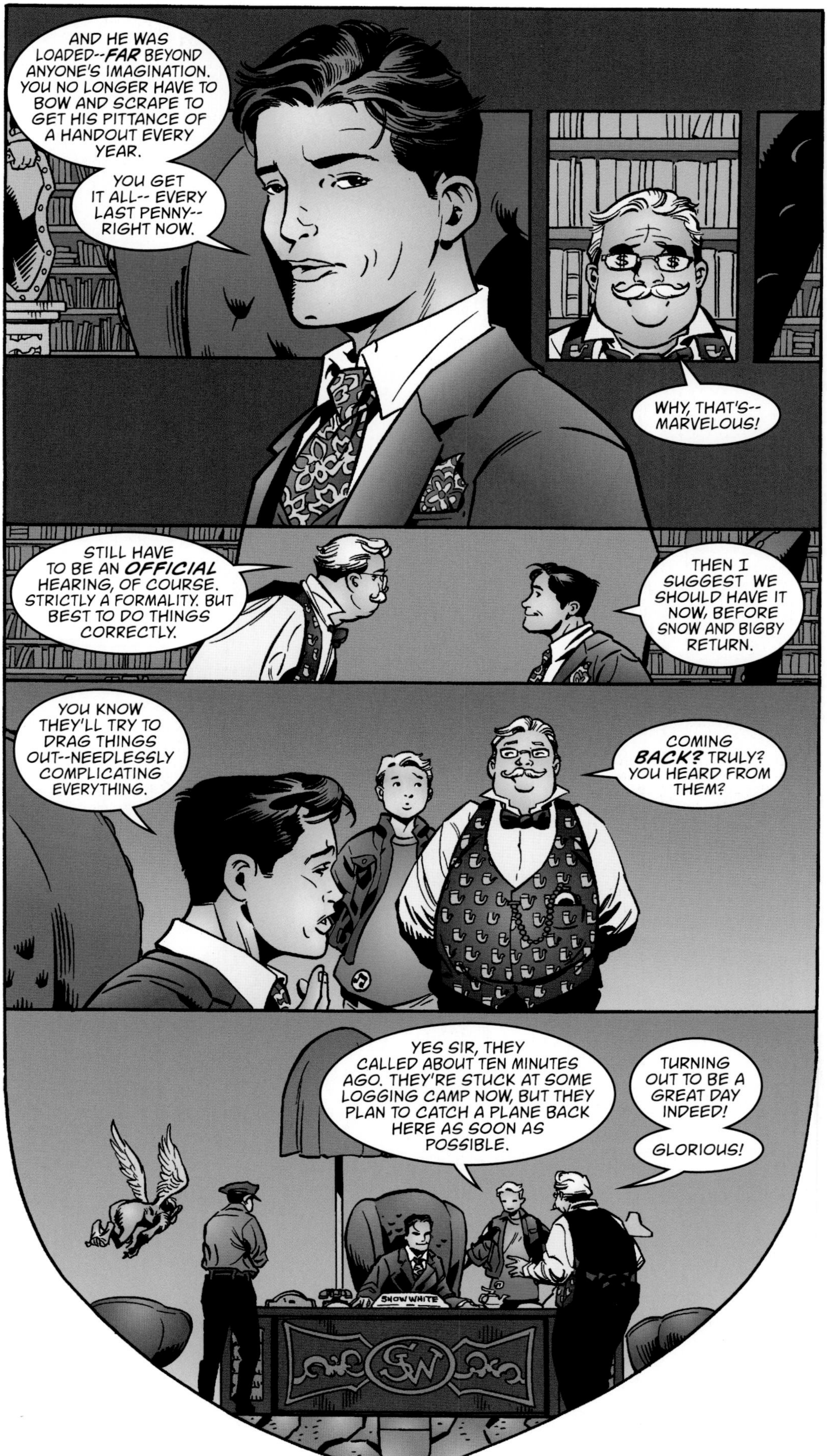
AND HE WAS LOADED--FAR BEYOND ANYONE'S IMAGINATION. YOU NO LONGER HAVE TO BOW AND SCRAPE TO GET HIS PITTANCE OF A HANDOUT EVERY YEAR.
YOU GET IT ALL-- EVERY LAST PENNY-- RIGHT NOW.
WHY, THAT'S-- MARVELOUS!
STILL HAVE TO BE AN OFFICIAL HEARING, OF COURSE. STRICTLY A FORMALITY. BUT BEST TO DO THINGS CORRECTLY.
THEN I SUGGEST WE SHOULD HAVE IT NOW, BEFORE SNOW AND BIGBY RETURN.
YOU KNOW THEY'LL TRY TO DRAG THINGS OUT--NEEDLESSLY COMPLICATING EVERYTHING.
COMING BACK? TRULY? YOU HEARD FROM THEM?
YES SIR, THEY CALLED ABOUT TEN MINUTES AGO. THEY'RE STUCK AT SOME LOGGING CAMP NOW, BUT THEY PLAN TO CATCH A PLANE BACK HERE AS SOON AS POSSIBLE.
TURNING OUT TO BE A GREAT DAY INDEED!
GLORIOUS!
SNOW WHITE
SW

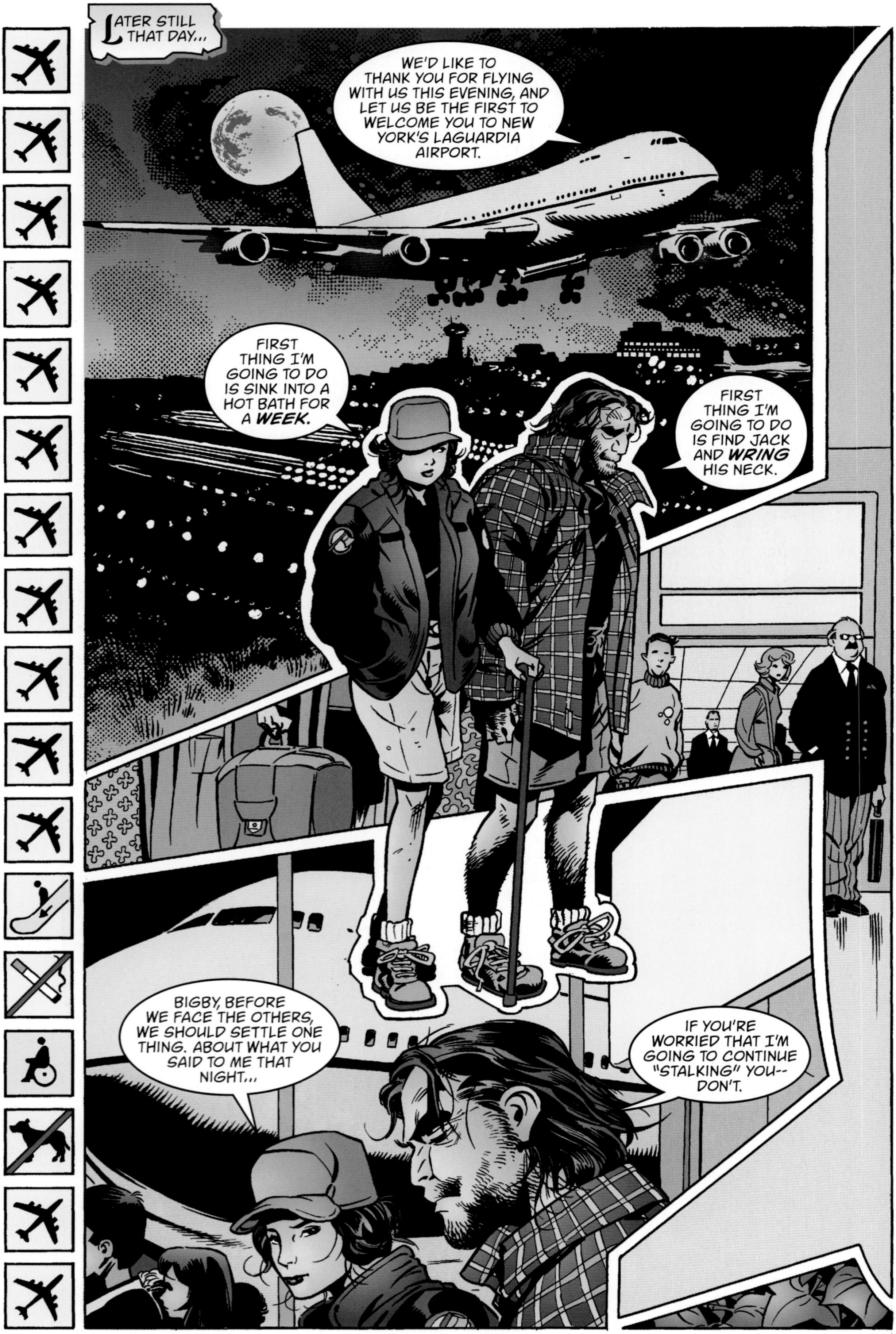
LATER STILL THAT DAY...
WE'D LIKE TO THANK YOU FOR FLYING WITH US THIS EVENING, AND LET US BE THE FIRST TO WELCOME YOU TO NEW YORK'S LAGUARDIA AIRPORT.
FIRST THING I'M GOING TO DO IS SINK INTO A HOT BATH FOR A WEEK.
FIRST THING I'M GOING TO DO IS FIND JACK AND WRING HIS NECK.
BIGBY, BEFORE WE FACE THE OTHERS, WE SHOULD SETTLE ONE THING. ABOUT WHAT YOU SAID TO ME THAT NIGHT...
IF YOU'RE WORRIED THAT I'M GOING TO CONTINUE "STALKING" YOU-- DON'T.

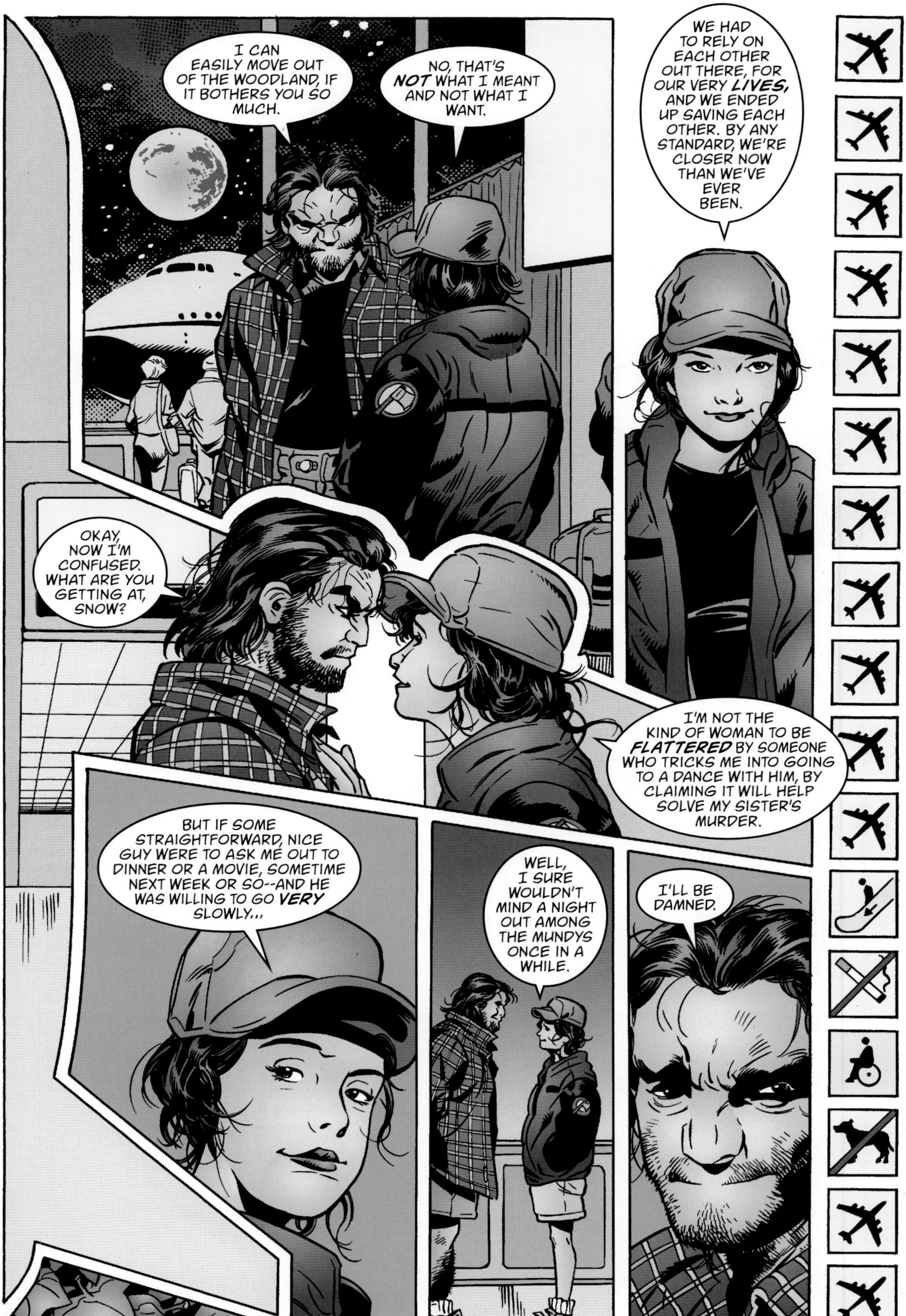
I CAN EASILY MOVE OUT OF THE WOODLAND, IF IT BOTHERS YOU SO MUCH.
NO, THAT'S NOT WHAT I MEANT AND NOT WHAT I WANT.
WE HAD TO RELY ON EACH OTHER OUT THERE, FOR OUR VERY LIVES, AND WE ENDED UP SAVING EACH OTHER. BY ANY STANDARD, WE'RE CLOSER NOW THAN WE'VE EVER BEEN.
OKAY, NOW I'M CONFUSED. WHAT ARE YOU GETTING AT, SNOW?
I'M NOT THE KIND OF WOMAN TO BE FLATTERED BY SOMEONE WHO TRICKS ME INTO GOING TO A DANCE WITH HIM, BY CLAIMING IT WILL HELP SOLVE MY SISTER'S MURDER.
BUT IF SOME STRAIGHTFORWARD, NICE GUY WERE TO ASK ME OUT TO DINNER OR A MOVIE, SOMETIME NEXT WEEK OR SO--AND HE WAS WILLING TO GO VERY SLOWLY...
WELL, I SURE WOULDN'T MIND A NIGHT OUT AMONG THE MUNDYS ONCE IN A WHILE.
I'LL BE DAMNED.

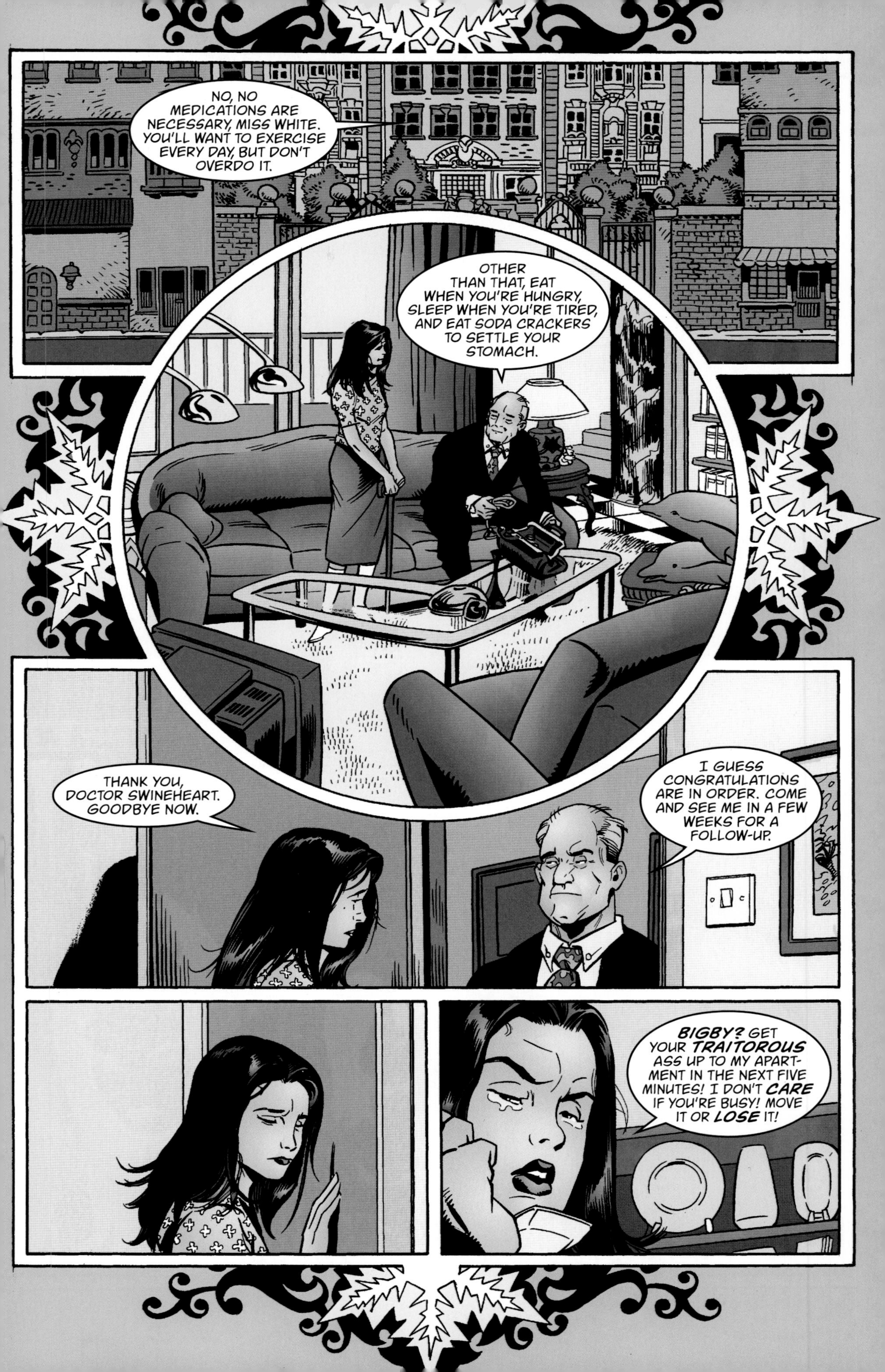

NO, NO MEDICATIONS ARE NECESSARY, MISS WHITE. YOU'LL WANT TO EXERCISE EVERY DAY, BUT DON'T OVERDO IT.
OTHER THAN THAT, EAT WHEN YOU'RE HUNGRY, SLEEP WHEN YOU'RE TIRED, AND EAT SODA CRACKERS TO SETTLE YOUR STOMACH.
THANK YOU, DOCTOR SWINEHEART. GOODBYE NOW.
I GUESS CONGRATULATIONS ARE IN ORDER. COME AND SEE ME IN A FEW WEEKS FOR A FOLLOW-UP.
BIGBY? GET YOUR TRAITOROUS ASS UP TO MY APARTMENT IN THE NEXT FIVE MINUTES! I DON'T CARE IF YOU'RE BUSY! MOVE IT OR LOSE IT!

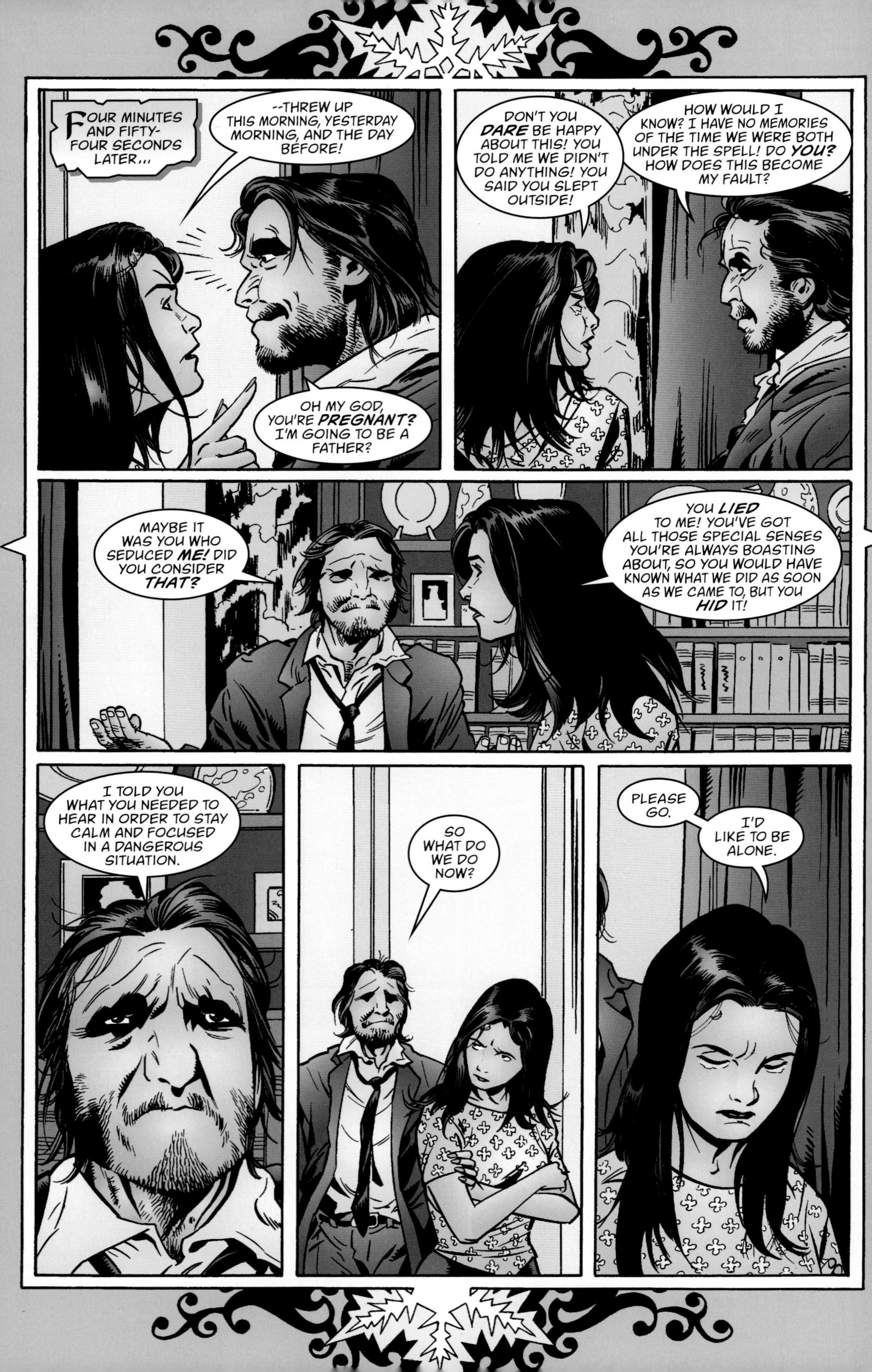
FOUR MINUTES AND FIFTY-FOUR SECONDS LATER...
--THREW UP THIS MORNING, YESTERDAY MORNING, AND THE DAY BEFORE!
OH MY GOD, YOU'RE PREGNANT? I'M GOING TO BE A FATHER?
DON'T YOU DARE BE HAPPY ABOUT THIS! YOU TOLD ME WE DIDN'T DO ANYTHING! YOU SAID YOU SLEPT OUTSIDE!
HOW WOULD I KNOW? I HAVE NO MEMORIES OF THE TIME WE WERE BOTH UNDER THE SPELL! DO YOU? HOW DOES THIS BECOME MY FAULT?
YOU LIED TO ME! YOU'VE GOT ALL THOSE SPECIAL SENSES YOU'RE ALWAYS BOASTING ABOUT, SO YOU WOULD HAVE KNOWN WHAT WE DID AS SOON AS WE CAME TO, BUT YOU HID IT!
MAYBE IT WAS YOU WHO SEDUCED ME! DID YOU CONSIDER THAT?
I TOLD YOU WHAT YOU NEEDED TO HEAR IN ORDER TO STAY CALM AND FOCUSED IN A DANGEROUS SITUATION.
SO WHAT DO WE DO NOW?
PLEASE GO.
I'D LIKE TO BE ALONE.

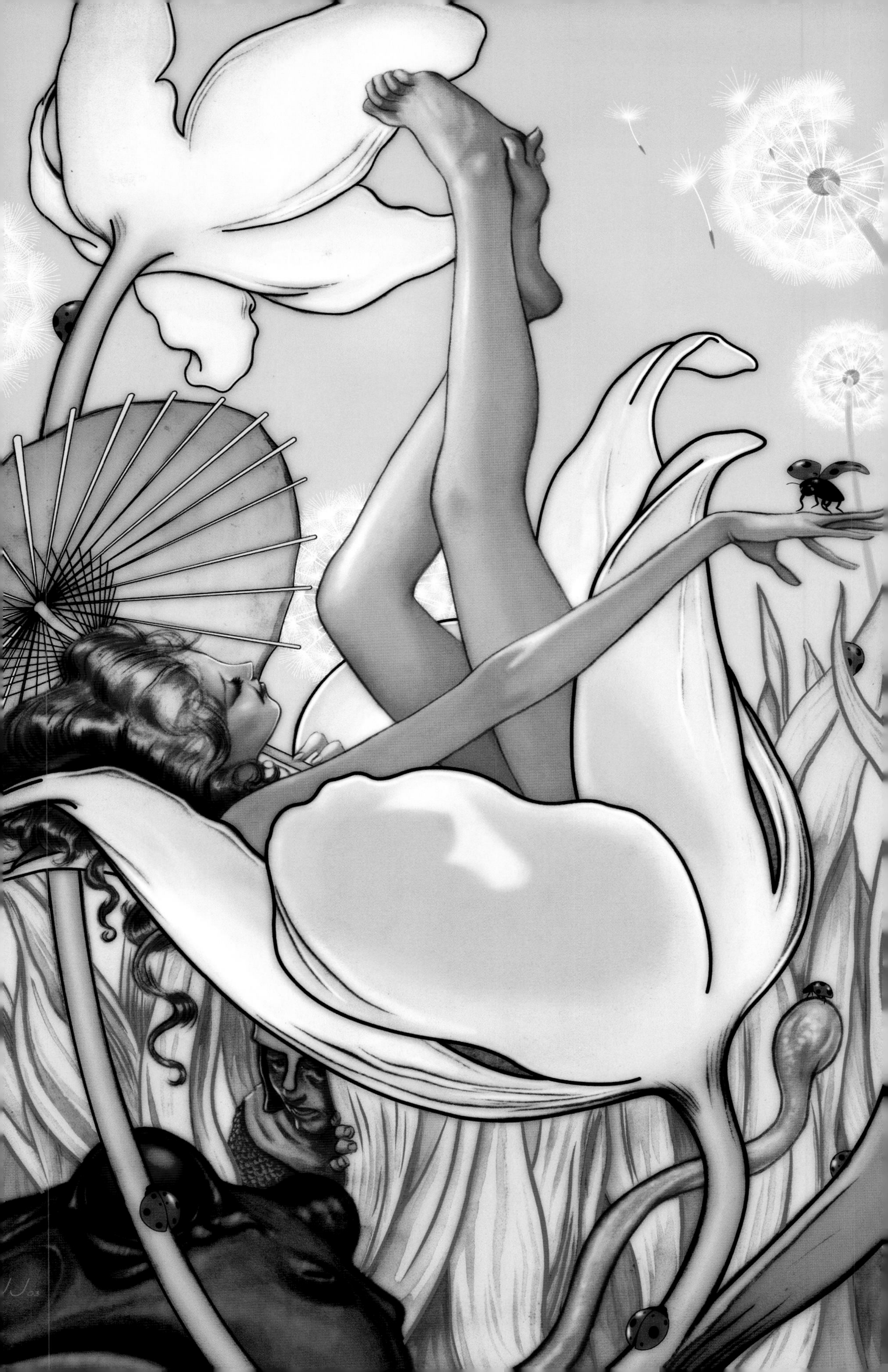

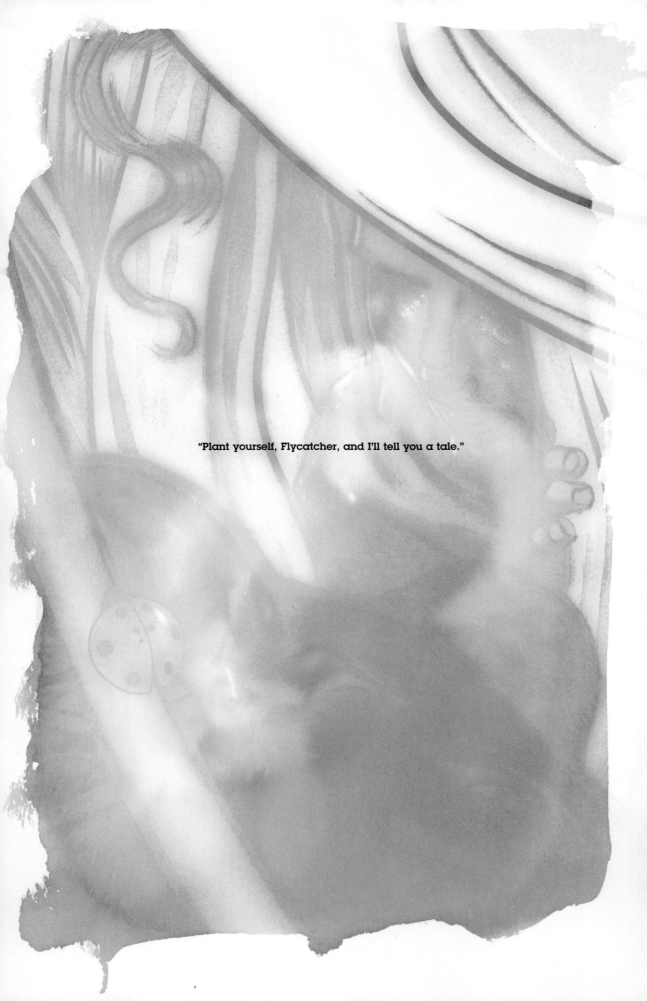

"Plant yourself, Flycatcher, and I'll tell you a tale."

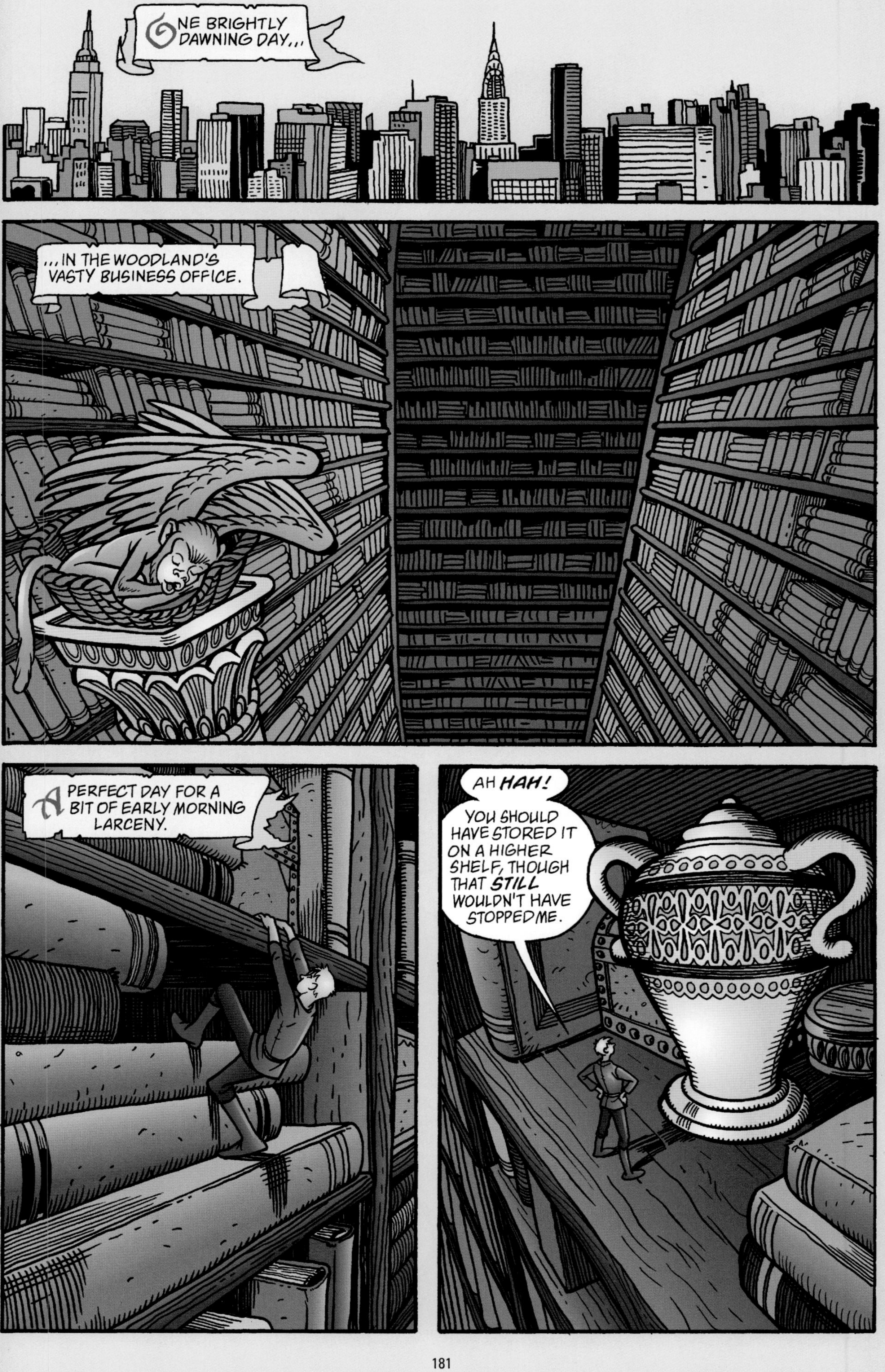
ONE BRIGHTLY DAWNING DAY...
...IN THE WOODLAND'S VASTY BUSINESS OFFICE.
A PERFECT DAY FOR A BIT OF EARLY MORNING LARCENY.
AH HAH!
YOU SHOULD HAVE STORED IT ON A HIGHER SHELF, THOUGH THAT STILL WOULDN'T HAVE STOPPED ME.

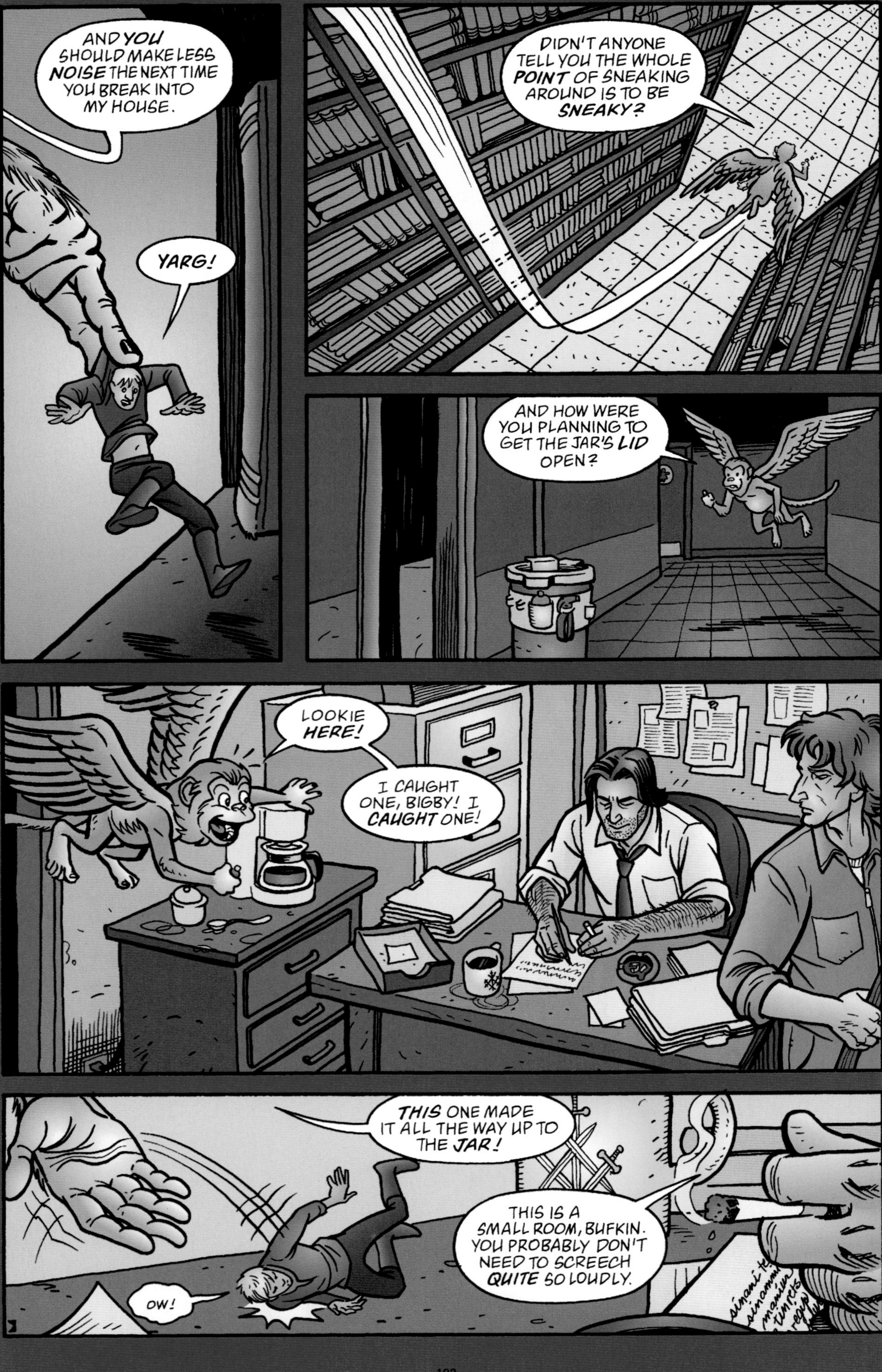
AND YOU SHOULD MAKE LESS NOISE THE NEXT TIME YOU BREAK INTO MY HOUSE.
YARG!
DIDN'T ANYONE TELL YOU THE WHOLE POINT OF SNEAKING AROUND IS TO BE SNEAKY?
AND HOW WERE YOU PLANNING TO GET THE JAR'S LID OPEN?
LOOKIE HERE!
I CAUGHT ONE, BIGBY! I CAUGHT ONE!
THIS ONE MADE IT ALL THE WAY UP TO THE JAR!
OW!
THIS IS A SMALL ROOM, BUFKIN. YOU PROBABLY DON'T NEED TO SCREECH QUITE SO LOUDLY.

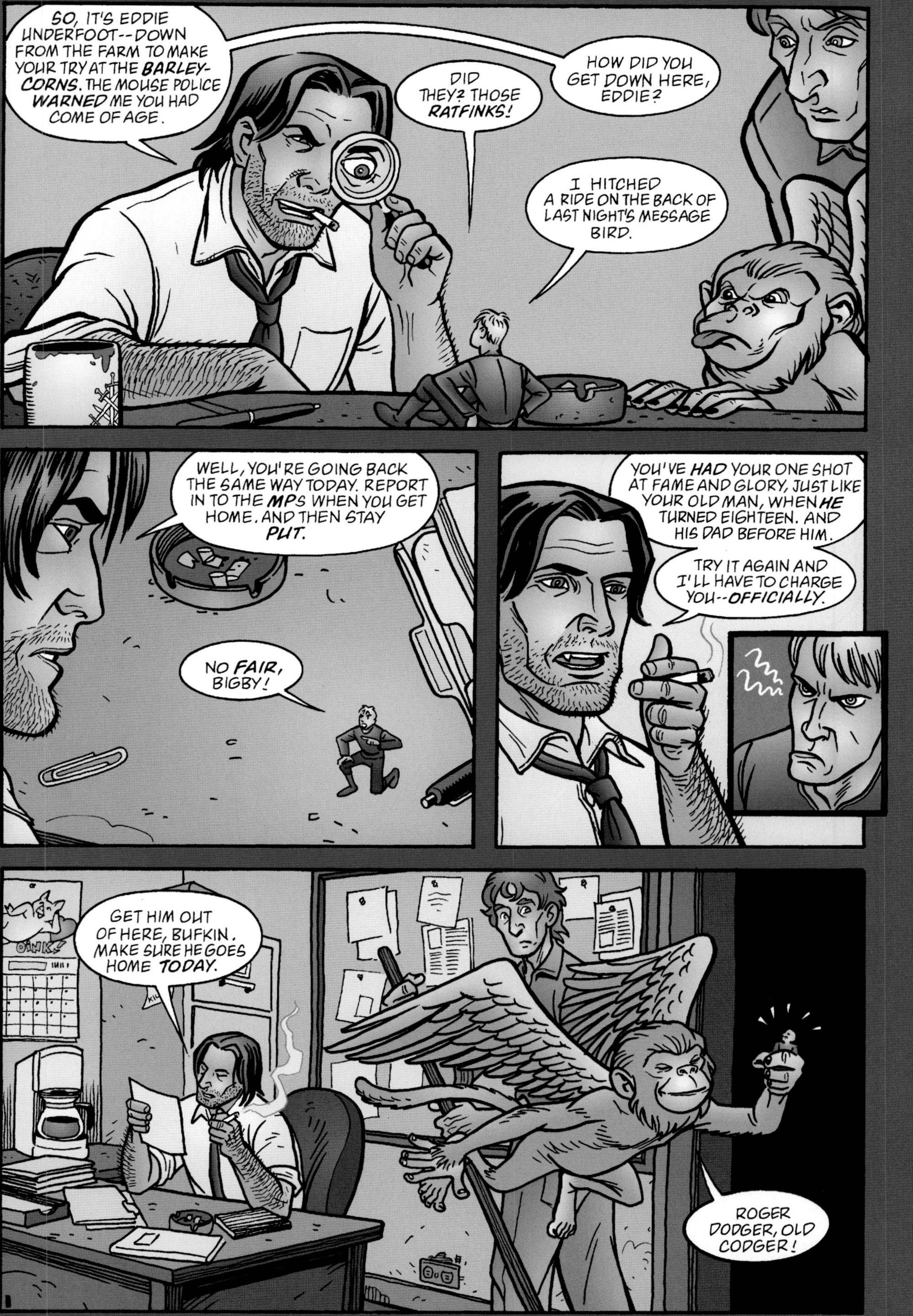

SO, IT'S EDDIE UNDERFOOT--DOWN FROM THE FARM TO MAKE YOUR TRY AT THE BARLEY-CORNS. THE MOUSE POLICE WARNED ME YOU HAD COME OF AGE.
DID THEY? THOSE RATFINKS!
HOW DID YOU GET DOWN HERE, EDDIE?
I HITCHED A RIDE ON THE BACK OF LAST NIGHT'S MESSAGE BIRD.
WELL, YOU'RE GOING BACK THE SAME WAY TODAY. REPORT IN TO THE MPs WHEN YOU GET HOME. AND THEN STAY PUT.
NO FAIR, BIGBY!
YOU'VE HAD YOUR ONE SHOT AT FAME AND GLORY, JUST LIKE YOUR OLD MAN, WHEN HE TURNED EIGHTEEN. AND HIS DAD BEFORE HIM.
TRY IT AGAIN AND I'LL HAVE TO CHARGE YOU--OFFICIALLY.
GET HIM OUT OF HERE, BUFKIN. MAKE SURE HE GOES HOME TODAY.
ROGER DODGER, OLD CODGER!

BIGBY?

HMMM?

I DON'T GET IT. YOU LET THAT KID GO WITH JUST A *WARNING*?

YEAH. SO *WHAT*?

YOU CHARGE *ME* EACH TIME YOU CATCH ME EATING FLIES, WHICH IS ONLY A *MINOR* OFFENSE, BUT TRYING TO STEAL *MAGIC* STUFF FROM THE BUSINESS OFFICE IS A GREAT BIG *CRIME*.

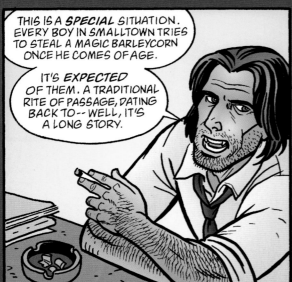

THIS IS A *SPECIAL* SITUATION. EVERY BOY IN *SMALLTOWN* TRIES TO STEAL A MAGIC BARLEYCORN ONCE HE COMES OF AGE.

IT'S *EXPECTED* OF THEM. A TRADITIONAL RITE OF PASSAGE, DATING BACK TO-- WELL, IT'S A LONG STORY.

I'VE GOT TIME.

WHAT THE HELL. WHY NOT?

PLANT YOURSELF, FLYCATCHER, AND I'LL TELL YOU A TALE.

184

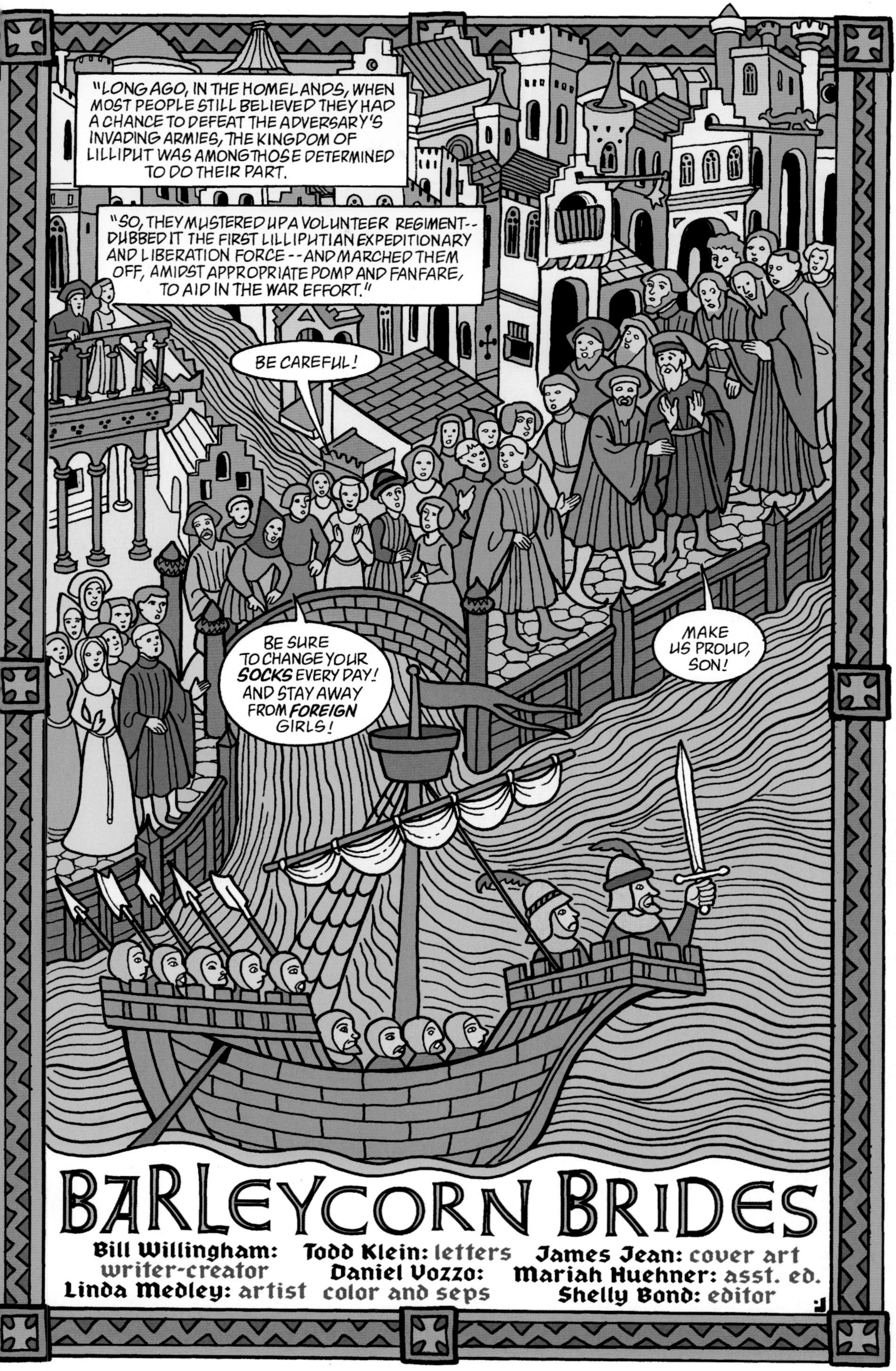
"LONG AGO, IN THE HOMELANDS, WHEN MOST PEOPLE STILL BELIEVED THEY HAD A CHANCE TO DEFEAT THE ADVERSARY'S INVADING ARMIES, THE KINGDOM OF LILLIPUT WAS AMONG THOSE DETERMINED TO DO THEIR PART.
"SO, THEY MUSTERED UP A VOLUNTEER REGIMENT--DUBBED IT THE FIRST LILLIPUTIAN EXPEDITIONARY AND LIBERATION FORCE--AND MARCHED THEM OFF, AMIDST APPROPRIATE POMP AND FANFARE, TO AID IN THE WAR EFFORT."
BE CAREFUL!
BE SURE TO CHANGE YOUR SOCKS EVERY DAY! AND STAY AWAY FROM FOREIGN GIRLS!
MAKE US PROUD, SON!
BARLEYCORN BRIDES
Bill Willingham: writer-creator
Linda Medley: artist
Todd Klein: letters
Daniel Vozzo: color and seps
James Jean: cover art
Mariah Huehner: asst. ed.
Shelly Bond: editor

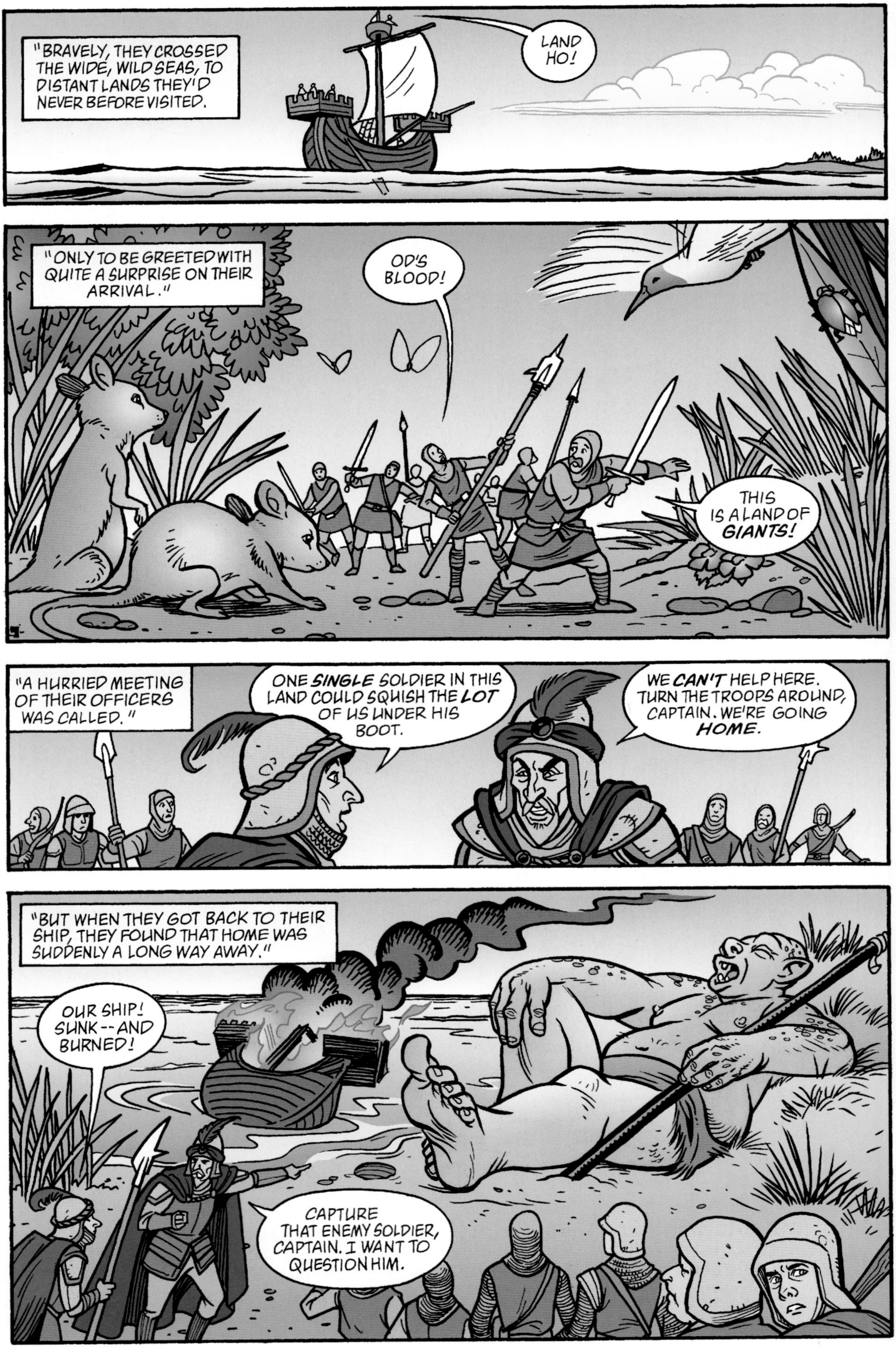
"BRAVELY, THEY CROSSED THE WIDE, WILD SEAS, TO DISTANT LANDS THEY'D NEVER BEFORE VISITED.
LAND HO!
"ONLY TO BE GREETED WITH QUITE A SURPRISE ON THEIR ARRIVAL."
OD'S BLOOD!
THIS IS A LAND OF GIANTS!
"A HURRIED MEETING OF THEIR OFFICERS WAS CALLED."
ONE SINGLE SOLDIER IN THIS LAND COULD SQUISH THE LOT OF US UNDER HIS BOOT.
WE CAN'T HELP HERE. TURN THE TROOPS AROUND, CAPTAIN. WE'RE GOING HOME.
"BUT WHEN THEY GOT BACK TO THEIR SHIP, THEY FOUND THAT HOME WAS SUDDENLY A LONG WAY AWAY."
OUR SHIP! SUNK--AND BURNED!
CAPTURE THAT ENEMY SOLDIER, CAPTAIN. I WANT TO QUESTION HIM.

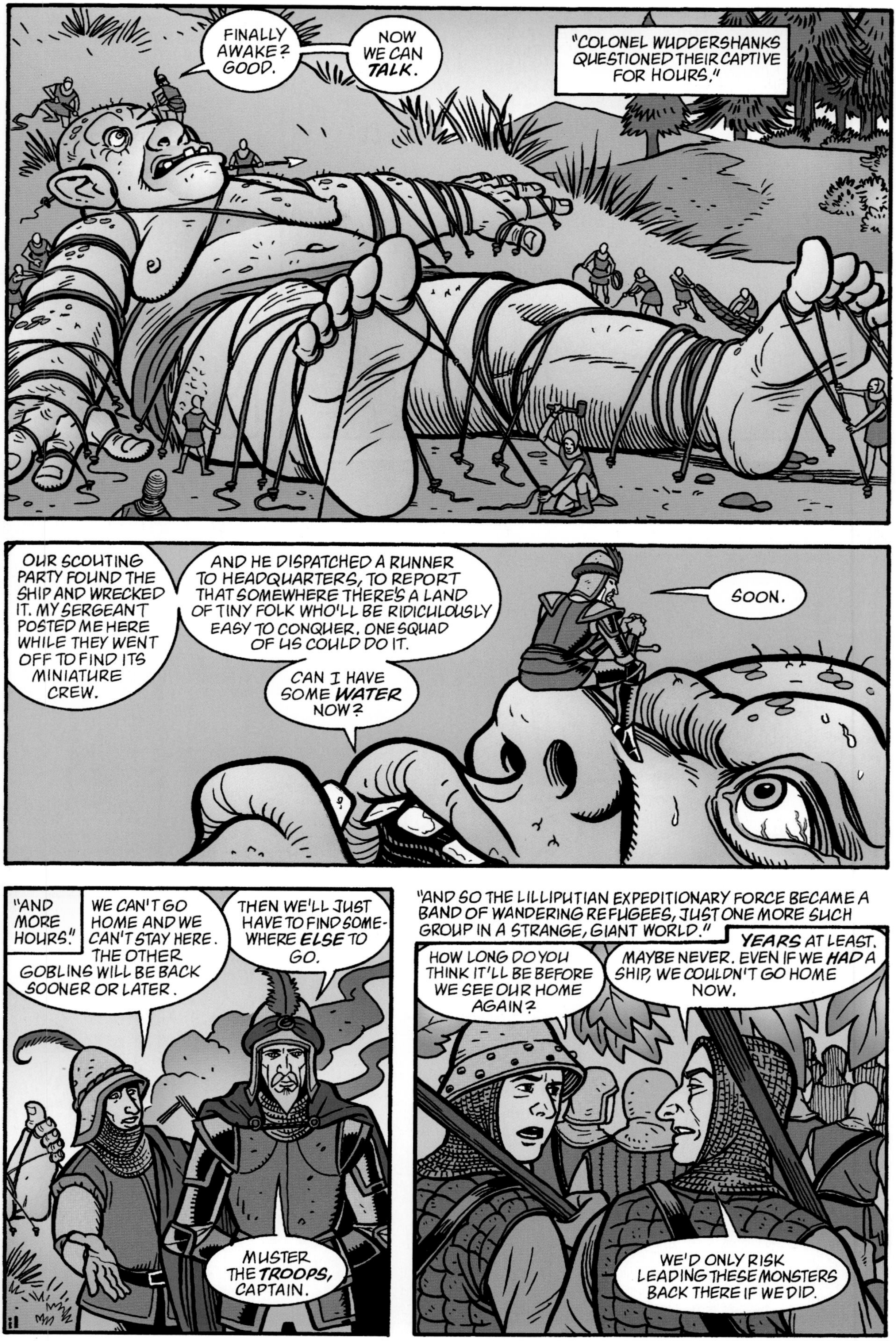
FINALLY AWAKE? GOOD.
NOW WE CAN TALK.
"COLONEL WUDDERSHANKS QUESTIONED THEIR CAPTIVE FOR HOURS."
OUR SCOUTING PARTY FOUND THE SHIP AND WRECKED IT. MY SERGEANT POSTED ME HERE WHILE THEY WENT OFF TO FIND ITS MINIATURE CREW.
AND HE DISPATCHED A RUNNER TO HEADQUARTERS, TO REPORT THAT SOMEWHERE THERE'S A LAND OF TINY FOLK WHO'LL BE RIDICULOUSLY EASY TO CONQUER. ONE SQUAD OF US COULD DO IT.
CAN I HAVE SOME WATER NOW?
SOON.
"AND MORE HOURS."
WE CAN'T GO HOME AND WE CAN'T STAY HERE. THE OTHER GOBLINS WILL BE BACK SOONER OR LATER.
THEN WE'LL JUST HAVE TO FIND SOMEWHERE ELSE TO GO.
MUSTER THE TROOPS, CAPTAIN.
"AND SO THE LILLIPUTIAN EXPEDITIONARY FORCE BECAME A BAND OF WANDERING REFUGEES, JUST ONE MORE SUCH GROUP IN A STRANGE, GIANT WORLD."
HOW LONG DO YOU THINK IT'LL BE BEFORE WE SEE OUR HOME AGAIN?
YEARS AT LEAST. MAYBE NEVER. EVEN IF WE HAD A SHIP, WE COULDN'T GO HOME NOW.
WE'D ONLY RISK LEADING THESE MONSTERS BACK THERE IF WE DID.

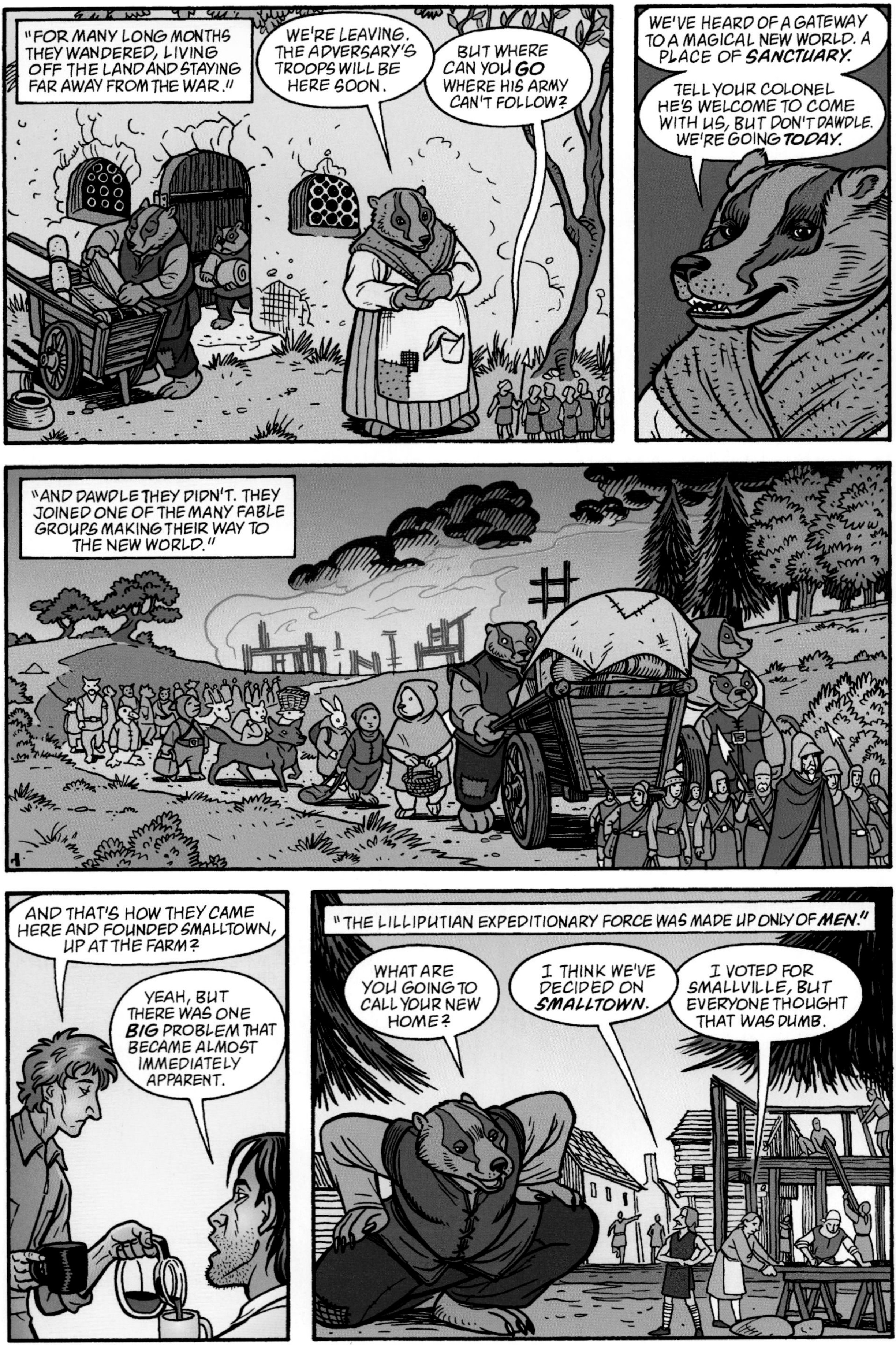
"FOR MANY LONG MONTHS THEY WANDERED, LIVING OFF THE LAND AND STAYING FAR AWAY FROM THE WAR."
WE'RE LEAVING. THE ADVERSARY'S TROOPS WILL BE HERE SOON.
BUT WHERE CAN YOU GO WHERE HIS ARMY CAN'T FOLLOW?
WE'VE HEARD OF A GATEWAY TO A MAGICAL NEW WORLD. A PLACE OF SANCTUARY.
TELL YOUR COLONEL HE'S WELCOME TO COME WITH US, BUT DON'T DAWDLE. WE'RE GOING TODAY.
"AND DAWDLE THEY DIDN'T. THEY JOINED ONE OF THE MANY FABLE GROUPS MAKING THEIR WAY TO THE NEW WORLD."
AND THAT'S HOW THEY CAME HERE AND FOUNDED SMALLTOWN, UP AT THE FARM?
YEAH, BUT THERE WAS ONE BIG PROBLEM THAT BECAME ALMOST IMMEDIATELY APPARENT.
"THE LILLIPUTIAN EXPEDITIONARY FORCE WAS MADE UP ONLY OF MEN."
WHAT ARE YOU GOING TO CALL YOUR NEW HOME?
I THINK WE'VE DECIDED ON SMALLTOWN.
I VOTED FOR SMALLVILLE, BUT EVERYONE THOUGHT THAT WAS DUMB.

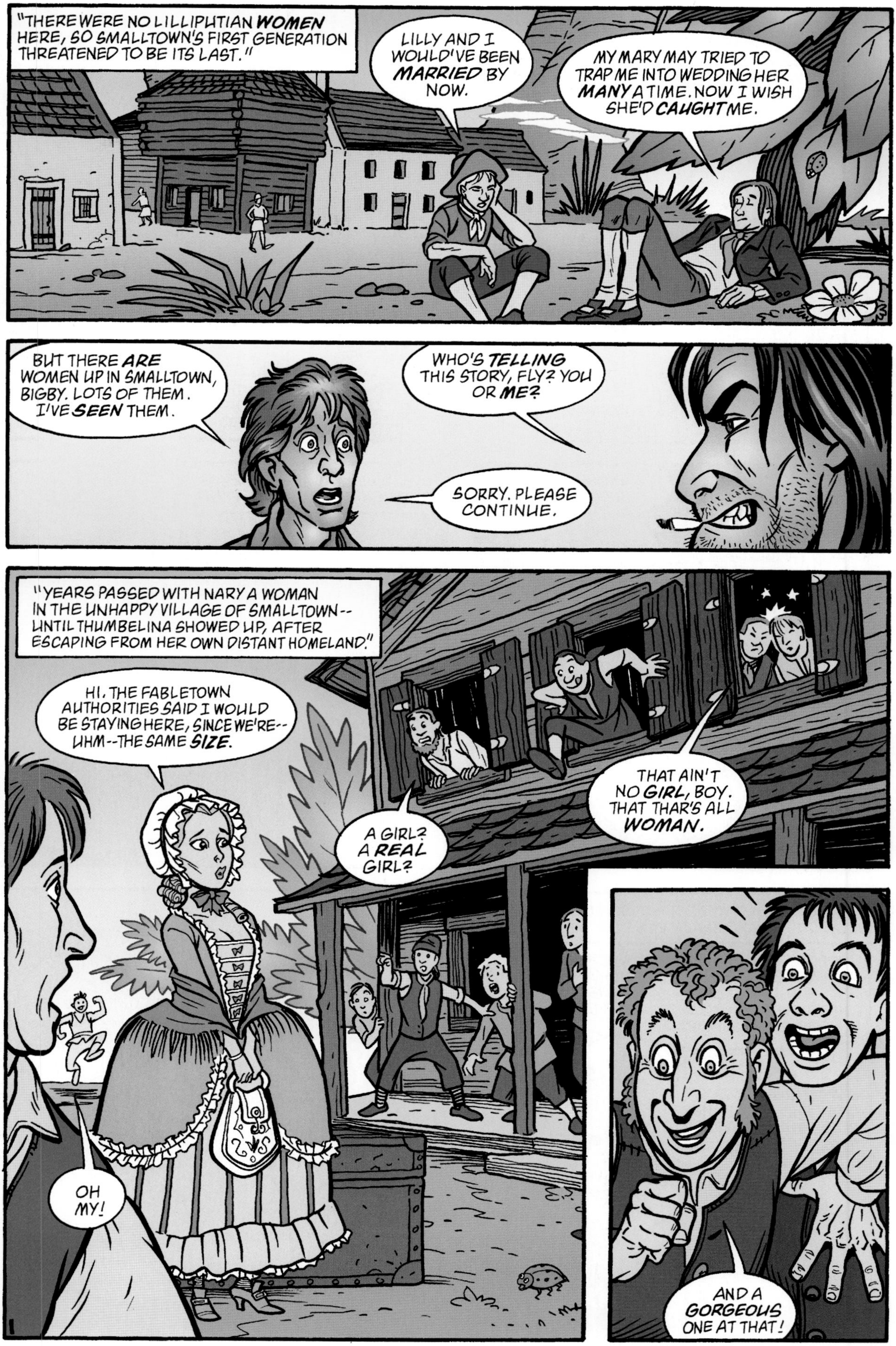
"THERE WERE NO LILLIPUTIAN WOMEN HERE, SO SMALLTOWN'S FIRST GENERATION THREATENED TO BE ITS LAST."
LILLY AND I WOULD'VE BEEN MARRIED BY NOW.
MY MARY MAY TRIED TO TRAP ME INTO WEDDING HER MANY A TIME. NOW I WISH SHE'D CAUGHT ME.
BUT THERE ARE WOMEN UP IN SMALLTOWN, BIGBY. LOTS OF THEM. I'VE SEEN THEM.
WHO'S TELLING THIS STORY, FLY? YOU OR ME?
SORRY. PLEASE CONTINUE.
"YEARS PASSED WITH NARY A WOMAN IN THE UNHAPPY VILLAGE OF SMALLTOWN-- UNTIL THUMBELINA SHOWED UP, AFTER ESCAPING FROM HER OWN DISTANT HOMELAND."
HI. THE FABLETOWN AUTHORITIES SAID I WOULD BE STAYING HERE, SINCE WE'RE-- UHM--THE SAME SIZE.
A GIRL? A REAL GIRL?
THAT AIN'T NO GIRL, BOY. THAT THAR'S ALL WOMAN.
OH MY!
AND A GORGEOUS ONE AT THAT!

"AND OF COURSE, THAT ONLY MADE THINGS *WORSE*."

PLEASANT DAY, MISSY THUMBELINA.

YOU'RE LOOKING AS *PRETTY* AS A STRAWBERRY *PIE*, THUMBELINA. MIGHT I CALL ON YOU LATER TO--

"NO WOMEN AT ALL WAS BAD ENOUGH. BUT ONLY *ONE* WOMAN--

"--WITH EVERY MAN KNOWING ONLY ONE OF THEM COULD EVENTUALLY WIN HER--WELL, THAT WAS INTOLERABLE.

ANYONE KNOW WHAT THEY'RE FIGHTING ABOUT?

TAKE ONE GUESS.

WHAT'S *EVERY* FIGHT ABOUT?

"EVERYONE WAS MISERABLE, NOT THE LEAST OF WHOM OUR PERPETUAL BELLE OF THE BALL.

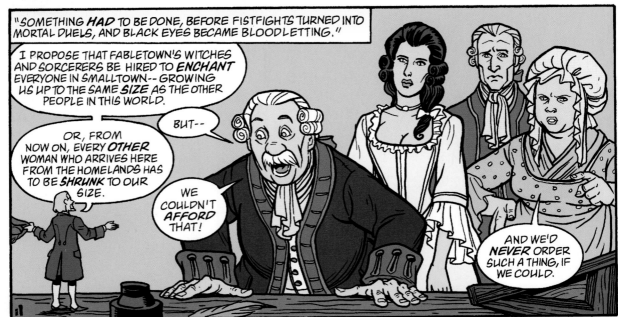

"SOMETHING *HAD* TO BE DONE, BEFORE FISTFIGHTS TURNED INTO MORTAL DUELS, AND BLACK EYES BECAME BLOODLETTING."

I PROPOSE THAT FABLETOWN'S WITCHES AND SORCERERS BE HIRED TO *ENCHANT* EVERYONE IN SMALLTOWN--GROWING US UP TO THE SAME *SIZE* AS THE OTHER PEOPLE IN THIS WORLD.

BUT--

OR, FROM NOW ON, EVERY *OTHER* WOMAN WHO ARRIVES HERE FROM THE HOMELANDS HAS TO BE *SHRUNK* TO OUR SIZE.

WE COULDN'T *AFFORD* THAT!

AND WE'D *NEVER* ORDER SUCH A THING, IF WE COULD.

"THE EVENTUAL SOLUTION TO THEIR DILEMMA CAME FROM AN UNEXPECTED CORNER."

SO MY MOTHER-TO-BE PLANTED THAT KERNEL OF BARLEYCORN IN A FLOWER POT.

"BY THEN, EVERYONE KNEW THUMBELINA'S STORY-- HOW SHE CAME INTO THE WORLD."

AND A *TULIP* GREW OUT OF IT AND I SPRANG OUT OF THE TULIP BLOSSOM.

"NOW THAT SAME VERY GOOD WITCH-- WHO GAVE THE BARLEYCORN TO THE WOMAN TO GROW HERSELF A DAUGHTER-- HAD ESCAPED THE ADVERSARY AND WAS EVEN THEN LIVING IN FABLETOWN."

OH YES, GAFFER WOLF, I HAD ME A WHOLE *JAR* FULL OF THEM MAGIC BARLEYCORNS--FULL TO THE *TOP.*

BUT I DIDN'T ESCAPE WITH THEM. I HAD TOO MUCH TO CARRY AS IT WAS.

I IMAGINE THAT JAR MIGHT STILL *BE* THERE, BACK IN MY OLD COTTAGE.

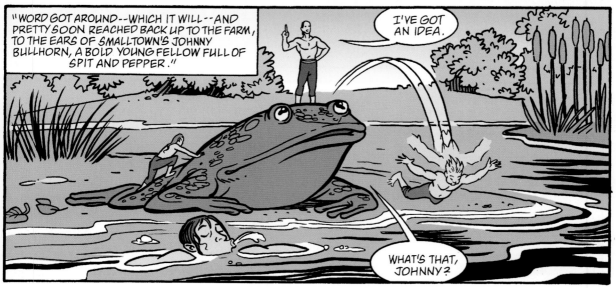

"WORD GOT AROUND--WHICH IT WILL--AND PRETTY SOON REACHED BACK UP TO THE FARM, TO THE EARS OF SMALLTOWN'S JOHNNY BULLHORN, A BOLD YOUNG FELLOW FULL OF SPIT AND PEPPER."

I'VE GOT AN IDEA.

WHAT'S THAT, JOHNNY?

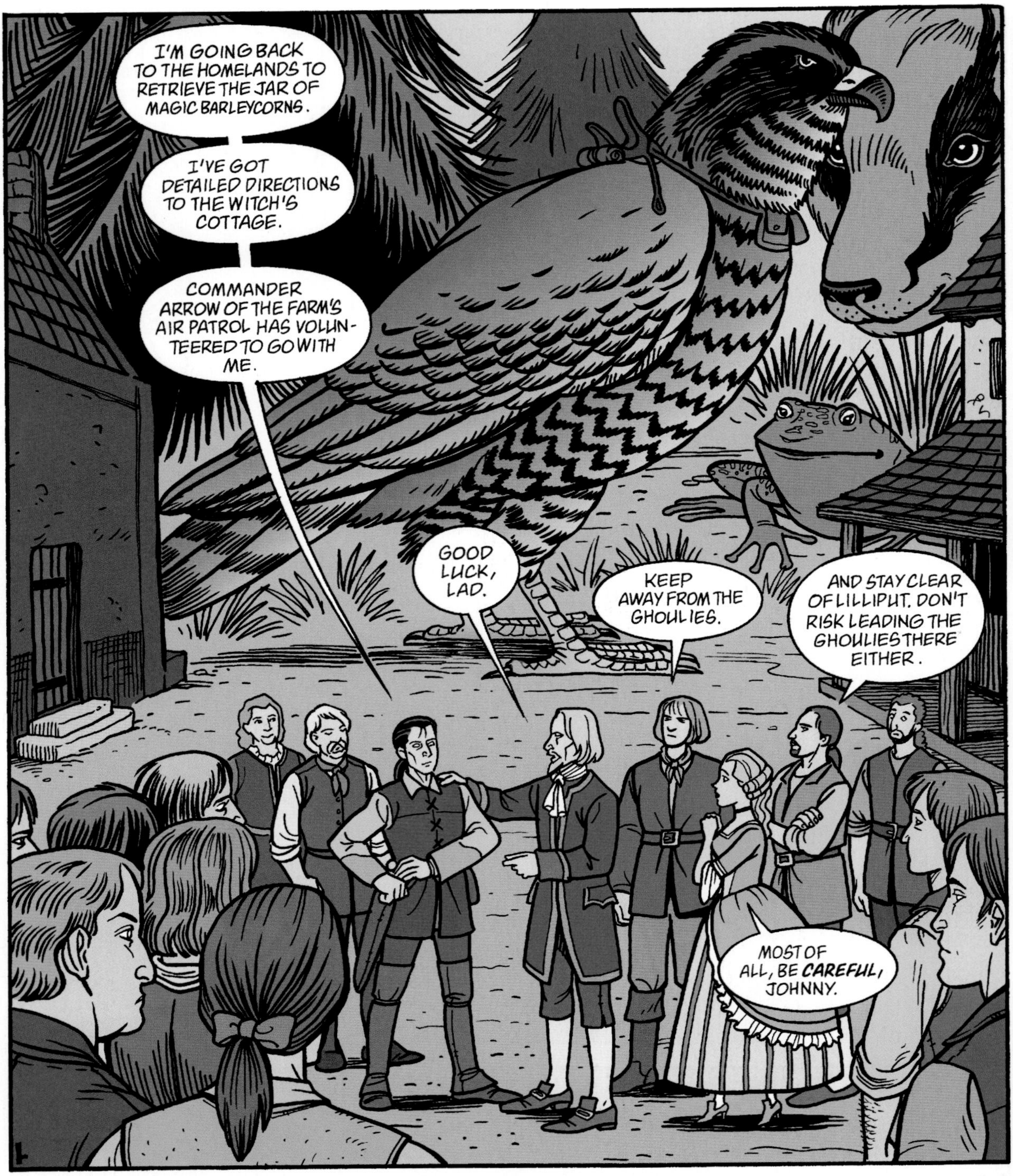
I'M GOING BACK TO THE HOMELANDS TO RETRIEVE THE JAR OF MAGIC BARLEYCORNS.
I'VE GOT DETAILED DIRECTIONS TO THE WITCH'S COTTAGE.
COMMANDER ARROW OF THE FARM'S AIR PATROL HAS VOLUNTEERED TO GO WITH ME.
GOOD LUCK, LAD.
KEEP AWAY FROM THE GHOULIES.
AND STAY CLEAR OF LILLIPUT. DON'T RISK LEADING THE GHOULIES THERE EITHER.
MOST OF ALL, BE **CAREFUL**, JOHNNY.

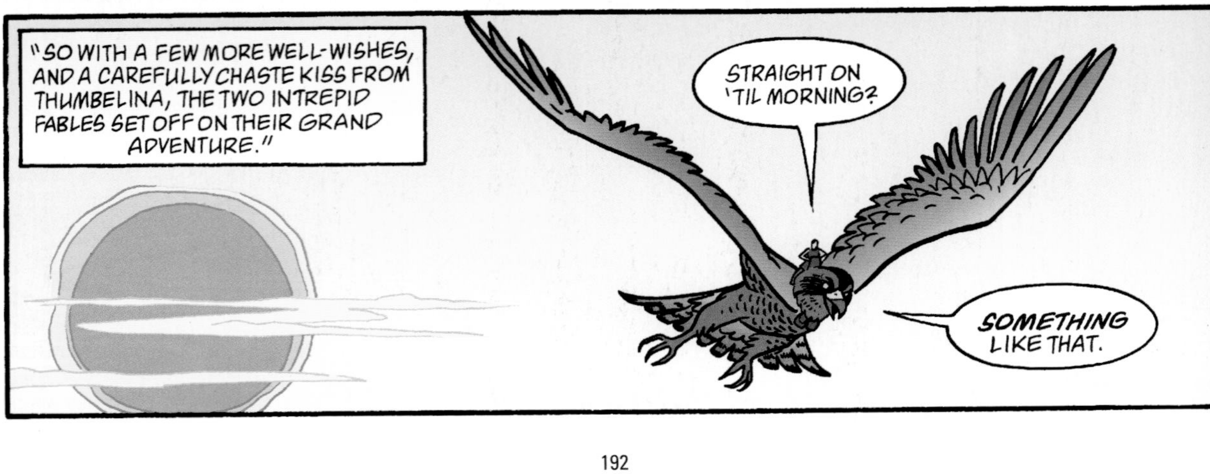
"SO WITH A FEW MORE WELL-WISHES, AND A CAREFULLY CHASTE KISS FROM THUMBELINA, THE TWO INTREPID FABLES SET OFF ON THEIR GRAND ADVENTURE."
STRAIGHT ON 'TIL MORNING?
SOMETHING LIKE THAT.

" THEY PASSED BACK INTO THE HOMELANDS THROUGH THE OAK HOLLOWS GATE. THIS WAS STILL CLOSE TO FORTY YEARS BEFORE THE ADVERSARY'S WARLOCKS WOULD FIND AND DESTROY IT.

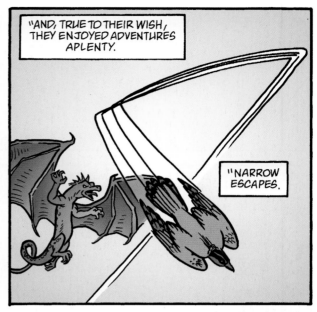

"AND, TRUE TO THEIR WISH, THEY ENJOYED ADVENTURES APLENTY.

"NARROW ESCAPES.

"INCLEMENT WEATHER.

"AND COUNTLESS OTHER HARDSHIPS."

YOU'LL HARDLY MAKE A MOUTHFUL.

COME ANY **CLOSER** AND YOU'LL NIBBLE ON AN INCH OF GOOD MILDENDAN STEEL.

WHAT WAS **THAT** ALL ABOUT?

A GUEST TO SHARE OUR **LUNCH**, BUT HE COULDN'T STAY.

BAH! HE WAS TOO SMALL TO BE RIPE YET ANYWAY.

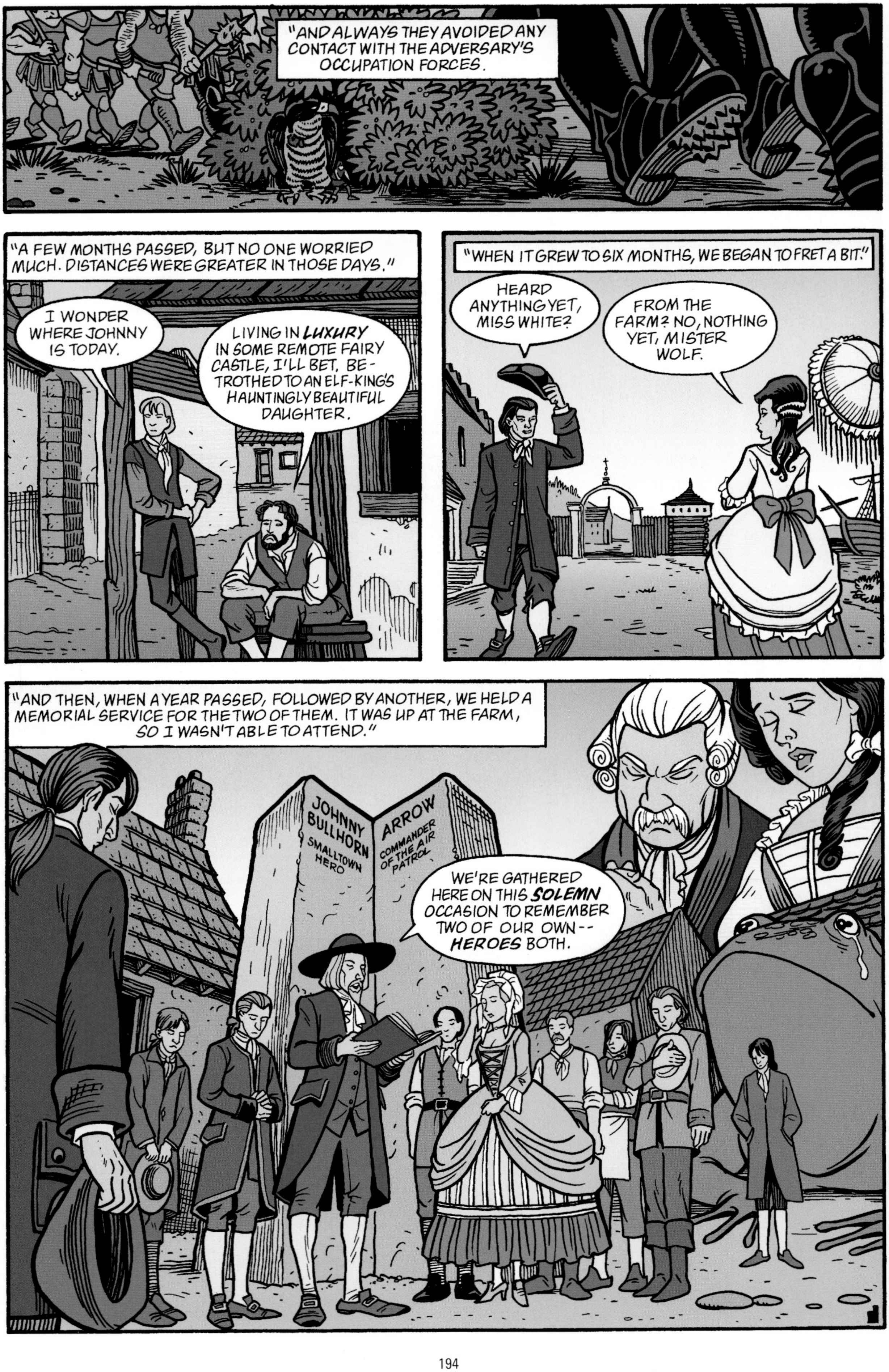
"AND ALWAYS THEY AVOIDED ANY CONTACT WITH THE ADVERSARY'S OCCUPATION FORCES.
"A FEW MONTHS PASSED, BUT NO ONE WORRIED MUCH. DISTANCES WERE GREATER IN THOSE DAYS."
I WONDER WHERE JOHNNY IS TODAY.
LIVING IN LUXURY IN SOME REMOTE FAIRY CASTLE, I'LL BET, BETROTHED TO AN ELF-KING'S HAUNTINGLY BEAUTIFUL DAUGHTER.
"WHEN IT GREW TO SIX MONTHS, WE BEGAN TO FRET A BIT."
HEARD ANYTHING YET, MISS WHITE?
FROM THE FARM? NO, NOTHING YET, MISTER WOLF.
"AND THEN, WHEN A YEAR PASSED, FOLLOWED BY ANOTHER, WE HELD A MEMORIAL SERVICE FOR THE TWO OF THEM. IT WAS UP AT THE FARM, SO I WASN'T ABLE TO ATTEND."
JOHNNY BULLHORN
SMALLTOWN HERO
ARROW
COMMANDER OF THE AIR PATROL
WE'RE GATHERED HERE ON THIS SOLEMN OCCASION TO REMEMBER TWO OF OUR OWN-- HEROES BOTH.

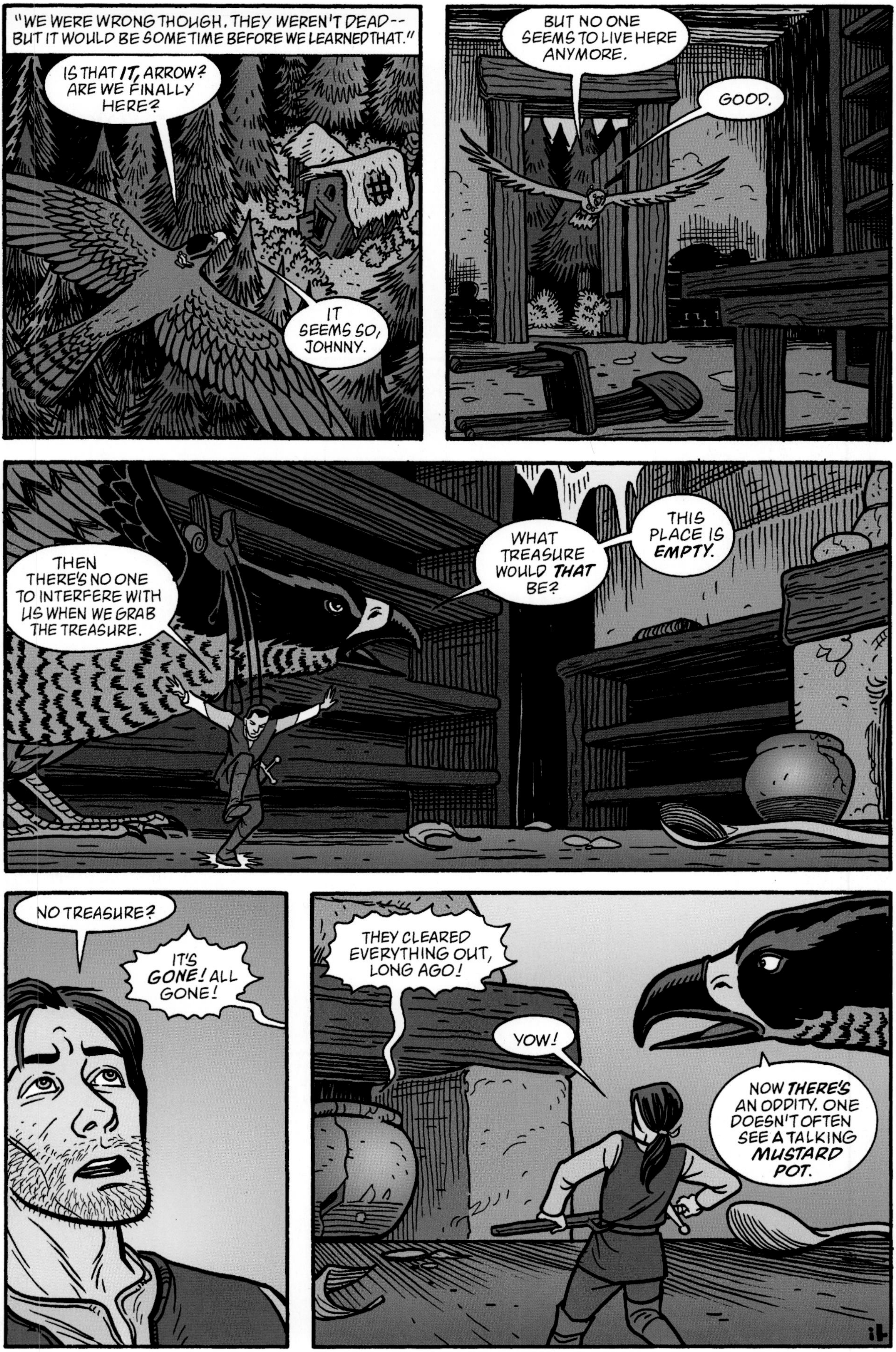
"WE WERE WRONG THOUGH. THEY WEREN'T DEAD-- BUT IT WOULD BE SOME TIME BEFORE WE LEARNED THAT."
IS THAT IT, ARROW? ARE WE FINALLY HERE?
IT SEEMS SO, JOHNNY.
BUT NO ONE SEEMS TO LIVE HERE ANYMORE.
GOOD.
THEN THERE'S NO ONE TO INTERFERE WITH US WHEN WE GRAB THE TREASURE.
WHAT TREASURE WOULD THAT BE?
THIS PLACE IS EMPTY.
NO TREASURE?
IT'S GONE! ALL GONE!
THEY CLEARED EVERYTHING OUT, LONG AGO!
YOW!
NOW THERE'S AN ODDITY. ONE DOESN'T OFTEN SEE A TALKING MUSTARD POT.

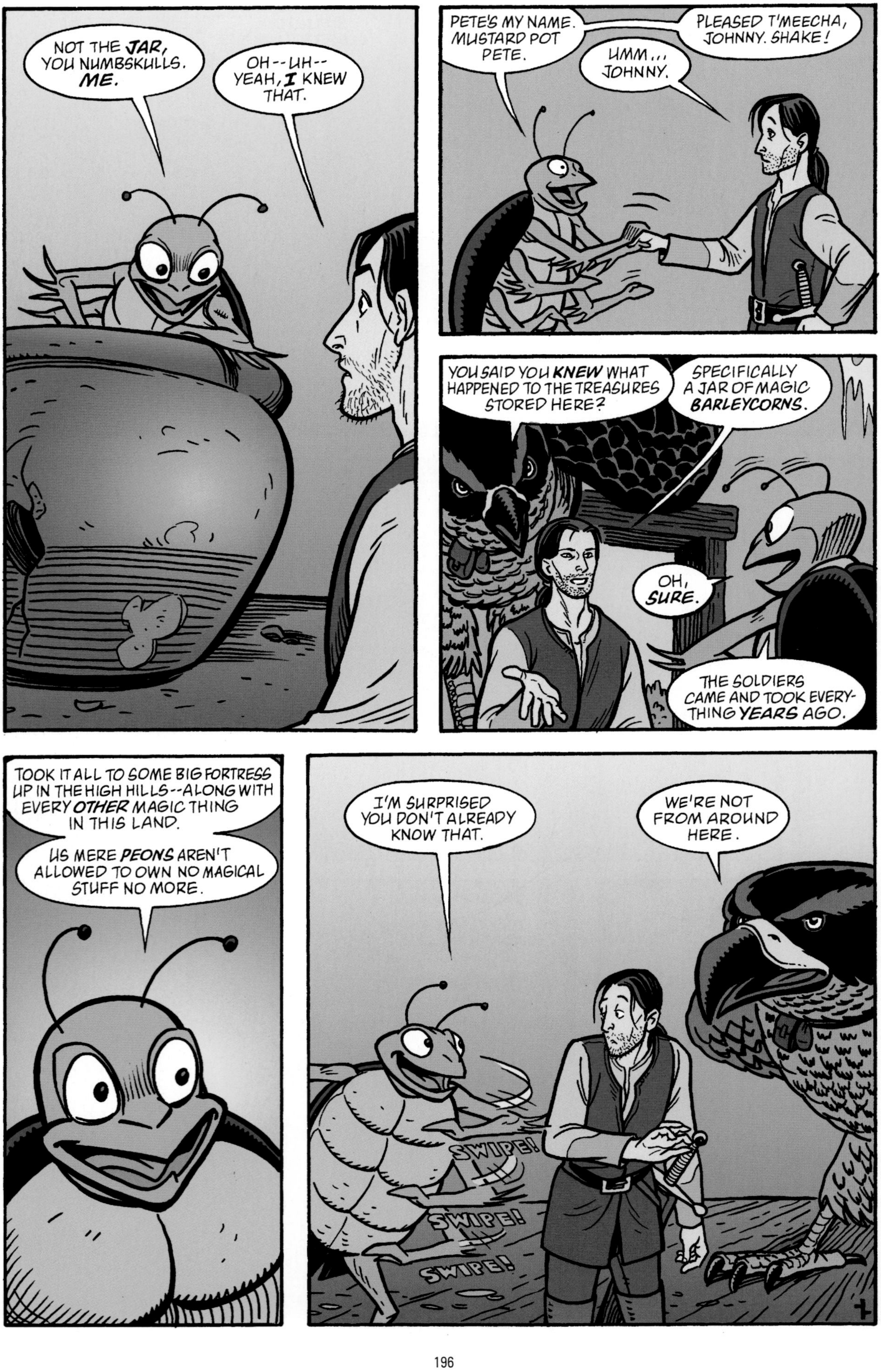
NOT THE JAR, YOU NUMBSKULLS. ME.
OH--UH-- YEAH, I KNEW THAT.
PETE'S MY NAME. MUSTARD POT PETE.
UMM... JOHNNY.
PLEASED T'MEECHA, JOHNNY. SHAKE!
YOU SAID YOU KNEW WHAT HAPPENED TO THE TREASURES STORED HERE?
SPECIFICALLY A JAR OF MAGIC BARLEYCORNS.
OH, SURE.
THE SOLDIERS CAME AND TOOK EVERYTHING YEARS AGO.
TOOK IT ALL TO SOME BIG FORTRESS UP IN THE HIGH HILLS--ALONG WITH EVERY OTHER MAGIC THING IN THIS LAND.
US MERE PEONS AREN'T ALLOWED TO OWN NO MAGICAL STUFF NO MORE.
I'M SURPRISED YOU DON'T ALREADY KNOW THAT.
WE'RE NOT FROM AROUND HERE.
SWIPE!
SWIPE!
SWIPE!

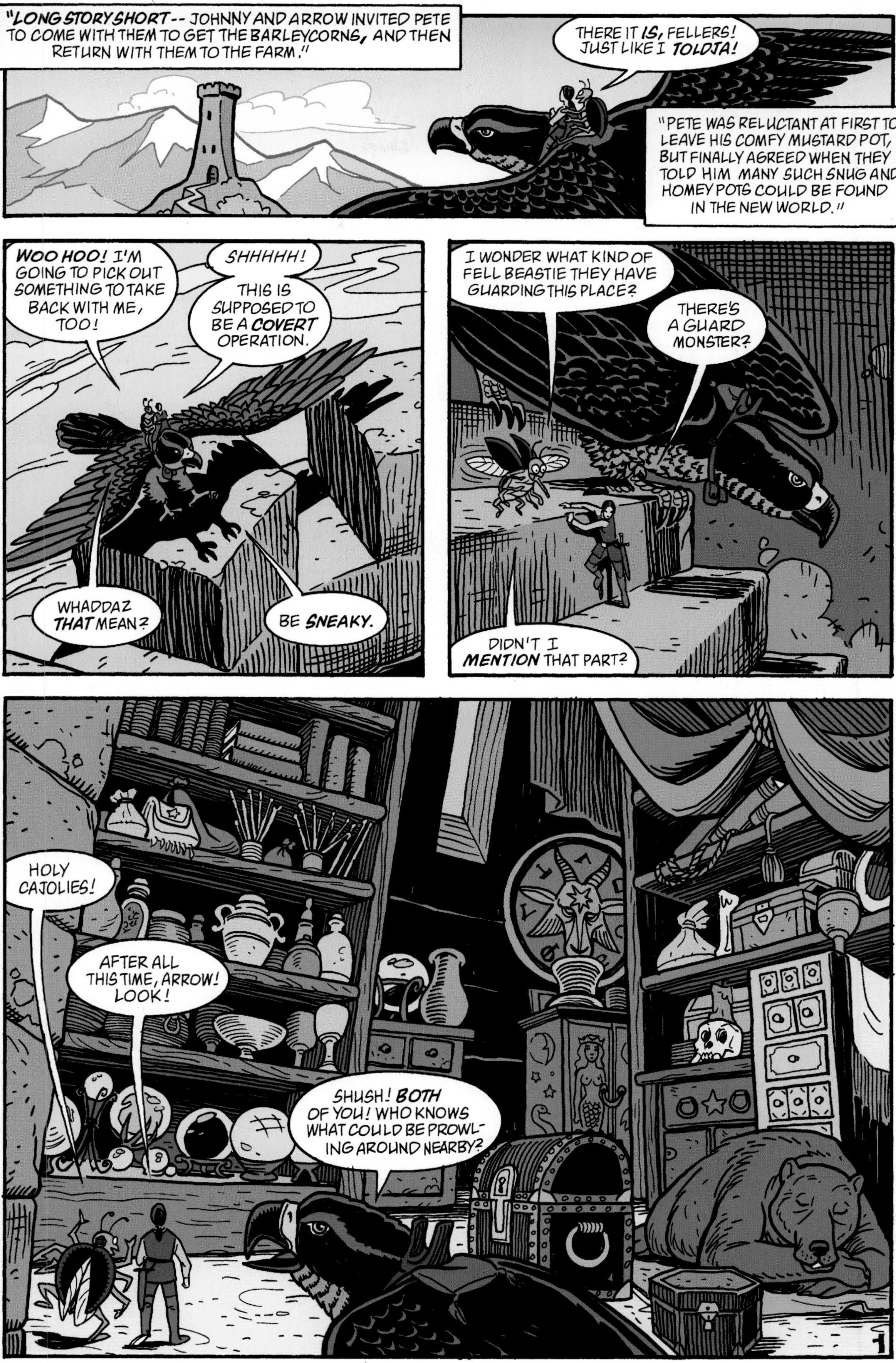
"LONG STORY SHORT -- JOHNNY AND ARROW INVITED PETE TO COME WITH THEM TO GET THE BARLEYCORNS, AND THEN RETURN WITH THEM TO THE FARM."
THERE IT IS, FELLERS! JUST LIKE I TOLDJA!
"PETE WAS RELUCTANT AT FIRST TO LEAVE HIS COMFY MUSTARD POT, BUT FINALLY AGREED WHEN THEY TOLD HIM MANY SUCH SNUG AND HOMEY POTS COULD BE FOUND IN THE NEW WORLD."
WOO HOO! I'M GOING TO PICK OUT SOMETHING TO TAKE BACK WITH ME, TOO!
SHHHHH!
THIS IS SUPPOSED TO BE A COVERT OPERATION.
WHADDAZ THAT MEAN?
BE SNEAKY.
I WONDER WHAT KIND OF FELL BEASTIE THEY HAVE GUARDING THIS PLACE?
THERE'S A GUARD MONSTER?
DIDN'T I MENTION THAT PART?
HOLY CAJOLIES!
AFTER ALL THIS TIME, ARROW! LOOK!
SHUSH! BOTH OF YOU! WHO KNOWS WHAT COULD BE PROWLING AROUND NEARBY?

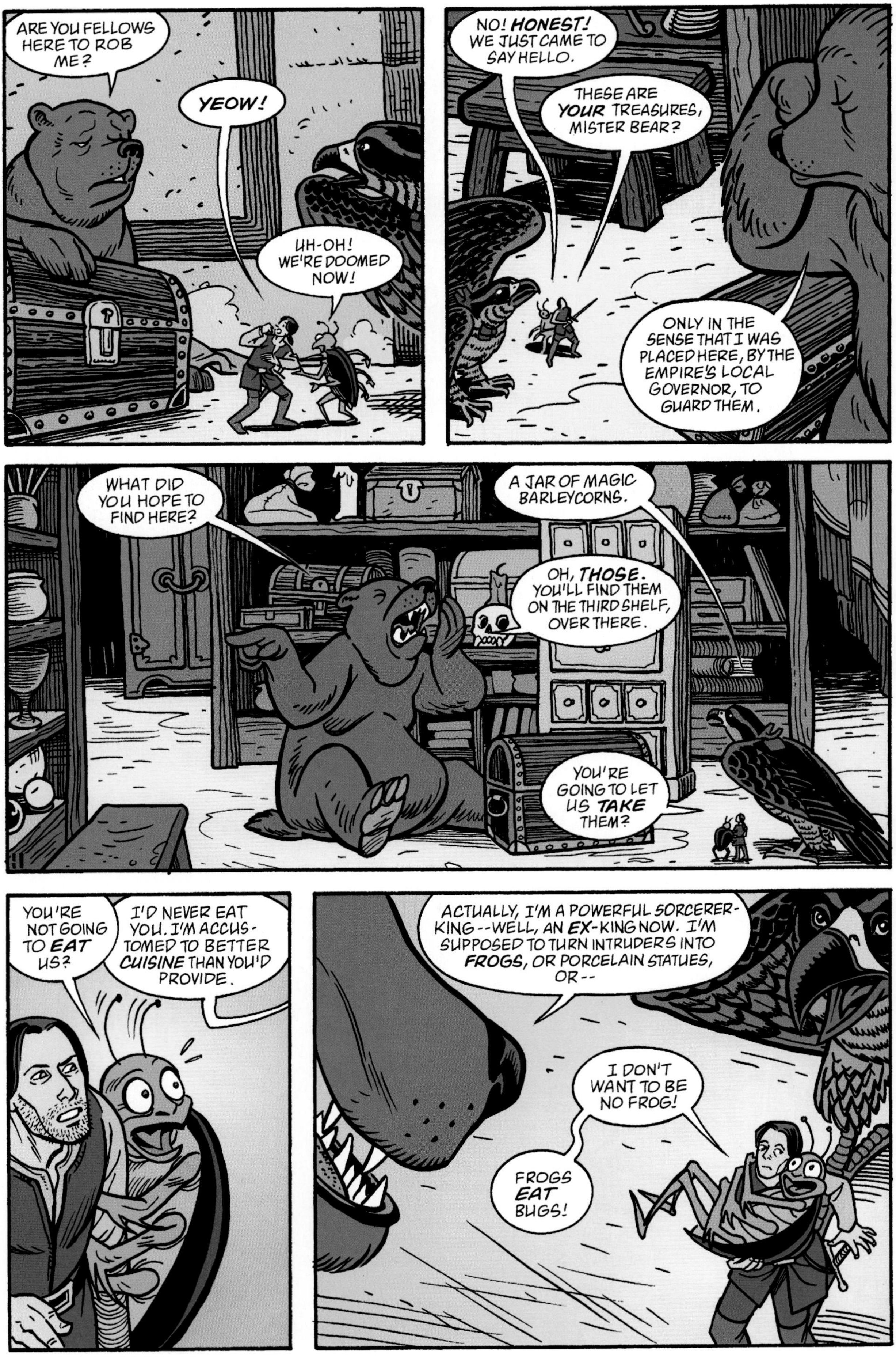
ARE YOU FELLOWS HERE TO ROB ME?
YEOW!
UH-OH! WE'RE DOOMED NOW!
NO! HONEST! WE JUST CAME TO SAY HELLO.
THESE ARE YOUR TREASURES, MISTER BEAR?
ONLY IN THE SENSE THAT I WAS PLACED HERE, BY THE EMPIRE'S LOCAL GOVERNOR, TO GUARD THEM.
WHAT DID YOU HOPE TO FIND HERE?
A JAR OF MAGIC BARLEYCORNS.
OH, THOSE. YOU'LL FIND THEM ON THE THIRD SHELF, OVER THERE.
YOU'RE GOING TO LET US TAKE THEM?
YOU'RE NOT GOING TO EAT US?
I'D NEVER EAT YOU. I'M ACCUS-TOMED TO BETTER CUISINE THAN YOU'D PROVIDE.
ACTUALLY, I'M A POWERFUL SORCERER-KING--WELL, AN EX-KING NOW. I'M SUPPOSED TO TURN INTRUDERS INTO FROGS, OR PORCELAIN STATUES, OR--
I DON'T WANT TO BE NO FROG!
FROGS EAT BUGS!

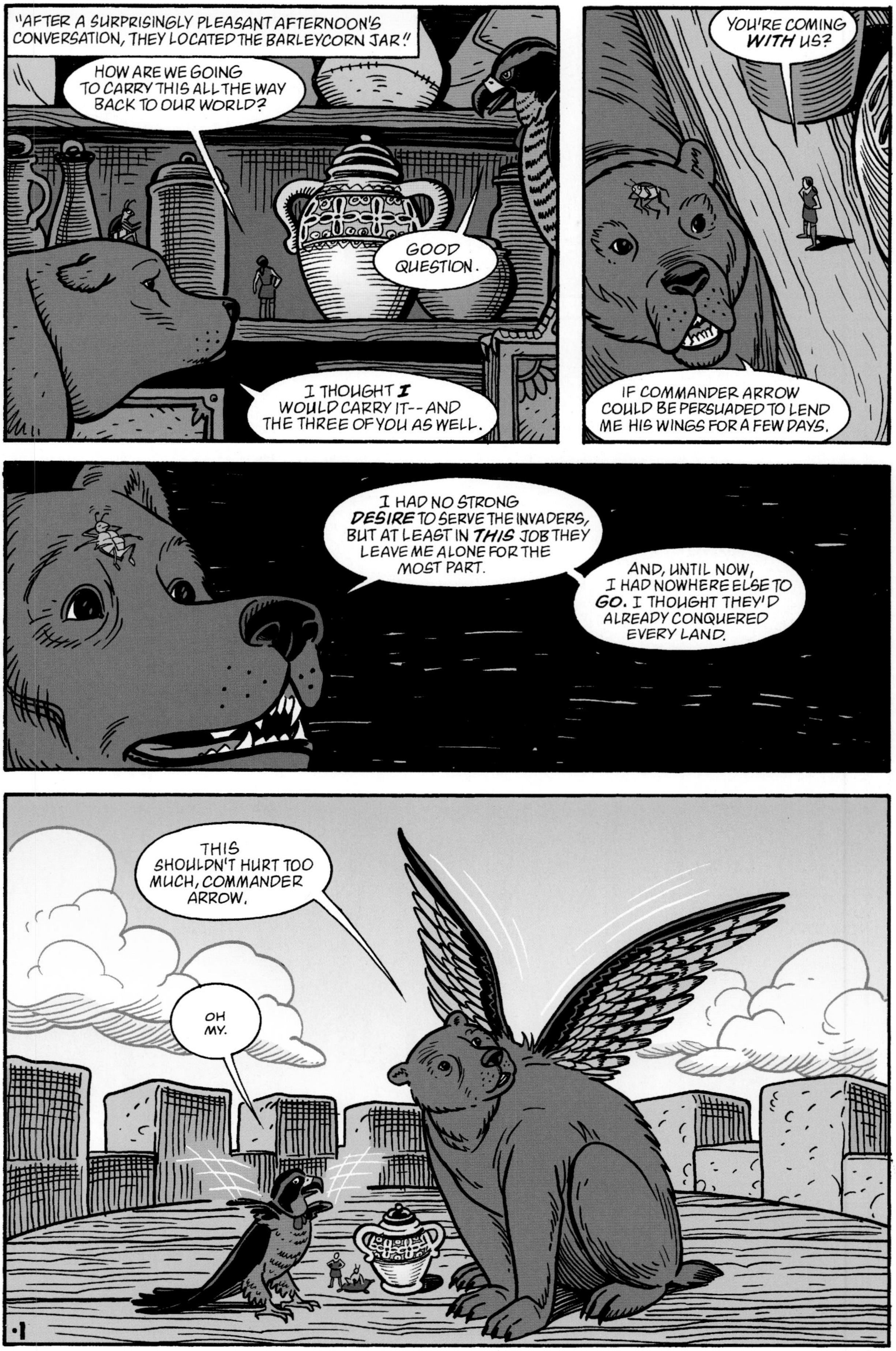
"AFTER A SURPRISINGLY PLEASANT AFTERNOON'S CONVERSATION, THEY LOCATED THE BARLEYCORN JAR."
HOW ARE WE GOING TO CARRY THIS ALL THE WAY BACK TO OUR WORLD?
GOOD QUESTION.
I THOUGHT **I** WOULD CARRY IT-- AND THE THREE OF YOU AS WELL.
YOU'RE COMING **WITH** US?
IF COMMANDER ARROW COULD BE PERSUADED TO LEND ME HIS WINGS FOR A FEW DAYS.
I HAD NO STRONG **DESIRE** TO SERVE THE INVADERS, BUT AT LEAST IN **THIS** JOB THEY LEAVE ME ALONE FOR THE MOST PART.
AND, UNTIL NOW, I HAD NOWHERE ELSE TO **GO.** I THOUGHT THEY'D ALREADY CONQUERED EVERY LAND.
THIS SHOULDN'T HURT TOO MUCH, COMMANDER ARROW.
OH MY.

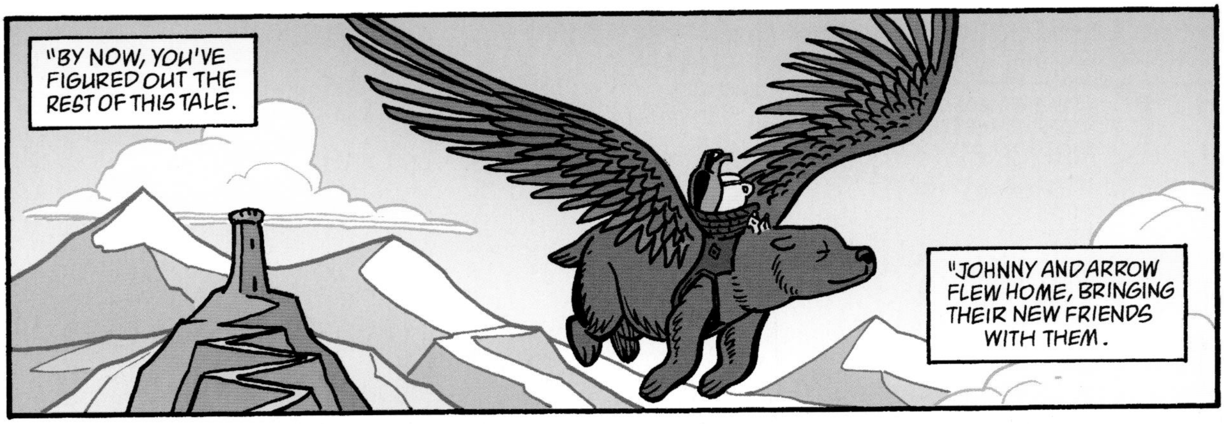
"BY NOW, YOU'VE FIGURED OUT THE REST OF THIS TALE.
"JOHNNY AND ARROW FLEW HOME, BRINGING THEIR NEW FRIENDS WITH THEM.

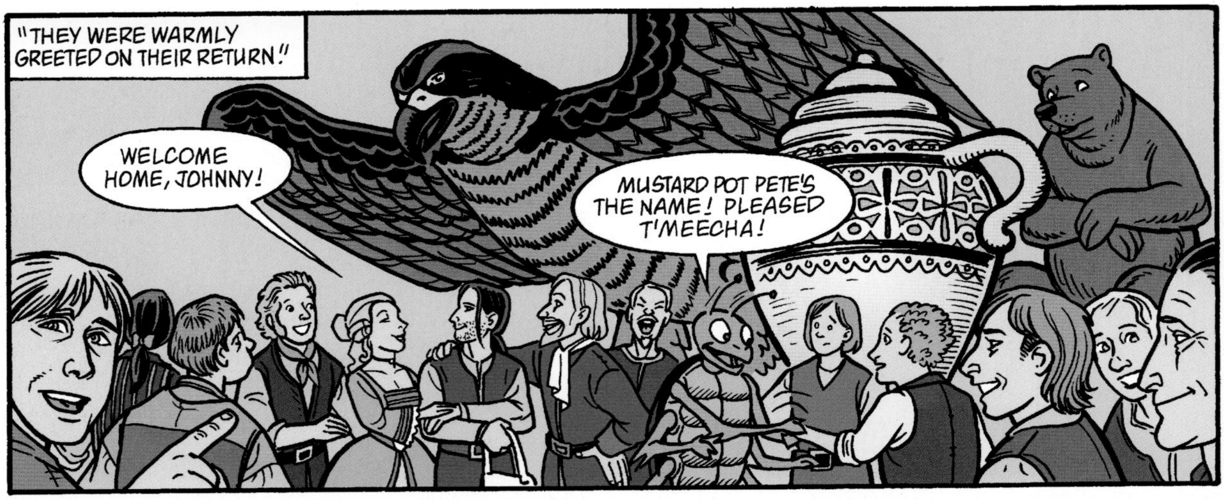
"THEY WERE WARMLY GREETED ON THEIR RETURN."
WELCOME HOME, JOHNNY!
MUSTARD POT PETE'S THE NAME! PLEASED T'MEECHA!

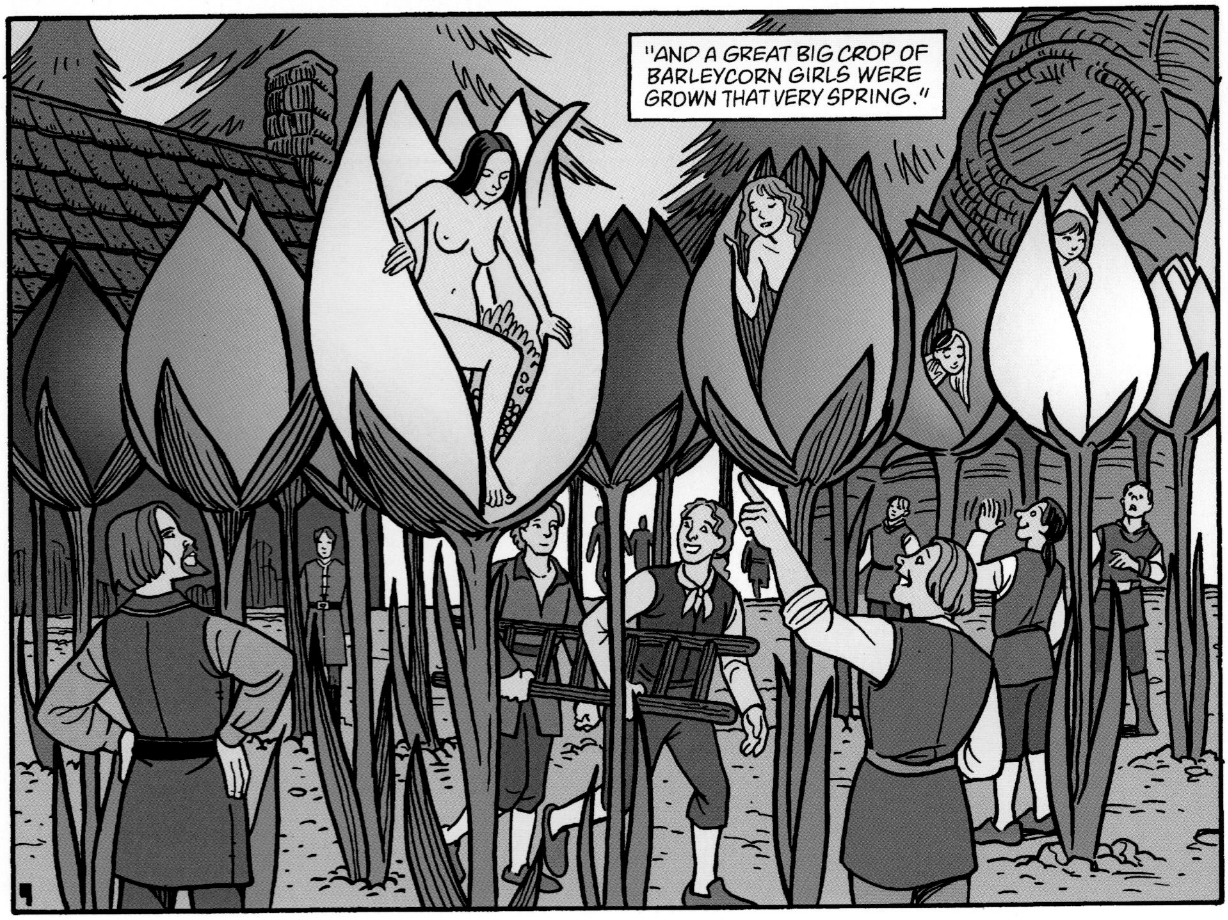
"AND A GREAT BIG CROP OF BARLEYCORN GIRLS WERE GROWN THAT VERY SPRING."

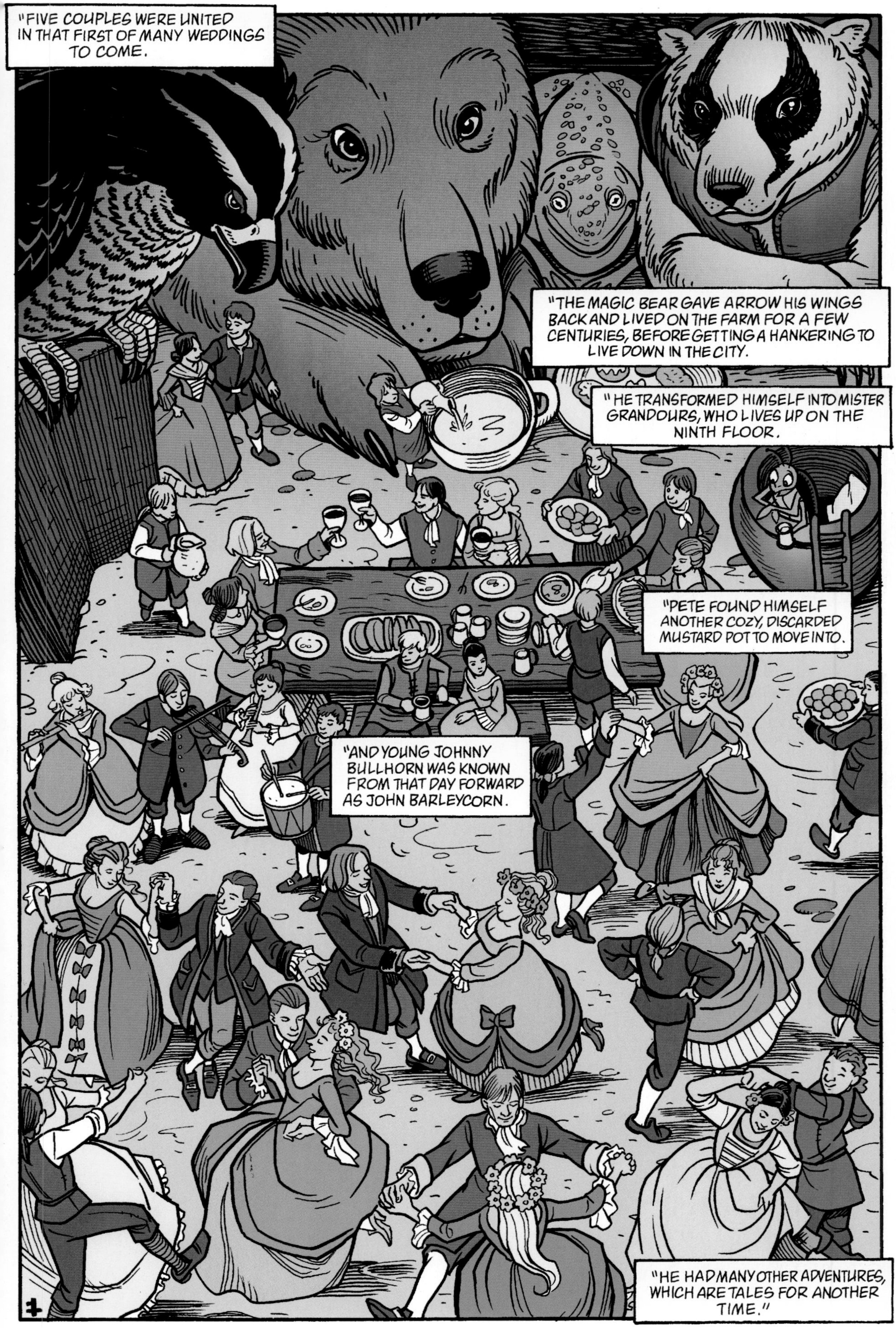
"FIVE COUPLES WERE UNITED IN THAT FIRST OF MANY WEDDINGS TO COME.
"THE MAGIC BEAR GAVE ARROW HIS WINGS BACK AND LIVED ON THE FARM FOR A FEW CENTURIES, BEFORE GETTING A HANKERING TO LIVE DOWN IN THE CITY.
"HE TRANSFORMED HIMSELF INTO MISTER GRANDOURS, WHO LIVES UP ON THE NINTH FLOOR.
"PETE FOUND HIMSELF ANOTHER COZY, DISCARDED MUSTARD POT TO MOVE INTO.
"AND YOUNG JOHNNY BULLHORN WAS KNOWN FROM THAT DAY FORWARD AS JOHN BARLEYCORN.
"HE HAD MANY OTHER ADVENTURES, WHICH ARE TALES FOR ANOTHER TIME."

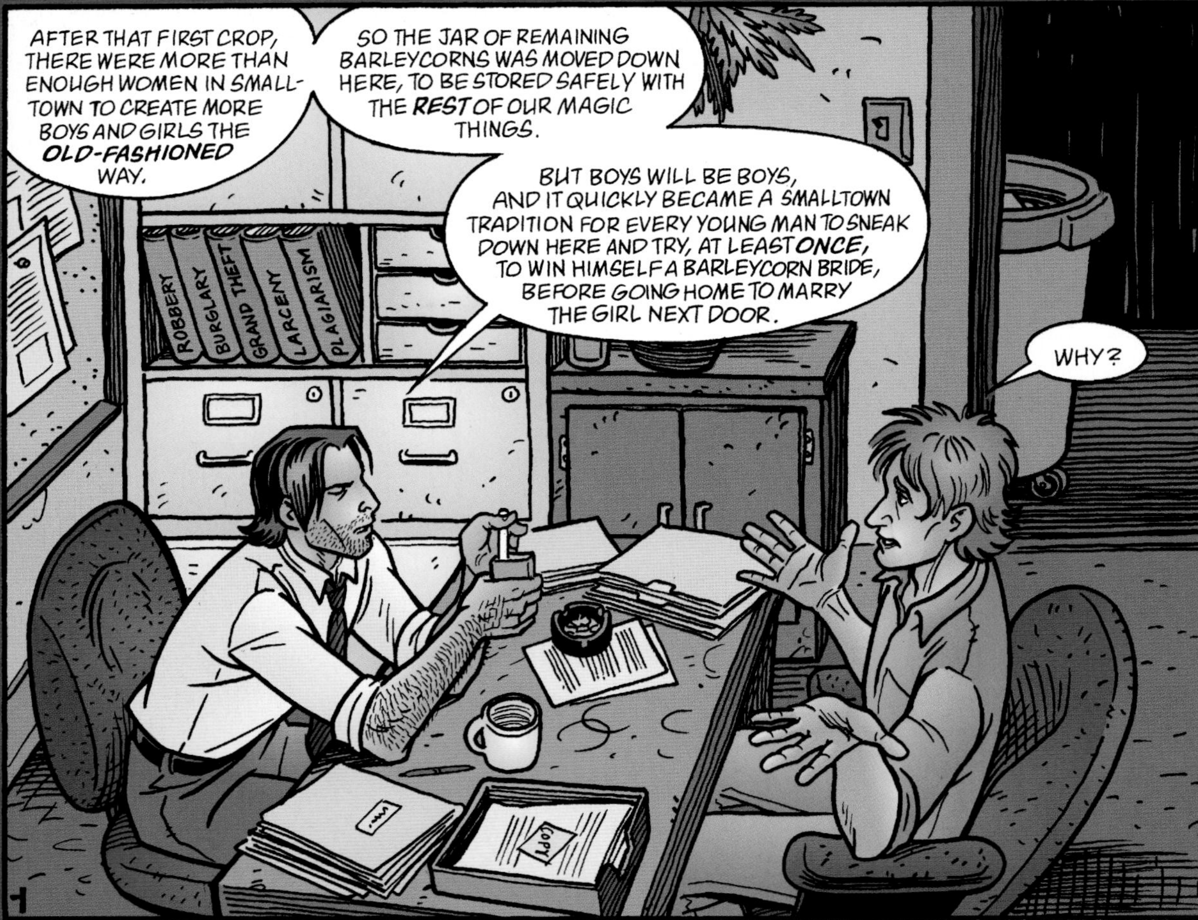
AFTER THAT FIRST CROP, THERE WERE MORE THAN ENOUGH WOMEN IN SMALL-TOWN TO CREATE MORE BOYS AND GIRLS THE OLD-FASHIONED WAY.
SO THE JAR OF REMAINING BARLEYCORNS WAS MOVED DOWN HERE, TO BE STORED SAFELY WITH THE REST OF OUR MAGIC THINGS.
BUT BOYS WILL BE BOYS, AND IT QUICKLY BECAME A SMALLTOWN TRADITION FOR EVERY YOUNG MAN TO SNEAK DOWN HERE AND TRY, AT LEAST ONCE, TO WIN HIMSELF A BARLEYCORN BRIDE, BEFORE GOING HOME TO MARRY THE GIRL NEXT DOOR.
WHY?
ROBBERY
BURGLARY
GRAND THEFT
LARCENY
PLAGIARISM
COPY

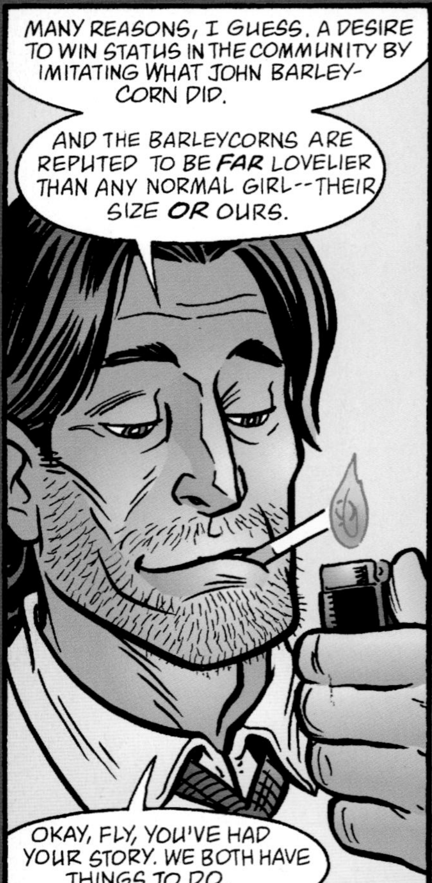
MANY REASONS, I GUESS. A DESIRE TO WIN STATUS IN THE COMMUNITY BY IMITATING WHAT JOHN BARLEY-CORN DID.
AND THE BARLEYCORNS ARE REPUTED TO BE FAR LOVELIER THAN ANY NORMAL GIRL--THEIR SIZE OR OURS.
OKAY, FLY, YOU'VE HAD YOUR STORY. WE BOTH HAVE THINGS TO DO.

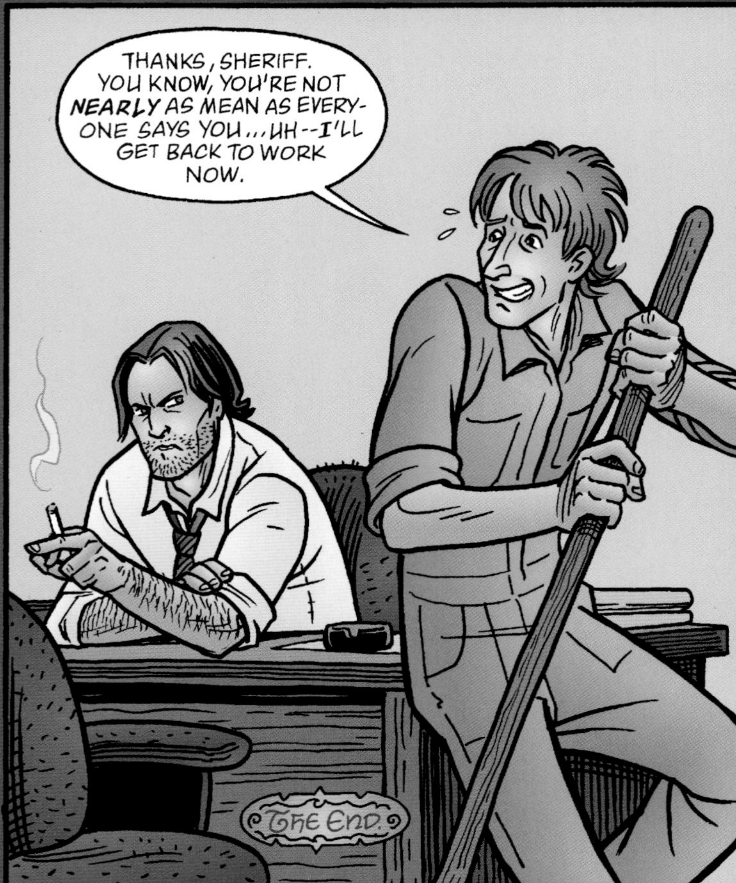
THANKS, SHERIFF. YOU KNOW, YOU'RE NOT NEARLY AS MEAN AS EVERY-ONE SAYS YOU... UH--I'LL GET BACK TO WORK NOW.
THE END.

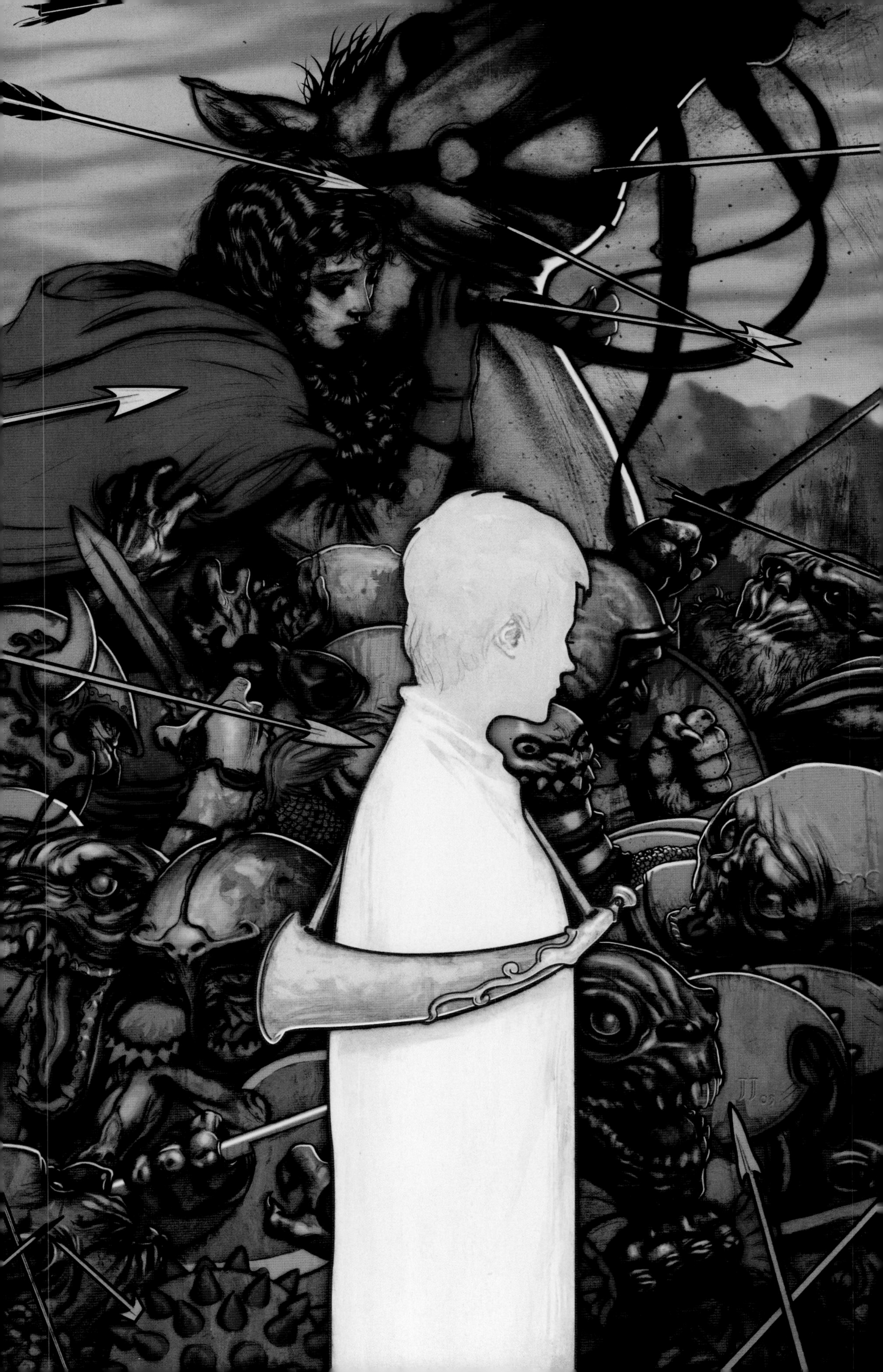

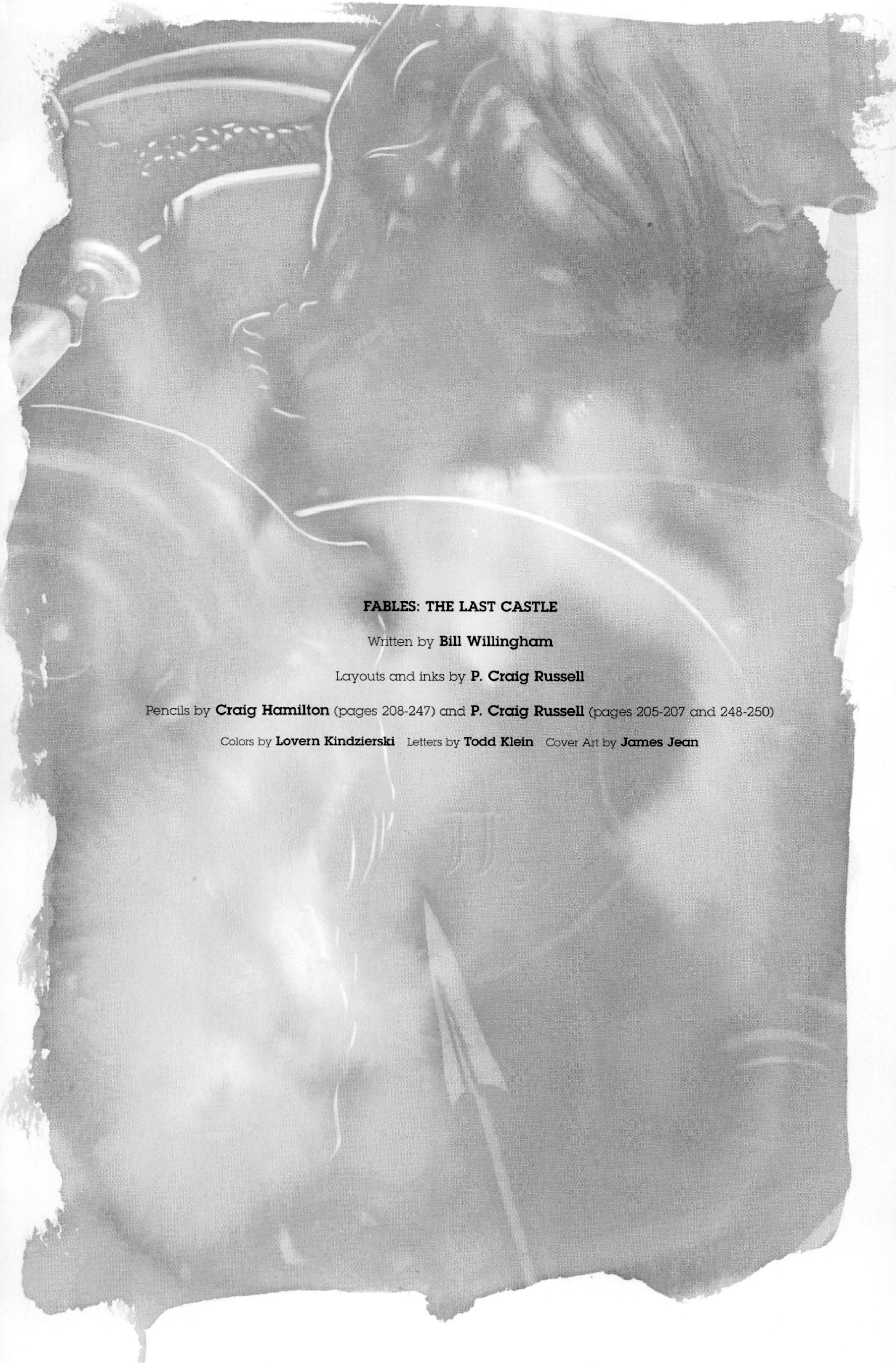

FABLES: THE LAST CASTLE

Written by **Bill Willingham**

Layouts and inks by **P. Craig Russell**

Pencils by **Craig Hamilton** (pages 208-247) and **P. Craig Russell** (pages 205-207 and 248-250)

Colors by **Lovern Kindzierski** Letters by **Todd Klein** Cover Art by **James Jean**

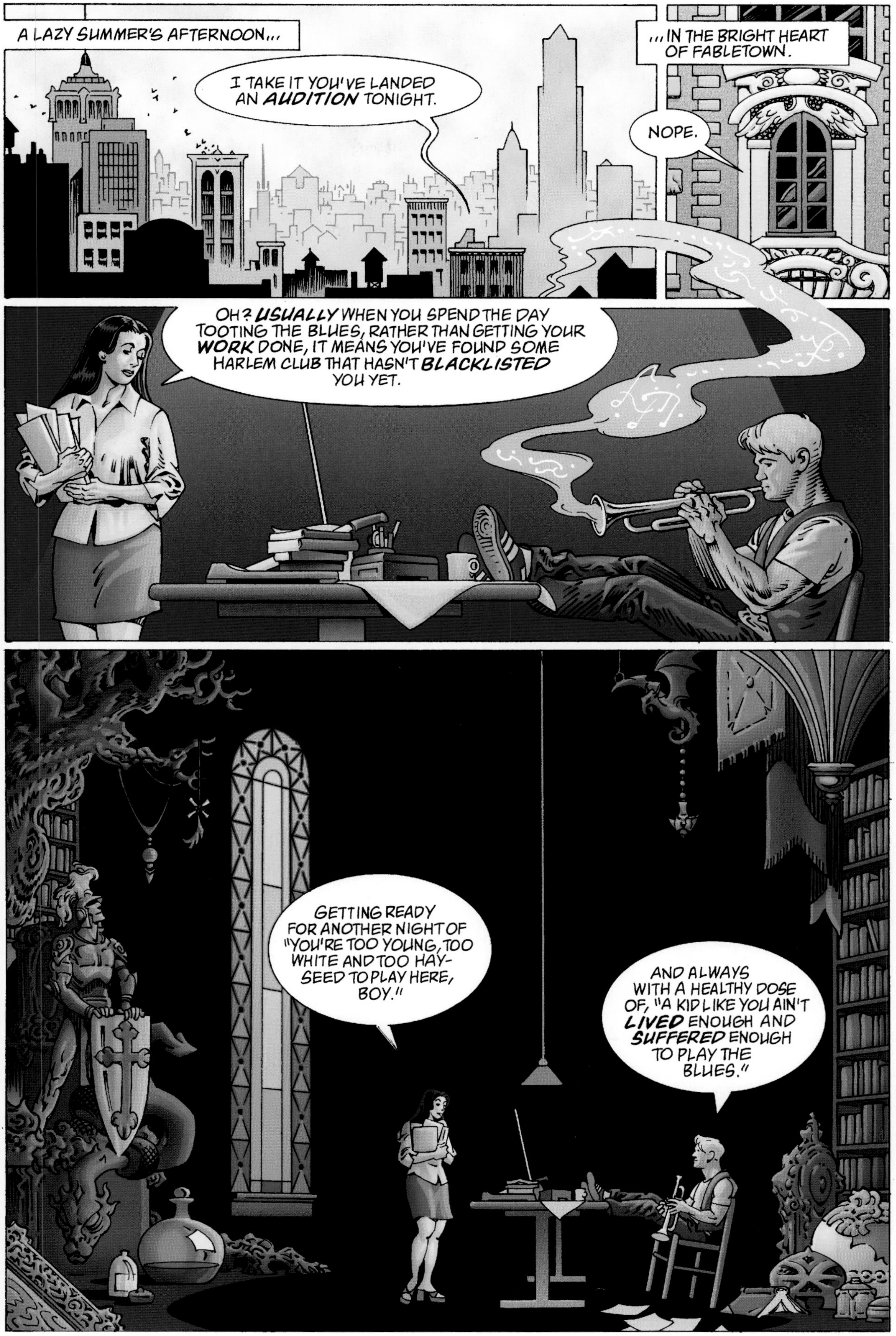
A LAZY SUMMER'S AFTERNOON...
I TAKE IT YOU'VE LANDED AN AUDITION TONIGHT.
...IN THE BRIGHT HEART OF FABLETOWN.
NOPE.
OH? USUALLY WHEN YOU SPEND THE DAY TOOTING THE BLUES, RATHER THAN GETTING YOUR WORK DONE, IT MEANS YOU'VE FOUND SOME HARLEM CLUB THAT HASN'T BLACKLISTED YOU YET.
GETTING READY FOR ANOTHER NIGHT OF "YOU'RE TOO YOUNG, TOO WHITE AND TOO HAY-SEED TO PLAY HERE, BOY."
AND ALWAYS WITH A HEALTHY DOSE OF, "A KID LIKE YOU AIN'T LIVED ENOUGH AND SUFFERED ENOUGH TO PLAY THE BLUES."

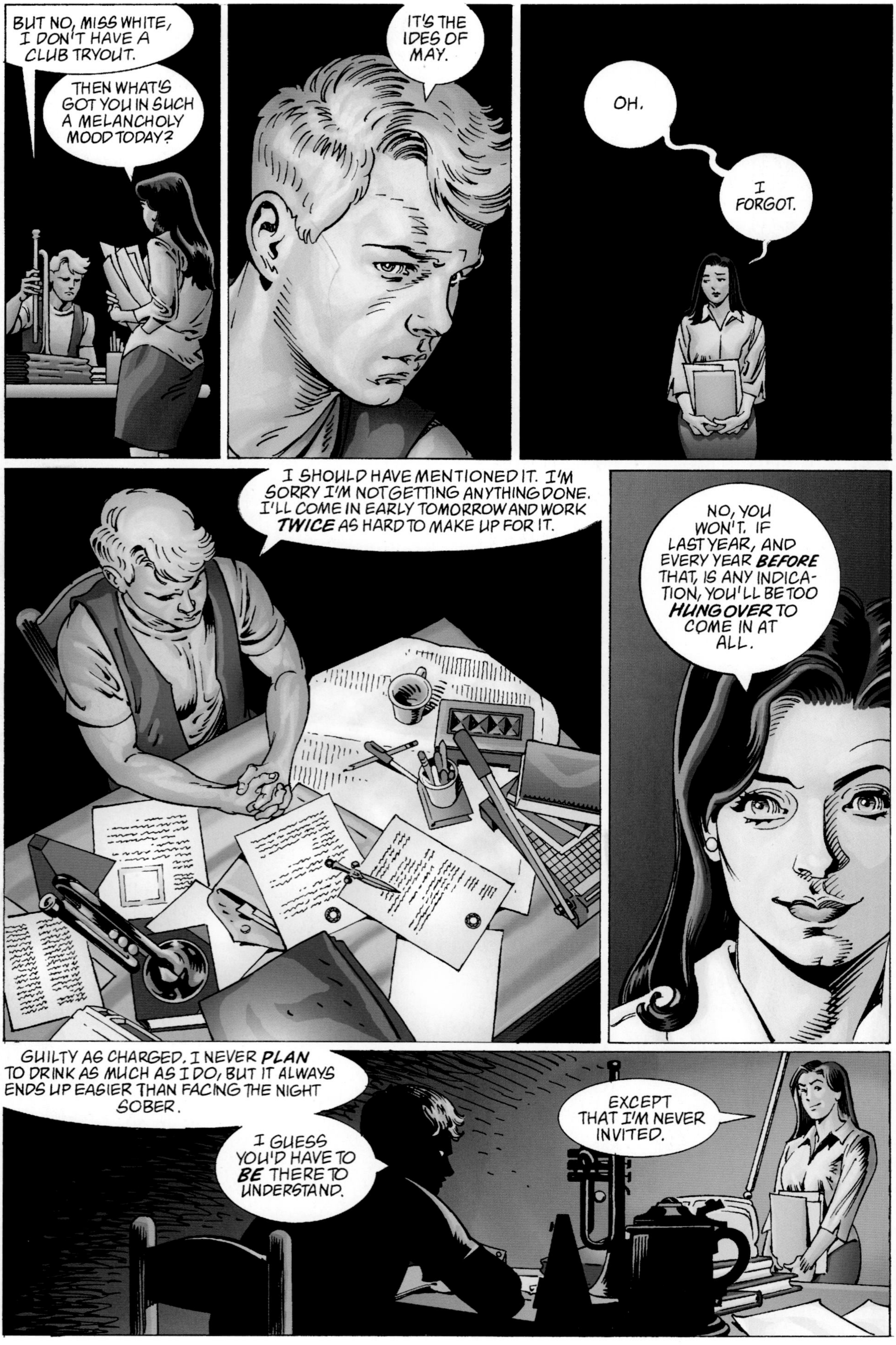
BUT NO, MISS WHITE, I DON'T HAVE A CLUB TRYOUT.
THEN WHAT'S GOT YOU IN SUCH A MELANCHOLY MOOD TODAY?
IT'S THE IDES OF MAY.
OH.
I FORGOT.
I SHOULD HAVE MENTIONED IT. I'M SORRY I'M NOT GETTING ANYTHING DONE. I'LL COME IN EARLY TOMORROW AND WORK TWICE AS HARD TO MAKE UP FOR IT.
NO, YOU WON'T. IF LAST YEAR, AND EVERY YEAR BEFORE THAT, IS ANY INDICATION, YOU'LL BE TOO HUNGOVER TO COME IN AT ALL.
GUILTY AS CHARGED. I NEVER PLAN TO DRINK AS MUCH AS I DO, BUT IT ALWAYS ENDS UP EASIER THAN FACING THE NIGHT SOBER.
I GUESS YOU'D HAVE TO BE THERE TO UNDERSTAND.
EXCEPT THAT I'M NEVER INVITED.

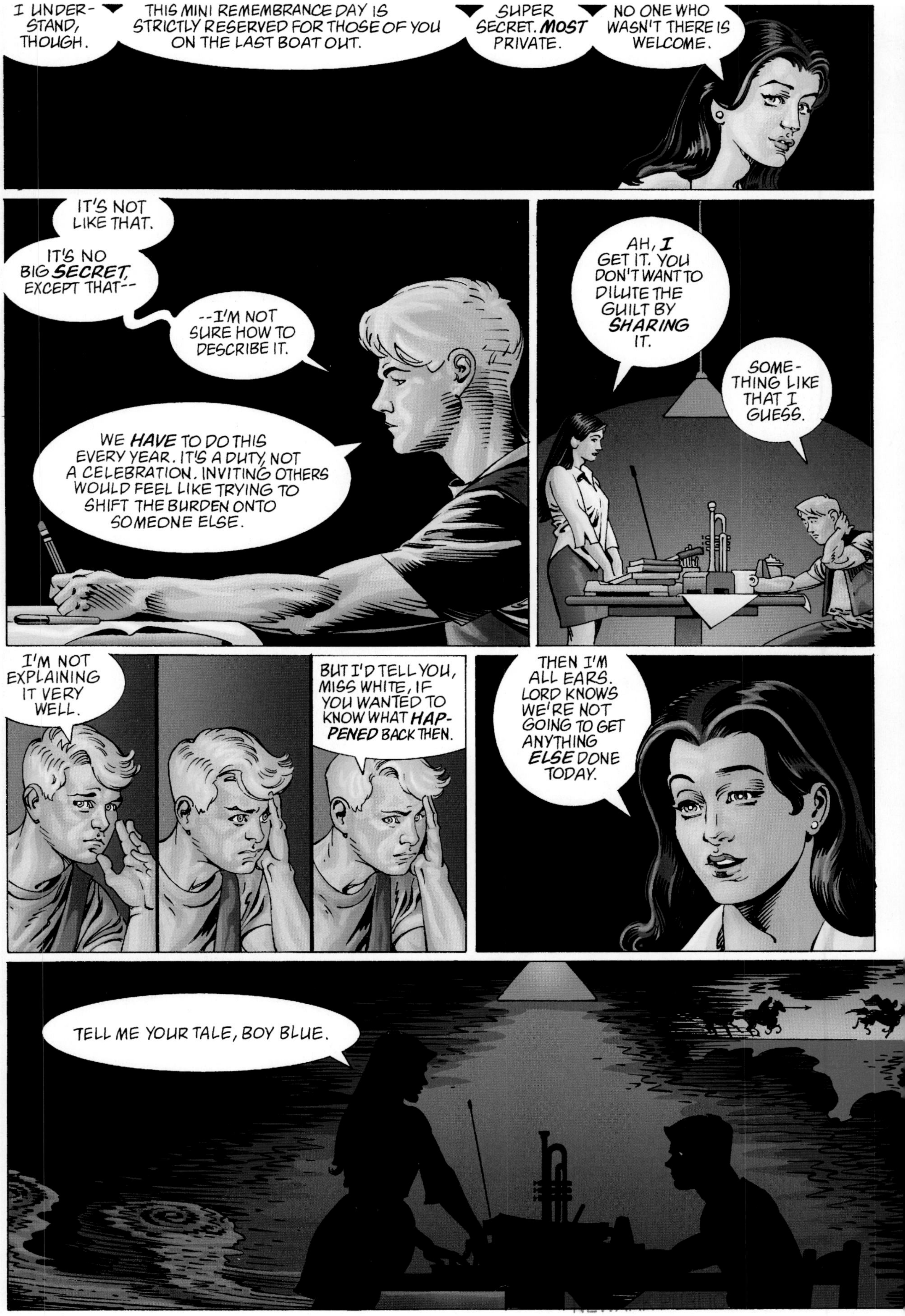
I UNDERSTAND, THOUGH.
THIS MINI REMEMBRANCE DAY IS STRICTLY RESERVED FOR THOSE OF YOU ON THE LAST BOAT OUT.
SUPER SECRET. **MOST** PRIVATE.
NO ONE WHO WASN'T THERE IS WELCOME.
IT'S NOT LIKE THAT.
IT'S NO BIG **SECRET**, EXCEPT THAT--
--I'M NOT SURE HOW TO DESCRIBE IT.
WE **HAVE** TO DO THIS EVERY YEAR. IT'S A DUTY, NOT A CELEBRATION. INVITING OTHERS WOULD FEEL LIKE TRYING TO SHIFT THE BURDEN ONTO SOMEONE ELSE.
AH, **I** GET IT. YOU DON'T WANT TO DILUTE THE GUILT BY **SHARING** IT.
SOMETHING LIKE THAT I GUESS.
I'M NOT EXPLAINING IT VERY WELL.
BUT I'D TELL YOU, MISS WHITE, IF YOU WANTED TO KNOW WHAT **HAPPENED** BACK THEN.
THEN I'M ALL EARS. LORD KNOWS WE'RE NOT GOING TO GET ANYTHING **ELSE** DONE TODAY.
TELL ME YOUR TALE, BOY BLUE.

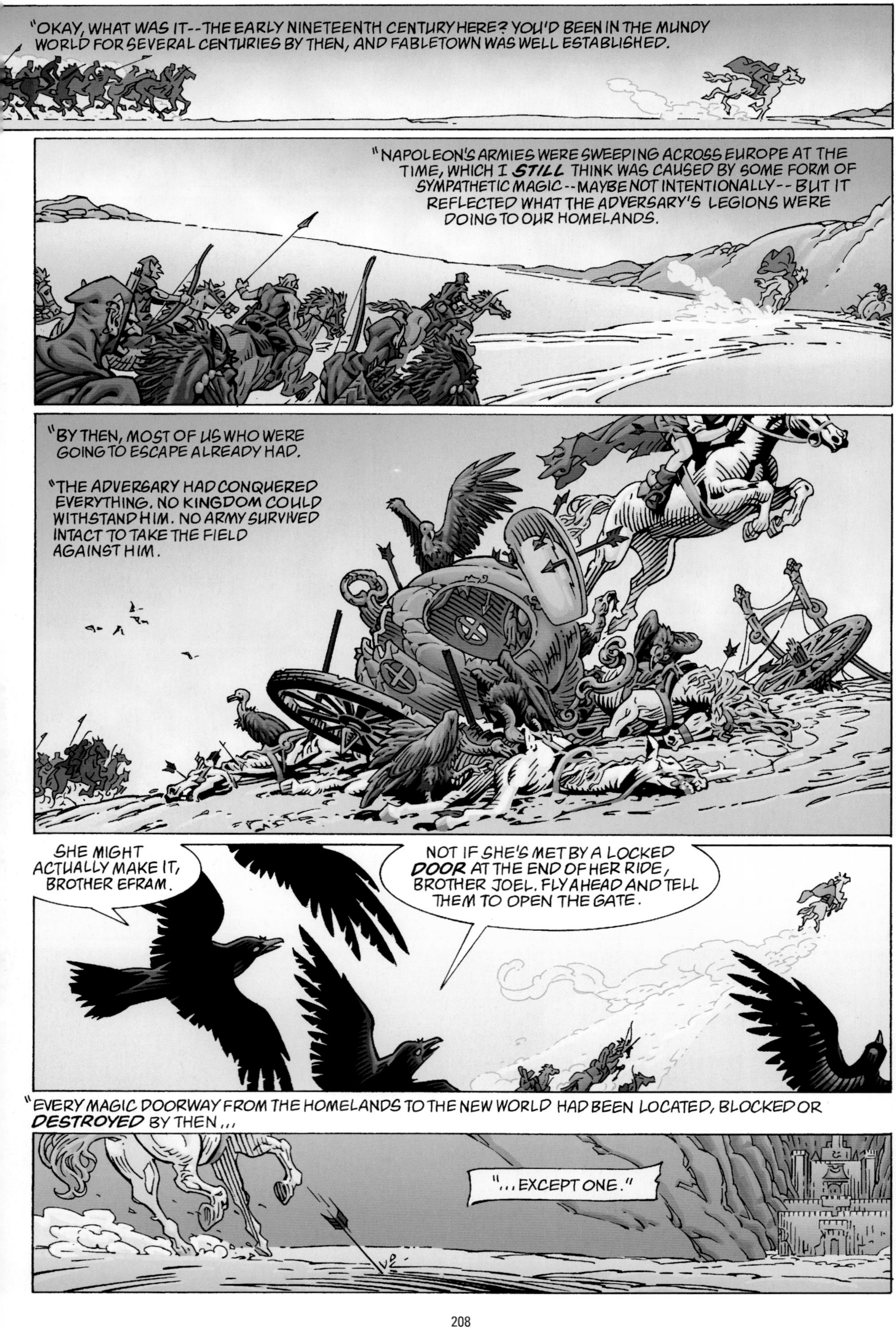
"OKAY, WHAT WAS IT--THE EARLY NINETEENTH CENTURY HERE? YOU'D BEEN IN THE MUNDY WORLD FOR SEVERAL CENTURIES BY THEN, AND FABLETOWN WAS WELL ESTABLISHED.
"NAPOLEON'S ARMIES WERE SWEEPING ACROSS EUROPE AT THE TIME, WHICH I STILL THINK WAS CAUSED BY SOME FORM OF SYMPATHETIC MAGIC--MAYBE NOT INTENTIONALLY--BUT IT REFLECTED WHAT THE ADVERSARY'S LEGIONS WERE DOING TO OUR HOMELANDS.
"BY THEN, MOST OF US WHO WERE GOING TO ESCAPE ALREADY HAD.
"THE ADVERSARY HAD CONQUERED EVERYTHING. NO KINGDOM COULD WITHSTAND HIM. NO ARMY SURVIVED INTACT TO TAKE THE FIELD AGAINST HIM.
SHE MIGHT ACTUALLY MAKE IT, BROTHER EFRAM.
NOT IF SHE'S MET BY A LOCKED DOOR AT THE END OF HER RIDE, BROTHER JOEL. FLY AHEAD AND TELL THEM TO OPEN THE GATE.
"EVERY MAGIC DOORWAY FROM THE HOMELANDS TO THE NEW WORLD HAD BEEN LOCATED, BLOCKED OR DESTROYED BY THEN...
"...EXCEPT ONE."

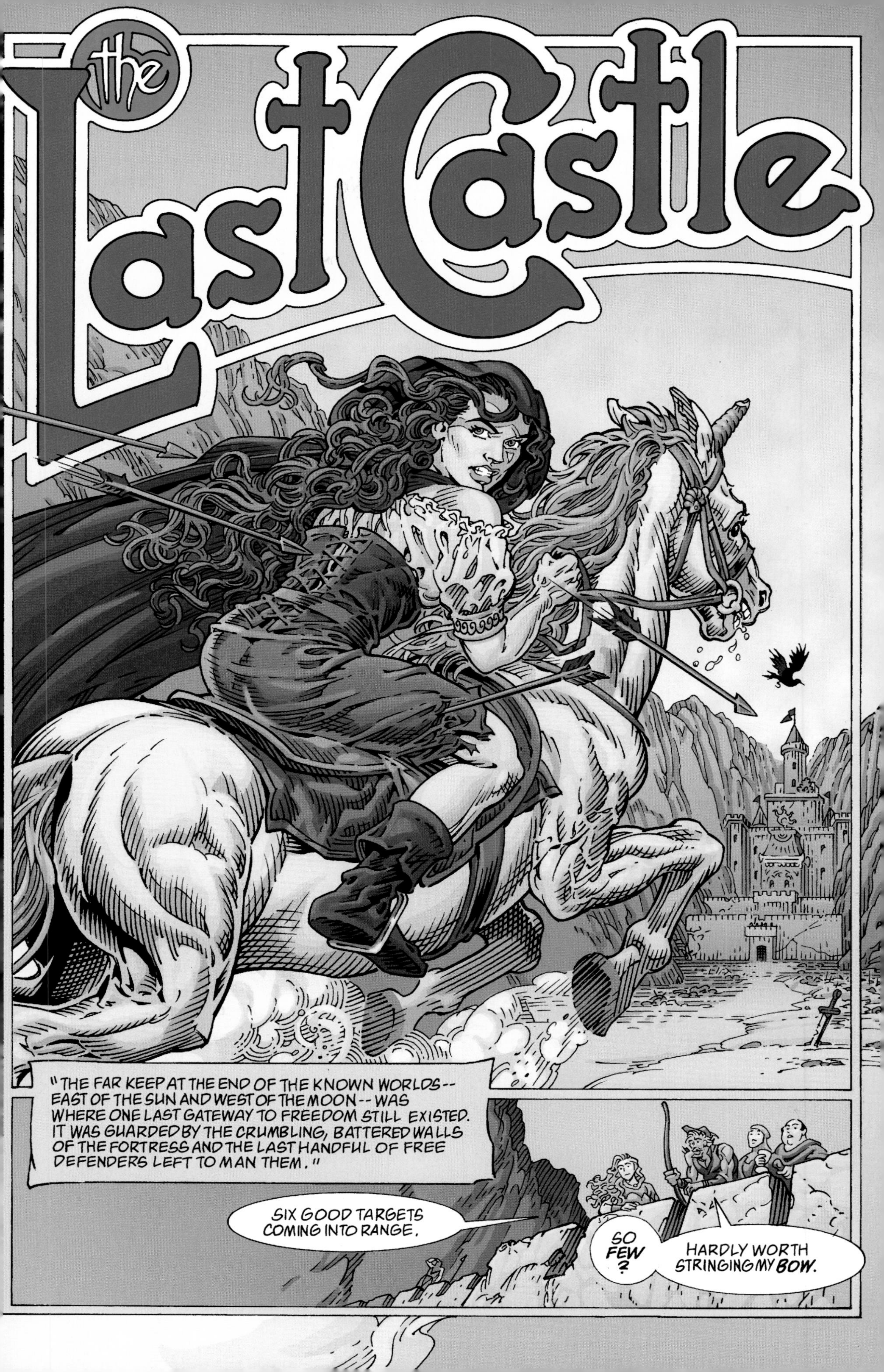
the Last Castle
"THE FAR KEEP AT THE END OF THE KNOWN WORLDS-- EAST OF THE SUN AND WEST OF THE MOON-- WAS WHERE ONE LAST GATEWAY TO FREEDOM STILL EXISTED. IT WAS GUARDED BY THE CRUMBLING, BATTERED WALLS OF THE FORTRESS AND THE LAST HANDFUL OF FREE DEFENDERS LEFT TO MAN THEM."
SIX GOOD TARGETS COMING INTO RANGE.
SO FEW?
HARDLY WORTH STRINGING MY BOW.

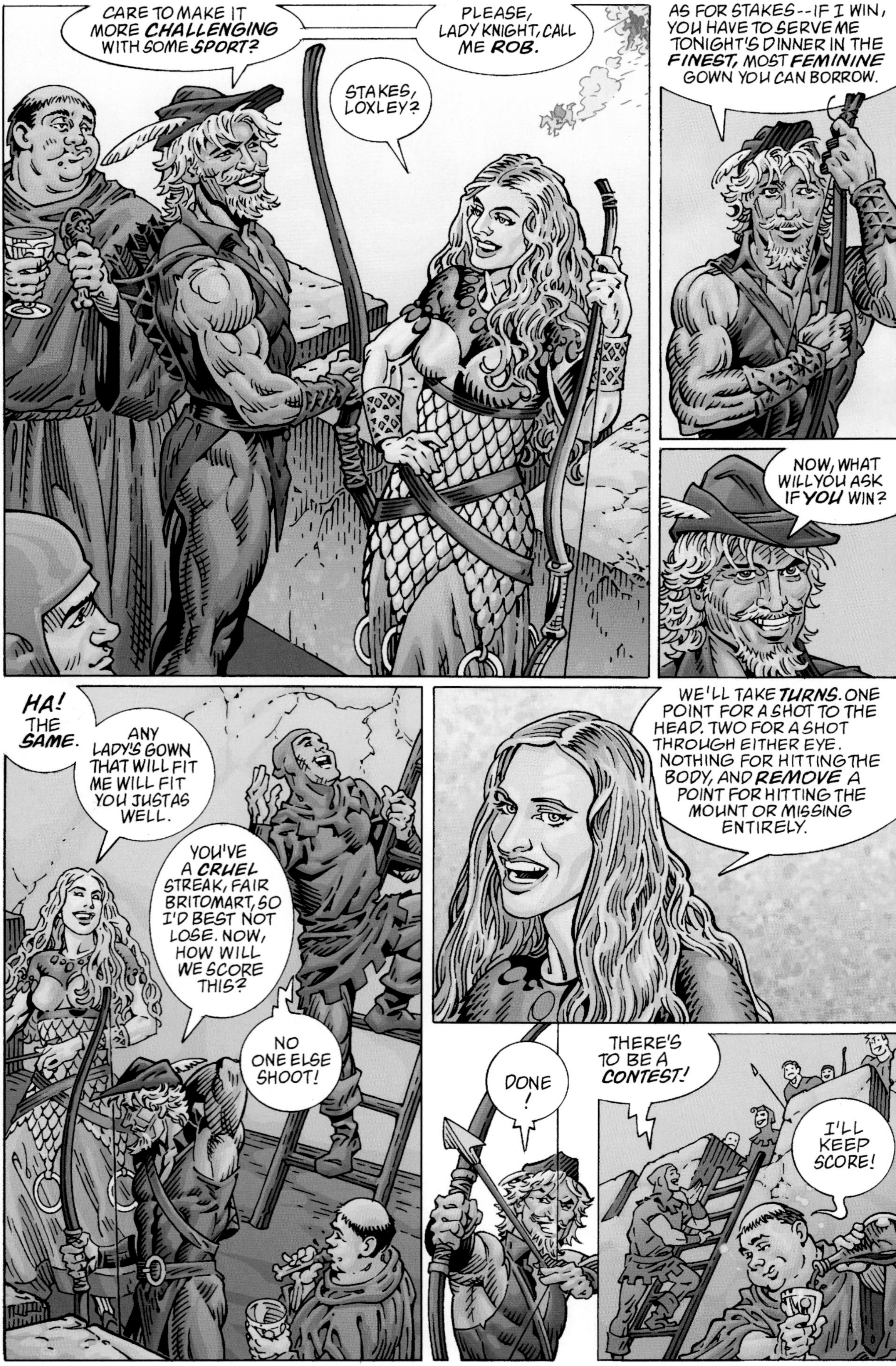
CARE TO MAKE IT MORE CHALLENGING WITH SOME SPORT?
PLEASE, LADY KNIGHT, CALL ME ROB.
STAKES, LOXLEY?
AS FOR STAKES--IF I WIN, YOU HAVE TO SERVE ME TONIGHT'S DINNER IN THE FINEST, MOST FEMININE GOWN YOU CAN BORROW.
NOW, WHAT WILL YOU ASK IF YOU WIN?
HA! THE SAME.
ANY LADY'S GOWN THAT WILL FIT ME WILL FIT YOU JUST AS WELL.
YOU'VE A CRUEL STREAK, FAIR BRITOMART, SO I'D BEST NOT LOSE. NOW, HOW WILL WE SCORE THIS?
NO ONE ELSE SHOOT!
WE'LL TAKE TURNS. ONE POINT FOR A SHOT TO THE HEAD. TWO FOR A SHOT THROUGH EITHER EYE. NOTHING FOR HITTING THE BODY, AND REMOVE A POINT FOR HITTING THE MOUNT OR MISSING ENTIRELY.
DONE!
THERE'S TO BE A CONTEST!
I'LL KEEP SCORE!

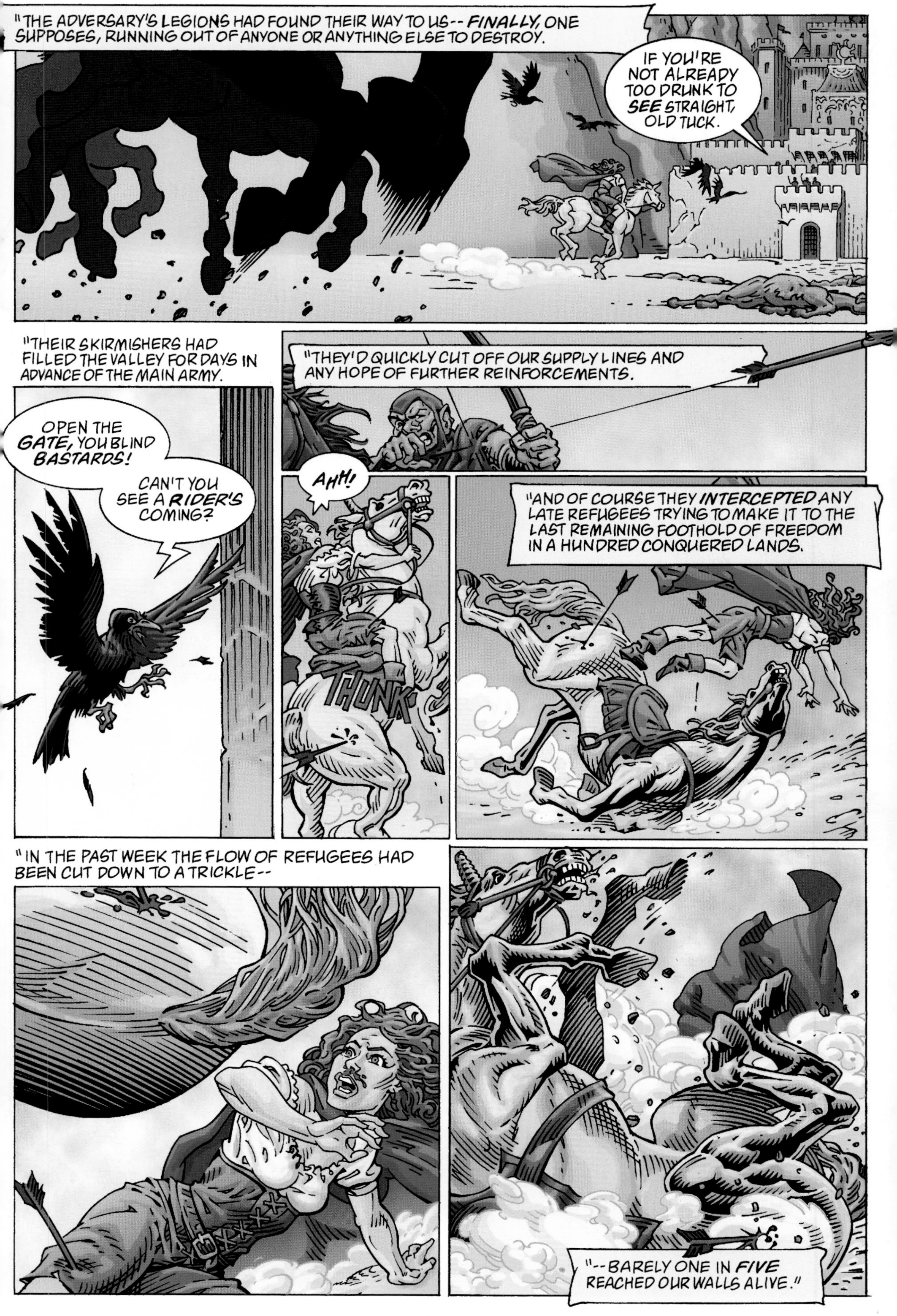
"THE ADVERSARY'S LEGIONS HAD FOUND THEIR WAY TO US-- FINALLY, ONE SUPPOSES, RUNNING OUT OF ANYONE OR ANYTHING ELSE TO DESTROY.
IF YOU'RE NOT ALREADY TOO DRUNK TO SEE STRAIGHT, OLD TUCK.
"THEIR SKIRMISHERS HAD FILLED THE VALLEY FOR DAYS IN ADVANCE OF THE MAIN ARMY.
OPEN THE GATE, YOU BLIND BASTARDS!
CAN'T YOU SEE A RIDER'S COMING?
"THEY'D QUICKLY CUT OFF OUR SUPPLY LINES AND ANY HOPE OF FURTHER REINFORCEMENTS.
AHH!
THUNK
"AND OF COURSE THEY INTERCEPTED ANY LATE REFUGEES TRYING TO MAKE IT TO THE LAST REMAINING FOOTHOLD OF FREEDOM IN A HUNDRED CONQUERED LANDS.
"IN THE PAST WEEK THE FLOW OF REFUGEES HAD BEEN CUT DOWN TO A TRICKLE--
"--BARELY ONE IN FIVE REACHED OUR WALLS ALIVE."

"AND NONE AT ALL IN THE LAST TWO DAYS."

HELP ME!

--ARRUP:-

"UNTIL *SHE* SHOWED UP, ALL ALONE, OUT OF THE BLUE."

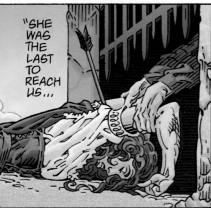

"SHE WAS THE LAST TO REACH US..."

"...ALIVE IN ONLY THE MOST *RUDIMENTARY* SENSE OF THE WORD."

ONE TO ONE SO FAR, MY LADY.

ONE TO *TWO*, LOXLEY, MY SHOT PIERCED HIS EYE.

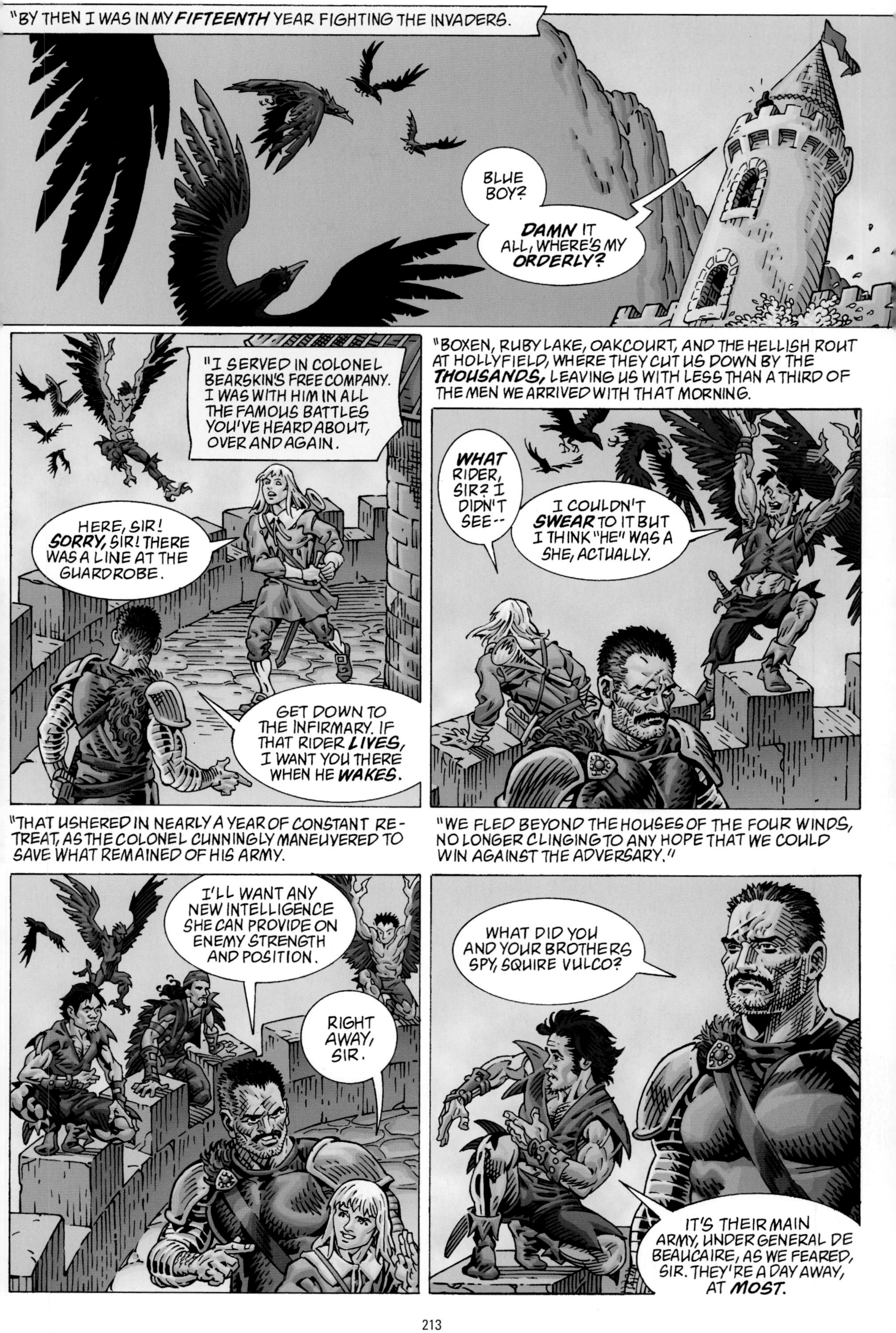
"BY THEN I WAS IN MY FIFTEENTH YEAR FIGHTING THE INVADERS.
BLUE BOY?
DAMN IT ALL, WHERE'S MY ORDERLY?
"I SERVED IN COLONEL BEARSKIN'S FREE COMPANY. I WAS WITH HIM IN ALL THE FAMOUS BATTLES YOU'VE HEARD ABOUT, OVER AND AGAIN.
HERE, SIR! SORRY, SIR! THERE WAS A LINE AT THE GUARDROBE.
GET DOWN TO THE INFIRMARY. IF THAT RIDER LIVES, I WANT YOU THERE WHEN HE WAKES.
"BOXEN, RUBY LAKE, OAKCOURT, AND THE HELLISH ROUT AT HOLLYFIELD, WHERE THEY CUT US DOWN BY THE THOUSANDS, LEAVING US WITH LESS THAN A THIRD OF THE MEN WE ARRIVED WITH THAT MORNING.
WHAT RIDER, SIR? I DIDN'T SEE--
I COULDN'T SWEAR TO IT BUT I THINK "HE" WAS A SHE, ACTUALLY.
"THAT USHERED IN NEARLY A YEAR OF CONSTANT RETREAT, AS THE COLONEL CUNNINGLY MANEUVERED TO SAVE WHAT REMAINED OF HIS ARMY.
I'LL WANT ANY NEW INTELLIGENCE SHE CAN PROVIDE ON ENEMY STRENGTH AND POSITION.
RIGHT AWAY, SIR.
"WE FLED BEYOND THE HOUSES OF THE FOUR WINDS, NO LONGER CLINGING TO ANY HOPE THAT WE COULD WIN AGAINST THE ADVERSARY."
WHAT DID YOU AND YOUR BROTHERS SPY, SQUIRE VULCO?
IT'S THEIR MAIN ARMY, UNDER GENERAL DE BEAUCAIRE, AS WE FEARED, SIR. THEY'RE A DAY AWAY, AT MOST.

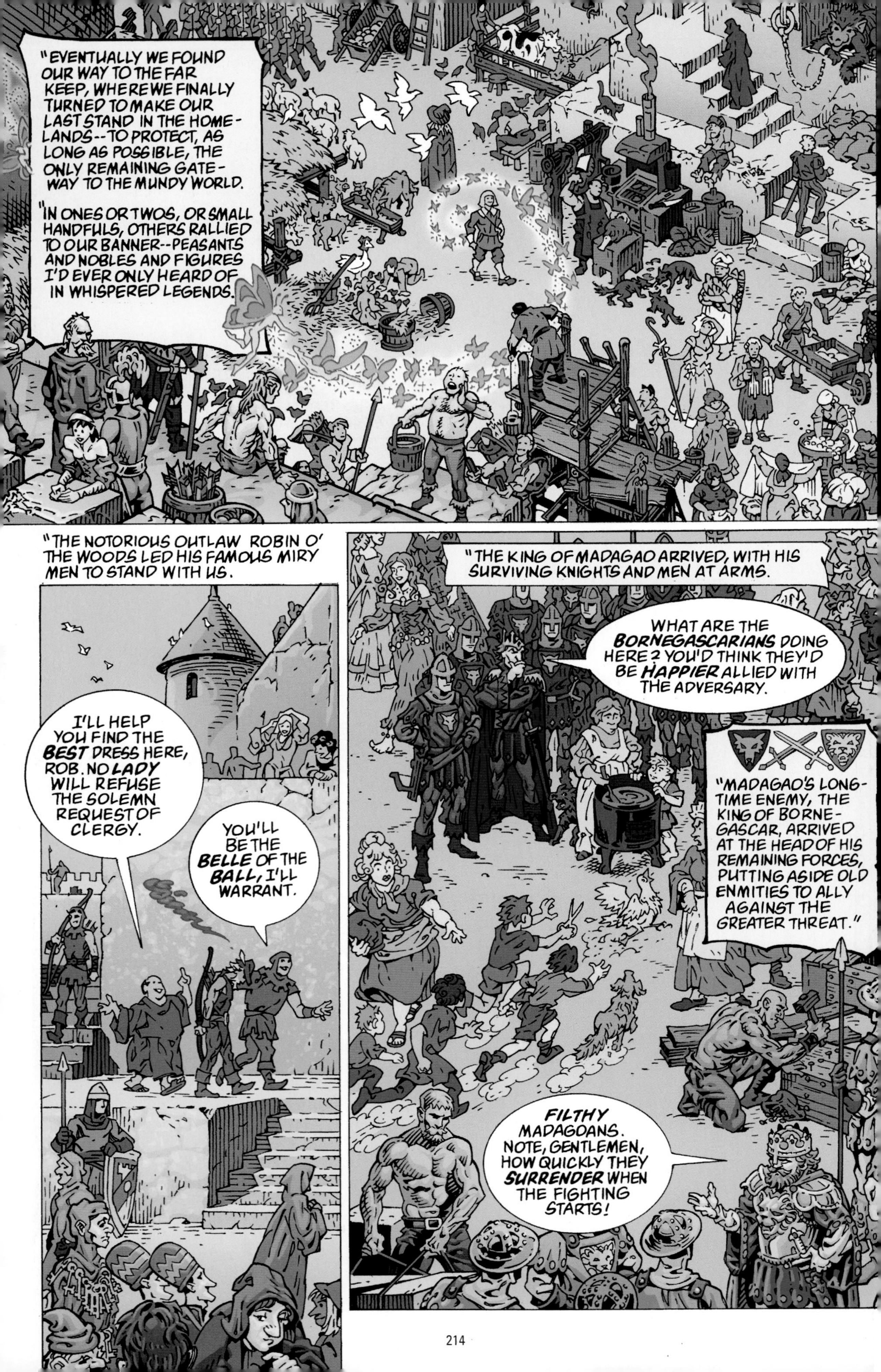
"EVENTUALLY WE FOUND OUR WAY TO THE FAR KEEP, WHERE WE FINALLY TURNED TO MAKE OUR LAST STAND IN THE HOMELANDS--TO PROTECT, AS LONG AS POSSIBLE, THE ONLY REMAINING GATEWAY TO THE MUNDY WORLD.
"IN ONES OR TWOS, OR SMALL HANDFULS, OTHERS RALLIED TO OUR BANNER--PEASANTS AND NOBLES AND FIGURES I'D EVER ONLY HEARD OF IN WHISPERED LEGENDS.
"THE NOTORIOUS OUTLAW ROBIN O' THE WOODS LED HIS FAMOUS MIRY MEN TO STAND WITH US.
I'LL HELP YOU FIND THE BEST DRESS HERE, ROB. NO LADY WILL REFUSE THE SOLEMN REQUEST OF CLERGY.
YOU'LL BE THE BELLE OF THE BALL, I'LL WARRANT.
"THE KING OF MADAGAO ARRIVED, WITH HIS SURVIVING KNIGHTS AND MEN AT ARMS.
WHAT ARE THE BORNEGASCARIANS DOING HERE? YOU'D THINK THEY'D BE HAPPIER ALLIED WITH THE ADVERSARY.
"MADAGAO'S LONG-TIME ENEMY, THE KING OF BORNEGASCAR, ARRIVED AT THE HEAD OF HIS REMAINING FORCES, PUTTING ASIDE OLD ENMITIES TO ALLY AGAINST THE GREATER THREAT."
FILTHY MADAGOANS. NOTE, GENTLEMEN, HOW QUICKLY THEY SURRENDER WHEN THE FIGHTING STARTS!

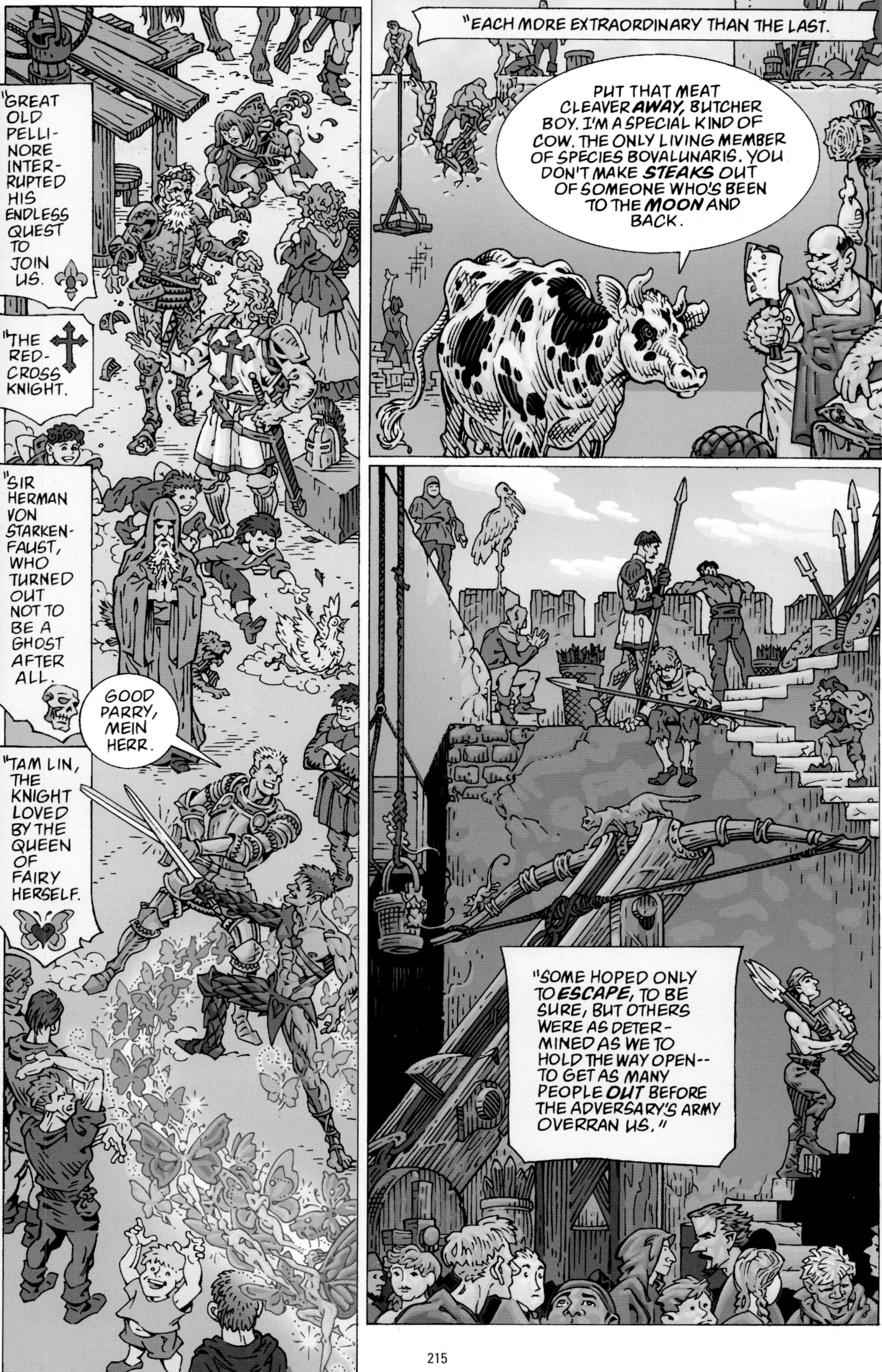
"GREAT OLD PELLINORE INTERRUPTED HIS ENDLESS QUEST TO JOIN US.
"THE RED-CROSS KNIGHT.
"SIR HERMAN VON STARKENFAUST, WHO TURNED OUT NOT TO BE A GHOST AFTER ALL.
GOOD PARRY, MEIN HERR.
"TAM LIN, THE KNIGHT LOVED BY THE QUEEN OF FAIRY HERSELF.
"EACH MORE EXTRAORDINARY THAN THE LAST.
PUT THAT MEAT CLEAVER AWAY, BUTCHER BOY. I'M A SPECIAL KIND OF COW. THE ONLY LIVING MEMBER OF SPECIES BOVALUNARIS. YOU DON'T MAKE STEAKS OUT OF SOMEONE WHO'S BEEN TO THE MOON AND BACK.
"SOME HOPED ONLY TO ESCAPE, TO BE SURE, BUT OTHERS WERE AS DETERMINED AS WE TO HOLD THE WAY OPEN-- TO GET AS MANY PEOPLE OUT BEFORE THE ADVERSARY'S ARMY OVERRAN US."

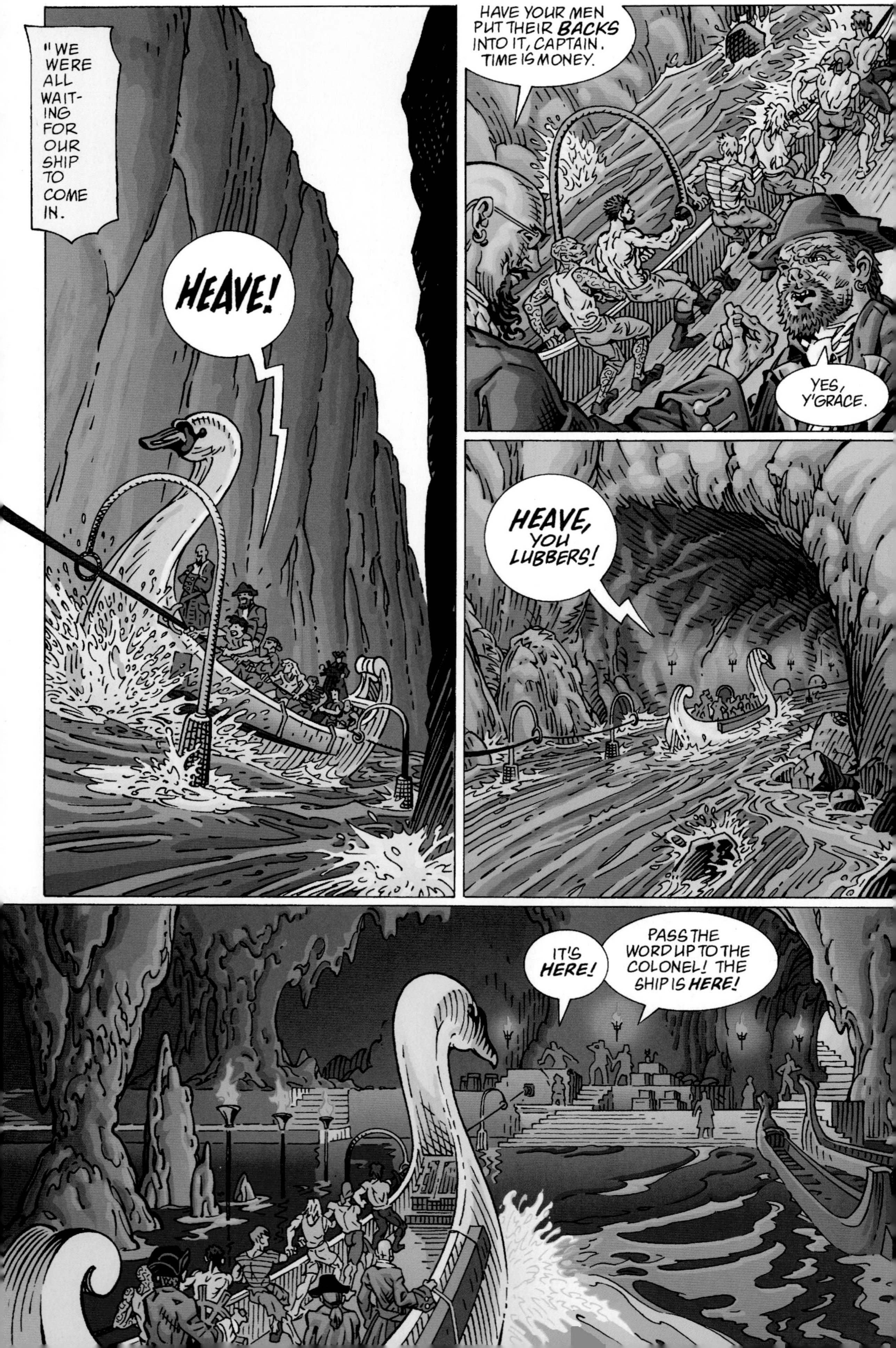
"WE WERE ALL WAITING FOR OUR SHIP TO COME IN.
HEAVE!
HAVE YOUR MEN PUT THEIR BACKS INTO IT, CAPTAIN. TIME IS MONEY.
YES, Y'GRACE.
HEAVE, YOU LUBBERS!
IT'S HERE!
PASS THE WORD UP TO THE COLONEL! THE SHIP IS HERE!

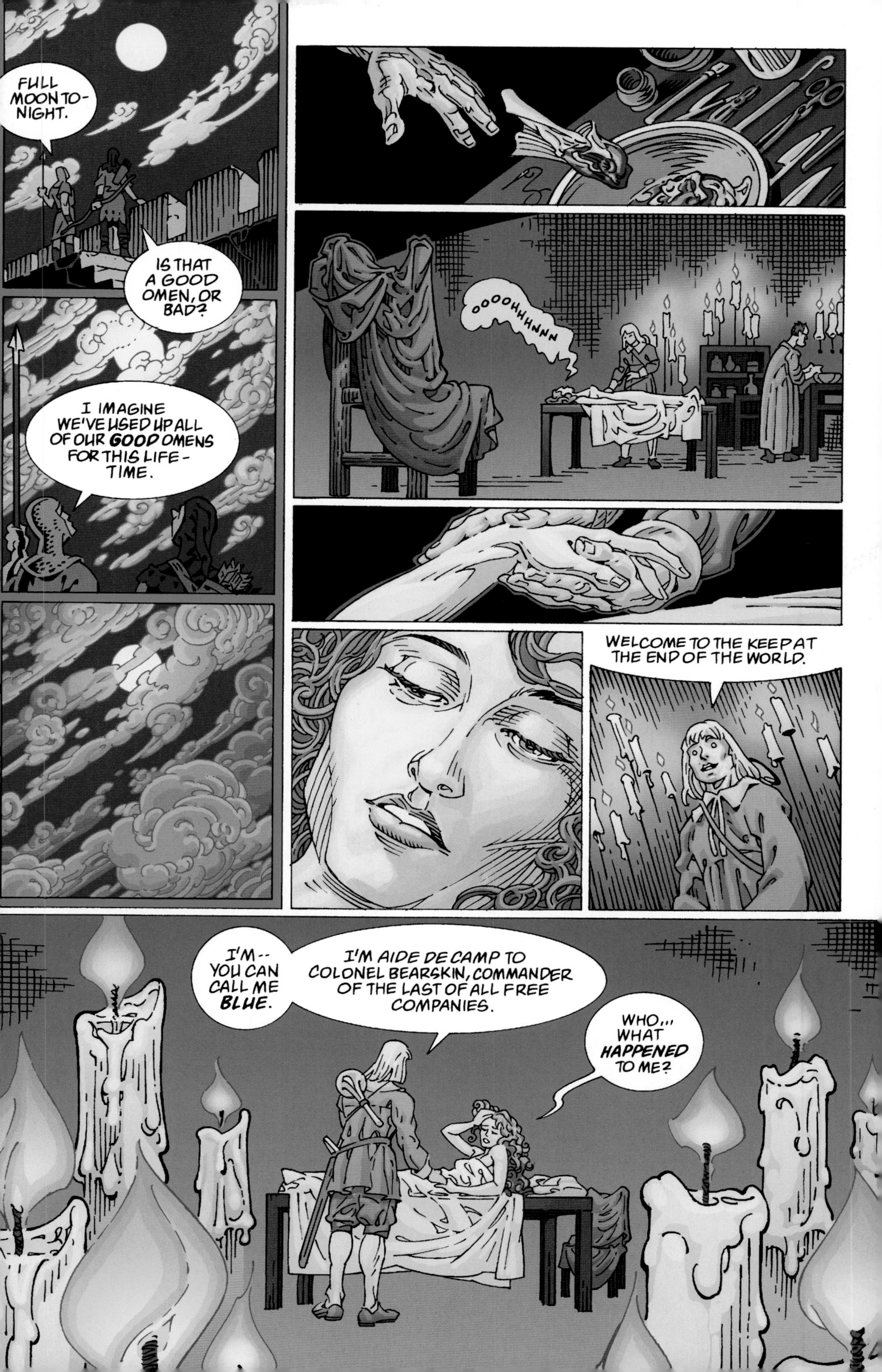
FULL MOON TO-NIGHT.
IS THAT A GOOD OMEN, OR BAD?
I IMAGINE WE'VE USED UP ALL OF OUR GOOD OMENS FOR THIS LIFE-TIME.
OOOOHHHNNN
WELCOME TO THE KEEP AT THE END OF THE WORLD.
I'M -- YOU CAN CALL ME BLUE.
I'M AIDE DE CAMP TO COLONEL BEARSKIN, COMMANDER OF THE LAST OF ALL FREE COMPANIES.
WHO... WHAT HAPPENED TO ME?

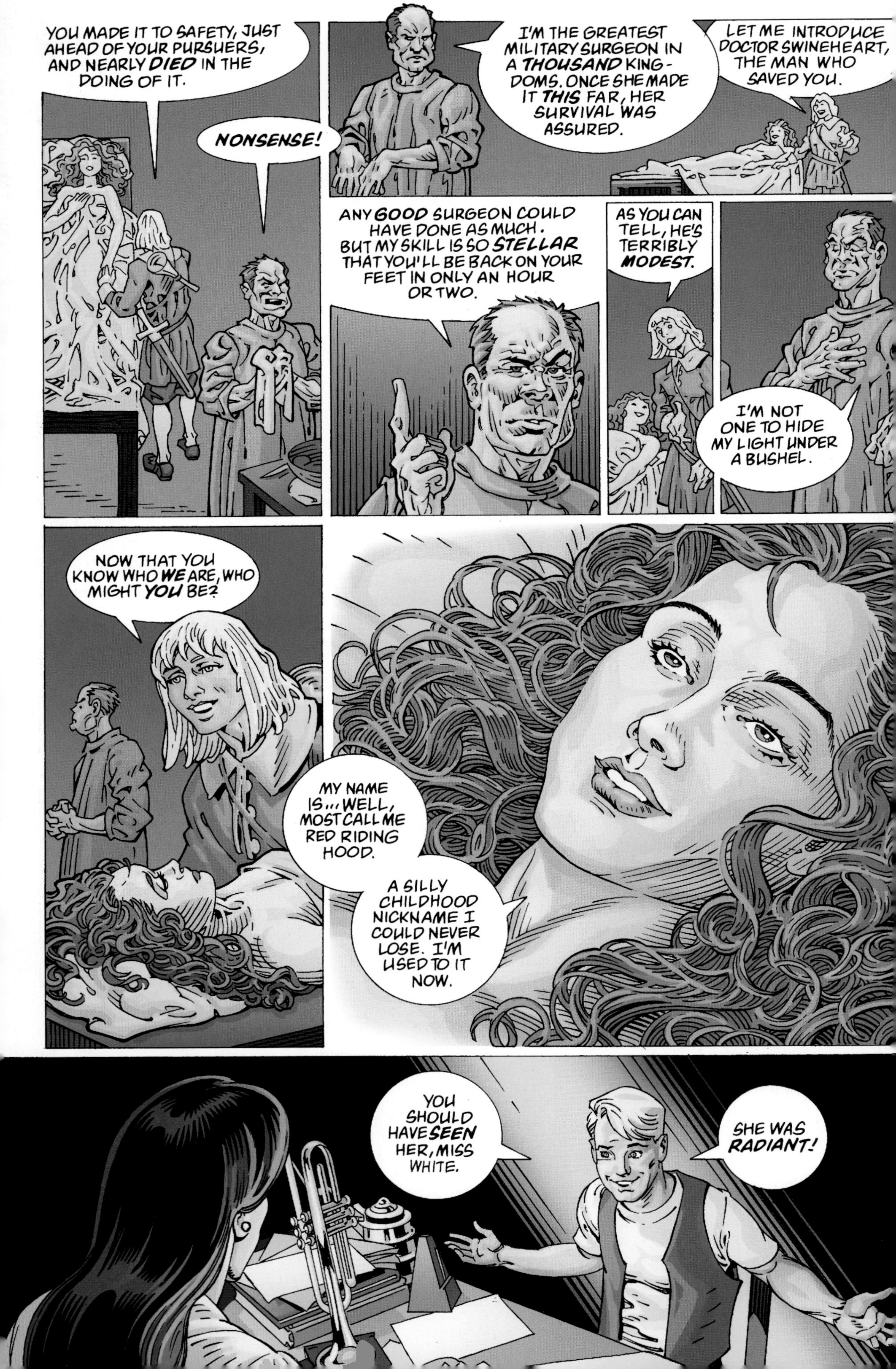
YOU MADE IT TO SAFETY, JUST AHEAD OF YOUR PURSUERS, AND NEARLY DIED IN THE DOING OF IT.
NONSENSE!
I'M THE GREATEST MILITARY SURGEON IN A THOUSAND KING-DOMS. ONCE SHE MADE IT THIS FAR, HER SURVIVAL WAS ASSURED.
LET ME INTRODUCE DOCTOR SWINEHEART, THE MAN WHO SAVED YOU.
ANY GOOD SURGEON COULD HAVE DONE AS MUCH. BUT MY SKILL IS SO STELLAR THAT YOU'LL BE BACK ON YOUR FEET IN ONLY AN HOUR OR TWO.
AS YOU CAN TELL, HE'S TERRIBLY MODEST.
I'M NOT ONE TO HIDE MY LIGHT UNDER A BUSHEL.
NOW THAT YOU KNOW WHO WE ARE, WHO MIGHT YOU BE?
MY NAME IS... WELL, MOST CALL ME RED RIDING HOOD.
A SILLY CHILDHOOD NICKNAME I COULD NEVER LOSE. I'M USED TO IT NOW.
YOU SHOULD HAVE SEEN HER, MISS WHITE.
SHE WAS RADIANT!

"I PASSED THAT EVENING WATCHING HER SLEEP. I DON'T KNOW WHAT OCCURRED IN THE REST OF THE KEEP.

WHY IS THAT **MAN** IN A **DRESS?**

I **ASSURE** YOU, LORD BLUEBEARD, I HAVE **NARY** AN IDEA.

THIS **RATHOLE** TURNS MORE CHAOTIC EVERY TRIP I **MAKE.**

WHERE'S YOUR COLONEL BEARSHIRT TONIGHT?

THAT WOULD BE **BEARSKIN,** SIR. HE TAKES HIS MEALS IN HIS QUARTERS, AND LACKING AN **EMERGENCY,** WON'T BE DISTURBED UNTIL MORNING.

NONSENSE. I WANT TO GET MY SHIP LOADED AND OUT OF HERE AT FIRST LIGHT.

NOT WITHOUT HIS LEAVE, SIR.

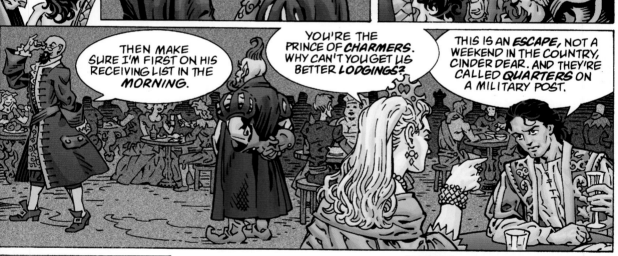

THEN MAKE SURE I'M FIRST ON HIS RECEIVING LIST IN THE **MORNING.**

YOU'RE THE PRINCE OF **CHARMERS.** WHY CAN'T YOU GET US BETTER **LODGINGS?**

THIS IS AN **ESCAPE,** NOT A WEEKEND IN THE COUNTRY, CINDER DEAR. AND THEY'RE CALLED **QUARTERS** ON A MILITARY POST.

AND DIDN'T I GET US **THIS** FAR WITH OUR SKINS INTACT? THAT'S **SOMETHING,** MY TURTLEDOVE.

WHAT WILL THIS MUNDY WORLD BE LIKE? IS IT TRUE THAT **BOTH** OF YOUR PREVIOUS WIVES ARE THERE ALREADY?

GOD, I **HOPE** NOT. IT'S SUPPOSED TO BE A **REFUGE** AFTER ALL.

THE NEXT DAY WASN'T SO ENJOYABLE.

THAT MORNING, THE ADVERSARY'S ARMY SHOWED UP.

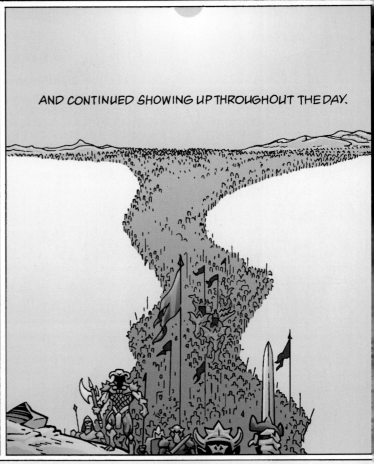

AND CONTINUED SHOWING UP THROUGHOUT THE DAY.

UNTIL, BY THAT EVENING, THEY FILLED THE LENGTH AND BREADTH OF OUR CORNER OF THE WORLD.

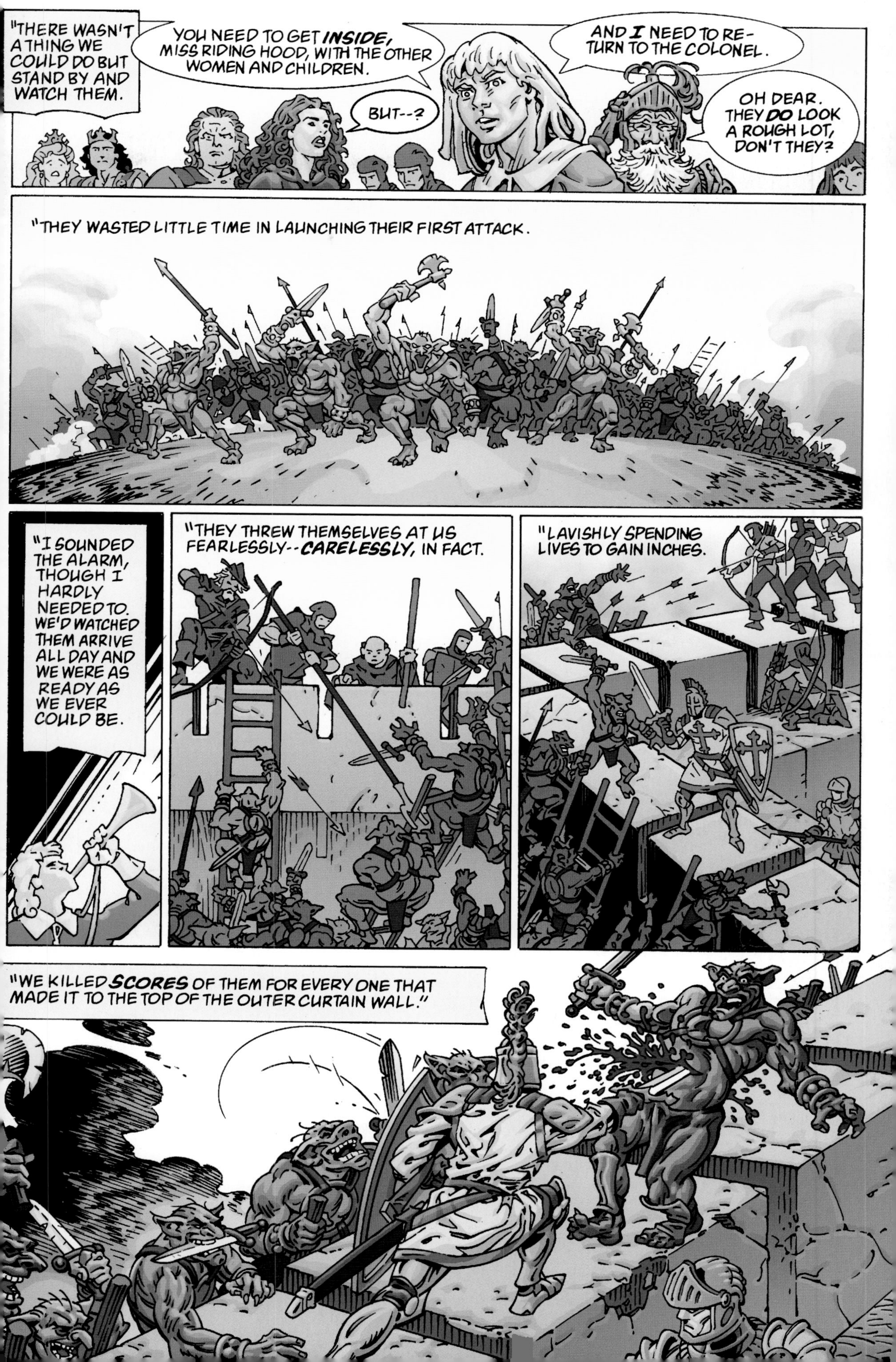
"THERE WASN'T A THING WE COULD DO BUT STAND BY AND WATCH THEM.
YOU NEED TO GET INSIDE, MISS RIDING HOOD, WITH THE OTHER WOMEN AND CHILDREN.
BUT--?
AND I NEED TO RE-TURN TO THE COLONEL.
OH DEAR. THEY DO LOOK A ROUGH LOT, DON'T THEY?
"THEY WASTED LITTLE TIME IN LAUNCHING THEIR FIRST ATTACK.
"I SOUNDED THE ALARM, THOUGH I HARDLY NEEDED TO. WE'D WATCHED THEM ARRIVE ALL DAY AND WE WERE AS READY AS WE EVER COULD BE.
"THEY THREW THEMSELVES AT US FEARLESSLY--CARELESSLY, IN FACT.
"LAVISHLY SPENDING LIVES TO GAIN INCHES.
"WE KILLED SCORES OF THEM FOR EVERY ONE THAT MADE IT TO THE TOP OF THE OUTER CURTAIN WALL."

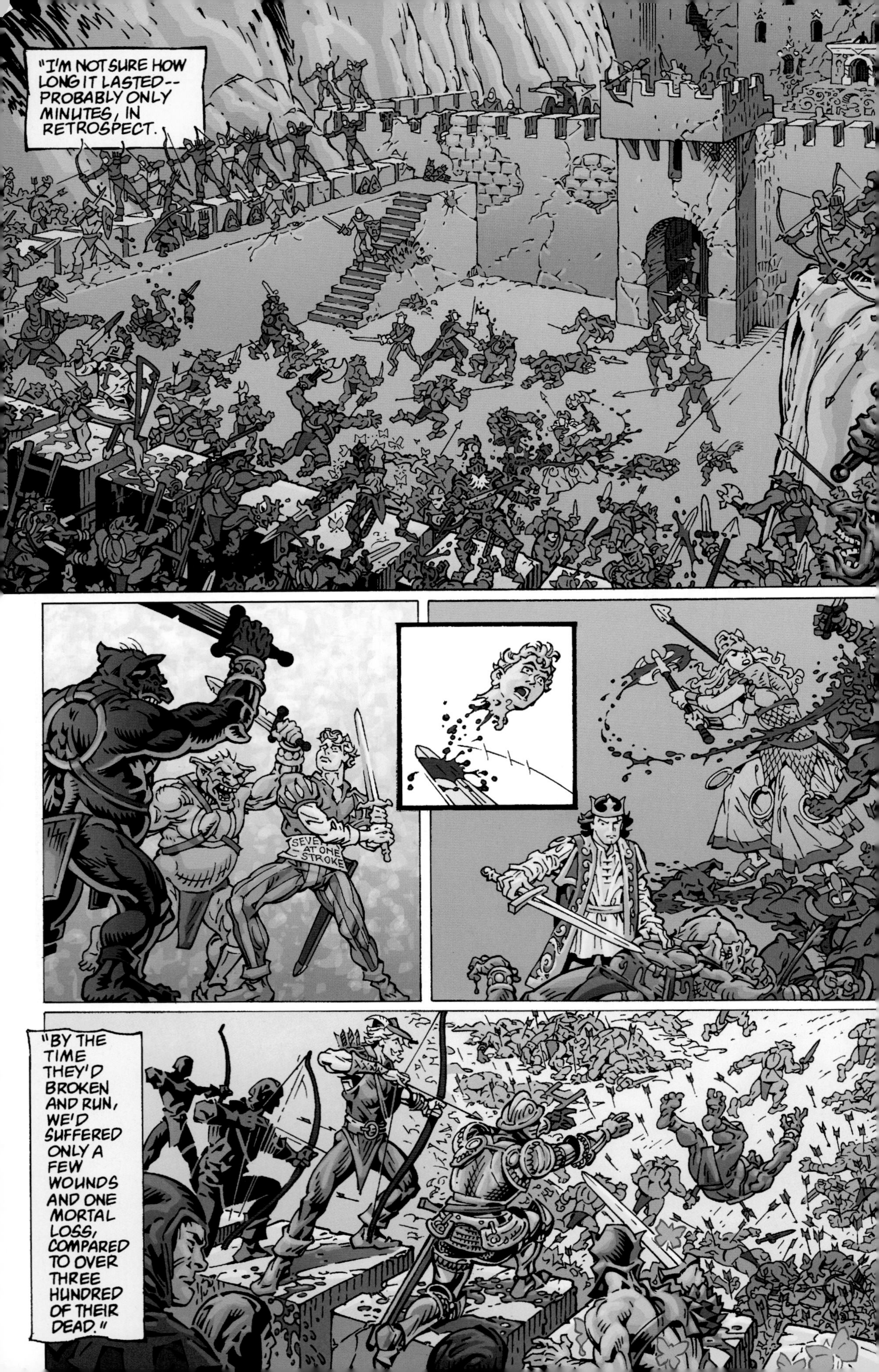
"I'M NOT SURE HOW LONG IT LASTED-- PROBABLY ONLY MINUTES, IN RETROSPECT.
SEVEN AT ONE STROKE
"BY THE TIME THEY'D BROKEN AND RUN, WE'D SUFFERED ONLY A FEW WOUNDS AND ONE MORTAL LOSS, COMPARED TO OVER THREE HUNDRED OF THEIR DEAD."

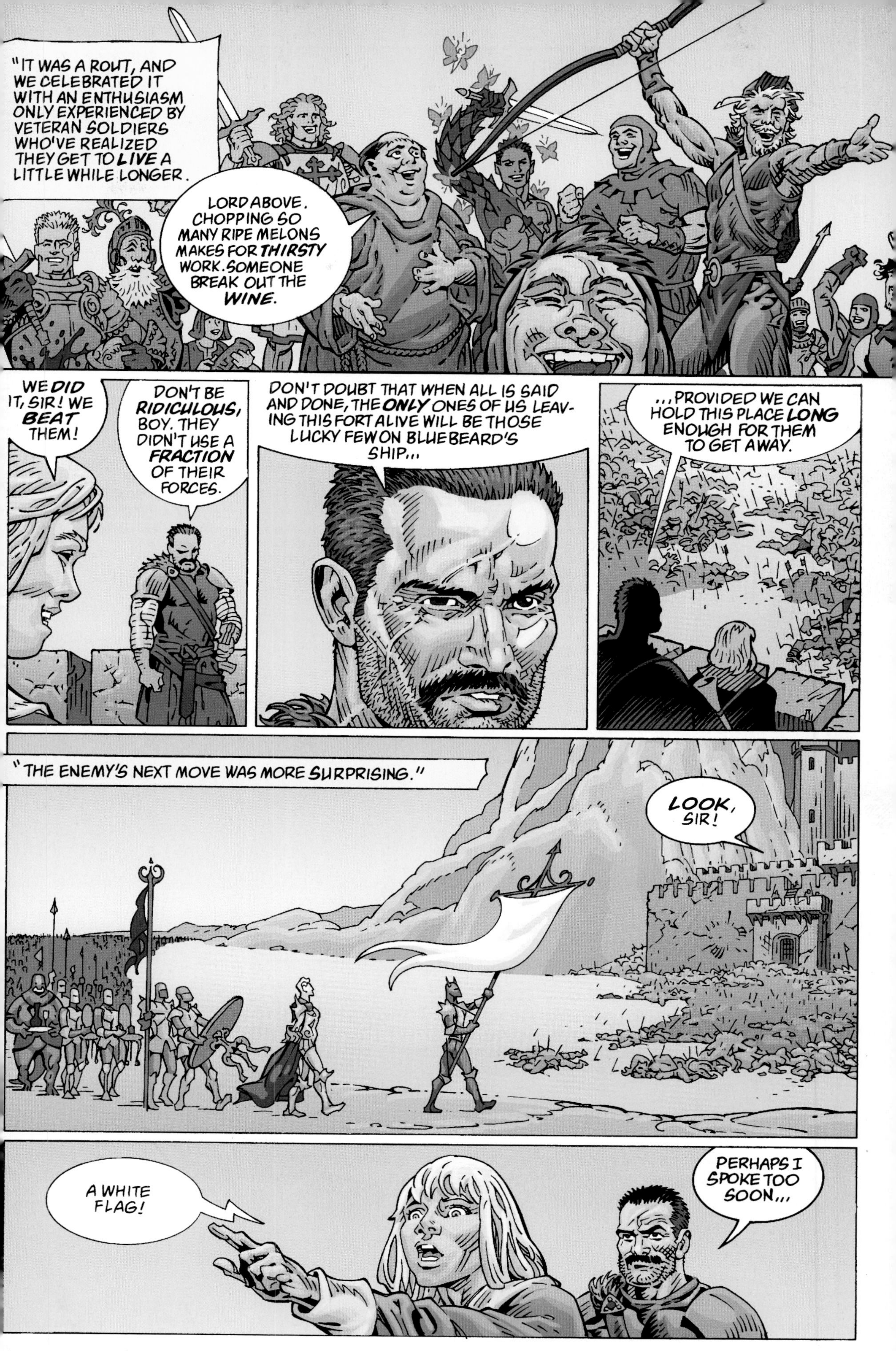
"IT WAS A ROUT, AND WE CELEBRATED IT WITH AN ENTHUSIASM ONLY EXPERIENCED BY VETERAN SOLDIERS WHO'VE REALIZED THEY GET TO LIVE A LITTLE WHILE LONGER.
LORD ABOVE. CHOPPING SO MANY RIPE MELONS MAKES FOR THIRSTY WORK. SOMEONE BREAK OUT THE WINE.
WE DID IT, SIR! WE BEAT THEM!
DON'T BE RIDICULOUS, BOY. THEY DIDN'T USE A FRACTION OF THEIR FORCES.
DON'T DOUBT THAT WHEN ALL IS SAID AND DONE, THE ONLY ONES OF US LEAVING THIS FORT ALIVE WILL BE THOSE LUCKY FEW ON BLUEBEARD'S SHIP...
...PROVIDED WE CAN HOLD THIS PLACE LONG ENOUGH FOR THEM TO GET AWAY.
"THE ENEMY'S NEXT MOVE WAS MORE SURPRISING."
LOOK, SIR!
A WHITE FLAG!
PERHAPS I SPOKE TOO SOON...

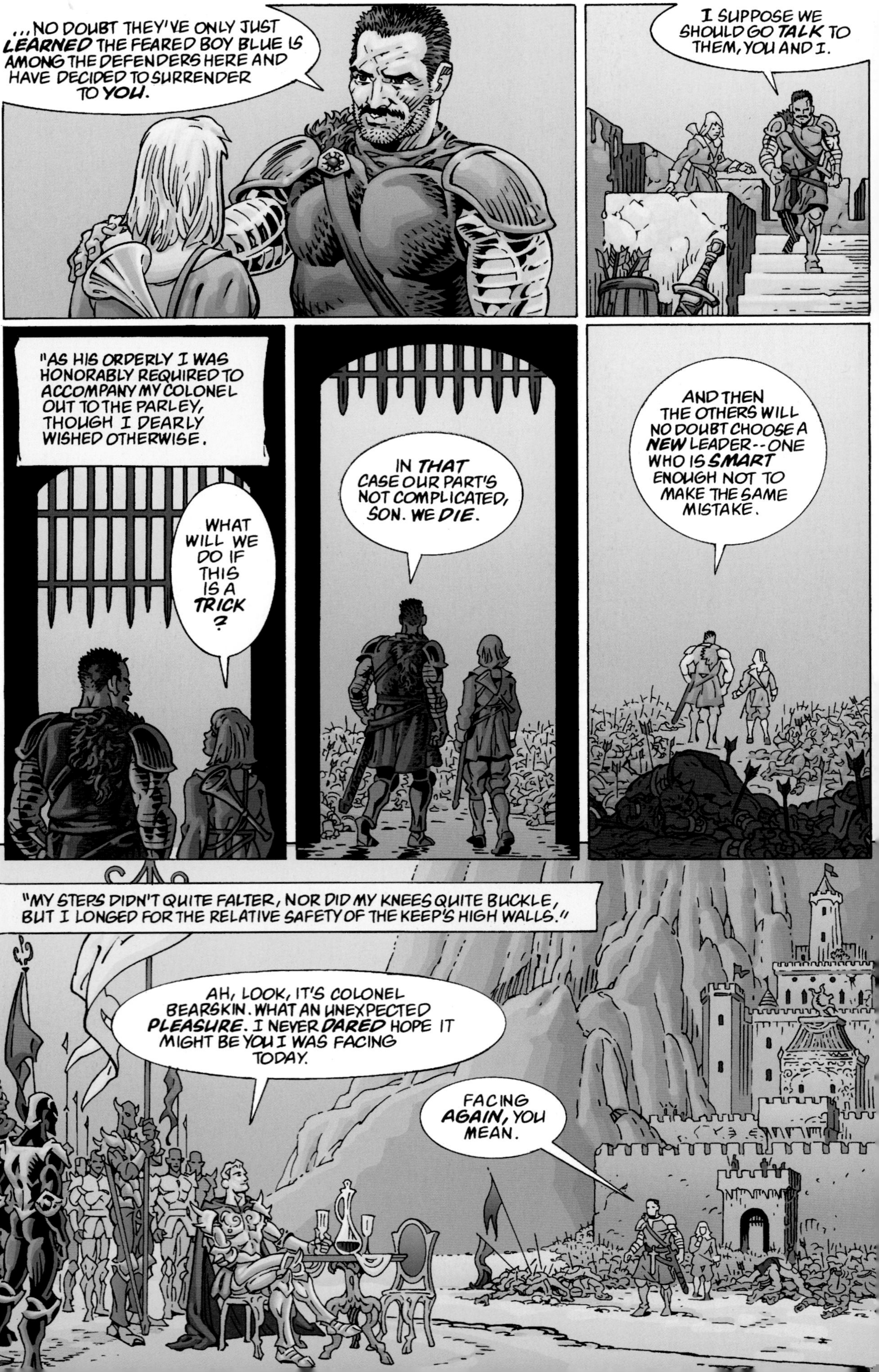
...NO DOUBT THEY'VE ONLY JUST LEARNED THE FEARED BOY BLUE IS AMONG THE DEFENDERS HERE AND HAVE DECIDED TO SURRENDER TO YOU.
I SUPPOSE WE SHOULD GO TALK TO THEM, YOU AND I.
"AS HIS ORDERLY I WAS HONORABLY REQUIRED TO ACCOMPANY MY COLONEL OUT TO THE PARLEY, THOUGH I DEARLY WISHED OTHERWISE.
WHAT WILL WE DO IF THIS IS A TRICK?
IN THAT CASE OUR PART'S NOT COMPLICATED, SON. WE DIE.
AND THEN THE OTHERS WILL NO DOUBT CHOOSE A NEW LEADER--ONE WHO IS SMART ENOUGH NOT TO MAKE THE SAME MISTAKE.
"MY STEPS DIDN'T QUITE FALTER, NOR DID MY KNEES QUITE BUCKLE, BUT I LONGED FOR THE RELATIVE SAFETY OF THE KEEP'S HIGH WALLS."
AH, LOOK, IT'S COLONEL BEARSKIN. WHAT AN UNEXPECTED PLEASURE. I NEVER DARED HOPE IT MIGHT BE YOU I WAS FACING TODAY.
FACING AGAIN, YOU MEAN.

YOU WERE IN COMMAND AT BOXEN, WEREN'T YOU? I BEAT YOU THEN, COUNT AUCASSIN DE BEAUCAIRE.

OUT-*MANEUVERED* ME, PERHAPS.

AND NOW YOUR LATEST ATTACK *FAILED*.

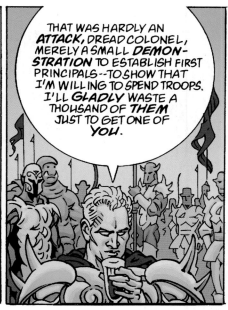

THAT WAS HARDLY AN *ATTACK*, DREAD COLONEL, MERELY A SMALL *DEMON-STRATION* TO ESTABLISH FIRST PRINCIPALS -- TO SHOW THAT I'M WILLING TO SPEND TROOPS. I'LL *GLADLY* WASTE A THOUSAND OF *THEM* JUST TO GET ONE OF *YOU*.

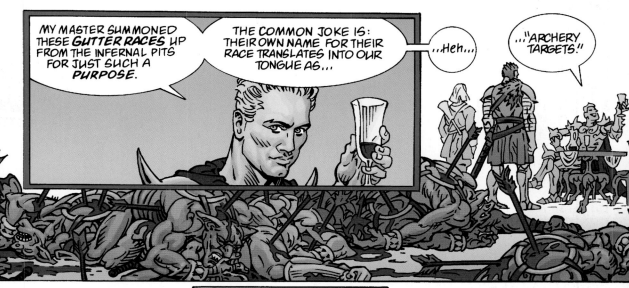

MY MASTER SUMMONED THESE *GUTTER RACES* UP FROM THE INFERNAL PITS FOR JUST SUCH A *PURPOSE*.

THE COMMON JOKE IS: THEIR OWN NAME FOR THEIR RACE TRANSLATES INTO OUR TONGUE AS...

...Heh...

..."ARCHERY TARGETS."

BUT I'M BEING *RUDE*. I'D INTENDED TO OFFER YOU *REFRESHMENT* BEFORE WE GOT DOWN TO BUSINESS. DO *PLEASE* SIT DOWN.

NO, THANK YOU. I'M *PARTICULAR* ABOUT WHO I DRINK WITH. WHY DON'T YOU JUST SAY WHAT YOU *INTEND* TO SAY?

VERY WELL, THEN. YOU'RE OUT-NUMBERED BY AN *OVERWHELMING* FACTOR. YOU CAN'T WIN AND YOU CAN'T GET AWAY. MY ORDERS ARE TO KILL YOU -- *ALL* OF YOU.

--EVEN UNTO THE SMALLEST CHILD.

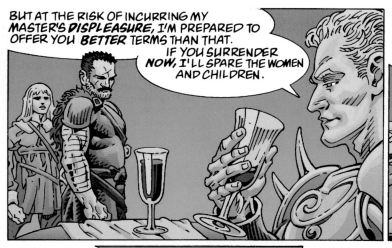

BUT AT THE RISK OF INCURRING MY MASTER'S *DISPLEASURE*, I'M PREPARED TO OFFER YOU *BETTER* TERMS THAN THAT.

IF YOU SURRENDER *NOW*, I'LL SPARE THE WOMEN AND CHILDREN.

THEY'LL LIVE IN DIRE CAPTIVITY...

...BUT AT LEAST THEY'LL *LIVE*.

HOW LONG DO WE HAVE TO DECIDE?

NO TIME AT ALL. CHOOSE *NOW*.

I CAN'T. THIS TIME I'M ONLY *NOMINALLY* IN CHARGE OF A MIXED FORCE. I'LL HAVE TO CONSULT THE OTHER COMMANDERS.

VERY WELL. GO BACK AND *TAKE* YOUR MEETING. DON'T DELAY, THOUGH. YOU HAVE UNTIL I BECOME *BORED* WITH SITTING OUT HERE.

"RETURNING--WITH MY UNPROTECTED *BACK* FACING THE ENEMY--WAS *WORSE*. I SWEAR I COULD FEEL THEIR ARROWS CENTERED ON ME."

YOU'LL *KNOW* THAT THE TIME HAS FINALLY RUN OUT WHEN YOU FEEL MY *SWORD* SLICE THROUGH YOUR OVER-LARGE NECK.

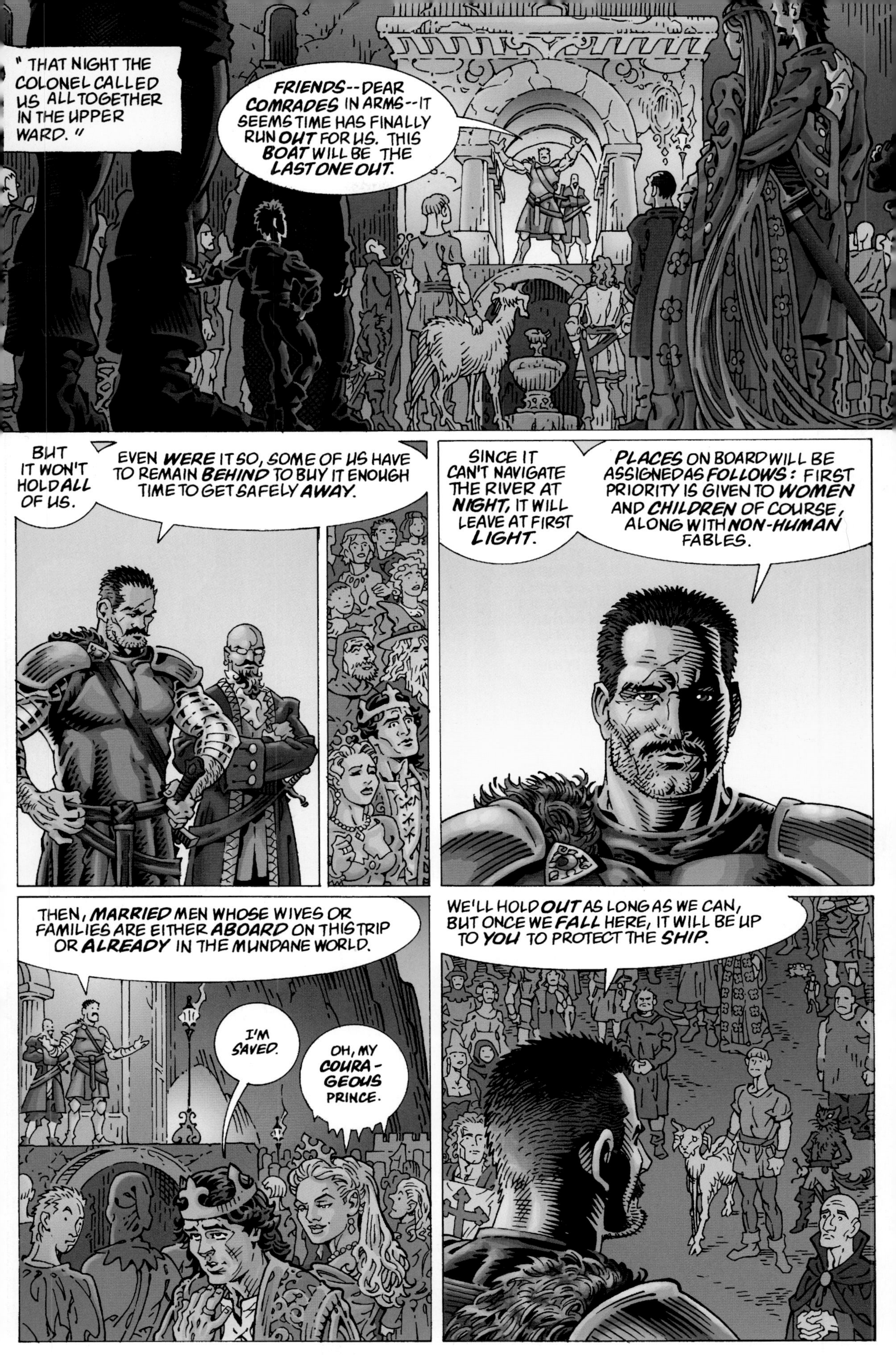
" THAT NIGHT THE COLONEL CALLED US ALL TOGETHER IN THE UPPER WARD. "
FRIENDS--DEAR COMRADES IN ARMS--IT SEEMS TIME HAS FINALLY RUN OUT FOR US. THIS BOAT WILL BE THE LAST ONE OUT.
BUT IT WON'T HOLD ALL OF US.
EVEN WERE IT SO, SOME OF US HAVE TO REMAIN BEHIND TO BUY IT ENOUGH TIME TO GET SAFELY AWAY.
SINCE IT CAN'T NAVIGATE THE RIVER AT NIGHT, IT WILL LEAVE AT FIRST LIGHT.
PLACES ON BOARD WILL BE ASSIGNED AS FOLLOWS: FIRST PRIORITY IS GIVEN TO WOMEN AND CHILDREN OF COURSE, ALONG WITH NON-HUMAN FABLES.
THEN, MARRIED MEN WHOSE WIVES OR FAMILIES ARE EITHER ABOARD ON THIS TRIP OR ALREADY IN THE MUNDANE WORLD.
I'M SAVED.
OH, MY COURAGEOUS PRINCE.
WE'LL HOLD OUT AS LONG AS WE CAN, BUT ONCE WE FALL HERE, IT WILL BE UP TO YOU TO PROTECT THE SHIP.

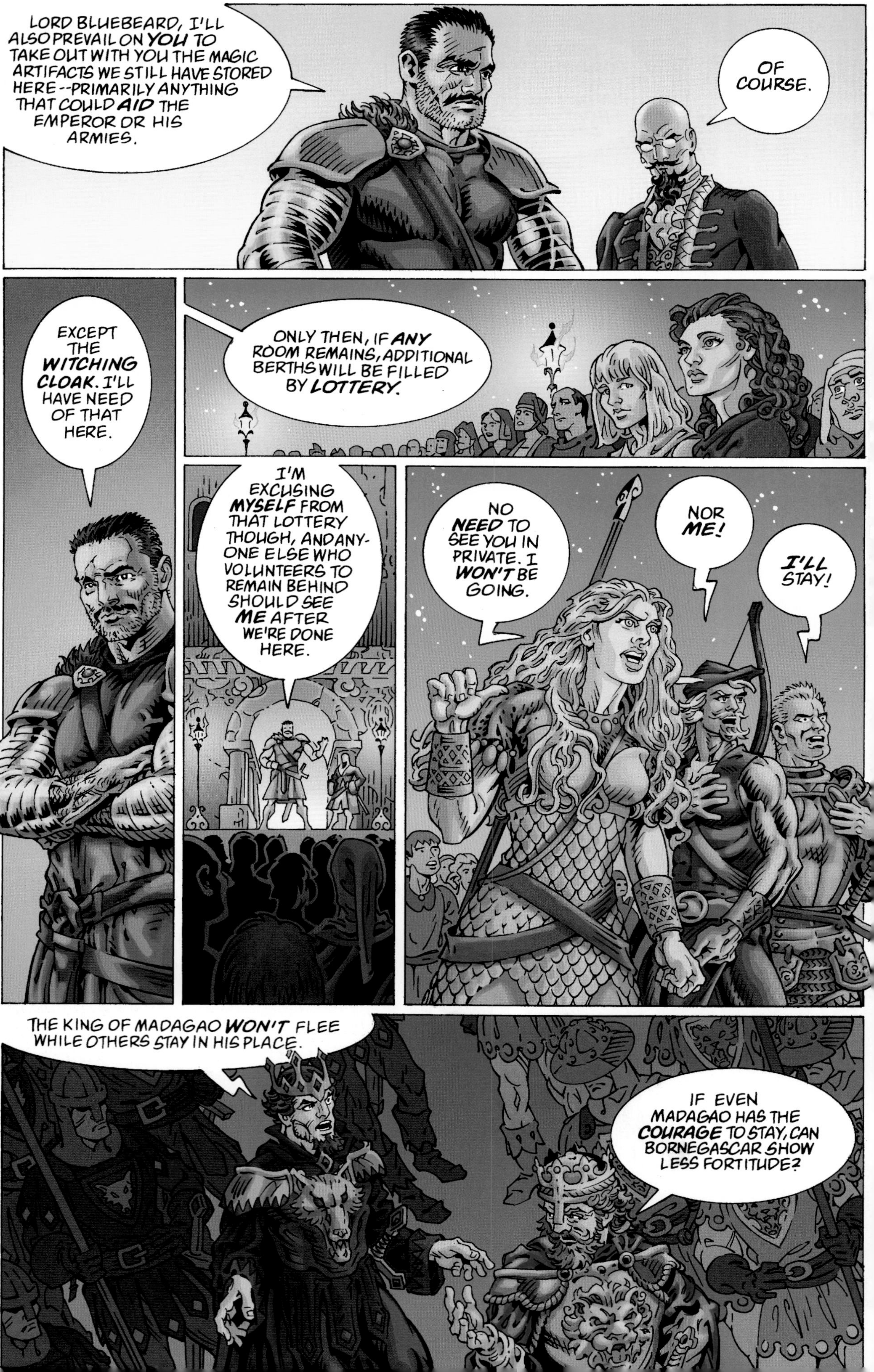
LORD BLUEBEARD, I'LL ALSO PREVAIL ON YOU TO TAKE OUT WITH YOU THE MAGIC ARTIFACTS WE STILL HAVE STORED HERE--PRIMARILY ANYTHING THAT COULD AID THE EMPEROR OR HIS ARMIES.
OF COURSE.
EXCEPT THE WITCHING CLOAK. I'LL HAVE NEED OF THAT HERE.
ONLY THEN, IF ANY ROOM REMAINS, ADDITIONAL BERTHS WILL BE FILLED BY LOTTERY.
I'M EXCUSING MYSELF FROM THAT LOTTERY THOUGH, AND ANYONE ELSE WHO VOLUNTEERS TO REMAIN BEHIND SHOULD SEE ME AFTER WE'RE DONE HERE.
NO NEED TO SEE YOU IN PRIVATE. I WON'T BE GOING.
NOR ME!
I'LL STAY!
THE KING OF MADAGAO WON'T FLEE WHILE OTHERS STAY IN HIS PLACE.
IF EVEN MADAGAO HAS THE COURAGE TO STAY, CAN BORNEGASCAR SHOW LESS FORTITUDE?

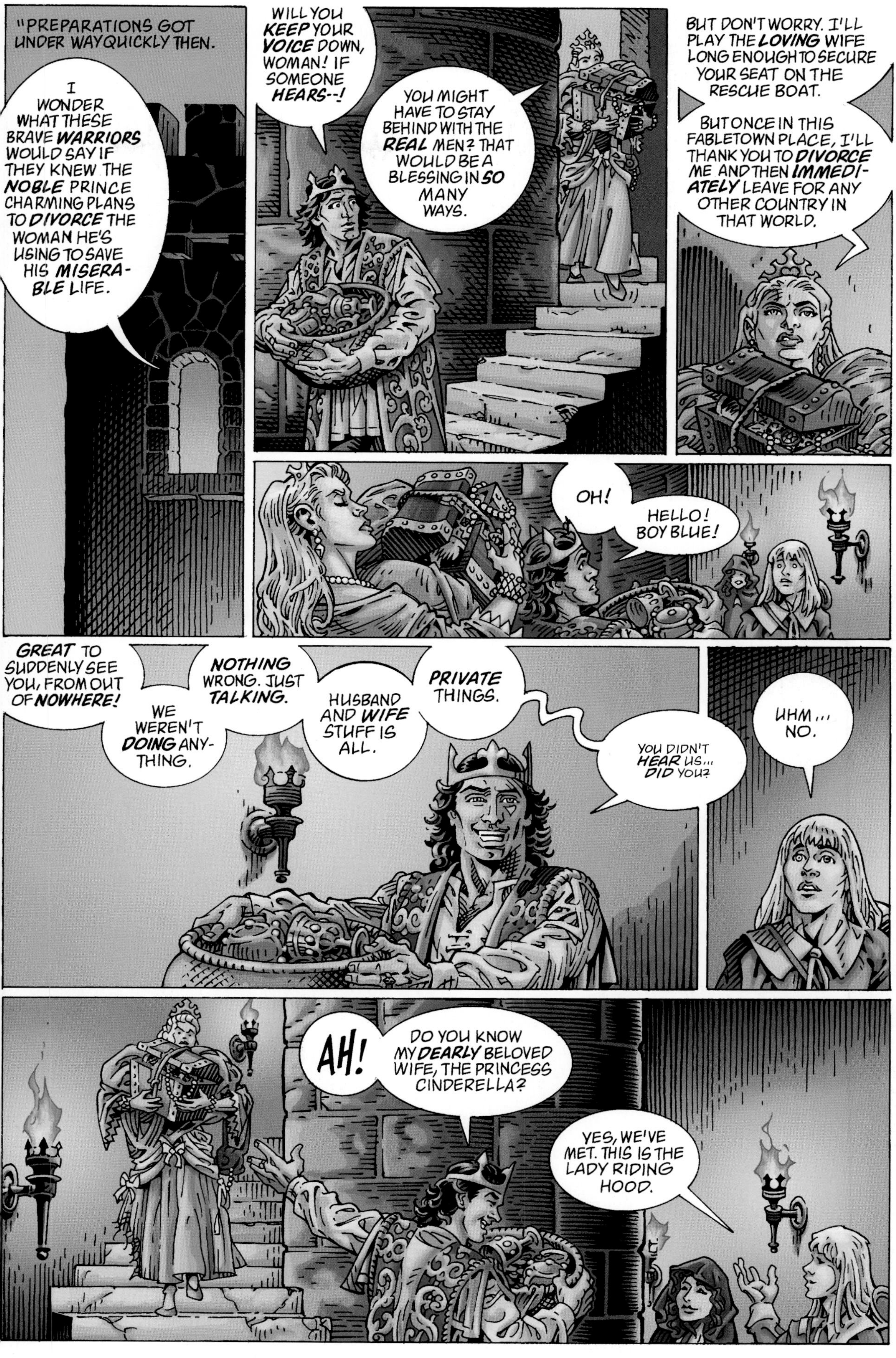

"PREPARATIONS GOT UNDER WAY QUICKLY THEN.
I WONDER WHAT THESE BRAVE WARRIORS WOULD SAY IF THEY KNEW THE NOBLE PRINCE CHARMING PLANS TO DIVORCE THE WOMAN HE'S USING TO SAVE HIS MISERABLE LIFE.
WILL YOU KEEP YOUR VOICE DOWN, WOMAN! IF SOMEONE HEARS--!
YOU MIGHT HAVE TO STAY BEHIND WITH THE REAL MEN? THAT WOULD BE A BLESSING IN SO MANY WAYS.
BUT DON'T WORRY. I'LL PLAY THE LOVING WIFE LONG ENOUGH TO SECURE YOUR SEAT ON THE RESCUE BOAT.
BUT ONCE IN THIS FABLETOWN PLACE, I'LL THANK YOU TO DIVORCE ME AND THEN IMMEDIATELY LEAVE FOR ANY OTHER COUNTRY IN THAT WORLD.
OH!
HELLO! BOY BLUE!
GREAT TO SUDDENLY SEE YOU, FROM OUT OF NOWHERE!
WE WEREN'T DOING ANYTHING.
NOTHING WRONG. JUST TALKING.
HUSBAND AND WIFE STUFF IS ALL.
PRIVATE THINGS.
YOU DIDN'T HEAR US... DID YOU?
UHM... NO.
AH!
DO YOU KNOW MY DEARLY BELOVED WIFE, THE PRINCESS CINDERELLA?
YES, WE'VE MET. THIS IS THE LADY RIDING HOOD.

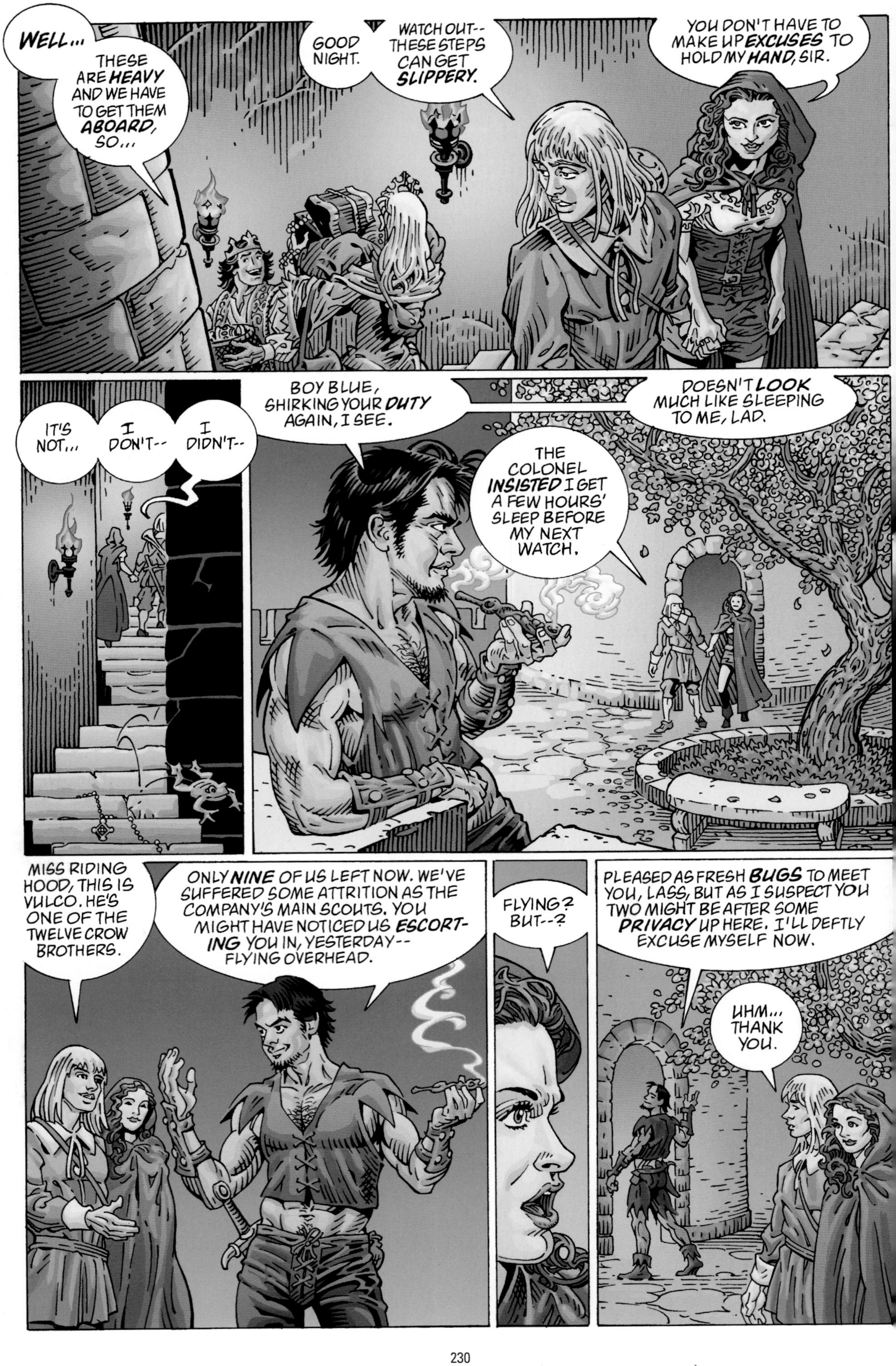
WELL... THESE ARE HEAVY AND WE HAVE TO GET THEM ABOARD, SO...
GOOD NIGHT.
WATCH OUT-- THESE STEPS CAN GET SLIPPERY.
YOU DON'T HAVE TO MAKE UP EXCUSES TO HOLD MY HAND, SIR.
IT'S NOT...
I DON'T--
I DIDN'T--
BOY BLUE, SHIRKING YOUR DUTY AGAIN, I SEE.
THE COLONEL INSISTED I GET A FEW HOURS' SLEEP BEFORE MY NEXT WATCH.
DOESN'T LOOK MUCH LIKE SLEEPING TO ME, LAD.
MISS RIDING HOOD, THIS IS VULCO. HE'S ONE OF THE TWELVE CROW BROTHERS.
ONLY NINE OF US LEFT NOW. WE'VE SUFFERED SOME ATTRITION AS THE COMPANY'S MAIN SCOUTS. YOU MIGHT HAVE NOTICED US ESCORTING YOU IN, YESTERDAY-- FLYING OVERHEAD.
FLYING? BUT--?
PLEASED AS FRESH BUGS TO MEET YOU, LASS, BUT AS I SUSPECT YOU TWO MIGHT BE AFTER SOME PRIVACY UP HERE, I'LL DEFTLY EXCUSE MYSELF NOW.
UHM... THANK YOU.

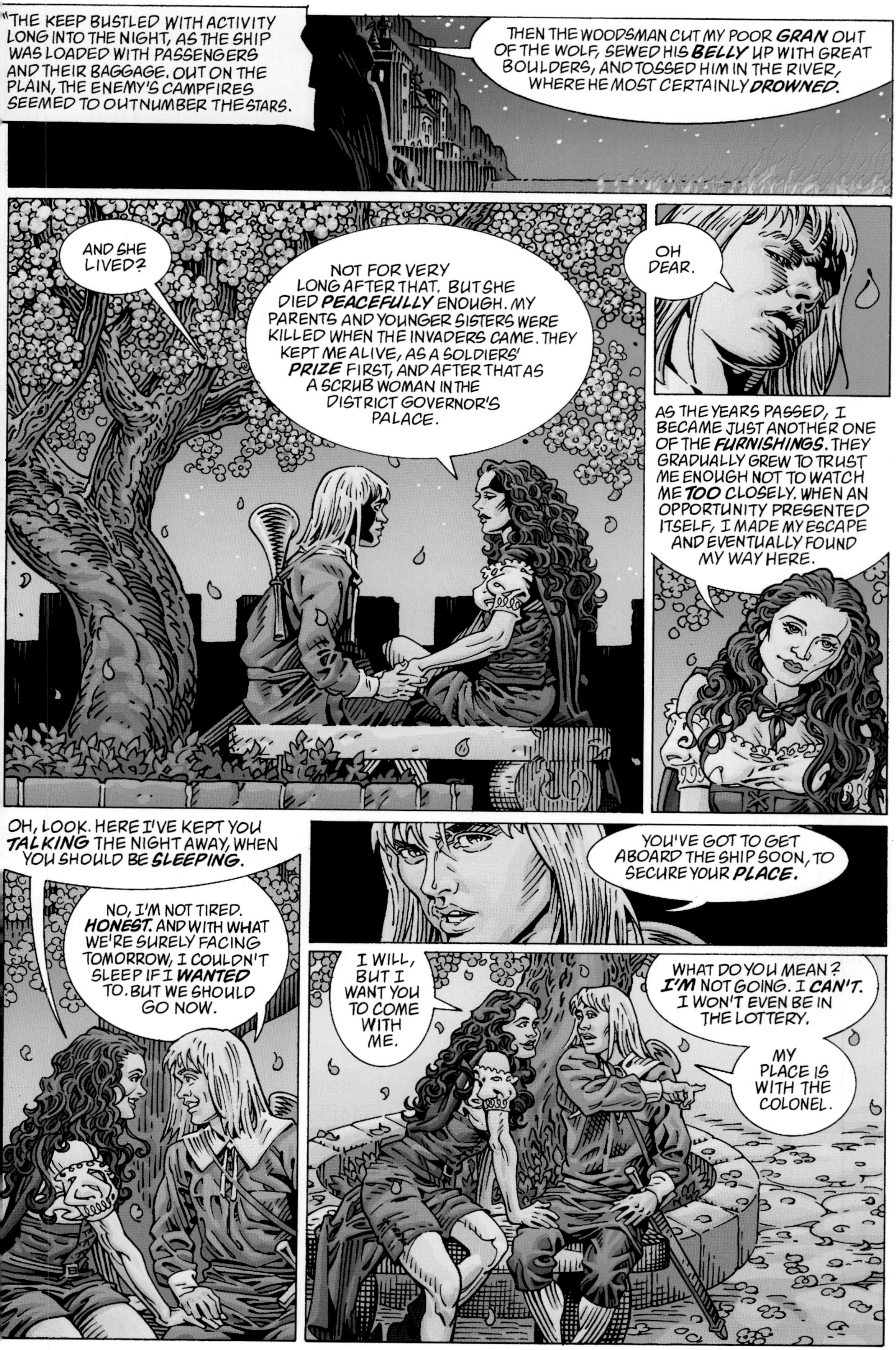
"THE KEEP BUSTLED WITH ACTIVITY LONG INTO THE NIGHT, AS THE SHIP WAS LOADED WITH PASSENGERS AND THEIR BAGGAGE. OUT ON THE PLAIN, THE ENEMY'S CAMPFIRES SEEMED TO OUTNUMBER THE STARS.
THEN THE WOODSMAN CUT MY POOR GRAN OUT OF THE WOLF, SEWED HIS BELLY UP WITH GREAT BOULDERS, AND TOSSED HIM IN THE RIVER, WHERE HE MOST CERTAINLY DROWNED.
AND SHE LIVED?
NOT FOR VERY LONG AFTER THAT. BUT SHE DIED PEACEFULLY ENOUGH. MY PARENTS AND YOUNGER SISTERS WERE KILLED WHEN THE INVADERS CAME. THEY KEPT ME ALIVE, AS A SOLDIERS' PRIZE FIRST, AND AFTER THAT AS A SCRUB WOMAN IN THE DISTRICT GOVERNOR'S PALACE.
OH DEAR.
AS THE YEARS PASSED, I BECAME JUST ANOTHER ONE OF THE FURNISHINGS. THEY GRADUALLY GREW TO TRUST ME ENOUGH NOT TO WATCH ME TOO CLOSELY. WHEN AN OPPORTUNITY PRESENTED ITSELF, I MADE MY ESCAPE AND EVENTUALLY FOUND MY WAY HERE.
OH, LOOK. HERE I'VE KEPT YOU TALKING THE NIGHT AWAY, WHEN YOU SHOULD BE SLEEPING.
NO, I'M NOT TIRED. HONEST. AND WITH WHAT WE'RE SURELY FACING TOMORROW, I COULDN'T SLEEP IF I WANTED TO. BUT WE SHOULD GO NOW.
YOU'VE GOT TO GET ABOARD THE SHIP SOON, TO SECURE YOUR PLACE.
I WILL, BUT I WANT YOU TO COME WITH ME.
WHAT DO YOU MEAN? I'M NOT GOING. I CAN'T. I WON'T EVEN BE IN THE LOTTERY.
MY PLACE IS WITH THE COLONEL.

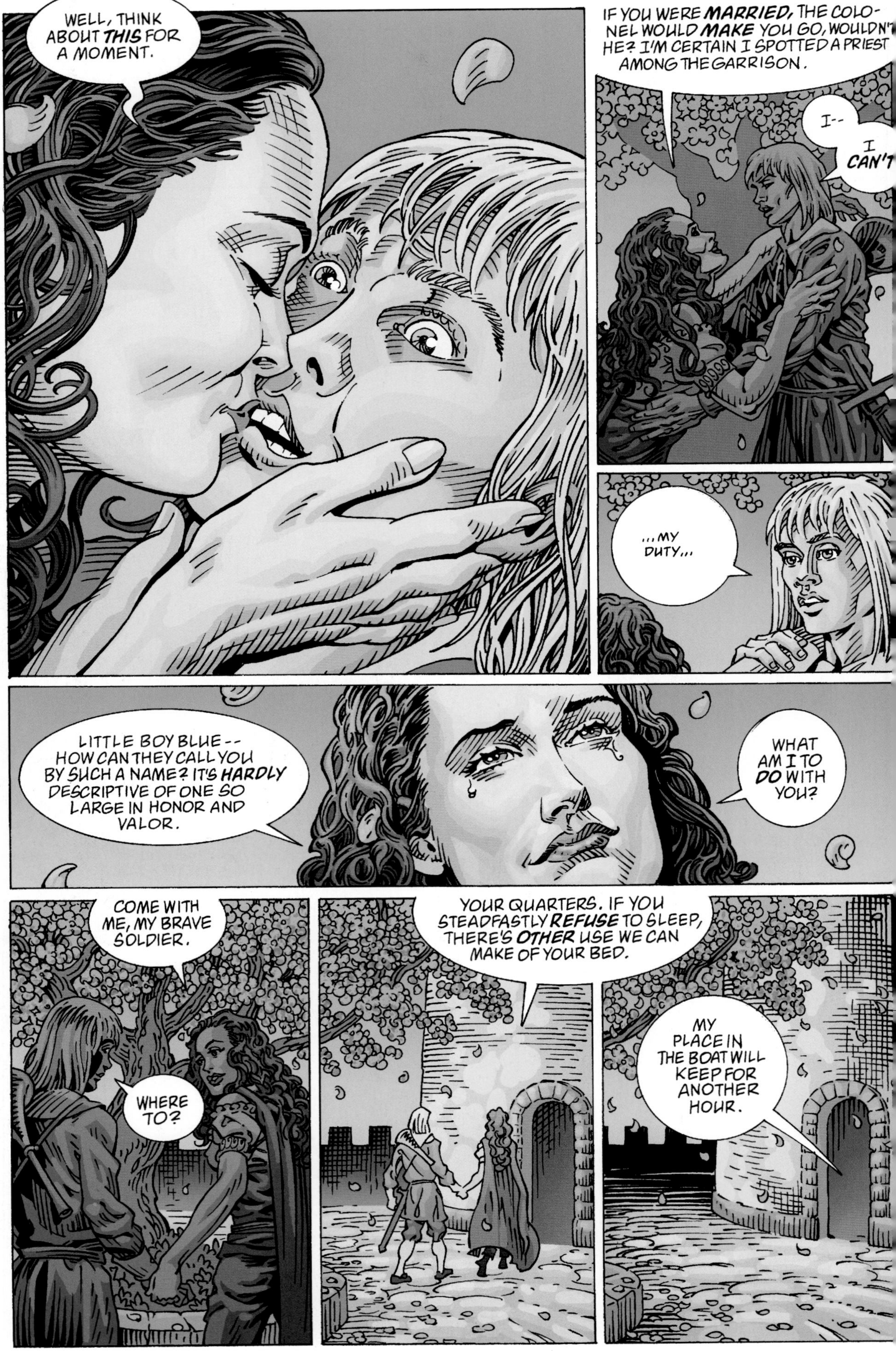
WELL, THINK ABOUT THIS FOR A MOMENT.
IF YOU WERE MARRIED, THE COLONEL WOULD MAKE YOU GO, WOULDN'T HE? I'M CERTAIN I SPOTTED A PRIEST AMONG THE GARRISON.
I--
I CAN'T
...MY DUTY...
LITTLE BOY BLUE -- HOW CAN THEY CALL YOU BY SUCH A NAME? IT'S HARDLY DESCRIPTIVE OF ONE SO LARGE IN HONOR AND VALOR.
WHAT AM I TO DO WITH YOU?
COME WITH ME, MY BRAVE SOLDIER.
WHERE TO?
YOUR QUARTERS. IF YOU STEADFASTLY REFUSE TO SLEEP, THERE'S OTHER USE WE CAN MAKE OF YOUR BED.
MY PLACE IN THE BOAT WILL KEEP FOR ANOTHER HOUR.

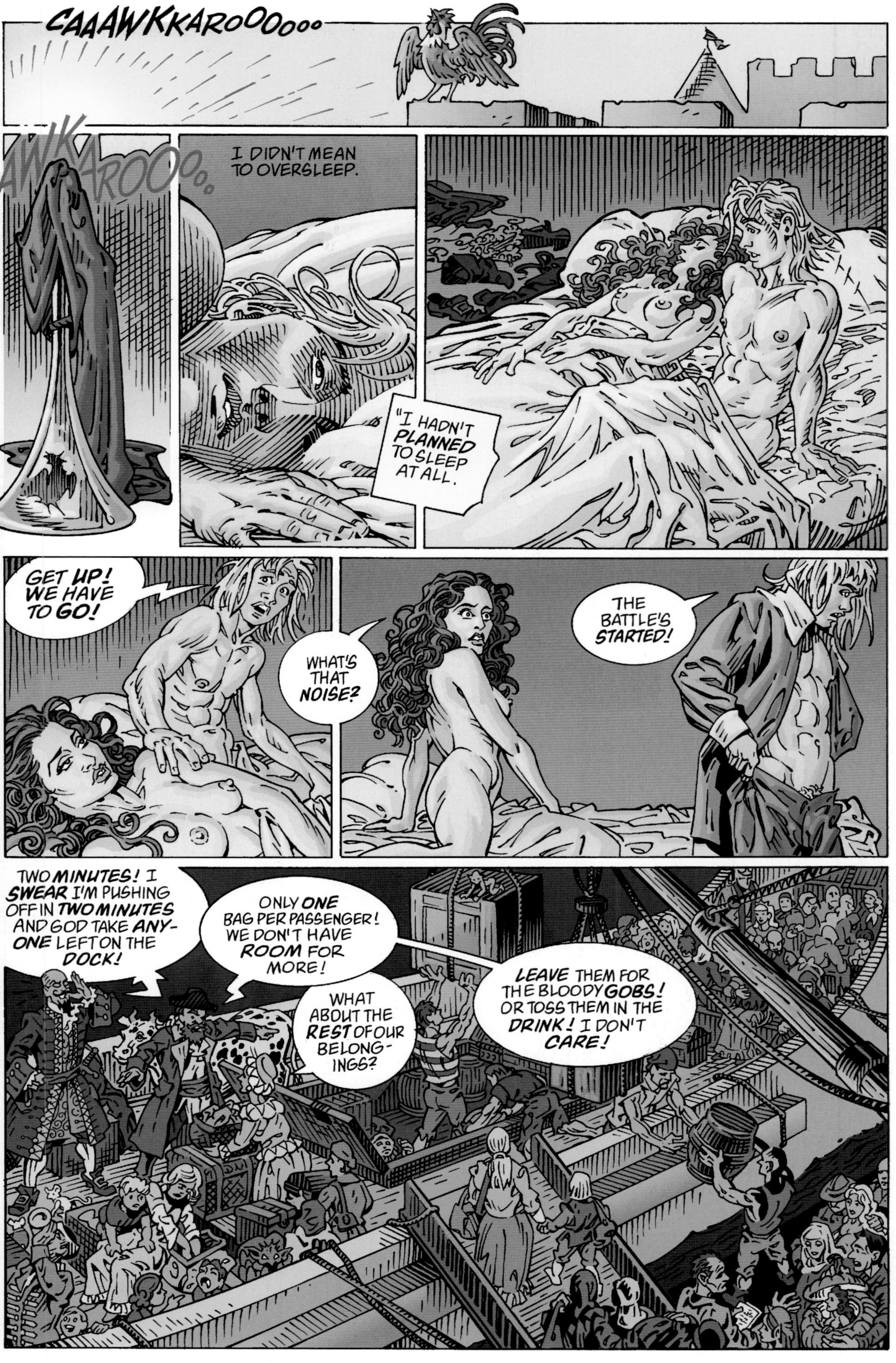
CAAAWKKAROOOooo
AWKAROOOoo
I DIDN'T MEAN TO OVERSLEEP.
"I HADN'T PLANNED TO SLEEP AT ALL.
GET UP! WE HAVE TO GO!
WHAT'S THAT NOISE?
THE BATTLE'S STARTED!
TWO MINUTES! I SWEAR I'M PUSHING OFF IN TWO MINUTES AND GOD TAKE ANY-ONE LEFT ON THE DOCK!
ONLY ONE BAG PER PASSENGER! WE DON'T HAVE ROOM FOR MORE!
WHAT ABOUT THE REST OF OUR BELONG-INGS?
LEAVE THEM FOR THE BLOODY GOBS! OR TOSS THEM IN THE DRINK! I DON'T CARE!

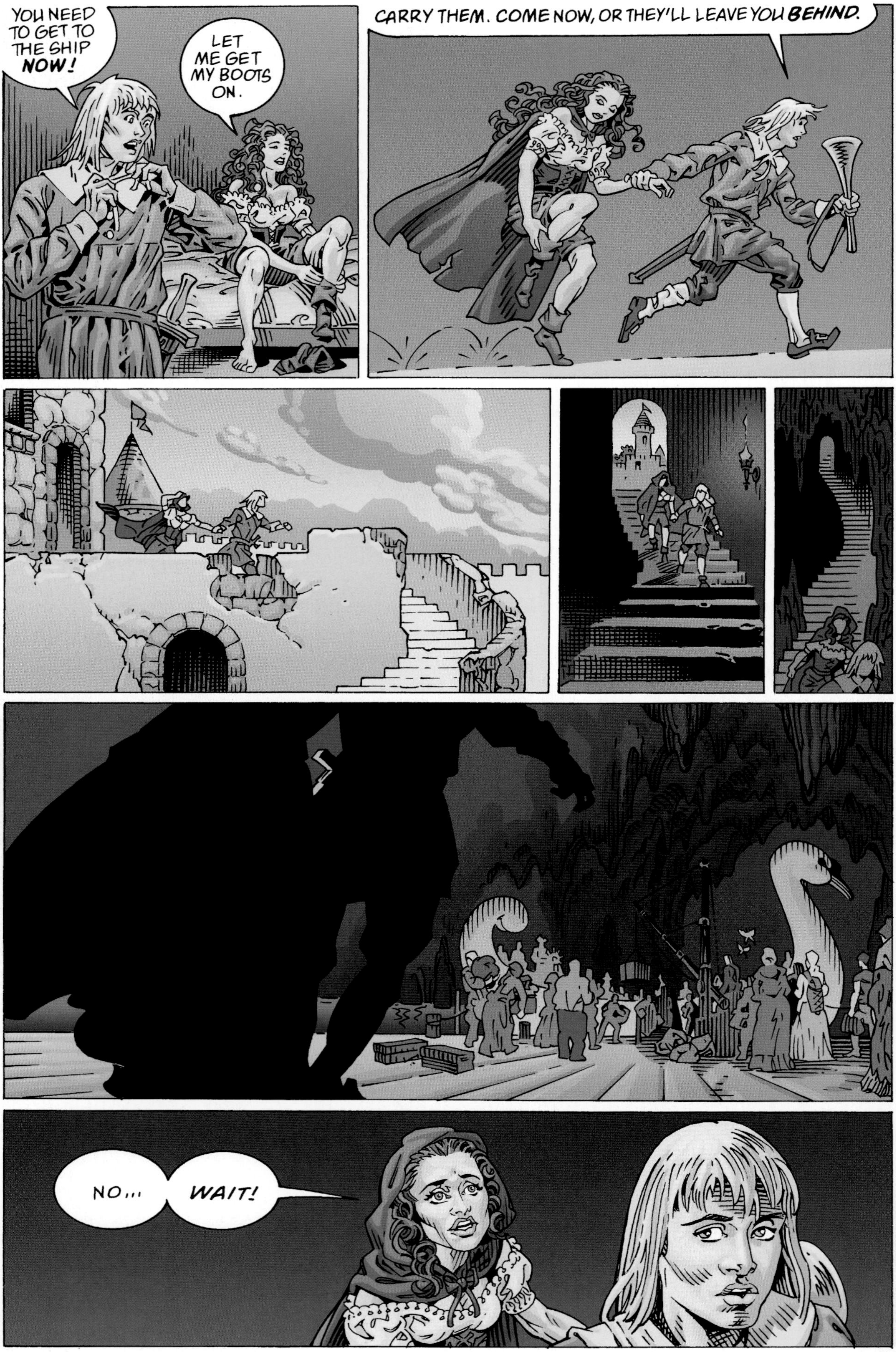

YOU NEED TO GET TO THE SHIP **NOW!**
LET ME GET MY BOOTS ON.
CARRY THEM. COME NOW, OR THEY'LL LEAVE YOU **BEHIND.**
NO...
WAIT!

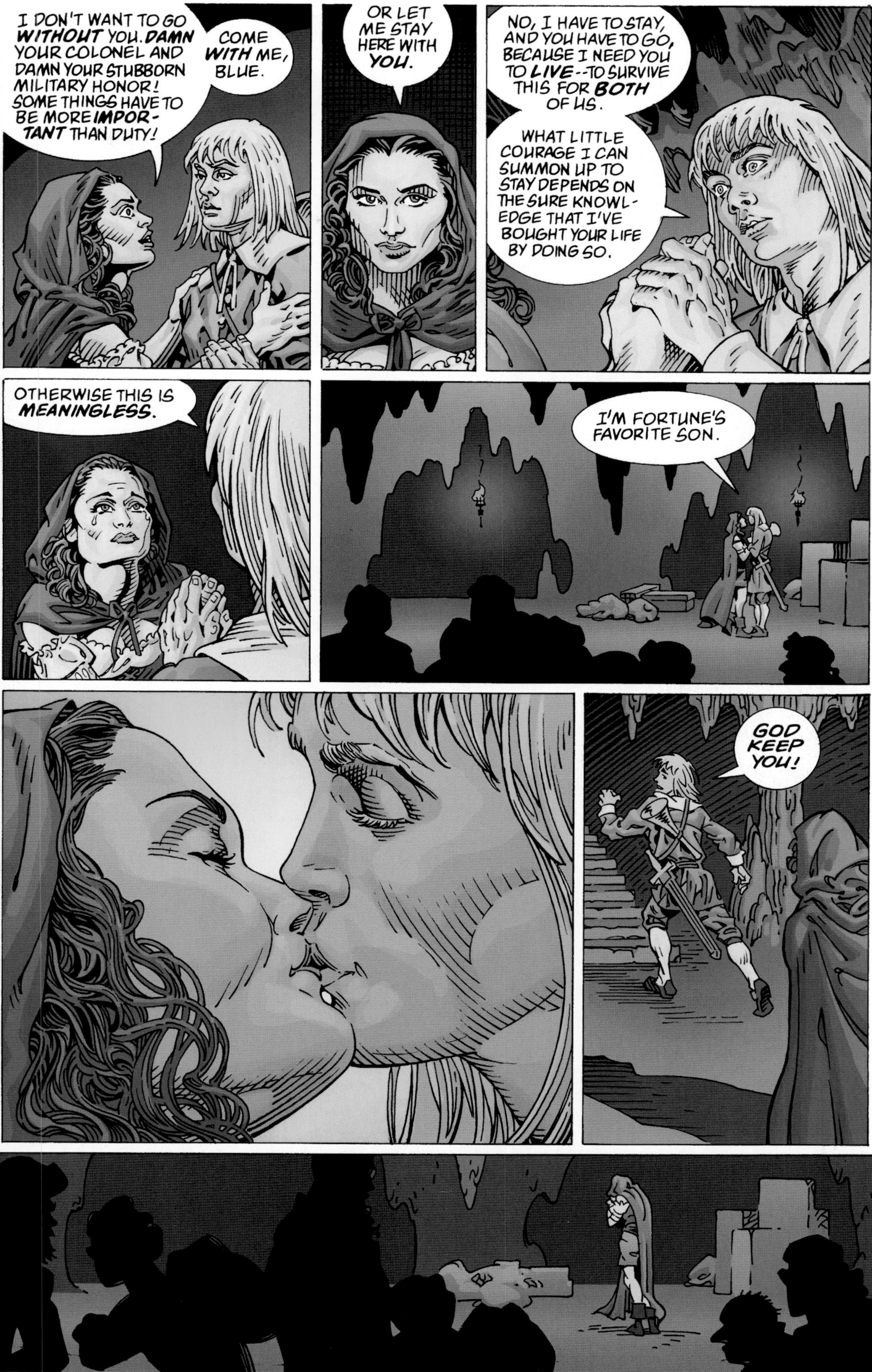
I DON'T WANT TO GO **WITHOUT** YOU. **DAMN** YOUR COLONEL AND DAMN YOUR STUBBORN MILITARY HONOR! SOME THINGS HAVE TO BE MORE **IMPOR-TANT** THAN DUTY!
COME **WITH** ME, BLUE.
OR LET ME STAY HERE WITH **YOU**.
NO, I HAVE TO STAY, AND YOU HAVE TO GO, BECAUSE I NEED YOU TO **LIVE**--TO SURVIVE THIS FOR **BOTH** OF US.
WHAT LITTLE COURAGE I CAN SUMMON UP TO STAY DEPENDS ON THE SURE KNOWL-EDGE THAT I'VE BOUGHT YOUR LIFE BY DOING SO.
OTHERWISE THIS IS **MEANINGLESS**.
I'M FORTUNE'S FAVORITE SON.
GOD KEEP YOU!

WHERE THE **HELL** HAVE YOU **BEEN?**

SEEING RIDING HOOD ON HER WAY, WHAT HAPPENED?

THEY'RE OVER THE FIRST WALL.

DON'T **BLOW** THAT THING! EVERYONE'S ALREADY WHERE THEY'RE SUPPOSED TO BE--

--EXCEPT **YOU.**

I WANT YOU UP ON THE TOWER TOP, WHERE YOU CAN SEE EVERYTHING.

WHY NOT WITH YOU, SIR? DID I--?

BECAUSE I **SAID** SO. HERE, TAKE **THIS.** IT'S THE WITCHING CLOAK. **WEAR** IT.

THE SHIP WILL NEED TO KNOW WHEN THE LAST OF US FALLS AND THEY'RE ON THEIR OWN.

THAT'S **YOUR** JOB.

WHEN THE ENEMY REACHES THE UPPER KEEP, WE'RE DONE HERE.

THAT'S WHEN YOU USE THE CLOAK TO **WITCH** YOURSELF ONTO THE SHIP.

BUT--

SOMEONE HAS TO DO IT, SON. I CHOSE **YOU.** DON'T SULLY A PERFECT MILITARY CAREER BY **DISOBEYING** MY FINAL ORDER.

SOME-ONE HAS TO SURVIVE TO TELL OUR STORY.

VULCO TELLS ME YOU'RE SWEET ON THAT GIRL-- GO **BE** WITH HER.

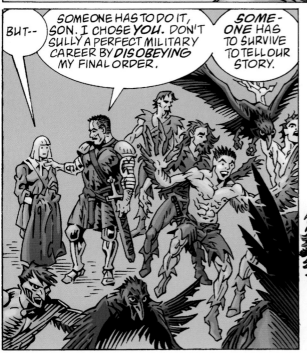

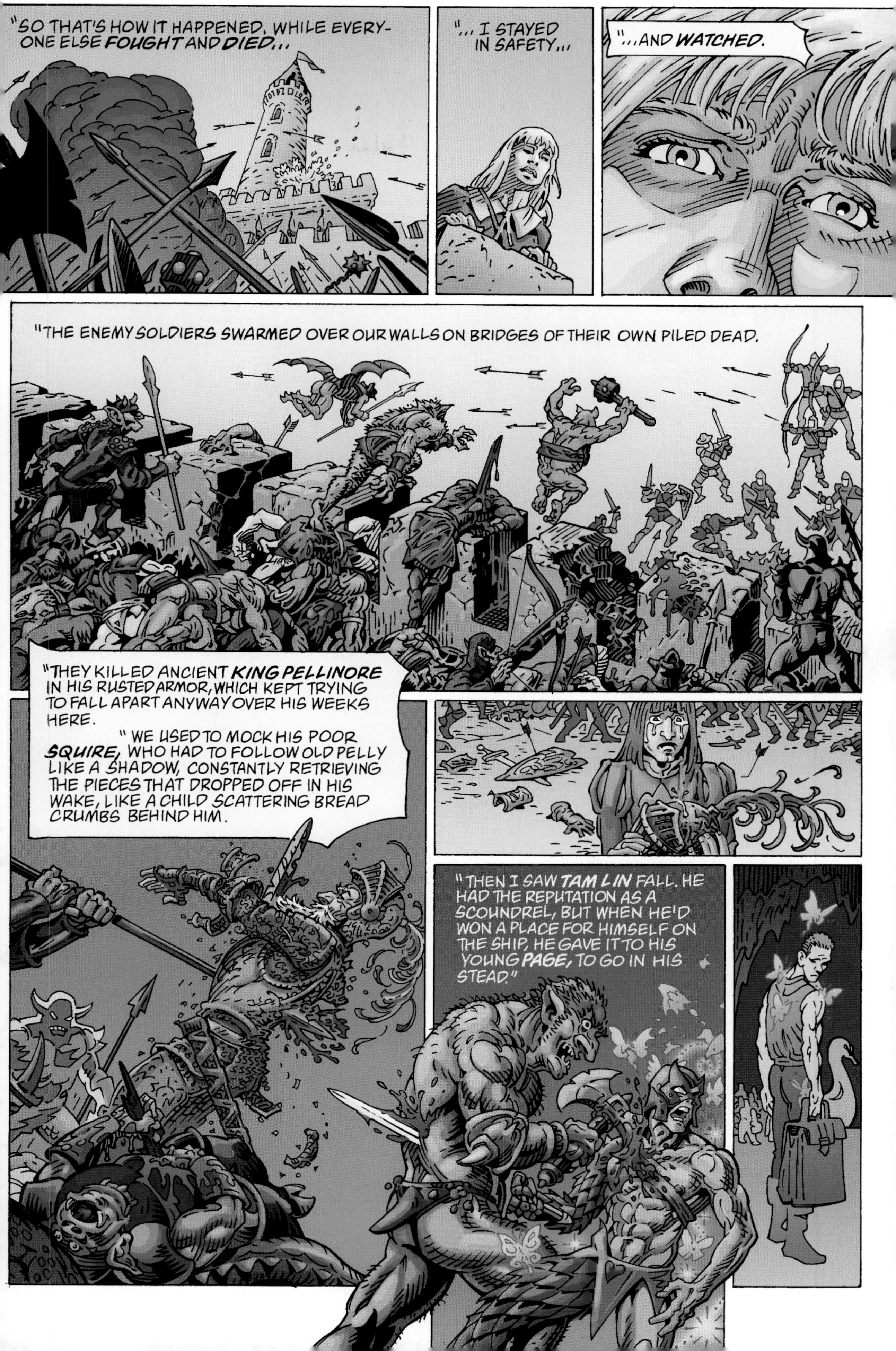
"SO THAT'S HOW IT HAPPENED. WHILE EVERYONE ELSE FOUGHT AND DIED...
"...I STAYED IN SAFETY...
"...AND WATCHED.
"THE ENEMY SOLDIERS SWARMED OVER OUR WALLS ON BRIDGES OF THEIR OWN PILED DEAD.
"THEY KILLED ANCIENT KING PELLINORE IN HIS RUSTED ARMOR, WHICH KEPT TRYING TO FALL APART ANYWAY OVER HIS WEEKS HERE.
"WE USED TO MOCK HIS POOR SQUIRE, WHO HAD TO FOLLOW OLD PELLY LIKE A SHADOW, CONSTANTLY RETRIEVING THE PIECES THAT DROPPED OFF IN HIS WAKE, LIKE A CHILD SCATTERING BREAD CRUMBS BEHIND HIM.
"THEN I SAW TAM LIN FALL. HE HAD THE REPUTATION AS A SCOUNDREL, BUT WHEN HE'D WON A PLACE FOR HIMSELF ON THE SHIP, HE GAVE IT TO HIS YOUNG PAGE, TO GO IN HIS STEAD."

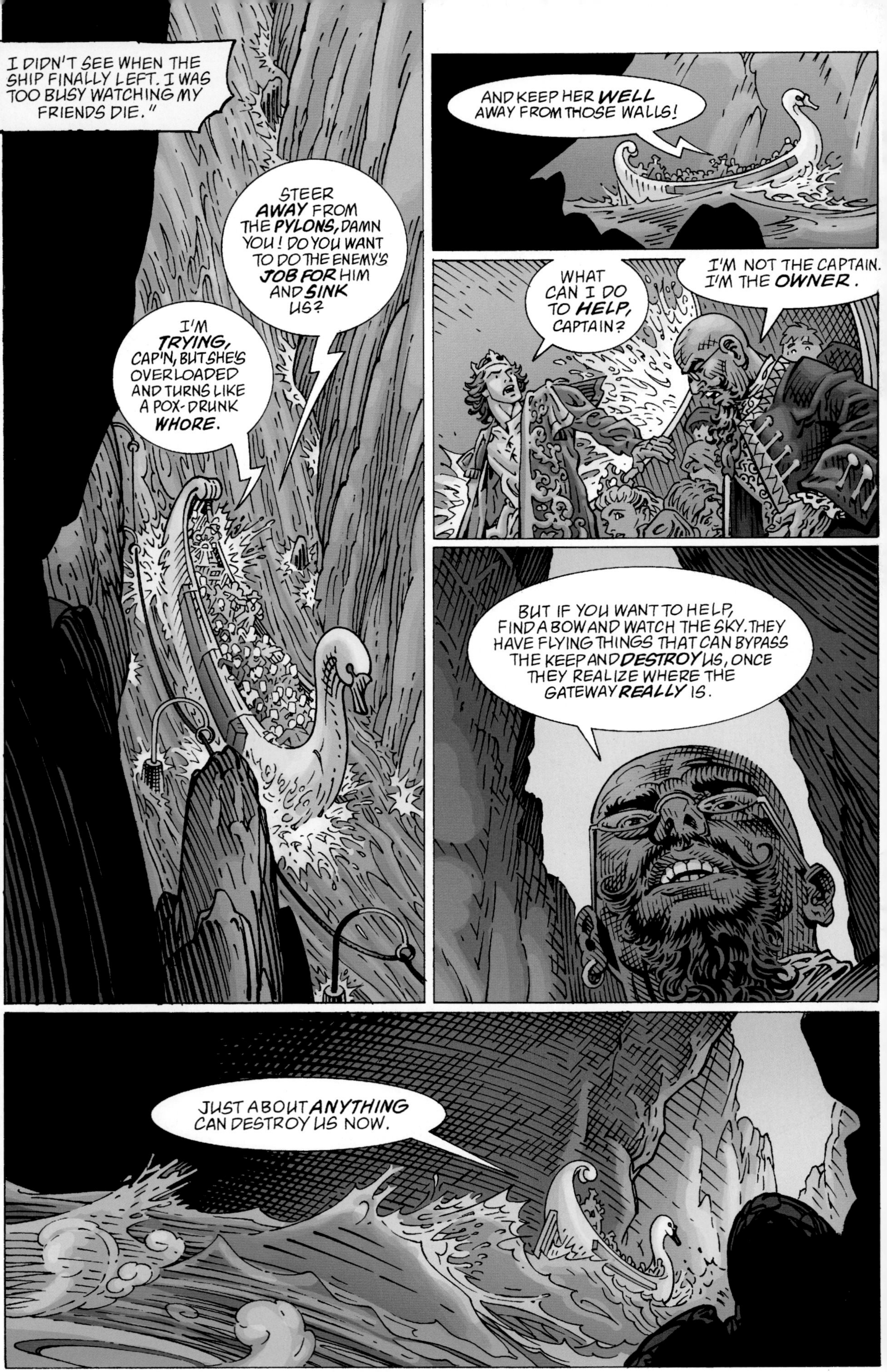

I DIDN'T SEE WHEN THE SHIP FINALLY LEFT. I WAS TOO BUSY WATCHING MY FRIENDS DIE."
STEER AWAY FROM THE PYLONS, DAMN YOU! DO YOU WANT TO DO THE ENEMY'S JOB FOR HIM AND SINK US?
I'M TRYING, CAP'N, BUT SHE'S OVERLOADED AND TURNS LIKE A POX-DRUNK WHORE.
AND KEEP HER WELL AWAY FROM THOSE WALLS!
WHAT CAN I DO TO HELP, CAPTAIN?
I'M NOT THE CAPTAIN. I'M THE OWNER.
BUT IF YOU WANT TO HELP, FIND A BOW AND WATCH THE SKY. THEY HAVE FLYING THINGS THAT CAN BYPASS THE KEEP AND DESTROY US, ONCE THEY REALIZE WHERE THE GATEWAY REALLY IS.
JUST ABOUT ANYTHING CAN DESTROY US NOW.

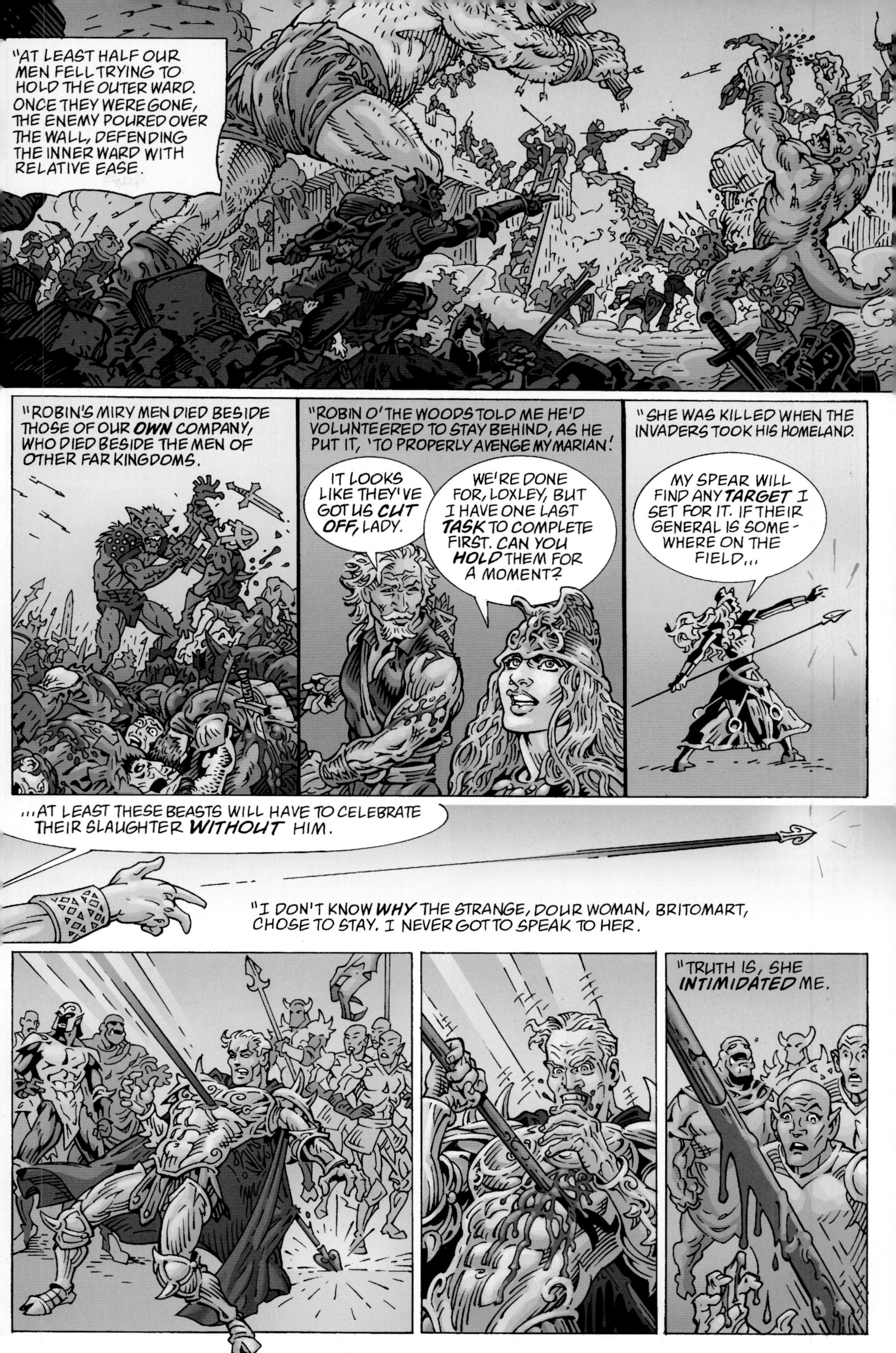

"AT LEAST HALF OUR MEN FELL TRYING TO HOLD THE OUTER WARD. ONCE THEY WERE GONE, THE ENEMY POURED OVER THE WALL, DEFENDING THE INNER WARD WITH RELATIVE EASE.
"ROBIN'S MIRY MEN DIED BESIDE THOSE OF OUR OWN COMPANY, WHO DIED BESIDE THE MEN OF OTHER FAR KINGDOMS.
"ROBIN O' THE WOODS TOLD ME HE'D VOLUNTEERED TO STAY BEHIND, AS HE PUT IT, 'TO PROPERLY AVENGE MY MARIAN.'
IT LOOKS LIKE THEY'VE GOT US CUT OFF, LADY.
WE'RE DONE FOR, LOXLEY, BUT I HAVE ONE LAST TASK TO COMPLETE FIRST. CAN YOU HOLD THEM FOR A MOMENT?
"SHE WAS KILLED WHEN THE INVADERS TOOK HIS HOMELAND.
MY SPEAR WILL FIND ANY TARGET I SET FOR IT. IF THEIR GENERAL IS SOME-WHERE ON THE FIELD...
...AT LEAST THESE BEASTS WILL HAVE TO CELEBRATE THEIR SLAUGHTER WITHOUT HIM.
"I DON'T KNOW WHY THE STRANGE, DOUR WOMAN, BRITOMART, CHOSE TO STAY. I NEVER GOT TO SPEAK TO HER.
"TRUTH IS, SHE INTIMIDATED ME.

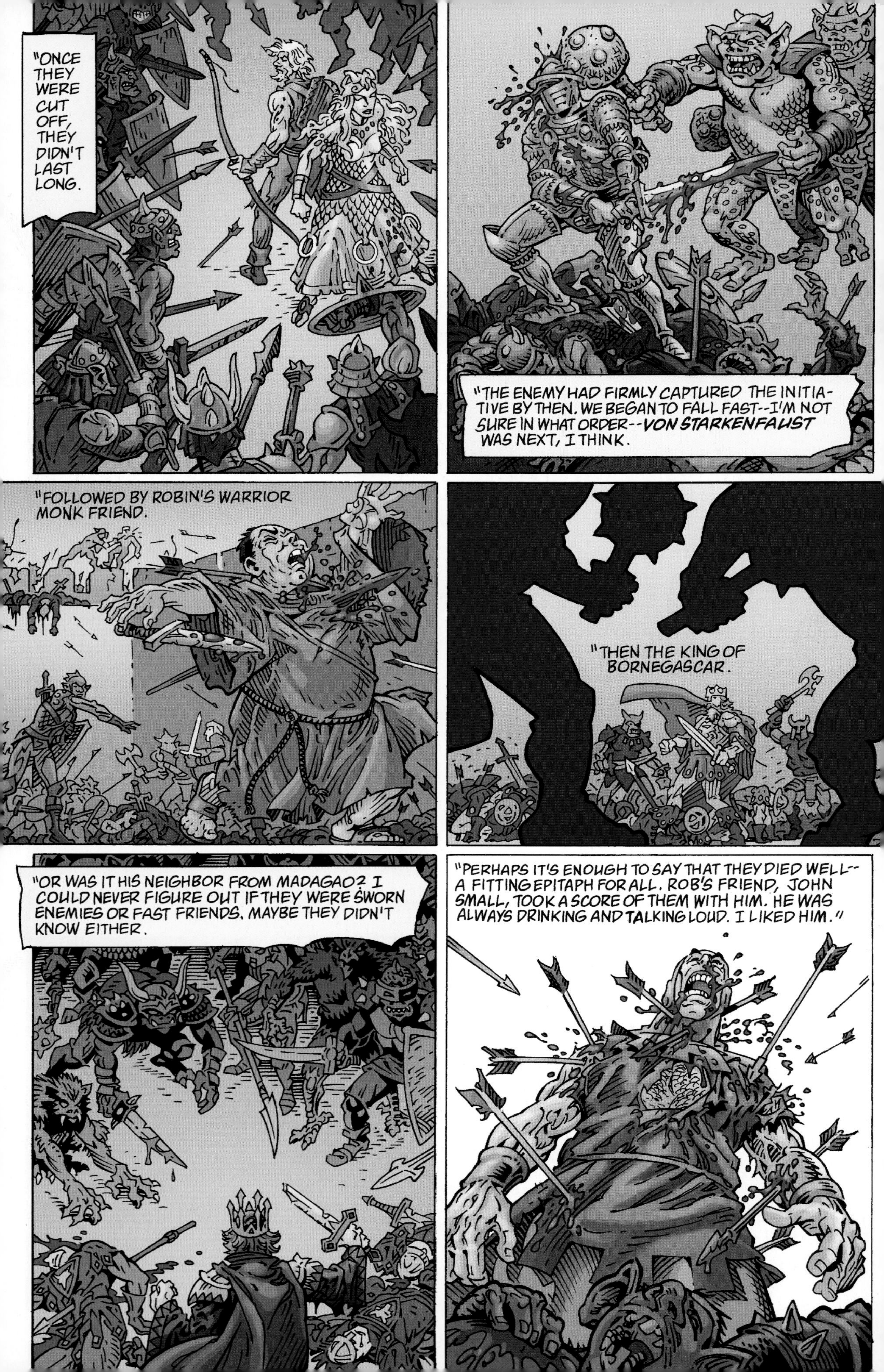
"ONCE THEY WERE CUT OFF, THEY DIDN'T LAST LONG.
"THE ENEMY HAD FIRMLY CAPTURED THE INITIATIVE BY THEN. WE BEGAN TO FALL FAST--I'M NOT SURE IN WHAT ORDER--VON STARKENFAUST WAS NEXT, I THINK.
"FOLLOWED BY ROBIN'S WARRIOR MONK FRIEND.
"THEN THE KING OF BORNEGASCAR.
"OR WAS IT HIS NEIGHBOR FROM MADAGAO? I COULD NEVER FIGURE OUT IF THEY WERE SWORN ENEMIES OR FAST FRIENDS. MAYBE THEY DIDN'T KNOW EITHER.
"PERHAPS IT'S ENOUGH TO SAY THAT THEY DIED WELL--A FITTING EPITAPH FOR ALL. ROB'S FRIEND, JOHN SMALL, TOOK A SCORE OF THEM WITH HIM. HE WAS ALWAYS DRINKING AND TALKING LOUD. I LIKED HIM."

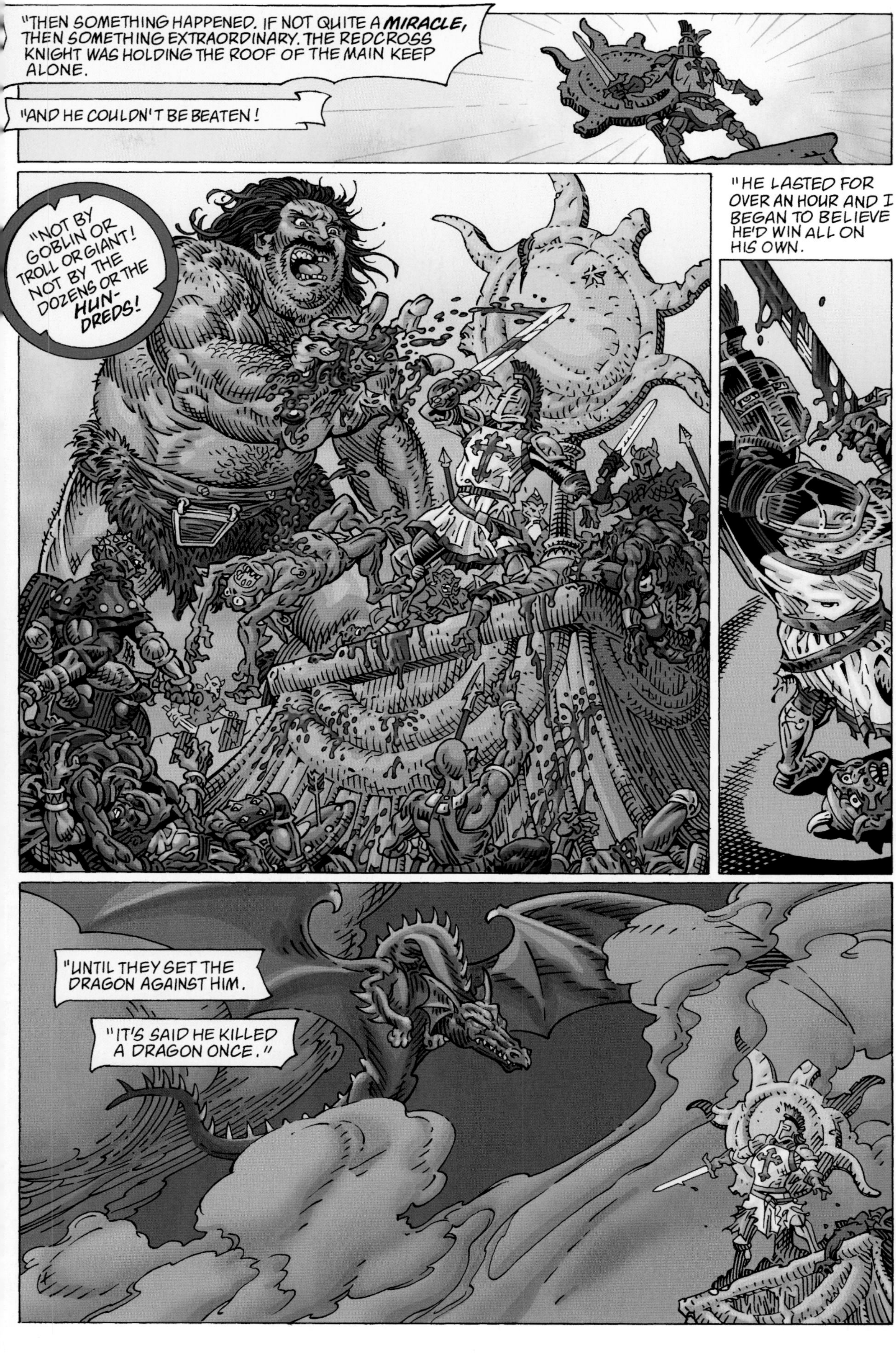
"THEN SOMETHING HAPPENED. IF NOT QUITE A MIRACLE, THEN SOMETHING EXTRAORDINARY. THE REDCROSS KNIGHT WAS HOLDING THE ROOF OF THE MAIN KEEP ALONE.
"AND HE COULDN'T BE BEATEN!
"NOT BY GOBLIN OR TROLL OR GIANT! NOT BY THE DOZENS OR THE HUN-DREDS!
"HE LASTED FOR OVER AN HOUR AND I BEGAN TO BELIEVE HE'D WIN ALL ON HIS OWN.
"UNTIL THEY SET THE DRAGON AGAINST HIM.
"IT'S SAID HE KILLED A DRAGON ONCE."

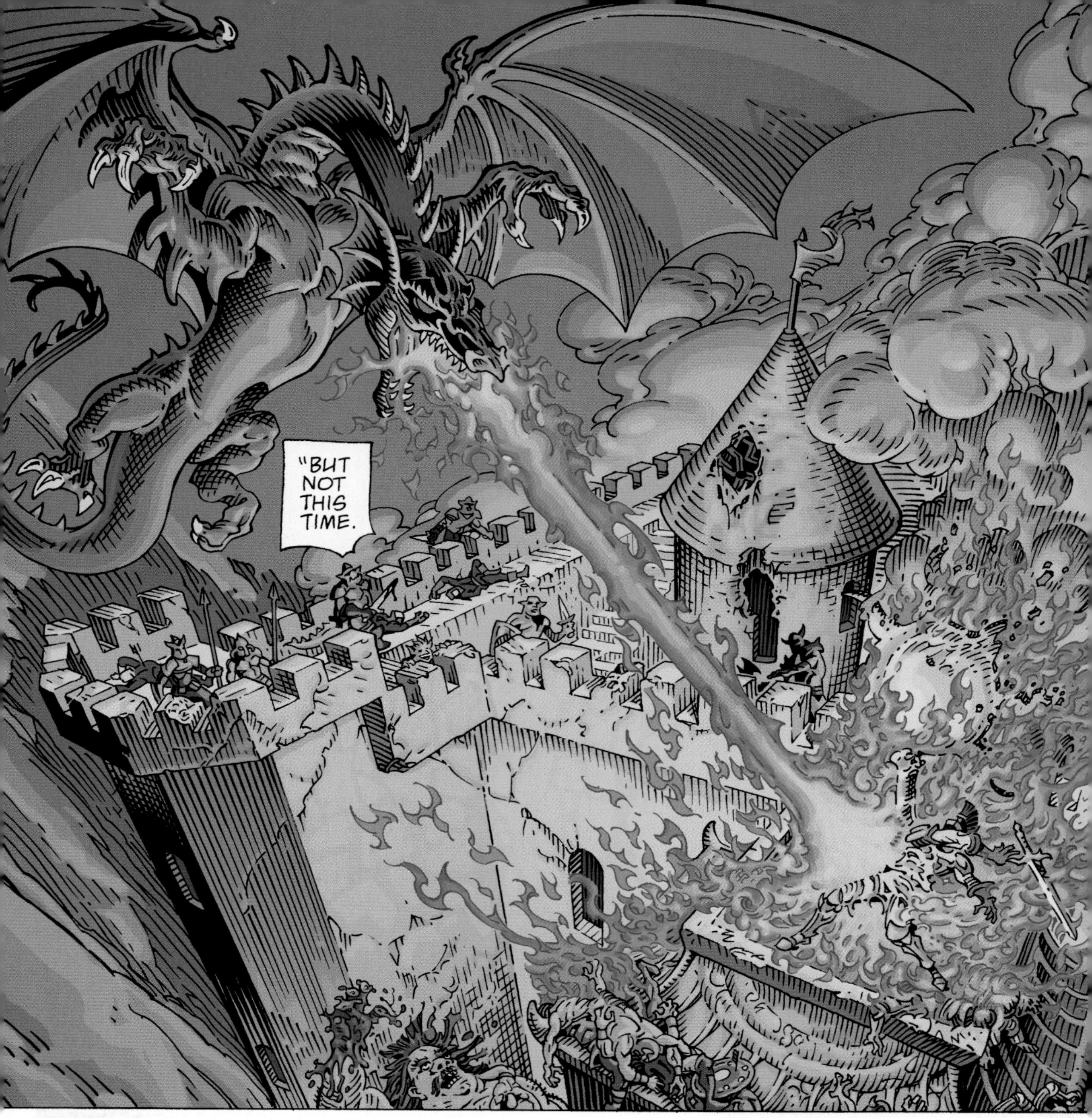
"BUT NOT THIS TIME.

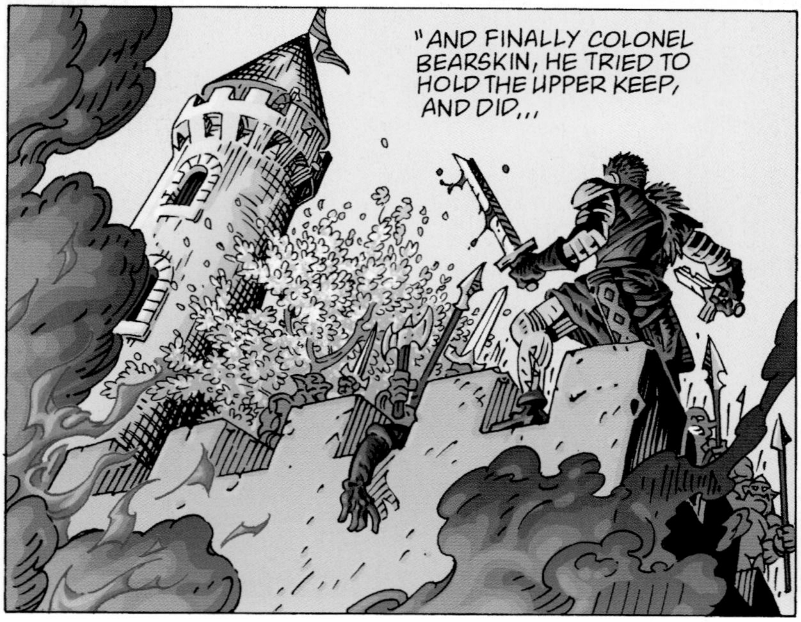
"AND FINALLY COLONEL BEARSKIN, HE TRIED TO HOLD THE UPPER KEEP, AND DID...

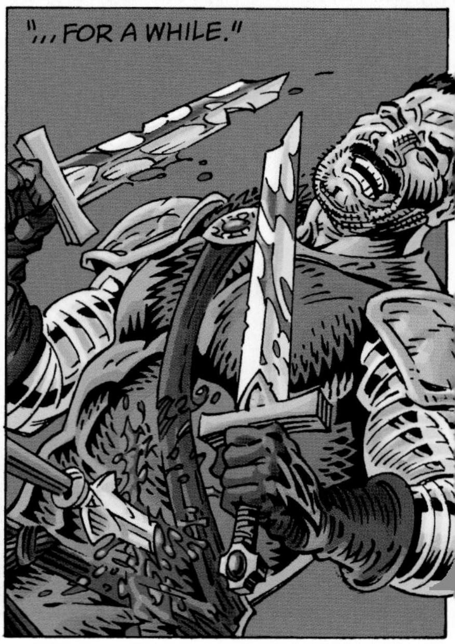
"...FOR A WHILE."

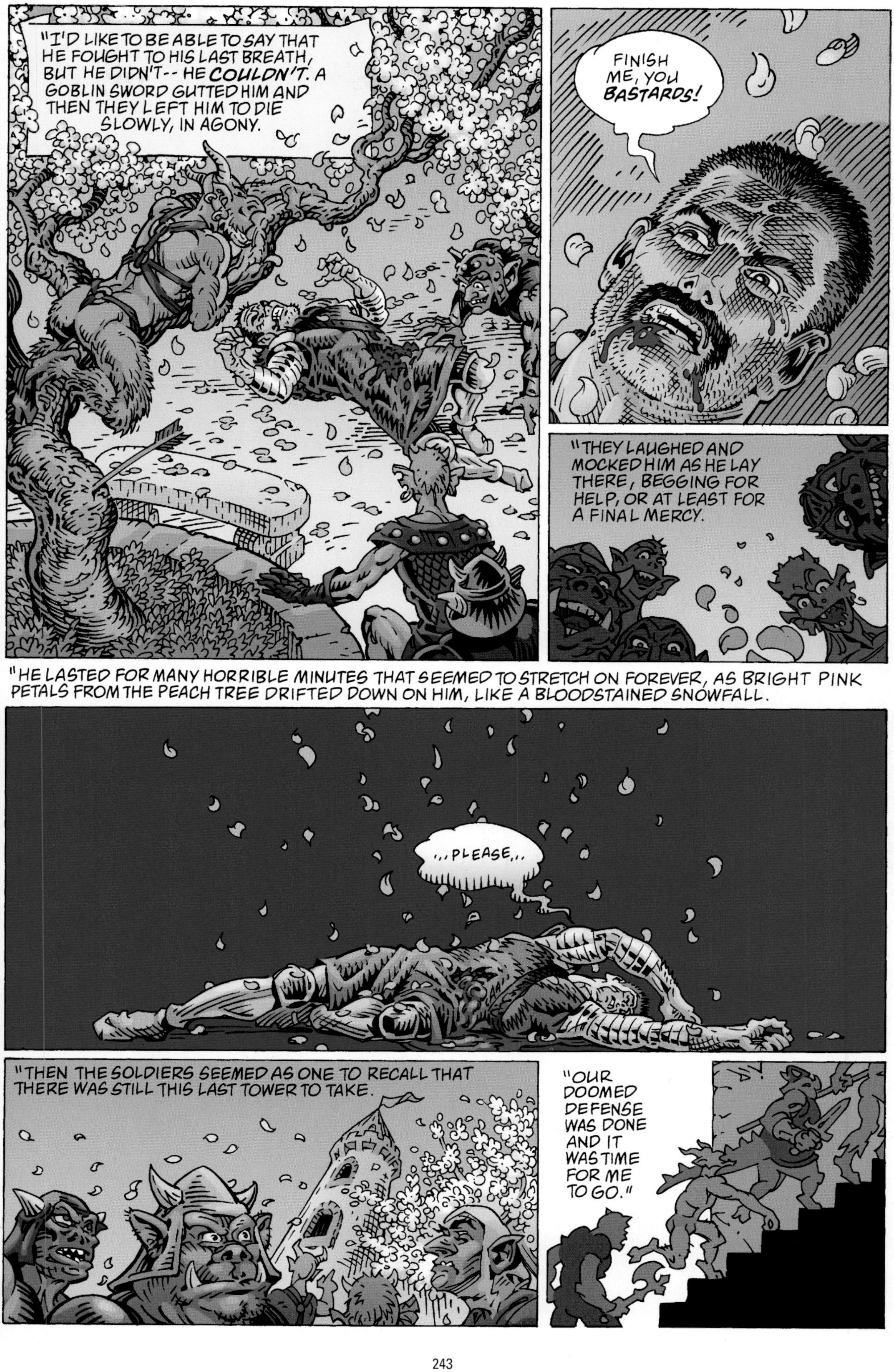
"I'D LIKE TO BE ABLE TO SAY THAT HE FOUGHT TO HIS LAST BREATH, BUT HE DIDN'T-- HE COULDN'T. A GOBLIN SWORD GUTTED HIM AND THEN THEY LEFT HIM TO DIE SLOWLY, IN AGONY.
FINISH ME, YOU BASTARDS!
"THEY LAUGHED AND MOCKED HIM AS HE LAY THERE, BEGGING FOR HELP, OR AT LEAST FOR A FINAL MERCY.
"HE LASTED FOR MANY HORRIBLE MINUTES THAT SEEMED TO STRETCH ON FOREVER, AS BRIGHT PINK PETALS FROM THE PEACH TREE DRIFTED DOWN ON HIM, LIKE A BLOODSTAINED SNOWFALL.
...PLEASE...
"THEN THE SOLDIERS SEEMED AS ONE TO RECALL THAT THERE WAS STILL THIS LAST TOWER TO TAKE.
"OUR DOOMED DEFENSE WAS DONE AND IT WAS TIME FOR ME TO GO."

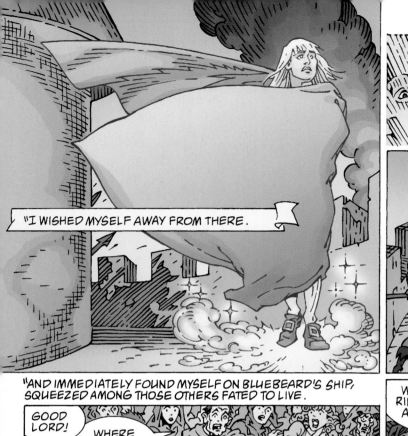

"I WISHED MYSELF AWAY FROM THERE.

"AND IMMEDIATELY FOUND MYSELF ON BLUEBEARD'S SHIP, SQUEEZED AMONG THOSE OTHERS FATED TO LIVE.

GOOD LORD!

WHERE DID *YOU* COME FROM?

FROM HELL. I'VE JUST COME FROM *HELL.*

WHERE'S MISS RIDING HOOD? DOES ANYONE *KNOW?*

IS SHE BELOW DECKS?

"I DIDN'T HAVE A CHANCE THEN TO LOOK FOR HER.

WE'RE APPROACHING THE *FALLS!*

ALL HANDS, *STAND BY* ON PORT AND STAR-BOARD! PREPARE TO *DEPLOY WINGS,* AS SOON AS WE CLEAR THE CLIFFS!

"THE SHIP WAS RUSHING HEAD-LONG DOWN THE RIVER RAPIDS AND, LIKE THE OTHERS, ALL I COULD DO WAS FIND SOME-THING TO HANG ON TO."

DEPLOY!

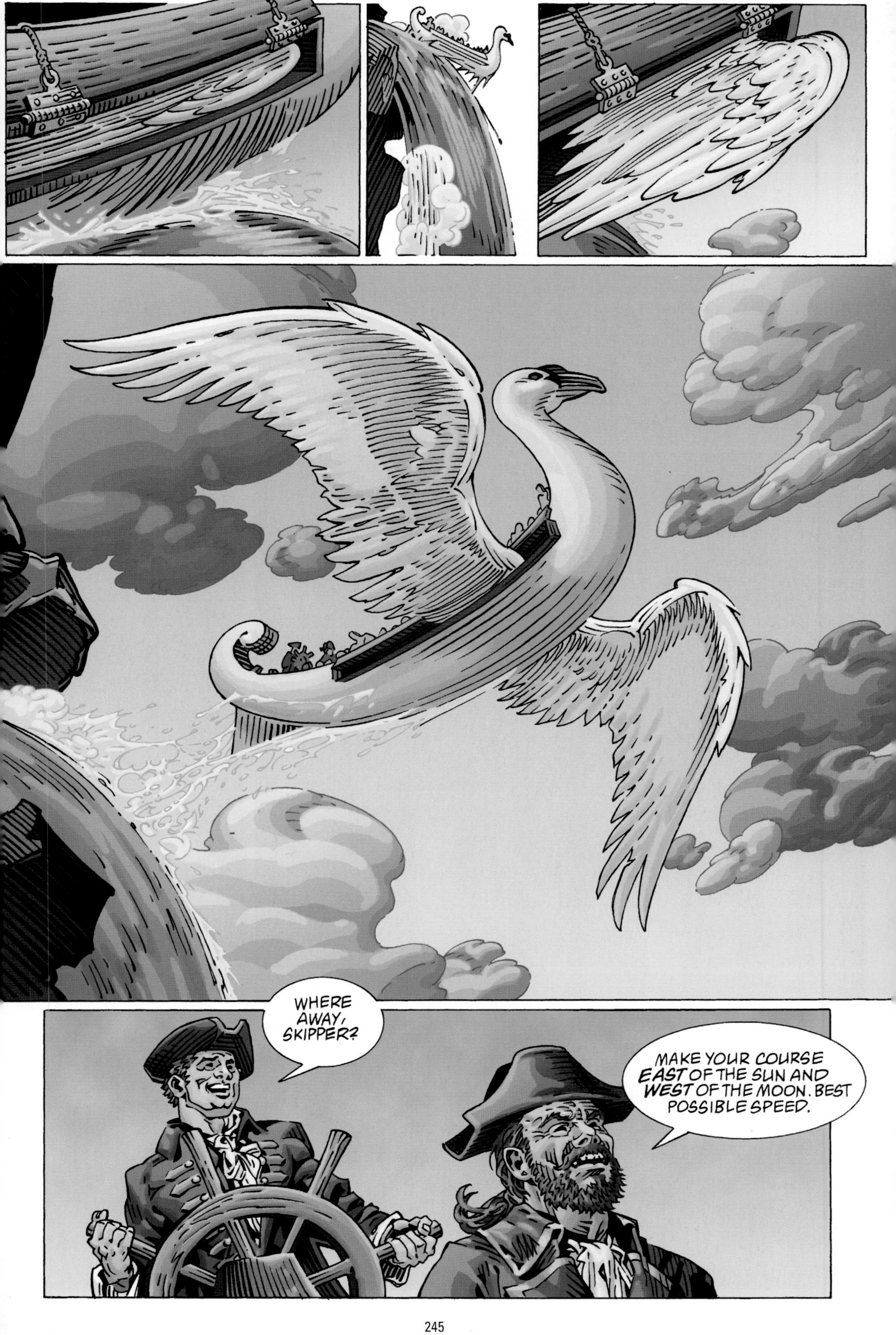
WHERE AWAY, SKIPPER?
MAKE YOUR COURSE EAST OF THE SUN AND WEST OF THE MOON. BEST POSSIBLE SPEED.

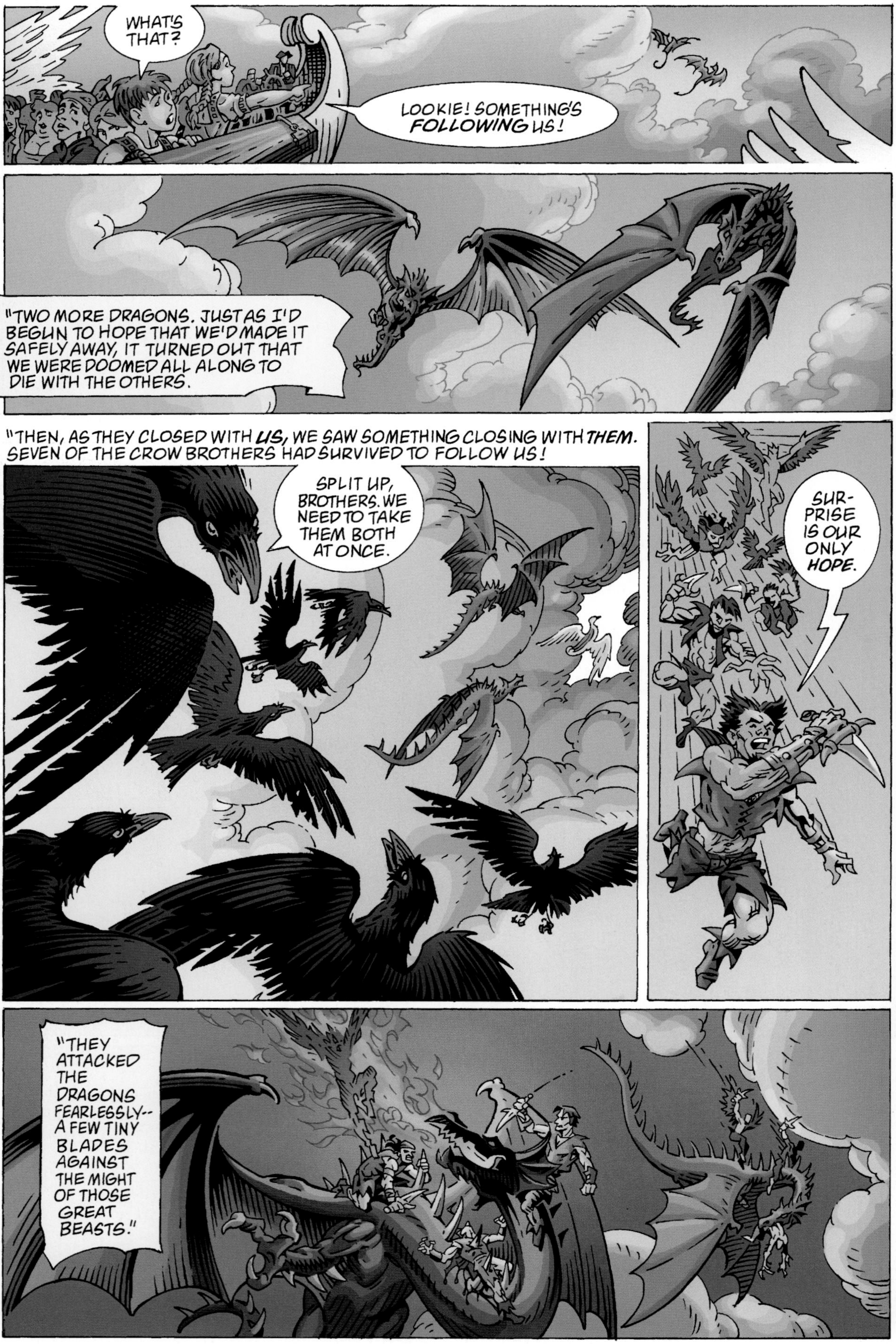
WHAT'S THAT?
LOOKIE! SOMETHING'S FOLLOWING US!
"TWO MORE DRAGONS. JUST AS I'D BEGUN TO HOPE THAT WE'D MADE IT SAFELY AWAY, IT TURNED OUT THAT WE WERE DOOMED ALL ALONG TO DIE WITH THE OTHERS.
"THEN, AS THEY CLOSED WITH US, WE SAW SOMETHING CLOSING WITH THEM. SEVEN OF THE CROW BROTHERS HAD SURVIVED TO FOLLOW US!
SPLIT UP, BROTHERS. WE NEED TO TAKE THEM BOTH AT ONCE.
SURPRISE IS OUR ONLY HOPE.
"THEY ATTACKED THE DRAGONS FEARLESSLY-- A FEW TINY BLADES AGAINST THE MIGHT OF THOSE GREAT BEASTS."

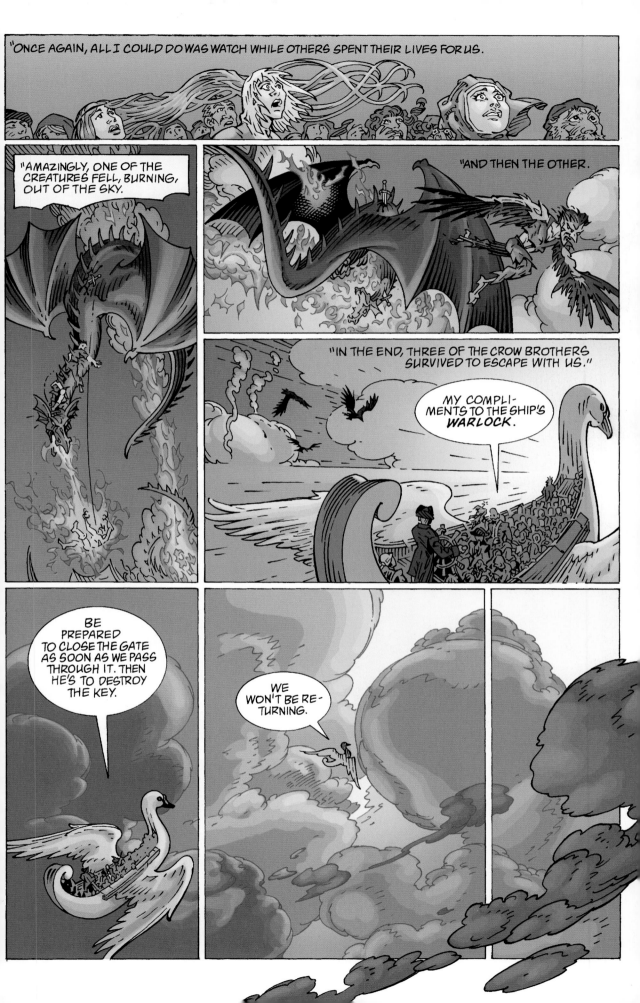

"ONCE AGAIN, ALL I COULD DO WAS WATCH WHILE OTHERS SPENT THEIR LIVES FOR US."

"AMAZINGLY, ONE OF THE CREATURES FELL, BURNING, OUT OF THE SKY."

"AND THEN THE OTHER."

"IN THE END, THREE OF THE CROW BROTHERS SURVIVED TO ESCAPE WITH US."

MY COMPLIMENTS TO THE SHIP'S **WARLOCK.**

BE PREPARED TO CLOSE THE GATE AS SOON AS WE PASS THROUGH IT. THEN HE'S TO DESTROY THE KEY.

WE WON'T BE RETURNING.

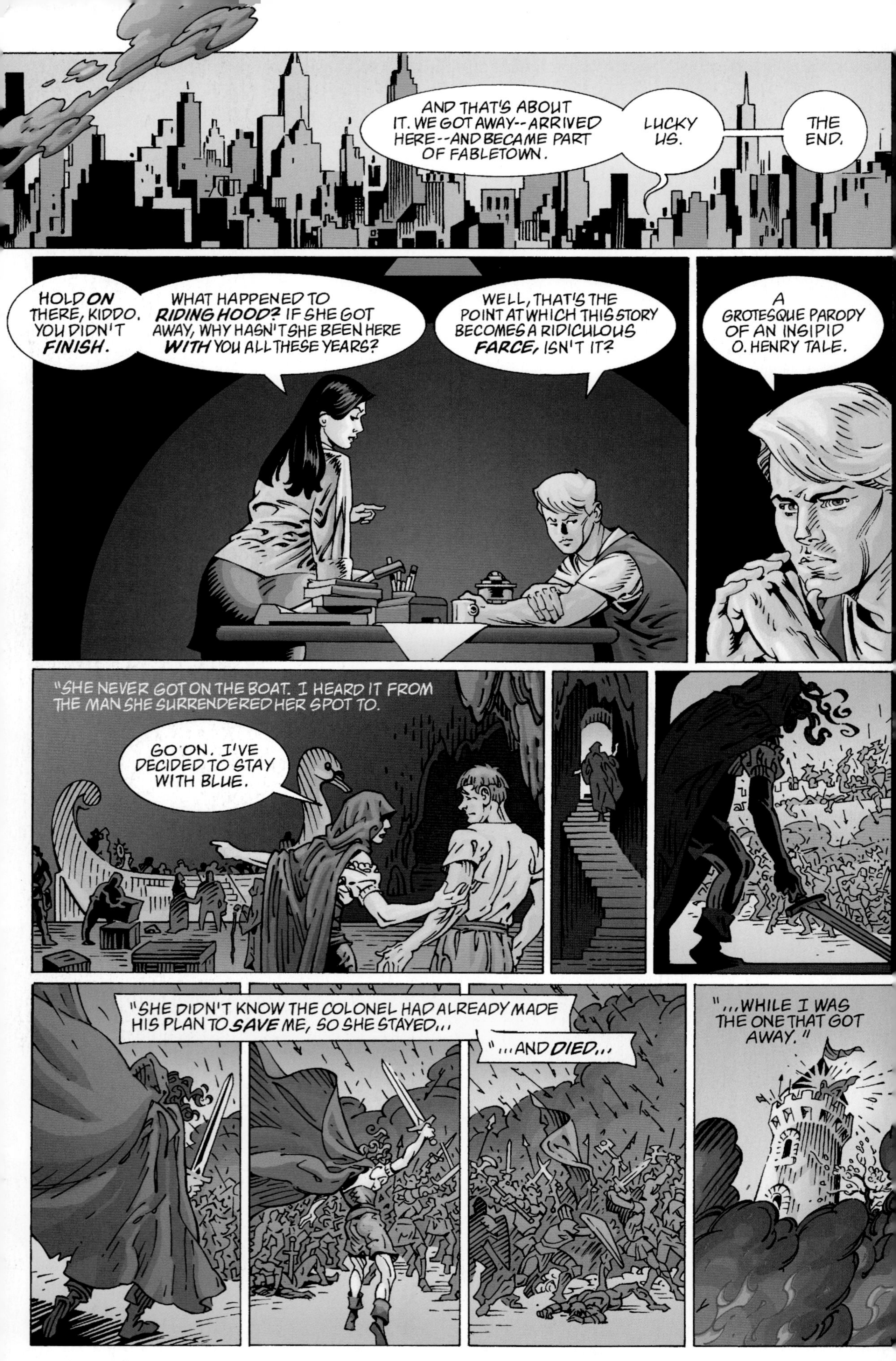
AND THAT'S ABOUT IT. WE GOT AWAY--ARRIVED HERE--AND BECAME PART OF FABLETOWN.
LUCKY US.
THE END.
HOLD ON THERE, KIDDO. YOU DIDN'T FINISH.
WHAT HAPPENED TO RIDING HOOD? IF SHE GOT AWAY, WHY HASN'T SHE BEEN HERE WITH YOU ALL THESE YEARS?
WELL, THAT'S THE POINT AT WHICH THIS STORY BECOMES A RIDICULOUS FARCE, ISN'T IT?
A GROTESQUE PARODY OF AN INSIPID O. HENRY TALE.
"SHE NEVER GOT ON THE BOAT. I HEARD IT FROM THE MAN SHE SURRENDERED HER SPOT TO.
GO ON. I'VE DECIDED TO STAY WITH BLUE.
"SHE DIDN'T KNOW THE COLONEL HAD ALREADY MADE HIS PLAN TO SAVE ME, SO SHE STAYED...
"...AND DIED...
"...WHILE I WAS THE ONE THAT GOT AWAY."

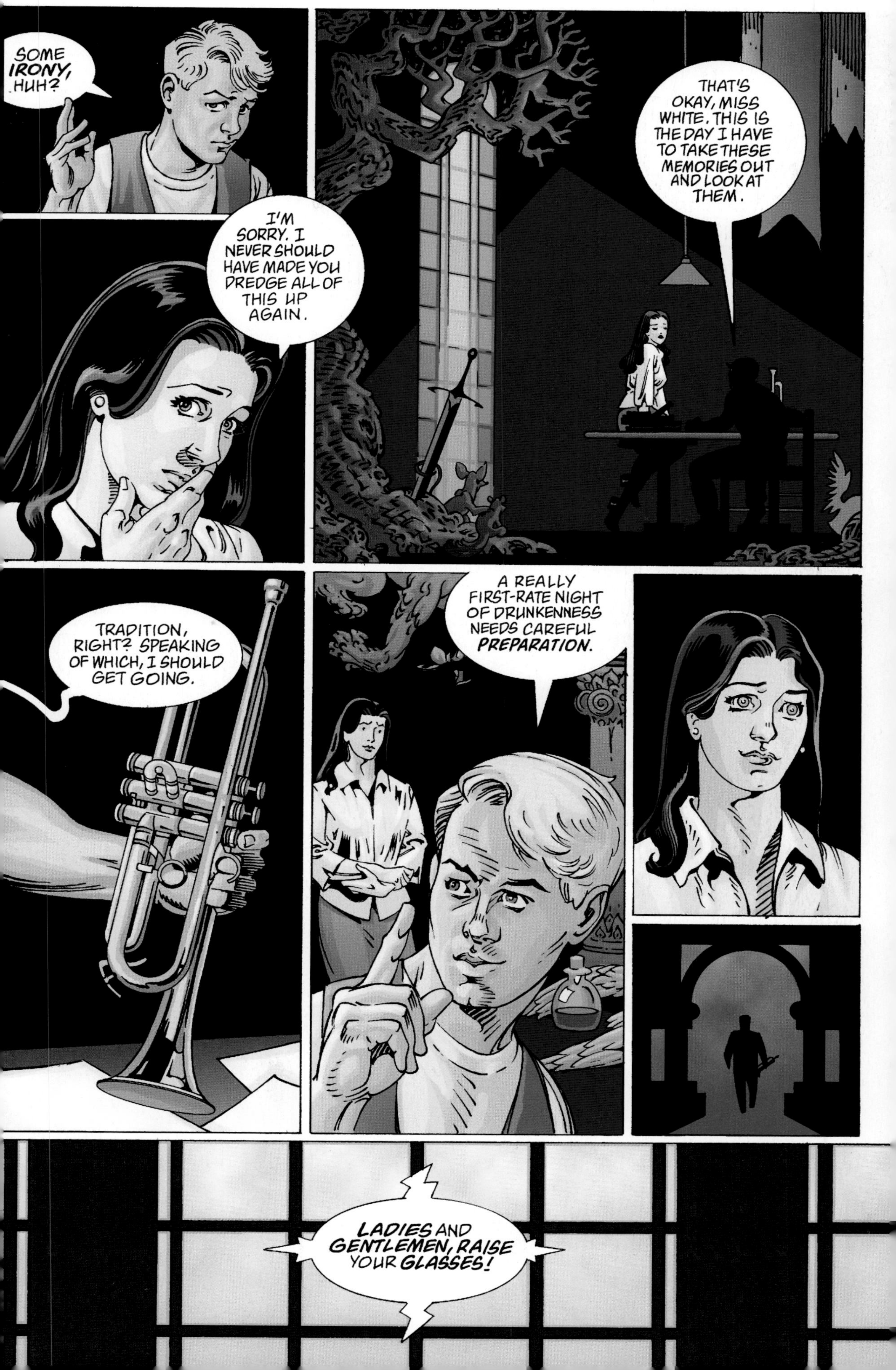
SOME IRONY, HUH?
I'M SORRY. I NEVER SHOULD HAVE MADE YOU DREDGE ALL OF THIS UP AGAIN.
THAT'S OKAY, MISS WHITE. THIS IS THE DAY I HAVE TO TAKE THESE MEMORIES OUT AND LOOK AT THEM.
TRADITION, RIGHT? SPEAKING OF WHICH, I SHOULD GET GOING.
A REALLY FIRST-RATE NIGHT OF DRUNKENNESS NEEDS CAREFUL PREPARATION.
LADIES AND GENTLEMEN, RAISE YOUR GLASSES!

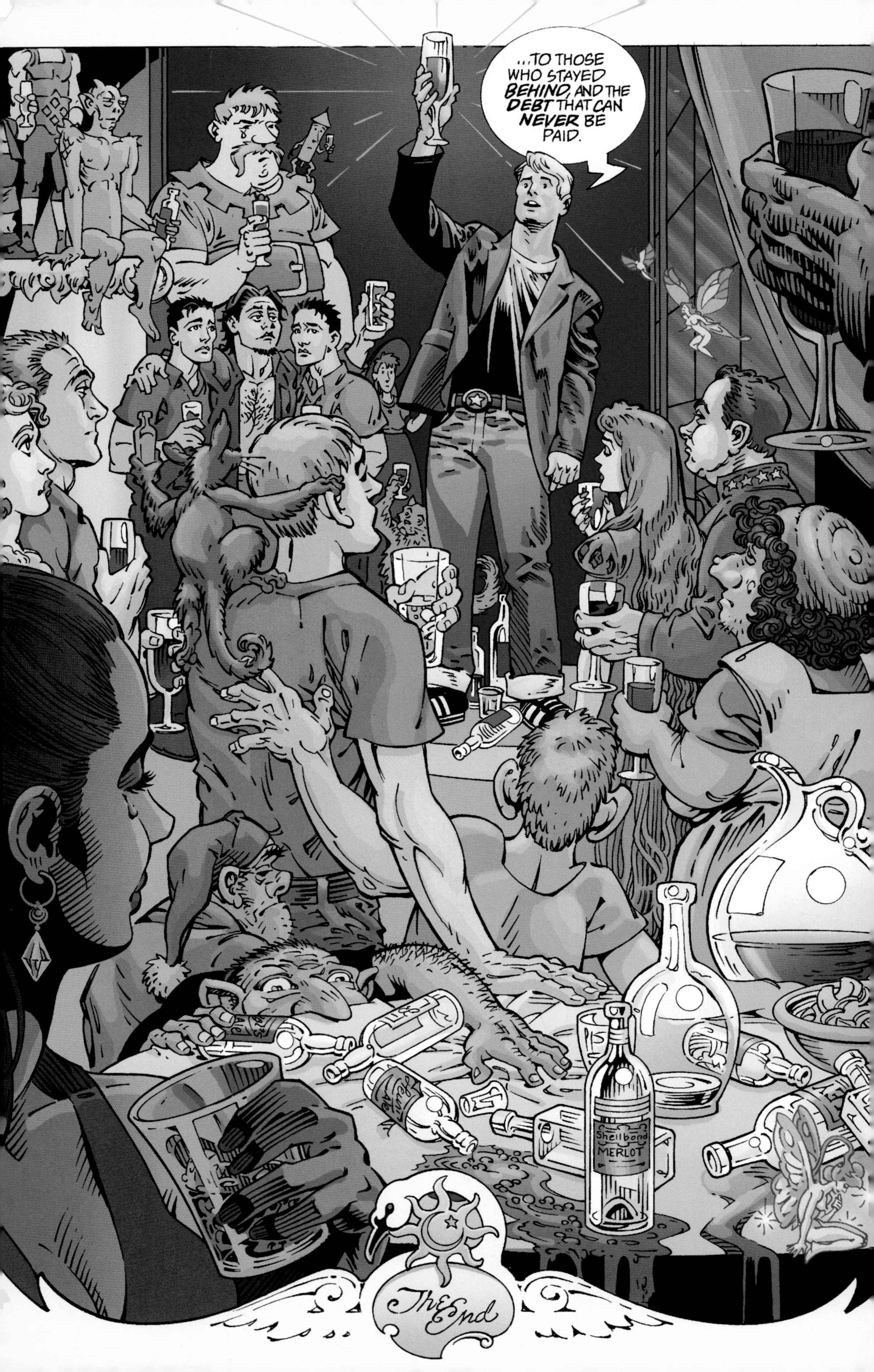
...TO THOSE WHO STAYED BEHIND, AND THE DEBT THAT CAN NEVER BE PAID.
Shellbond MERLOT
The End

A Wolf in the Fold

By Bill Willingham

When the invaders flooded into the valley, the old wolf came down from his warm den in the high hills to see what all the fuss was about. It didn't take him long to find the alien soldiers, for they tended to call attention to themselves. They wore suits of dark iron and marched in long, clattering ranks. They burned and pillaged wheresoever they went, enslaving those they could easily capture, while putting all others to the sword — those who resisted, to be sure, but also those who were too lame, too old, or too well educated to make able and subservient workers. The wolf took umbrage at these uncouth intruders, not only because they had the temerity to enter his territory uninvited, but also because they murdered wantonly, without craft or subtlety. In addition they killed or spirited away many of those living in the wooded valley that the wolf had marked in his mind to dine on one day, and such a breach of etiquette could not be endured.

In those days the wolf was still largely ruled by his belly, so he decided to sample a few of the invaders. They were easy enough to bring down, because, for all of his monstrous size, the wolf could strike with great stealth and cunning. In the deep woods between one isolated village and another, he picked off two stragglers as they marched behind a long column, biting easily through their shells of thick plate and the ring-mail hauberks underneath like a child crumbles autumn leaves. Once he'd stripped away the outer wrappings, he discovered misshapen, yellow-tusked gobliny things within. They screamed and pleaded and writhed well enough as he savaged them, and their bones crunched satisfyingly, but their green and warty flesh was foul. Carrion three weeks rotting in the heart of summer tasted better than this!

That night, silent as a shadow, he crept into the army's sprawling encampment, thinking that their more human-looking captains might prove more suitable to his refined palate. He whispered past the watch-fires, ragged troop tents, and posted sentries — both sleeping and alert — until, quite undetected, he reached the camp's innermost ring, where the silken

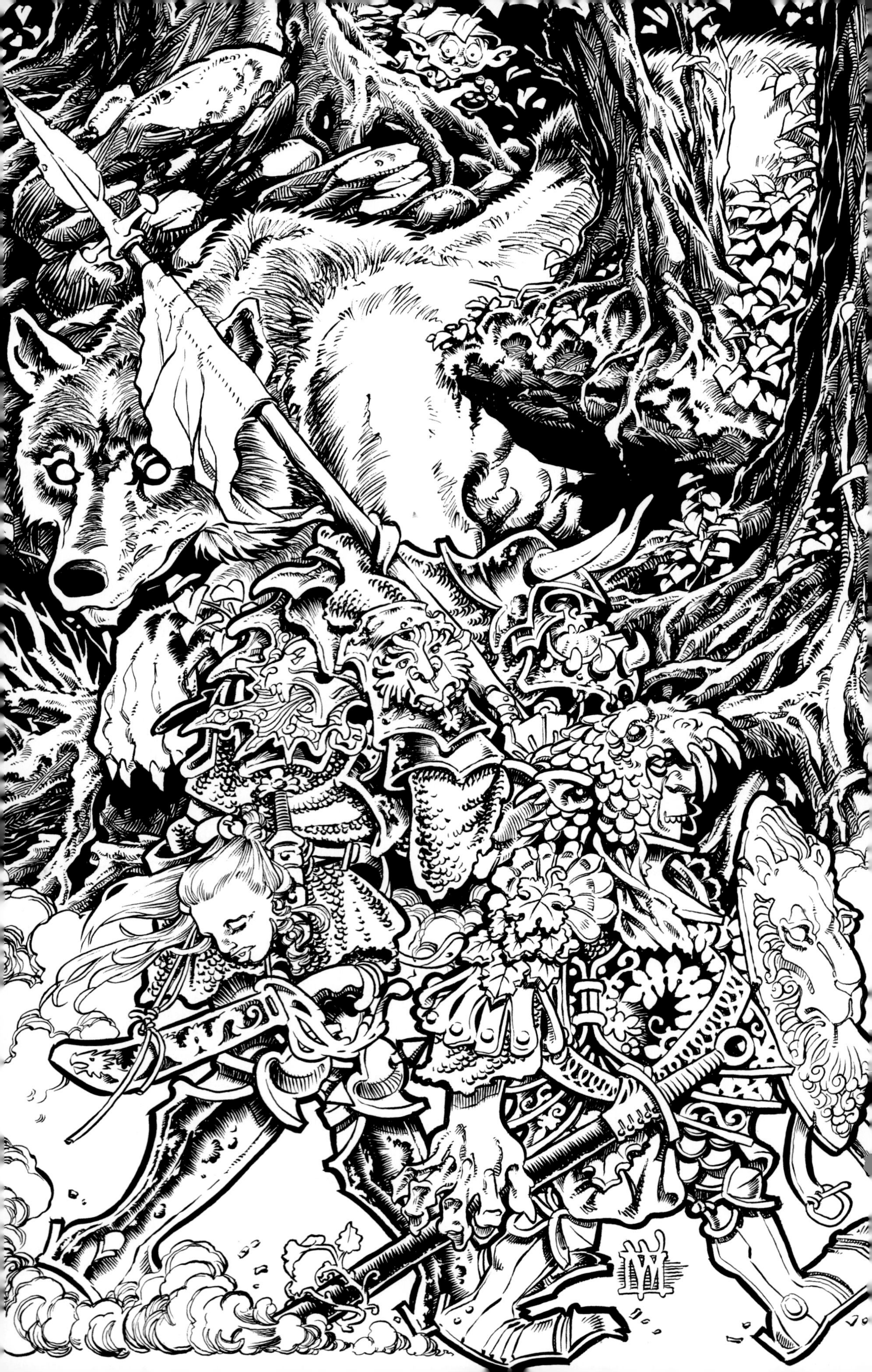

pavilions of the officers could be found. Choosing the biggest tent as the one most likely to house the sweetest confection, he leapt in, without so much as a breath of sound, and surprised a sleeper in his bed. He crunched the man's head first, like a red ripe apple, stifling any possibility of alarm, and then settled in for a long, leisurely repast. But after only a few bites, even this man's flesh proved unsuitable. It was tan and unblemished, but still carried a disturbing taint of corruption. The audacity of these people! Not only do they rob him of his preferred provender, but in turn they fail to provide anything approaching a suitable substitute?

The wolf's rage grew and long into the night he pondered what to do about it.

In the days that followed the wolf made himself a determined enemy of the invaders. He ranged far and wide, striking in this place and that, in the dead of night, or under the bright daytime sun. There seemed no pattern to his predations, which only increased the dread sown amongst his new adversaries. Relentlessly he hunted the soldiers and their masters, wherever he could find them — and he found them in abundance, infesting every land and kingdom, no matter how far afield he wandered from his own familiar territory. He slaughtered most of those he caught without hesitation or mercy, but spared a few long enough for questioning. From these he learned little of value. They were the advance forces of a remote and unnamed power — known only to the troops as their emperor — for he was by all accounts a creature bold with ambition and sorcerous might who'd decided to carve for himself a single, grand empire out of all the disparate kingdoms of fable.

"Why do you contend so against us?" one captive pleaded as he struggled helplessly under the wolf's massive forepaws. "For you are the very sort of monster we are commissioned to recruit into our ranks. You could rise high in the empire, commanding legions, or more!"

"Not interested," the wolf growled in return. "Even the highest office in service to another is too low a station for me." And with that the wolf sank his fangs into the captive's neck. A single, irresistible shake ended the soldier's tremors, instantly transforming living flesh into wet carcass.

Years passed in this fashion. The wolf hunted where he would and the invaders trembled in their tents. But for all of his rapacious success, the wolf was but a single creature, where the Emperor could field seemingly endless battalions. Lands were methodically conquered and consolidated into the empire, despite his constant harassment. At best he was but an irritant in his unseen adversary's vast game of thrones.

Which isn't to say that his personal campaign went unnoticed in whatever distant country that had spawned the invasion. Entire companies of the Emperor's most diabolical soldiers — trolls, giants and worse — were tasked with his capture or destruction. And when he eluded those, fell sorcerers and black-hearted warlocks were dispatched. He led them all a merry chase, and reflected from time to time that his life was good, all things considered.

One day, in the shadow of a range of tall white mountains that looked like the fangs of the Earth, bared to rend the heavens above, the wolf encountered a small force of the Emperor's soldiers escorting a much larger group of captives. They were led in heavy rattling chains, down out of the mountains' girdling foothills, where many tried to escape in recent years. From a concealed spot above the winding trail, the wolf watched them as they passed. The prisoners were wretched and dirty things, dressed in old rags for the most part, and new scars, no doubt received during the rough business of their capture. They stumbled along with bent backs and blank faces, sure signs that they knew, and finally surrendered to, the fate that awaited them — days of torture, to wring from them any information about other fugitives, followed by public execution. It seems the Emperor didn't believe in redemption. Those who resisted the all-too-generous initial welcome into his new regime were never offered a second chance. The guards for their part merely looked bored. They could hardly even be bothered to whip the slowpokes and those who stumbled on the trail's sharp stones. This had become routine duty to them, for many fugitives from many countries converged on this land, believing whispered rumors of a magic avenue of escape hidden somewhere in these rugged and forbidding hills. They arrived in droves and the soldiers captured them — most of them anyway — with ease.

From his hiding place the wolf patiently watched and waited as he sniffed the cold pre-winter air for signs of a larger, hidden force. This wouldn't be the first time the enemy had tried to lure him into a trap with such inviting bait as this. He'd grown quite wary over the years. Eventually though, with no sign of other threats in the air, he padded down to the trail and followed the slow procession, silently closing the distance between them.

Nearly midway in the prisoner train, two sisters were chained to the line, one in front of the other. They were both lovely young women — though it was hard to be sure under the dirty clothes and half-dried mud that covered them from head to toe — and resembled each other, except that one had hair as dark as night while the other's was as red as the morning sun. In one other way they differed as well. The dark-haired sister wore a gown of rich velvet and white linen, bespeaking nobility, while the red-haired sister wore a simple peasant dress of rough homespun. Of course, the great leveler of extended hardship and adversity had so reduced each garment to egalitarian rags and tatters that only close and careful examination could determine their disparate origins.

Like the other captives, the sisters marched silently — except for the rattling chains manacled to each wrist and ankle — alone in their thoughts, until a sudden clamor of dying men startled them out of their private reveries. The commotion came from the back of the prisoner train, which abruptly compressed in the center, as those in front stopped to see what occurred in the rear, while those in the rear rushed forward to escape whatever it was back there that was killing the guards and filling the air with such feral, bestial sounds as to chill anyone's soul to the core.

Within the tangled press of panicking captives the dark-haired sister couldn't make out any details of what was happening behind them, other than the occasional glimpse of armored guards rushing from the head of the line towards the screams and clamor at its rear. For the moment she concentrated on holding onto her sister, as they worked together to keep upright, so as not to be trampled underfoot. Then the worst of the sounds died away, leaving only the whimpers of the chained prisoners, and while she was still being jerked and tugged, first one way and then the next, by the chains that attached her to everyone else, the mass of shuddering bodies opened up enough to finally reveal their new danger. A wolf had come amongst them, and such a wolf it was! On all fours it stood as tall as a yearling colt. Its fur was black, shading to brownish-gray on its flanks and belly, but at the moment most of its front end was painted red with the blood of the dozen guardsmen who'd so ruthlessly ruled their lives for many days past — right up until a moment ago. To a man they were all dead — savagely dismembered — their parts scattered up and down the trail, and the beast that destroyed them now stood no more than a pace or two from the center of the line, and the two sisters caught there. The women were held in place, stretched out to the limits of their shackles, as their chained companions on each end of the line tried to rush away

from the middle, in an attempt to escape the terrible thing that stood amongst them. Some tried to run or crawl away, in both directions on the trail, while others tried to claw their way up the steep embankment on its hill-ward side. Still others simply surrendered to their certain doom and dropped where they were, trying to curl up or cover themselves as best they could. But the sisters didn't attempt to run or crawl or in any other way try to escape. Perhaps they knew that such attempts would be futile, or they found reserves of courage, or perhaps they simply knew something of what the cornered deer knows after the long chase, when it has finally resigned itself to becoming food for the lion. Whatever the reason, they stood where they were and stared into the yellow eyes that seemed to impale them in place. Entranced, they watched the steaming vapor of recent murder rise from each side of its red-wet muzzle. They listened to each ragged breath that issued from the bellows of its massive chest.

Then a sudden loss of tension in the chains seemed to break the dark one out of her spell — if only for a moment — but that was long enough for her to reach down by her feet where one of the guard's swords had landed during the carnage. She deftly snatched up the curved blade, slippery with its former owner's blood.

"Stay back, dire beast!" the dark sister cried. "My husband taught me well how to use this!" She held it in both hands, boldly brandishing it towards the wolf.

"I don't believe you," the wolf replied, and was that a tone of humor that colored its deep voice? It didn't attack her, but neither did it back away, or in any way seem concerned about the threatening blade held in a young woman's trembling hands.

"You will if you come closer and I chop you down."

"You misunderstand," the wolf replied, the grin of his long muzzle revealing rows of sharp fangs — the largest longer than a grown man's fingers. "I don't believe you've a husband. Though you're clearly no maiden, I can tell with a whiff and a sniff that it's been long years since you've visited anyone's marriage bed."

"My *former* husband!" the woman said. Under the caked grime, twin apples of ripening anger colored her alabaster cheeks.

"Put down your sword, woman. I doubt you could hurt me with it. But if you'll hold out your arms, I'll bite those shackles off of you. Quit trembling so! I'm not going to eat you, or these other mewling creatures. It amuses me much more these days to frustrate the Emperor and his legions by spiriting his desired conquests safely out from his clutches. You two aren't from this land — your accents mark you as distant strangers — and yet here you are. I'll bet you've come hoping to find a certain witch's cave of legend. One with many twisting passages that lead to many distant worlds — at least one of which is far beyond the Emperor's reach and possibly even his knowledge."

"I'm amazed that you would know of such a place." This time it was the red-haired woman who spoke. Imitating her sister, she had taken advantage of the moment to look for weapons within reach, but no other such device had fallen close enough.

The wolf ignored their efforts at self-defense, but suddenly dashed to nip at those on either end, still stretching out the chains in their efforts to escape. Eventually he herded them back into a loose and fearful cluster that for the most part left the long central chain hanging limp between each captive. Finally, when this was done, he returned to his former place, sat where he had been standing, and answered the red-haired sister.

"I not only know of it, I'm the only one who can still find it, for the witch that made it is long gone, having passed through it to safety many years ago. And because she wanted none of the Emperor's minions following after, she left it cloaked in myriad spells and glamours that cause anyone seeking it to become misdirected and turned around so thoroughly as to be completely frustrated. But I can go there, straight and true, because I secretly followed the old hag that long-lost day and marked the trail as only a wolf can."

"Then you are the one that we heard of — the great and terrible guardian of the way," the dark sister said. She hadn't lowered the point of her borrowed blade.

"You look like you expected someone else."

"We'd heard that you were a giant."

"I'm hardly tiny."

"And that you had at least three heads," the red-haired one said, "and by merely looking at you directly, we would be turned to stone."

"Stories do grow in the telling."

"And is the legend also false that you charge a dear price from those you allow to pass on to safety — to the unreachable world?" the dark one said.

"Not entirely, but it's not a matter of payment so much as precaution. The Emperor and his sorcerers have many devious ways to disguise his agents. He's often tried to slip one by me and there's only one sure way to tell if you're genuine refugees, or more of his creatures in sheep's clothing."

"And what would that be?"

"I'll need a taste — just a little nip from each of you. No matter what shape they began in, or what form in which they present themselves, all of his minions have an unmistakable taint to their flesh. Since you two are so fair, under the accumulated dirt and grime of your recent trials, you'll want to pick a spot where the scar won't show."

"How are we to know that we can trust you, dread wolf?"

"I have no idea, but you'd better decide soon, or any number of bad things could happen. More soldiers could arrive, too numerous for me to overcome, I could grow bored and decide to leave all of you here, to your own devices — or I could grow hungry again and decide to stay."

For the first time since picking it up, the dark woman let the point of her blade drop, perhaps just an inch or two, as her look of fear and determination slowly, reluctantly gave way to something else.

* * *

Two long centuries later the wolf was prowling the deep dark woods of his new home, in a wild land called Carpathia, when a quiet rustling of underbrush alerted him to the approach of two people. Even from downwind their scents reached him long before they did, identifying one as a stranger and one who seemed distantly familiar.

"You might as well finish coming forward," the wolf grumbled. "You've no chance of out-running me now, should I decide to eat you, no matter what your starting distance."

The underbrush parted enough to admit two people into the small glade in which the wolf paused, under the spreading canopy of a great oak — a giant of lost ages that painted everything below in deep shadow. The first of the wolf's visitors was an achingly beautiful woman, with skin of whitest porcelain and silken hair darker than a raven's secret heart. She wore an expensive gown of charcoal gray, embroidered in dancing loops and swirls of burgundy thread. It was bowed out by any number of petticoats beneath — a ridiculous contrivance, the wolf thought, in which to go tramping through the woods. Over the dress she wore a long traveling cape, lined in white silk.

Her companion was dressed in similar opulence. He was a tall, slender, aristocratic fellow in matching breeches and waistcoat of powder blue, decorated with enough golden buttons, at the breast, waist and cuffs, to sate the avarice of ancient Midas himself. His vest was also of gold cloth and sported twin rows of even more gold buttons. He wore a broad-brimmed cap, set just so at a jaunty angle. It was of midnight blue, trimmed in more gold, and there was a long feather stuck through its band. He carried a long clay pipe and smoked it furiously, puffing an endless fog of white smoke into the air, almost obscuring his too-handsome features.

"Once long ago you promised not to eat me, Gaffer Wolf," the woman said, through a shy and tentative smile. In that instant the wolf recognized her.

"Only because sparing you then served a higher purpose," the wolf said. "But I no longer spend my days confounding the wishes of that hidden adversary in his far-off empire. I've returned to my former ways, and you're no longer guaranteed safe passage."

Leaving his pipe firmly clamped between his white and perfect teeth, the gentleman's hands drifted down to hover around two bulges distorting his waistcoat that the wolf hadn't noticed at first glance.

"Do you imagine you can retrieve whatever weapons you've concealed there, before I can close my jaws around your throat?" the wolf said.

"I doubt you'll find my neck to your taste," the gentleman replied, showing not a hint of fear, "but try it if you must. It won't do me any permanent harm and you'll be too close to avoid the twin shots of lead I've prepared for you."

"Stop such talk this instant," the woman said. "We didn't travel all this way for anyone to end up shot or eaten."

"Nature will win out," the wolf growled.

"Perhaps so, unless one has a way to change your nature," the woman said. "In any case I'm glad you finally decided to come over to this world."

"I had to. The Emperor's pet warlocks refined their methods of locating me over the years, until it finally became too dangerous even for me to remain there, prowling the numberless lands that had fallen under his heel. And since by that time there were rumors that other passageways to this world had been discovered, I decided my duty was done and it was time to see what sort of place I'd been sending folks to."

"And yet you chose to remain alone, in such a remote land as this?" the woman said. "We had the devil's own time finding you."

The wolf noted that the man moved each time he did, always shifting so as to keep positioned close enough to quickly interpose himself between wolf and woman. The fellow was a puzzle. For the first time in his memory he couldn't decipher a potential opponent's mood and intentions by the scent he gave off. There was a gentleman's cologne of course, but that couldn't mask his natural telltale musks — or at least it couldn't in any past encounter with such men. But

beneath this man's sickly sweet perfume the wolf detected nothing — no fear at all, which was surprising enough, but nothing else either. He turned to the woman again, whom he could still read easily.

"I purposely chose a home far away from those I'd sent here," he said, "so as not to let my hunger undo all of the work I'd done to save them. Here I'm free to hunt the mundane people of this land. They're a superstitious folk that blame everything I do on some fanciful local count who's rumored to be some fell spirit returned from the dead. It means I'm left alone for the most part, and he actually enjoys the notoriety. We visit from time to time. He's not a bad fellow and a good conversationalist, for when I want news of the wider world."

He faced the woman, but all of his attention was focused on her strange companion. He'd seen what these new things — these guns could do. He had no doubt they could do him great harm. If violence was required, he decided he'd first spring at the fellow's waist, rather than his neck. If he could crunch the pistols first, then he'd likely have the two of them in his power — no matter what his strange nature.

"You saved so many of us over the years — the centuries in fact," the woman said. "I don't believe anyone who could do so much good can be such a monster as you present yourself to be. You belong among us, Gaffer Wolf, among those you saved and other refugees from the lost lands. That's why we've come here, to invite you to take your rightful place back among your own kind. We've started something in the far colonies — the New World. We've formed a community of Fables — two communities actually — separated by distance, but as one in spirit and purpose. Those of us who can pass as normal humans live together in a remote town called New Amsterdam, far away from the hustle and bustle of this world. Those of us who can't pass as human live in a secret colony deep in the wilderness, in a place so remote that civilization will never overtake it."

"So you long for my company, woman, but plan to send me off to live amongst the animals, far away from you?"

"Not at all," she said, and began to blush with embarrassment. "There have been dissenting opinions, threatening to destroy our community before it begins. In point of fact the experiment is about to fall apart over the matter of what to do with you. On one hand you saved so many of us. On the other hand, your predations in the homelands were truly monstrous, and it's for those crimes that the wilderness colony won't have you. Of all the fell creatures who've escaped to this world,

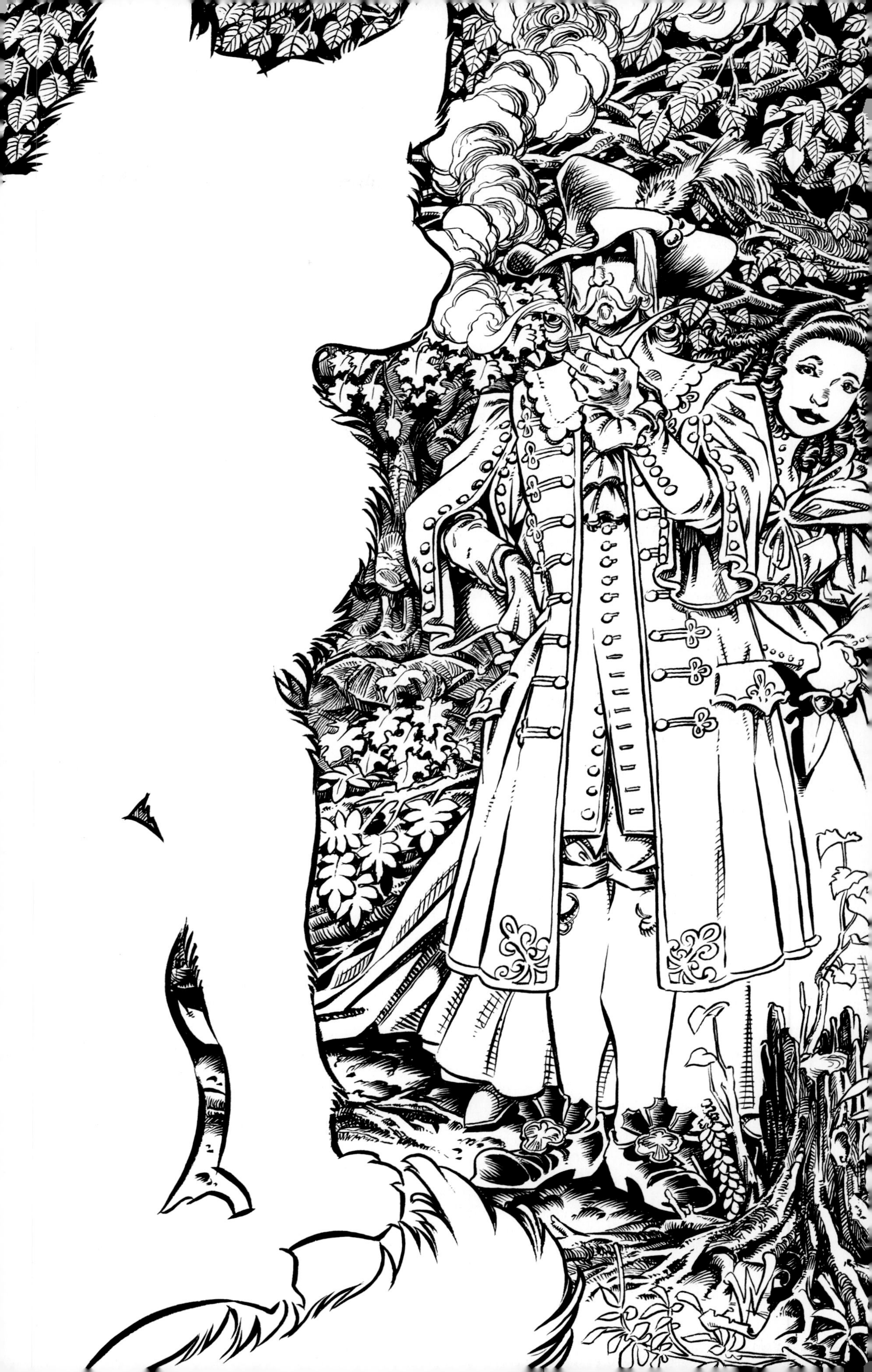

they fear you the most. But what we're attempting is predicated on the notions of equality for all, beginning with a universal pardon of all past crimes, debts and grievances. If one of us is singled out as not worthy of amnesty, then we're back where we started: picking and choosing and counting up past crimes. The community is still fragile and will surely crumble because of this division amongst us, perhaps not this year or the next, but inevitably. Since one colony won't have you, the other one must — but you'll have to be able to pass as human."

"And there's the rub," the wolf said.

"It can be done," the woman said. "You can live as a human, if you choose to." From under her cape she withdrew an ancient iron knife. Its blade was pitted and scarred and looked ready to crumble away in the next breeze. The wolf stiffened when he spied it, reflexively gathering himself to spring — either at her or at the man (or away as fast as he could run) he didn't know yet.

"What's the purpose of that?" he said.

"You found it necessary to bite me once long ago," she said, "so now it's my turn to bite back. This blade is tainted with an ancient magic — an enchantment that lets men walk as wolves."

"I've encountered those impostors, once or twice. They didn't impress me."

"The witch who sold this to me — at a very dear price I might add — said the curse... uhm, the enchantment should work as well in the other direction. A wolf can walk as a man."

"Why should I ever want to do that?"

"That's what we're here to discuss," she said. "And we're prepared to stay long enough to resolve it one way or another. Our hired coach is parked on the roadway down below. Can you direct us to nearby lodgings?"

"Perhaps his friend the count will volunteer shelter to a pair of noble cousins from distant lands," the gentleman said.

*　*　*

The wolf was still getting used to all of the manifest irritations of his new shape when they made the sea crossing. He continuously tugged at and scratched under his woolen frock coat when he'd take his turns on deck. The woman — who turned out to be named after a type of weather in which hunting was typically bad — seldom left her cabin. She didn't like sea travel and claimed the constant pitching and rolling worked ills on her stomach. The wolf discovered he rather enjoyed it. He often encountered the strange gentleman on deck, who seemed not to be bothered by anything, as long as he could keep his ever-present pipe lit. He claimed to have too many names and titles to bother the wolf with and invited him to use Feathertop, which is how he was known amongst most of the Fables. The wolf never felt entirely at ease in the man's company, which Feathertop also noticed and remarked upon one day on the pitching deck.

"I was chosen to accompany the princess on this journey because, of all of the Fables living in this world, I'd be the one most safe from you, if you truly turned out to be monstrous again. I'm not really made of the sorts of things you like to eat." He wouldn't expand on those cryptic comments.

"But as long as we're trading personal secrets," he went on to say, "why don't you tell me why you really chose to come back with us? Though I fancy myself no mean rhetorician, I don't believe either her ladyship or myself argued you into doing anything you hadn't already set your mind to do. The truth now. Why are you here?"

The wolf didn't answer. Instead he turned his face into the gusting rain of a summer squall that had overtaken them, and he thought again about the tiny wisp of a girl, cloaked in equal parts caked grime and foolish bravado, on that long ago mountain trail, prepared to fight off a ravening monster with but a thin sliver of borrowed steel. And he wondered why, of all the people he'd encountered in his long life, he couldn't quite get her scent out of his mind, no matter the passing of years. He stayed late on deck that night as the tiny wooden ship rode bravely over the rolling swells towards the New World.

Treasures from the Woodland Vaults

Above: Bryan Talbot's first sketch of Jack of the Tales.

Following pages: Pencils by Bryan Talbot for the epic title spread from FABLES #11.

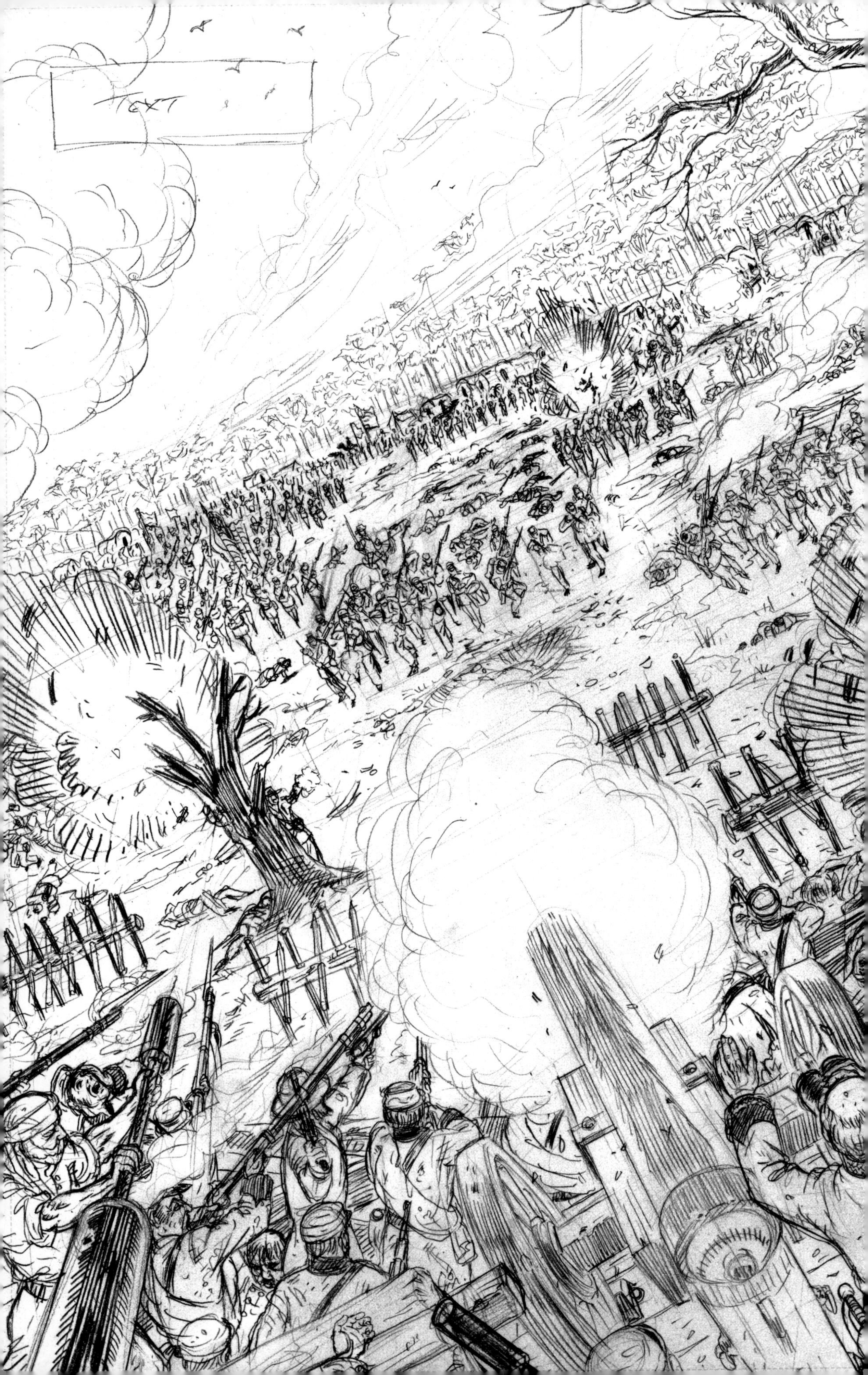
TEXT

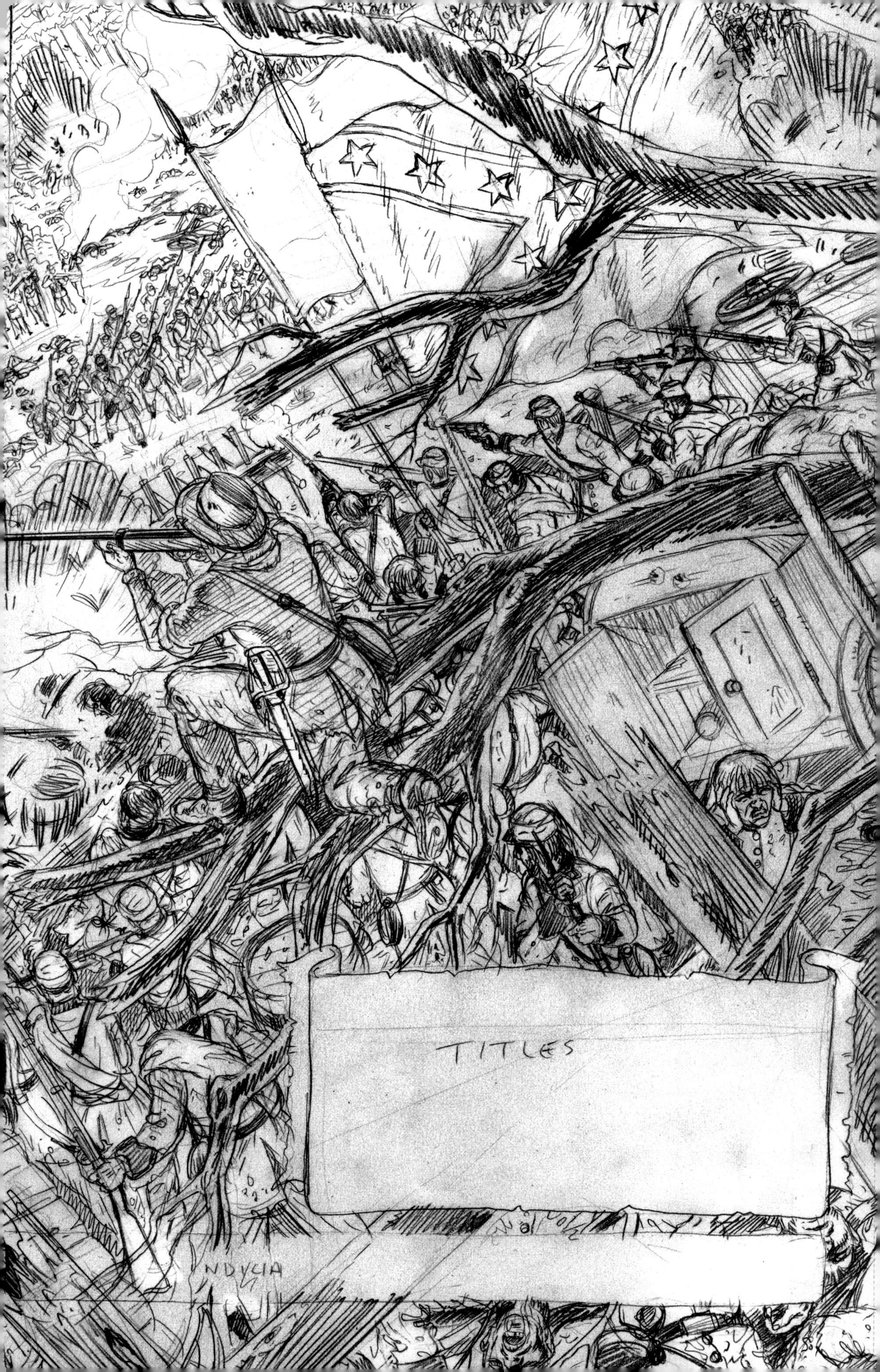
TITLES

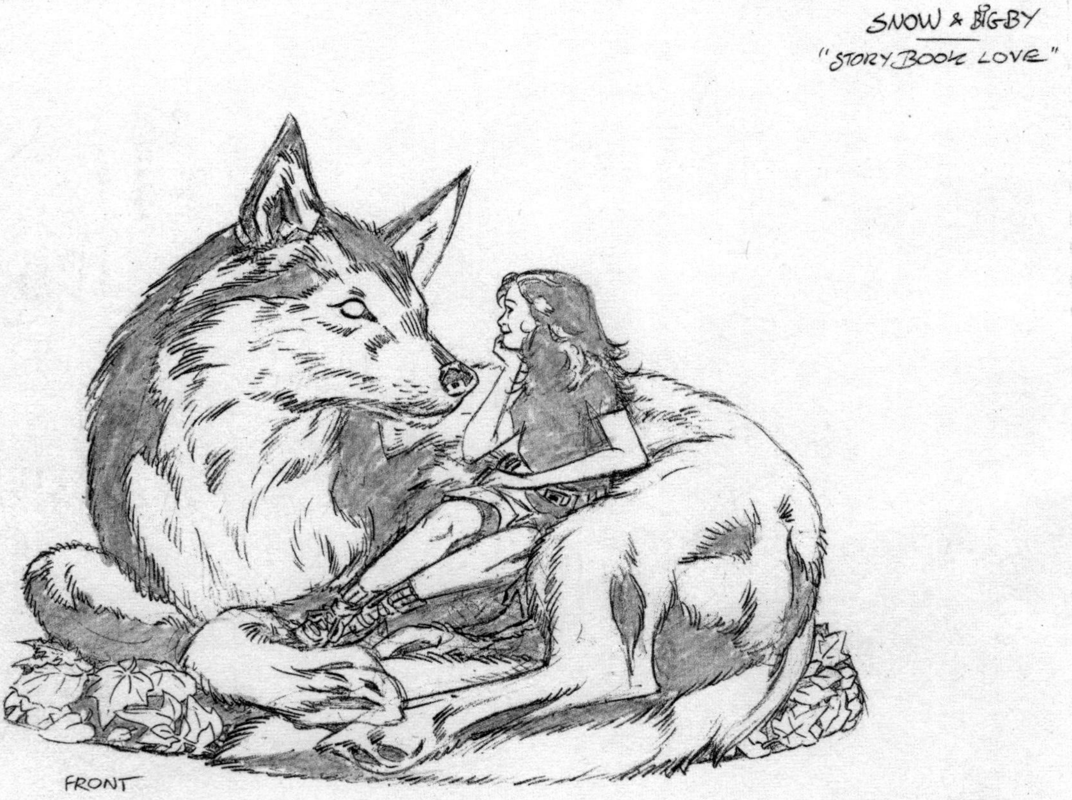
SNOW & BIGBY
"STORY BOOK LOVE"
FRONT

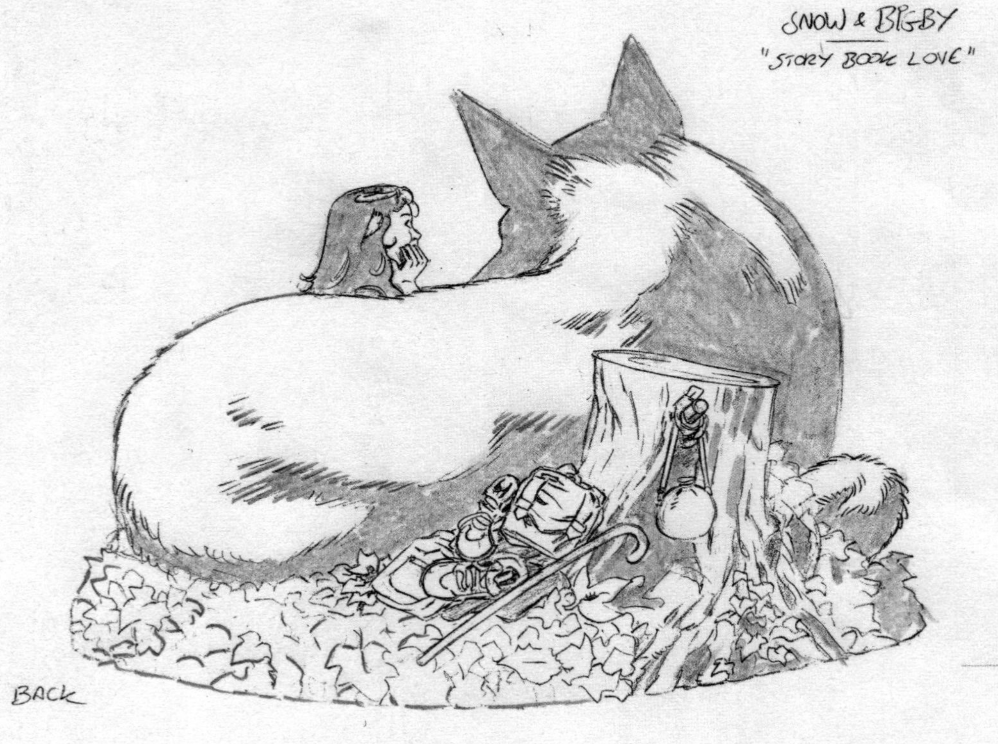
SNOW & BIGBY
"STORY BOOK LOVE"
BACK

Above: Conceptual designs for an unproduced "Storybook Love" statue of Bigby and Snow White by Mark Buckingham.